THE
CREATURE
CHRONICLES

Interview Books by Tom Weaver

Universal Terrors, 1951–1955: Eight Classic Horror and Science Fiction Films (2017)

A Sci-Fi Swarm and Horror Horde: Interviews with 62 Filmmakers (2010)

*I Talked with a Zombie: Interviews with 23 Veterans of
Horror and Sci-Fi Films and Television* (2009; paperback 2014)

Earth vs. the Sci-Fi Filmmakers: 20 Interviews (2005; paperback 2014)

*Double Feature Creature Attack: A Monster Merger of
Two More Volumes of Classic Interviews* (2003)
(A combined edition of the two earlier Weaver titles
Attack of the Monster Movie Makers and
They Fought in the Creature Features)

*Eye on Science Fiction: 20 Interviews with Classic
SF and Horror Filmmakers* (2003; paperback 2007)

*Science Fiction Confidential: Interviews with
23 Monster Stars and Filmmakers* (2002; paperback 2010)

*I Was a Monster Movie Maker: Conversations
with 22 SF and Horror Filmmakers* (2001; paperback 2011)

*Return of the B Science Fiction and Horror Heroes: The Mutant
Melding of Two Volumes of Classic Interviews* (2000)
(A combined edition of the two earlier Weaver titles
Interviews with B Science Fiction and Horror Movie Makers
and *Science Fiction Stars and Horror Heroes*)

*Science Fiction and Fantasy Film Flashbacks: Conversations with 24 Actors,
Writers, Producers and Directors from the Golden Age* (1998; paperback 2004)

*It Came from Horrorwood: Interviews with Moviemakers
in the SF and Horror Tradition* (1996; paperback 2004)

*They Fought in the Creature Features: Interviews with
23 Classic Horror, Science Fiction and Serial Stars* (1995; paperback 2014)

Attack of the Monster Movie Makers: Interviews with 20 Genre Giants (1994; paperback 2014)

*Science Fiction Stars and Horror Heroes: Interviews with Actors, Directors,
Producers and Writers of the 1940s through 1960s* (1991; paperback 2006)

*Interviews with B Science Fiction and Horror Movie Makers: Writers,
Producers, Directors, Actors, Moguls and Makeup* (1988; paperback 2006)

Other Books by Tom Weaver

John Carradine: The Films (1999; paperback 2008)

*Poverty Row HORRORS! Monogram, PRC and
Republic Horror Films of the Forties* (1993; paperback 1999)

By Tom Weaver with Michael Brunas and John Brunas

Universal Horrors: The Studio's Classic Films, 1931–1946, 2d ed. (2007; paperback 2017)

All from McFarland

THE CREATURE CHRONICLES

Exploring the Black Lagoon Trilogy

Tom Weaver
David Schecter and Steve Kronenberg

Introduction by Julie Adams

McFarland & Company, Inc., Publishers
Jefferson, North Carolina

The present work is a reprint of the library bound edition of The Creature Chronicles: Exploring the Black Lagoon Trilogy, *first published in 2014 by McFarland.*

Chapter 7, "A Brief History of the *Black Lagoon Bugle*," copyright © David J. Schow, 1999, revised 2014. All rights reserved. Used by permission.

Chapter 8, "Revenge of the Return of the Remake of *Creature from the Black Lagoon*," copyright © David J. Schow, 1993, revised 2014. All rights reserved. Used by permission.

LIBRARY OF CONGRESS CATALOGUING-IN-PUBLICATION DATA

Weaver, Tom, 1958–
The creature chronicles : exploring the Black Lagoon trilogy / Tom Weaver, David Schecter and Steve Kronenberg ; introduction by Julie Adams.
 p. cm.
Includes bibliographical references and index.

ISBN 978-1-4766-7386-8
(softcover : acid free paper) ∞
ISBN 978-1-4766-1580-6 (ebook)

1. Black Lagoon films—History and criticism.
I. Schecter, David. II. Kronenberg, Steve, 1950– III. Title.
PN1995.9.B58W43 2014   791.43'75—dc23   2014024003

BRITISH LIBRARY CATALOGUING DATA ARE AVAILABLE

© 2014 Tom Weaver, David Schecter and Steve Kronenberg. All rights reserved

No part of this book may be reproduced or transmitted in any form or by any means, electronic or mechanical, including photocopying or recording, or by any information storage and retrieval system, without permission in writing from the publisher.

Designed by Kelly Elliott with Jessica Wilcox, David Alff and Robert Franklin
Typeset by Jessica Wilcox
Front cover design by Kerry Gammill

Printed in the United States of America

McFarland & Company, Inc., Publishers
Box 611, Jefferson, North Carolina 28640
www.mcfarlandpub.com

Dedication

Ned Comstock of the USC Cinema-Television Library. I've been writing about the monster oldies for 30 years, and Ned has to be *the* most bend-over-backwards-nice guy I've ever encountered…. Welllll, alongside of:

Bob Burns, the heart and soul of the Monster Kid Universe. Schecter, Kronenberg and I could have done this book without Bob. The book would have turned out sucktacular, but we coulda *done* it.

David J. Schow, another great "go-to guy" for all things Creature—and yet again, a guy with a heart big as a lagoon.

Dr. Robert J. Kiss, an amazingly resourceful researcher, and the kind of guy who cannot respond to a movie-related question with anything less than four or five pages of wonderful information!

Ricou Browning. The fact that he played the Gill Man has never meant the Earth, moon and stars to him and yet he's put up with 1000 questions from me, 900 of them quite inane, over a span of more than two decades, with never a peep of complaint. Thank you for the thousandth time, Ricou!—Tom Weaver

Table of Contents

Acknowledgments — xi
Introduction by Julie Adams — 1

Part One

1. *Creature from the Black Lagoon* (1954) — 11
2. *Revenge of the Creature* (1955) — 139
3. *The Creature Walks Among Us* (1956) — 227

Part Two

4. The Official Gill Man Guide to the Sunshine State — 303
5. Aquatic Kith and Kin — 305
   - **The Return of the Creature** (1954) — 305
   - **Curucu, Beast of the Amazon** (1956) — 310
   - **The Monster of Piedras Blancas** (1959) — 312
   - **Octaman** (1971) — 315
6. Creature Conversations — 319
   - Ginger Stanley — 319
   - Mike Gannon — 337
   - Vikki Megowan — 342
7. A Brief History of *The Black Lagoon Bugle* (David J. Schow) — 349
8. Revenge of the Return of the Remake of *Creature from the Black Lagoon* (David J. Schow) — 353

Chapter Notes — 363
Index — 387

Acknowledgments

No evidence of aquatic humanoids has ever been found.
—U.S. National Oceanic and Atmospheric Administration (2012)

You know, sometimes I theenk all North Americanos are crazy!
—Lucas in *Revenge of the Creature*

No evidence of an aquatic humanoid?? Our little friends at National Oceanic are wrong. They have been affected by the skepticism of a skeptical age. They do not believe except they see. They think that nothing can be which is not comprehensible by their little minds.

Yes, National Oceanic, there *is* a Gill Man. He exists as certainly as fannish love for him exists in the hearts of Baby Boomer Monster Kids who saw his movies theatrically back in the Fabulous '50s and/or on TV. Alas! how dreary would be the world if there were no Gill Man! It would be as dreary as if it were without the wonderful folks who went above and beyond for this book:

Everett Aaker, Susan Acosta, Julie Adams, Ron Adams, John Agar, John Alland, Susan Alland, William Alland, Arthur Anderson, John Antosiewicz, Brad Arrington, John Athanason, Buddy Barnett, Mike Barnum, Sally Baskin, Marty Baumann, Jere Beery, Jr., John Beifuss, Judeena Blackmer, Michael Blake, Larry Blamire, Ted Bohus, Gibby Brand, Patrick Briggs, Ricou Browning, John Brunas, Michael Brunas, Jon Burlingame, Bob Burns, James H. Burns, Kathy Burns, James Caperton, John Carcaba, John Carpenter, Sandy King Carpenter, Chris Casteel, Ben Chapman, Didier Chatelain, Lissa Morrow Christian, all the marvelous folks on the Classic Horror Film Board, Jim Clatterbaugh, David Colton, Ned Comstock, Heidi Conley, Dick Contino, Ann Cullen, Glenn Damato, Dennis Daniel, Joe Dante, Janlou de Amicis Silva, Richard Denning, Maury Dexter, Frank Dietz, Henry Escalante, Harry Essex, Julian Fant, Michael Fox, Robert M. Fresco, Bob Furmanek, Scott Gallinghouse, Kerry Gammill, Mike Gannon, Beverly Garland, Dick Gautier, Dorothy Gertz, Irving Gertz, Brett Halsey, Susan Hart, Irma B. Havens, Richard Heft, Tom Hennesy, Charles Henson, John Herbert, Dee Denning Hewett, D.J. Hoek, Robert Hoy, Kathleen Hughes, Jeffrey Hugo, Cortlandt Hull, Marsha Hunt, Joe Indusi, Jeff Janeczko, Jeff Joseph, Joe Kane, Steve Kaplan, Larry Kartiganer, Dr. Annette Kaufman, Merrilee Kazarian, Doug Kennedy, Jack Kevan, Bob King, Robert J. Kiss, Richard Kline, Hal Lane, Harris Lentz, Renee Le Feuvre, Tim Lilley, Terry Lipsit, Gary Lockwood, Donna Lucas, Greg MacAyeal, Adie Grey Mackenzie, Boyd Magers, Ginny Mancini, Henry Mancini, Greg Mank, Maurice Manson, Mark Martucci, Richard Matheson, Elizabeth Maury, Kathleen Mayne, Dave McDonnell, Charles McNabb, Greg Megowan, Jan Merlin, Bob Meyer, John Morgan, Jeff Morrow, Bruce Mozert, Kristina Murphy, Edward Mussallem, Dave Narz, John Narz, MaryLou Narz, Robert Neill, Lori Nelson, Ted Newsom, Greg Nicotero, Vikki Megowan Noblitt, Gregg Palmer, Cynthia Patrick, Delee Perry, Joseph Pevney, Mark Phillips, William Phipps, the Photofest Gang, Ina Poindexter, Gary Prange, Kenisha Ramsay, Frederick Rappaport, Rex Reason, Shirley Ann Reason, David Redman, Joe Reiner, William Reynolds, Alan K. Rode, Allan Rosen, Arthur Ross, Robert Rotten, Mary Runser, Hans J. Salter, Mikki Sampo, John Saxon, Dan Scapperotti, Joe "Sorko" Schovitz, David J. Schow, Rich Scrivani, Gloria Selph, Curt Siodmak, Dennis Skotak, Robert Skotak, Ginger Stanley, Richard Stapley, Herman Stein, John Stephens, Bonnie Stevenson, Stephen Strimpell, Larri Thomas, Tony Timpone, Charles A. Tingley, Laura Wagner, Clint Walker, Michelle Weis, Craig Wichman, Lucy Chase Williams, Wade Williams, Mark Wingfield, Annie Wollock and Jack N. Young.

Introduction by Julie Adams

When I was in grade school and growing up in Jonesboro, Arkansas, I loved watching horror pictures at the local movie theater. My parents let me see them because I never let on that they frightened me. But once I was inside the theater, I would crouch down on the floor and peek through the two seats in front of me during the really scary parts. I remember seeing *Frankenstein* (1931) that way and being scared to death, but it was worth it. Because for a mere quarter I not only saw all the movies being shown that day, but I could also afford popcorn and a "Coke ice."

Despite my early love of horror movies, after I arrived in Hollywood I acted in a very small number of such films. And that probably comes as a surprise to those who know me primarily for one particular monster picture I made back in the 1950s.

In 1954, the year *Creature from the Black Lagoon* was released, Universal-International produced close to 30 feature films. At the time I was a contract actress with the studio, and I was appearing in about my twentieth movie. Over my long career I have acted in over 200 television episodes, movies and plays, but in terms of popularity, nothing rivals that little horror picture I was in way back when. And to call it a "little" picture is not to demean it, but simply to state that at the time it was made, *Creature from the Black Lagoon* did not necessarily stand out from other films I had done. Because as much as I enjoy and admire it now, back then it was just another movie that Universal had assigned to me.

I can say with absolute certainty that back in 1954 I never thought we'd still be talking about the picture all these years later. There was no reason to believe it would have more long-term popularity than other films I had made around the same time, such as *The Stand at Apache River* (1953) and *Six Bridges to Cross* (1955). Back then there was no home video or films you could watch on the not-yet-invented Internet. While some movies were being broadcast on television, few or none were from major studios like Universal. Motion pictures were produced, shown in theaters, and soon replaced by the next films to come off the studio assembly lines. And after that, for the most part they were pretty much forgotten.

Julie Adams rings in 1954, the year when one of her movies, Creature from the Black Lagoon, would be enough of a hit to make Variety's list of top domestic grossers.

If anyone working on *Creature from the Black Lagoon* had any inkling at the time that it would still be popular in ten years, let alone six decades later, I'm sure they would have wanted to take home some souvenirs from the set. In my case, I probably would have asked if I could keep the white bathing suit so I could store it safely for future generations to admire. Alas, almost everything associated with the production of the film has disappeared over time.

INTRODUCTION BY JULIE ADAMS

We weren't making the picture "for the ages." We were just making a simple monster movie. That it has become a classic does not mean that any of us approached it differently from any other film we worked on. Regardless of the project, whether it was a movie, live television, a series or acting on the stage, it was my job to always try to give the best performance I could. And the others who made their living in Hollywood put their very best into everything they worked on. Working on *Creature* was a few weeks out of my life, and when it was finished, the entire cast and crew moved on to different projects.

As for why *Creature from the Black Lagoon* and its sequels are being watched again and again by fans after all this time, many theories have been offered. They range from the Gill Man being a tragic figure who elicits sympathy, the Beauty and the Beast aspect, the wondrous design and execution of the monster suit, the scary musical theme, and the well-written script. And how much of the film's appeal has to do with the beautifully executed sequence where the monster swims in harmony with Kay in the lagoon? That episode combined a few shots of me taken in Hollywood with second unit underwater shots of Ricou Browning (the Gill Man) and my underwater double Ginger Stanley in Florida, which were then edited into a seamless whole that is probably the most visually stunning sequence in the picture.

Whether it's one of those reasons or something else entirely, it's a mystery to me, and I doubt anybody will ever know for sure. And I think it's probably better that way. Why one work of art, be it a painting, a musical composition or a motion picture, resonates with an audience while another one doesn't is part of what makes art such a fascinating topic. There were many other excellent science fiction movies made at the same time as *Creature*, so I think it only adds to the mystique of our little picture that it has such a fervent following while many other equally well-made movies do not. I've always considered the work to be the reward, and whatever people choose to like the best, that's okay with me. I am both surprised and happy that so many people still seem to enjoy our little monster movie so much.

Those who work on motion pictures have very different perspectives about their experiences than film historians wish we did. As a working actress, I never had the time or opportunity to stand back and reflect upon the making of a film from start to finish, and to therefore file everything away in my memory for easy recall. My job is to study my role by reading the script and learning my lines, and then to follow whatever specifics the director might suggest during shooting. I'm seldom around for scenes that don't include me, and I've never been privy to behind-the-scenes talks between producers, cinematographers, set designers, effects technicians and others working on a film. Just as those people are focused on their own areas of expertise and probably have no idea what the actors are experiencing. Production schedules on a film

Bud Westmore, Ricou Browning, Julie Adams and Jack Arnold atop the Underwater Tank, preparing to test the first monster suit made for Browning. Its hands and feet look like the eventual Gill Man; the rest, not so much!

have been worked out in detail in advance, so while you can have some fun on the set, you have to make sure all your scenes are completed on time so the picture makes its deadline.

The things that stick out about making a movie are seldom what you might think. While all actors are different, we often remember the personal things that directly affected us during production, rather than larger issues that influenced the picture as a whole. We might recall if we were feeling a little under the weather during shooting, or whether it was extremely hot or cold on location. Were there problems with the wigs or costumes we wore? Even though I could have been working with a famous movie star, I might have had a closer friendship with a supporting player in the film, simply because we had a lot in common or because we were old friends or becoming new ones. My recollections of the Gill Man's first cinematic adventure are almost entirely of this personal nature, and all concerning the people with whom I was in direct contact during production. So it is within this very limited framework that I look back on *Creature from the Black Lagoon* after this long passage of time.

Before the Creature entered my life, I was happy where my career was going. I had already gotten to work with such accomplished actors as Richard Conte, Arthur Kennedy, Tyrone Power and James Stewart, and watching them perform helped lift my work to a higher level. And with Raoul Walsh and Mark Robson having directed some of my recent pictures, I was working with some of the most respected men in the business.

When I received the screenplay for *Creature from the Black Lagoon* and was told it would be my next assignment, my first thought was to turn it down. Not that I had anything against monster movies, but it just surprised me because I wasn't expecting it. After all, Universal wasn't considered the "monster" studio the same way it had been back in the 1930s and 1940s, as *Creature* was only their second such movie in the decade, coming after *It Came from Outer Space* (1953).

However, because I was under contract, I knew that if I refused to do the project I would be put on suspension, and that didn't seem like such a good idea. I loved being a working actress, which is the reason I almost never turned down any opportunities that came my way during my career. Also, I was basically a "good kid" while under contract, as I was only in my third year with Universal. I've always been a very positive person and an optimist; otherwise, I couldn't have left a small town in Arkansas to pursue my dreams of becoming a Hollywood actress. So I usually met new ideas and adventures in an upbeat fashion, and being the love interest to a scaly monster was certainly a novel idea. And a big part of the fun of being an actress is playing different roles. Universal had been very nice in giving me a wide variety of parts, so I never had to worry about being typecast the way many actors did.

There were other reasons why I became convinced that acting in *Creature from the Black Lagoon* might not be such a terrible idea. The first thing I noticed was that the screenplay was well-written and logical. It pretty much laid everything out in as believable a fashion as you could expect in a movie like this. That realism is probably one reason the film still stands up so well today. I also liked that my character Kay Lawrence was a scientist. She wasn't just some dope along for the ride. Not that Kay does too many scientific things in the film, but she was an intelligent woman, and I enjoyed playing characters like that. And as somebody who never really liked to travel, I also appreciated the fact that I didn't have to go off to some crazy location to make the movie.

As if I didn't have reason enough to jump on board the *Rita*, I liked the choice of Jack Arnold as the film's director. I had attended the premiere of his *It Came from Outer Space*, so I knew that *Creature* would be in good hands with him. Universal was making fairly good movies then, and even their programmers were a far cry from the Lippert Westerns I had done a few years earlier. So all things considered, I said to myself, "What the hey—it might be fun!"

When you're working for a big studio like Universal, almost everyone you encounter on the lot is a total professional. Otherwise, they wouldn't have been hired in the first place. There are few surprises because everyone knows how to do his or her job, and do it well. In the case of *Creature*, as with most of my pictures, it was a thoroughly professional venture all around. If there were major problems occurring behind the scenes on any of the studio's pictures I worked on, it's doubtful I would have known about them. Universal was very low-key in terms of drama, so any such situations that might have arisen on any of my pictures likely would have been handled without the actors being aware of them.

I enjoyed working with Jack Arnold a lot. He didn't rehearse the actors the way directors like Mark Robson and Rudolph Maté did in *Bright Victory* (1951) and *The Mississippi Gambler* (1953), but the type of acting we were doing on *Creature* didn't require the same type of run-throughs those more realistic dramas did. For the most part, Jack left the actors alone during filming, as we were all experienced professionals and he had more pressing matters to attend to. I liked and respected him because his direction made sense. The camera moves he made and the way he blocked the scenes were always logical. That didn't happen with every director I worked with during my career. Even though we all knew we weren't making an A-picture, right away you could tell, "This guy knows what he's doing. He's going to make a pretty good movie." He was easy to work with, and I felt comfortable with him in charge.

I don't recall much about producer William Alland, who worked on three other pictures I made at Universal, other than that he was a pleasant individual. That I don't know more about him has nothing to do with him as a person, but it's simply because actors seldom interact much with producers. They do their jobs and you do yours, and if you do run into them on the set from time to time, you have a very simple and professional relationship. The same goes for technical people like cameramen and set decorators. Other than saying "Good morning" or "Good evening," you rarely have anything to do with them on a deeper level. I'm not sure I ever ran into an art director or an editor, as the former would have already done his work before I arrived on the set, and the latter would be working on your scenes after they were shot.

Although I didn't personally know people like *Creature*'s art directors Hilyard Brown and Bernard Herzbrun or set decorator Russell Gausman, they were obviously very talented individuals, as Universal was very skilled at designing and making sets. While you have to use your acting skills to bring a character to life, your imagination also plays a large part in the process, and realistic sets can certainly help you feel more comfortable in your role. The sets in *Creature* were all superb, especially our wonderful boat, the *Rita*. These people I almost never met helped bring to life many of the films I made at the studio.

There were a few technical people that I did have personal contact with on *Creature*, as their jobs involved the actors. Makeup man Bud Westmore or members of his team were usually hovering somewhere around us. I was extremely lucky because Bud and I just hit it off—we were pals, and he often did my makeup during my tenure with the studio. I felt very privileged to be in this position, as it was an honor to have the head of the department doing my makeup in the morning. He was extremely talented and I always loved when he'd do my face. Bud was a delightful man and easy to be around, with a good sense of humor. We'd talk about life while he was working on me, although I had to be careful not to talk when it would affect him applying my makeup. Morning on the sets was a very lively time with all the actors being made up at the same time breakfast was being served!

Rosemary Odell was a clothes designer, and she handled my wardrobe on *Creature* and other pictures. She designed my custom-made bathing suit, something that was never done for me before or since. I remember seeing the sketch and it looked great. I was happy they didn't put me in a two-piecer because my ribs stick out. The only racy thing about the suit was that it was pulled up on the leg, but even that wasn't too risqué for the time. The suit was made of good latex and it fit my form perfectly. It felt good and I enjoyed wearing it very much. To this day, the question I probably get asked more than any other is, "Whatever happened to that white bathing suit?" My answer is that it probably went the way of all latex!

One of my fondest memories of working at Universal was a temperamental fitter by the name of Idabelle. She took my measurements for my various costumes and for my *Creature* swimsuit. Idabelle was about five feet tall—much shorter than me—but, boy, was she tough! Although she thought I had a pretty good figure, that didn't stop her from pointing out every last flaw in me! This shoulder

Julie Adams joins Ricou Browning in the tank. Would Creature *have become the hit it did with a monster that looked like this? We'll never know ... but we can probably make a safe guess!*

Introduction by Julie Adams

Man movie, I don't recall, but we had a very friendly relationship at Universal and she was just a wizard with hair. There are many times these days when it would have been wonderful to have her around to fix me up!

Although my two male co-stars in *Creature* weren't as famous as some of the stars I had already worked with, such as Jimmy Stewart, Rock Hudson, Robert Ryan and William Powell, they were both fairly well-known. Richard Carlson was a respected actor and I found him to be a real gentleman. Richard Denning was a charming guy. Both Richards were very professional, I liked them both, and enjoyed working with them.

Creature from the Black Lagoon was more of an action film than an "actor's picture," and Universal hired both Carlson and Denning because they wanted them to play their "types," just as I was chosen because the studio wanted me for my "type." There wasn't a lot of difference between the personalities they were playing in the movie and their personalities in real life. They were basically nice-looking men who happened to be a scientist and a businessman, and both of them were pros at these sorts of roles. You knew what you would get from each of them, and indeed they delivered the goods. Their battles over me and the Gill Man drive the plot, and they both have a determination and intensity that adds to the drama. Being an actress can be a very rewarding experience, because when you're working with actors such as these and getting paid for it every week, what's there to complain about? Although I hadn't

Whether in an Amazon lagoon or on the Universal back lot, how could Julie Adams not turn the Gill Man's fish head? A Ramona, California, exhibitor offered his opinion of Black Lagoon *in* Boxoffice *magazine's May 8, 1954, issue, writing in part, "Enough gruesome details and situations to satisfy anyone—and plenty exposure of Julia Adams—wow!"*

was higher than the other. My legs weren't the same exact length. When she was done with my fittings, I'd walk away feeling completely deformed. Idabelle didn't have much of a sense of humor, and I think that added to the experience. It was actually funny to partake in one of her fittings because I always knew what was coming before I even saw her.

Hair stylist Joan St. Oegger was a terrific woman and another wonderful friend. She designed whatever hair styles were needed on a film, and if you were doing a period picture, she would be in her element. However, if you were doing a modern picture, hairdressers on the set would help to maintain the proper look for continuity. For *Creature*, they wanted me to use my real hair, especially as they liked the "wet hair" look in certain scenes. Whether I had any contact with Joan during the shooting of the Gill

For publicity photograph purposes, Julie Adams gasps at the nightmare in scaly armor (Ben Chapman). In real life she and Chapman were friends on the set and even better friends in the 2000s, when they saddled up and rode the autograph show trail together.

acted with a monster before, I don't recall worrying about figuring out my motivation. The script pretty much gave me a solid framework within which I could practice my craft.

I have good memories of all the other actors in *Creature*. Antonio Moreno was a very nice person, and we had already worked together in the Mexican adventure *Wings of the Hawk* (1953). I loved Nestor Paiva, and we used to kid around with him, saying, in a thick Spanish accent, "Good morning, Captain *Loo*-kus!" We teased him, but he had a great sense of humor. I was fond of him, and he was fun just to be around. Whit Bissell, who played a sort of father figure to my character, was simply adorable and I just loved him. He was relatively small, extremely funny, and I remember that we always laughed. I don't recall what we laughed about, but we laughed a lot and I was delighted to see him every day during the shoot. He was a lovely man, and I considered him a great friend. He had what they call in the business today a very high "likability factor." I was always delighted whenever we ran into each other later in our careers.

As for my other main co-stars—the land and the water Creatures—I have very fond and special memories of Ben Chapman, with whom I filmed most of my monster scenes. He was a big guy, but very gentle, with a sweetness about him. I seem to recall meeting him before he was in his suit. He had a good sense of humor and was a lot of fun to be around. Just a lovely fellow. The first time I saw the suit was when Ben came out of makeup, and it was really awesome. An impressive creation, and I must say I was surprised it looked so good. There was something magical about it at the time, there has seldom been anything quite like it since, and its ability to convey a realistic living, breathing monster is extraordinary to this day.

During filming, Ben and I got into this routine where every day I'd say, "Good morning, Beastie," and he would laugh back. We couldn't talk much, as he was enclosed in his rubber suit, but I could occasionally hear some muffled mutters coming from inside. We didn't see each other after filming until many decades later, when I began doing some film conventions with him. From then on we became the very best of friends, and I loved being with him. I still miss him very much to this day.

While I didn't have as much to do with Ricou Browning, who was off filming in Florida during much of the shoot, we still managed to see each other on occasion and I liked him. Over the past few years we have done a number of conventions and we consider ourselves to be dear friends. A couple of memories that remain etched in my memory involve Ricou. I remember one day during *Creature* production when I was told that the rushes from Florida were going to be shown, and some of the other actors and I excitedly went to the screening room to watch the footage of Ricou swimming in the Creature suit. The dailies were long, silent takes of him and Ginger Stanley deep in the crystal clear water of Wakulla Springs. They'd swim

After her Universal stay came to an end, Julie Adams built up an enormous TV résumé that today looks like the history of the medium itself.

for a while, get some air from an air hose, and then go back and resume their action. It was so exciting seeing the Gill Man brought to life by Ricou's unique swimming style, and I was captivated. Even before the screening, I think we all had a sense that *Creature from the Black Lagoon* was going to be a pretty good movie, but after seeing the dailies, which I think I might have watched over a few days, I had an inkling that the movie would be better than expected and nothing to be embarrassed about.

As I stated, when you're working with professionals, there are seldom major things that go wrong. The only really serious problem I recall was when the initial Creature suit was rejected. But that led to what was probably my best memory of the entire time I spent on this assignment, and again Ricou was involved.

I had met "Scotty" Welbourne, who designed and operated the 3-D underwater camera used in the movie, when he and Ricou were in Universal's Underwater Tank testing out the Aqualung. At the time I didn't know

Introduction by Julie Adams

"Scotty" was a technical wizard or anything—we were just friends on the picture. I asked him if I could try out the scuba equipment and spend a few minutes underwater, and he kindly let me. I loved the experience of breathing freely underwater, even though it was just in a tank on the studio lot.

Looking back, it's not surprising that I wanted to use the Aqualung, because I had spent a lot of my youth in the water. Along with riding horses, one of my real joys was swimming, and I could often be found at the nice-sized municipal swimming pool in Blytheville, Arkansas, which was only a couple of blocks from my home. They charged 15 or 20 cents to go in, and you could stay in the water for six hours. I was a good swimmer and passed the junior lifesaving test, and for the life of me couldn't figure out why the older girls spent a lot of time outside the pool preening themselves in the sun. Of course, I was pretty skinny then, so nobody was paying much attention to me. During much of my childhood, swimming was just about the most fun I could possibly have.

After Universal realized it needed a better design for the Creature suit, the production start date was delayed for a few weeks. Again I asked "Scotty" about using the Aqualung, only this time I wanted to go into the ocean. I didn't want to go locally to Santa Monica or any place like that, where you couldn't see diddly. I had previously been on a glass bottom boat farther out in the ocean, so I knew how pristine the water could be. "Scotty" suggested we take a boat out to nearby Catalina Island. I asked Ricou to go along with us, which made me feel really safe having two capable guys along who wouldn't let me drown.

The experience of going underwater in the Pacific and breathing freely was unbelievable, even better than I had imagined. I was released from the force of gravity and living among the denizens of the ocean. I got to investigate a sunken yacht and I walked on the ocean floor. It was an amazing experience to be swimming within a school of big fish, to be among them, to feel like you were one of the crowd. They were so casual, and many of them came so close to me I could almost reach out and touch them, although they always moved a little bit away to keep some distance between themselves and their strange two-legged visitor. It was an incredible adventure, one I went cuckoo over. I was so in love with being underwater, and through the years I learned a lot about life under the sea, much of it by reading Jacques Cousteau's books. Years later when I was visiting Hawaii I repeated my scuba diving experience, but that phenomenal holiday with "Scotty" and Ricou during my break from *Creature* was something I have never forgotten.

Even though I didn't make more than a handful of horror or science fiction movies, I have accepted the fact that I will forever be linked to this little picture we made 60 years ago. And when I think about it, from the standpoint of my love of swimming and all things underwater, perhaps you could say that I was indeed made for *Creature from the Black Lagoon*.

According to the movie, the Gill Man has been around since Devonian times. And from what I can tell, it looks like he's still going to be around well into the future.

Julie Adams at the Festival of the West in Scottsdale, Arizona, in March 2013.

PART ONE

CREATURE FROM THE BLACK LAGOON

And awaaaay we go!

Creature from the Black Lagoon Full Credit Information

A note on this book's lists of crew members: Universal's production paperwork for the Gill Man movies designates uncredited workers by last name only ("Script Clerk: Hughes," "Makeup: Hadley," etc.). I've included them anyway, and in many cases made parenthetical guesses as to who the people might be; for instance, there was at that time a Hollywood makeup man named Joe Hadley, so you'll see on the following crew list "Makeup: Hadley (Joe Hadley?)." Perhaps some future researcher will dig deeper and improve upon the three crew member lists.

CREDITS: Produced by William Alland; Directed by Jack Arnold; Underwater Sequences Directed by James C. Havens; Screenplay: Harry Essex and Arthur Ross; Story: Maurice Zimm; Photography: William E. Snyder; Special Photography: Charles S. Welbourne [aka "Scotty" Welbourne][1*]; Editor: Ted J. Kent; Art Directors: Bernard Herzbrun and Hilyard Brown; Set Decorators: Russell A. Gausman and Ray Jeffers; Sound: Leslie I. Carey and Joe Lapis; Music Director: Joseph Gershenson; Julie Adams' Wardrobe: Rosemary Odell; Hair Stylist: Joan St. Oegger; Makeup: Bud Westmore; Assistant Director: Fred Frank; **Uncredited:** Story Idea: William Alland; Contributors to Screenplay: Ernest Nims and Leo Lieberman; Music: Hans J. Salter, Herman Stein and Henry Mancini; Tracked Music: Robert Emmett Dolan, Milton Rosen, Herman Stein, Henry Mancini and Hans J. Salter; Orchestrator: David Tamkin; Tuba Player: Jack Barsby; Creature Costume Designer: Milicent Patrick; Creature Costume Makers: Jack Kevan, Chris Mueller, Jr., Milicent Patrick, Tom Case, Rudolph Parducci, John Kraus, Elmer Balogh, John Phiefer and Frank Acuna; Production Manager: Gilbert Kurland; Assistant Directors: Russ Haverick and Kenny (Joseph E. Kenny?); Sound Editors: Ray Craddock and Al Kennedy; Unit Manager: Foster Thompson; Camera Operators: Kyme Meade and Lathrop (Philip Lathrop?); Assistant Cameramen: Charles Alder, Robert Hager and King (James King?); Optical Department Supervisor: Roswell Hoffman; Cameraman ("Nebula & Explosion" sequence, "Gill Man on Fire" trick shots *et al.*): David S. "Stan" Horsley; Mechanical-Visual-Special Effects Supervisor ("Nebula & Explosion" sequence): Charlie Baker; Pyrotechnic Supervisor ("Nebula & Explosion" sequence): Eddie Stein; Still Photographer: Bert Anderson; Script Clerks: Luanna Sherman and Hughes (Dorothy Hughes?); First Grips: Everett Brown and Wes Thompson; Second Grips: Les Neal and Cowie (Charles Cowie?); Gaffer: Norton Kurland; Best Boy: Lester Burnette; First Prop Man: Harry Grundstrum; Assistant Prop Men: Burke (Ross Burke?), Barrett (Hoyle Barrett?), Murdock (Robert Murdock?), Martino (Solly Martino?) and Neel (Roy Neel?); Wardrobe Woman: Rosamonde Prior; Wardrobe Man: Roger J. Weinberg; Makeup: Frank Westmore, Bob Dawn, Perrell (Sidney Perell?), Hadley (Joe Hadley?) and Marcellino (Nick Marcellino?); Hair Stylists: Lillian Burkhart and Kirkpatrick (Sue Kirkpatrick?); Recorder: Donald Cunliffe; Mike Men: Jack Bolger and Strong; Mixer: Freericks; Cable Men: Frank Artman, Marks and Healey; Dialogue Director: Irvin Berwick; Coordinator: Ray Gockel; Lily Boy: Egan (William Egan?); Stand-ins: Sue Curtis, Joe Walls, Harold Lockwood and Otto Malde; Propmaker: Fred Knoth; **Unconfirmed:** Production Coordinator: Ellis Coleman; **Florida Crew:** Assistant Director: George Lollier; Unit Manager: James T. Vaughn; Script Clerk: Jack Herzberg; Assistant Cameraman: Walter Bluemel; Camera Crew Member: Clifford Poland; Still Photographer: Harry Walsh; Underwater Still Photographer: Bruce Mozert; Camera Mechanic: F. McConihay; First Grip: Fletcher; Makeup: Tom Case and Mark Reedall; Propmaker: Frank Brendel; First Aid Man: R.A. Guyer; Diving Trainer for Jack Betz and Stanley Crews: Fred Zendar; Safety Divers: Fred Zendar, Charles McNabb, Patsy Boyette, Robert Lee Tinney, Frank Den Bleyker; **Unconfirmed Florida Crew:** Underwater Cameraman: Bruce Mozert; **Inserts Crew:** Cameraman: Robinson (George Robinson?); Camera Operator: Coopersmith (William Coopersmith?); Assistant Cameraman: Wyckoff (Robert Wyckoff?); First Grip: Hawkins (Ben Hawkins?); Technician: Schwartz; Battery Man: McCathy; 79 minutes.

CAST: Richard Carlson (*Dr. David Reed*), Julia Adams [Julie Adams] (*Kay Lawrence*), Richard Denning (*Dr. Mark Williams*), Antonio Moreno (*Dr. Carl Maia*), Nestor Paiva (*Lucas*), Whit Bissell (*Dr. Edwin Thompson*), Bernie Gozier (*Zee*), Henry Escalante (*Chico*), **Uncredited:** Ben Chapman, Ricou Browning (*The Gill Man*), Al Wyatt (*The Gill Man on Fire*), Rodd Redwing (*Luis*), Julio Lopez [Perry Lopez] (*Tomas*), Sydney Mason (*Dr. Matos*), Stanley Crews (*Richard Carlson's Underwater Double*), Ginger Stanley (*Julie Adams' Swimming Double*), Helen Morgan, Polly Burson (*Julie Adams' Stunt Doubles*), Jack Betz, Frank Den Bleyker (*Richard Denning's Underwater Doubles*); **Unconfirmed:** Richard Cutting (*Narrator*); **In unused footage:** Cliff Lyons (*Richard Carlson's Stunt Double*), Allen Pinson (*Richard Denning's Stunt Double*).

*See Chapter Notes beginning on page 363.

Production History
By Tom Weaver

The idea for Universal's final blue-chip movie monster grew out of an after-dinner conversation that took place more than a decade before the beastie ever surfaced on theater screens. The year was 1940 and the place was the home of Orson Welles, the stage and radio wunderkind turned Hollywood picturemaker, then in the midst of crafting his movie masterpiece *Citizen Kane* (1941). Present at the gathering were Welles; his girlfriend, Mexican actress Dolores del Rio; Mexican cinematographer Gabriel Figueroa[2]; and 24-year-old William Alland, a member of Welles' renowned Mercury Theatre, now playing in *Kane* the small but pivotal part of the shadow-shrouded *News on the March* newsreel reporter Thompson. In 1995, Alland recalled for me:

> In idle conversation, Figueroa told the story about the fact that there is this creature that lives up in the Amazon who is half-man, half-fish. Once a year he comes up and claims a maiden, and after that, he leaves, and the village is then safe for *another* year. We just looked at him. He said, "You people think I'm joking, don't you?" and he then *insisted* that this was absolutely true, that he could produce *photos* and this and that…! He went on and on and on and on and we said, "Yeah, yeah, yeah, yeah…" [*laughs*], and we went on to other things. But he, for about five *minutes* there, held forth about how this was *not* a myth, that there really was such a creature, that the Amazonian people talked about him all the time, etc.

Possible? Well, who can say? Remember that there are more species of fish in the Amazon River (perhaps as many as 8000) than in the Atlantic Ocean … north *and* south.

Fast-forward to 1952, past Alland's war service as a combat pilot (56 South Pacific missions) and award-winning radio career, and we find his shingle hanging at Universal-International: associate-producing the Robert Louis Stevenson–based outdoor drama *The Treasure of Lost Canyon* (1952), providing the story for the prizefight yarn *Flesh and Fury* (1952), taking story *and* producing credits on director Raoul Walsh's Western *The Lawless Breed* (1953)—and first setting foot on terror turf with *The Black Castle* (1952). Forever trying to dream up new screen tales, his mind flashed back to the night of the Welles dinner party and Figueroa's strange account. With a few clever embellishments, he put it down on paper as

"THE SEA MONSTER"
A Story Idea
By
WILLIAM L. ALLAND

The date on this three-page document, October 2, 1952, goes down in horror film history as a red-letter day for the genre. This memo was the first step toward creating one of *the* touchstone monster movies of the decade—a horror adventure that begins with a team of fossil hunters deciding that they're gonna take a sedimental journey to the Amazon River's fabled Black Lagoon…

"The Sea Monster"

Alland's "Sea Monster" memo begins by describing the night of the Welles party. Figueroa's already tall tale reaches new heights in the retelling: Alland wrote that he had once had dinner with a South American movie director [*sic*] who revealed that, living underwater and on the banks of the Amazon River, there exists a race of beings that resemble humans in shape but have gills in place of ears; webbed hands and feet; and fishlike skin:

> [A] friend of my informant organized a small expedition and proceeded up the Amazon to find these creatures. He was never heard from again. However, many months later some natives found and brought back to civilization a camera which was identified as belonging to the explorer. There was some film in this camera and when developed—there it was, big as life, a seven-foot creature with gills, webbed hands and feet, and a scaly skin. My informant swore he has been shown this photograph and promised me that some day he would send me a print.

Alland went on to write that he complimented the storyteller on his "fine imagination" and yet continued to wonder if such creatures could actually exist. At this point in the memo, he proposes a film called *The Sea Monster*, which would open with a scene of just such an after-dinner conversation and one character regaling his listeners with the story of the Amazon fish-men. Another expedition ("with

Makeup lab technician Jack Kevan and the Pollywog prototype. Producer William Alland never lost faith in his idea that Black Lagoon *should have featured a much more human-looking man-fish, and told me, "We'll never know whether 'my' version would have become a classic, as [the on-screen Gill Man] did."*

a beautiful girl along, of course") sets out in a small boat, their arrival in the fish-men's Amazon waters watched by "a strange pair of eyes glistening under water." The beautiful blonde sees the eyes ("filled with lust and desire") and screams. Shots are fired but nothing is found.

The scientist of the expedition turns heavy, sends the blonde's boyfriend off on a wild goose chase, then "overpowers the girl, chloroforms her, ties her, semi-nude, onto a raft, [and] sets a snare-trap around the raft...." As he watches, the webbed hand of the monster reaches up and drags the unconscious girl into the water. From here, Alland suggested two possible story directions: (1) The boyfriend succeeds in rescuing her, and the monster is killed, or (2) the monster is captured and brought to a small South American seaport, but it escapes and terrorizes the area. "Needless to say," Alland concludes, "the monster's end is brought about by his desire for the blonde-haired girl of the expedition."

The second proposed ending instantly calls to mind

King Kong (1933), and in fact makes any worth-his-salt Monster Kid realize that "The Sea Monster"'s *whole plot* is lifted from *Kong*. When I asked the always forthright Alland about the similarities, he made no effort to deny it: "Absolutely! As a matter of fact, [reusing *Kong*'s basic plot] was the whole idea. Oh, sure, that was my idea!" he laughed. (*Kong*, it should be mentioned, didn't have the most original plot in the world either, being itself a close echo of the 1925 movie version of Sir Arthur Conan Doyle's novel *The Lost World*.) Surely not coincidentally, RKO's summer-of-'52 theatrical reissue of *King Kong* had just been a big success, racking up gross profits of $2,500,000.

The job of turning Alland's idea into a treatment went to 43-year-old Maurice Zimm, a longtime writer but a newcomer to the movies. A native of Waterloo, Iowa, the son of an Austrian-Jewish foundry laborer-cum-broom salesman, Zimm (real name: Maurice Zimring) had moved to Los Angeles in the 1930s, adopted the pseudonym Maurice Zimm and written mystery and suspense stories for radio. MGM bought and adapted one of his radio plays into *Jeopardy* (1953), a suspenser about a woman (Barbara Stanwyck) trying to find help for her husband (Barry Sullivan) whose foot is caught underwater just off a deserted Mexican beach, before the tide rises. Zimm's submission *Black Lagoon,* dated November 8, 1952, was his first written-for-the-movies story to reach the screen. It was followed by MGM's Biblical spectacle *The Prodigal* (1955) and a few others, plus many TV credits.[3]

Black Lagoon
(treatment by Maurice Zimm)

A winch cable lowers a bathysphere from a trawler into whitecapped ocean waters, a TV camera covering the activity. An on-camera announcer says into his hand-mike that famed undersea explorer Dr. Lyman Reed has reached a depth of 4000 feet—well on his way to establishing a one-mile record for underwater descent. Kay Lawrence, a headstrong blonde heiress, reaches Reed via radio and warns the man she loves that the seas are getting too rough, and that she's about to order that the bathysphere be brought back up. Over a speaker comes Reed's retort: "*I* give the orders, Kay. And if you even try, this will be the last time I ever let you talk me into bringing you along." Another sudden lurch of the ship cuts off communication and prompts Reed's assistant Donovan to order that the winch be reversed. The crane hoists the bathysphere back aboard the trawler and a groggy, shaken Reed emerges. He's thankful to have been rescued and vows that tomorrow he'll make another attempt at breaking the record.

That night, in the trawler's main cabin, Reed explains to Kay the reason for his recent, reckless behavior: He needs to break the record in order to get money from the TV network, and from product endorsements, in order to finance a South American expedition. From his coat pocket he produces a letter from his explorer-friend Carl Sloan, but before he reveals its contents he tells her that "there are fish that walk, fish that climb, fish that drown," and reminds her of her own amateur-ichthyologist father's statement, "There are stranger things beneath the water than man has ever dreamt of." With the stage ominously set, Reed explains that Sloan recently organized an Amazon River expedition, and that near the junction of Colombia, Brazil and Peru they "stumbled upon something. Something which bore out, backed up, *proved* a ... native legend.... The

(above) Ricou Browning submits to having a mold of his face and shoulders made by Jack Kevan (right) and an assistant (love the surgeon-white gowns). Molds were made of all parts of the bodies of Browning and Ben Chapman, the movie's Creatures; the molds were then used to create plaster replicas, and Creature body parts were sculpted on those replicas. The result: Gill Man suits that fit like a second skin.

(right) After the plaster set, the mold was split and removed from Ricou Browning's body. To keep his hair from being pulled, he wore a skullcap (according to Bob Burns). Browning's memory is that Jack Kevan (left) "put a gel of some sort" in his hair.

legend is … this. That there exists today in the Amazon a species which Sloan has named 'Pisces Man.' … Like the human race. Except for such things as gills." Reed needs $64,000 to organize an expedition to come to Sloan's aid with special equipment that will enable them to capture a specimen. Kay offers to foot the bill but Reed refuses with a smile. Later, out on the deck, she uses a chisel to damage the portable generator that powers the bathysphere equipment. Reed, arriving too late to stop her, groans, "You wrecked the Field Coils."

"Which means, Lyman, that you'll have to take my money—for the Expedition."

Kay, "looking like a couturiere's daydream," arrives at the office of her estate handler Miles Faraday, a "fat, fussy old bachelor [who] feels very fatherly toward her." Her request for a $64,000 check to finance the expedition outrages Faraday, and he offers to write the check on the condition that she stay behind, but she wraps him around her finger. Faraday later phones Ted Clayton, a Lawrence Oil Company oil field superintendent in Venezuela; the broad-shouldered Clayton sports a day's stubble on his bronzed chin, "rolls his own" and is the troubleshooter the company sends to one forsaken part of the globe after another. At first he balks at Faraday's request to infiltrate the Reed expedition in order to keep an eye on Kay ("I'm not playin' nursemaid to any skirt—especially a harebrained heiress!"), but the promise of a substantial bonus changes the he-man's mind.

Clayton makes his way to the docks of the South American town of Leticia and locates the *Pongo*, the battered sternwheeler chartered by the Reed expedition. In the pilot house he encounters a barefoot man wearing a greasy T-shirt and greasier dungarees, an unruly mop of hair shielding his unwashed forehead. He is Tasha, the Mittel European captain of what he calls the "old wessel." (Part of the character description: "His 'V's always give him trouble. So do most of the other consonants.") Clayton offers his services as mate (or engineer or steward), but Tasha has one man, Joe, filling all those positions. (Tasha: "This way I balance my budget—sometimes.") Behind Tasha's back, Clayton bribes Joe to quit without notice.

At the Leticia airfield, Tasha and his new mate-engineer-steward Clayton meet the just-arrived Reed, Kay, Kay's secretary Winifred "Winnie" Adams ("considerably past the bloom of youth") and Donovan. Tasha assumes the two women are the men's wives until Reed corrects him; "Ah-ha!" Tasha says, glancing meaningfully at Ted. "Not even wives! Ho-ho!" Later, on the *Pongo*, Clayton warns Kay against going for a swim, telling her that piranha may be in the water, but she ignores him and dives in. Later, as she climbs back aboard, Clayton uses a knife to cut a few strips from a hunk of blood-red beef and lets them fall overboard; almost instantly, the water begins to churn. "If you'd have had as much as a scratch, that would have happened to you. Blood will always bring them if they're anywhere around. Even one drop of blood," he tells the now white-faced girl.

That night, a cadaverous-looking man in torn clothes, toting a canvas-wrapped package, shuffles weakly up the *Pongo* gangplank and demands to see Reed. Clayton escorts the sinister-looking stranger to the salon, where Reed instantly recognizes him as Carl Sloan. Sloan says that the other two members of his expedition are dead; they'd tried to capture the Pisces Man alive, without traps and nets. Sloan grows angry when he thinks he sees mockery in Clayton's eyes: "You wouldn't be so smug and superior if you'd seen those bodies lying there, crushed to a pulp, on the banks of the Black Lagoon." Muttering "Proof! Proof!," the half-mad scientist opens the package, revealing the petrified forearm and webbed, taloned hand of a monster, unearthed by his men before they died. "And now there's only one specimen left. One. A male," says Sloan. Kay appears in the salon doorway, wearing a robe and slippers, her silken hair falling voluptuously to her shoulders. When Sloan sees her, his eyes become sly and crafty ("*You're … going along on the Expedition?*").

Soon the *Pongo* is en route to the Black Lagoon; Clayton, in the pilot house steering the boat, still can't bring himself to accept the existence of a Pisces Man, and becomes annoyed when Donovan declares himself a believer: "Look, Mister, this is the Twentieth Century!"

"The Twentieth Century of the modern calendar," Donovan reminds him. "But how many centuries were there before the birth of Christ?"

Meanwhile, in the galley, comedy relief is rearing its ugly head as Tasha tastes from a pot of soup, then pours half of a good-sized salt cellar and nearly an entire pepper-shaker into the cauldron. Luis, the ship's combination stoker and chef, looks on in disbelief. Winnie storms in, saying that she is now in charge of the cooking. When Tasha objects, she stomps on one of his bare feet; he backs away, howling in pain. When we return to the galley a scene or two later, it's spic and span (Winnie made Luis scrub it), and a now surprisingly clean-looking Tasha is on his best behavior with her. Tasha: "I only come to ask … maybe you know how to make a kugel? … For a taste of kugel, I would be wery … grateful." (Scene description: "No man has ever talked to her like this before, looked at her like this before. She drops her eyes.")

The *Pongo* arrives at its destination, a point five miles from the Black Lagoon. In a series of trips aboard an outboard motor–powered dugout canoe, Reed, Sloan and Donovan bring traps and special nets of spun steel to the Lagoon via an Igarape (water trail), "so narrow that the trees

1. Creature from the Black Lagoon (1954)

on its banks almost meet overhead…. The atmosphere here is eerie and forbidding, and the wildly overrun banks rise so sharply that sounds bounce back in a haunting echo." After a week of nothing but empty nets and traps, Reed is becoming frustrated. One day he is convinced to let Kay accompany them to the Lagoon. Determined to get her man (Reed), she is at her most enticing as she sits in the bow of the canoe, "her stunning figure arrayed in an abbreviated sunsuit." A pair of human-and-yet-not-human eyes peer at her from below the surface of the water but only Sloan notices them, holding his breath as "the demon-eyes" draw closer. "Let's start back," Reed says suddenly, and the eyes disappear into the depths. During their next trip to the Lagoon, a webbed hand silently breaks the surface and reaches for Kay, but it disappears when Clayton shouts a warning cry from the bank. The fact that Clayton surreptitiously followed them makes him a suspicious character to the others.

For the next two weeks, Sloan haunts the lagoon watching for some further sign of the Pisces Man. Romance blooms as Tasha (who has exhumed an old uniform from mothballs) is served kugel by an increasingly giggly and girlish Winnie. Reed, sick with fever, wonders if Kay can not only overlook the difference in their ages but also the fact that his first love will always be science. Consumed by his hatred for Clayton, Sloan throws a spear from ambush, knocking him into the water. He's saved from the piranha by Tasha and Donovan.

Ricou Browning watches as makeup department majordomo Bud Westmore fiddles with the life-cast plaster bust of Browning's head; the makeup department's Chris Mueller, Jr., will sculpt the Creature head on it. On the left, notice on the table a Pollywog maquette and, in front of it, a Creature prototype that looks almost like the *20 Million Miles to Earth* Ymir, complete with tail.

The next day, Sloan asks a hesitant Kay to accompany him to the Lagoon. There he chloroforms her, places her on a raft, and conceals himself in the branches of an overhanging tree. When the Pisces Man climbs onto the raft and caresses her blonde hair, Sloan drops a net over him and jumps down. The monster tears the net apart like it was gossamer thread and then crushes Sloan to death. Clayton arrives to see the Pisces Man drop into the water with Kay in his arms. He swims after them, to the floor of the Lagoon ("like an underwater fairyland") and then into a tunnel which leads up into a grotto "as enchanting as a child's dream. It's bathed in the soft glow of luminous, multi-colored rocks which decorate the walls in designs reminiscent of the first artistic strivings of the human race. The floor of the grotto is cushioned with exotic flowers and plants, and at the far end is a shadowy recess in which can be seen decorated mounds resembling graves."

The Gill Man places Kay on the "floral carpet" and then backs into the shadows, his gaze still fixed on her. When she wakes and is startled by the sight of the Gill Man, he approaches slowly, making a crooning sound that is almost human, a look of pleading in his eyes. Clayton attacks the Gill Man with a machete, but the creature knocks it from his hand and the fight is on. Clayton applies a headlock, closing off the creature's gills until he drops unconscious.

Kay and Clayton flee, bringing the news of the Pisces Man's grotto lair to Reed, who immediately begins to lay plans to capture him. Kay's pleas to leave the Pisces Man in peace ("The last of an ancient species that in so many ways became … so human!") falls on deaf ears. Under Reed's supervision, the grotto's underwater tunnel entrance is dynamited, forcing a weakened, gasping-for-air Pisces Man to crawl to a surface entrance, struggling to get to the life-giving water. Instead he is seized by the men and placed in an enormous water-filled tank on the *Pongo* afterdeck.

On the third night of the voyage back to Leticia, Kay is drawn to the prison-tank and looks in at the Pisces Man, whose eyes are "so human, so tortured, so pleading…. Why should they affect her so? What had come over her that day in the grotto beneath the Black Lagoon?" Reed ignores her suggestion that they allow the Pisces Man to return to his grotto and the graves of his ancestors.

Crowds swarm on the Leticia docks trying to get a look at the creature; to Kay, it's all as "tawdry and revolting" as a freak sideshow. That night, in the airfield hangar where a cargo carrier (with the tank aboard) are stored, she again looks in at the Pisces Man, whose eyes seem to say, "It's now or never … now or never." Making up her mind, she unbolts the tank door and stands unafraid as the grateful creature gently touches her as he leaves the plane. Reed sees the Pisces Man entering the jungle and begins shouting orders that he be recaptured. At military headquarters, Col. Harbus mobilizes the entire male population and organizes lines of defense throughout the eight miles of jungle between the airfield and the river. The colonel is visiting the second line of defense when a sentry is strangled by the passin'-through Pisces Man. Later, on a shadowy Leticia side street, the Pisces Man realizes that the soldiers conducting a house-by-house search are getting too close:

> The eyes of the hunted creature dart frantically in every direction. Can this be the end? How many hundreds of millions of years have led to this moment? The death of a species. For in his very bearing, the last of the Gill Men makes it evident that he'll never let himself be taken back to his prison-tank alive…

The Pisces Man climbs through the unlocked window of a house into the barren room of a sleeping blonde child ("Just such a child as Kay might have"); he hides behind the door as soldiers search the room and somehow miss him. On his way out, the Pisces Man smoothes the coverlet over the child.

Wielding a rifle, the obsessed Reed is waiting on the Amazon shore as the Pisces Man, weak after four hours on land, staggers out of the jungle. Reed realizes that no one is close enough to stop him from getting to the water and begins firing. Riddled with bullets, the Pisces Man crawls into the water, which begins to churn as piranha converge. Clayton must prevent the frenzied Reed from jumping into the river after him.

The next morning, Kay is seated aboard the cargo carrier, waving out the window at Tasha ("He looks like he'd just stepped out of a Mail Order Catalog, his civilian wardrobe is so completely and uncomfortably new") and Winnie (who now sports a ring on her third finger, left hand). Kay turns to Reed, seated beside her, and he promises that what happened last night won't stand between them. But she knows it will. And when she sees Clayton boarding a passenger plane across the field, she bolts from her seat and runs to him.

Among the writing contributors to *Black Lagoon* (Alland, Arthur Ross, Harry Essex), Zimm has always received short shrift in the fan press. And, judging from his 72-page treatment, perhaps deservedly so! If filmed, his would been a very different type of movie from the monster-rific, kiddie-thrill-packed *Creature from the Black Lagoon*; Zimm's treatment is as much about the Reed-Kay-Clayton triangle (with the comic-relief Tasha-Winnie romance thrown in) as the sea monster. Not until page 49 are we given our first partial glimpse at the Pisces Man (his "demon-eyes," underwater); on page 50 we get to see his hand, and finally on

1. *Creature from the Black Lagoon* (1954)   19

Pollywog on Parade: Accompanied by Bud Westmore (trailing the pack), Julie Adams et al., Ricou Browning is on his way to Universal's Underwater Tank to try out his monster suit.

Zimm's treatment gave Alland the aquatic variant on *King Kong* he wanted: Dr. Reed, a Carl Denham–like adventurer and publicity hound, organizes a shipboard expedition to search unexplored territory for a prehistoric monster, and allows a beautiful blonde to accompany them. The girl is abducted by a heavy and delivered into the clutches of the monster, but rescued by the virile male lead. Later, the monster itself is captured and brought to civilization, but manages to escape. Even *Kong*'s "Beauty and the Beast" angles are intact, with Zimm overdoing it almost shamelessly, as in the scene where the Pisces Man adjusts the blanket of the sleeping child. (Zimm alternates between "The Pisces Man" and "The Gill Man" as the name of the monster.)

In the entire Zimm treatment, the Pisces Man only kills two people (Sloan in the lagoon and a sentry in Leticia—the latter "off-camera"), even though there are extraneous, ripe-for-the-plucking characters (Tasha, Donovan, Luis) galore. In the movie, the Gill Man has taken two lives by the 11-minute mark and then proceeds to nearly triple the gore score.

When the writing of this book was in the homestretch, co-author Steve Kronenberg purchased an original copy of this treatment from a Baltimore rare-books dealer. On page eight, the Pisces Man is first mentioned in dialogue … and on the back of that page is a pencil drawing. Presumably it's somebody's best shot at drawing what he or she thought the creature should look like. But who was the "artist"? Zimm? Alland? Yes, probably one or the other, most likely Alland. Then again, it also could have been

page 54 (exactly the three-quarters mark) he climbs onto the raft and we see him for the first time.[4] Although violent when provoked, Zimm's Pisces Man is in his own way civilized and, with Kay, almost courtly. Zimm mentions his scalloped gills which at a distance "resemble the bobbed hair of a knight of old"; if he'd looked like that in the movie, it might have added to the subliminal impression that this horror hails from the royal family of movie monsters. In short, Zimm's descriptions and depiction of the Pisces Man make him seem more human than monster. And this appears to be exactly the type of "monster" that Zimm's boss Alland wanted. Alland told me,

> I had an idea of how this creature should look—I wanted him to look much more human. I had a marvelous sculptor create [a small statue of] a very sad, beautiful monster—in fact, it *wasn't* a monster, it was far more "attractive," more "romantic-looking" than the beast we ended up with. While it had fish lips and this, that and the other, *my* creature was all done as a sort of an aquatic development of a *man*. And I was so pleased with it! It would still frighten you, but it would frighten you because of how human it was, not the other way around.[5]

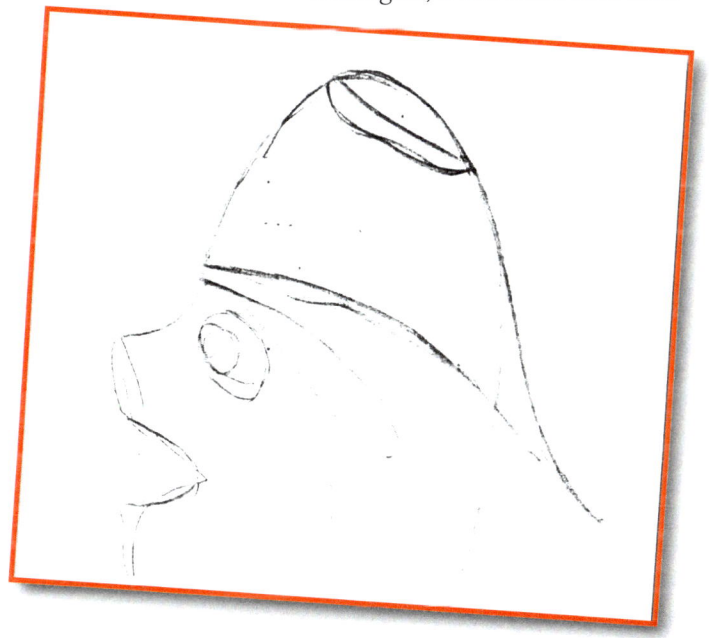

A crude pencil sketch found on the back of a page of William Alland's copy of Maurice Zimm's November 8, 1952, Black Lagoon treatment.

drawn in 2006 by ten-year-old Rufus T. Fishtwanger IV, who hypothetically could have read and doodled on this copy when it hypothetically passed through the hands of his dad, hypothetical Creature connoisseur Rufus T. Fishtwanger III. We'll never know.

The Zimm treatment was analyzed "in-house" and critiqued in a one-page December 11 memo. (It's not signed but I've got a feeling the memo writer was Ernest Nims, Universal's editorial department head.) "This treatment seems to hold promise of becoming an excellent horror-suspense film," the memo writer began. "The handling of the monster and his surroundings is first-rate." Then came the Howevers, beginning with the fact that the stage-setting goes on too long, that the leading man is not introduced "until considerably too late," and that there's just too much of Tasha and Winnie. Additionally:

> I question the value of having Reed parallel the insanity of Carl in his effort to obtain the monster and return same to civilization. Would suggest that he play it somewhat more straight-line and let his avarice and compelling personal desires be the motivation for his insistence that he take the monster back with him.
>
> I would like to suggest that a brief scene be inserted in which the monster, apparently capable of some reasoning power, as indicated by his relationship with the girl, hates Reed because he senses him as a nemesis. Then, too, this would personalize some of the relationships and would also make it possible to pay off his hatred for Reed near the end of the story, which I think would greatly strengthen the impact of the ending of the story. It is apparent the monster does not necessarily have a lust to kill everyone he meets, but has a rather human-like hatred or love for those he meets.

The writer closes by saying that he discussed his ideas with Alland, who was in "general agreement" about them. He continues, "[Alland] further indicated that he would change the ending to provide a means of possibly continuing this into sequels by keeping the monster alive, or at least leaving his fate in doubt at the end of the picture. I believe this should be done." It's interesting to learn that, right from *Creature from the Black Lagoon*'s earliest stages, Alland could see far enough ahead to sense that his fantastic man-fish might deserve its own Dracula-Frankenstein-Mummy (etc.)–type *series*.

Alland and director Jack Arnold spent part of the next ten months making the 3-D *It Came from Outer Space*, adapted by writer Harry Essex from treatments by Ray Bradbury. During that time, tinkering continued on the *Black Lagoon* script. In that era of six-day work weeks, Zimm, a $250-a-week writer, labored over his treatment from October 23 to December 2, 1952, earning $1,458. Leo Lieberman, whose

"Made it, Ma! Top of the world!" Ricou Browning, wearing the Pollywog head, hands and feet, waves down from the top of the tank.

weekly paycheck was $50 fatter than Zimm's, worked over the course of the following two months. Lieberman was also something of a newcomer to the movies, his one pre–*Black Lagoon* screenplay credit being the inane comedy-fantasy *Bonzo Goes to College* (1952). Arthur Ross ($500 a week) left his mark between March 2 and April 30, 1953; his second-draft screenplay, dated March 19, is a veritable "Missing Link" script, partially spanning the gap between the Zimm treatment and the final Harry Essex screenplay in *Creature*'s "evolution." According to Ross, he had already written the Western *The Stand at Apache River* (1953) for Alland when the producer came to him claiming to be "in terrible trouble" with *Black Lagoon*. Ross told me,

> [Alland] had a draft, and it was just impossible—the front office turned it down, they weren't gonna do the picture. Bill said, "Would you look at it?" and I said, "Let me read it and see." At that same time, I had just finished reading Jacques Cousteau's *The Silent World*, his first really big important book, and it occurred to me that what was wrong

1. Creature from the Black Lagoon (1954)

with [the script] was that it was an imitation of films that had been made in that genre at Universal for 25 years. The only difference was that it was an underwater creature instead of a mummy or Frankenstein or Dracula. I said, "Bill, you've got a mad scientist in your story, and that's passé.... It seems to me that what should be at work here is the fact that it is a scientist curious about the forces of nature, and how nature evolves, and nature's relationship to Man. What he is trying to demonstrate is that nature can be *examined*, but it cannot be *troubled*, it cannot be *dislocated*. The more you attack what is natural in the world, the more likely it will do something to protect itself." That, I thought, should be the essential viewpoint: the scientist warning others not to make a freak out of the Creature. The conflict was that, when they *did*, the Creature became something dangerous to all of them.

... *The Silent World* gave me the most *profound* idea for *Creature*, the idea that the scientist is the hero, not the villain. The scientist is a humanist who *inquires* of nature rather than dictating to it or exploiting it. He's the one who holds out for not harming the Creature.

... [Alland] was very nice, and he understood what I was trying to do. He knew that the first approach had failed terribly, the old-fashioned script that he had. Universal had a history of that kind of story—Frankenstein attacks, the Mummy attacks, the *dummy* attacks [*laughs*], any number of things like that, and there was always a mad scientist doing something crazy that provoked it. But I said, "No, we're living in another era, we're living in another time." That was the giant step that I took, and it made *Creature* something quite different.

Black Lagoon
(second-draft screenplay by Arthur Ross)

This screenplay is a lot closer to the eventual movie than the Zimm treatment, but I'm not in a position to credit all (or *any*) of the changes to Ross, since Leo Lieberman worked on the project for two months during the interim between Zimm and Ross, and I don't know what Lieberman's contributions were.[6] According to Ross, quoted above, he changed the tenor of the whole script, but until and unless Lieberman's work comes to light, we're taking Ross' word for that.[7] Another elusive item is Ross' earlier (April 17) stab at an acceptable screenplay. An original copy which once belonged to Alland was (probably still *is*) available from a rare-books dealer, as part of a package with some other *Black Lagoon*–related items, for an asking price of *$11,500*. BAH-BAH-BAHHH!

That 108-page April 17, 1953, screenplay was the basis for budgets compiled by Universal's Estimating Department on May 20, when the studio decisionmakers were still up in the air whether the movie would be color or black-and-white, 2-D or 3-D. Amidst a lot of ifs, ands and buts, the bottom line was that a black-and-white 2-D would have total allocation of $600,000, an Eastman Color 2-D $675,000, a black-and-white 3-D $650,000 and an Eastman Color 3-D $750,000.

According to the May 28, 1953, memo headlined "Meeting and Review of Producer's Picture Assignments," a verdict had been reached:

Bob Burns doesn't know who sculpted the Pollywog head but thinks Jack Kevan ("He was a fine sculptor") would be a safe guess. Wouldn't ya just love to see test shots of Ben Chapman wearing his version of this get-up?

> It was decided that this picture [*Black Lagoon*] would be done in color (Eastman) and 3-D with an allocation of $650,000 (total cost).
>
> The present story was discussed and the general outline for some story changes was agreed upon, and also the different and modified Gill Man will be incorporated in the revised script. [Universal executive William] Goetz's suggestion of shooting the underwater scenes in black and white, with subsequent printing with Technicolor blue tint process, was considered as extremely satisfactory and will be adopted, thereby effecting an appreciable saving in operating cost.

Needless to say, this "verdict" (shooting in color) would soon be overturned.

We now return you to your regularly scheduled script

nd-draft screenplay opens with a "bright, scene of a speedboat roaring across the s of a Southern California cove and stopping beside the empty motorboat of David Reed, a Pacific Institute of Marine Life ichthyologist who, clad in the gear of the lung-diver, is working 40 feet below. The speedboat driver is Kay Lawrence, a lovely young woman who gives the impression of "great assurity ... especially with men," and her passenger is Reed's colleague Edwin Hempstead. Summoned to the surface, Reed is introduced to Kay; a daughter of privilege, she is proposing to make a $50,000 endowment to the Institute. (This is the only version of the script I've found where the male and female leads are initially strangers to each other.) In long-standing movie tradition, they "meet cute," Kay impressed by what she sees ("I didn't expect a guard on the varsity water polo team") but also doing a bit of needling that leads to some verbal sparring. This sets the tone for most of their exchanges throughout the story. (Truth be told, their talking-in-circles, "point-counterpoint-*counter*counterpoint" conversations, all quite lengthy, are deadly reading.)

At the Institute,[8] Reed talks about the Brazilian trip that Kay's money will finance. He and fellow scientists intend to study a particular specie of lungfish, and many other fish, to learn how life evolved; "Then maybe we can help man adapt to *new* worlds [other planets]—without waiting twenty million years." Kay, who paints, plans to tag along: "New sights—new ideas," she shrugs.

On a wharf in Manaus, Brazil, we meet two more expedition members, zoologist Dr. Sansoni and geologist Dr. Mark, as well as the slovenly, slow-moving Tasha, captain of the *Pongo* (still a weather-beaten sternwheeler). Accompanying the group is Kurt Dreier, a hunter who will take them to the native Indian village where they can examine a pointy-headed skeleton that recently washed up from the river. Characters talk about the Amazon and its animals, with Dr. Mark pointing out that the area is "less than primitive. Geologically, we call this a half-formed land. It belongs more to the Devonian era of 150,000,000 years ago than it does to the present day." At the village, the skeleton lives up to the hype; the script describes it as "a large skeletal form of the torso, neck and head of an animal. Except for the large size, the rib-cage and spinal column and pelvis bone look almost human. The head, however, is like the skull of [a] prehistoric thing. It is tapered, has a mouth more like a beak." More mammal than fish, it resembles a pirarucu and, according to Sansoni, "It could stand at over eight feet tall."

The first sign of trouble comes when a net is dropped off of the moving *Pongo* to drag the river, and it catches something that puts up a fight that damages the boat. Hauled up, the net now has a gaping hole in it. (Reed: "It would take a pair of hands to do that—powerful hands.") The *Pongo* pulls into a lagoon so that repairs can be made. That night, standing at the railing, Reed and Kay discuss Dreier, who in movie fashion is constantly living up to his German name with talk of the survival of the fittest and the mindset of kill-or-be-killed.

KAY: Nothing will ever change Dreier—will it?
REED: Unless something stronger than he is beats him—or kills him.

As they continue to talk, we vaguely discern underwater the face of a fish looking up; when it moves closer to the surface, the outline of the Gill Man's face is seen. Kay spots it and throws herself into Reed's arms. Reed is leaning out over the side, trying to get a look, when "with a terrible churning of water," the amphibian rears out of the water and knocks the burning lantern from his hand. The script specifies, "The Gill Man's leap into the scene and descent out of it should be so rapid that his general features should not be clearly discernable." It's hard to mentally envision this scene and *not* be reminded of *Jaws*' (1975) startling shot of the great white shark breaking the water's surface behind Chief Brody ("Come on down and chum some of *this* shit!").

The next day, Reed and Dreier don aqualungs and descend in search of the humanoid. In the dark water, they dimly spot the monster and Reed takes pictures, the camera flashes giving them split-second glimpses of him. Dreier fires his harpoon gun, and gets the Gill Man in the side, before Reed yanks the weapon from his hands. Later, below decks on the *Pongo*, Reed puts the negative of one of his photos in a slide projector and shines the image on a white wall: "[There,] in clear sight, is the Gill Man. The structure, his webbed feet, his head, the gills, the webbed hands—all clear and sharp." (This seems like an un-dramatic way for audiences to get their first good look at the monster.)

Rotenone, a drug that paralyzes fish, is put into the lagoon in an effort to catch the amphibian man. Finally he emerges from the water near the shore and disappears into the jungle growth. Carrying heavy nets, some of the men chase after him into a densely overgrown area, and are soon reacting as though they were the hunted and not the hunters. The Gill Man fights and mangles a jaguar and then runs like a trapped animal, "throwing aside trees." When he reappears on the shore, he stumbles after a hysterical Kay before collapsing. When the men appear out of the jungle, Reed has to hit Dreier to stop him from shooting the Gill Man.

The Gill Man is loaded into a steel tank on the *Pongo* stern. That night, looking at him through a viewing porthole, Kay observes, "It seems to look at us with a kind of sullen accusation because it's imprisoned." Reed and Kay talk, the latter beating herself up over a failed marriage, and then they have their first kiss. Suddenly the Gill Man pushes the tank apart and, grabbing one of Tasha's native boat hands, raises him over his head and fatally smashes him to the deck. He then dives into the lagoon.

The expedition members' planned getaway lasts only as long as it takes them to get to the entrance to the lagoon, which is now blocked by a log barricade below the surface.

> KAY: This was built by "*him*"—wasn't it?
> REED: Seems the only explanation.
> KAY: He's smarter than we thought…
> REED: … A lot…

Again putting on their diving gear, Reed and Dreier make a series of attempts to fasten a winch chain to the logs, so that the *Pongo* can pull them away, but the Gill Man thwarts them time and again. On the next attempt, Reed can't stop Dreier from chasing after the Gill Man. Reed quickly returns to the boat to get a harpoon gun, but Kay talks him out of going back into the water ("You're trying to get Dreier out in the same stupid way he got into this!"). Realizing that she's right, Reed merely stands on the deck looking out at the water while, below, Dreier and the Gill Man play a sub-aquatic cat-and-mouse game. It ends when they go *mano a claw-o*, the Gill Man tearing out Dreier's air hose and mouthpiece and continuing to hold him while he drowns.

With escape uppermost in everybody's minds, Reed decides that they must force the Gill Man aboard the *Pongo* in order to kill him. Rotenone is mixed with water, and then with radium compound, and put in an air tank so that it can be fired under pressure; armed with this unusual weapon, Reed again descends into the deeps. More sub-aquatic encounters with the Gill Man ensue, with Reed warding him off with the luminous rotenone. The Gill Man finally retreats onto the shore but that night climbs silently and undetected onto the *Pongo*. Sansoni wanders into his clutches and is grabbed, lifted overhead "like a sack of meal" and lethally thrown down onto the deck. There's now some round-and-round-the-deck hide-and-seek–style suspense but eventually "the numbers game" catches up to the Gill Man as our heroes come at him from all directions: Tasha and Mark put many bullets into him, and Reed shoots a harpoon at him. Finally, as the badly wounded, faltering monster is closing in on Mark, Reed comes up behind him with a fire axe and delivers a fatal blow:

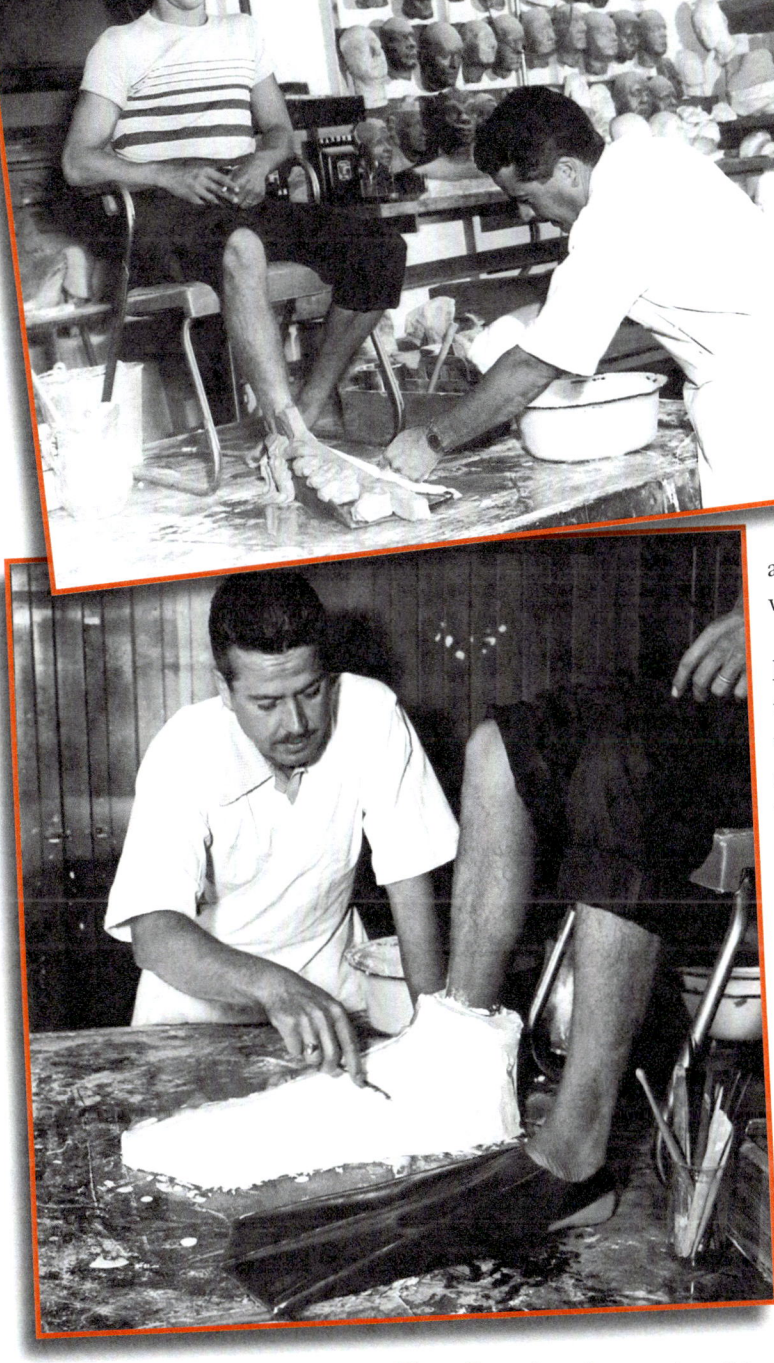

Ricou Browning sits wearing diving flippers as Jack Kevan, covering them with plaster, begins the task of creating Creature feet.

The axe, protruding from the neck of the Gill Man, apparently embedded there, cutting the spinal cord. As the Gill Man falls, the axe is pulled from Reed's grasp.

The last scene is set on the foredeck of the *Pongo* as it makes its way back to civilization. Reed says he wishes they could have taken the Gill Man alive and blames Dreier for all that happened; Kay keeps telling him it isn't nice to talk about Dreier like that but Reed still badmouths him, calling him "as much a dead end of nature as the animal he fought." He finally changes the subject, mentioning how "very affectionate" Kay has gotten a few times over the last 24 hours, and the movie fades out as he takes her in his arms and kisses her.

This script is a step in the right direction but, if I may act as the unelected spokesgeek for Creature fans, still not what the ichthyologist ordered. First and foremost, the Beauty and the Beast touches, introduced on Day One in Alland's "The Sea Monster," have all gone missing: In their brief encounters, the Gill Man doesn't react to Kay any differently than he does to any of the men—or, for that matter, to the jaguar! And aside from Kay's comment that the Gill Man, imprisoned inside the *Pongo*'s steel tank, wears an accusing look, she obviously regards him as nothing more than a monster and an object of terror. Without the Beauty and the Beast angle, the story might as well be about an expedition or safari encountering any powerful *real-life* wild animal.

Discussing the movie with me, Ross said that Alland

> wanted to put in *more* of the woman. Here comes this big Creature with his cock four feet long, he's going to fuck her, and she gets away just in time—but she *does* think about him [*laughs*]! … I had done as much [Beauty and the Beast] as I thought it was correct to do, because essentially that wasn't the story. The fact that the Creature was attracted to the woman was not the reason he fought back.… But Bill wanted more of the *King Kong* element in *Creature*, so [Harry Essex came in]. Really, all he did was add more of the girl. Underwater shots, the Creature sees her, the Creature gets an erection [*laughs*].… I rather felt that the nature of the Creature's relationship to the woman in the picture was quite simplistic.

(Two years later, when Ross soloed as screenwriter of *The Creature Walks Among Us*, there wasn't an iota of Beauty and the Beast to be found in his finished script.)

Not only doesn't this Ross script give us the Creature we expect, we don't even get much of a Black Lagoon: Damaged by the caught-in-the-net Gill Man, the *Pongo* limps into the first lagoon it subsequently comes to. The place is not described as attractive or mysterious or in *any* way unusual, there's no legend about it, there's no indication that the amphibious man *comes* from there (or has ever even *been* there before), and it's never once *called* the Black Lagoon. In this script, it's just the place where the *Pongo* happens to make an unscheduled pit stop, and the Gill Man follows them there.

Absent, too, is the Kay of the movie-to-come. Once the Gill Man turns up in this draft, *this* Kay becomes a bundle of nerves, alternating from a frightened and defeatist attitude ("I knew something would go wrong … I knew it wouldn't work" regarding the attempt to capture the monster with rotenone) to complete hysteria. Kay's fear of the Gill Man is so strong and so sustained, she becomes pitiable. Monster movie fans might have to go back as far as *King Kong* to find a quote-unquote heroine with a more powerless, panic-stricken outlook. (And to make things worse, Kay is also a basket case on the subject of her past marriage, getting stressed and flagellating herself whenever the subject arises.) Reed is more of a hero than Kay is a heroine, so it comes as a surprise that while Dreier is underwater fighting the Gill Man, Reed (aboard the *Pongo*) allows Kay to talk him out of going down with a harpoon gun to help. It's certainly "lifelike" that Reed is made aware that he can opt *out* of risking his life to save Dreier, who's only in danger because he's a kill-crazy "idiot" (Reed's word) who *put* himself in that position; but it's certainly not "movie-like" for a

The foam rubber feet are put in an oven for baking. A contemporary Collier's *article on the U-I "monster mill" (its makeup department) called the place "the cauldron in which most of today's horror creatures are brewed … with death masks lining its shelves, a huge black oven for baking monstrous beings and a few partially decomposed ogres hanging from the walls."*

loaded-for-bear hero to abruptly decide that one of his comrades isn't worth trying to help, and to walk away from the battle.

Dr. Mark stops the story cold every time he opens his mouth ("[A] mineral called zircon is in this sediment. It will be drawn off by this magnetic separator," "One million grams of uranium convert to 1/7,400th of lead per year," "This gelatinous substance dissolves in water one cubic inch per minute," more), not a good thing in a script that's already action-lite the same way Zimm's was. In this 107-page script, the first excitement, such as it is, comes when the off-screen Gill Man gets caught in the *Pongo* net (page 24–26), the next when he rises from the water near the *Pongo* to knock the lantern from Reed's hand (page 31); after that, it's the Gill Man–jaguar fight (page 51). The Gill Man's only victims are the *Pongo*'s native crew member and Dr. Sansoni, both killed identically (picked up and slammed down onto the deck) and Dreier, held underwater to drown. Most of the action involves the extremely repetitive multiple attempts to move the log barricade, which are unexcitingly described on paper. And the Gill Man's death scene sounds like it would have been grim viewing, as the poor creature is surrounded and ganged-up on by men with guns and a harpoon gun and, while on its last legs, is gruesomely Pearl Harbor–ed by the axe-wielding Reed. (The no-doubt-about-it killing of the Gill Man would have eliminated the possibility of sequels—at least sequels with the *same* Gill Man.)

Arthur Ross seemed rather pleased with his contribution to the series of scripts, telling me:

> No matter what I'm doing, whether I'm writing something just to make a living or something I really believe is important, I never write *down* to an audience. I don't *believe* in that—audiences are not stupid. They may not be geniuses, they may not be specialists in fields, but they are reasonably intelligent people in the main. And for that reason, I always felt that I would present what I thought was not only a melodramatic device, but also a study of characters in conflict. The conflict in this case would be these people versus the Creature—the more they attack him, the more he attacks *them*. I just re-read the script—I hadn't read it in God knows how long—and I was pleased at least to see that I had done what I set out to do. I wrote intelligent people doing intelligent things—everyone, that is, except for the aggressive person who wanted the Creature dead and mounted, considering that just as good as live and left alone. He was *un*intelligent and arrogant and caused the difficulties. And those difficulties finally had to be rectified in violence, because by that time the Creature was a violent and beset thing that had no choice but to fight them.

You can read this entire script draft in my 1992 MagicImage book *Creature from the Black Lagoon*.

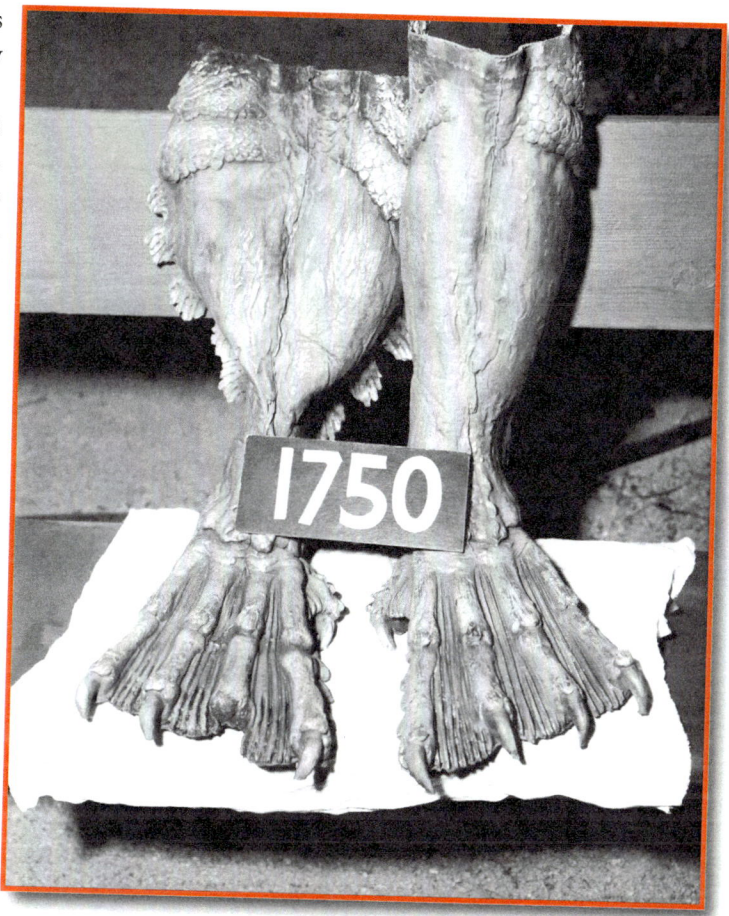

How's this for exemplary attention to detail? Since the film's story called for the Gill Man to lose a toenail in the Rita *net before his first on-camera appearance, the right foot was made minus a toenail! This was pointed out by the Classic Horror Film Board's Chris Casteel, aka The Mighty Bongo. We could have watched the movie 10,000 times and never noticed.*

Black Lagoon
(step outline of proposed changes by Harry Essex)

In the pool of *Black Lagoon* writers, "the last one in" (and you know what they say about the last one in) was Harry Essex, who in the months since working on *It Came from Outer Space* had conspicuously kept his wagon hitched to the tri-dimensional star: He co-wrote the 3-D Westerns *Devil's Canyon* (1953) and *Southwest Passage* (1954), the latter an unusual post–Civil War story (based on the real-life U.S. Army Camel Corps) about these "ships of the desert" and their Arab herders employed in a frontiersman's California-bound caravan. Essex also scripted *and* directed *I, the Jury* (1953), the feature film bow of novelist Mickey Spillane's private detective character Mike Hammer. With pint-sized TV actor Biff Elliot portraying the shamus as a loutish loudmouth, this adaptation of Spillane's same-name bestseller stood out dimensionally but in no other way; it's nearly incoherent and yet it was a moneymaker. Spillane found Essex to be obnoxious and disrespectful. Cinematographic great John Alton was behind the 3-D cameras.[9]

Black Lagoon–wise, the earliest Essex contribution I have seen is a 17-page June 8, 1953, composition titled "Step Outline—Proposed Changes for *Black Lagoon*," which reads like a synopsis. I am not in a position to ascribe everything (or *anything*) new or different in the following synopsis to Essex, without knowing what writing (if any) Ross and/or others did in the interim. Common sense dictates that *some* of the changes are Ross', since his second-draft script was dated March 19 and he was employed on the picture until April 30; one assumes he did a good bit of additional writing in all those weeks.

Put on the *Black Lagoon* payroll on June 1, Essex was the priciest of *Black Lagoon*'s writers, making $750 a week as opposed to Maurice Zimm's weekly $250, Leo Lieberman's $300 and Ross' $500, so by working on the movie for 11 six-day weeks plus two days he made $8500. (On July 17, just past the midpoint of Essex's *Black Lagoon* writing gig, Hollywood columnist Edwin Schallert mentioned that Essex was currently busy writing the movie, "which he might also direct." One wonders if Schallert was supplied that tidbit by Universal or by Essex.)

Essex's step outline opens (like the movie) with a look-back at the formation of the Earth, with narration complete

It looks like an AARP art class but it's actually Universal makeup room wizards up to their dewlaps in sculpting chores: John Kraus, John Phiefer, Rudolph Parducci (with Jack Kevan behind him), Chris Mueller, Jr. (with Elmer Balogh behind him), and Bud Westmore. Kraus is pretending to be sculpting the prototype Creature head for the purposes of this photograph; that head was the work of Mueller.

with Genesis quote.[10] From here we fast-forward several billion years to modern times and an Amazon beach where geologist Jose Malona and his native guides are examining the skeleton of what appears to be a prehistoric fish five feet in length. Malona snaps a photograph which, in an insert shot, we see published in *Life* magazine; and then through the insert whips a speedboat, racing across a Southern California bay. Driver Kay Lawrence has a copy of *Life* in her hands as she arrives at the spot where David Reed and an assistant are diving for fish specimens. She brought Reed the magazine because the article supports some of Reed's thoughts on evolution, and his theory that an even more completely developed human form of marine life could conceivably still exist.

Reed and Kay return to the Marine Institute where both are employed by Mark Williams, Kay's fiancé. Businesslike and humorless, Williams appreciates Reed's excitement over the fossil find and says that he's managed to get the Institute to finance a trip to South America so that Reed can get a first-hand look at it.

Reed, Kay, Williams and Williams' physician Dr. Sansoni are soon in Brazil, heading up the Amazon aboard a beat-up fishing boat, the *Pongo*, captained by Tasha. En route, Williams senses that Reed and Kay are attracted to one another. In Malona's tent, the geologist shows the expedition members the bones of the fish, which turns out to have been a coelacanth. Reed drops the bombshell that the bones are not prehistoric but contemporary; this marine animal had been alive as recently as a year ago. On the beach where the coelacanth bones were found, there's agreement that it came from somewhere up the river, probably some inland stream. As they talk, the camera pans over the water until we get a quick glimpse, just the impression, of the Gill Man beneath the surface. From the script:

> NOTE: The views of the creature should be progressive ... possibly the first time a webbed hand poking out of the water ... or foot ... then face.

That night, back in the tent, there's a discussion as to whether to continue the search or return home. Williams is against proceeding; he says he thinks it's a wild goose chase but actually he doesn't want Reed and Kay to continue to be together. Malona says he suspects that the coelacanth came from "a lost lagoon" several hundred miles upriver; if Williams won't join them, then Malona would like to go there with Reed. When Kay volunteers to accompany them, Williams is forced to go along (to keep tabs on Kay).

At the lagoon, Reed dons an aqualung and goes underwater to pick up some sample bits of rock; we now get our second semi-glimpse of the Gill Man, who is watching from concealment. When Kay goes for a swim, the Gill Man reaches up and touches her, causing her to scream and make a hasty return to the *Pongo*. The Gill Man follows and gets caught in a *Pongo* net, tearing a giant hole in it in order to escape.

Later, on deck, Kay tells Reed that she met Williams when she was a university student and he was an instructor; he aided her financially, helped her carve out a career in zoology and even gave her her present job. As they talk, the Gill Man swims close to the boat in order to get a look at Kay. She sees him and lets out a scream. The next morning, Reed is preparing to dive down to try to take pictures of the creature in his natural habitat; Williams, who has decided to accompany him, arms himself with a harpoon gun. Underwater, Reed manages to take only one picture before the panicked Williams fires a harpoon into the man-fish. Topside, Reed takes him to task for his hostile behavior. In the developed photograph, we get our first good, complete look at the Gill Man: seven feet tall, earless, with arms and legs "and a tail not unlike the shark."

Set on capturing the creature, Reed drops rotenone into the lagoon. By that night, the Gill Man is forced to come to the surface in shallow water; in this scene, his Mole People–like aversion to light is established when he flees from the boat's spotlight. In pursuit, Reed and Williams swim down to the spot where he disappeared and come up through a submerged entrance into an air-filled grotto described as an "an under-world fairy-land" that "offers the feeling of a cathedral" and even "gives off music" (?!). In the grotto, the creature and "some animal" [*sic*] have a struggle to the death (the animal's), after which the Gill Man darts through an opening and comes out a cave entrance onto the beach where Kay is sitting in a rowboat. Desperate to get back to the water, he staggers to the edge and collapses inches from Kay. Williams is all for killing the helpless creature, aiming his rifle between the Gill Man's "pleading eyes." Reed knocks him down to stop him.

The creature is put in a tank on the *Pongo* deck. As Sansoni keeps vigil, Kay comes along and they have a long talk about her strained relationship with Williams (pretty much the same one that Kay and Dr. Thompson have in the movie). With the harpoon head still embedded in his side, the Gill Man lets out a moan; Kay asks Sansoni to help her get it out. Sansoni draws the bolt to open the tank cover and the creature leaps out. Sansoni blocks his path and tries to reason with him(!), and gets himself knocked down. The creature is starting toward the screaming Kay as Reed and others appear on deck. Reed's flashlight has the Dracula-and-crucifix effect on the merman, who hurdles the rail and drops back into the drink.

Reed comes up with a plan to go to the nearest native village for more rotenone. As they attempt to leave the lagoon, they see that the Gill Man has set up a barricade (a huge log) across its narrow entrance. The Gill Man thwarts their attempt to pull the log away with a cable, and Reed and Williams must descend into the water to re-attach it. As Reed is working, Williams looks at Reed's back, tempted to send a harpoon through his rival—and then takes aim and lets one fly. Reed hears it and moves clear. The Gill Man watches as Reed and Williams proceed to stalk one another in a harpoon duel. When the Gill Man feels threatened, he grabs and kills Williams.

On Reed's next dive, he's armed with a solution of rotenone (to paralyze the Gill Man) and radium (its light will frighten him). A few squirts buy him enough time to secure the cable around the log, which now can be pulled away. The Gill Man, dazed, climbs aboard the *Pongo* to get out of the poisoned water, heading toward Reed until he sees Kay and changes course. Reed fires several bullets point blank into the monster but cannot prevent him from grabbing Kay and going over the rail. Armed with a knife, he follows them down through the water to the grotto, where Kay is unconscious and the Gill Man is lying in wait in the darkness for Reed. Kay wakes and screams, alerting Reed to the monster's presence. Reed throws rocks and a knife to hold off the Gill Man but he continues to advance, backing Reed up against a wall. Death seems imminent until Tasha and Sansoni come in through the beach entrance and fire a barrage of shots into the Gill Man. The monster now moves toward them but they stand their ground, firing away and "literally tearing [the Gill Man] apart." The Gill Man drops into a well-like pool of water, sinking into it as the expedition members stand in hushed silence.

Aboard the homeward-bound *Pongo*, Kay mentions Williams' death while Reed remains silent, unwilling to mention Williams' murderous attack. From the bottom of the 17th and final page: "In some ways the fish has it all over man. No memory of the past. All future—and as she goes into [Reed's] arms, Sansoni sees them and nods approvingly."

Interesting variations from previous drafts, and from the movie, are found in this version. The fossil bones which provide the story's takeoff point are those of a coelacanth rather than those of a merman.[11] Reed and Kay are back to knowing each other prior to the start of the story, but Kay now has as a fiancé her boss Mark Williams, whose obsession in this draft is not capturing or killing the Gill Man (as in the movie) but separating Reed and Kay—or, if all else fails, killing Reed. The centerpiece of the movie, the Black Lagoon swim with Kay above and the Creech below, is now penciled in, but in preliminary, perfunctory form: When Kay unknowingly happens to swim right to the spot where he's submerged, his webbed hand (all we see of him) reaches out and touches her, prompting her to frantically swim back to the boat. One assumes he'd have done the same thing if, say, Tasha was the innocent swimmer.

An on-deck discussion between Reed and Kay provides us with a bit of Kay–Mark Williams backstory (he was her university instructor and benefactor, and guided her career) that, truth be told, the movie probably could have used. In the movie, Williams regularly makes it obvious that he plainly resents that she and Reed are an item, and their reaction to his attitude is never what it should be. As one sneak preview audience member ranted on his or her Preview Comment Card, in answer to the question "Were all the story points clear to you?":

> No—what was the deal with R. Denning? I didn't quite get it. Was he in love with J. Adams? Was he just mad at R. Carlson? Was he just after the recognition? If so, why take it out on J. Adams and Richard Carlson?

In the Ross draft described above, we got our first clear and complete look at the Gill Man as a slide image projected on a wall; here it's in a photograph displayed by Reed. The Gill Man's shark tail sounds like a terrible idea[12]—I'm picturing a two-legged Gill Man with the ass-end of a shark sticking out his butt, and not liking what I see. Another bad addition: the way the monster can be driven off with a spotlight, a flashlight and even the glow of radium. Worst of all is the idea that the Gill Man's grotto somehow produces its own bizarre muzak—but, instead of being discarded right away, this innovation survives into future drafts where even *the Gill Man himself* is some kind of music machine! More on this is ahead.

The Ross script's "Gill Man vs. jaguar" jungle clash has been changed to a grotto fight between the man beast and some unspecified animal. Eventually *Black Lagoon* would become the one Creature movie with*out* a fight of this sort; in 1955's *Revenge of the Creature* he fights a German Shepherd and in 1956's *The Creature Walks Among Us* a mountain lion.

Kay's desire to remove the harpoon head from the captured Gill Man makes the reader think that an "Androcles and the Lion"–type moment is in the offing, but the beastie is up and out of the tank as soon as Sansoni draws the bolt, before the Gill Man can know *why* he opened it. (The Beauty and the Beast moments have begun to creep back into the storyline, but they're minor and inconsequential until the Creature's abduction of Kay in the final pages.) Williams' underwater attempt to harpoon Reed was another plot embellishment wisely smothered at birth; for one thing, the ensuing harpoon duel, with the divers stalking each other in and out of shadowy water, sounds like a blueprint for sheer boredom because after a while, few audience members would know who was who—the downfall of nearly all such multi-character sub-aquatic action scenes.

Essex's first-draft screenplay has eluded me, so next in the evolutionary chain we have…

Black Lagoon
(revised second-draft screenplay by Harry Essex)

First, however, a few words about Ernest Nims.

Hailing from Des Moines, Iowa, Nims was the editor of dozens of Republic features of the 1930s and '40s, from deep-dyed dreck to some of their cut-above John Wayne vehicles (*Flying Tigers, In Old Oklahoma*). "He was the great supercutter," Orson Welles once said of Nims, who even did some pre-production pruning of the *script* of *The Stranger* (1946) to improve director Welles' chances of finishing on schedule and under budget. According to Welles, "[Nims] believed that nothing should be in a movie that did not advance the story."[13] Nims' "how to make a movie" notions led to disagreements between the two men on *The Stranger* but for Welles the *real* grief came about a dozen years later when Nims, by now Universal's post-production head, famously re-edited the writer-director-star's *Touch of Evil* (1958) into exactly the sort of straightforward movie that Welles hadn't set out to make. Welles called Nims "the supersurgeon" and, according to Welles biographer Barbara Leaming, Nims came to embody what Welles perceived as Hollywood's inclination to hack apart his films.

I've seen *Touch of Evil*, I *know Touch of Evil*, and *Creature from the Black Lagoon* is no *Touch of Evil*. And *Black Lagoon*–wise, Nims collaborated on a list of script suggestions that went a long ways toward making it the favorite that it is.

On Saturday, July 25, 1952, Nims and William Alland got together to discuss the latest version of the *Black Lagoon* script (presumably one by Harry Essex, since he had been assigned to the movie since June 1). Nims subsequently sent Alland a six-page list of the changes discussed in that meeting. The very first suggestion was to establish the Creature to a greater extent in the opening sequence; Nims wrote, "Once we have [done this], the quicker we can get the expedition back to the camp and the hand in the water[,] the better off we are." Among the many other items mentioned in Nims' memo:

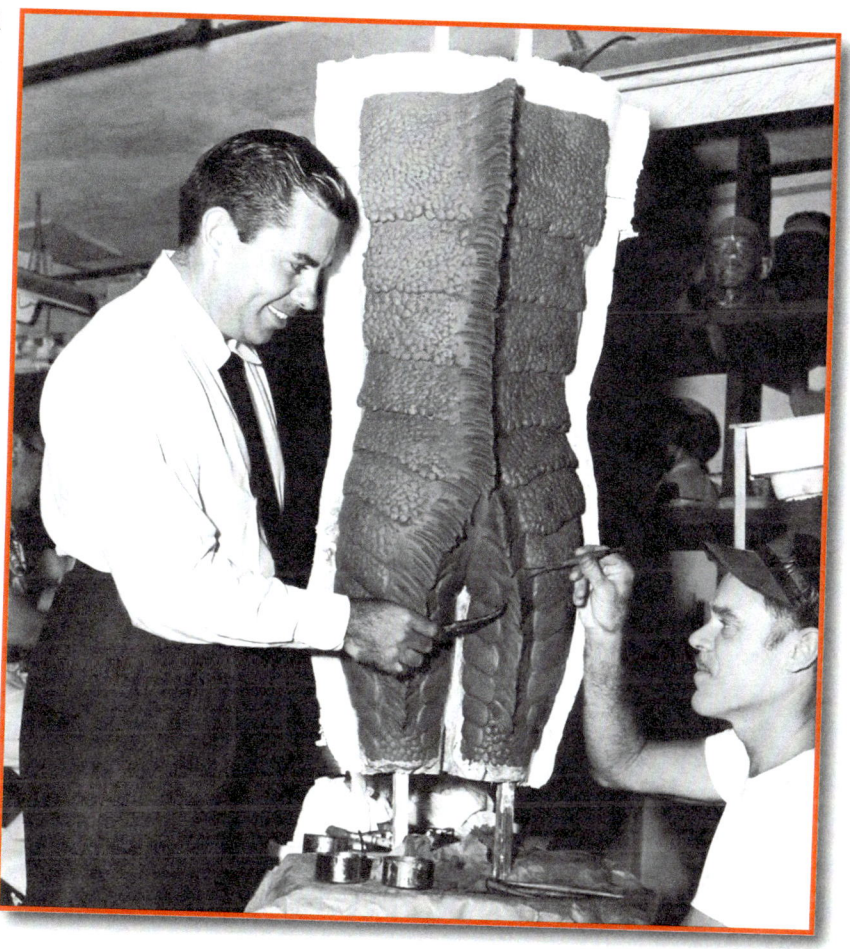

Bud Westmore and Chris Mueller, Jr., pose for a photograph with the clay sculpt of the Creature's back. Mueller is holding an actual sculpting tool while Westmore grips what appears to be a paint brush, which is odd because there'd be no need for a paint brush yet ... plus the fact that he's holding it all wrong!

- It suggests that "the travelogue" up the Amazon River to the geologist's camp be shortened;
- it recommends that "unusual scales or some small part of the creature" be found in the torn-apart trawling net;
- it advises that we *see* the Gill Man's deadly attack on the native on the *Pongo* deck, rather than letting his death be indicated by his off-camera scream;
- and, because of an *It Came from Outer Space* audience's shocked reaction to a desert roadside scene of Ellen unexpectedly coming up behind Putnam and touching his back, the Nims memo suggested adding an identical moment to *Black Lagoon*, and they did: Williams makes a startling appearance behind Reed in the first cave scene. At *Creature*'s January 7, 1954, preview, many audience members wrote on their preview cards that this was one of the big thrills of the picture.[14]

Amidst many other modifications, *the* major proposal in this memo was a build-up of the scene in which Kay's lagoon dip is disrupted by the Gill Man below. To the best of my knowledge, in all pre–July 25 scripts, the scene had entailed nothing more than Kay coincidentally swimming to the spot directly above the submerged Gill Man, who has observed her from this fixed position and now touches her leg; in a fright, she immediately returns to the boat. The memo advised "[dramatizing] to a greater extent this section of the script where Kay is swimming toward the boat" with an underwater shot of a "shadow effect of [the] creature following Kay" and a "down-shot" into the water of the creature approaching her. These may be the first-ever suggestions to build up the scene that would become the movie's undisputed highlight.

Essex's August 7 revised second-draft screenplay reflects Nims and Alland's changes and additions and therefore greatly resembles the coming movie, but still contains some notable variations. The idea of shooting in color hadn't yet been vetoed and Essex emphasizes things like "the greens and blues of the crystal-clear lake water," "the patches of rose, mauve," the luminous, multi-colored rocks of the Gill Man's lair, etc.

As well-read fans of *It Came from Outer Space* know, Essex told interviewees (including me) the outrageous lie that he, not Ray Bradbury, was principally responsible for the writing of that movie. The Truth got another black eye whenever Essex talked about *Black Lagoon*. He told me that when he was assigned to it, it was a very, very poorly written short story—just the basic idea of a fish that had been discovered in the jungle. Universal had bought the story for very little money and assigned me to it, and I was bitter and angry. I didn't want to do anything with a title like *Creature from the Black Lagoon*, it was an embarrassment to me. But they pleaded with me to do the picture, and so I began to redevelop the whole damn thing. It's pretty much formula, for the kind of horror stories we used to do in those days, except in this particular case I added the Beauty and the Beast theme.

Where to begin? When Essex was assigned, it wasn't just "a short story," he had the Zimm treatment and everything written by Leo Lieberman and Arthur Ross to work from, and there was *much* more to it than just "the basic idea of a fish that had been discovered in the jungle." Universal hadn't "bought the story," it was created in-house by producer Alland. At the point when Essex was engaged, the title wasn't *Creature from the Black Lagoon*, just *Black Lagoon*. He didn't add the Beauty and the Beast touches, they were part of the yarn right from the get-go, in Alland's "The Sea Monster." As for Universal having to plead to get him to grace their project with his participation … you make the call.

"Harry was so full of shit," Arthur Ross told me. But Ross went a little overboard in his criticisms: He said that Essex did nothing to his (Ross') draft but add more scenes with Kay, which is incorrect. Ross ranted that Essex

Front and side views of the painted-up Gill Man head that was in contention to be the head. It was sculpted by Chris Mueller, Jr., who also sculpted the Creature head that ended up in the movie.

later went around claiming that he did it all [all the scriptwriting]. That's all bullshit. All you have to do is look at my script and look at the final script, and the main difference is that in the final script there was more of the girl. That's it, *period*—nothing more than that.... When I found out how much Essex was taking credit for it, it irritated me only because I don't *believe* in that sort of thing. You take credit for what you do and you let it go at that. But I think he led such a *small* life that [*Black Lagoon*] was the only thing of any real significance that he could point to.

Similar to Essex, *Creature from the Black Lagoon* director Jack Arnold used latter-day interviews as an opportunity to claim credit for ideating the movie, when in fact he had less to do with it writing-wise than Essex—probably nothing at *all*. He told interviewer John Landis that Universal asked him and Alland "to please make another 3-D movie [after *It Came from Outer Space*]. It was in '53 or '54 that they discovered the coelacanth off the coast of Madagascar. I said, 'Hey, instead of a coelacanth, a *man-fish*.' ... So we kicked that story around and we got a-hold of two good writers at the time, Harry Essex and Arthur Ross, and we sat down and made up the story." His version of events sounds plausible unless you know that the *Black Lagoon* story idea was cooked up by Alland (in his memo "The Sea Monster") in 1952, prior to the coelacanth discovery, and not as a result of the success of *It Came from Outer Space* but months before *It Came from Outer Space* even began shooting! It's also telling that Arnold doesn't mention the writers who worked on the story in the early months, just the ones who came along last, probably around the time that *he* (Arnold) first became involved. His name is conspicuous by its absence from all of the extant memos written by the movie's script consultant or consultants, which mention only discussions with Alland.

Arnold receives on-screen writing credit on only two movies, 1955's *Tarantula* and 1957's *The Monolith Monsters*, both featuring the line "Story: Jack Arnold & Robert M. Fresco." But to hear Fresco tell it, Arnold muscled in on him, a twentysomething wet-behind-the-ears Hollywood beginner, and contributed not one word or idea. "Look, Arthur Ross and Harry Essex wrote *Creature from the Black Lagoon*, but you wouldn't think so if you talked to Jack Arnold," Fresco told me. "That's 'cause he was desperate. You know who he was? Sammy Glick, the character in the great Budd Schulberg novel *What Makes Sammy Run?* Sammy Glick, the ultimate hustler who ends up on top of the heap *all alone*, 'cause he's alienated everyone on the planet." When I mentioned to Alland that interviewee Arnold was a perennial credit-grabber, he couldn't have been more unsurprised:

> I got out of the picture business when I was still young—I was about 50 when I retired. And later I began to get feedback: "You know, Jack is taking all the credit for all the pictures he made for you." According to Jack, they were his *ideas*, his *this*, his *that*, on and on. When he'd mention me—if he mentioned me at all!—I was nothing but a front office man. But it didn't bother me, it didn't bruise my ego. I never called Jack and said, "What the hell are you doing? These were all my ideas, for God's sake—you came aboard and did the scripts that I gave you. Where do you get off saying that you were strictly a one-man band?" I never did say anything about it. I gather that he was *very* egotistical that way, and apparently *no*body did anything on his pictures except him.
>
> ... But he was not that way with me *personally*. That was one of the reasons I hired him so often, because I could depend on him doing *my* movie the way *I* wanted it done! I'm finding out more and more, talking to people like yourself, that after I left the business, people like Jack had a feeding frenzy on my corpse because I was not around to refute *any*thing.[15]

Alland used Arnold as director on seven of his movies—*It Came from Outer Space, Creature, Revenge of the Creature, Tarantula, The Lady Takes a Flyer* (1958), *The Space Children* (1958) and *The Lively Set* (1964)—the reason being

> that he had very little ego when it came to working for me. He was very controllable. I would say that that was both good for him and good for me. He would come aboard perhaps a week or two before we started shooting, and he was not involved in re-writing or any of that. The casting had been pretty much done, the art direction, the camera, just about everything was in place. And I could count on Jack *not* upsetting the apple cart, *not* saying, "Wait a minute, let's change this whole thing." He was very, very amenable to shooting my pictures, and so I was very confident in him. I liked Jack because he never got original ideas! I didn't *want* creative directors, because *I* was a creator.... He knew how to get a little shock out of the audience, by revealing a hand, or this, or that—although all that stuff was *in* the script. But he could accent that with the way he shot it, so I don't want to take anything away from his ability in *that* regard. But he was, himself, *not* a storyteller. He was a *director*.

Interviewed on-camera in the documentary *The Man Who Pursued Rosebud: William Alland on His Career in Theatre and Film*,[16] Alland made it clear that the directors of *all* of his Universal pictures were usually in that same, near-zero-input boat: "[Universal] had *so* much control," he said. "They decided what scripts were going to be shot, who was going to be the art director, who was going to do [this and that]. By the time we put a director aboard, he had *very* little to say about *any*thing. If he wanted a few script changes, all right, but if he wanted to [change] *too* much: '*No!*'"

Getting back to Essex's August 7 draft...

The Nims-Alland suggestion to better establish the Creature in the opener is the first order of business that

Essex handles: During the introductory "morning of time" sequence, as the narrator describes the birth of life in the sea, Essex suggests the use of 16mm stock footage of a creature with "paddle-like fins and long appendages, which provide land locomotion, as it moves [from the water's edge] up on the beach." One wonders what 16mm stock footage he was referencing.

On the banks of the Amazon, geologist Carl (changed from Jose) Malona has found in a limestone wall the fossilized skeleton of a prehistoric hand and forearm. Nearby, a green, mossy hand with webbed talons pokes up out of the water and rests on the bank. The Creature is still afraid of light, now ridiculously so: The flash of Malona's camera, photographing the fossil, causes the hand to quickly withdraw, as though *it* can see! In this draft, the action starts early: Up next is the night scene of Malona's native worker Luis, alone in a camp tent, being accosted by the Gill Man. Luis tries to chop at him with his machete, but the monster grabs and drags him off. (Again in this draft, we don't get a real look at the man-fish until late in the game.)

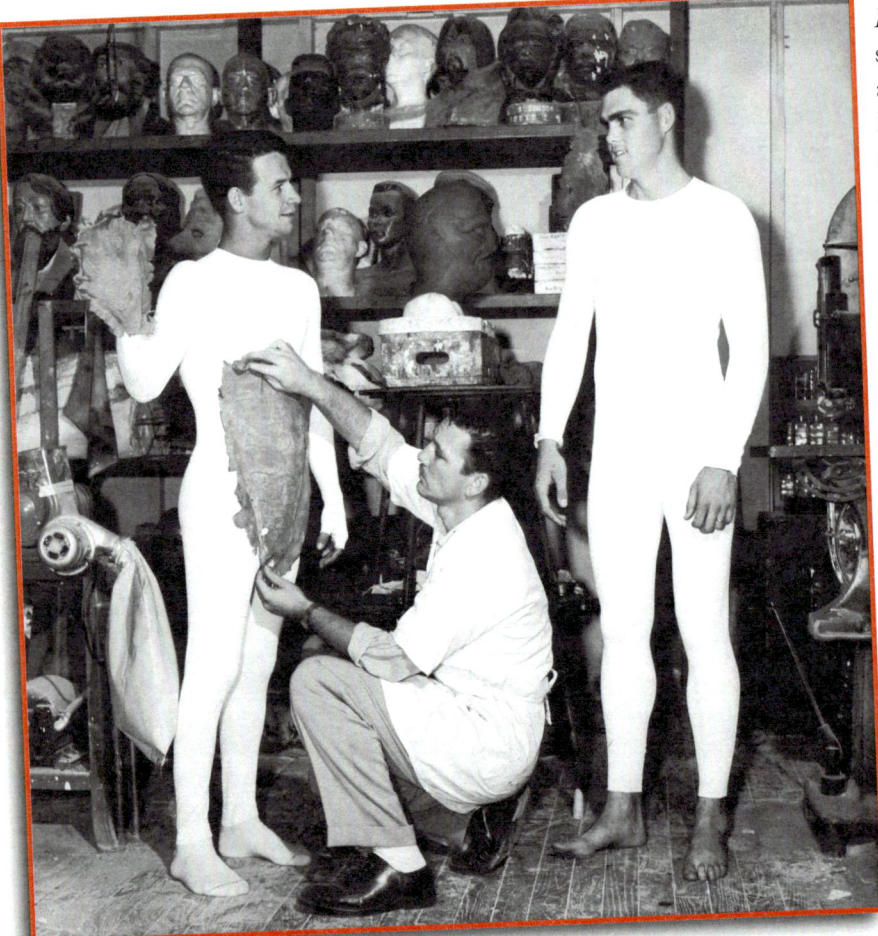

After the aquarium "Let's put on an expedition!" scene, we find its members Reed, Kay, Williams and Sansoni aboard Tasha's creaking, groaning boat. Reed's movie soliloquy about the area's oversized critters ("The Amazonian rat is as big as a sheep," etc.) is now divvied up between Reed, Malona and Sansoni, and interspersed with stock footage of Indian natives paddling a canoe, a giant anteater, a foot-long centipede and a capybara (a rat). When they get to the geological camp, Malona's two native guides are missing. In the tent is found an ouanga—several twigs bound together by hairs. "It's a tribal charm to ward off— demons," says Malona. "Apparently something frightened my boys."

Following an unsuccessful attempt to find more of the fossil, Reed advances the theory that part of the limestone wall may have long-ago dropped into the water and been carried up river. As the boat heads in that direction, just under the surface a long, shark-like shadow can be seen in its wake; a hand reaches out of the water so that we recognize it as the green, taloned thing we saw at Malona's camp.[17] A Reed–Kay conversation on the *Pongo*'s prow is intercut with stock footage shots of a boa constrictor, a giant spider, and alligators in combat. (If Essex's directions had been followed, surely by this point the surfeit of stock shots would have given *Black Lagoon* the feel of a Sam Katzman movie or even a *Ramar of the Jungle* TV episode!) As they near the lagoon, a storm rises and a 3-D lightning bolt strikes out into the audience.

At the Black Lagoon, Reed and Williams put on aqualungs and go down for rock samples while, topside, Sansoni bores Tasha (and the reader): "[T]he world was formed out of a gas that turned into uranium. Then particles of it turned into radium, and finally, lead," etc., etc. At the lagoon bottom, the Gill Man, unseen by Reed and Williams, watches the men from a forest of ribbon weeds. After Reed and Williams return to the boat, Kay takes her imprudent swim, and this time (per Nims and Alland) the Gill Man—seen as a shadow effect in an underwater shot and as a silhouette in a down-shot—follows her back to the *Pongo*. The incident with the torn trawling net is capped by the discovery of a finger with web portion attached. Reed and Williams descend again, the former toting a camera, the latter a harpoon gun, and when the Gill Man

Ricou Browning (left) wears the leotard to which the various pieces of the Gill Man costume will be glued.

1. Creature from the Black Lagoon (1954)

appears, both take a shot. As Reed's photo is being developed in the *Pongo*'s bunk room, the Creature comes up on deck and kills Tasha's Indian guide Mala. Dreamily looking off into space, Tasha tells Sansoni,

> There are many strange legends in the Amazon.... There is the legend of the beautiful mermaid, who lived in one of the hidden lagoons of the Amazon. It was a very beautiful legend ... about how this mermaid, she fall in love with a man on a ship, and nobody will believe him.... And then one day when the time came for him to go away, she follow him ... far out into the Amazon ... only to lose her way ... and be devoured by the crocodiles.

As Tasha related the story, we were to have seen a montage of images of the placid surface of the lagoon, the inlets overrun with plants, and the thick jungle fringing the body of water.

An attempt to drug the Creature with rotenone leads to the discovery of his grotto; as in earlier drafts, it's still the type of "enchanting" spot where a Disney-cartoon princess might hang her tiara. As they search it, Reed and Williams find a portion of the shirt of Malona's native worker and an ouanga, proof that *both* of Malona's men are dead (and that the Gill Man likes to take souvenirs of his kills). In a nearby section of the grotto is the Creature, who we in the audience were now to clearly see for the first time: "He's some seven feet tall, a giant, his webbed hands reaching ahead of him." Rotenone-drugged, he painfully staggers out onto the beach and makes a beeline for Kay, who's sitting in a *Pongo* rowboat. Also on the beach is Garu, the native brother of Mala, who gets between the monster and the girl and pays with his life.[18] The Gill Man picks up Kay, carrying her with

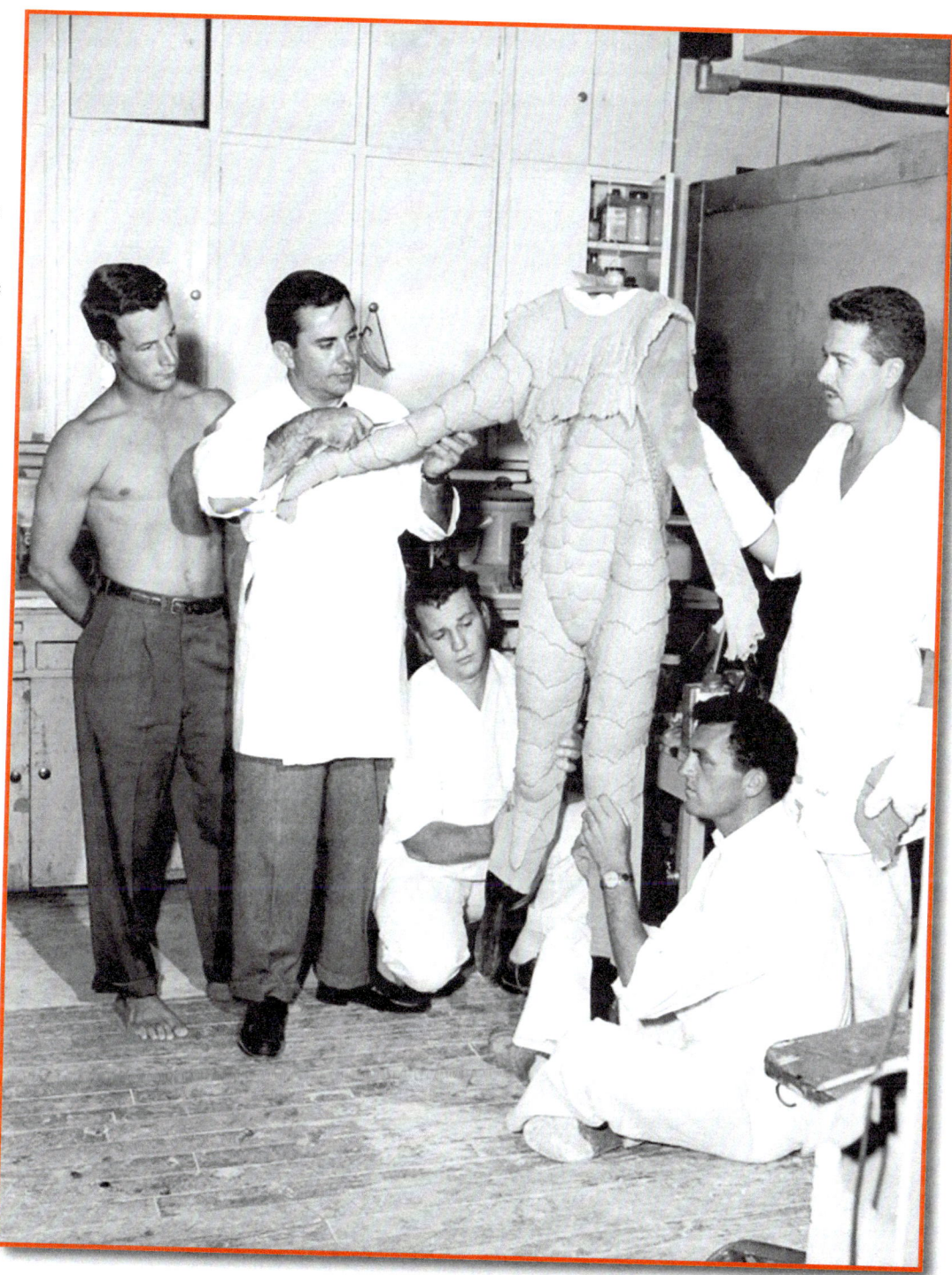

Standing left to right, Ricou Browning, Bud Westmore and Jack Kevan admire their work, the Gill Man costume complete with most of the glued-on pieces (but still no left arm).

his taloned fingers open so he doesn't hurt her, when the rotenone at last takes effect. But even when he finally falls, "his concern for the safety of the girl is predominant." Williams appears on the beach and gives the beast a shot to the head with his rifle butt, leaving a gash.

The captured Creature has a brief stay in a makeshift tank on the *Pongo* deck before busting out and going after Kay. Sansoni steps in with a kerosene lantern while Kay, now behind the Creature, picks up a rifle, aims and pulls the trigger; we hear a click but no explosion. Again she pulls the trigger, with no result. The ammo is wet. (One wonders how the Beast would have felt about his Beauty if he'd observed this.) Though mauled by the Creature, Sansoni manages to drive him off by shattering the lantern against him and setting him afire.

The single-minded Williams is all for trying to re-capture the man-fish but he's overruled, and soon the *Pongo* is headed for the lagoon entrance. But a huge dead-tree barricade now lies horizontally across the narrow opening. Reed goes below to attach a winch cable to the tree, and Williams joins him to stand watch. When the Creature appears, Williams takes off after him, bent on taking him single-handedly. The Creature catches him and won't let go, tearing the air hose from his mouthpiece. Reed is too late to prevent Williams' drowning.

From here to the end, the script mirrors the movie almost exactly: the Gill Man vs. Reed and his rotenone spray gun, the abduction of Kay, Reed's attempt at a rescue in the grotto, and the last-second arrival of Malona and Tasha, their automatic rifles firing a deadly barrage.

Again we get a few steps closer to the movie-as-produced, especially with Kay's lagoon swim starting to build toward what it eventually became, and with Williams now hard-driving and possessed by the need to capture the Creature. (In the words of the trailer narrator, his "scientific passion turned to the fury of revenge.") There's not much trace of Williams the Sometimes-Coward of Essex's step outline; in fact, he now has some of the qualities of the uber-hunter Dreier of earlier drafts. In this draft, as the Creature stalks Williams at the bottom of the lagoon, Williams "senses he's being followed and almost enjoys it."

Essex weaves a few above-and-beyond suggestions into the draft, frequently specifying the use of stock footage from *Amazon Head-Hunters* (he must have meant the 1951 RKO release *Jungle Headhunters*) and, for the aquarium interior scene, proposing either Hermosa Beach or Scripps Institute in La Jolla as the shooting location. He also specifies which shots need to employ the tri-dimensional effect: the footage of the lungfish, leopard sharks, eel and octopus in the aquarium tank, various shots of underwater swimmers Reed, Williams and the Creature (he wants them to appear to be "seemingly swimming into the audience"), the lightning bolt, Garu being thrown by the Creature, the Creature jumping off the boat on fire, harpoons piercing the water, etc.

There's also the usual attempt to build suspense by giving us nothing but partial glimpses of the merman for most of the movie; Essex takes it too far by having the Creature do ridiculous things like swim with one hand reaching out of the water (picture it). As the expedition arrives at Malona's camp, on the spot on the bank where we earlier saw the Creature's hand emerge, now we see its *foot* poke up from the water and rest on the bank. (From the "Just when you think it can't get any worse" department: On my copy of this script, the lines about a foot appearing out of the water and resting on the bank are X-ed out, and someone wrote off to the side **Shoulder!**)

But the worst new idea was for the Creature to be one part fish, one part man and one part music machine: In this draft, nearly every time the Creature is nearby, we hear its music, *and sometimes the characters seem to hear it, too*. In the early scene at Dr. Maia's camp, after the Creature's hand slides back into the water: "Seemingly out of the water comes a strange music now ... unearthly ... unknown ... as though the sound of waves lapping up against rock." When Kay is standing on the bank and the Creature is poised to reach for her ankle, "[s]he seems to be listening to the odd sound of the music again, the effect almost hypnotic"; he withdraws but the music continues to play. In an underwater scene where the Creature sticks his hand out of a patch of ribbon weeds, we again hear "the strange music ... almost the sound of a voice." Kay considers a swim as the music comes out of the water, "as though beckoning." As the rotenone-drugged Creature pulls itself onto the boat, Reed seems to hear the music before anybody sees the Creature. The music follows the amphibian as he walks on to the beach toward Kay, with the girl "listening ... almost hears it." This identifying music is also heard over Tasha's mermaid story, as the Gill Man looks up at Kay's floating cigarette, and at several other spots. In 1971 when Essex amateurishly semi-remade *Black Lagoon* as *Octaman*, it *did* have a B.Y.O.M. (Bring Your Own Music) Monster.

The evolutionary chain of *Black Lagoon* scripts appears to have reached its dead end with a *revised* revised version of Essex's second draft; my copy has "August 28, 1953" handwritten on the bottom of the title page, and it's filled with many pages of "Changes" dated September 22 and 23. The most notable "Changes" pages add to the Kay–Creature swimming scene, calling for an "almost playful" Gill Man to swim upside-down beneath her in the lagoon as he follows her back to the boat. Another "Changes" page includes a description of an underwater shot of the Gill Man following the boat from Maia's camp to the Black Lagoon. After he "porpoises" to the surface, we were to then get a camera-out-of-water Gill Man p.o.v. shot of Kay standing at the stern.

The Beauty and the Beast touches, which Alland included from the get-go but which went AWOL in several of the scripts, were now all in place; in fact, the Gill Man's infatuation with Kay was now *too* obvious for the MPAA's Joseph Breen, who had a September 1, 1953, confab with Universal's William Gordon to stress that care be exercised in the Kay–Gill Man scenes, "to avoid any sexual emphasis that might suggest bestiality" (as Breen phrased it in a next-day letter). "We have in mind the various scenes in which he is shown carrying her off, and also the dialogue on pages 82–83, 'And he'll keep trying to come aboard until he gets what he wants,' 'Can't you understand he's after Kay?'"[19] In the same letter, Breen also asked for Gordon's assurance "that there will be no problem with the Gill Man's costume"—a reminder that the Gill Man was, after all, a male, naked and obviously love-starved fellow. (There was, of course, no problem with the Gill Man's costume. As one wag put it, "Call it a triumph of the censors over the ichthyologists.")

The idea of making the movie in Technicolor was "on the table" as prep work proceeded. On August 17, the studio's Sam Israel wrote a letter to the New York office in which he mentions that it had not yet been definitely decided whether the movie was going to be in black-and-white or in Technicolor, or even whether it would be in 3-D.[20] In the midst of my 1995 interview with William Alland, I mentioned that the Gill Man movies, *Tarantula* and other Alland sci-fi flicks would have been better in color and he emphatically agreed, singling out *Black Lagoon* as a movie that would have been "fabulous" in color; "As a matter of fact," he added, "I'd like to see them colorize it." If a good job could be done of it, so would I. In the meantime, you can get an idea how the Creature movies' underwater scenes might have looked in color by watching such films as 1951's Technicolor *Crosswinds* (shot at Weeki Wachee Springs) and 1955's Eastman Color *Jupiter's Darling* (shot at Silver Springs and Weeki Wachee Springs).

Some Early Casting Ideas

Through these months of script evolution, the casting process was also underway. The earliest casting-related paperwork I've found, dated May 22, 1953, gives the movie's title as *The Black Lagoon* and it indicates that three Universal contractees were under consideration for the top role of Dr. David Reed: Gregg Palmer, Bart Roberts (aka Rex Reason)

Riciou Browning tries out the two "competing" Gill Man heads at the bottom of the Underwater Tank. The most amazing thing about his ability to hold his breath underwater is that he started smoking around 1949, one or two packs a day—and eventually got up to five a day! He quit in the 1980s.

and Richard Long. (Palmer and Reason would both appear in the second *Black Lagoon* sequel, *The Creature Walks Among Us*.) Julie Adams is already listed as playing Kay, and Richard Denning has the role of Dr. Mark Williams earmarked for him. The part of Dr. Sansoni (a character name later changed to Dr. Thompson) was up for grabs between Donald Randolph and Paul Cavanagh. Confusingly, on this paper, Ramon Novarro seems to be "up" for either the part of Reed's mentor Carl Malona or the villainous Kurt Dreier. Novarro in the cast *would* have been a mark of distinction for *Black Lagoon*; the singing waiter-turned-silent movie headliner played the title role in Metro's 1925 super-production *Ben-Hur* and was second only to Rudolph Valentino as a Hollywood "Latin Lover" in the pre-talkie era.

August 4 is the date on the next casting memo I've seen, and there's now a semi-major name in the *Black Lagoon* lead: For the role of Reed, Universal had lined up Frank Lovejoy, the Bronx-born actor then finishing a good run of starring and co-starring roles at Warner Brothers—including that studio's big 3-D horror hit *House of Wax*, which was still playing in the summer of 1953 as *Black Lagoon*'s cast selections were being made. Five thousand dollars a week for five weeks was set aside for Lovejoy salary-wise. This August 4 memo has Julie Adams, Richard Denning and Nestor Paiva listed for their eventual screen roles. (From the "Some Typos Are Funnier Than Others" Dept.: The memo says that Denning will play *Mary Williams*.) Randolph and Cavanagh are both still in the running for the job of playing Dr. Sansoni, and Novarro is now listed only for the role of Carl Malona; he was to have received $1250 a week for three weeks work. Evidently *someone* involved on the movie had their heart set on a silent-era romantic star in this role, as Antonio Moreno wound up with the gig.

I've never read or heard anything that indicated that anyone other than Julie Adams was ever in contention for *Black Lagoon*'s female lead. (Ultimately she was the one and only Universal contractee to appear in the movie. Everyone else was "outside talent.") But another actress set her sights on it: Universal contractee Suzan Ball, who got "Introducing…" billing for playing a treacherous dance hall wench (at age 17!) in the studio's *Duel in the Sun*–like Western *Untamed Frontier* (1952). First, some backstory: While Ball was rehearsing for an Oriental dance scene in the studio's *East of Sumatra* (1953), she did a dip and accidentally clunked her knee on the concrete floor. A form of cancer resulted, and soon she was being told that amputation of the leg was necessary. Instead she got a second opinion from a doctor who felt he could treat her and save the leg. This was the point in her medical history at which Ball spoke with Hollywood journalist Bob Thomas over a Universal lunch table; his syndicated column of August 4, 1953, described the meeting, with Ball quoted as saying that she felt everything was going to be all right. "Now I want to do a picture," the 19-year-old added. "There's a script here called *The Black Lagoon* and a part in it for a girl who doesn't have to walk. I'm going to hound every executive in the studio until I get it." Yes, conceivably she could have played it: In the movie, we seldom see Kay walk more than a few steps, so a Ball double could have taken her place in these infrequent instances and for part of the swimming scene. Sad to say, Ball *did* lose the leg and then also lost her cancer battle. She died at age 21 two years (almost to the day) after the publication of her "It looks as though everything is going to be all right" interview with Thomas.[21]

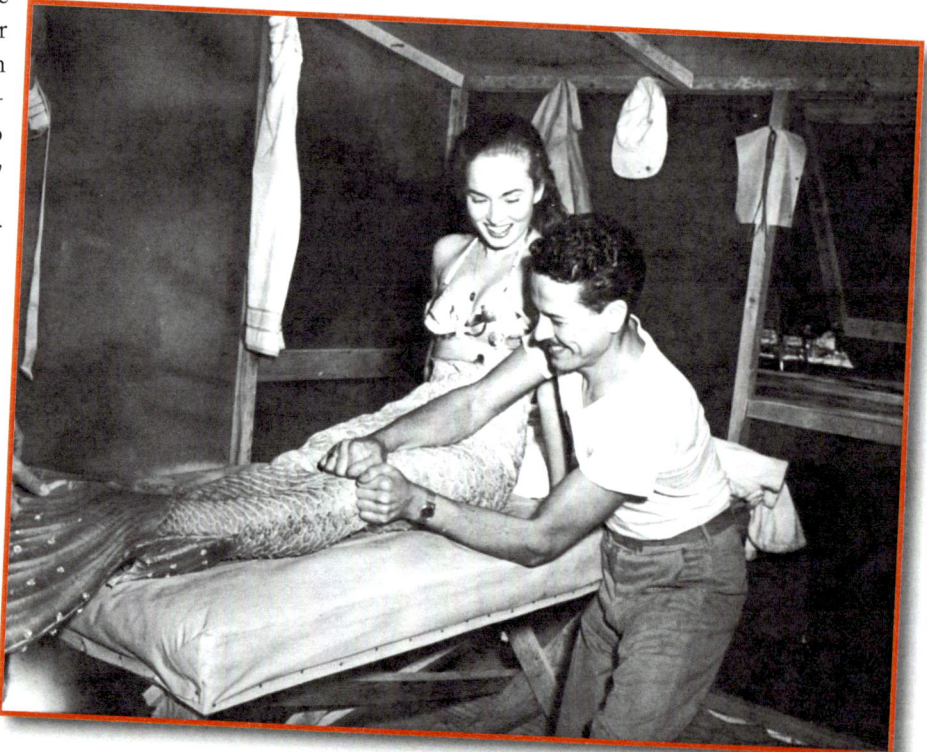

Six years before helping Ricou Browning squeeze in and out of Gill Man suits, the Universal makeup department's Jack Kevan had more fun getting Ann Blyth into her mermaid tail for *Mr. Peabody and the Mermaid* (1948) (courtesy State Archives of Florida).

Location Location Location

When it came time to select a spot to shoot *Black Lagoon* scenes of the Gill Man's underwater realm, thoughts turned to Florida, perhaps because someone recalled that their then-recent *Mr. Peabody and the Mermaid* (1948) was partly shot below the surface of the Sunshine State's Weeki Wachee Springs. In that Irving Pichel–directed fantasy-comedy, William Powell starred as a Bostonian, vacationing in the British West Indies, who finds at the end of his fishing line a beautiful mermaid (Ann Blyth with a large foam rubber and latex tail). Unlike the Gill Man and Kay, the attraction between Powell and Blyth soon becomes mutual, and hilarity ensues (or not, depending on your sense of humor; I find it to be quite a dreary one-joke movie).

In late July 1953, a *Black Lagoon* location scouting crew prepared to leave for Florida to find a body of water where these underwater scenes—nearly a quarter of the film—could be shot. Among the spots under consideration: Wakulla Springs, one of the world's largest and deepest freshwater springs, located in Wakulla County cypress swamps several miles south of the state capital Tallahassee. ("Wakulla" is supposed to be an Indian word that means either "river of the crying bird" or "mysterious waters.") In common with the fictional Black Lagoon, Wakulla Springs was the home of prehistoric animal life; in newsreels from the 1930s, we can see mastodon bones discovered there. More pertinently for the *Black Lagoon* crew, its waters were perfect for their purposes. Vodka-clear and anesthetizingly cold, they come gushing up from an underwater cave (perhaps the world's deepest), hundreds of thousands of gallons a minute. From the four-acre bowl of the spring, they then flow into the Wakulla River, which after nine miles joins the St. Marks River, which empties into the Gulf of Mexico.

The Wakulla Springs area remained primitive right up into the mid–1930s when it was purchased by Edward Ball, brother-in-law of industrialist Alfred I. du Pont. Developing it became a passion for Ball, who promptly began construction on Wakulla Springs Lodge, a two-story marble-and-masonry hotel.

In 1941, Ball hired Newton Perry (1908–1987) to manage Wakulla Springs. A product of southern Georgia, Perry had come to Florida as a kid in the days when the state had a population of less than one million people (it'll soon be America's third-most populous state with approximately 20 million). Nearly every day Perry would walk the six miles from his Ocala home to Silver Springs, and he was soon as much at home in the water as on land. He went from a 14-year-old giving 25-cent swimming lessons at Silver Springs, to Ocala High School's 16-year-old swim coach, to the state's top collegiate diver. In 1923, when the owner of Silver Springs asked Perry to teach his wife to swim, she became the first of an estimated 120,000 people Perry taught. In a 1982 *Ocala Star-Banner* article, Ray Washington wrote about the way Perry hitched himself to Florida's burgeoning tourist industry:

> At springs around the state he performed what were to become the first underwater tourist shows. The idea of breathing through underwater tubes was his. Riding bicycles, foot racing, teaching class—anything that could be done on land, he proved it could be done underwater too.
>
> Newt Perry was in demand across the state. He shuttled back and forth between the springs as they developed—Silver Springs, Wakulla Springs, Cypress Gardens, Weeki Wachee. He was the king of the springs. He loved Rainbow Springs. He discovered Hart Springs. He seemed to be everywhere there was a spring that needed swimming.

But prior to the tourist show activity mentioned above, Perry was the manager of Wakulla Springs, luring MGM moviemakers there to shoot above- and below-the-water

Ungawa! Behind the scenes on Tarzan's Secret Treasure *(1941), Wakulla Springs manager Newt Perry poses with locals portraying Bantu warriors in the movie. Perry, nicknamed "The Human Fish," once held his breath for a record-setting three minutes and 50 seconds, according to his daughter Delee (courtesy State Archives of Florida).*

scenes for 1941's *Tarzan's Secret Treasure* with Johnny Weissmuller and Maureen O'Sullivan. He became the go-to guy for movie studios in need of water scenes; he also served as liaison between the moviemakers and the local black community when blacks were needed to play natives in, say, Tarzan movies.

During this era, someone who got to know Perry, and to know Wakulla Springs, was a Tallahassee kid named Ricou Browning—soon to achieve movie immortality as the Creature from the Black Lagoon.

In November 2003, 73-year-old Browning gave an extensive interview to Wakulla Springs State Park Ranger Mike Nash, describing his nearly lifelong "history" with the place. He began by talking about one of his first-ever visits[22] to Wakulla:

> I think we were on the back of a truck, maybe 15 or 20 kids out of Tallahassee's Leon High School…. We came to the springs and I fell in love with it. It was just beautiful. As it is right now, it was full of squirrels, full of fish, full of eelgrass, and the water was freezing. We spent, I think, the entire day here and from then on I came every weekend. And I got to know Newt Perry very well. His wife … trained all of us in diving. He taught us in swimming, and at that time he had an air compressor and a pump right next to the diving tower and an air hose that ran out from that. He taught us all how to hose-breathe [while underwater]. It's kinda like drinking water out of a hose. You drink the water you want, and you let the rest spill on the ground. Well, breathing from a hose is the same way. You take what air you want and let the rest just spill out.

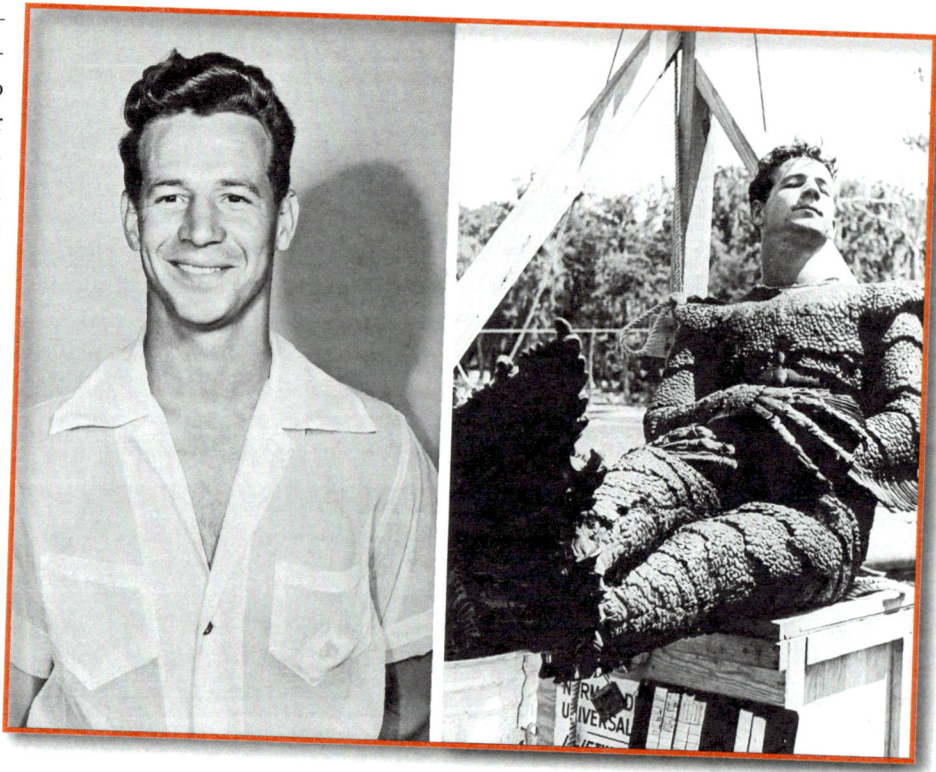

On a Florida junket, Black Lagoon location scouts' efforts were crowned with double success: They selected Wakulla Springs and found the ideal guy to play their Gill Man, Ricou (pronounced like Rico) Browning. The accomplished swimmer-diver was named after his maternal grandfather Ransom Ren "R.R." Ricou (1867–1925), a commercial fisherman whose company became the South's largest wholesale fish dealer.

Browning told me about his boyhood experience of working for the first time as a "performer" at Wakulla:

> One of the glass bottom boats would go from a dock area out over the spring, hand-rowed by a boat captain—they were all colored guys in those days. Today the boats have electric outboard motors, but in those days they rowed with oars. The boat captain had a speech that came out kinda like a song, about the spring and things that were done there, movies that were made there, Henry the Pole-Vaulting Fish and all of those various things.
>
> Then he'd row over near the diving tower, where the other kids and I would be waiting, and tell his passengers, "I can get one of those boys to swim underwater with an air hose, and you folks can watch him." He would yell out to one of us and we'd go in the water with an air hose, swim down … the deepest would be about 80 feet. We'd swim around and then work our way all the way back up to the boat. And the captain would say, "Give him applause" and "If you want to give this boy some money, just throw it on the glass," and then *he* would throw a quarter onto the glass bottom of the boat so that it'd make a sound. The passengers didn't know that *he* threw that first coin, 'cause they'd be looking out of the boat at the kid in the water. They'd hear the clink of the quarter and *they'd* take out money and throw it onto the glass. The captain would collect the money, and at the end of the day he'd split it with us. Some of us kids would earn 30, 40 dollars a day, and that was big, big money.

Sportswriter-movie producer Grantland Rice shot some of his short subjects below the surface of Wakulla's teeth-chattering cold waters. The documentary *The Wonders of Wakulla Springs* features clips from Rice shorts, among them the comedic *What a Picnic!*: In that 1945 release, the driver of a filled-with-teens Model T convertible (Ricou Browning's brother Clement Walker "Buddy" Browning, Jr., with high schooler Ricou sitting right behind him) drives into the water until it, and *they*, are completely submerged.

The kids then bail out and, at the bottom of the spring, begin to roast frankfurters, have a picnic, smoke a cigarette, dance, etc.[23] This is just one of several Rice shorts in which Browning can be seen.

Perry's promotional skills made the picnic and recreational areas of Wakulla Springs a real "hot spot" in the '40s: All day long, kids from Tallahassee, soldiers from Dale Mabry Field and gals from Florida State College for Women, wall-to-wall people, would swim, dance to jukebox music, etc. "Buddy" and Ricou worked there: In the summer, they were lifeguards, soda jerks, ticket sellers, grass mowers, whatever needed to be done. In cooler weather, when business was slow, they went underwater with air hoses and, in shallow areas where eelgrass interfered with swimmers, they pulled it up until the chilliness of the water forced them to retreat inside the Lodge and warm up beside its big fireplace.

In 1947, 17-year-old Browning enlisted in the Air Force, rising to the rank of corporal before leaving in 1950. At 20, while attending Florida State University, he worked in his first "Hollywood movie": The Pine-Thomas adventure *Crosswinds* (1951) was made in Florida and Browning got the job of underwater double for Forrest Tucker in scenes shot at the bottom of Weeki Wachee Springs. (Sharing the screen with Ricou: *Crosswinds* star John Payne, who did his own underwater swimming.) A few months later he married, and at the end of 1952 his son Ricky was born. During this period he supported himself by producing and performing in Newt Perry's underwater "mermaid shows" at Weeki Wachee; read the interview with "mermaid" Ginger Stanley (in Chapter 6, "Creature Conversations") for the full story on that unusual roadside attraction. Browning also worked at a Tampa state fair, acted as chief lifeguard of a pool in a Tallahassee park, etc., and resumed his FSU studies.

Then, in July 1953, came The Phone Call. He told me that Newt Perry

> phoned me and said that he had received a call about showing some Hollywood people [*Black Lagoon* location scouts] Wakulla Springs. He couldn't make it, he was busy in Miami doing *some*thing, so he asked me if I wouldn't mind showing it to them. I said fine. So these people called me and told me when they were coming into town, and I met 'em at the airport in Tallahassee. It was Jack Arnold and the cameraman, "Scotty" Welbourne, and a couple other people, I just don't remember who they were.[24] I took them to Wakulla Springs and showed 'em the area, and they loved it. "Scotty" had his underwater camera and he asked me if I would get in the water with him and swim in front of the camera so they could get some perspective. [With a person in the shot, viewers would have some idea of the size of the fish, eelgrass, logs, etc., they were also seeing.] I said sure, so I did. They saw the spring and the river and loved 'em. We had dinner that night, talked a little bit about the Springs, and they left. The kind of movie they were planning to make—not once did the subject come up. Just that there was going to be a lot of underwater.

The moviemakers did decide to utilize Wakulla Springs for *Black Lagoon*'s underwater scenes; it was picturesque, its water was transparent and, at its bottom, caves and cliffs offered ideal crannies for a Gill Man to lurk. Wakulla shooting would be done by a second unit working at the same time that the main unit was busy at Universal, which meant that underwater doubles would be needed for Reed, Kay, Williams—and the Gill Man. Some time after the location scouts' departure, Ricou's phone rang once again, and it was Jack Arnold on the other end. The director asked, "How would you like to be the Creature?"

"Creature? *What* creature?"

"We're doing a film about an underwater monster," Arnold explained. "We've tested a lot of people for this part, but I'd like to have you play the Creature—I like your swimming. Do you want to do it?"

Browning said, "Sure!"

According to the minutes of an August 5, 1953, Studio Operating Committee meeting, "The swimmer will arrive at the studio next Monday to be outfitted for the part." Twenty-three-year-old Browning, FSU physical education major, husband and father of an eight-month-old, indeed was on a Sunday, August 7, flight to the movie capital, and the makeup department's work on the Creature costumes to be worn by Browning and the "on-land" Gill Man Ben Chapman (much more on him later) went into high gear. Starting early in this chapter is a series of behind-the-scenes photos of the process, every one of them worth 1000 words.

The Creature Costume

For years, *Creature* fans have been under the impression that the first monster suit was made after Ricou Browning arrived at the San Fernando Valley lot. As already mentioned in this chapter's endnote 12, that was not the case: Weeks prior to the "discovery" of Browning in Florida, the minutes of the Studio Operating Committee's July 14 meeting included the line, "We are shooting underwater tests tomorrow of the 'lagoon man' in both 3-D and 2-D." Who designed that suit? What did it look like? Who wore it in the tests? These, and a dozen other fun questions, will probably never be answered.

> Monster-making is easy after 21 years. You just read a lot of books on life in the lower depths of the ocean, a couple of dozen books on zoology, and an assortment of medical treatises on human anatomy; you become an expert on insect life, read up on psychology, study every picture of pre-

historic monsters you can lay your hands on; you use a little common sense—and then let your imagination run riot … in a controlled sort of way, of course.—Bud Westmore, quoted in the December 10, 1954, *Collier's* article "Monsters Made to Order"

Creature from the Black Lagoon's sole on-screen credit for makeup ("Make-up: Bud Westmore") notwithstanding, many hands and minds were involved in the ideation and fabrication of the eventual Gill Man outfit. The paper trail extends all the way back to its sketchy description in William Alland's October 2, 1952, memo "The Sea Monster," itself possibly based on Gabriel Figueroa's "word picture" ("painted" at the 1940 Orson Welles party) of the supposedly true-life fish-men of the Amazon. Various screenwriters starting with Maurice Zimm added their own details. But the foam rubber didn't hit the road until the process of building a costume actually began.

Bud Westmore's brother Frank was one of many makeup men who worked on *Black Lagoon*: Wardrobe man Roger J. Weinberg had the job of drying out the actual perspiration on the wardrobe of various players, and Frank's job was to then apply *synthetic* perspiration to the dried-out clothes, to match the perspiration stains in previous and following shots! Two decades later, Frank wrote the "warts and all" book *The Westmores of Hollywood*, a look-back at his family's movieland history. He devotes several pages to *Black Lagoon*, mentioning that Alland initially

> assigned the special effects department and the staff shop (which makes statues and other props) to develop his concept of what the sea creature should look like. The movie had a budget of only $650,000, and Alland was trying to circumvent the makeup department to save both time and money. For two months they wrestled with the problem. When they finished, [Ricou Browning] put on their handiwork and got into the Underwater Tank on the back lot. Instead of projecting menace, he looked like a man swimming around in long rubber underwear with black hair stuck to it.

Frank writes that the tank was on the back lot. He was there and I wasn't, but I have a 1951 map of Universal that shows that it was then on the *front* lot, practically in the shadow of the Phantom Stage and not far from Stage 21 where most of *Black Lagoon*'s interiors were shot.

The "black hair" part notwithstanding, Frank is obviously describing the fish-faced, mostly smooth-skinned outfit matching Alland's mental picture of what the Creature should look like: "much more human" than the eventual Gill Man, "very sad, beautiful," "far more 'attractive,' more 'romantic-looking'" than the beast we ended up with." For years, Monster Kid Numero Uno Bob Burns was friends with Universal makeup department sculptor Chris Mueller, Jr., who worked on *Black Lagoon*[25]; Burns has a memory of Mueller dismissively calling that incarnation of the Creature "The Pollywog," a nickname that Burns assumes Mueller concocted himself. If "The Pollywog" was good enough for Mueller, that's good enough for this book; hereinafter, that's what we'll call it too.

In an August 22 memo, unit manager James T. Vaughn wrote that the Pollywog suit was estimated to be ready for testing on September 2. He continued:

> Tests should include underwater shots in a suitable location such as Catalina where foliage and underwater growth can be found to determine the 3-D effect upon the spectator.
> … The monster should be photographed both under water and on land. Mr. Arnold is afraid that on land the absence of live eyes will give the mask a Mardi Gras feeling.
> … Re the monster double for land work, an extra outfit has been ok'd. Mr. Alland wants a man as tall as possible[26] and is looking at athletes for this purpose. It is my opinion that a professional stuntman should be employed, since certain of the work requires the knowledge and timing of a professional. He should also have acting ability in other scenes not of a stunt nature. Arnold is in agreement on this. The Makeup Department estimates they will require ten days with the new monster to develop the outfit, and the cost consideration of employing a stuntman for this purpose enters into the decision.[27]

The Pollywog suit, with Browning inside, got its first and probably last on-camera workout on September 5, when a test was shot—not at Catalina, as Vaughn suggested, but in the Underwater Tank (round 30' deep, 20' in diameter). There was a 12:36 p.m. crew call (director Arnold, 3-D underwater cameraman Welbourne, the makeup department's Jack Kevan, unit manager Sergei Petschnikoff, assistant director Fred Frank, more) and a 1:00 set call for actors Julie Adams and Ricou Browning. Adams showed up on time, wearing *a* bathing suit but not *the* hubba-hubba bathing suit she wears in the movie. (She was there for publicity photo purposes.) Browning was 45 minutes late, perhaps due to unexpected delays involving the costume. Browning and Welbourne got in the water, the latter shooting approximately 1400 feet of film as Browning gracefully swam. Intrigued, Adams asked to be allowed to put on an aqualung and swim a bit; Welbourne, concerned for her safety and initially hesitant, finally agreed. With Browning standing by in case anything went wrong, the actress got into the tank. In her 2011 autobiography *The Lucky Southern Star: Reflections from the Black Lagoon* she wrote that she loved the experience of "being released from gravity and breathing freely underwater":

> I could have stayed down there forever, but I could tell "Scotty" and Ricou were ready to call it a day. I got out somewhat reluctantly and dried off, babbling about how much fun I'd had. I was already racing ahead mentally,

thinking about going into the ocean with it. Of course, we did have a movie to make, so my dream of taking the aqualung out to sea would have to wait at least six weeks, until we wrapped principal photography.

Browning and Adams were dismissed at 3:45, the crew sticking around to shoot "tests on air gun and spears."

According to Adams, Universal exec Edward Muhl "hated" the look of the Pollywog suit on film. Browning was there when it happened: He told me,

> We all went into the screening room, people sat down and started watching the test footage they had filmed. I was there watching, along with the makeup guys and—well, *every*body was in there who had anything to do with the suit. Then when the thing was over, there was kinda silence until [James] Pratt and Muhl, two guys that I guess were the heads of the studio, spoke up and said, "That *sucked*!" Then everybody chimed in and said about the same thing.

Alland told me that when studio brass insisted that "his" non-monstrous monster, the Pollywog, wasn't sufficiently scary (and/or that it "sucked"), he stepped back and allowed Westmore and Co. to take over completely. "I just turned that over to them," Alland recalled, adding:

> I cannot take credit or blame for how the Creature's appearance turned out. To me, it was a cartoon, but apparently all of *you* people [adult-olescent Monster Kids] thought it was great. As I said, my concept originally was of a much more poetic and strangely beautiful—although frightening—kind of a being, who could become angry, who could become friendly, who could love. [The eventual costume] was just beyond my pale. But I'm wrong, everybody else loved it.

So who designed the "classic Creature"? Its creators began to die before most monster-movie fact-finders were born, so the complete story is lost to time. A still-existing Universal memo shows that Jack Kevan got a one-week's-pay bonus for the outstanding job he did "designing and working extremely long hours" on the Gill Man, so obviously he had no small hand in the matter. Bob Burns picked the brain of Gill Man

While working on Against All Flags *(1952), El Paso native Milicent Patrick sketched four portraits of Errol Flynn, who then purchased them for himself. Pictured: Bud Westmore, Patrick, Flynn.*

sculptor Mueller,[28] and according to Mueller, the humanoid we know and loved was designed by artist-actress Milicent Patrick.

On her résumé from the late 1960s (or later), she gives her name as

BARONESSA di POLOMBARA
Milicent Patrick
Formerly
Mildred Elizabeth Fulvia di Rossi

and claimed to have been born an Italian baroness. She was raised in South America and in San Simeon, California, where her father C.C. Rossi spent ten years "building the William Randolph Hearst Estate, as engineer, architect and superintendent of construction." Patrick won "three scholarships in Art at Madam Chouinard's Art Institute" and claims to have been the first woman animator at Walt Disney Studios; according to an article in an unidentified 1954 magazine, she was "sketching film fashions for Paramount Pictures" at age 15. She later turned to modeling and then, in the late 1940s, to acting in the movies, debuting in 1947 in the Danny Kaye comedy *A Song Is Born*.[29]

According to a *Creature* publicity story on Patrick, she was playing a small and uncredited role in Universal's costume adventure *The World in His Arms* (1952) when, anxious to resume her artist career, she showed some of her drawings to Westmore. As a result, she won the assignment of creating the "pirate faces" for actors who would be appearing opposite Errol Flynn in the studio's upcoming *Against All Flags* (1952). Subsequent subjects for "makeup illustrator" Patrick included Jack Palance (and all the character parts) in *Sign of the Pagan* (1954); she also contributed to the creation of the *It Came from Outer Space* Xenomorphs and, according to *Mirror* magazine, to the look of Mr. Hyde in 1953's *Abbott and Costello Meet Dr. Jekyll and Mr. Hyde*.

Burns didn't think to ask Mueller if Patrick had any input on the Pollywog but he, Burns, feels she probably did. "Chris Mueller said that Milicent was the sweetest lady in the world and that she was in [on *Black Lagoon*] from the very beginning," said Burns, "and as far as he was concerned, *she* designed the whole thing. I got that right from Chris, and he wasn't the kind of guy to lie. Chris said that Bud Westmore had nothing to do with the design of the Creature. The way Chris put it was, 'Westmore signed the checks and got in the pictures

Westmore and Kevan *hope* to have one suit for the monster and the two heads ready to test about October 3rd. Should this suit be o.k., it will take three or four more days to make another underwater suit to take to Florida. They are also making bits and pieces for the land monster, which they hope to have ready about a week after the water monster is o.k'd.

Westmore would like to test the water suit at Catalina. I would like to discuss this with you, as I think a test of this nature would run into considerable money.

The original plan, according to a July 2, 1953, *Hollywood Reporter* item, was for *Black Lagoon* to roll in late August or early September, but the need for the design and fabrication of an all-new monster suit delayed the start of filming for weeks. This benefited at least one person: Julie Adams. She called Welbourne and said that, because there was nothing to do during this unexpected hiatus, she'd like to use the aqualung in the ocean. To her delight she found herself, a few days later, en route with Welbourne and Browning to Catalina, where they met friends of Welbourne's who had a boat. She described the adventure in *Southern Star*:

> We all got rooms on the island and then went out on the boat each day. My first underwater adventure was a dive down to a sunken yacht that had been taken over by a school of very large fish that permitted us to swim among them as we explored the shipwreck. The next day we went even deeper to take a look at the ocean floor. On our slow ascent back to the surface, we drifted into a school of thousands of small fish. They gave way just enough to let us through, but they didn't wish to be touched.
>
> On our final day, I was offered the opportunity to put on a real diving suit, complete with a helmet and heavy shoes for walking on the ocean floor. I took them up on it. They put me into the suit, which was connected by a hose to a pump on the boat, and explained that the pump would keep air going into the suit continuously.
>
> … All set, down I went. I was lowered off the boat into about 30 feet of water. The ocean floor was a gradual downward slope, which made walking easy. Some colorful fish swam by; I walked past some sea urchins. All the while, my friends "Scotty" and Ricou, equipped with aqualungs, swam along beside me. Everything was going fine, but we

Milicent Patrick, the Creator from the Black Lagoon, told *Mirror* magazine, "Let the other gals have the Hollywood wolves. I'm very happy with my monsters" (Frankenstein, Mr. Hyde, the Gill Man).

[the still photographs of the makeup men at work]. That's about it.'"[30]

In a September 21 inter-office memo, unit manager Petschnikoff wrote to production manager Gilbert Kurland:

1. Creature from the Black Lagoon (1954)

were getting a little too far away from the boat, so "Scotty" signaled that it was time to go back. I turned around and started to head back up the gentle slope. The problem was that the heavy shoes were much happier going downhill than up. There was no traction, and the harder I tried to walk, the deeper my boots dug into the sand. I was getting nowhere.

"Scotty" and Ricou swam to the surface and signaled to the boat that I needed help. Suddenly, [the ropes] that had lowered me down were now pulling me back toward the boat, as I accumulated a lot of kelp along the way. Finally they hauled me up, diving suit, kelp and all. It was a rather ignominious end to my diving adventure.

It always looked so easy when I saw it in the movies but, as I discovered that day, real life could be more complicated than screen life. Still, we all had a good laugh at my expense. That was the first and last time that I ever went down in a diving suit. At least I can say that I did it once.

Although this was Browning's first time in California, the Catalina adventure was about the only "getaway" he had during the month he spent there during *Black Lagoon* pre-production. "I did *that* [Catalina], and I went to the observatory," he told me. "Other than that, I didn't really get to *do* much or *see* much, 'cause I had to be at the studio every day, working on the building of the suit or doing *some*thing." Even in his off-hours, he didn't get far from the lot: Universal had him staying in an old hotel right across the street.

Finally, on October 5, *the* Creature suit we all know and love was ready for its 3-D closeups: Back at the Underwater Tank, director James Havens was scheduled to shoot "Photo Water Tests" of Ricou Browning in his new "Water Gill Man" suit, plus footage of Julie in her bathing suit. The Daily Production Report shows that work began smoothly with a full shot of Adams "as she dives into water. Shooting up from in water. She comes f.g. toward camera and swims away to exit b.g."; next they got a shot of Browning's Gill Man "in water shooting up as he swims around." But Welbourne's underwater camera stripped a gear and landed in the studio's machine shop from 11:30 a.m. to 1:30 p.m. Later in the day, it stripped another gear. In defeat, one of the production people wrote on the Report, "Unable to finish scheduled tests due to loss of light and fatigue of Rico [*sic*] Browning."

One problem that needed to be resolved quickly: The costume for this underwater beast was made of foam rubber … and foam rubber *floats*. Jack Kevan told me, "We found out that he couldn't get underwater because the sponge had so much air in it, so we developed a system of weights and so on. We used lead weights to counter-balance the sponge; also, the suit would absorb a lot of water, which also lent weight to it."

"I wore a chest plate that was thin lead," Browning told

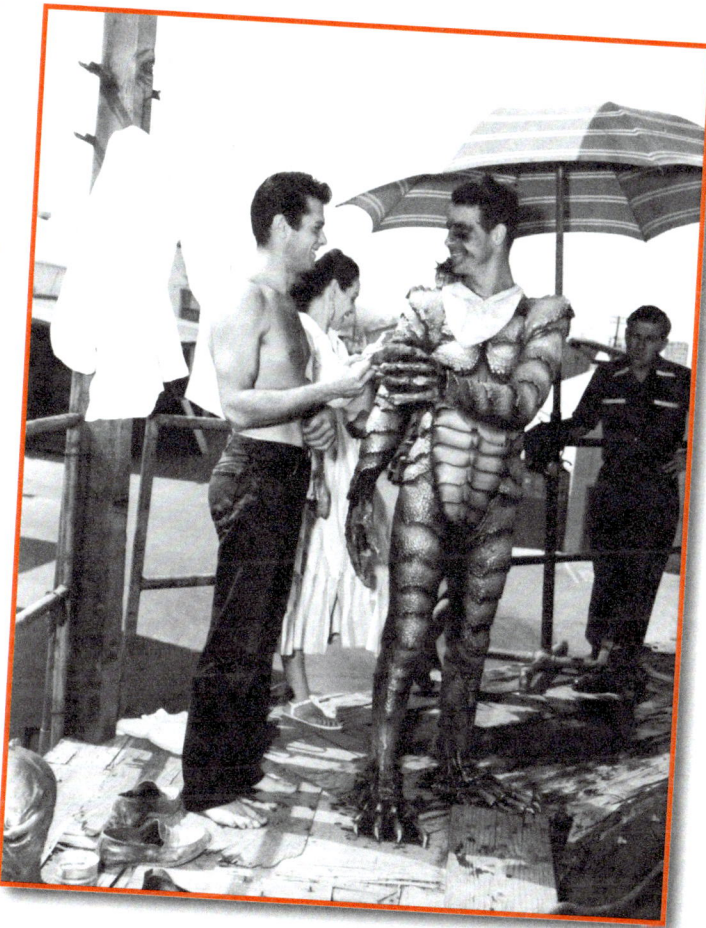

When Ricou Browning worked in the Underwater Tank, he was visited by a few actors then making other movies on the lot, among them Tony Curtis (pictured giving Browning a cigarette) and Audie Murphy, who according to Browning "sat down and talked for a little while." Curtis and Murphy were then making Johnny Dark *and* Drums Across the River, *respectively.*

me. "It had straps permanently attached to the lead on one side, and the loose ends of those straps went around my back and over my shoulders and hooked to the *other* side of the chest plate and held it in place. The same thing with thigh weights. Same thing with ankle weights."

Also on October 9, on Stage 9, wardrobe tests were being photographed. Among the six players modeling their threads was the movie's star, no, not Frank Lovejoy, but Richard Carlson, the leading man in Universal's still-in-theaters *It Came from Outer Space*. Lovejoy was "out" because, according to a September 8 Hedda Hopper column, he got his wires crossed and committed himself to two pictures whose shooting schedules overlapped, *Black Lagoon* and MGM's *Men of the Fighting Lady* (1954). Lovejoy ended up in *Fighting Lady* while Carlson took over in *Black Lagoon*.[31] Hopper added, "Dick had got three months ahead in shooting his television series [*I Led 3 Lives*] and was preparing to take a vacation. But he couldn't resist the picture, since it's another science fiction story being made by the same group that did *It Came from Outer Space*."[32] Carlson is 41 in Universal's *Creature from the Black Lagoon*, exactly one day older than the studio where he was working: The actor was born on April 29, 1912, and the Universal Film Manufacturing Company was incorporated by Carl Laemmle the very next day.

On October 6, Havens and Welbourne again shot Gill Man test footage: First they photographed Browning on land, then coming out of the U-I back lot's Park Lake and finally in the Underwater Tank. The actor wore as many as three different Creature heads that day, the one he sported in the tank designated in paperwork as the "#3-Head." (While at the Underwater Tank, Havens and Welbourne also made photographic tests of the "rotenone.")

Vision was a problem for Browning. Inside his Gill Man head he tried wearing goggles, the type that pearl divers wear, but water would get into them and then there was no way to get it out. A face-mask made the Gill Man face bulge too much. Ultimately it was just his naked eyes seeing out through the eyeholes in the Gill Man helmet.[33] "It was kind of like looking through a keyhole," he told me. "And looking through an underwater keyhole without a mask on, your vision is blurred—*very* blurred. It was very awkward seeing, and a lot of it was kind of hit and miss."

Universal publicists claimed that the Gill Man suit seen in *Black Lagoon* was the result of eight months' work, and over the subsequent decades, many fan-writers bought into that. The *truth* is even more impressive: Once the Pollywog was rejected and the makeup department had to start from scratch, less than *one* month passed before the all-new, now-iconic suit was being screen-tested.

As *Black Lagoon*'s start date neared, preparations also continued to be made in other departments; for example, Production Service Memos show the acquisition of acacia trees, cottonwood trees and a eucalyptus tree, plus loads of live oak, sumac, juniper, bamboo and carpet grass for Set 1 (the Black Lagoon), 1000 feet of snake grass and a load of tea trees for Set 2 (Dr. Maia's camp), etc. The (sound) stages were being set. Soon it would be time for cameras to roll … time for Universal, the House That Horror Built, to add another bold-faced name, **The Gill Man**, to the monster field.

Many fans consider him to be one of Universal's very best Classic Monsters—and to be their very *last* Classic Monster.

Synopsis

The action begins in outer space with a shot of a ball of smoke meant to depict Earth's materialization out of gaseous material. A stentorian narrator[34] opens with a quote from Genesis as fiery explosions rock the nebula and send sparks and rocks into the 3-D camera. The narrator then gives us a crash course on the formation of the Earth and the creation of life in the young planet's oceans, and we see a long trail of imprints of a monster's feet leading from the water's edge up a sandy beach. "The record of life is written on the land," the narrator continues, "where, 15 million years later, in the upper reaches of the Amazon, Man is still trying to read it."

After some aerial stock footage of a jungle, we cut to the river's-edge camp of Brazilian geologist Dr. Carl Maia (Antonio Moreno), where there's excitement in the air: Extending out of a limestone wall is a just-unearthed, claw-like skeleton hand and forearm,

No nerds need apply: The Maurice Zimm treatment described the Reed character (ultimately played by 41-year-old Richard Carlson) as "a distinguished, dynamic-looking man in his early forties, with a touch of gray at his temples. There's nothing bookish or professorial about him. He belongs to the virile breed of Scientist-Adventurers."

with webbed fingers suggesting a prehistoric amphibian. What happens next is described in Jim Shepard's humorous February 2002 *Playboy* magazine article "Reflections from the Black Lagoon," the story of *Creature from the Black Lagoon* as told *by* the Creature:

> The doctor took pictures, his flash redundant in the sunlight. He said he thought [this archaeological find] was very important. He set the camera aside and pickaxed the fossil arm right out of the rock. So much for the preciousness of the find.

Maia tells his native helpers Luis and Tomas (Rodd Redwing and Perry Lopez) that he is leaving for the Instituto de Biología Marítima in Morajo Bay to get help for the job of digging out the rest of the skeleton. Unnoticed by Maia and the natives, bubbles are surging to the surface of the water just a few feet off-shore, and then a huge, web-taloned hand—the live counterpart of the fossil—reaches out of the water and rakes its claws along the bank. Listen close and you can hear, buried by music, the sound of scratching. And notice the (rubber) pinkie claw bending as it drags along the hard surface!

The scene switches to Manaus in Northern Brazil, where Dr. Maia and ichthyologist Kay Lawrence (Julie Adams) race in a speedboat from the Instituto's Morajo Bay pier to an anchored barge: Kay's boyfriend David Reed (Richard Carlson) has descended from the barge via aqualung to look for specimens of lungfish. Summoned to the surface, Reed is happy to see his old teacher Maia, who asks, "Are you two married yet?"

"No, no," Kay says wearily. "David says we're together all the time anyway. 'Might as well save expenses.'"[35] Maia shows Reed a photo of the petrified hand, which fascinates him. Later, in a combination office-aquarium at the Instituto, the fossil (now mounted on a stand) is the center of attention as Reed, Kay, their boss Mark Williams (Richard Denning), Maia and Dr. Thompson (Whit Bissell) decide to comprise an expedition and recover more of the skeleton. Reed is especially keen on learning more about this "missing link" between land and marine life, as it may lead to a means for modern-day man to adapt to the rigors of future life on other planets with different atmospheres and pressures.[36]

Meanwhile, back at Maia's camp, the webbed hand again reaches out of the water (same shot as before, just day-for-night); the camera now "becomes" the Gill Man and approaches the tent occupied by natives Luis and Tomas. Antagonized when Luis throws a lantern, the monster piefaces the quailing, whimpering native with his baseball mitt-sized hand, then turns his attention to Tomas.[37] From outside, we watch as the tent shakes as the Gill Man's boar-like roars and his victims' screams fill the air (along with Herman Stein's music cue "That Hand Again"). We don't see the carnage, nor even the Creature, and yet it might be the scariest scene in the picture.

A ramshackle fish-hauling boat, the *Rita*, chugs up the Amazon; according to the *Black Lagoon* review in the magazine *The Skin Diver*, "[It looks] like a resurrected *African Queen* left over from a previous picture of that name." *Black Lagoon*'s nod to comic relief, the grizzled, greasy Lucas (Nestor Paiva), is the captain, and his crewmen are brothers Zee and Chico (Bernie Gozier, Henry Escalante). (From the script: "[Lucas] speaks with a slight Portuguese accent.... He's a little too easy-going, bordering on the lazy.") The weather is hot, Williams is hotter ("Couldn't Maia find anything better than this *barge*?!") and we get a foretaste of the way the very different Reed and Williams tend to squabble and how Kay tries to act as peacemaker. (We also get the idea that part of the reason for Williams' irritability is the fact that longtime colleague Kay has gone for Reed rather than for him.) A groundwork is also laid for the 20th-century existence of the movie's monster as Reed soliloquizes that the Amazon is "exactly as it was 150 million years ago.... Even the animals here grow as they did in Devonian forests."

When the party arrives at Maia's camp, the natives' bodies are discovered, their ripped-up condition prompting Lucas to suggest they were killed by a jaguar. Yet again the webbed hand reaches out of the water, this time for the unsuspecting Kay's ankle, but she walks away in the proverbial nick of time. A montage of pickaxe, shovel and sift box activity indicates the passage of eight sweltry, sweat-stained days of excavation into the limestone wall; Williams is angry and disappointed over their failure to find the skeleton and makes no bones about it. Reed suggests that in the distant past, part of the bank may have fallen into the river, with the current breaking it up and carrying it away. According to Lucas, this tributary dead-ends at a lagoon. "My boys call it 'the Black Lagoon,' the paradise," he says, adding with a laugh, "Only, they say, nobody has ever come back to *prrrrove* it!" With hopes of finding more of the fossil at the bottom of the lagoon, Williams growls, "We'll *do* it!"

The Black Lagoon, accessible through a narrow inlet, is eerie and otherworldly, with glass-like water and banks overrun with jungle fringe. Reed and Williams don aqualungs and descend in quest of rocks to compare to those in the limestone wall.[38] *BAH-BAH-BAHHH!*: Our first look at the Gill Man comes when Williams swims over his hiding place and the monster unexpectedly rises up into the shot. He's got a man's body, a fishy face, scales and fearsome claws.[39] Unaware of his presence, the two men return to the *Rita* where Reed's description of the lagoon depths ("Like another *world*") gives Kay ideas. Unobserved, she sheds her shirt to reveal a snug-fitting one-piece white bathing suit and dives in for a swim.[40] In an amazing scene that probably elicited oohs'n'aahs and squeals of terror in equal number in 1954, the captivated Creature backstrokes through the water directly beneath her, "obviously as taken up with her figure as any mere man might be" (to quote a sneak preview audience member's preview card). Kay is unaware that anything is below, and even does some Esther Williams–like underwater rolls, until the Creature mischievously pokes at her ankles. When she returns to the *Rita*, the Gill Man follows and gets tangled in a trawling net hanging over its side. His efforts to escape rock the boat and crack the boom. When the ruckus subsides and the net is brought up, the onlookers see a Gill Man–sized hole in it plus a torn-off claw. Kay, examining the claw and remembering being touched during her swim, lets out a gasp. In the movie it's an effective moment but the assistant director's Daily Production Report describes the shot most mundanely: "Kay as she reacts to Gill Man's toenail."

Preparing to dive and investigate, Reed is packing a camera[41] and Williams a CO_2 speargun.

> REED: Mark, we're out for photographs for study, not trophies. This—this thing *alive* and in its natural habitat is valuable to us.
> MARK [*condescending*]: Why settle for a photo when we can get the real thing?
> REED: You don't sound like a scientist, you sound like some big game hunter out for the kill!

Underwater, Williams swims around trying to poke out the eye of every 3-D viewer with his speargun as the unseen Creature watches and semi-playfully tries to avoid them. But Williams finally catches sight of the fleeing fishman and puts a spear in him. In the *Rita*'s bunk room, as Reed develops a photo he hopes will feature the Creature, Lucas mentions that an old native woman once told him the legend of a man who lives underwater. ("But she was crazy," he adds with a bellylaugh. "'Crazy Goole,' everybody call her!") Unbeknownst to them, the Creature is prowling the deck, and pounces upon the screaming Chico (the monster's one unprovoked killing in the movie). "Chico is *gone*!" cries Zee. "My brother was dragged down into the water by a *demon*!"

A plan is hatched to capture the Creature by dropping into the lagoon sacks of rotenone, a drug that native fishermen make from roots to paralyze and catch fish. Throughout the day and that night, as the motionless bodies of small fish dot the water's surface, a watch is kept for a similarly smashed Creature. The marine monster attempts to climb aboard the *Rita* but is scared off by a hanging lantern. Hoping to catch him while he's still groggy, Reed and Williams hit the water in pursuit, trailing him down to the underwater entrance to an air-filled grotto. The Creature exits the grotto through a beach entrance, strikes a Menacing Monster pose and begins walking toward an unsuspecting Kay who is sitting nearby. His machete raised high, Zee races to her rescue, but the Creature fatally throttles him. As the Creature attempts to carry off the yelping Kay, the rotenone kicks in and he collapses. Williams, arriving on the scene, becomes maniacal and beats the kayoed Creature with a rifle until Reed intercedes.

After sealing the unconscious Creature in a water-filled tank on the *Rita* deck, Reed quite stupidly insists on

Julie Adams, Richard Denning and Richard Carlson examine a Gill Man toenail found in the Rita net. Early script drafts called for it to be a torn-off finger with attached web portion, but apparently it was decided not to have the Gill Man visibly minus a finger throughout the movie.

revisiting and photographing the grotto. Quite stupidly, *everyone* goes with him except Kay and Thompson, the latter left to stand guard over the Creature. Thompson is dispensing avuncular advice Kay's way when the Creature awakens and (off-camera) smashes his way free. Thompson tries to keep him at bay with a lantern, but the monster lunges forward and begins to maul the scientist. Whacked with the lantern, the Creature is engulfed in (superimposed) flames and dives overboard. Thompson writhes on the deck, his face (seen for a split-second) a bloody mess, and his agonized groans continue to be heard even after the scene fades to black.

The Alpha Male Olympics recommence when Williams announces that he wants to try to recapture the Creature, and Reed insists that they leave now (and then come back properly equipped for monster-fighting). Reed prevails with a bit of help from Lucas, who draws a knife on the unreasonable Williams. But the Creature, with a human canniness, prevents their departure by placing a dead tree horizontally across the lagoon inlet's narrow entrance. Reed realizes he must go into the water and wrap a cable around the half-submerged tree so that it can be winched aside; Williams, consumed by the thought of killing the Creature, tries to get Reed to let him tag along. A bunk room fistfight ensues, with Williams coming out on the losing end.

Reed descends into the water and Williams follows, again going after the Gill Man. This time the hunter becomes the hunted, and Williams quickly finds himself in an aqueous court of no appeal: Underscored by Henry Mancini's pulse-pounding cue "Monster Gets Mark," the hand-to-claw clash between the Creature and his tormentor goes from "mid-water" to lagoon bottom where the combatants roil up an impressive cloud of mud and silt before the Gill Man uses his teeth to tear out Williams' air hose. Speargun-toting Reed chases off the Creature as Williams' air tanks pull his lifeless body to the surface.

For his next descent, Reed arms himself with a jerry-rigged rotenone "spray gun" to keep the Creature at bay; this time his attempt to attach a cable to the tree barricade is successful. The Devonian Don Juan will not be denied: He creeps aboard the *Rita*, seizes Kay and dives overboard, swimming with her down to his grotto entrance. Reed makes the same descent, enters the grotto and finds the unconscious Kay in a partially flooded cave chamber, ceremoniously draped across a slab of rock. Laying in wait for Reed's arrival, the Creature moves in on him.[42] Reed is about to lose a knife-to-claw battle with the beastie when Maia and Lucas enter the grotto via the beach entrance, their rifles blazing. Bleeding from multiple bullet holes, the gurgling Gill Man staggers out of the cave and toward the water's edge. Maia is taking careful aim at his back, about to go for the kill, when Reed reaches out and pushes down his rifle. The Creature wades into the water, swims through some weeds and, in the final shot, limply drifts down into inky darkness.

Bios from the *Black Lagoon*
By Tom Weaver

Richard Carlson as Dr. David Reed

In her May 7, 1953, column, filmland's Hedda Hopper drew attention to the extent to which Richard Carlson had become immersed in movies with "adult science themes": She revealed that he'd had a busy day the previous Monday (May 4) finishing work on the Gothic horror–SF *The Maze* at 7:30 p.m. and then, skipping a party thrown by his wife Mona, going directly to the airport and thence to New York to help kick off his movie *The Magnetic Monster* (which he also co-produced). While he was in the Big Apple, Universal put him on salary to stay a while longer in order to help publicize the coming release of his film *It Came from Outer Space*.

All the activity and attention would probably please most people, but according to actor Richard Stapley, Carlson—who began his career working with some top stars at top studios—might actually have felt that he'd let himself down. Stapley, star of *The Strange Door* (1951) and therefore Universal's first '50s horror hero, was friendly with Carlson, Universal's first sci-fi hero, and also with William Holden—and felt that Carlson was the better actor of the two. He told me,

> In addition to being just a great guy—one of the nicest people I ever met—Carlson was a really terrific actor. I don't think he ever got the break he should have gotten, 'cause he was probably a better actor than Bill Holden. But Carlson drank a lot. I don't think he ever drank [while working], he was very, very strict with himself. But I think he was kind of disappointed with his career. It started off

Richard Carlson in a starlet-like "lounging-seductive" pose(!). By all reports, he did like hitting on the ladies ... starting with his long-suffering wife Mona's best friends.

drooled over for the last ten years…!'" But the date was Friday the 13th (of February 1953) and, as far as working with Carlson was concerned, the day lived up to its unpleasant reputation:

> Our dressing rooms were right next to each other on the set, and I found out he was *not* a nice person. He told me some really nasty stories, mean-spirited stories [about other Hollywood people] that made me *really* dislike him. I did not like him at all.
>
> I must tell you about the "date," if you could call it that, that I had with him. Oh! I guess he had just had a fight with his wife or something, and he asked me if I would go out for a drink with him. I wasn't doing anything special that night so I said, "Well … sure." And he drank, and he drank, and he drank, and he drank. And I *didn't* drink. I thought he was taking me out to dinner or something. [*TW: Did you get a dinner out of it?*] Just drinks, I don't remember ever getting *any*thing to eat, unless there were nuts at the bar! Then he took me to another place, a very famous place at the corner of Sunset and Crescent Heights, the Garden of Allah. I'll tell you one disgusting thing: After he parked his car and we were walking into the Garden of Allah, all of a sudden he stopped by some bushes, whipped it out and *peed* into the bushes. Without a word, he came to a stop and hosed down the bushes! And then at the Garden of Allah he drank, and he drank, and he drank…
>
> Well, it was *the* most boring evening of my life, it was like an evening from Hell. I was so glad when it was over.

The actor died as a result of his alcoholism according to Curt Siodmak, writer of *The Magnetic Monster* and *Riders to the Stars* (1954)—the latter co-starring and directed by Carlson. Siodmak told me, "They're all unhappy people, actors. Most of them start to fade, and they cannot take it."

In *Western Clippings* magazine, actor-writer Warren Douglas was quoted as saying that Carlson "fancied himself rather superior intellectually and culturally to most of his peers," and actor Michael Fox (*The Magnetic Monster, Riders to the Stars*) told me,

> Richard was a Phi Beta Kappa. I happen to have some collegiate honors as well.… He was used to being the intellectual limelight on a set. He did not like to share it with someone who was, in his opinion, lesser than he.… It was sad, because he was a good-looking man, he was bright, he was quite well read in many areas, but the moment he thought that somebody else was in authority, he would tell you how to do the job.

Some descriptions of Carlson as a person make you wonder if *Black Lagoon* would be just a little bit better with Carlson as the bossy, high-handed Mark Williams and real-

much higher, then he didn't become a star. I think that he and Holden were good friends, and … you know how it is, you see somebody taking off and you're *not*.

"When I was a child, I had a crush on him, I just thought he was the *handsomest* guy I had ever seen," gushed Kathleen Hughes, who was under contract to Universal in 1953 when *Black Lagoon* was made. "My uncle, [screenwriter] F. Hugh Herbert, was a friend of his, and when I was a kid, he used to take my cousins and me by Richard Carlson's house, when we were on our way somewhere. I know I was at his house a couple of times and, oh!, I just thought he was a dreamboat."

Hughes had one scene in *It Came from Outer Space* and was excited to know she'd be acting with Carlson: "I felt so *lucky* when I heard that I was gonna work in a picture with him, I thought [*she sighs rapturously*]: 'Oh, this man I have life nice guy Richard Denning as Nice Guy Scientist David Reed.

Born in Albert Lea, Minnesota, the son of a Danish-born attorney, Carlson (1912–1977) read *Amazing Stories* as a kid and remained a science fiction fan, according to his Forry Ackerman–written *Famous Monsters* obit. While attending the University of Minnesota he wrote, produced and directed a pair of well-received plays; after graduation he opened a Minneapolis theater where he wrote, directed and acted in three flops. From here he went to the Pasadena Playhouse and then to Broadway, where he not only acted in plays but also wrote and directed one, *Western Waters*—at age 24![43]

Carlson went into the movies when screen mogul David O. Selznick spotted him in an unsuccessful Broadway play and brought him out to Hollywood as an actor-writer-director. Arriving in the film capital by train on April 21, 1938, Carlson made his film bow in Selznick's charming comedy *The Young in Heart*, playing a good part as Janet Gaynor's impecunious Irish-accented beau. After *The Young in Heart* was previewed at a Riverside theater on September 25, Selznick perused the 400 preview cards and ordered his story department to search for starring vehicles for Carlson (and others). But *Young in Heart* wound up being Carlson's *only* Selznick picture. In March of 1939 it was announced that Carlson would play the title role in Columbia's *Golden Boy*, an adaptation of Clifford Odets' recent Group Theatre play—but then the role went instead to (uh-oh!) William Holden![44] Carlson picked up a consolation prize in June: a beautiful 20-year-old wife, Mona Mayfield. Their honeymoon had to wait a few months as Carlson was making four pictures consecutively.[45]

In the beginning, Carlson would get the best male role in every B picture and the second-best in A pictures. He was in good company in the latter: Bette Davis in *The Little Foxes* (1941), Charles Boyer and Margaret Sullavan in *Back Street* (1941), Hedy Lamarr and Walter Pidgeon in *White Cargo* (1942), Judy Garland in *Presenting Lily Mars* (1943), etc., and he played all these parts with considerable second-lead charm. There were also roles in the kind of pictures "we" like: Bob Hope's *The Ghost Breakers* (1940) and Abbott and Costello's *Hold That Ghost* (1941). Speaking of ghosts, the bleak and gooey fantasy film *Beyond Tomorrow* (1940) co-stars Carlson as an aw-shucks too-polite Texas lad, stranded in the snowy Big Apple at Christmastime, who becomes a popular radio baritone—and then a ghost himself in the closing reel.

In the supporting cast of one of Carlson's early movies, *Winter Carnival* (1939), was Marsha Hunt; "We became acquainted on the show, and after that I knew him *very* well over a number of years," she told me.

A Hold That Ghost *shot of Richard Carlson and Evelyn Ankers—later Mrs. Richard Denning. Foreshadowing scientist roles to come, the twentysomething Carlson's character in* Ghost *is a boyish, bespectacled doctor ("I'm doing some special research on glands and their vitamin consumption"), alternately diffident and bold.*

Richard was brand-newly married to Mona Mayfield from Texas, a very stunning and appealing person to me. Richard and Mona rented a guest house from … I think it was Jimmy Bush, who had been a young juvenile actor and kept working in films into adulthood. He had a home off Laurel Canyon with a guest house, which the Carlsons rented, and where they entertained a few friends every Sunday. My husband Jerry Hopper and I became regulars there and enjoyed, many a Sunday, meeting interesting, stimulating people.

Richard and Mona were starting to think about a house of their own; Jerry and I were renting an apartment and also dreaming of a place of our own. So we looked together for available land, and the Valley appealed to us because it was wide open and unsettled country. We found a package of acreage, two parcels adjoining, on a hillside overlooking the Valley. Well, they bought one and we bought the other, so we were next-door neighbors. We had our homes designed and custom-built to our own needs, and we saw a great deal of each other and it was compatible and charming.

In 1942 came MGM's *The Affairs of Martha* with Hunt and Carlson top-billed (in that order), "directed by the great

Jules Dassin and a charming experience," said Hunt. During the war years, there were changes in Hunt's life (she remarried)—and perhaps even more of a change in Carlson, personality-wise:

Richard Carlson and wife Mona at a 1950 cocktail party. Alongside other Hollywood wives, Mona appeared as herself on a 1955 *I Love Lucy* episode. She also played herself in her husband's 1952 TV pilot *Richard's Almanac*, shot in the study of their Sherman Oaks home: Carlson read passages of poetry and prose, Mona and their two kids came in and out, and neighbors dropped by to kibitz.

He was very bright, very analytical, and he enjoyed [determining] *why* things were the way they were, or people were the way they were ... but without being emotionally involved. He was sort of like the detached scientist. And I'm afraid that friendships were kind of the same: Richard didn't have warmth personally. Mona remained very dear to me, and I just didn't see them as a pair any more. Richard was drinking ... and he was *far* from a faithful husband. This really affected my estimate of him. I had been so fond of him, and I was really so disappointed at the change that occurred over the years.

Afterwards I hardly saw Richard again except by chance, and then it was really not much more than a greeting. I was just so disappointed in the change in the person. Years after Richard died, I went to Mona's funeral and I found it a very sad business. Mona was a lonely and sad lady.[46]

I think Richard was gifted with looks, personality, intelligence ... he did good work on the screen, but I don't think it was very emotional or very deep. It was *proficient*.

I guess this is not a very good portrait, is it?, that I'm giving you of Richard Carlson...?

Perhaps part of the reason for the change was that, after his return from naval wartime service, there were fewer movie offers; he supplemented his income by writing magazine articles and other activities. When he did get film roles, he was no longer working with (say) Hedy and Judy at MGM or Bette at Goldwyn; now it was usually on the level of Lynn Bari and Turhan Bey at Eagle-Lion (*The Amazing Mr. X*, 1948), Greta Gynt at Hammer (*Whispering Smith Hits London*, 1951), Sterling Hayden and Bill Phipps at Monogram (*Flat Top*, 1952). In 1952 he had his first go at TV when he produced two 15-minute pilot films called *Richard's Almanac*; the series was considered "too erudite for the commercial market" and went no further. He had better luck with Ziv's syndicated series *I Led 3 Lives* (1953–56), a weekly dose of skullduggery based on the autobi-

Richard Carlson (right) with Herbert A. Philbrick, who for nine years posed as a Communist agent on behalf of the FBI; in the spring of 1949 his surprise testimony helped convict 11 top Commie leaders on trial for conspiracy to overthrow the U.S. government. Based on Philbrick's book, the Carlson-starring teleseries *I Led 3 Lives* was a favorite of Lee Harvey Oswald's (courtesy Photofest).

ography of Herbert Philbrick, who led parallel lives as (Life #1) a Boston family man and advertising executive, (Life #2) a top member of the New England chapter of the Communist Party, and (Life #3) a U.S. government spy, secretly keeping the FBI posted on his Commie cohorts' activities.

Then, suddenly, Carlson began casting a long shadow across the sci-fi movie landscape: Within a space of perhaps only 12 months, one after another, came *The Magnetic Monster* and *Riders to the Stars* for Ivan Tors, *It Came from Outer Space* and *Black Lagoon* for Universal, and *The Maze* for Allied Artists—the latter screen-pairing him for the *first* time with a frog-faced, web-fingered marine monster. Carlson was working in moneymaking movies but if he expected critical plaudits (which he probably didn't), there weren't many to be had. In his *Black Lagoon* review, *Pacific Stars and Stripes* entertainment editor Al Ricketts encapsulated Carlson's recent work in a humorous vein:

> Richard Carlson seems to be Hollywood's favorite when it comes to probing into outer space, under water and into the past.
>
> In the last year "Dauntless Dick" has battled with moon men, globs of Jell-O and frog-like critters that turn out to be his uncle.
>
> [In *Black Lagoon* he is] assisted by several types of "ologists" plus a shapely gal (Julia Adams) who trots around in shorts and plants a kiss on his forehead every time he dons his aqualung for a dip into the deep.

In the *Video Watchdog* article "They Did Science!" Baby Boomer Monster Kid Larry Blamire wrote of Carlson,

> As a sci-fi salesman bar none, he convinced us something vital to the Earth's survival was happening and if we don't concentrate on our TV screen really hard, *Earth ain't gonna make it, okay? So you better keep watching, okay?* And I did.
>
> In the dictionary next to the word "earnest," there's a picture of Richard Carlson. The man had focus. He was driven.... [W]e genuinely believed he was a learned man. There seemed an innate intelligence there.

Indeed there did seem to be. Carlson is the best of the three Gill Man leading men, serious and forthright about the business of science (and the business of Creature-fighting), and also effective in his tender scenes with Julie Adams. His successors came across quite differently: Although ready to put his life on the line in dicey situations, *Revenge*'s John Agar too often comes across as the class clown of the science set, and *Creature Walks*' Rex Reason is holier-than-thou and more than a little dull.

After the wrap-up of *Black Lagoon*, Carlson went right back into his TV series *I Led 3 Lives*—and, movie-wise, right back into the supporting player ranks. Except for Bert I. Gordon's "haunted lighthouse" tale *Tormented* (1960), there were no more leads. But maybe in some ways, that suited him. Asked in a *Photon* magazine interview if he enjoyed playing heavies, he responded, "I enjoy acting. I don't care if it's a heavy or what as long as it's not the straight leading man—I'm not cut out for it."

Julie Adams as Kay Lawrence

Not every performer can specify exactly when that old clichéd "acting bug" bit, but Julie Adams can: when she was in a third grade play, *Hansel and Gretel*, and a jug of milk was spilled too soon. Other cast members stood frozen in fear, unsure what to do next, while she surprised herself by ad libbing and saving the day—and receiving some audience applause. "This gave me a flush of power—in the third grade—and I think that's where it all began!" she told me with a smile in her voice.

Creature came early in Adams' eventual movie career, and starring in that cult classic (and becoming sci-fi fans' first pin-up girl) proved to be a mixed blessing. She's demonstrated her dramatic worth in dozens of movies, several plays and enough TV to fill a back lot Black Lagoon, but this one monster movie managed to put everything else she did, past and future, in the shade. She told me,

> Once I was working in Chicago in a play, *Father's Day* by Oliver Hailey, and I was peeved when I got this review that said, "Julie Adams shows more depth than one would have suspected from the star of *Creature from the Black Lagoon*." No matter what you do, you can act your heart out, but people will always say, "Oh, Julie Adams—*Creature from the Black Lagoon*."

She said this back in the early 1990s, at a time when she sometimes seemed to be keeping *Creature* fanatics at arm's length, and even though she laughed as she said it, I wondered aloud if she wasn't crying on the inside. She insisted that she was not: "Oh, no, no, no. One must take all these things with humor. After all, it's amazing that the film connected with that many people. To be so closely connected with it is fine, just fine."

The only child of alcoholic parents, she was born Betty May Adams in Waterloo, Iowa. In her self-published 2011 autobiography *The Lucky Southern Star: Reflections from the Black Lagoon* she writes in a humorous way about the fact that she was conceived out of wedlock, her parents rushing to the altar, fibbing about her birth date, etc., back in the days when such things mattered greatly. Just days after her third birthday, what little money the family had went "poof" in the 1929 stock market crash. In *Southern Star* she wrote that, as a result, her mismatched parents moved from town to town as my father earned a living as a cotton buyer for a large textile company. Our transient lifestyle and the brutal economics of those trying times meant that we never owned a house. Rather, we lived in a series of rented houses or apartments. Throughout my childhood, I seemed to be always walking into new classrooms full of strange faces.

Her father died when she was 15 (cirrhosis of the liver), leaving Adams and her mother with very little. As a consequence of the mother's heavy drinking, the two ended up living apart from each other, Mom moving in with her own sister in Iowa, Julie living in Arkansas with an aunt (her father's sister) and uncle who treated her like a daughter. After being crowned Miss Little Rock, and coming "thisclose" to becoming Miss Arkansas, she got the idea that she might have the looks needed to make it in the movies. Flying to California was the 19-year-old's first-ever time on an airplane.

While waiting for studio doors to swing open for her, Adams worked as a secretary and lost her Southern accent with the help of a speech and acting coach. She made her TV bow on the anthology series *Your Show Time*; the first time she was seen in a movie, it was just a photograph of her, on the cover of a magazine in the Betty Hutton vehicle *Red, Hot and Blue* (1949).

B-movie stardom came suddenly, and in spades, when she landed the female lead in a cheapie Western, *The Dalton Gang* (1949) with Don "Red" Barry, and the producers then asked her if she'd star in their next *six* Westerns—which were all to be made simultaneously! James Ellison, Russell Hayden, Raymond Hatton and Fuzzy Knight were the stars of all six; Adams played a different character in each but, presumably to avoid confusion, all were named Ann:

> I was The Girl in all of them, so I had three outfits. I had a riding outfit, a stagecoach "dress-up" outfit and a "farm" girl outfit. We'd shoot all the farmhouse scenes for all six movies at once, then all the stagecoach scenes. I had a hard time remembering who I was. "Am I the farm girl this time, or the cow girl?" It was very funny!

Universal's *Bright Victory* (1951) was the story of a World War II veteran (Arthur Kennedy in an Oscar-nominated performance), permanently blinded by a sniper's bullet, returning home to try to adapt to a new type of life; Adams, third-billed, plays the fiancée he left behind—who now can't see spending her life with him. At a sneak preview where audience members filled out Comment Cards, enough of them praised Adams that Universal put her under contract at $150 a week. In *Bright Victory* she used the screen name Julia Adams, and retained it for several years (even in *Black Lagoon*) before it was changed to Julie Adams. Apparently Universal didn't think much of her B-Western past, declaring *Bright Victory* her film debut.

For over six years Adams "had a place where I felt like I belonged" (Universal), playing in movies with stars ranging from James Stewart, Tyrone Power, Charlton Heston and fellow Hollywood newbie Rock Hudson to Francis the Talking Mule and, yes, the Gill Man (played by Ben Chapman). She told *Psychotronic Video* magazine interviewer Dennis Daniel that, when assigned to *Creature*, she thought, "I don't know if I really want to be in a monster picture," but she *also* didn't want to go on suspension so she forged ahead with it, swimsuit scene and all. So many of her other Universals were Westerns and other period pieces that *The Hollywood Reporter*'s Milton Luban

From mid–November to mid–December 1949, new-to-Hollywood Julie Adams played six different characters in six different cheapie Westerns being made simultaneously, a baptism of fire perhaps unique even in Hollywood. ("It was crazy!" she told me.) She's pictured here with James Ellison in West of the Brazos.

wrote in his *Creature* review, "Lovely Julia Adams, finally out of crinoline costumes, reveals a gorgeous pair of gams." (Actually, audiences had already gotten some good long looks at them in *The Lawless Breed*.) In 1953, for publicity purposes, Universal had her legs insured for $125,000 by Lloyds of London.

When New York actor Ray Danton screen-tested for a role in *Six Bridges to Cross* (1955), Adams appeared in the scene with him; they then acted together in *The Looters*, shot in the Colorado Rocky Mountains in the summer of 1954. It was the story of greed on a mountaintop, with hunting guide Rory Calhoun and ne'er-do-well Danton hiking to a plane crash site and finding a handful of survivors *and* a quarter million dollars in a cash box. As a former model touchy about her tarnished past, Adams gives an especially good performance (and shows off a lot of cleavage and leg). By the time *The Looters* began playing in the spring of '55, she was Mrs. Danton.

After *Slim Carter* (1957), Adams' run at Universal came to an end. In the years that followed she made a handful of additional movies, including the sci-fi *The Underwater City* (1962), but spent much more time working in TV, including "our" kind of stuff (*Alfred Hitchcock Presents, One Step Beyond, Kolchak: The Night Stalker*, etc.). Son #1, Steven Danton, is now a busy assistant director and Son #2 Mitchell Danton, named after Robert "Mitch" Mitchum, is an editor; the latter co-wrote her autobiography.

Before her marriage to Danton ended in divorce, they acted together several more times, including a *Night Gallery* episode; he also directed her both pre- and post-split, mostly in TV episodes but also in the feature *Psychic Killer* (1975), a violent and gory (and surprisingly PG-rated) horror flick.[47] For more upscale audiences, "guest artist" Adams played leading roles in more than a dozen stage productions throughout the country, some in conventional theaters, others in dinner theaters and one in a theater-in-the-round dinner theater. Among these stage credits: *The Prime of Miss Jean Brodie* (as Jean Brodie, complete with Scottish accent), *The Glass Menagerie, Butterflies Are Free, Auntie Mame* (in the title role), *Forty Carats, Long Day's Journey into Night* and *Mary, Mary*. She was Miss Daisy in an early '90s Denver production of *Driving Miss Daisy*, her last time "treading the boards" to date.

After years of ducking the celebrity autograph scene (and/or, perhaps, her more fervent *Creature* fans), she finally dipped a toe into those dark waters in the 2000s at the behest of Ben Chapman. It began with an appearance at 2002's Creaturefest, an event held at the Wakulla Springs State Park and Lodge with Adams, Chapman and Adams' underwater double Ginger Stanley in attendance. (Ricou Browning opted out, but he joined them the following year for the movie's 50th anniversary, and the two Gill Men, Browning and Chapman, met for the first time.) Adams told me that it did take "a little persuasion" from Chapman to start going the convention-and-autograph route:

> Yes, I dragged my feet, I was not too enthused about doing it, but once I got started, it was really fun, because you are meeting people who like movies and they're all enthusiastic. I enjoyed kinda getting in touch with the audience directly, as opposed to just hearing about their reaction. So it did turn out to be fun, especially with Ben, who was a wonderful pal to *be* with. We would have fun meeting the people, and we would "play off each other" in talking with them and so on. I miss him a lot!

After Chapman died in 2008, she continued down the autograph show road, always accompanied by a relative or friend. On October 27, 2011, her book *The Lucky Southern Star* debuted at the Egyptian Theatre on Hollywood Boulevard; Adams was in attendance, and the appropriately all–Julie double bill that night was *Creature* (in 3-D) and her James Stewart Western *Bend of the River* (1952). Sons Steven and Mitch both have two kids, making her the grandmother of four. The last time I phoned her in connection with this book, she had one foot out the door, leaving for a book signing and *Creature* 3-D screening at a theater in Jacksonville, Florida—spitting distance from the spot where *Revenge of the Creature*'s Lobster House scenes were shot. For Julie Adams, there *is* no escaping the Gill Man!

Richard Denning as Dr. Mark Williams

By every report, Richard Denning was a nice guy in real life, and he had no trouble making this come across on movie and TV screens. In his first monster movie *Unknown Island* (1948) he had to work his way into viewers' good graces because at the outset his character was a denizen of Singapore barrooms, driven to drink by a horrific past experience on a Pacific island crawling with prehistoric monsters; but he does a 180 when forced to return to the island and becomes the movie's thoroughly likable hero. From then on, Denning was among the most genial of sci-fi he-men, proving in picture after picture that even Mr. Nice Guys can take command in situations charged with danger: *Target Earth* (1954), *Creature with the Atom Brain* (1955), *The Black Scorpion* (1957), etc. In the post-atomic Armageddon *Day the World Ended* (1956), he's not only the apple of leading lady Lori Nelson's eye but also that of her dad (Paul Birch), who pushes for them to get right down to the business of repopulating the planet!

But Denning could also score as cowardly and disagreeable knaves, and he was at his least likable in the $1100-a-week role of *Black Lagoon*'s publicity-starved Mark Williams. First he gets our hackles up with his open resentment of the relationship between Reed and Kay; and then his failure to bag the Gill Man sends him over the edge from Type A to A-hole, his singleness of purpose costing him his life. (As a member of *Black Lagoon*'s sneak preview audience wrote on a Preview Comment Card, "Denning is a real stinker for a change.") In 2001, writer-producer Frederick Rappaport (*The 4400, The New Twilight Zone, Star Trek: Deep Space Nine*) posted on the Classic Horror Film Board (www.monsterkid.com), "So I'm watching *Creature from the Black Lagoon* for the umpteenth time the other night…

> … when it suddenly occurs to me that a solid and understated Richard Denning is making off with the acting honors. As the trigger-happy and glory-hungry Mark, the film's one thoroughly unsympathetic character, Denning also serves as an interesting physical counterpoint to the punier Richard Carlson. My guess is that had it not been for the success of *It Came from Outer Space*, the actors would have switched roles. Me, I like it this way just fine. The strapping, jockish Denning comes off as a spoiled, selfish, to-the-manor-born bully whose sense of privilege and entitlement (hell, Mark's old man probably bought him his doctorate) creates interesting tension within the research group, and whose premature departure leaves a definite hole in the film.

Born in Poughkeepsie, New York, Denning (real name: Louis Albert Denninger, Jr.) was 18 months old in 1915 when his garment-manufacturing father moved the family to Los Angeles. He attended business college and was expected to take over from his dad, but once he began working with little theater groups, the idea of continuing to work as an on-the-road garment salesman lost what little appeal it had. He and 12 other actor-wannabes were the winners of a radio contest that earned them Warner Brothers screen tests; all 13 tested the same morning, and Denning suspected that there was no film in the camera. He was told that he was not hired because he was too much like one of their newer contract players, Errol Flynn. A few years before Hal Roach's *One Million B.C.* (1940) was made, Denning was offered the lead, but his agent told him he wasn't ready for it. Instead the blond, blue-eyed Denning signed with Paramount, where the juvenile player received training and tackled roles big and small in almost 50 movies, from college boys in comedies to gang members in the crime flicks *Persons in Hiding* (1939, based on Bonnie and Clyde's

Clad only in leopard skin trunks, Richard Denning co-starred in Paramount's Beyond the Blue Horizon *with sarong queen Dorothy Lamour—not to mention Lamour's character's faithful tiger Satan. It was his favorite of his own movies (courtesy Photofest).*

exploits) and *Queen of the Mob* (1940, based on the career of Ma Barker and her boys).[48]

On loanout to Columbia, Denning made a good showing in *Adam Had Four Sons* (1941) as part of the title quartet, unable to resist the aggressive charms of a brother's sexually eager wife (Susan Hayward) and regretting it afterwards ("She's *monstrous*!"). Back at Paramount, he was second-billed as a Tarzan type in the Technicolor jungle adventure-romance-comedy *Beyond the Blue Horizon* (1942); then he was the ill-fated, no-good gambler brother of Veronica Lake in the same year's *The Glass Key*. (Alan Ladd to Lake: "That crummy brother of yours *needed* killing!")[49] Also in 1942 he married Chilean-born Englishter Evelyn Ankers, then building her reputation as Universal's "Queen of the Horror Movies." While Evelyn fought monsters on soundstages, Denning stood up for democracy: A few weeks after their Las Vegas elopement, he enlisted in the wartime Navy and became the submarine service's newest first class petty officer. He was a yeoman, third class, by August 1943 when he had his first leave after almost a year; he returned to Hollywood to take Evelyn to Seal Beach on an overdue honeymoon.

By the time Denning left Uncle Sam's payroll, his career momentum was gone and Evelyn, now the mother of their daughter Diana Dee, was no longer a Universal contractee. To help make ends meet, they lived during the summer in a Paradise Cove, Malibu, house trailer and set 100 lobster traps on the beach; they ate some of their catch and sold the rest to buy other food. In the winter, the Dennings, house trailer and all, moved to Palm Springs. Their total housing expense was $40 a month. "Evie and I often would look back, years later," he told me, "and realize that was the happiest time we had."

Eventually more movie roles started coming his way, including 20th Century–Fox's cloying *Black Beauty* (1946) in which Denning must choose between horse-crazy teen Mona Freeman and ... Ankers (and ends up with the former!). Most of the rest of Denning's '40s films were undistinguished mysteries and actioners that clocked in at an hour or so. Radio fans will recall that he played the husband of Lucille Ball on *My Favorite Husband*, an airwave series which, when it crossed over to television, became *I Love Lucy*. It made the crossing without Denning:

On TV, Ball's real-life hubby Desi Arnaz had the role of her spouse.

By the start of the 1950s Ankers was slowing down career-wise. Denning, however, was busier than ever in films and on radio and TV. Often he was the B-movie hero but there were exceptions, among them a coward in the Western *Hangman's Knot* (1952) and encore boozehounds in *Jivaro* (1954) and *The Magnificent Matador* (1955).[50] In *Western Clippings* magazine, Ankers' friend and fellow Universal actress Anne Gwynne told Michael Fitzgerald that there was a time when Denning himself had what she called "a fondness for the grape":

> One night the police found him butt naked in the middle of the street. They asked what he was doing, he told them the world is constantly moving and he was waiting for his house to come by so he could go in. Later, he and Evelyn became super-religious, but by this time the cigarettes and booze had destroyed his looks and health.

Despite these bumps in the road, the marriage remained strong; in fact, for the first 25 years or so, Denning and Ankers exchanged monthly anniversary cards.

Someone in Universal's casting department must have thought Denning did "obnoxious" better than "heroic": He made his debut at the studio in the annoying comedy *Week-End with Father* (1951), playing a musclebound summer camp counselor who does Tarzan yodels; he encored as a Nob Hill nincompoop with inheritance on the brain in *Scarlet Angel* (1952), a stereotypically slick TV exec in *The Glass Web* (1953) and then the Goofus to Richard Carlson's Gallant in *Black Lagoon*. Carlson had his own television series *I Led 3 Lives* at the same time he did *Black Lagoon* but Denning outdid him: Denning's mystery-comedy *Mr. & Mrs. North* was a TV *and* radio series before and after *Creature*. He later played the title roles in the series *Michael Shayne* and *The Flying Doctor*, the latter shot in England and in the Australian Outback.

By the 1960s the Dennings had residences in both California and Hawaii; the Hawaiian home was purchased, Denning said, because "[m]y wonderful wife suggested that, since we had worked and saved together since our marriage, perhaps the time had come to do the things we really enjoyed and at a comfortable tempo." (He'd first taken a liking to Hawaii in 1956 on his Kauai location junket for producer-director Roger Corman's *Naked Paradise*.) He described their Maui home as "about as close to

Richard Denning made his sci-fi movie debut in Unknown Island, *set in a Black Lagoon–like "land that time forgot." In a funny switch on* Black Lagoon, *his* Unknown Island *character is sensibly insistent on immediately leaving lest The Girl fall victim to a prehistoric beast—but he is constantly overruled by publicity- and money-hungry "Mark Williams types"! Pictured: Denning, Barton MacLane.*

A goofy gag shot of Richard Denning caught between the Venusian robot and the gun-toting producer (Herman Cohen) of Target Earth *(1954).*

Richard Denning couldn't catch a man-fish (in Creature*) but he landed a fish-fish at the Sportsmen's Lodge trout pond between takes on* Day the World Ended *(1956).*

Richard Denning and his wife, Evelyn Ankers, costumed as pioneers at a party at Ciro's, the Hollywood nightclub.

Paradise as we could find on Earth—and we love it more each day." Eventually Hawaii won out, partly because the movie business had, in their opinion, gone to pot in more ways than one: In 1968, Ankers told *Film Fan Monthly*'s Doug McClelland,

> [Denning] and I—Dick especially—have both turned down scripts for movies and plays because we felt they had been written under the influence of LSD. Maybe we are squares, but we also can't stand the filth and perversion that are now showing as "entertainment." … [That is] one of the main reasons we want to move over to Hawaii permanently, to get away from it all, to live a life more like we think God intended us to live: quiet, clean, healthy, but most of all peaceful—away from the man-made rat race!

Denning told interviewer Harold Heffernan in 1970 about one worry he had about life in Hawaii:

> More and more we notice the hippies being attracted from the mainland.
> Only a few stay on and the natives do their best to discourage permanency. This is a clean place and while everyone goes casual in dress, the long-hairs and the raggedy, filthy outfits stand out like sore thumbs.

If there is one danger the islands face, it is a concerted drive on the part of these people. And it's a real danger because the climate is perfect for the drones.

Unexpectedly, there was acting work for Denning in the Aloha State: the role of the state governor on CBS-TV's crime-adventure series

Hawaii Five-O with Jack Lord.[51] Ankers nixed offers to appear as the governor's wife on the show, preferring to go shopping in Honolulu while her husband acted. She told Denning, "Somebody's gotta spend it if you're making it!"

Not long after the end of *Five-O*'s final season, Ankers contracted cancer and battled it for two years. Describing the awful experience to interviewer Greg Mank, Denning revealed that, near the end, Ankers told him, "I just want to go up to our country place in Haiku and be out there alone with you and wait until the Good Lord calls me." Denning gave her shots every half-hour for the pain; Dee told *Famous Monsters*' Ray Ferry that she (Dee) was there too, in the final days, when Ankers was hallucinating because of the combo of painkillers and medication. "Her lips were all dried out," Dee recounted, "and I was putting an ointment on her lips and she said, 'That's not my good side—please—do the other side.' In her mind she was back at the studio having her makeup put on. I just thought that was so very sweet and telling."

Ankers died in August 1985 and Denning remarried several months later. By 1990 when I met and interviewed him, he and second wife Pat were living in San Diego and he seemed to be in good shape, but years of heavy smoking eventually took their toll. Despite his having quit in the '60s, he got "severe emphysema," Dee told me, adding with a rueful laugh, "Emphysema, which we all think of every time we see him smoking in old movies." By 1997 he was in a wheelchair most of the time and on oxygen "100 percent of the time" according to Dee, in addition to regular use of inhalers and a nebulizer. When Gill Man Ben Chapman tried to entice Denning to join him in New Jersey at one of Chiller Theatre's celebrity autograph shows, the actor had to beg off, explaining, "Ben, I can't even leave the house."

Toward the end, Denning and the missus were living in a Rancho Bernardo condo, right on a golf course. Dee and her oldest daughter Summer were visiting on Sunday, October 11, 1998:

> Summer and I went to church, and then we were going to go to brunch afterwards, and *both* of us felt … Summer even more than me … she felt an urgency to get home. So we went home, and sure enough, Dad was in his bedroom gasping for air, and his wonderful certified nurse's aide Cecilia was trying to calm him down. He kept wanting a puff off his albuterol, his inhaler, and you're only supposed to do like two or three but he was *so* desperate for air that he kept *doing* it. That is probably what killed him, because if you overuse it, your chest just constricts. Cecilia had been wanting to call 911, but he wouldn't go for it, he didn't want to go through the whole ambulance thing … typical stoic German "Oh, I'll be okay" attitude. And he *wasn't* okay.
>
> I called 911 and they came and got him, and I rode in the ambulance with him. I wanted to sit in the back with Dad but they wouldn't let me, they had an EMT back there taking his blood pressure and so on. The closest hospital that could provide *immediate* help was Escondido. They took him into the emergency room, and … it *haunts* me: They started to wheel him off to the room where they were going to work on him, and they wouldn't let me come along … and he kinda leaned up and he looked at me, and I can still remember that look … it was like, "Well, you're in charge now." [*Choking up*:] I didn't even get to kiss him goodbye!

Denning was buried in the Maui Veterans Cemetery in Makawao, Hawaii, next to Evelyn, who had been there "waiting" for him since her death 13 years earlier. Not long after Denning's passing, Pat began suffering from radiation dementia as a result of throat cancer treatments. It was Pat's wish to eventually be buried next to her husband but that was against Veterans Cemetery rules. She died in July 2012.

Antonio Moreno as Dr. Carl Maia

Surely the behind-the-camera crew of Universal's *Creature from the Black Lagoon* included a few oldtimers who felt

Like Rudolph Valentino and Ramon Novarro, Antonio Moreno (seen circa 1920) was one of the silent screen's great Latin lovers. On September 14, 1953, while he was in Canada with U-I's *Saskatchewan* troupe, he was cast as the archaeologist in *Black Lagoon* (courtesy Photofest).

they "went way back" with the company. But it's a safe bet that not one of them went back as far as Antonio Moreno, who got his first acting job in a Universal picture by going to a studio on 43rd Street and 11th Avenue in Manhattan— in *1912*. It was as a "Latin lover" type that he first came to movie prominence; in a Moreno career article that ran in *Films in Review* just a few months after his February 1967 passing, writer DeWitt Bodeen pointed out that many of the great female stars of the silent screen's golden era had appeared opposite popular leading man Moreno, among them Mary Pickford, Dorothy and Lillian Gish, Pearl White, Norma and Constance Talmadge, Gloria Swanson, Pola Negri, Clara Bow, Marion Davies and Greta Garbo.

Born in 1886 Madrid, he was the son of Juan Moreno, a non-commissioned officer in the Spanish Army. The father died when Antonio was young, so the boy had to start working evenings in a bakery (for one peseta a night) to help support his impoverished mother Ana. He entertained boyish dreams of being a bullfighter and of going to sea as a sailor— and then, when he began seeing shows at various theaters, he saw a way to do *both*. In the 1924 article "The True Story of My Life" in *Movie Weekly* magazine, he wrote that in the theaters,

> I sat enthralled. Why, I thought, in the theater one *can* be all of the things one has dreamed about. One can be buccaneer and torero, sailor and poet, lover and adventurer. I had often wondered how, in one lifetime, I could ever manage to achieve all of the roles I, at various times, saw myself enacting. The stage was the solution. Yes, in the theater all things were possible.… [T]hese occasional and enchanted glimpses were what bred in me my first desire to go on the stage.

While still a teen, "picking up odd pennies and an even odder education about the streets and byways of a rather unenterprising little town" (*Movie Weekly* article), Moreno met two American men making a grand tour of Europe and became chummy with them; they decided to sponsor him and later cabled him the fare to sail to New York. Here in what Moreno called "The Promised Land," he finished school and began working at various jobs, including gas company meter reader in Northampton, Massachusetts. In *Movie Weekly* he told the story of visiting a Chinaman's Northampton store to examine the gas meter; according to Moreno, "The shop was always brilliantly illuminated but the meter, mysteriously, never contained more than two or three coins. As it was impossible for anyone to tamper with the meter without being detected through the mechanism, the superintendent couldn't for the life of him make out what was wrong. I looked over the meter carefully but could find no signs of manipulation. And yet I was sure that the Chinaman was getting a big return of gas on a very small investment." Turning detective, Moreno decided to spy on "Mr. Chinaman," and at dusk caught him putting something in the meter "that illuminated the shop like a cathedral at Easter time." Moreno immediately opened the meter and found that the store owner had stocked it with a piece of ice the size and shape of the required coin! "After serving its purpose the ice, of course, melted and drained away, leaving only—the mystery."

Moreno's dream of becoming an actor began coming true the summer he played small roles with a Northampton stock company. After that modest start came acting jobs with other troupes, and even on Broadway. Then he met an old English actor, fresh off of an Edison Picture Company production, who advised him to try the movies. Moreno's

Antonio Moreno made his Universal Horrors debut in *La Voluntad del Muerto* (1930), the studio's Spanish-language version of their simultaneously shot *The Cat Creeps*, both based on the popular mystery play *The Cat and the Canary*. It's a lost film so who can be sure, but leading lady Lupita Tovar appears to be refereeing an argument between Moreno (left) and Paul Ellis (courtesy Photofest).

1. Creature from the Black Lagoon (1954)   59

Many of the roles Moreno played in the second half of his movie career were characters who looked as if they just stepped out of the mists of Spanish or Mexican history, for example the Mexican ranch owner in 1941's Fiesta *(courtesy Photofest).*

first job was "doing 'atmosphere'" (translation: working as an extra) in the aforementioned Universal film, the two-reeler *The Voice of the Millions* (1912), and he soon decided that films was where he belonged. Moreno started working as an extra for D.W. Griffith and was soon a $40-a-week member of Griffith's stock company. Starring roles followed, plus enough serials that he earned the title "King of the Cliff-hangers."

Movie star Moreno married wealthy socialite divorcee Daisy Canfield Danziger in 1923, and on a six-acre estate on a hill overlooking L.A. they built one of *the* show-homes of the era, a villa they called Crestmount. When the talkies came in, bilingual Moreno began acting in the simultaneously made Spanish versions of Hollywood films, among them the Español counterpart of Universal's *The Cat Creeps* (1930). In the early 1930s he even did some directing of Mexican movies, including the country's first talkie, 1932's *Santa*, which still looms large in Mexi-movie annals.[52] By this time Moreno was separated from wife Daisy, who died in 1933 when, coming home from a Hollywood party, her car went over a 300-foot cliff. To this day her ghost reportedly haunts Crestmount, which is now a recording studio called the Paramour Mansion.

Time marches on and Moreno began playing smaller parts; in the '40s he even did some uncredited acting in movies both major and minor. In the early '50s his film were almost exclusively Universals; he played a Mexican priest in the tri-dimensional *Wings of the Hawk* (1953) with Julie Adams and an Indian chief in *Saskatchewan* (1954), which wrapped shortly before *Black Lagoon* started. His last Hollywood film role was in director John Ford's *The Searchers* (1956) as the unctuous, white-bearded Mexican working with title characters John Wayne and Jeffrey Hunter: "At your service ... *for a price. Always* for a price!"

By the 1950s, Moreno was doing a lot of "dining out" on his status as the director of Mexico's first talkie *Santa*: In 1951 there was a week-long Mexico City celebration of that movie's 20th anniversary, and the Mexican government picked up the tab to fly in guests Moreno and the movie's star Lupita Tovar—plus Tovar's agent-husband Paul Kohner, Groucho and Harpo Marx, Marta Toren, Lex Barker and wife Arlene Dahl, Craig Stevens and wife Alexis Smith, David Wayne, Don Taylor and Patricia Neal. In 1957 there was a two-day Mexico City ceremony for the silver anniversary of the country's first *two* talkies, *Santa* and *Águilas frente al sol* (1932), the latter *also* directed by Moreno, and again he headed "Down Mehico Way" to participate. In between, in 1956, Hollywood's Masquers Club gave Moreno, one of its founders, a testimonial dinner—which was probably the *least* the theatrical club could do for him, seeing as the Masquers Club was housed in a former home of the actor's, which he had *given* to them!

Toward the end of his life came a lengthy period of illness for this pioneer of the American and Mexican movie industries. In 1965 he was invited to yet another *Santa* commemoration, its 35th anniversary, but *Variety* reported that he was lying gravely ill in New York City and that the celebrations "now lie under a cloud." Mexican journalist Fernando Morales Ortiz declared:

> Just as it is true that Antonio Moreno is closely linked with the birth of Mexican sound pictures, he also forms part of that glorious U.S. movie era, when his performances with Pearl White, Greta Garbo, Alice Terry and so many others, raised him to the status of the most famous Latin lover of his time. Moreno was, with Valentino and Ramon Novarro, the idol of all women all over the world.

Moreno died at home in February 1967. According to his *Variety* obituary—which began by saying that he'd retired in 1950!—he had lost much of his wealth in an unsuccessful real estate venture but at the end was still a man of considerable means, "estimate running anywhere from $800,000

Ben Chapman as the Creature

Despite the popularity of *Creature from the Black Lagoon*, for decades little was known about the man in the foam rubber suit in the on-land scenes, and to the movie's fans, "Ben Chapman" remained nothing but a name.[53] That began to change when my interview with him appeared in the July 1992 *Starlog*, and then, much more dramatically, once the Honolulu resident became the Kahuna (star attraction) at autograph shows throughout the United States. Tanned, silver-haired, hard-to-miss at 6'5", and *harder* to miss with that big voice and bigger personality, Chapman was a monster-sized hit at cons coast to coast—the first classic Universal movie monster portrayer ever to appear on the circuit, most of the others having died decades before. Children were gently fussed over, female fans came away charmed and, behind the scenes, adult male Monster Kids got a hilarious, sometimes profane earful of Tales from the Hollywood Trenches as only "Uncle Benny" could tell 'em.[54]

Ben Chapman was as Tahitian as a grass skirt and yet that *was* his real name—*Benjamin Franklin* Chapman, Jr., in fact. He was born in Oakland, California, in 1928; his parents Benjamin Franklin and Valentine Irene Chapman later left the Bay Area to go back to their native Tahiti where in his youth, Chapman told me, he "spoke English at home, French at school, and Tahitian and Chinese in the streets." He went to school in Papeete and then, after a *return* to California, various schools here, graduating with honors from San Francisco's Bates High School. Chapman claimed that one of his cousins was movie and TV star Jon Hall, that one uncle was *Mutiny on the Bounty* co-author James Norman Hall, and that *another* uncle was William Bainbridge, who in the 1935 movie version of *Mutiny on the Bounty* played Hitihiti the kindly Tahitian chief and breadfruit-tree provider ("Bligh! You got *fat*!").

According to some of Chapman's obituaries he appeared in *Wake of the Red Witch* (1948), a John Wayne adventure saga with a South Pacific setting, but I don't know if he did; he told me that working as a dancer in nightclubs led to his first movie role, dancing in MGM's *Pagan Love Song* (1950). Next came a stint with the 1st Marine Regiment in Korea; talking to fans, Chapman spun yarns of finding himself in such harrowing Korean War hot spots as the Yalu River and the Chosin Reservoir. For his service, he added, he received a Silver Star, a Bronze Star and two Purple Hearts. More on this later.

During his life, Ben Chapman held many jobs, from bartender to 7-Up executive, and from Beverly Hills cop to Creature. He would boast "I swam before I walked," a talent that helped him land the role of the Gill Man.

Back on U.S. soil, Chapman was part of an "all–Polynesian revue" in a nightclub called the Islander Room. Universal producer-director Will Cowan cast Chapman and his dance partner Tani Marsh in his 3-D musical short *Hawaiian Nights* (1954) which also featured Pinky Lee, Mamie Van Doren, Lisa Gaye and some Miss Universe contestants. According to Chapman, Universal liked what they saw of him in *Hawaiian Nights* and gave him a $125-a-week stock player contract; but if that's true, he was no longer on the studio payroll when *Black Lagoon* came along because he had to sign a Screen Actors Guild Inc. Minimum Free Lance contract to join that movie's cast. He got the role of the "Land Creature" thanks to Universal's Jonny Rennick, a redhead who cast wranglers, cowboys and stunt people: Rennick became aware of the search to find an appropriate person for the monster role and thought Chapman was right for it. "She knew I was a diver, a swimmer, etc., etc.—I had all the qualifications to portray the Gill Man," he told me. "So eventually we went off and met with a group of people to talk about this…. Jonny really went to bat for me, she told 'em, 'This guy here *is* actually part-fish!'"

Chapman went through the messy process of plaster casts and all the other ordeals involved in making the skin-tight full-body Creature suit, then dove into production. With the Creature helmet on, the 6'5" actor was now closer to 6'7". The problem for an *out*-of-the-water merman, he told me, was:

Front and side views of Ben Chapman as the Creature. Throughout Black Lagoon's *weeks of shooting, every person mentioned in the Daily Production Reports' section "Remarks and Explanation of Delays" is called by name but not Chapman, who is instead called "The Gill Man," as on the report from October 27, 1954: "Gill Man not ready on set until 8:37 a.m. His call was 8:15." It's as though there was a nameless monster being used in the movie!*

I *would* heat up, because I had a body stocking on and then the foam rubber [Gill Man] outfit over it…. On days when we worked on soundstages, what they would do was set up hoses, and there was someone there I could go to between takes and say, "Hey, do me a favor, hose me off." Because once you were into that suit, there was no taking it off! On the back lot, I would just stay in the lake to keep cool.

Post-*Creature*, there was only one more movie appearance in his future, a native killed by pygmies' poison darts in the *She*-like Johnny Weissmuller adventure *Jungle Moon Men* (1955); for the first and only time in his movie career he received on-screen billing (as Benjamin F. Chapman, Jr.). A few additional TV roles ensued, then some jobs outside of show business. Eventually he moved to Hawaii where he landed more TV parts (*Hawaii Five-O* and even a *Six Million Dollar Man* episode where he played a spaceman) but he was much more active in working as a public relations person for a tour company, selling real estate, etc.

In his retirement in the mid-1990s, Chapman began headlining autograph shows with a vengeance. A big fish in that ink-stained pond, he drew long lines, and sometimes drew stares (he wore shorts even in the wintry Northeast!) as he energetically loped about dealer rooms and hotel hallways, and delighted fans with his "Which way to the party?" high spirits. Autograph buyers also got freebies such as a Xerox copy of his original *Black Lagoon* contract (even though it belied his claim of being a Universal contractee), a "Gill Man dollar," etc. Merrilee Kazarian, Ben's companion for his last 25-plus years, told me, "He was very *proud* of the fact that he had played this classic Universal monster of the '50s and that he could spend his golden years, his retirement years, going to autograph shows and conventions. He really enjoyed them." Laughing, she added, "You know what he always used to say when he would get money on this autograph thing? He'd say, 'It's better than robbing banks!'" (Merrilee became known to fans of Ben and *Black Lagoon* as "Mrs. Creature," which she also regularly used as the signature on her emails.)

There was a scare in 2001 when 72-year-old Chapman, attending a show called Horrorfind Weekend at a hotel outside Baltimore, walked backward while moving a dealer room table, fell and painfully snapped his hip in half. The Creature from the Black-and-Blue Lagoon underwent hip replacement surgery a week later, then physical therapy; according to his website the-reelgillman.com, he was soon "95 percent healed" and Merrilee was posting that he looked better than when he left for the con! "Ben refuses to use a walker—uses only a cane occasionally," she revealed. "He is really making a remarkable recovery! I really believe he *is*

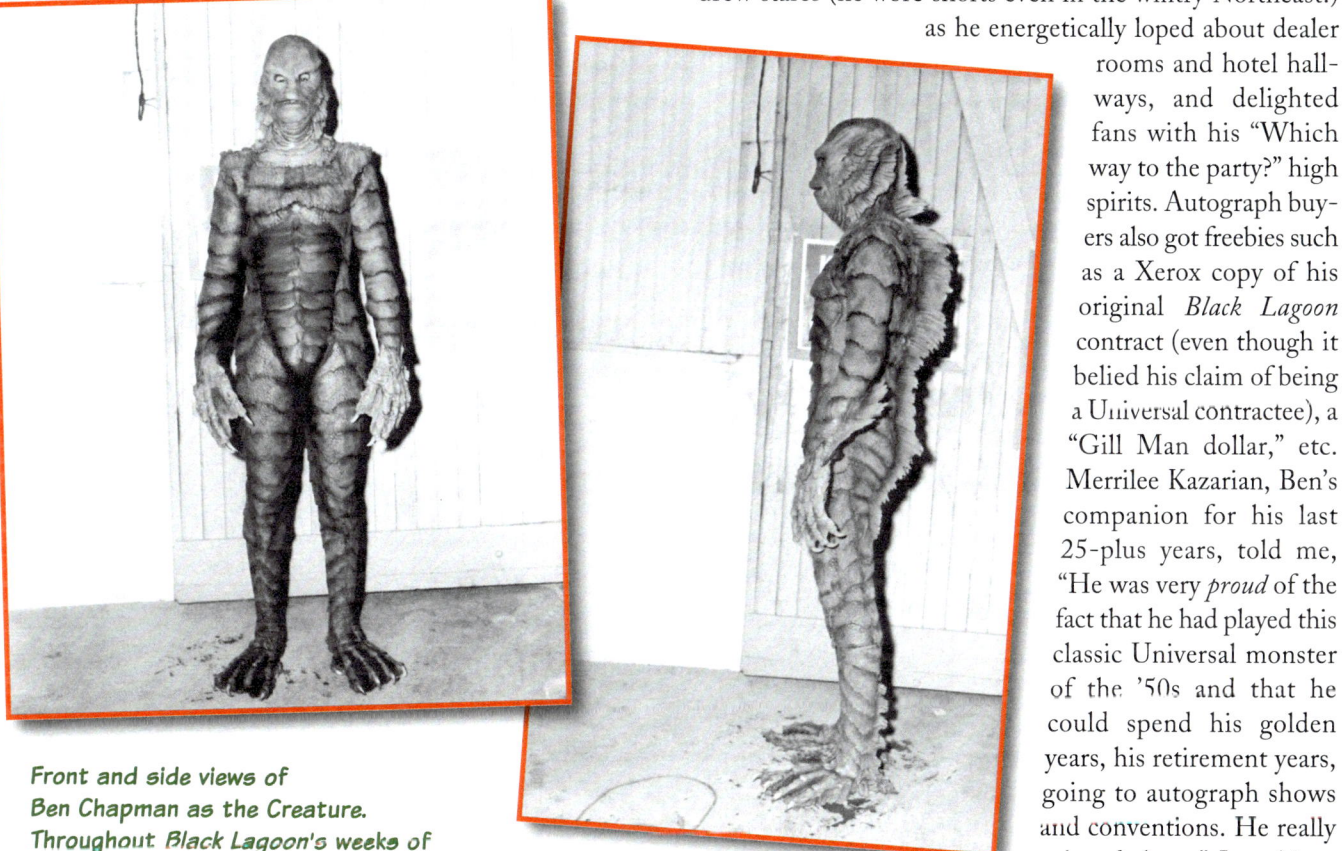

the Creature from the Black Lagoon (indestructible)!"

As mentioned earlier, Julie Adams had no interest in monster movie conventions and their sights, sounds ... and smells ... until Chapman got her to join him at the 2002 Creaturefest in Wakulla Springs; she had such a great time that she was soon accompanying him hither and yon to other cons. "He was always such fun at these shows," she told me. "And he was so *good* at them, too: He would go [to our signing tables] and set up all the pictures, he would hang up posters for us to have as a background—oh, he was *very* particular! He loved the fans and the fans loved him."

Eventually the *two* Creatures were united: Chapman and Ricou Browning, who apparently never met in 1953 when the movie was made, first pressed the flesh 50 years later at the 2003 Creaturefest at Wakulla. "We became friends immediately," Browning told me, "and subsequently did several other shows together. Ben was a bubbling personality, very appreciative of all the fans that the Creature had. He was a fun person to be around, never seemed 'down.' Even when he was sick [at shows]—a coupla times, he didn't feel too good—he covered it up pretty well. A very enjoyable person."

As Browning reported, there *was* a decline in Chapman's health. At the June 2007 Monster Bash, held at Pittsburgh's Airport Four Points Hotel, a now much-thinner, thin-voiced Chapman became sick on the morning of the second day; paramedics were summoned and swarmed into his room. It was not a heart attack as feared but the 78-year-old was too weak to stray far from his bed the rest of the weekend. Late Sunday night, sitting on the edge of his bed looking frail and shaken, he pulled up his shirt to show me a deck-of-cards-sized bulge in the skin over his heart (his defibrillator), told me about his recent heart problems and glumly said that this would have to be his last public appearance.

After his return home to Hawaii, I phoned him and he said he was going to try to rally his strength and do a few more cons, starting with the March 2008 Monster-Mania (Cherry Hill, New Jersey) where he would again appear alongside Browning. But according to Merrilee, Chapman became increasingly unwell in the early part of '08, and on the morning of February 20, she had to call 911 for an ambulance for her unconscious mate. She rode with him in the ambulance to the Tripler Army Medical Center, a pink hilltop facility overlooking the city of Honolulu; he was taken off life support around noon but lingered another 12 hours. Merrilee and Benjamin III, his one biological son (from a past marriage), were at his side the entire time. At 12:15 a.m., right after being given last rites by a Catholic priest, "The REEL Gill Man" drew his last breath, a victim of congestive heart failure.

Ben Chapman gets the Bob's Basement tour in 2004 and poses among some familiar items. As the first line of Chapman's 2008 Los Angeles Times *obit pointed out, he had "achieved a degree of movie immortality—and he did it without uttering a word of dialogue or even showing his face."*

Shock and Aw-kward! About four weeks after Chapman's obituaries appeared in newspapers countrywide, Creature fans were rocked when those same papers ran a correction: Marine Corps officials had alerted the media that Chapman was *not* a decorated veteran as he had maintained in numerous interviews. Uncle Benny caught in a Semper *Lie*? Yes, according to Dan Lamothe of the weekly newspaper *Marine Corps Times,* which broke the story:

> The late Ben Chapman ... didn't confine his acting to playing the part of a classic movie monster.
>
> He also fictionalized parts of his own life, telling family and fans alike that he had earned medals for valor.... [He] never received the Silver Star, Bronze Star and two Purple Hearts he had claimed for decades, according to Marine Corps officials and a copy of Chapman's military Report of Separation.

Using as his source a 2005 Chapman interview on the Icons of Fright website, Lamothe quoted the late actor as saying that he arrived in Korea as part of the Inchon Landing, and was surrounded by 20 divisions of Chinese soldiers during the Battle at Chosin Reservoir; Lamothe then pointed out that official records prove that in 1950 when those clashes took place, Chapman was at California's Camp Pendleton. Documentation showing that Chapman's highest rank was corporal contradicted Chapman's claims to have left the Corps a sergeant.

Semper *Defy*: Chapman's family disputed the charge that he was a pretender, with Ben III insisting, "It must be wrong. I have a box with all of his awards."

Semper **sigh**: But Ben III—himself a former Marine sergeant—ultimately had to admit that his dad had no documentation for his medals. Nor could verification be found in the database of Silver Star recipients at the Marine Corps Awards branch in Quantico, Virginia.

Appalled by the *Marine Corps Times* story, Merrilee wrote them a long letter that began, "You are talking about a time in history before computerized records. It is very likely records from that long ago could be mixed up, missing, distorted." That same idea was advanced on the Internet's Classic Horror Film Board by former child actor Donnie Dunagan (1939's *Son of Frankenstein*): The retired Marine spoke from firsthand experience about how easily paperwork of this sort can be lost in the fog of war. To show the seriousness of what Chapman is accused of doing: The Stolen Valor Act of 2005, which passed Congress with overwhelming support, calls for fines and even imprisonment for the crime of "falsely representing oneself as having been awarded any decoration or medal authorized by Congress for the Armed Forces or any of the service medals or badges." There are increased penalties if the offense involves a Silver Star, a Purple Heart *et al.*[55]

The Classic Horror Film Board's Butcher Benton (Alan K. Rode) ruefully opined:

> Ben is gone and all his family and friends have left is his good name and the memories that go with it. Mr. Chapman's reputation is under a dark cloud and I certainly hope it is resolved in his favor. I personally lean towards serious doubt though, when not only the awards but the actual dates and locations of his reputed time in country and in combat don't jive with his service record. Not good.
>
> Aside from slighting the people who earned these awards, I think people who make up these lies and live with them for decades never pause to consider how damaging it will be to their families and their own reputations when these hoaxes are inevitably exposed. After enough time passes, perhaps they even believe the invented events actually happened. And that may be the worst aspect of this sad syndrome.

The hottest feedback to Lamothe's article may have appeared on the *Military Times* website. One unregistered poster asked,

> How many service members that abruptly left the military at the end of their contracts have had their records screwed up?
>
> While it is possible that Ben Chapman made up those awards, it is also possible that Ben Chapman actually did receive those awards in formations with his commander, and kept those awards close to his heart, while the paper-

In the sunset of his life, Ben Chapman had fun with Creature fans at autograph shows and at Christmas sent some of them "Mele Kalikimaka" cards; this photograph was included with one of them. Pictured right to left: Merrilee Kazarian with her companion Ben, Ben's biological son Ben Chapman III, and Ben's "hanai'ed" (informally adopted) son Grant Chapman.

work got lost or screwed up somehow. Usually those who receive awards related to combat and do not plan on re-enlisting do not bother to get their paperwork fixed. Going into admin to fix paperwork related to combat awards is embarrassing, in that it is selfish compared to those who died in combat, and it usually takes a long time.

A poster calling himself Concerned Marine chimed in:

> Obviously Mr. Lamothe has never been a part of the bureaucracy that is the United States Military. Where so often one hand doesn't know the other is wiping its own ass. How plausible is it that a military that routinely shoots at its own troops does not have the most accurate recordkeeping from 60 years ago. I think it is very sad that the issue would surface in such a manner as to tarnish the image of a person who championed for the same USMC that is currently slandering his name in multiple papers…

Again taking aim at Lamothe, Concerned Marine asked whether the writer "realizes the effect his slanderous words have on those friends and family of the deceased. Walk a mile in another man's shoes, sir, before you begin to tell me who deserves what." An equally irate commenter asked Lamothe, "How dare you drag an American veteran through the muck post-mortem?! Is this what our current Marines have to look forward to in their old age, should they be lucky enough to reach it? A reporter spitting on their grave via a scathing obituary?"

In Waikiki on March 29, 2008, Chapman family members and friends gathered to memorialize him. On the beach across the street from the St. Augustine by-the-Sea Church, there was a brief service with Ben's actor friend Don Stroud delivering a eulogy, and then the participants climbed into three outrigger canoes and paddled out onto the ocean. "I was the only one not paddling," said Merrilee. "I was carrying the ashes in a lauhala basket covered with a Tahitian cloth. When we got to the designated spot, Ben III took the ashes and dove into the ocean, releasing them underwater. This is done so winds won't blow the ashes back on the canoes. Then everyone threw in flower petals. It was beautiful." During the first week of April 2013, additional ashes made a one-way trip to Tahiti with Ben III and his girlfriend Jessa. And in the interim between Waikiki and Tahiti, there was another memorial gathering, this one on the Universal back lot, with family members, plus a few of Ben's L.A. area fans, giving a small amount of his cremains a new home there … *in the Black Lagoon*.

Said Merrilee, "Ben is now in his three favorite places—Hawaii, California and Tahiti."

Production

Black Lagoon's pre-production shooting phase began one year, almost to the day, after William Alland wrote "The Sea Monster." On the morning of Wednesday, September 30, 1953, director Jack Arnold, Julie Adams and a small crew shot at the Hermosa Beach Aquarium, then one of the largest and best attractions of its type in the world.[56] For the camera's looking-out-of-the-aquarium shot of Kay (Adams), there were multiple takes on one slate.

Members of the camera unit remained at the aquarium to photograph plates and other fish footage while Arnold *et al.* headed off to Portuguese Bend for the shooting of Morajo Bay speedboat scenes. A crew was already there waiting, those men having "gotten up with the birds," driven to San Pedro, loaded a boat and sailed to the location. Despite heavy fog throughout the entire day, they got their shots of Kay (stuntwoman Polly Burson[57]) at the wheel of the speedboat, leaving from the Instituto de Biología Marítima pier with Dr. Maia (an extra); arriving at the barge; and then shoving off from the barge with Maia and Reed (another extra). Hats off to whoever took the trouble to hang a Brazilian flag from the mast on the pier. But a light slap on the wrist to whoever translated "Institute of Marine Biology" into "Instituto de Biología Marítima" for the signs on the pier and barge; that's Spanish, and the movie is set in Brazil where the language is Portuguese. Janlou de Amicis Silva, New York–based spokesperson for the consulate-general of Brazil, tells me that in Portuguese the signs would read "Instituto de Biologia Marinha." Incidentally, what a funny coincidence that the scene should happen to be shot at a shoreline spot called Portuguese Bend.

On Saturday, October 3, a budget meeting was held and a *Black Lagoon* budget of $595,000 was set. On Monday October 5, a small crew returned to Portuguese Bend to shoot process plates of the area. Cameras also rolled at Universal: As mentioned previously, at the Underwater Tank "Photo Water Tests" were made of Browning in the new'n'improved Gill Man outfit plus, on Stage 9, wardrobe and makeup shots of Carlson, Adams, Denning, Moreno, Paiva and Bissell. The six actors struck poses and did turns for William E. Snyder's camera as they modeled various costumes, including (for Carlson and Denning) trunks and diving equipment and (for Adams) bathing suit. The six players were also examined for insurance purposes.

October 6 was the last day of second unit tests, with Havens and Welbourne shooting Gill Man Browning in a

1. Creature from the Black Lagoon (1954)

The Gill Man came "thisclose" to being human but instead became "a poster boy for [the 1950s'] new brand of scientific monster—a group that drew upon the lower, more abhorrent forms of life (reptiles, fish, insects, even plants) for their aesthetic makeup" (Bill Cooke, Video Watchdog magazine).

dry suit on land and then coming out of Park Lake. At the Underwater Tank, they photographed him wearing his #3-Head (whichever one *that* was) and made tests of the rotenone. Also on this day, "the Makeup Department was commended for the excellent job they have done in developing the Gill Man outfit for this picture. The head was particularly difficult to construct because of its size which presented problems in providing vision for the Gill Man. Other complications resulted from the underwater requirements." (Quote taken from the minutes of the October 7, 1953, Studio Operating Committee meeting.)

The sixth was also Day One of Arnold's first unit production. The work was scheduled to take 21 days, rather a long time considering the fact that he was making, in effect, a one-hour movie. (The Florida unit's footage, plus opening and closing credits, etc., would bring the running time up to 79 minutes.) Arnold had an expert d.p. in William Snyder, who had the distinction of having been Oscar-nominated for his very first movie *as* d.p., *Aloma of the South Seas* (1941). He received two more nominations for *The Loves of Carmen* (1948) and *Jolson Sings Again* (1949).

On this first day, there was a crew of 65 and a company shooting call of 8:45 a.m.; all the players were there early (Julie Adams the earliest, at 6:45). The first shot of principal photography: a "full moving shot" (the camera on the deck of the *Rita*, shooting past the smoking funnel and cast members standing in the forward section) as the boat squeezes through the narrow passage and into the lagoon. Throughout pre-production shooting, it seemed as though nothing had gone exactly right, and that went for this first shot also: There was supposed to be a fog effect but they couldn't make it happen, and apparently the cable towing the boat came loose, necessitating repairs.

Various *Rita* deck scenes were shot throughout the day: the lowering of the trawling net, Maia's explanation of the uranium-lead test, Reed climbing aboard and presenting Kay with the bottom-of-the-lagoon "bouquet," etc. "Bad light" put an end to things at 4:55. Most of the next two days were spent on the same location photographing Adams cavorting in the water for the topside half of the Kay–Gill Man swim scene[58] and footage of the *Rita* rocking as the Gill Man attempts to escape the submerged net. On the 8th, *Black Lagoon*'s second unit, headed by director James Havens, planed out for the Florida Panhandle for two weeks of filming underwater footage.

On October 9, the entire on-screen-credited cast was at Park Lake in plenty of time for their 7:45 set call but director Arnold's car broke down on his way to the studio and he made his appearance at an unfashionably late 8:40. Among the scenes put on film on that date: the Creature's legs and feet as he walks the *Rita* deck, and the Creature descending upon the screaming Chico. Ben Chapman did *not* work, according to the Daily Production Report, so it's anybody's guess as to who wore the Creature costume in those two shots.

The doomed Chico was played by Henry "Blackie" Escalante, a Mexican actor-stuntman hailing from a family of circus trapeze artists. (And apparently a rather prominent one; his 2002 passing rated a *Los Angeles Times* obit page story.) In my neverending quest for *Creature* minutiae, I once telephoned Escalante out of the blue, expecting little or nothing from someone who had played such a small part—and he flummoxed me by saying he played the Creature! According to Escalante,

> I had to put on a rubber suit. It was hotter than a pistol [*laughs*]—it was *awfully* hot. I tore a hole in the mouthpiece, so I could *breathe*. I couldn't breathe otherwise! And it was a lot of fun. A lot of people were very nice; they knew that I was in turmoil there and they gave me all the things that I needed. I had a guy come there with a fan and fan me all the time....

Escalante didn't claim to have done the underwater Gill Man scenes, telling me that *that* job went to "other guys"; that was one of several offhand comments that got me to thinking he might possibly be legit. Just when I was on the verge of taking him at his word that he did briefly "suit up," he threw me again when he began to reminisce about "swinging in the trees" as part of his Gill Man job! "My background was as a flying trapeze man," he enthusiastically continued. "Anything to be done with swinging from tree to tree and stuff like that, it was, 'Let Henry do it!'" Escalante couldn't have been nicer or more nonchalant as he talked to me; in fact, he sounded like he was either cooking or washing dishes at the same time. And throughout the entire session, he had the very casual attitude of a guy talking about something he really did, and never attached any importance to.

Nothing in Universal's production paperwork backs up his claim; and of course his comment about tree-swinging adds a deafening note of confusion. But *some*body was in the monster suit (or parts of the suit) on days when production paperwork indicates the *absence* of Ben Chapman; the scenes in question also include the Gill Man's arm reaching out of the water at Maia's camp, his arm coming through the bunk room porthole, and more. So with a big question mark and an even bigger grain of salt, put the name of "Blackie" Escalante on the list of people who might have played Blackie LaGoon in some of those shots. Although certainly not the shot where the Gill Man kills Chico—because Chico *was* Escalante!

On the morning of Saturday, October 10, the first unit moviemakers were in Sierra Canyon, a rugged back lot spot first seen in *Sierra* (1950), a Western with Wanda Hendrix and her husband Audie Murphy. In February 1953, director Arnold and Richard Carlson were there filming the meteorite crater scenes for *It Came from Outer Space*; now in *Black Lagoon* the area represented Dr. Maia's geological camp. The day began with delays (waiting for light, repairing the camera) but then proceeded smoothly: The scene depicting the discovery of the fossilized hand was shot,[59] plus part of the later scene where the expedition members arrive and find the bodies of Luis and Tomas. Shot but not used in the movie: footage of Reed noticing and reacting to rips in the canvas of the dead men's tent (obviously the Gill Man's handiwork ... or claw-iwork). I cannot recall seeing that vignette in any version of the script, so it might have been ad libbed. Ben Chapman's name isn't on the list of players who worked that day, and yet a river's-edge scene of the Gill Man hand reaching out of the water for Kay's ankle was photographed.

On the morning of Monday, October 12, overcast skies and poor light meant that additional electricians and artificial light were needed to continue shooting the above-mentioned scene. Work commenced with more footage of the Gill Man hand reaching for Kay's leg—and again, according to the records, Chapman was not present. Also put on film was a shot ultimately not used in the movie: a closeup of the surface of the river as a rock (thrown by Williams) hits it—and then bubbles surge up to that spot, indicating the presence of the Gill Man below.

Hollywood columnist Harrison Carroll was on the set that Monday, making the first of at least two visits, and talked to Arnold. "Our Gill Man will make your blood run cold," the director predicted. "He has a fish-like head and fish eyes, arms and legs a little longer than a crocodile's and a body covered with thick tough scales. The head, of course, is a rubber mask.... I wouldn't want to get in that mask and even stick my face under a faucet."

On Tuesday, October 13, the fistfight between Reed and Williams was shot on Stage 21's "Interior Cabin and Dark Room" set. Stunt doubles Cliff Lyons and Allen Pinson were on hand, but the brawl as seen on film is all Carlson and Denning. It's a fight that, if it had taken place between kids in a schoolyard, would have left young onlookers wanting more; Williams punches Reed, Reed shakes off the cobwebs, rushes Williams and jacks him back. But a Universal publicity item makes it sound like the Battle of the Century: "[The sequence has] all of *The Spoilers*' thrills in an area one-tenth the size of that famous fight," the publicist raved. The story additionally says that for Carlson, the staged fistfight was a "harrowing experience" and "the most grueling experience he had ever undergone" because it took place in a confined area.

That same day's production report includes the note, "Per arrangement with management Miss Julia Adams excused at 8:30 a.m. to go to Santa Monica on personal business. Company shooting around her. She returned at 11 a.m. ready." Not only "ready" but a hundred and some-odd pounds lighter, as that was the morning she shed her screenwriter-husband Leonard Stern. They'd met and married in 1950 when both were working at Universal; now, nearly three years after they exchanged their "I do"s, her testimony included the tidbit that he once told her that she didn't have the acting ability to go with her well-publicized, well-insured legs. She additionally charged him with being rude and disagreeable to her friends. Stern also wrote for TV, including the well-loved series *The Honeymooners, The Phil Silvers Show, Get Smart et al.*; in later years he became a producer and director as well.[60]

With Adams back, the *Black Lagoon* company went on to shoot more cabin scenes, including the memorable vignette when the Gill Man's hand reaches through the open porthole and hovers over the bandaged and bedridden Dr. Thompson. Several of the folks who caught *Black Lagoon*'s January 7, 1954, sneak preview wrote on their Comment Cards that this was the scene they liked most in the picture; for actor Whit Bissell's daughters, it was the scene they probably liked the *least*. "Those claws coming in through the window were just horrible," Bissell told *Filmfax* interviewer Pat Jankiewicz. "My daughters were very young at that time, and when that scene came on the screen, my youngest daughter screamed, right in the middle of the theater, 'It's going after Daddy!' It was very realistic."

Meanwhile, 2260 miles away (give or take), the *Black Lagoon* second unit was arriving at their home for the next few weeks, the Wakulla Springs Lodge, 80 or 100 yards from the edge of the body of water where they'd be shooting. Some of the guest rooms, plus the dining room and terrace, had (and *have*) a view of the Spring and River. They grabbed a noon-to-one lunch and then, typical of this problem-plagued production, found themselves unable to get the 3-D camera to operate. They then set up a process camera on a boat, in order to shoot plates of river and jungle backgrounds—and had trouble with the camera's batteries! By 5:12, less than an hour after they'd finally started shooting, they called it quits. The next morning, Gill Man Ricou Browning officially started working, but only appeared on-camera for a few minutes at the very end of the day.[61] In order to play an aquatic monster without the use of air tanks, he used the amazing "hose-breathing" techniques he'd been taught during his teen years by Newton Perry. What this involved, Browning told me, was:

> Coming down from a compressor on the surface, I'd have an air hose, the air coming out of it with some force. I'd stick the air hose in my mouth and breathe from it, like you would drink water from a hose in your backyard. There's kind of a little knack to it, but I learned it when I was very young, at Wakulla Springs.... It was something I did very naturally, and so it came easy for me. I could insert the hose in the mouth of the Creature, then I'd have to go a couple of inches further, to get to my own mouth, and then breathe.
>
> Let's say we were ready to do a scene: With me, I would have a safety man with an air hose and I'd be breathing, and when I was ready to go, I'd give the cameraman "Scotty" Welbourne the okay sign—hand signals—and I'd keep breathing. When he would give me the signal he was rolling the camera, I would release the air hose, giving it back to the safety man, and then (if it was just a swim-through) I would swim by camera. On the other side, there'd be another safety man who'd give me a different air hose. So I had safety men in various places in order to get air. The compressor on the surface supplied air to my safety men's multiple hoses ... sometimes more than one compressor.
>
> If I got to where I was really desperate for air, I would just stop everything and go limp, and the safety man would swim in to me and give me an air hose. Or if I was in a fight

Julie Adams and Richard Carlson at Park Lake. Notice in the background, beyond the trees, the castle set built for Tower of London *(1939). In the '50s, the new breed of Universal Monsters worked amidst the haunts of the old.*

On the water at Wakulla, the moviemakers worked from a glass bottom boat with an attached raft. To keep them from floating downstream, cables were tied to boat and raft, with the other ends tied to secure spots on shore (for example, Wakulla's three-deck, 32-foot diving tower). Wakulla "work boats" like the one on the left transported people to and from the raft (courtesy State Archives of Florida).

On the right is Charles McNabb (1927–2012), a member of Ricou Browning's safety team on all three Creature movies. He was also a World War II naval aviator, a crop duster, professional scuba diver, feature film stuntman, location scout and a pilot for the state of Florida Bureau of Aircraft, flying department heads and governors for 33 years. From right to left, the others pictured are safety diver Frank Den Bleyker, underwater doubles Jack Betz and Stanley Crews and their trainer Fred Zendar (courtesy State Archives of Florida).

scene, I would just stop fighting and not do anything, and then they would come in and give me an air hose. I had people that I had worked with underwater for years prior to this, so I had a lot of confidence in them. They were very good and it worked fairly well.[62]

Browning got to pick the members of his safety team; some were co-workers from water shows (like Patsy Boyette, a Weeki Wachee "mermaid") and others were people with whom he'd gone cave-diving. One safety man, his longtime friend Charles McNabb, took part in all three Gill Man movies. In 1983 when Browning was profiled by newspaper interviewer Bill Luening, McNabb was quoted in the article and described working with the man (Browning) whose life was often in his hands: "You've got to know Ricou. He'd push himself to the absolute limit. He's like that. And when he needed air, he needed it now. Or he died."

The second unit crew's "workplace" was a boat-and-raft set-up; the raft was held up by six air-filled 55-gallon drums. An upcoming shot would be discussed and rehearsed on the raft, and then the cast and underwater crew would go down and shoot. "And if we screwed up *real* bad, we'd come up and rehearse again," Browning said. "*Or, we'd try to solve the problem underwater."* The compressors pumping out the air for Browning's underwater hose-breathing use were noisy and would have interfered with rehearsals, so they were kept on a second boat and/or raft.

Also shot underwater in Wakulla on October 14 was the footage where Reed (played by FSU student Stanley Crews), working at the bottom of Morajo Bay, notices the jiggling 40-foot marker. It's not hard, in the new millennium, to take some of the underwater scenes in *Black Lagoon* and the other Gill Man movies for granted, but in the mid–1950s they were real attention-getters: Scuba-diving was a newish phenomenon and public interest was at its peak. Truth be told, these scenes were movie history-makers: It was the first time that a 3-D camera had gone underwater *and*, as William Alland pointed out to me, it was a *free-floating underwater camera in a natural environment*, practically unheard-of prior to *Black Lagoon*. "Scotty" Welbourne, *Black Lagoon*'s second unit d.p., was its inventor. As Alland told me,

> [He] was an old Hollywood type, famous for being a still photographer—Greta Garbo always insisted on having him, he was her favorite still photographer. Anyway, he had branched out and had gotten into scuba, and he developed an underwater camera to use with scuba gear. He had a little inner tube that was tied to the bottom of the camera, and with a CO_2 cartridge he could inflate or deflate that, and get neutral buoyancy with it and swim all over the place and take movies. "Scotty" had already done some free-swimming movie photography in the ocean—nobody had ever done that before.

According to Ricou Browning, cameraman "Scotty" Welbourne would sometimes need to have someone hold him (as pictured) because moving a camera underwater is "like being in outer space": When you try to pan, water resistance pushes the body in the opposite direction. In this Revenge of the Creature *shot, Welbourne is steadied and balanced by expert swimmer Charles McNabb on the bottom of Silver Springs.*

A *Revenge of the Creature* publicity item pointed out that the filming of pictures underwater, which had been going on for 40 years,[63] was revolutionized by "lens artist" Welbourne when he did *Creature from the Black Lagoon*. In 1954 when *Revenge* was made, there were only three of Welbourne's tri-dimensional cameras in existence: The first was built by Welbourne in his shop, the second was built in a Universal shop from Welbourne's specifications, and the third was built at Disney, again from his specifications. Powered by a battery unit inside it, it weighed 200 pounds but it could be pushed or pulled through water, always floating on an even keel. (A *Black Lagoon* article in the magazine *The Skin Diver* described the camera as "self-pressurized by a miniature lung" and said it had "perfect weight neutrality.") It rose or sank in the water, still always on an even keel, by responding to either of two buttons pressed by the operator. The speed of its ascent or descent was regulated by the amount of pressure on the buttons. "It was a big monster of a camera," Browning told interviewer Mike Nash. "And to handle that camera, 'Scotty' did a magnificent job."

"'Scotty' was an absolute artist, he was tremendous," Alland said in *The Man Who Pursued Rosebud*. "All the underwater stuff in [*Black Lagoon*]—hey, I've seen nothing done since that's any more artistically beautiful than the stuff in that."

At Universal, the 14th began with the usual difficulties (a heavily overcast sky, poor light and a camera in need of repair) and then several scenes were shot at a variety of locations. The entire morning was spent at Park Lake shooting rowboaters Reed and Williams dropping rotenone sacks into the lagoon and discussing the Gill Man. Then in the afternoon, on Stage 21, parts of two cabin scenes were shot, starting with the tail end of the developing-the-photo sequence. Put on film but not used in the movie: a shot of Williams talking, with the camera dollying in to show us, through a porthole behind him, the legs of the Gill Man going past the opening. (Chapman again is *not* on the list of actors present.) Other shots made that day but not seen in the movie: a closeup of Kay screaming (in reaction to the Gill Man reaching through the porthole) and a medium closeup of Kay rising from her bunk, putting on her shoes and exiting her cabin.[64] Lastly, in front of a process screen, the scene of Reed, Kay and Maia in the Morajo Bay speedboat was performed. The 14th, incidentally, was Jack Arnold's 41st birthday.

"Perhaps Jack's greatest characteristic was his very cool demeanor," Julie Adams wrote in *The Lucky Southern Star*, continuing:

> No matter how complicated the shot was, or how difficult the staging appeared, he somehow managed to make things look easy. He also created a terrific environment for everyone to work in. The cast and crew were always happy on his set, and enjoyed coming to work every day. [Carlson, Denning, Moreno] and I all developed a nice camaraderie, which I think translates into how well our scenes together play for an audience.

There was an 8:15 call on the morning of the 15th but Adams was late; her makeup, which normally took 45 minutes, took an hour due to the fact that a new makeup man (last name: Hadley; possibly Joe Hadley) was preparing her for the cameras for the first time. More Park Lake scenes were committed to film that day, including the drugged fish floating on the lagoon surface and the flareup between Williams and Lucas, who holds a knife beneath Williams' chin. In North Florida the morning's work was lost due to yet more camera problems. The afternoon was devoted to shooting the last of the plates and a test of Dottie Kulick,

"In the know" *Black Lagoon* fans will watch the scene of Reed in his makeshift darkroom and recall the real-life incident of Gabriel Figueroa telling William Alland *et al.* that he could actually produce photographs of an Amazon man-fish. Pictured: Richard Denning, Julie Adams, Antonio Moreno, Richard Carlson, Whit Bissell, Nestor Paiva.

1. Creature from the Black Lagoon (1954)

Dottie Kulick, seen with first aid man R.A. Guyer and Ricou Browning, auditioned for the job of double for Kay. For five minutes the underwater camera filmed her (from two different angles) doing a "straight stroke," then the backstroke, and executing a turn in the water. For whatever reason, she didn't get the job (courtesy State Archives of Florida).

who was auditioning for the job of underwater double for Kay.

There was an addition to the small Wakulla cast that day: 27-year-old Jack Betz, yet another FSU student, who had the job of doubling Richard Denning's character Mark Williams. Credit producer William Alland with the bright idea of having one of the Wakulla underwater doubles (Betz as Williams) use a single tank, the other (Stanley Crews as Reed) two tanks, so viewers had a way to tell them apart in all the below-surface scenes.

One of the reasons Betz and Crews were hired: At Universal the Land Creature (Ben Chapman) was going to tower over his human co-stars, and so the Underwater Creature played by the average-height Ricou Browning also had to look big. This was achieved by selecting underwater doubles who were on the short side.

Betz grew up in Sarasota and later became three-time mayor of that city. His friend Brooksie Bergen, a Sarasota newspaper columnist, did a story on him in the 1990s and concentrated on his early-in-life career as an occasional movie stuntman (or, more accurately, stunt*kid*). According to Betz, he was the high-diving double for Johnny Sheffield as Boy in Tarzan movies partly shot in Florida, and also worked in the Florida-made scenes of *Sunday Dinner for a Soldier* (1944) and *On an Island with You* (1948). By the time *Black Lagoon* came along, he was a Navy veteran (two and a half years of submarine service) attending the University of Florida. He told Bergen that he auditioned for his *Black Lagoon* job at Silver Springs, where he "had to work with a lot of experimental underwater equipment, stuff we weren't familiar with. It was probably a test of endurance and swimming ability." Beating out a large number of aspirants, he landed the gig—but didn't like the next step, getting his hair dyed peroxide blond in a local beauty parlor, to match the color of Denning's: "In those days, being seen in a beauty parlor was as bad for a man's image as going into a lingerie shop." He also mentioned that the application of heavy body makeup took an hour and a half each morning. (Underwater without body makeup, a white man's skin looks *bright*-white on film.)

Betz told Bergen that money attracted him to the job. "Going back to school on the G.I. Bill with a wife and two kids was pretty tough. The $275 I got from Universal each week for a total of four and a half weeks was a fortune in those days. It was a lucky break." One of Sarasota's best-loved residents, Betz died of emphysema in 1998.

In the vast Wakulla wetlands, there was more aggravation for the *Black Lagoon* crew on the 16th, with *two* camera breakdowns and then heavy rain making the waters too dark. Well in advance of the start of shooting, "Scotty" Welbourne had made *Black Lagoon* unit manager James T. Vaughn aware that this could happen, and back on August 22 Vaughn had addressed the subject in an inter-office communication to production manager Gilbert Kurland:

> Welbourne advises me that if it rains, the water in the springs remains murky for as long as a week. He suggests that we figure on shooting alternate locations in that event, such as Silver Springs [about 170 miles from Wakulla Springs], since the rainfall is generally spotty and limited to a narrow area. This, of course, would involve delays and additional costs not anticipated in our budget.

Incidentally, no "crowd control" measures needed to be taken while *Black Lagoon* was shot publicly at Wakulla Springs: The place was a magnet for locals in the summer but much less so in colder months like October. As the *Black Lagoon* crew went about their business, Wakulla would have no more than six or eight visitors at any one time, and these visitors paid almost no attention to what the moviemakers were doing.

At Universal on October 16, the morning was spent trying to get the shot in which the *Rita*'s attempted escape from the Black Lagoon ends at the tree barricade. On the first attempt, the *Rita* was being towed by cables attached to a winch, but the winch couldn't pull the boat fast enough for the action to look realistic. As most of the company members had lunch, prop shop men re-rigged things so that the *Rita* would now be pulled by an off-screen, on-shore truck. Again things went awry. In order *not* to have to wait as the boat was *re*-re-rigged, Arnold and Co. jumped ahead in the script and shot an on-deck discussion *of* the tree barricade plus the reaction to the Gill Man's smashing of the rowboat. The light was lost at 4:05, so the company shot some silent test footage of the Gill Man. According to production paperwork, Chapman still had not worked a single day on the set so who knows who was in the suit.

Saturday, October 17, 1953, Julie Adams' 27th birthday, was another day that began with grief: According to the minutes of a subsequent Studio Operating Committee meeting, "The company had an exterior call, but the boat had been pulled on shore to rig the underwater cable for positive stopping of the boat [as it hit the barricade, I assume]. While on shore the water in the boat sank the stern and more water rushed in and the boat tipped over." Hastening to a Stage 21 cover set, the moviemakers photographed a variety of silent shots of the Gill Man's hand coming through the porthole. (Is it Chapman's hand? Who knows? He signed his contract to join the picture's cast that day, but apparently had not yet been fitted for his Creature costume.) Then, after *more* camera problems, they tackled the Instituto de Biología Marítima office-aquarium scene where, with rear-projected fish as a backdrop, the movie's leading characters examine the skeleton hand. (Speaking of hands: Early in the scene, watch Carlson's hand twitch. An alcohol withdrawal symptom?) It was a "one-and-done" day for unbilled actor Sydney Mason, who plays Dr. Matos; Mason also appears in *Revenge of the Creature*, there as a different character. Not surprisingly, given all the unexpected snags, *Black Lagoon* was now two days behind schedule and approximately $6000 over budget.

Richard Crosby of the magazine The Skin Diver *wrote in the August 1954 issue that Browning's in-water style "greatly contributed to the Gill Man's possession of a character all its own, with its strange method of swimming in a rocking fashion from side to side." Browning said, "I* do *have a unique stroke when I swim underwater, and I think that's what appealed to Jack Arnold."*

As mentioned above, October 17 was the date on Ben Chapman's "Screen Actors Guild Inc. Minimum Free Lance Contract" which called for him to play the role of "Gill Man" at a salary of $300 a week; "The terms of employment hereafter shall begin on the 17th day of October 1953, and shall continue thereafter until the completion of the photography and recordation of said role." It shows Chapman's address as 18670 West Topanga Beach Road, right on the beach in Malibu, and his phone number as Globe 62485. Needless to say, the contract's seventh clause—that the player agrees to furnish all "wearing apparel reasonably necessary for the portrayal of said role"—wasn't applicable in Chapman's case!

1. Creature from the Black Lagoon (1954)

In Florida the cameras worked well that day, but on Sunday, October 18, there were more breakdowns, and yet again "The Sunshine State" failed to live up to its nickname as heavy rain caused blackness underwater. Mechanical defects and bad weather weren't the only on-location difficulties: According to William Alland, second unit director James C. Havens didn't turn out to be much of a second unit director. Alland told me,

> After we picked the locations in Florida and everything, we sent "Scotty" Welbourne down there to shoot second unit stuff, underwater. And we sent down a very famous second unit director named James Havens to direct it. Well, after they were there a few days, I got a call from the production manager: "You'd better come down here, there's all hell breaking loose. Havens and Welbourne are not getting along." So I went down, and what I found out was that Havens was scared to go underwater! What he did was, he would swim on the surface with a snorkel, and look *down* 50 feet to see what was going on [*laughs*]! That's the God's truth! Havens had sketched out how he wanted the thing to be shot and everything, and Welbourne was saying, "Hey, I can't do it that way. He can't see what's down there, and I can't do things based on a sketch that he might show me. I gotta take advantage of what's there." Havens' position was, "Look, he won't do the scenes as I instruct him." But Havens wouldn't put on scuba and go down!
>
> Now I'm there, see, so what I did was, I tried to *shame* Havens into doing it. I put on scuba gear and went down there with "Scotty" and watched him doing his stuff and so forth, then came out and said to Havens, "Listen, either you go down and see what he's doing and work with him, or you've just got to get out of the way." And he said, "Well, I'll just get out of the way, that's all." He *stayed* there, but he did not have a damn thing to do with any of the stuff that went on underwater.

Considering the fact that almost one-fourth of the movie takes place underwater, I asked Alland if fans talking about the direction of *Black Lagoon* should say that it was directed by Jack Arnold and "Scotty" Welbourne. His emphatic reply was, "Absolutely. 'Scotty' Welbourne directed the underwater stuff."

Wanting more than one take on this situation, I also put the question to Ricou Browning, who looked at things differently. He disputed Alland's memory that Havens was "scared" to go underwater, saying that Havens simply "wasn't *capable*, in other words, he wasn't *trained* to go underwater. He was topside on an inner tube, looking down wearing a facemask, watching as much as he could what was going on. And that was *it*. He depended a great deal on 'Scotty' Wel-

"Scotty" Welbourne's 3-D camera is transported through Wakulla's crystal water. In 1954 when the Creature trailer narrator promised, "You'll see the most amazing underwater photography that the screen has ever known," that wasn't much of an exaggeration.

bourne, and 'Scotty' was a pretty sharp character. [Havens] kind of just left it to him and us to do our thing. And he would watch, and comment now and then." More recently I put the question to him again, and he added a few more particulars:

> We would stand on the raft with Havens and we would talk about and rehearse the scene that we were about to do, "Creature swims after girl" or whatever. Then when the rest of us [without Havens] got underwater, we'd have to figure out *how* to swim after the girl, or *how* to do whatever it was we had to do. "Scotty" and I would figure that out. If it looked good, "Scotty" and I would come up and say "It was great!" and Havens would say "Fine!," and then we'd go on to the *next* sequence.

On the question of who should receive credit for the direction of the underwater scenes, Browning replied, "I would just say a combination of people. I would give Havens credit."

In 1997 I tried to find and contact Havens and get his side of the story, and instead found myself talking on the phone to his widow Irma B. Havens. Married to him for 65½ years, she spoke of Havens (1902–90) with enthusiasm and knew a great deal about his career. According to Mrs. Havens, in 1924 they eloped and came to California where Havens met a fraternity brother employed at MGM. As a result, Havens went to work as an MGM art director; said Mrs. Havens, "They said they'd give him two weeks, and ten years later he had his first vacation!" During his 45 years in the business, Havens segued from art director to "marine director" to second unit action director. (In 1941, he and a Technicolor camera crew were on an American warship off Hawaii, getting background shots for Fox's *To the Shores of Tripoli*, when the Japanese attacked Pearl Harbor. The film they shot that day was seized by the Navy, and they were all made to sign a promise not to talk about their experiences.) No slouch in the bravery department, Havens was a Marine captain and demolition expert; for *Mogambo* (1953), made in Africa during the Mau Mau rebellion, he surveyed locations in a Land Rover and photographed animal scenes. According to Mrs. Havens, he knew a lot about boats starting in his teenage days when he worked at the submarine-manufacturing Lake Torpedo Works in Bridgeport, Connecticut; during their life together, he "always had a boat—a sailboat first, without any engines or anything, and then ketches and motorboats." For the 1962 Marlon Brando *Mutiny on the Bounty*, she said that he went to Nova Scotia, built the three-mast replica of the *Bounty*, trained the crew and sailed it to Tahiti![65] Mrs. Havens did confirm for me that her husband had no interest in diving: "He didn't like going under the water at *all*." Mrs. Havens passed away the same year I talked with her.

On Monday, October 19, the long arm of the law—Murphy Law's—again reached out for the Florida company: At a depth of 60 feet they were shooting Reed and Williams' second dive when water pressure cracked the glass in the camera's watertight housing, creating a hour-long setback.[66] The gang at Universal again attempted to get the jinxed shot of the *Rita* ramming the half-submerged tree barricade; they also shot subsequent scenes of Our Heroes trying to move the tree with cable and winch. Chapman is listed on production paperwork for showing up on the lot that day to be "fitted in Makeup." "Fitting in Makeup" is written next to Chapman's name on the Production Report for October 20, and then he did work on-camera that

night: Standing in knee-deep waters near the jungle-like edge of Park Lake, he played the scene where the Gill Man is blinded by the *Rita*'s spotlight, snatching at the empty air in front of him, and then sinking into the water to exit. This scene was then shot two more times, the third and last time with tubes hooked up to the Creature gills to produce the breathing effect.[67]

Bob Burns agrees that this was probably the first time Chapman was in front of the camera and that in all previously shot footage of the Creature, someone else was inside the world's weirdest onesie. "By the time Ben finally came on, they *had* to have demos of his suit already, they had to have pieces put together just to see what it was going to look like. So in those other scenes [the Creature's arm reaching out of water and through the porthole, the Creature's legs and feet as he walks the *Rita* deck, etc.], we're probably seeing some extra that they hired. I don't think it was even a stuntman, they wouldn't *need* a stuntman, I'm sure it was just an extra they got and said, 'Okay, we want you to put your hand through here' or 'Walk over here, we need to see your feet walkin' by,' stuff like that." Chapman did claim to have done the Gill Man scenes shot prior to October 20 but the Production Reports contradict him. For example, on the October 9 Production Report's list of actors, his is one of several names scratched out (meaning that

From right to left, underwater doubles Stanley Crews and Jack Betz learn scuba techniques from Fred Zendar. The Swiss-born Zendar (1907–90) was raised in France and, before his movie career as a "water specialist," competed as a swimmer in the Olympics of 1924 (Paris) and 1928 (Amsterdam) (courtesy State Archives of Florida).

1. Creature from the Black Lagoon (1954)

none of them worked on that date)—and that was the day the Gill Man attacked Chico. A $25 extra *did* work that day, from 9 a.m. until 11:50, departing minutes after the completion of the attack scene.[68]

Richards Carlson and Denning were also in Park Lake on the night of the 20th. (Reed: "That's where [the Gill Man] went under." Williams: "I'm going to take a look. You wait here.") Denning recalled the ordeal for me, admitting that he and Carlson were able to stay in the water until 8:00 partly thanks to some potent potables:

> It was October and it was freezing cold. We were out in the water and we were tired and it was late, and the prop man kept bringing us brandy to keep us from freezing to death. It worked great, and we were going just fine. And then we finally wrapped it up and we went to the dressing rooms—they were nice and warm. All of a sudden [*slurring his words*], that brandy just hit like a sledgehammer! But out in the cold and the wet and wind, it didn't bother us at all![69]

"That happened to me also," cross-country Creature Ricou Browning admitted to me:

> It can get quite cold in North Florida. We were shooting at Wakulla Springs and everybody was trying to be nice and they kept giving me a shot of brandy. And pretty soon they had a drunk Creature on their hands! So I had to cut that out!
>
> They had a heater on the boat 'cause the air temperature at that time was around 48 or 50. Pretty chilly! It didn't make much difference to me 'cause I was in the suit and the heater couldn't warm me up [in a cold-water–soaked foam rubber outfit], but the other divers would go in there and get warm.

"We spent a lot of time trying to shake off the chills after being submerged in those icy depths for long periods of time," Denning's underwater double Jack Betz told interviewer Brooksie Bergen. "We took a lot of hot showers and drank hot coffee by the gallon." According to Betz, the Wakulla water temperature during production was 49 degrees. "I'm sure the water *felt* like 49 degrees," Wakulla Springs festival faciliator Jeffrey Hugo emailed me, "but I am very skeptical of that being the actual temperature. To my knowledge, the water is and has been about 69 degrees year round. About five years ago I interviewed one of the lifeguards who worked here in the late '40s. He told me that he enjoyed swimming in Wakulla Springs in the winter because on a cold day the water felt warm." Bruce Mozert, *Black Lagoon*'s underwater still photographer, also told me that Betz's 49-degree claim was off-beam; Ginger Stanley recalled that 72 degrees was the year-round temperature of Wakulla Springs back in *Black Lagoon* days. *However* … 69 degrees and even 72 degrees is cold. Swimming in the average swimming pool feels a little chilly if the water is much less than about 85 degrees.

At Universal, cold water wasn't one of Ben Chapman's worries; he faced other trials. Talking about getting back and forth from the makeup department to the back lot location, Chapman said in our interview,

> [The makeup guys] would get me into the complete costume—complete, that is, except for the boots, gloves and helmet. Then I would go down the stairs and onto one of the little trams that they used to use to transport actors to and from the sets. I would have to stand up on the tram—in fact, I could never sit down once I was in the suit. They would put the rest of the stuff on me on the set itself. And once I was in that outfit, I'd stand anywhere between 12 to 14 hours a day.
>
> [At lunch time,] I'd take the helmet, the boots and the gloves off, get onto a tram and go in for lunch. They had for me what they called a "stand-up" chair: It looks like a chaise lounge, except it stands straight up and has arm rests on it. I'd get into that, and there would be a very high table for me to eat off of.

A Universal press release, stamped with the date October 20, advanced the following fishy story:

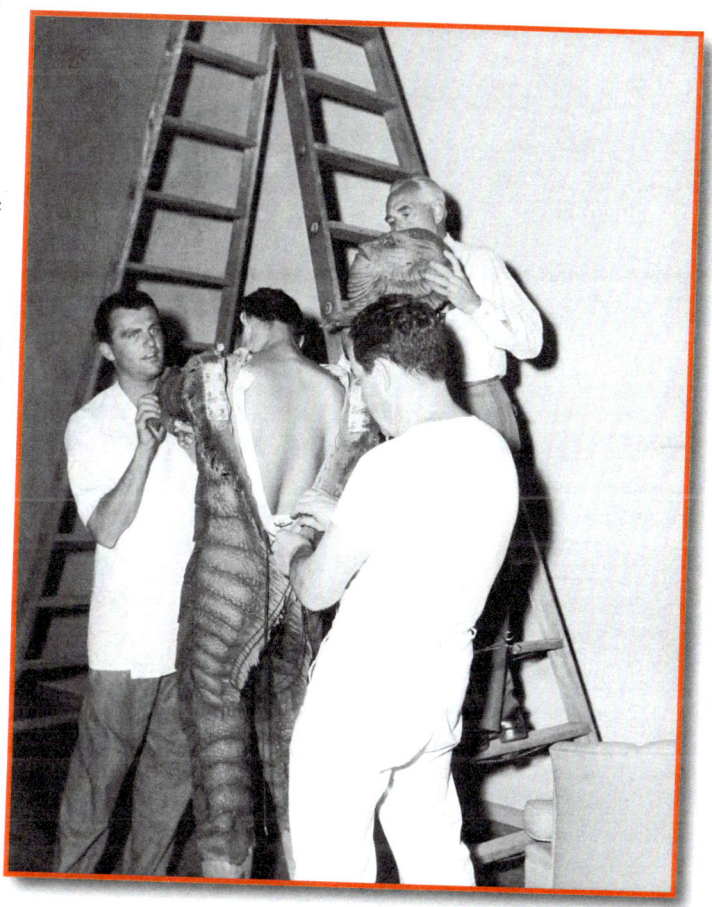

The time-consuming process of threading the drawstrings and tightening them is underway. The long fin down the Creature's (Ben Chapman) back will hide the seam.

A ghoulish monster, half-man and half-fish, rested comfortably in the dark recesses of a Universal-International studio vault today while filmmakers pondered its publicity future with the astute wisdom of a war strategy board.

The big question of the day was this: Would publicity aid or hinder his performance in the 3-D science fiction thriller *Black Lagoon*?

Dream Boy, as the scaly monstrosity has been dubbed by the film crew, is the product of eight months of experimentation by the studio's top artists and technicians. His ancestral tree includes 13 predecessors who failed to scare studio executives enough to win the important screen role.

Made of specially treated foam rubber, Dream Boy becomes the outer skin of a professional swimmer who will cavort before the 3-D cameras, both above and under water. Among a list of Universal-International's monsters which already include Frankenstein's brainchild, Dracula, the Wolf Man and the "It" from *It Came from Outer Space*, Dream Boy has already been voted the most frightening of them all.

Although his public debut would undoubtedly create a considerable stir in public print, Dream Boy's unveiling, on the other hand, may detract from the spine-tingling effect his first appearance on the screen is expected to generate.

So, until the movie moguls make a decision, Dream Boy will remain in the dark, under lock and key, appearing only for testing on closed sets before members of the crew.

Like most publicity items, this one flies in the face of reality: Photos of the Gill Man costume were already starting to appear in print. A cute UPI photo of Julie Adams alongside Ben Chapman in the Gill Man suit *sans* headpiece ran in newspapers in October 1953; the *Hollywood Citizen-News* published it on October 24 and a copy of that paper could conceivably been on the set that day during the shooting of *Black Lagoon*'s beach scenes (the Gill Man killing Zee, the bullet-riddled Gill Man climactically walking into the water, etc.).

Everybody got along well on Universal's *Black Lagoon* set, according to Adams, and when Chapman finally joined the gang, things got even better: "It was a very harmonious company, really, and he was a big part of it," she told me. "He was wonderful, he was funny, he was dear, he was considerate. We became great friends. I would come in in the morning and he would be in the outfit and I'd say [*Adams now speaks in a 'little girl' voice*], 'Good morning, *Beastie*!' [*Laughs.*] So he was part of what made that picture such a joy to make." She could not remember Chapman ever beefing about the challenges of wearing the Creature suit, adding with another laugh, "Oh, no, *no*, no. *Nothing* fazed Ben!"

Well, *one* thing that fazed him was Universal keeping his name out of the on-screen credits. Ben told me that Universal's head of publicity was responsible for this:

> It was his idea not to credit either Ricou or myself. He wanted to give the illusion that Universal had actually gone to South America, to the Amazon, and captured a creature that they later named the Gill Man. He didn't want the audience to see in the credits that the Creature was a guy in a suit; he wanted 'em to look for that credit, *not* find it, and say to themselves, "They didn't say who played the Creature. They must've got a real one." That was [Universal's] thinking. I didn't go along with it; I mean, don't underestimate people, they're not so stupid that they'd believe this was a real monster [*laughs*]!

While Chapman was of course correct about receiving no on-screen credit, he certainly got his share of plugs in the press, which belie his claim that Universal wanted to keep people in the dark

This photograph of Julie Adams and Ben Chapman ran in newspapers while Black Lagoon was still in production. Chapman's cloth hood keeps his hair contained and out of his eyes under the Gill Man helmet.

1. Creature from the Black Lagoon (1954)

about the Gill Man being an actor in a suit. The abovementioned UPI photo, published while the movie was in production, shows him in costume with the head off, and his name and Korean War service are mentioned in the caption. The *Long Beach Independent* (February 21, 1954) article "Hollywood Movie Monsters" *twice* credits Chapman with playing the Creature, in the story and in a photo caption. Not long after the movie's release, the May 17, 1954, issue of *Life* magazine revealed, "The Gill Man is 6'5" 25-year-old Ben Chapman, a dancer who was brought up in Tahiti and now specializes in 'Tahitian rhythms.' An ex–Marine, he was wounded in Korea. He has a French wife and a seven-year-old son."[70] On the castlist that appears with the *New York Herald Tribune*'s *Black Lagoon* review, Chapman as "Gill Man" is listed alongside the other stars; the reviews in *Motion Picture Exhibitor* and *Harrison's Reports* work Chapman's name into their synopses; etc., etc.

October 21 began at Park Lake the way *many* days began ("8:40: Camera breakdown discovered; 8:40–9:15: Camera being repaired"), and then the troupe got down to the business of shooting a day's worth of scenes and individual shots for various parts of the picture. In North Florida, however, Monster Movie History was being made: Ginger Stanley, Julie Adams' 21-year-old double, was now part of the unit as they began shooting "the underwater ballet" with Ricou and Ginger becoming the *Fred* and Ginger of sci-fi. (My interview with Stanley appears in Chapter 6, "Creature Conversations.")

The first shot committed to film that day was shortened for inclusion in the movie: "[Medium shot] Shooting up to bottom of boat ladder and net—Kay dives in to make big underwater arc—[Camera tilts down] with her dive to big [closeup] of Gill Man watching—he swims out over [camera]." In the edited version, the camera does begin to tilt down after her entrance into the water, but the shot ends before it gets to the Gill Man. (Having the merman *right there with her* from the first moment of her swim would have reinforced an idea briefly considered during the writing process: that the Gill Man has an influence over Kay, his "music" coming out of the water to beckon her.) Then more of this unforgettable, hypnotic Kay–Creature swim sequence was filmed. It's impressive that the Florida-made "synchronized swimming" part of the scene (the Gill Man directly below Kay) came out as well as it did considering the challenges faced by Browning, who was required to swim upside-down, holding his breath, hoping water didn't go up his nose, swimming the same speed as Stanley and maintaining the same short distance from her without ever touching her—all while being unable to properly see! ("Too bad the fish man isn't identified in the cast," wrote *Black Lagoon*'s *Los Angeles Times* reviewer. "He certainly had a tough job.")

According to *Time* magazine stalwart Richard Corliss' June 27, 2005, article "6 Best Sea Monster DVDs Ever," *Creature from the Black Lagoon* is one of 'em; he writes, "A half-century later, one image sticks to the moviegoer's retina: Julie Adams in a bathing suit of iconic white, swimming gracefully in an Amazon lagoon and, unseen by her, the Gill Man miming her strokes a few feet below, like the hidden id ready to surface. In this eerie pas de deux, the creature's attentions are both predatory and appreciative. He could be her destroyer or her lover: Swamp Thing or Wild Thing."[71]

A lot has been written about *Black Lagoon*'s water ballet, some of it kinda hifalutin (hidden id? pas de deux?). In Universal's made-for-DVD documentary *Back to the Black Lagoon* (2000), Adams said all that really needs to be said in just three words: According to Julie, it's "a love scene." In *The Lucky Southern Star* she wrote about seeing that footage for the first time:

An expert hose breather, Ginger Stanley got her feet wet in the entertainment field as a teenager in 1950, appearing in underwater shows at Weeki Wachee Springs.

For me, one of the more exciting moments during [*Black Lagoon*] production was when we all went to see the Florida unit dailies, with Ricou and Ginger doing their beautiful "water ballet." The way he mimicked her every move was mesmerizing, and even more amazing when it was cut together with the first unit shots of me swimming on the surface. I still love seeing it.

As marvelous as the Kay–Gill Man swim scene is, it does include one moment that can elicit unwanted audience laughter: Kay doing an elegant ballet knee back roll ... fine for pretty underwater pool swimmers in, say, a 1930s Busby Berkeley production number, but humorously out of character for a lady scientist in an Amazon lagoon in a horror movie. One also has to wonder how many 1954 audience members watching the Kay–Gill Man synchronized swim instantly thought of Esther Williams' then-newish (1953) *Dangerous When Wet*, and its scene of Williams (in a very Kay-like white bathing suit) swimming underwater with cartoon cat and mouse Tom and Jerry and other animated characters!

Reminiscing about his friend Ginger Stanley, *Black Lagoon* underwater still photographer Bruce Mozert told me,

> She knew about those movie people [she knew their reputations as womanizers]. When she was at Wakulla doing *Creature from the Black Lagoon*, she said ... and I was there, standin' there, when she told 'em ... "I want you to know, all of ya, that I'm a virgin. And I'm gonna be a virgin when I marry!" [*Laughs.*] That's what she told 'em, right to their faces! 'Cause those movie guys are bad that way. Not so much the actors, but the goldarn guys that worked on the crew. They would promise girls all *kinds* of stuff, and have their fun, and then they'd go back home to Hollywood to their wives!

"I think I *did* say that," Stanley said between hoots of laughter, when I relayed to her the Mozert anecdote above. "I was aware that movie people made passes and that they thought we [local Florida girls] were 'fair game.' Well, most of these guys couldn't get a girl otherwise. Just the fact that they worked on a movie didn't mean *they* were anybody important, but *they* thought it made them important, and so they would use that. And some girls might have been stupid enough to fall for it ... but they were girls who were going to fall for stupidity anyway [*laughs*]!"

Human nature being what it is, it's one's own work that one tends to most admire; and Ben Chapman, being human, liked to think of himself, and to publicize himself, as "The REEL Gill Man":

> If you'll look at the film, you'll see that Ricou's stuff was kind of ... I'm not going to say *easy*, but it was a little bit more simple. Swim this way, swim that way; that great water ballet scene where he comes up underneath the girl; the scenes where the guys are shooting [spears] at him. There wasn't that much. Playing the Creature on land involved a lot more work.

What Chapman's Gill Man did, and how he did it, were of course determined by script and director. But for some fans, his is strictly a standard issue monster performance, complete with Mummy gait and Frankenstein-like, arms-outstretched stalking poses, whereas the Gill Man scenes with Browning give the movie its magic and take it to a whole 'nother level. As David J. Schow wrote, "Ricou's dynamic swimming technique—a genuine performance as opposed to a lumbering guy in a monster suit—was fundamental to the film's visual punch."[72]

Jack Arnold wanted the Gill Man to have a gliding walk, for Chapman to walk without picking his feet up, and Arnold sometimes ordered that heavy pieces of lead be put in the bottoms of Chapman's Gill Man boots as a reminder. Chapman told me that, in the beach scene where the Gill Man approaches Kay, Arnold instructed him "to do no 'act-

Bathing Beauty and the Beast: The Gill Man apparently has a lidless eye for the female form divine, showing a mixture of awe and masculine appreciation when Kay intrudes upon his primordial paradise. Pictured: Ginger Stanley, Ricou Browning and the camera operators.

ing' other than to just extend my arms forward; he wanted no animation on my part, he said it would be more eerie his way."

Even compared to the other "on-land Creatures," Chapman might come up short. It isn't fair to stack him up against *Creature Walks Among Us*' Don Megowan, whose eyes showed and who was therefore able to give a bit more of a performance; but Chapman might also be less colorful on-camera than *Revenge of the Creature*'s fast-moving, high-steppin' Tom Hennesy, whose Gill Man often flailed his arms in a "swimming stroke" sort of way, as though this would help locomote him through the air the same way it would in the water. The fact that *Revenge of the Creature* has a more vigorous Land Creature makes me think that Arnold came to realize that "his way" (Arnold's way)—the slow-moving, Frankenstein-like, "eerie" Gill Man—could be improved upon.

On October 22 the Florida unit wrapped up the Gill Man–Kay swimming scene, while at Universal there was more Park Lake activity, including the scene of the Gill Man climbing aboard the *Rita*, grabbing Kay and jumping overboard with her in his clutches. Chapman did the "stunt" himself but Adams was replaced by stuntwoman Polly Burson the two times it was photographed: The first time was the shot we see in the movie, the second time (after Burson's hair dried) a reverse full shot of the boat, the camera panning down with them to the water. Again Harrison Carroll was on the set and very engagingly described the action in his syndicated column:

> Set builders have wrought wonders in turning this section of the U-I back lot into a tropical lagoon with jungle foliage crowding thick and lush to the very banks of the waterway.
> As the players get set in their positions, Arnold says, "Okay, bring on the Gill Man."
> First thing I see is a green, fish-like head that appears over the top of the rail.
> Its mouth is open, gasping for breath. Its scaly throat is throbbing. As the head turns, glassy fish eyes stare toward the figure of the girl.
> The creature pulls itself up over the rail onto the deck.
> An electrician behind me says in a low voice:
> "When you touch that thing, it's even more horrible. It is not hard. It's made of sponge rubber. Your fingers stick into it."
> The voice of director Arnold suddenly is rapping out instructions to the man inside the monster suit.
> "Benny," he says, "don't forget the labored breathing. As you walk up the deck keep the mouth opening and closing. You are out of the water. You have no lungs. Each step you are getting more toxic. You are reeling."
> The creature moves ponderously forward.
> "You are getting close to her," snaps Arnold. "Lift up your arms."
> The monster raises its claws and Arnold calls:
> "Okay, Julia, turn and see him. Scream!"
> Even though I am waiting for it, Julia's hysterical shriek sends shivers down my spine. At the same instant, the creature leaps forward and seizes her.
> "Cut!" shouts Arnold. "That's as far as we'll go in this shot."

Most of the actors were dismissed between 4:00 and 4:25. The actors playing Maia's native helpers Luis and Tomas, Rodd Redwing and Perry Lopez, stuck around a few more hours for Sierra Canyon shooting of the Creature's-eye-view scene of the man-fish advancing on their tent, and the full shot of the tent quaking as the unseen Gill Man wreaks havoc inside. (Monster's-eye-view shots were big at Universal in the 1950s, starting with *It Came from Outer Space*, with an eye superimposed over what each Xenomorph sees; then *Black Lagoon*, *Cult of the Cobra* [1955] and *Tarantula*.) Hollywood newcomer Lopez, who played Tomas, was uncredited here, but by 1955 he was a busy Warner Brothers contract player and even received top

Ben Chapman and Julie Adams' stuntwoman Polly Burson plan to make their dive over the Rita's side.

billing in one of that studio's pictures, the suspenseful prison melodrama *The Steel Jungle* (1956). Dozens of movie and TV roles followed, most notably Lt. Lou Escobar in *Chinatown* (1974) and *The Two Jakes* (1990). He died of lung cancer in February 2008, one week before Ben Chapman's passing.

On the morning of October 23, Arnold got a shot not used in the movie: the Gill Man emerging from the lagoon and climbing aboard the *Rita* (Lucas, standing watch in the background, doesn't see him) just prior to the reaching-through-Thompson's-porthole scene. While they were preparing to get that shot, there was an 11-minute delay for "Painting Gill Man's feet"! Later, on the beach, they shot day-for-night footage: the Gill Man making a beeline for Kay, scuffling with Zee, picking up and carrying Kay, collapsing and being beaten by the rifle-swinging Williams, etc. Adams remembered standing over the "dead" Zee (played by Bernie Gozier) and told me:

> We were looking down at the body and there was this moment where we were all very still. Richard Carlson was in his bathing trunks and he had the facemask on his forehead, and in just the way people take off their hats for the dead, he reached up and took off his facemask and bowed his head with the mask at his chest. He doffed it so seriously that we all started to laugh, and it took us a long time to come back together again. It was just too absurd [*laughs*]!

Carlson doesn't remove the facemask in the movie, so the shot must have been cut short.

Meanwhile, in the Florida Panhandle, swimming scenes featuring Reed, Williams and the Gill Man were photographed, plus *out*-of-the-water shots of Wakulla's primeval-looking banks and of an alligator diving off a log into the water,[73] a bird on a log doing the same, and vultures flying out of a tree. The good news: The 23rd was very productive for *Black Lagoon* units on both coasts. The bad news: The movie was now *three* days behind schedule and approximately $12,500 over budget.

It was a "gang's all here" day at Universal on Saturday the 24th with the entire screen-credited cast (plus Chapman, Rodd Redwing and Julio Lopez) on the Park Lake set. There was *of course* a hold-up in getting started: Chapman was late because the makeup department was repairing his damaged Gill Man suit (the second one wasn't yet ready). On the beach, the first order of business was to get a shot of the Gill Man lifting Zee (Gozier) and flinging him into the camera. Apparently Gozier was going to do the stunt himself, as no stuntman's name appears on the day's paperwork. Gozier was supposed to hang from a wire strung from the up-out-of-camera-range arm of a crane, but the wire broke in a rehearsal. Due to the length of time needed to fix the problem, a decision was made to get that shot later. But the moviemakers must have known that there was a possibility that they'd never get around to it, because later

Wakulla cameraman "Scotty" Welbourne and, on the right, his assistant Walter Bluemel. Welbourne started his career as still photographer on many Warner Bros. movies of the 1930s, among them The Public Enemy (1931), Doctor X (1932), Mystery of the Wax Museum (1933) and a couple Busby Berkeleys (courtesy State Archives of Florida).

that morning they shot a less spectacular death scene for Zee (the Gill Man choking and dropping him). Ultimately the lifting-and-throwing shot *was* never filmed.[74] Gozier, incidentally, was the son of Hawaiian-born bit player Al Kikume; horror and sci-fi fans might recognize Kikume from his roles as half-dressed island natives in dozens of features (including *The Mad Doctor of Market Street* and *Bela Lugosi Meets a Brooklyn Gorilla*) and serials (*Adventures of Captain Marvel*, *Jungle Girl*, *Perils of Nyoka*) with exotic settings.

While shooting the Gill Man–Zee run-in, Chapman had his one and only on-set mishap. He said in our interview,

1. *Creature from the Black Lagoon* (1954)

"The Creature became quite a story on the lot; my God, did it!" Chapman told me:

> I was visited just about every day: Universal stars would bring guests onto the lot and say, "Let's drive out to the back lot and see the Creature." Someone would phone ahead and say that (for instance) Rock Hudson or Tony Curtis was bringing people back to see us. They'd have me swim out to the middle of the lake, and I would float there with just the top of the helmet and the eyes showing. I would look until I'd see them arrive, then I'd go underwater and come bursting up of the water like a porpoise, then back under again. It would be tough for the people to get a good look at me. Then I would swim in towards them with just the eyes and the top of the head showing. I'd swim in this way, getting as close to shore as I could—of course it's becoming shallower and shallower. I'd swim in to where it was about a foot and a half deep and then all of a sudden I would stand right up and RRROOOAAARRR! Some of the guests would just about wet their pants [*laughs*]!

The Gill Man (Ben Chapman), with "bullet wound" on forehead for his death scene, is perhaps asking for some script revisions. A 2002 issue of MakeUp Artist *magazine listed the 50 Greatest Make-Ups of All-Time, as determined by an online poll of readers, and the Gill Man came in at #37: "It was the first monster suit that lavished the artistry normally limited to the face or head on the whole body."*

Bernie Gozier was supposed to swing at me with his machete, and I was going to counter by grabbing his hand. We rehearsed it, and I told him he was going to have to help me; with the helmet on, I couldn't see that well. Well, he came down with the machete, I reached up and I missed his hand—and *bang*, right on top of my head. Of course, the blade was dull and the top of the helmet was quite thick, so there was no damage.

Before and after lunch, they filmed part of the movie's final scene: the shot of the bullet-riddled Gill Man staggering into the water, followed and watched by David, Kay, Maia and Lucas. Next came shots of the *Rita* heading toward Maia's camp and then, after a 12-minute break while Julie Adams changed her costume, shots of the *Rita* en route *to* and arriving *at* the Lagoon. When you watch the latter scene in the movie, listen for Reed's line "It's tight over *here*": In the next shot, you'll easily spot in the Amazon jungle ("This is exactly as it was 150 million years ago…") what must be a 150 million-year-old telephone pole.[75]

To emphasize to this book's readers how up-to-the-minute-new scuba diving was in 1953: Black Lagoon *scripts put the words "skin diver," "flippers," etc., in quotation marks because they were then unfamiliar and the air tank and hose set-up is described in detail so the reader could envision it, etc. Pictured: The Gill Man (Ricou Browning) pulls Williams (Jack Betz, future mayor of Sarasota, Florida) down to his doom.*

Producer Alland would frequently take his young daughter Susan to work with him; she still remembers the day he brought her to a soundstage (presumably the Process Stage) during *Black Lagoon* shooting. "We walked in," she told me,

> and Dad left me for a minute and walked over to an area where I could see that there was some kind of an enclosure, full of water. I didn't know what he was doing. Then he came back to me and he had me walk up to this water-filled enclosure. And then this sea monster *leaped* out at me with arms raised and a *big*, bellowing voice—and scared the *shit* out of me [*laughs*]! I was nine at the time, and I was really upset by it![76]

In Florida, October 24 began with the shooting of various point-of-view shots of Wakulla plus a few more "wildlife shots" (a bird or two, baby alligators on a log). Then the camera was changed over for underwater and the below-the-waterline brawl between Williams and the Gill Man was filmed: Browning and Jack Betz fought and rolled, battled at the top of a cliff and raised a mud cloud as they tussled in weeds. The muddiness of the water necessitated a halt in shooting at 4:12.

On Sunday, October 25, the moviemakers finished the underwater Gill Man–Williams fight scene. On Monday they filmed "rotenone sacks" spiraling down into the depths;

Blooper! In the movie, Williams says "How do you do?" to the fish-man (Ricou Browning, pictured) by putting a spear in his upper belly—but when we see the man-fish in a different shot seconds later, the spear is in his lower back.

the *New York Herald Tribune* reviewer cited this shot as "superb." Also put on film that day: unused Creature p.o.v. shots of moving forward through reeds and rising to the surface; a shot of the "dead" Gill Man floating down toward the camera; another version of that scene in which he swims feebly down to a ledge and then dies, floating off the ledge and into the depths; and the shot of the Gill Man, with Kay under his arm, making his lengthy swim down to the submerged entrance to his cave. (There *was* no cave entrance there; it was just a limestone rock formation with a ledge they could duck under.) Julie Adams told me that, during *Black Lagoon* production at Universal, "they ran some rushes of the Florida second unit stuff for us, and they were so wonderful. Especially the dive that Ricou Browning made, kidnapping the girl who was doubling me [Ginger Stanley]. A 50-foot dive! … It was very exciting."

According to Browning, it was more like an *80*-foot dive—and quite challenging. For one thing, during their long straight-down descent, he and Stanley had to hold their breath and clear their ears multiple times (in order to prevent water pressure from bursting their eardrums) without letting the audience *see* that they were clearing their ears.[77] Below, unseen under the ledge, aqualung-wearing safety divers waited to provide them with air hoses when they arrived. But for as long as it took Ricou and Ginger *to* arrive, these divers also had to hold *their* breath, so that their air bubbles wouldn't be inexplicably emanating from under the ledge in the shot. But everything was perfectly timed: Ricou and Ginger swam under the ledge and were handed air hoses, and now the safety divers themselves could resume breathing. The long descent by Browning and Stanley was shot twice, the first time right before lunch, Take #2 about two hours later. Additionally, the moviemakers got a camera-pointing-up medium shot of Browning and Stanley making their descent, but it became a casualty of the cutting room.

In the movie, after the Gill Man dives with Kay off the *Rita*, there's no follow-up underwater-camera shot of them breaking the surface. A from-below shot of the Gill Man and Kay hitting the water *was* on the location troupe's To-Do List but the filmmakers didn't get the necessary instructions. From Florida, unit manager Vaughn fired off an October 23 telegram to George Golitzen at Universal, pointing out to him, "For [the scene of] monster and girl leaping into water urgently need full description of action and air mail special delivery action still. What part of boat is leapt from? Do they hit feet or head first? Is girl facing him or back to him? No action scenes received for any part of picture." They may never have received the needed information.

The first unit spent Monday, October 26, on the Process Stage, their home for the next (and last) six days of production. Activity on the cave set began with the scene of Reed entering for the first time; he's getting an eyeful of his weird (and unaccountably well-lit) surroundings when Williams' hand suddenly enters the frame from the right and touches his shoulder. Later in this chapter you'll read about the *Black Lagoon* preview audience's reaction to that scare tactic. The next shot that morning was one that Julie Adams was *not* looking forward to. She wrote in *The Lucky Southern Star*:

> We had shot the scene where the Creature picks Kay up in his arms and sweeps her off the deck of the boat into the water. This morning we would be shooting the scene of our surfacing into his air-filled cave.... [The shot] called for the Creature to be emerging from the water with Kay unconscious in his arms.
>
> ... We went over to the water we were to come out of. I put a foot in to test temperature and immediately took it out again. It was freezing cold! Someone had forgotten to heat the tank and now there was no time to do so.
>
> Though we complained a little, Ben and I were both troupers: We stepped into the frigid water and Ben submerged with me in his arms. The assistant director signaled "action" to Ben and we slowly rose up out of the water into the misty cave. I concentrated hard on not shivering and breaking out in goose bumps.

There was more grief for poor Julie later that morning during the shooting of the scene of the Gill Man walking sideways through a tight cave passage with Kay in his arms. "The cave set was very dimly lit," Chapman said in our interview, "and very narrow for two people to try to get through—especially with one carrying the other!" He went on,

> The cave walls looked like rock, but they were made of plaster—but, still, it was very hard, like a wall. It was just one of those things: I was wearing the "medium eyes," trying to carry her through there, when all of a sudden, *clunk* [he hit the wall with her head]! And she let out a yelp, let me tell you—she saw stars!

Chapman put her down carefully and, according to Adams, was very upset. Her abrasion was bandaged by a uniformed nurse, although just for the purpose of getting a fun publicity photo of the procedure (with Adams and the nurse flanked by director Arnold, stars Carlson and Denning, and Chapman still fitted out cap-a-pie in his Gill Man get-up). To promote the movie, a story went out that she was treated at the studio hospital for the abrasion and a minor concussion (!) but the truth is that the incident was so minor that the Daily Production Report doesn't even mention it. In fact, the bandage had to have been removed just moments after it was applied, because the retake was done immediately.

Just before lunch, the company filmed the shot of Kay awakening on the altar-like rock and Reed coming in from the foreground to embrace her. Notice that in this part of the grotto, a painted backdrop features a few white pillars with ornate bases. Whether they were meant to be spotted by audience members is open to conjecture but, if you *do* notice them, they add to the "storybook" look of the place; and they certainly make well-versed *Black Lagoon* fans think back to earlier script drafts that describe the grotto as cathe-

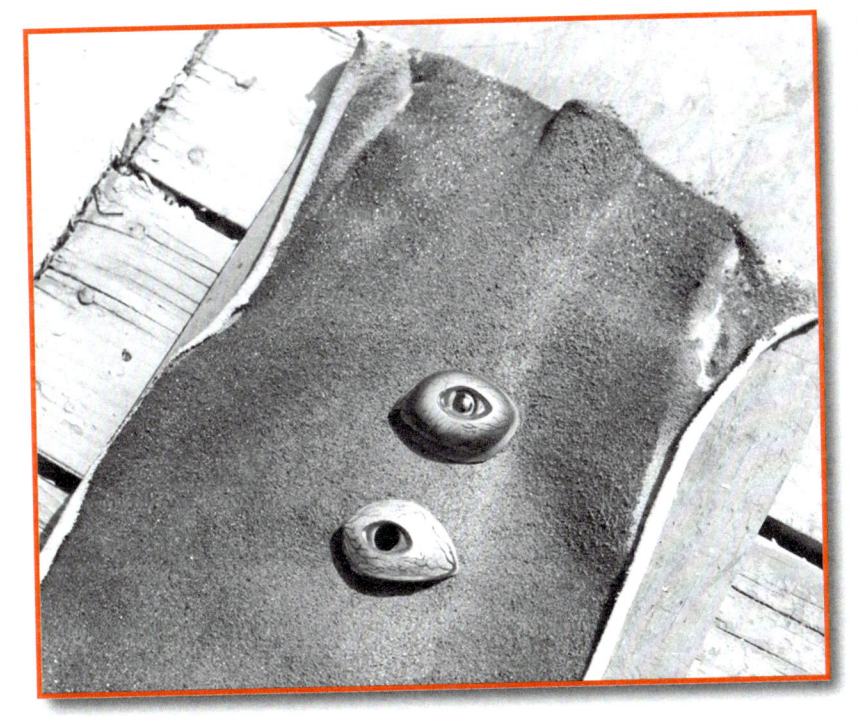

A great look at the eyes that could be popped in and out of Ben Chapman's Creature head. In medium shots he could wear the ones with holes in them and see fairly well, but in closeups and publicity shots he had to wear ones with no holes and couldn't see at all.

dral-like. For viewers who make out the pillars, they reinforce the sense that the Gill Man is 1950s monsterdom's uncrowned royal—or, at the very least, that he subscribes to *Better Caves and Grottos* or *Good Cavekeeping*. (Mark Wingfield, "blackbiped" of the Classic Horror Film Board, points out that the same backdrop of pillars was used in some of the Venus scenes of 1953's *Abbott and Costello Go to Mars*.)

Bob Skotak interviewed William Alland long before I did, and in 2013 emailed me,

> Did Alland ever allude to you his idea of a Gill Men pre-civilization, pre-human and prehistoric? I can't find the specific notes after so long, but I *do* recall him mentioning that he wanted to find a way to indicate that these creatures once ruled the Earth. I have to think that those strange pillars might have been intended to indicate the remains of the creature's long-lost ancestral civilization. Never came to a conclusion about this. Damn, wish Alland was still around!

You and me both, Bob.

After lunch, the rest of this climactic scene was shot amidst short breaks whenever the stage needed to be smoked up (for a mist effect) and whenever the smoke needed to be cleared. During Carlson's knife-to-claw tussle with the Gill Man, Carlson (rigged with wires attached to a crane) was grabbed by the waist and "lifted" into the air by Chapman; in all subsequent shots, Carlson has bloody claw wounds on his back and "claw thumb wounds" on his sides. The perks of stardom: Except for the wounds on Carlson's sides, no Gill Man movie hero is ever scratched or bruised in their lengthy fights with the monster, nor are the manhandled leading ladies marred in any way. But supporting characters (Thompson in *Black Lagoon*, Pete in *Revenge of the Creature*, Morteno in *The Creature Walks Among Us*, etc.) are invariably a mangled mess afterwards.

Part of October 27 was also spent on the cave set, doing a few bits of action a second time and shooting some new action, like Carlson ducking the swooping bat. Chapman was 22 minutes late getting to the set, having had trouble in the makeup department squeezing into "the #2 Gill Man suit" which was being used for the first time that day. About an hour later, Chapman's stand-in Otto Malde[78] tripped over a heater pipe and injured his left arm. He went to the studio hospital, and was sent from there to nearby St. Joseph's Hospital (on the corner of Olive and Buena Vista in Burbank) for x-rays. After the mishaps of Adams (her bumped head) and Malde, columnist Harrison Carroll wrote, "U-I's *Black Lagoon* company is wondering who'll be the next to make the hospital."[79]

After lunch, natives Luis and Tomas met their doom: On an interior tent set, actors Rodd Redwing and Perry

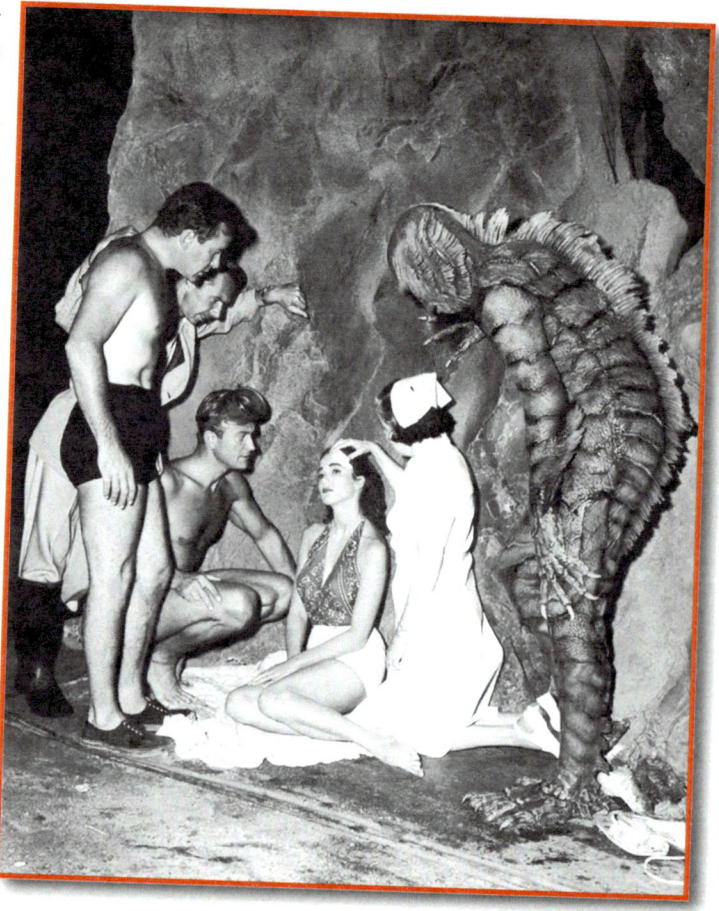

Lady sings the bruise: After Gill Man Ben Chapman inadvertently banged Julie Adams' head against a plaster "grotto wall," this publicity picture was taken even though she was unhurt. According to a spaced-out press release, Adams' "injury" was caused by a jut of real rock, and this led to the invention of foam rubber rocks that wouldn't injure actors. This innovation was called "The Julia Adams Blow Softener." (Left to right, Richard Carlson, Jack Arnold, Richard Denning, Adams, nurse, Chapman.)

Lopez were set upon by Gill Man Chapman. One shot taken that day and not used: a reverse angle shot (Luis' point of view) of the Creature's hand clawing at the camera (i.e., Luis' off-screen face).

As a kid, future shock rocker Alice Cooper loved the all-day-every-Saturday monster movies at Detroit's East Town Theater, and was unfazed by all of them until *Black Lagoon*, the first and only one that ever scared him out of the theater—with his sister right behind him! He told the *Miami New Times* in 2011 that he was about eight at the time: "It was the scene where the guy is in the tent and you see from the Creature's point of view, and the guy turns around and the Creature takes his face right off with his claw. And I ran out of the movie theater." That same year (2011), Cooper was in London, talking to an BFI Southpark

1. Creature from the Black Lagoon (1954)

A backstage peek at activity on the Process Stage, where some Rita-in-motion and Rita-at-night scenes were shot on a lookalike "boat." Sections of soundstage floor could be pulled up and the enormous well underneath filled with water, as it was for Black Lagoon (Reed, Kay and Maia on the Morajo Bay barge, the fiery Gill Man diving off the Rita, etc.), Revenge of the Creature (the Gill Man and Helen at the buoy and other scenes), Creature Walks (many shots of the Gill Man hunters in their dinghy), The Land Unknown (all lake scenes), etc. (courtesy Robert Skotak).

audience about his passion for horror flicks, and again the Creech came up: "I had already digested Frankenstein and Dracula and the werewolf ... I could deal with them, that was fine ... but there was this *new* thing [the Gill Man] that was half-fish, and it has *claws*, and [*repeatedly reaching out one arm at a time*] it was *just* missing her foot when she was swimming, *juuuust* almost getting there. It was *really* a pretty good movie!"

At the Wednesday morning October 28 Studio Operating Committee meeting, it was mentioned that *Black Lagoon* was now approximately $19,000 over budget. That day on the Process Stage, the players enacted scenes on the deck of a duplicate *Rita*, including the one where Reed tells Kay that the Amazon is still exactly as it was when it was part of the Devonian era "150 million years ago." This is "off" by only ... well, a couple hundred million years. A hundred fifty million years ago was the Jurassic era; Mother Earth went through her Devonian phase about *400* million years ago. Hearing Reed set the date as "150 million years ago" makes you wonder if he's the ideal choice to lead this search for Devonian fossils. And Kay, who doesn't bat an eye at his mega-million-year gaffe, doesn't inspire us with confidence either!

More *Rita* deck scenes were shot on the Process Stage on October 29 (Chapman's 25th birthday) and then the scene of Reed, Kay and Maia on the Morajo Bay barge. ("*Carl Maia*! It isn't *you*!" "What's *left* of me, Dr. David Reed!"[80]) It must have been a long day for Antonio Moreno, who blew enough lines that on the Daily Production Report, a special note is made of the fact that his gaffes set the company back four minutes and 28 seconds. For some reason, when Moreno's "off day" was discussed at the next morning's Studio Operating Committee meeting, the amount of time lost had ballooned up to *44 minutes*. Alland's one comment to me concerning Moreno: "I thought he was a little bit inept, but not a lot."

The Wakulla unit continued to make haste slowly: October 27 was a washout due to continuous heavy rain, muddy water and cold. On October 28, rain, cold and wind prevented shooting until almost noon, and then they had to stop at 4:12 due to "murky and dirty water." They finally got in a fairly full day on October 29, shooting from 9:29 a.m. to 3:32 p.m., including scenes of Reed repelling the Gill Man with sprays of rotenone. The Daily Production Report shows that William Alland arrived on the Florida set that day, but I don't think this could have been the visit he mentioned above (in connection with the "Scotty" Welbourne–James C. Havens battles); who'd travel cross-country to try to settle a dispute on the next-to-last day of shooting? The Daily Production Report of October 29 also reminds readers of the hazards of underwater work with its list of cast and crew members who, over the course of shooting, needed to visit Tallahassee physician Edson J. Andrews[81] for ear and nose injuries, among them Welbourne, safety diver Fred Zendar, still photographer Bruce Mozert and more.

The shoot was coming to an end at Universal as well: October 30 was the last day for Carlson, Denning, Moreno, Paiva and Gozier. On the Process Stage, various night scenes on the *Rita* deck were shot, among them the Gill Man appearing out of the water and climbing a rope up the *Rita*'s side; he gets as far as hooking one arm over the rail, and then the light from a lantern frightens him and he falls back into the water. Notice that, after the Gill Man lets go of the rail, he *stands on the water's surface* and then falls sideways into the water. As Chapman explained to me, even though he was young and strong there was no way for him to pull himself up a rope wearing slippery wet Gill Man gloves, and in a waterlogged Gill Man costume. So as he pretended to climb the rope, he actually scaled a submerged ladder. Once he let go of the rail, straight down was a direction he *couldn't* go, with the ladder beneath him, so instead he fell away from the boat from what looks like a "standing-on-water" position.

In Florida, they shot on October 30 from 9:56 a.m. to 4:25 p.m., and then the words "2nd Unit—Finished This Date" were written across the top page of the Daily Production Report. It had been over two weeks of nearly seven-days-a-week work, with much agita due to camera breakdowns and Mother Nature, plus plenty of breaks for medical attention. (Even on this last day, five people including Ricou Browning were examined for ear infections.) But the end results of their waterlogged labors were most of the best scenes from one of the best science fiction-horror-adventure films of the era.

October 31 (Halloween) was the final day of Universal shooting, with the cast's last Three Little Indians, Adams, Bissell and Chapman, on the Process Stage shooting a *Rita* deck scene (Thompson guards the tank containing the unconscious Gill Man, Kay comes up from below to join him, they talk, the Gill Man awakens and attacks). Prior to photographing the shot of the Gill Man unconscious in the tank, there was a 27-minute hold-up while his breathing apparatus was repaired; on the Daily Production Report was written the explanation "This was a very close shot—necessary for gills and throat to work." In the movie, the Gill Man's escape from the tank is off-camera, but a bust-out scene *was* shot: Crew members spent from 1:20 to 1:35 "[r]igging tank cover for special effect" and then, all in a single shot, the following action was shot: "[T]he GILL MAN leaps out of tank and THOMPSON pushes KAY out of way. THOMPSON picks up a lantern and scares the creature into backing up. The GILL MAN comes for THOMPSON then and claws his face."[82] For interviewer Dennis Daniel, Adams reminisced, "When Whit Bissell came out from makeup with his face all bloodied up…, the guy who put the clapper in front of the camera asked, 'How are you fixed for blades?'" (a line made famous by Gillette shaving razor ads of that era).

Black Lagoon wrapped two days behind schedule and over-budget by approximately $14,000. The Florida underwater unit was three days behind schedule by the time they finished.

On November 3, Army Archerd mentioned in his *Variety* column that Ben Chapman, "who plays the underseas monster in *Black Lagoon*, will be tested for a term contract—he looks good without gills, too." I never saw an interview where Chapman mentioned that, and don't know whether it actually happened. On November 10, a week and a half after the movie completed production, part of the abovementioned Kay–Thompson–Creature deck scene was re-shot. Adams, Bissell and Chapman returned to the Process Stage, where Arnold directed Kay's entrance, her chat with Thompson and their reaction to the sound of the off-screen Gill Man bursting out of the tank. It's a safe bet that the conversation we see in the movie (Thompson advising Kay about her relationships with Reed and Williams) was what was shot on the 10th because their dialogue in the movie isn't in the script. What *is* in the script, and what was presumably filmed on October 31 and then discarded, is the short-and-simple exchange that follows:

KAY (*reacting to the sound of hunting calls in the jungle*):
: Some of them are cries of fear.... Like people who whistle in the dark.... The law of the jungle—survival of the fittest—of the strongest.
THOMPSON: Darwin only claimed that survival belonged to those who adapt best to new surroundings.

In the script, this is the point at which they're interrupted by the sounds of wood-snapping, cord-ripping and the gush of water, and Kay and Thompson whirl about to see the tank with its "cover torn open—the Gill Man standing on the deck, water receding around him."

Kay and Thompson's longer, more interesting conversation (about her career and love life) is a nice scene to have in the movie if only because, *finally*, Thompson gets to speak more than just a few words at a time; the rest of Bissell's performance consists almost entirely of one-liners, making it obvious that the character is in the movie only to give the Gill Man an extra victim. "I liked Whit Bissell very much and thought he was a good performer—an interesting actor with an interesting face," actor William Phipps (*Five, Cat-Women of the Moon*) told me. He continued,

> We worked together several times, and one time—on the set of a TV show, I think—he and I were sitting in canvas chairs on the set, having coffee and shooting the breeze. He was sort of pensive that day, and he got philosophical about his life and his career. He started naming some of his contemporaries—actors and actresses that he was once in stock with or once on Broadway with. All the people he named were now *stars*, while Whit Bissell was an actor who played a lot of small parts. He wasn't complaining, he wasn't kvetching, he wasn't bitter or angry, but the gist of it was that it puzzled, or *disappointed* him. I thought the same thing about him and about many, many other actors I've worked with: "Why in the hell aren't these people doing a whole lot *more*? They're just *terrific*." He was almost wistful in talking about it and I was touched, because he was being genuine. I understood exactly what he was saying and how he felt. In his book, and in my book too, he was on a par with the people he was naming. But that's the way the cookie crumbles.

In *Black Lagoon*, we don't find out whether the mauled Thompson ultimately lives or dies (Reed: "If infection doesn't set in, he may pull through"). He does live. In *Revenge of the Creature*, Lucas says that the first movie's Gill Man mayhem resulted in "five persons" dead—and, in order of elimination, that'd be Luis, Tomas, Chico, Zee and Williams.

Before and after shooting the Kay–Thompson deck scene, the November 10 crew also photographed insert shots: the bat flying into camera, wet Gill Man footprints on the *Rita*'s deck, the harpoon hitting the *Rita*'s mast. After lunch, they moved to the Underwater Tank, adding some milk to the water to make it look a bit murky and then photographing a Gill Man dummy "as he is shot in back with spear" and "as he is shot in chest with spear" (shot descriptions from the Production Report). Then it was back to the Process Stage to get a shot of the Gill Man (Chapman's) hand "as it reaches out of water. There is a flash and the hand retreats, clawing the bank." (The flash was the flash of Dr. Maia's camera, photographing the fossil claw in the first scene at the geological camp; this shot wasn't used in the movie.) Then they got a few more insert shots: the photo of the fossilized claw, the photo taken by Reed underwater, etc.

During *Black Lagoon* pre-production, the name of the movie was up in the air: As early as September 1, publicity man Archie Herzoff was asking his colleagues to propose other titles. Staffers were told that the title needed to suggest "the shock and mystery value—and perhaps the prehistoric implications—of the story. However, we have been asked to stay away from words like 'monster' or 'beast' to avoid a title that might downgrade the picture." As of September 11, the list of offered-up titles included:

Amazon
The Amazon Man
The Being from the Dawn of Time
The Black Pool
The Chain of Life
Cruise of the Pongo
Curse of the Amazon
Expedition Terror
The Fossil That Lived
Grotto of Fright
The Hand from the Past
Jungle Nights
Lost Age
The Lost World (a bit much, taking that earlier novel and movie's basic story and Amazon setting, *plus* its title!)
The Man-Fish of Horror Lagoon
The Morajo Man
Mystery Man from the Amazon
Pongo
Since the Dawn of Time
The Stone Claw
Thunder Over the Amazon
Thundering Waters
Water Demon

Even William Alland got in on the action, sending publicist Clark Ramsay a September 18 memo with a list of six titles, five concocted by him (*The Demon of the Deep, The Sea Demon, The River of Terror, It Walks the Sea* and *It Came from Out of the Sea*) plus somebody else's *The Web and the Claw*. (*Black Lagoon* publicist Ramsay went on to become the #2 man at MGM.)

Black Lagoon remained the title right up to the first day of production, and onward *through* production. On October 19 one of the matters under discussion at the Operating Committee meeting was the name of their new monster movie: Studio brass, not happy with the title *Black Lagoon*, decided to register the replacement title *River of a Million Years*. But on November 12, Universal's Sam Israel addressed the following memo to "THE STAFF": "Hereafter please refer to *Black Lagoon* as *The Creature from the Black Lagoon*...."

I thought it was the most tawdry, cheap title I ever heard!—William Alland

Meanwhile, there was still more filming to do. Among the items on a November 23 work requisition order were black velvet ($50), a "boiler & steam setup" ($100), dry ice, powder and other miscellaneous materials ($200) for the movie's "Nebula & Explosion" sequence. "Stan" Horsley was the cameraman for this short scene, which begins behind the main titles. Visual effects artist Robert Skotak talked about this sequence with grip Wes Thompson and mechanical-visual special effects supervisor Charlie Baker, and in an email he passed along to me some specifics:

Black Lagoon's opening shots of the Earth surrounded by clouds were achieved by Horsley rigging a camera high on the Process Stage and descending vertically toward roiling, low-lying dry-ice fog being generated by foggers across a large area of stage floor, with flash powder intermittently triggered under the fog to produce the violent outbursts. A large wood disc was cut out to represent the Earth in one of the shots—I'd guess it was maybe 12, 15 feet across—using the same fog effects as above. In one of the images, the trick unit pyrotechnic supervisor Eddie Stein triggered high explosives to produce those "chaos" shots. In all of these, it is likely the camera was counter-weighted as a means to lower it in a controlled manner slowly toward the floor, especially effective as Stein's pyro erupted and sent great blasts of flaming material at the camera in 3-D. Some of this footage was tinted yellow and reused in *This Island Earth* in the scene where the spaceship approaches the surface of Metaluna.

Horsley was again in charge of the camera on November 24, when a trick unit trekked to Santa Monica's Will Rogers Beach (a bit west of Universal) to get the opening reel's shots of a long trail of Gill Man footprints in the sand starting at the water's edge. The *Black Lagoon* crew had long-ago been disbanded, so members of the crew of the jungle adventure *Tanganyika* (1954) did this work. In the movie it couldn't look more like night, but this beach footage was actually shot between 2:30 and 4:00 in the afternoon. Will Rogers Beach today, according to Wikipedia, "is popular within the LGBT community and is therefore considered Los Angeles' unofficial gay beach." *BAH-BAH-BAHHH!*

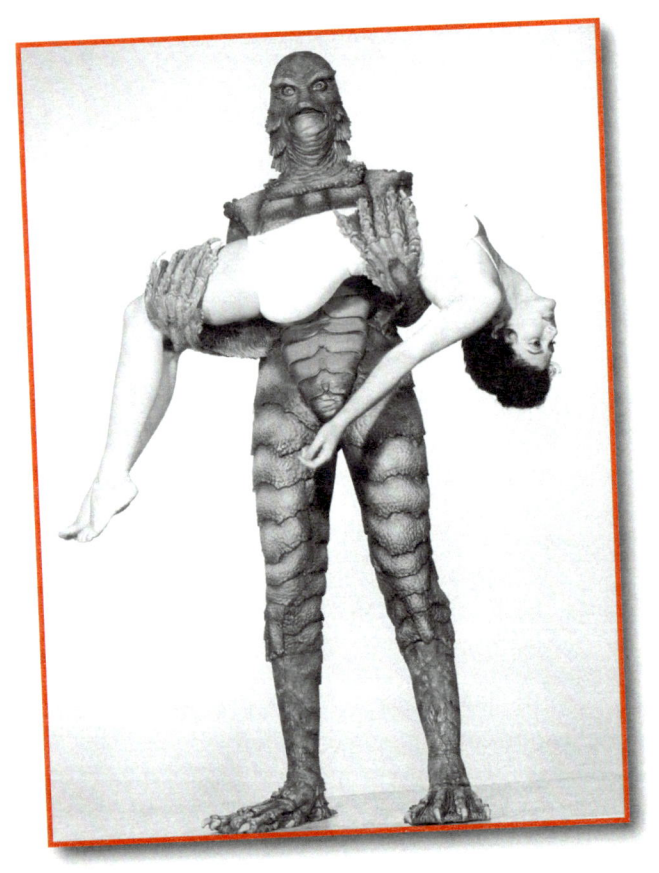

Alongside an unidentified woman, Ben Chapman appeared in a fun series of "Monster and the Girl"–type publicity photographs.

Bill Alland says he quit the commies in 1949. How come the party line against religion shows up in 1953's *Lawless Breed*?—*The Hollywood Reporter's* "Rambling Reporter" Mike Connolly, December 1, 1953

In late November, Alland had more on his mind than putting the finishing touches on his movie. It was the 37-year-old producer's turn to sit in the House Un-American Activities hot seat: He was one of five witnesses appearing at a closed-door hearing into possible Communist infiltration of the entertainment field.[83] Some of the colorful comments he made to reporters after the confab ran in the papers. According to Alland, loneliness prompted him to join the Party in 1946 and he was a member until 1949, in the interim forming the opinion that 95 percent of the Communist Party members were mentally and emotionally disturbed. When his Red friends found out that he was visiting a psychoanalyst, they told him not to attend any more meetings. Committee member Donald L. Jackson said that Alland had furnished several new identifications in the radio and TV fields; Alland said to me that the things he told them were "not very revealing." He also strongly encouraged me to take advantage of the Freedom of Information Act to obtain a transcript of his testimony so that I could see that he provided *no* new names. I never pursued it.

The Sneak Preview

Creature from the Black Lagoon had its first sneak preview on Thursday, January 7, 1954, at Los Angeles' United Artists Theatre, following a regularly scheduled showing of Universal's Tony Curtis–starring action drama *Forbidden*. The *Black Lagoon* print shown ran 7142 feet, which corresponds to a length of 79 minutes. Since the eventual release version runs 79 minutes, probably little or nothing was changed as a result of audience members' comments, which were written on preview cards. These cards were collected after the screening, distilled into a ten-page inter-office communication and sent to over two dozen interested parties, from Universal president Milton R. Rackmil on down. Here are the questions and some of the answers from 134 respondents:

How Would You Rate the Picture?

OUTSTANDING	27
EXCELLENT	30
VERY GOOD	45
GOOD	19
FAIR	13

Whom Did You Like Best in the Picture?

Respondants were instructed to list the characters in their preferred order from 1st to 6th. The numbers under each name show the number of votes they received for each ranking.

Richard Carlson
70
24
7
4
0
2

Julia Adams
18
29
30
15
4
1

Richard Denning
7
14
24
29
14
4

Antonio Moreno
3
5
9
18
21
27

Nestor Paiva
2
14
8
6
32
22

The Creature
33
16
15
10
8
15

Which Scenes Did You Like Most?

[Author's note: What follows here, and in other spots below, is a cherry-picked list culled from three pages of audience member comments.]

Underwater scenes.

When the creature died and when they shot the creature.

The creature putting his hand through the porthole in the cabin of the boat.

The scene where the injured man couldn't talk and the creature tried to get him through the porthole.

All the underwater scenes and the scene where the creature drowns Richard Denning.

Where David swam to the island and Mark put his hand on David's shoulder.

Every inch of film in scenes underwater was superb not to mention the swimming fish within the theater. The "creature" gave an "outstanding" performance. I didn't, and couldn't relax.

All underwater scenes. Scenes of the creature and jungle. All scenes of Julia Adams.

Underwater scenes. They kept people in their seats. I don't think there was a single person that got up and walked out.

Very hard to pick, so many excellent ones.

The tap on the shoulder in the cave.

Kay swimming under water and creature swimming with her.

When Kay is swimming in the Lagoon.

The one where the monster died.

The scene where Kay was swimming was particularly good also the one where Mark laid his hand on David's shoulder in the cave.

Julia Adams swimming and the creature tries getting her—especially when he touched her feet.

Next to the last scene when they were all in the cave.

The one where Julia Adams is swimming and the creature is trying to copy her.

For sheer suspense—the scene in which the girl swims around the lagoon and the monster is trailing her.

Bathing suit scene (seriously, not only in relation to her beauty, but the tense scenes with the monster). Showdown scenes.

All scenes of creature in and out of water. Every scene of Julia Adams especially swimming.

When the monster carried Julia Adams up on shore and when she was swimming they were terrific scenes.

Aqua-lung swimming scenes.

The scene in the cave where R. Denning tapped R. Carlson on the shoulder—thrilling.

No outstanding scenes.

Fight scene between creature and swimmers when they used spears and opening scenes of formation of earth.

In the cave when they go after the creature and R.D. puts his hand on [Carlson's] shoulder.

Underwater—without creature.

None outstanding.

Love scenes.

When the creature jumped off the boat with the girl.

Creature in net—boat being rocked.

Which Scenes, If Any, Did You Dislike?

NONE	39
ALL	3
NO COMMENT	60
INDIVIDUAL COMMENT	32

When David and Mark were fighting as to who would go in—been down [in the water] so often.

The scene where they were lifting the creature in the net with the stern hoist. I can see where he could have torn the net but his weight would not have cracked the boom.

In some of the scenes they were too obviously careless in looking out for the monster.

The first ascension of the creature into the camp where he killed the two Indians. It was very blurry and hard on the eyes.

I thought it was stupid the way they didn't notice the creature when she was sitting on the rock near the end of the movie.

Opening dialogue about marriage: "We are together all the time anyway."

I was a little disgusted with the fact that with practically every new scene, J. Adams had another costume on. How much changing of clothes can a woman do on a small boat? Ridiculous!

The dialogue about living together but not being married left a sour taste.

Most underwater scenes were not lighted up enough and tend to be hazy and indistinct.

The ones with only people.

The ones without the creature.

The silly way the people stood around without looking about them.

All of it, especially when Kay made like Esther Williams—not the time or place for it.

Were All the Story Points Clear to You?

YES	106
NO	1
NO COMMENT	13
INDIVIDUAL COMMENT	14

Yes and if I may add, if more pictures like this were made you'd have me at the shows every night of the week.

Need this require an answer—the story was excellent in every respect.

Amen!

Yes but I object to a picture of this type which always arrives at the nothing it sets out from. They could at least have gotten a picture of the creature to back up their story.

Her feeling toward Mark.

Yes, but the scientific possibility of such a creature might be emphasized more. The theories could be repeated as the story progresses to keep it from becoming fantastic.

Picture showed too much illogic. It was not good science fiction.

1. Creature from the Black Lagoon (1954)

Did the Picture Hold Your Interest Throughout? If Not, Where Did It Fail to Hold You?

YES	108
NO COMMENT	9
INDIVIDUAL COMMENT	17

Suspenseful throughout.
Yes, very good suspense build up.
There seemed to be too much of the same kind of suspense.
Yes—except the ending when they let the creature go, was a big letdown.
Fairly well.
Half-way.
It did, but I didn't like the way it did it.
Repetitious.
The picture was drawn out too much.
Very tight.

Would You Recommend This Picture to Your Friends?

YES	112
NO	17
NO COMMENT	2

Yes—those that like science fiction.
No—because they don't like this kind.
Yes and no.

Did You Like This Picture in 3-D?

YES	96
NO	28
NO COMMENT	4
INDIVIDUAL COMMENT	6

Only parts because I don't care for 3-D.
I don't like 3-D but this was O.K.
No—account of poor quality of glasses furnished.
Ambiguous question.
Yes and no.

Any Added Comment?

The spookiest picture I have ever seen and screamed throughout.
Most exciting picture I ever witnessed.
I'd like to know the name of the actor who played the part of the creature.
It is better than any other picture I've seen on that order.
For me this was an unusual experience, being my first "3-D." I hadn't anticipated anything quite like this. Keep up the good work.
Give us more pictures like this only in color.
It drew a lot of people. I have seen a lot of pictures in my days, but this beats them all.
Without question 3-D added plenty to the picture. Too bad it wasn't in color.
Powerful.
As a result of this picture we have ulcers.
Kay was too stiff in creepy scenes.
Why not in color?
Would have loved it in color. Very good underwater photography.
I'd like to know the name of the creature. He did a wonderful job of swimming as did all the rest.
Excellent—should make more pictures like it.
I enjoyed it very much. People around me got a few good scares whether they liked it or not. At least they will talk about it.
The 3-D in my opinion and of friends doesn't do anything to improve the quality of the picture.
Prefer a gayer subject matter, less grotesque. Scientific viewpoint to plot is good but don't care for science fiction. Why not try to please the audience rather than scaring them half to death.
Should have been in color. Please make more out of this world pictures.
I'm a bundle of nerves, I'll never go swimming in a lagoon.
Should have been in color. Well done.
3-D movies hurt my eyes even with those glasses. To whom it may concern: 3-D movies would be fine, if we didn't have to wear glasses to see them. Why can't you take the lens of those glasses and make a big screen and put it in front of the 3-D movie then no one would have to wear glasses. If this deserves an answer my name is Elanie Gennawey 1143 W. 64th Str.
Would be great in color. More animal life along water banks.
It would have been wonderful in color and the monster had moving gills.
A little too much like The Thing *in plot.*
I like 3-D as a medium of entertainment but for its continued success as far as I'm concerned you will have to produce a more permanent type of glasses. I would prefer to be able to buy my own and keep them. I want a pair that the lenses can be cleaned as the last five or six 3-D pictures which I attended I have received glasses which were dirty and had fingerprints on lens from handling by doormen and ushers.
Would prefer to see it in Technicolor.
3-D is no good. Bad for the eyes.
Brother.
Color would have helped.
Without 3-D would have been just another picture.
The makeup on the creature was excellent.
Music crescendo bit too obvious as crisis approaches from time to time.
Too many shots of the creature.
Yes, why waste talent like Messrs. Carlson and Paiva in such B type movies.
3-D needs better stories. There is too much play on the sensational. 3-D could be good because of the fact it adds a life-like quality. Also the glasses are annoying.
Why don't you tell who played the creature?
It's not the kind of picture a man of my age likes to see.
The story would come under Class "B."
Story not realistic—who would dive in the lagoon knowing a huge monster was lurking there?

WE DON'T NEED TO KNOW YOUR NAME, BUT WE WOULD LIKE TO KNOW THE FOLLOWING FACTS ABOUT YOU:

MALE	74
FEMALE	59
NO CHECK	1
BETWEEN 12 AND 17	9
BETWEEN 18 AND 30	93
BETWEEN 31 AND 45	21
OVER 45	10
NO CHECK	1

Assuming that this United Artists Theatre *Black Lagoon* preview was the only *Creature* preview, then it's the one Arthur Ross described to me. His main memory of that night involved Universal production chief Edward Muhl, and how "high" he was on *Black Lagoon*'s prospects:

> Ed was a *very* bright man, highly intelligent, well-read. We got along well—we sort of liked each other. He sensed something in *Creature* that nobody else did, and they sort of laughed at him. But he said, "This is going to be an absolute *smash*." They used to have previews: They would take the main participants in the picture to dinner at, say, the Beachcombers or Chasen's or somewhere, and then they would go to the theater. Well, for the preview of *Creature*, there were three buses filled with people, they took us to dinner at the Beachcombers and then downtown for the preview. Ed made *every* executive, *every* contract producer, *every* contract director come watch *Creature* because, he said, "This is going to be the pattern and form and intent of our future films." At that point, Harry Essex and I looked at each other and said, "He must be crazy!" [*Laughs.*] But off it went!

William Alland recalled for me a different Universal honcho with ideas about how to attract audiences:

> Somewhere in this period when I was really bangin' 'em out, a fellow named Blumberg, one of the stockholders, kept saying to me, "Bill, *you* know what to do. You gotta stick yer hand in there and grab 'em by the balls!" [*Laughs.*] I swear it, *that* was his advice to me! They were crude, *Jesus*, they were a crude bunch—*some* of them, that is. They saw the business in a light that absolutely used to kill me!

How to Market a Monster

While *Black Lagoon* was still in production, Universal's great pretenders (i.e., the publicity department) were cooking up dozens of stories about the making of the movie, most of them with little or no basis in fact. In one of them, the *Rita* "went aground" one day because it collided with a submerged Alaskan gunboat that had sunk in that lake two years earlier during the shooting of Gregory Peck's *The World in His Arms* (1952). According to another, Richard Carlson did all of his own underwater scenes (126 of 'em!), registering "surprise, anger, fear, determination, exhaustion, pleasure and concern through a diving mask strongly enough for the 3-D underwater camera to register each emotion clearly." Then there's the one where Fritz, an ancient Airedale (dog) that had been hanging around the back lot for years, got a look at Ben Chapman in his Gill Man get-up, snarled and bit his leg, cutting through to the skin (the suit needed repairs and Chapman required first aid): "Producer Alland was overjoyed and hoped human audiences would react the same as Fritz."

Prepared around this same time, a six-page list of campaign suggestions was the usual assortment of the good, the bad and the ugly. Among the ideas for exploitations and tie-ups:

- "William Alland was production manager of the Mercury Group when Welles did the *War of the Worlds* broadcast. His *It Came from Outer Space* is one of the few films to ever please science fiction fans. Now, with *Black Lagoon*, he is out to shock 'em again. Should make a good feature."
- "Symposium on famous monsters and who has played them. Several actors have gotten their start as monsters (James Arness as 'The Thing,' Karloff, Lugosi, Chaney, etc.)."
- "Oldtime actors are money savers. Hung on Tony Moreno, Jack Arnold could talk about how oldtime actors actually save the company money because they are so sure in their scenes that they help speed up production. This could be in the form of a story that more of the oldtimers should be put to work."
- "We should dig up a good technical name for our frogman on the order of the Xenomorph of *It Came from Outer Space*. How about a combination of man and halibut called the XENOBUT."
- "[A] roundup on monsters highlighted by our Gill Man from this picture, and including King Kong, the WereWolf of London, Frankenstein, Buddy Hackett [*sic*!], etc."
- "There is always suspense attached to being under water. Richard Carlson might 'save' Julia Adams from drowning!"
- "Carlson, a good writer of short stories, might be talked into writing a by-liner for the *New York Times* on underwater third-dimension and the picture in general."
- "Might sell the wire services a story that while on location a panic was narrowly averted several times when people saw the Gill Man emerging

from the water—but didn't realize that a movie was being filmed."
- "Second unit has 152 scenes to film in Florida. Both James Havens and Cameraman 'Scotty' Welbourne should make good interviews for *N.Y. Times*, trades, magazines, etc., telling of their experiences."
- "When the picture is completed, cameraman 'Scotty' Welbourne and 'monster' Rick Browning plan to swim under water from Wakulla Springs, Florida … to the Gulf. This is a distance of 18 miles, and should take from 4 to 6 hours. Using their aqualungs, they must remain under water at all times, or will be disqualified. They will encounter alligators, which should add to the suspense. Such an underwater swim has never been attempted, so whatever they accomplish will be a record. Also, it would be a new twist, and a relief from the raft of ocean swimmers. They will bring along official timers, who can watch them from an accompanying boat, since the water is crystal clear. This should make a good newsreel. Suggest sending Julia Adams to ride in the boat and periodically dive in to furnish the swimmers with fresh air bottles whenever their supply of air runs out." [Ricou Browning's 2013 reaction to reading the above paragraph: "This is the first time I heard of it."]
- "There is great interest in skin diving. Suggest 'how to' feature by Julia Adams, showing each step in learning, what to look out for, etc. Good chance for leg art at the same time."
- "Picture of director Jack Arnold, at studio underwater tank, leaning over and sticking head beneath the surface to show 'how a director has to operate to direct a film such as *Black Lagoon*.' Might be incongruous enough to grab some space."
- "Do we publicize our Gill Man? If so, how about getting our cute starlets to surround him for cityside photo plant on Hollywood's latest leading man?"
- "Bob Thomas of the A.P. or one of the other wire boys or gals might get a hell of a story by putting on an aqualung and 'covering' a scene below the surface. This would be a first time for such a thing and the story, with appropriate art, ought to get a big break."
- "Richard Carlson has been a scientist in one picture after another. In view of his glamorizing of such folks, couldn't we get a scientific fraternity or club to give him an honorary membership or title?"
- "Maybe make miniature rubber or plastic Gill Man for exploitation and mailing piece."
- "Display the Gill Man costume—or replica—in lobbies of larger theaters where the picture plays. Perhaps use as an advance gimmick."
- "The kids should have worn out their cowboy and space men suits by now—or be ready for something new. Why not turn them all into little monsters by putting 'Gill Man Suits' on the market. Or, as Disney did with his Peter Pan beanies, sell fake Gill Man masks or claws in the theater lobbies … good for nightmares."

According to the 2012 online article "An In-Depth Look at *Creature from the Black Lagoon*" by Bob Furmanek and Greg Kintz, while *Black Lagoon* was in post-production, the U-I publicity department

> designed a series of teaser ads which helped to prepare moviegoers for a new type of monster from the studio that had cornered the horror market in the 1930s. They also selected seven scenes from the movie to be used in a ViewMaster display cabinet utilized in theaters throughout the country. Even though it was promoted in the pressbook, these promotional reels were never issued.
>
> … They also prepared a full line of 3-D posters. However, at the last minute, these designs were scrapped and they opted to distribute snipes for the 2-D posters instead. The only original poster to have 3-D text actually printed on it was the 14 × 22 window card.

Following a mid–January meeting in the office of publicist Clark Ramsay, his colleague Archie Herzoff recorded the minutes of that meeting in a two-page memo packed with suggestions for exploitation:

- "TOUR 'SOUTH AMERICAN BEAUTY.' The thought here … would be to find a 'South American' girl who has descended from one of the tribes that inhabit the Amazon jungle, to talk about 'the legend which has persisted for centuries' that a fanciful creature such as ours inhabits remote tributaries of the Amazon and that records of the creature's depredations exist in tribal lore."
- "PREHISTORIC DISPLAY. It has been suggested that, through studio sources, or that New York, through the Museum of Natural History, get together a display of plaster-of-Paris, or similar, casts of prehistoric footprints, fossils, and other curiosa to emphasize the never-ending scientific search for a link between the far past and the present."

- "'COMING OUT PARTY.' As a one-shot national publicity stunt, possibly for TV, it has been suggested that the Gill Man be introduced to the public by recreations of other film monsters, such as Frankenstein and the Wolf Man."
- "GILL MAN MASK. We are working on a manufacturer to recreate the head of the monster in Latex, as was done with the Frankenstein masks. (Unfortunately, the Frankenstein mask manufacturer has gone out of business.)"
- "TOUR OF 'SCOTTY' WELBOURNE. The underwater photography was done by the noted underwater cinematographer, Charles C. ('Scotty') Welbourne. It has been suggested that the possibility of touring Welbourne be investigated. However, there was some feeling that such publicity might detract from the aura of terror which we are trying to establish in connection with the picture."

Herzoff named a number of L.A.–based network TV programs which could be approached for stunts, interviews or the use of filmclips (*Art Linkletter's House Party*, *Place the Face*, *You Asked for It*, *Queen for a Day* and *Juke Box Jury*) and also provided a list of network radio possibilities. "Interviews on the above could concentrate on Julia Adams, Bud Westmore, 'Scotty' Welbourne, producer William Alland, director Jack Arnold and possibly Richard Carlson."

Another Herzoff proposal was a personal appearance tour of Ben Chapman: "Chapman at the aquarium and zoo or at the fish market offer solid possibilities for newspaper space," he wrote in a memo. "Papers would treat it with tongue in cheek, which, of course, would make no difference."

Herzoff continued,

> THIS REQUIRES A DIVER and is a bit wild, but I submit it because of its potential showmanship possibilities. If practical, we might equip Chapman's costume with a small oxygen tank and tube on the inside of the suit. We plant the diver aboard a boat in shallow water. Donning Chapman's suit, he "walks out of the sea" at a specified time. Radio spots, news stories and, perhaps, an ad invite the public to come to the harbor and meet the CREATURE FROM THE BLACK LAGOON as he emerges from the water.

Universal had acceded to the MPAA edict that the Gill Man's scenes with Kay never suggest bestiality, but the Creature's amorous intentions were clear in the poster taglines…

> MONSTER FROM A LOST AGE! …
> RAGING WITH PENT-UP PASSIONS!
>
> CREATURE FROM A MILLION YEARS AGO!
> … every man his mortal enemy … and a woman's beauty his prey!

… and in their radio spots…

> From fish-like thing to mammal…from mammal to a man-like horror of the sea…with the heart of a human, filled with hate and a man-like instinct to love.
> … Julia Adams as the exciting beauty who stirred savage emotions in the Creature from the Black Lagoon!
> Its [the Creature's] heart filled with strange man-like passions…

… and in their pressbook articles…

> [The Creature is] aroused to strange emotions by its first sight of a woman…

… and in their trailer narration:

> Lovely Julia Adams, her beauty a lure even to the man-beast from the dawn of time!

… and in *another* trailer:

> A woman's beauty the bait that brought it out of its lair!

In late January 1954, with *Black Lagoon* just days away from its first playdates at various Michigan theaters, newspaper readers got their first gander at the syndicated story "Film Makeup Wizards Have Tough Jobs," on the manufacture of the Gill Man suit:

> Universal-International Makeup Chief Bud Westmore and his assistant, Jack Kevan, have computed that "more blood, sweat and tears" went into the designing of the Gill Man, half-fish–half-man monster in [*Black Lagoon*], than were ever spilled on any U-I freak of nature in the studio's long history of shockers.
> Westmore and Kevan studied 25 volumes on strange creatures of the deep, ancient mammals and eerie drawings by some of the world's great artists who dabbled in such fantasies.
> Westmore submitted a total of 76 different sketches of the body and 32 of the head to producer William Alland and director Jack Arnold. They used a total of 167 lbs. of rubber and plastic in making life-sized models of the monster's sea-green "body," a covering for an actual man who would be cast to size after the creature was perfected. The "skin" is so designed that every muscle ripple of the man wearing it will appear to be that of the creature itself.
> "Even the Frankenstein monster," said Westmore, "Lon Chaney's Hunchback of Notre Dame and the wolf-man in *WereWolf of London* did not take half the time to create that we have put in on the Gill Man. When you get one who lives on land half the time and in the water the other half, you've really got a problem."

The above story is yet another that contradicts Ben Chapman's claim that Universal's head publicist tried to make the public believe that the Gill Man was an actual monster.

One of *Black Lagoon*'s obvious plusses was a monster with pathos but apparently Westmore thought otherwise

1. Creature from the Black Lagoon (1954)

time tone for his closing comment, "Westmore needn't worry. [The Metaluna Mutant] will restore his reputation as a monstrosity-maker."

Westmore's unexpected "dissing" of the Gill Man suit couldn't have pleased whichever Universal honchos read Thomas' story. And then, for sheer swinishness, he outdid himself with what we'll euphemistically call "the Milicent Patrick incident."

Probably because Patrick was a knockout (a pretty brunette, statuesque, 40–25–38), *Black Lagoon* publicists proposed that she be sent to various cities where the movie was about to open, make appearances at theaters and give interviews about the creation of the Gill Man outfit.

But the mere suggestion that the movie be represented by this beauty brought out the beast in Westmore. When Clark Ramsay discussed with Westmore

Daylight rubbery: Bud Westmore complained to an interviewer that the Creature was photographed in broad daylight, which he thought you shouldn't do with monsters: "You have to keep them in the shadows." The sunlit shots didn't faze the DVD Savant, Glenn Erickson, who has declared the Gill Man "perhaps the best rubber-suited thing Hollywood ever turned out."

because he was discouraged by preview audience members who had empathy for "the Creech." *So* discouraged, in fact, that he badmouthed the star attraction of Universal's as-yet-unreleased movie! Syndicated columnist Bob Thomas visited the U-I makeup department in February 1954, watched as some finishing touches were put on *This Island Earth*'s Metaluna Mutant, and talked to Westmore for his story "Bud Westmore Enjoys Doing Horror Makeup." And when the conversation turned to *Black Lagoon*, the department head came out with the surprising statement, "We sort of fell down on that one"!

"He wasn't frightening enough," Westmore continued. "The preview cards indicated that some people in the audience sympathized with him. The trouble was that they photographed the frog man in the bright sunlight. You can't do that with monsters. You have to keep them in the shadows." Apparently taking Westmore at his word that the Gill Man costume was a flop, Thomas adopted a better-luck-next-

Milicent Patrick's work area is nicely decorated with "spooky stuff" in this publicity photograph.

the idea of a Patrick tour, the makeup department bigwig made it plain that he resented the use of the tie-in phrase "The Beauty Who Created the Beast." Ramsay described their conversation in a memo to the Universal New York office's director of publicity and exploitation Charles Simonelli:

His point was that the eventual creation of the beast of the Black Lagoon was completely his own work. He pointed out that many people had been involved in the original sketches and thinking, but had all dropped out of the project when it became difficult and complex. As a result he spent four or five weeks, himself, developing the model which was eventually used.

Particularly because of these circumstances, I am afraid he would be a little upset if we credited his creation to someone else. He pointed out he would be quite willing to do anything we insisted upon, but honestly felt that since this involved his professional talents that crediting the work to someone else was not the thing to do.

Inasmuch as we depend upon Westmore for some rather close cooperation we felt it would be best if we tried to develop another tie-in line. We held a staff meeting and came up with a line we think will do as well. We will call Miss Patrick "The Beauty Who Lives with the Beasts."

It was felt that this would provide an opportunity to send her out, not only to discuss the Gill Man, but with some of the masks and photographs of the other horror creatures which our Makeup Department has turned out over the years. Her basic story could be that she is not only a creative designer of such creatures but another of her tasks is their care and preservation. In other words, "she lives with them." The newest in her colony of monsters is, of course, the Gill Man. We feel that this would not only provide excellent photographic material, but would certainly give her a good line for newspaper, TV and radio interviews.

We can also get some photographs of Miss Patrick at work here at the studio surrounded by either the actual horror costumes of Frankenstein, the Wolf Man, etc., or all of the heads.

It was also suggested that Miss Patrick might make a good plant on *What's My Line*, as a kick-off to her tour.

… Westmore feels that there will be no problem in sending Miss Patrick out during the first two weeks of February and perhaps even longer, if necessary.

I have discussed the proposed trip with Miss Patrick. On her current arrangement with the studio (which is on a freelance basis) she averages around $250 a week. She feels that she should be guaranteed at least $300 a week if we are to send her out on tour since she will have to not only give up any current assignments here, but will also have to forego any assignments from other studios during the period she is gone. She also wishes to check with her family and will let us know tomorrow.

Even when it appeared as though all of the bugs had been ironed out of the plan, things were still not All Quiet on the Westmore Front: Evidently Bud had come to realize that the Gill Man was one of the finest feathers in his department's cap and wanted all the credit. This black hole of need next stormed into the office of Sam Israel; Israel described their meeting in a January 26 letter to Eastern publicity manager Philip Gerard of Universal's 445 Park Avenue, New York, office:

> [Westmore] made it very clear that he resented this whole project, although he denied it and put it on a different basis. He is perturbed, he says, by the fact that Milicent will claim credit for what he has achieved in putting these monsters together, and he would like us to make sure that as far as possible the interviews stress the fact that he is the one who supervises the creation of these creatures from start to finish. Milicent's job, he says, is merely to put his ideas in the form of sketches. It is a battle of credits, of course, and I would suggest we be guided by his wishes if they do not get in our way. Frankly, I am getting a little fed up with these squawks from people who are paid to do a job, and from what I hear, Milicent's contribution in this work is very important.[84]

Three days later, Israel sent Simonelli the following one-sentence letter: "Just to make sure that Milicent Patrick does not go off the deep end in interviews, I am showing her a work print of the picture tomorrow and have supplied her with a synopsis of the story, the credit listings and the production notes on the picture." By this time, Patrick already had a fairly full schedule of appearances to make in New York: NBC-TV's *The Today Show* with Dave Garroway, WPIX's *The Eloise McElhone Show*, ABC-TV's *Your Show* with Robert Alda, Dumont's *Broadway to Hollywood* with Conrad Nagel and more.

When she toured on behalf of Black Lagoon, Milicent Patrick had to credit no one but Bud Westmore as creator of the Creature, but on her résumé from the late 1960s (or thereabouts) she says that she "helped design" the Gill Man and did the final painting on the costume.

1. Creature from the Black Lagoon (1954)

> Milicent Patrick, sketch artist and actress, has been engaged by U-I to aid in the coast-to-coast promotion campaign on *Creature from the Black Lagoon*, first 3-D production with extensive underwater sequences. Miss Patrick, working under the supervision of U-I makeup chief Bud Westmore, planes out Sunday for New York.—*The Hollywood Reporter*, January 28, 1954

She did "plane out" that Sunday, January 31, and just four days later she was getting rave reviews: On February 4, Gerard wrote Israel that Patrick was turning out to be an ideal personality for their *Black Lagoon* promotional activities:

> We have had excellent response from the press, radio and TV, and she comes off extremely well in all of these interviews. By the way, in addition to the original schedule I sent you last week, we have added an AP interview and photo layout in the Sunday *Mirror*, and a photo press conference for all New York papers.

Patrick then began touring with the movie itself, making appearances in numerous Michigan cities several days in advance of its first playdate there. As of February 4, her itinerary included Lansing (February 6), Bay City (the 8th), Grand Rapids (the 9th), Flint (the 10th), Detroit[85] (the 11th and 12th), Saginaw (the 13th), Kalamazoo and Battle Creek (both on the 14th). By the 16th she was back in New York and supplementing her original press, radio and TV schedule with interviews with Mel Heimer of King Features, Hope Johnson of the *World-Telegram and Sun* and ABC-TV's Henry Morgan, Jerry Lester and (wait for it) Ern Westmore, brother of Bud! (Read more about Ern below.) In total, according to Patrick's résumé, on her *Black Lagoon* tour she "guest starred on 40 TV and radio shows" in New York and Michigan.[86]

No good deed goes unpunished: Even though Patrick had sallied forth with Westmore's imprimatur, and conducted herself strictly according to Hoyle, the kudos she received must have stirred the soup of his discontent and he continued to raise hell about it. Ramsay wrote Simonelli on March 1:

> The Milicent Patrick tour on behalf of *Creature from the Black Lagoon* has apparently placed her in a rather awkward position here at the studio. I think that you can be of considerable help.
>
> As I told you prior to the tour, Bud Westmore was very sensitive in the matter of credit for the designing of the Creature. Apparently under rather difficult circumstances he did it himself and Milicent Patrick's sketches were copied from the original design rather than the basis for the original design. You will recall that we had to switch our copy slant from "The Beauty Who Created the Beast," to "The Beauty Who Lives with Beasts."
>
> Apparently Westmore went to the trouble of getting hold of newspapers from a number of the cities that Miss Patrick visited and discovered that she was being credited as the designer of the Creature with no mention of Westmore. He has let it be known in a general way that he is not going to use her as a sketch artist any more.
>
> Even were the company to force Westmore to hire her the circumstances would be such that it would be impossible for her to do a satisfactory job for him. Somehow Westmore will have to be made to understand that she, herself, did everything possible to credit Westmore on radio and newspaper interviews. If there is any blame in the matter, I think we will have to take it ourselves or place it on the newspapers.
>
> I think that we all will agree that Westmore is being a little childish over the entire matter but at the same time I dislike very much having her penalized, for a situation in which she is not the responsible party.
>
> I think it might be very well if you "spontaneously" sent a letter to Bud Westmore complimenting him for the wonderful person he selected for the tour and also telling him what a "loyal" person she was to the Westmore organization. You might also accompany the letter with a number of the releases which we gave out (crediting Westmore—I hope!).

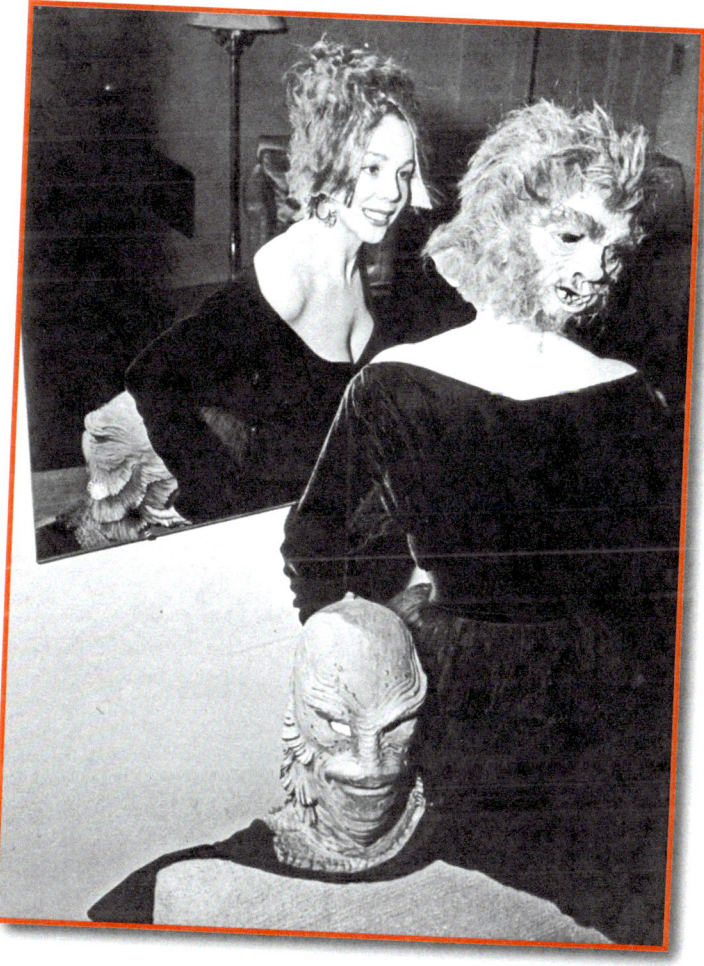

The heads of two of the monsters that Milicent Patrick helped design: the Gill Man (on chair arm) and, worn backwards by Patrick, an Abbott and Costello Meet Dr. Jekyll and Mr. Hyde *mask.*

I am sure you see the point of the letter and can devise something that will help smooth Mr. Westmore's ruffled feelings. Ordinarily I would be in favor of telling him to go jump, but under the circumstances this would undoubtedly only widen the breach between Miss Patrick and himself.

I leave it to your good judgment.

Whatever additional action was taken may not have been enough to get Westmore to stop lashing out from his hurt locker. Patrick's résumé reveals that she did makeup illustrations for Universal's *Captain Lightfoot* (1955), a movie whose production postdated the *Black Lagoon* controversy; her sketches might not have. Apart from that, she may never again have worked in a makeup or sketch artist capacity at Universal.[87] According to Bob Burns,

> Westmore was so afraid, when Milicent was out on her tour, that she was gonna "tell" on him [reveal that she, not Westmore, was the Creature costume designer]. But she didn't, she followed the rules, she said, "Bud Westmore created it." She did what she was supposed to do but he *still* got her fired, which is really sad, just not right at all. But he was not a "right" person. One thing I'll say on his behalf, he was a good *straight* makeup artist, he was good at beauty makeup. In the beginning, that's what the Westmores were known for, beauty makeup. He was pretty good at that, but he was *not* good at monster stuff.

The Bud Westmore dossier bulges with similar stories of unabashed attempts to gain, and maintain, a clawhold on his rep as Hollywood's master of makeup. For members of his staff, complete compliance was the only means of staying on his slim sunny side. And, just like in the old movies, he eventually reaped the bitter harvest he had sown.

Frank Westmore's book *The Westmores in Hollywood* pulls few punches as it describes how his five-years-older brother Bud, and some of his other siblings, put the -nasty in dynasty. According to Frank, their British dad George Westmore founded *the* first movie makeup department in 1917 and, even more impressively, fathered *19* children, of which only seven survived: daughter Dorothy and sons Monte, Perc, Ern, Wally, Bud and Frank. At one time or another, a Westmore was in charge of the makeup departments at Paramount, Universal, Warners, RKO, 20th Century–Fox and over a dozen more companies. In the mid-1940s, twentysomething Bud was doing makeup at PRC (including their 1946 horror flicks *The Flying Serpent*, *Strangler of the Swamp* and *Devil Bat's Daughter*); when PRC morphed into Eagle-Lion, he became head of its makeup department. In the late 1940s, Universal needed a new head of makeup and considered Ern Westmore, but Ern's twin brother Perc decided out of sheer spitefulness to keep Ern from landing that position. Perc knew of Ern's tendency to tarry too long at the wine and so, the night before Ern's interview at Universal, Perc invited him to a celebratory restaurant dinner and got him drunk. Then, during some subsequent bar-hopping, Perc got him drunk*er*. Ern showed up blotto at Universal the next day, as Perc planned that he would, and he didn't get the job. Studio head William Goetz still wanted a Westmore in the post and, at Perc's suggestion, hired Bud.

Milicent Patrick's Universal bio quotes her as saying, "I spent six weeks with the Gill Man. He changed his shape three times before he was able to win the approval of the executives who inspected him. No matter how badly he scares people, I think he's cute."

"It would take a psychiatrist to figure Bud out," Frank wrote in *The Westmores of Hollywood*,

> but knowing him as well as I did, I don't think he ever got over feeling guilty about the way he had become the head of the Universal makeup department instead of Ern. Although Bud had not conspired with Perc to get Ern drunk the night before his interview, he had tacitly gone along with the ploy and said nothing in Ern's defense. Bud did his work as well as anyone else, but I could sense his insecurity. Whenever someone he had hired began to show signs of independent inventiveness, Bud would either fire him or resort to his famous "silent treatment," making the makeup artist's life so miserable in general that he would quit.

Frank writes that Tom Case was one of the victims of the "arrogant, power-driven" Bud. Even though Case was almost-a-Westmore (he married the sister of a Westmore wife), three years of working with the caustic Bud was enough and he quit "at the height of the Creature triumphs." Bud fired another makeup artist because he couldn't stand the way the guy laughed. Frank continued, "At our increasingly infrequent family gatherings, Bud exhibited outright contempt for Perc, oblivious to the agony Perc was going through after his fall from power or, perhaps, trying to compensate for his own guilt. Whatever the reason, it was uncomfortable to be present when Bud grew insultingly silent and wouldn't even answer a direct question from Perc. Even the usually impervious Wally squirmed."

Actor Jan Merlin was a veritable prisoner in the Universal makeup lab in 1962 as he was being prepared to play several heavily made-up characters in *The List of Adrian Messenger* (1963)[88] and got a long look at the shabby way Westmore treated his employees. While shooting part of the picture in London, Merlin watched in dismay as, at the end of a long day, makeup men John Chambers and Nick Marcellino began doing humiliating janitorial-type work because Bud had made that part of their makeup room duties and they didn't dare leave it undone. Merlin told me, "I began to realize fully that the sly rumors and hints I'd been getting from people about Bud were actually quite true. He *wasn't* the charming, sweet little guy that you met with the big smile and the laugh like the bray of a donkey. He was really quite … nasty." At one point during the making of *Adrian Messenger*, Chambers prevented an irate Merlin from charging at Bud, at a later point, Merlin stopped Chambers from mixing it up with Bud. After the picture wrapped, Merlin and Westmore avoided each other at Universal to the extent that Merlin never laid eyes on Westmore again.[89]

In the mid–1960s when tours of Universal became popular, Perc was hired to entertain tourists with twice-a-day lectures and makeup demonstrations. He and his presentations were well-attended and well-liked while Bud chewed on his resentment like a piece of tough meat. And the longer he chewed it, the bigger it got. Perc was later given other, different responsibilities at the studio, including the job of applying Al "Grandpa" Lewis' makeup for TV's *The Munsters*. Wrote Frank,

> Bud, watching stars flock to Perc's office instead of his own, couldn't stand it any more. Working behind the scenes, he did just what the old Perc would have done at Warner Brothers 20 years before: He got Perc fired. I still don't know how Bud managed it, but it was obviously a masterpiece of undercover manipulation.

Bud climbed the ladder of success wrong by wrong, probably never realizing that all his employee abuse was drawing a figurative rope around his neck. This noose began to tighten when Universal came to the realization that it no longer needed a deluxe "Old Hollywood"–style makeup department with a high-salaried czar. According to Frank, by 1970 "[t]here were too many freelance makeup men like myself on call for contract work on specific shows and films, too many stars who now demanded their own favorite artists to do their makeup. Suddenly Bud was the target not only of a cutback in the Universal makeup department's budget but also of a revolt from below by those assistants he had ground down." When Bud was fired, he became a recluse for two years, unwilling to be seen in public because he knew that his appearances would prompt people to say he got what he deserved. He turned down producer Ross Hunter's offer of a makeup job on *Lost Horizon* (1973) because he felt he didn't know how to *do* daily makeup any more, but dwindling funds forced him to grit his teeth and accept work on *Soylent Green* (1973).

When all Hollywood production closed down during a writers' strike, panic set in for the insolvent Bud, he offered to sell Frank a skiff which Frank didn't need but agreed to take, because Frank knew that Bud could use the 300 bucks. It was the hardest 300 bucks Bud ever earned: Lifting the boat was strenuous work that gave him heart palpitations and landed him in the hospital. Just a few days after his hospital release (and after his last makeup job, two days' work on a Ford TV commercial), 55-year-old Hamilton Adolph "Bud" Westmore died while watching TV on the couch of his Sherman Oaks home. Ten days later, Wally Westmore died after two years of hospital bed vegetation, making Frank the last of the Westmore brothers—and free to tell the tale of his brothers' near-monopoly on the film makeup biz and their dysfunctional lives.

Bud and Lou—and TV Censors—Meet the Creature

On Saturday, February 20, 1954, Julie Adams plugged *Creature from the Black Lagoon* during CBS's national telecast of the Heavyweight Championship Wrestling Match. The following night, TV viewers got their first coast-to-coast glimpse of the Gill Man during an episode of the NBC variety show *The Colgate Comedy Hour* (available for viewing on YouTube). An on-camera announcer introduces Abbott and Costello, who come out on stage where Bud tells Lou that they need to go to the Universal-International property department to get some "real funny props." The curtain behind them opens to reveal a storeroom with full-sized figures of Dracula and Mr. Hyde (the latter from *Abbott and Costello*

Meet Dr. Jekyll and Mr. Hyde) *et al.* and some medieval weapons. A creepy property man with thick glasses (Bud's real-life nephew Norman Abbott) says that this is where Universal keeps all its horror figures and then, looking directly into the camera, adds, "But wait—wait until you see our *latest* horror creature: the Creature from the Black Lagoon!" While Bud and the property man are in and out of the room, Lou contends with a self-moving inkwell, watches as the Invisible Man makes off with Bud's cigarette, hears sounds that no one else hears and has an encounter with the Frankenstein Monster (Glenn Strange in a Jack Kevan–made over-the-head mask). In the big finish, the Creature (Ben Chapman) bursts onto the scene and Lou faints, sliding down the Creature's body and lying on the floor at his feet for the fadeout. Chapman said in our interview,

> I remember standing around backstage with Glenn Strange and, being a buff of thriller movies, I knew that he had played Frankenstein in some of the old classics. So I asked him about that and we talked about it, and he asked me about the Creature. We talked about our careers in general and horror films particularly; he told me how he liked working with Boris Karloff. General chitchat about our careers—and hoping that we would go on to bigger and better things!

According to the next day's *Variety*, this *Colgate* episode featured Costello's first appearance "since illness dry-docked him last October." *Variety* reviewer Helm liked the spooky sketch, calling it "a howler [that] touched off a laugh barrage."

Small screen-wise, the Gill Man was also being seen on local stations paid to play commercials for the movie. Twenty- and sixty-second ads began running in the L.A. area in late February—and, going by Universal's placement of these ads, the studio must have decided that their best bet was to court the blue-collar and kiddie crowd. Some of the L.A. ads ran during boxing, basketball and wrestling events, and before, during or after episodes of the juvenile series *The Cisco Kid*, *Sky King*, *The Joe Palooka Show* and *Ramar of the Jungle*. One spot followed an episode of Richard Carlson's *I Led 3 Lives*. But their most frequent appearances were between episodes of the favorite shows of the Pampers and pabulum set, *Howdy Doody* and *Peanut Circus*!

The *Howdy Doody–Peanut Circus* gang may have had the grit to endure *Black Lagoon* ads but at least one TV censor was set back on his heels. On March 9, NBC's Stockton Helffrich, "America's First Network TV Censor" (also the title of the 2010 book on his life and career), wrote an inter-department memo in which he claimed to be "appalled at what motion picture interests submitted as suitable for general family viewing":

> Trailers from *Creature from the Black Lagoon* submitted on the coast started out with explosions depicting the creation of time, screams from male and female abductees in sync with video of creature surrounding the heroine on the banks of his lagoon and ichthyotic hands, with thorns yet, engulfing a man's head, "Creature" latching on to the heroine below the "line of decency" and plunging into the lower depths of the Black Lagoon, full front view of "Creature" being broiled to such an extent he (or she) has to plunge into the lagoon to extinguish himself, and … don't go away … narration inferring that the creature's strange emotions are being aroused by the sight of a woman after 150,000,000 years in sync with creature carrying limp heroine through his habitat under the lagoon.

According to the memo, with "some really drastic cutting," some TV spots for *Black Lagoon* and for *Phantom of the Rue Morgue* (1954) were now acceptable for "some late evening scheduling." Universal's Duke Hickey took a look at the NBC-edited *Black Lagoon* spots, didn't like them and did his *own* re-editing, resulting in spots that NBC agreed to show. Hickey wrote in a memo to the Universal advertising department's Guy Biondi, "I feel that we have not lost too much because on the re-edit they [NBC] made several concessions, and the station is too important for our area coverage to leave out of the schedule."

In a February 26, 1954, inter-office communication, publicist Herzoff showed that he had a good attitude about situations like these:

> I can't think of higher praise for what we have to sell on TV for *Creature from the Black Lagoon* than to have a station refuse a spot because it considered the material "too scary." We have had two such incidents locally, one with KTTV which is a Dumont affiliate and KNBH, the NBC station. In both instances, it related primarily to placement between programs with large juvenile followings. We finally won our point with KNBH, but it took considerable haranguing.[90]

The theatrical trailer is also fairly intense. To the accompaniment of the movie's *BAH-BAH-BAHHH*mbastic music, we get to see the best parts of almost every action scene, plus a great trailer-made shot of the Gill Man on a "limbo set" approaching us through a dense fog, and a closeup of his clawed hands enveloping the camera. Any viewer, especially young ones, would get the idea that the movie was the ultimate cinematic test of courage.

Studio publicists also had the print media spilling gallons of ink reminding readers that Universal was the home lamasery of all things movie-monstrous. The *Long Beach Independent* (February 21, 1954) was one of no doubt many papers that ran the article "Hollywood Movie Monsters" with photos of Chaney's Phantom, Chaney Jr.'s Wolf Man, Lugosi's Dracula, Glenn Strange's Monster (the actor misidentified as Boris Karloff in the caption, natch) and, largest of all, the Gill Man, with the accompanying text setting the scene for his imminent unveiling:

1. Creature from the Black Lagoon (1954)

For a quarter of a century, one Hollywood movie studio (Universal-International and, earlier, the old Universal Co.) has periodically shocked the wits out of movie fans—and delighted exhibitors—with movie monsters, horror creations which have, in their own way, provided competition with the glamour queens! Some of these have been star-making in their success; in other cases the monster itself has outshone the player involved and outlasted him in memory.

The monster matter comes up at the present moment because of the entry upon the movie scene of a new contender for horror "honors"—the Gill Man, a creation which lives and breathes on land—or under water.

The Release

Today is a red-letter day for horror film fans. Universal—who gave us the Frankenstein Monster, Dracula and the Wolf Man—has come up with another animated gargoyle: half human, half-fish and all horrid.

—from the New York Herald Tribune review

You'll find March 1954 as *Creature from the Black Lagoon*'s release date in the reference books, but they're all wet. Michiganders got an advance look at the newest addition to Universal's monster franchise as multiple prints of the movie played in that state in February. According to ace researcher Robert J. Kiss, the movie was released early to Michigan theaters belonging to the Butterfield chain, world-premiering at Detroit's 2700-seat Broadway-Capitol Theater on February 12 and then appearing at other Butterfield theaters. For five days (February 13 through 17, 1954) the doors of the Michigan Theatre in Traverse City opened at 11:15 p.m. for "midnight screenings" of *Black Lagoon*. It was a stand-alone feature there, as it was at the Lyric in Ludington (three screenings daily for two days, February 14 and 15) and at Center Theater in Holland (five daily for three days, February 18 through 20). *Black Lagoon* had another early playdate at State Theatre in Benton Harbor; for two days, February 19 and 20, it shared the screen with a "2-D co-hit," *Donovan's Brain* (1953). Kiss writes,

Within the sample of around 900 movie theaters across the U.S. during this period, 57 percent of all screenings of *Black Lagoon* took the form of a stand-alone presentation supported only by "selected shorts." This form of presentation was equally common in large cities, average-sized towns and rural communities throughout the entire period from February to September 1954. In a tiny number of instances (around two percent), the

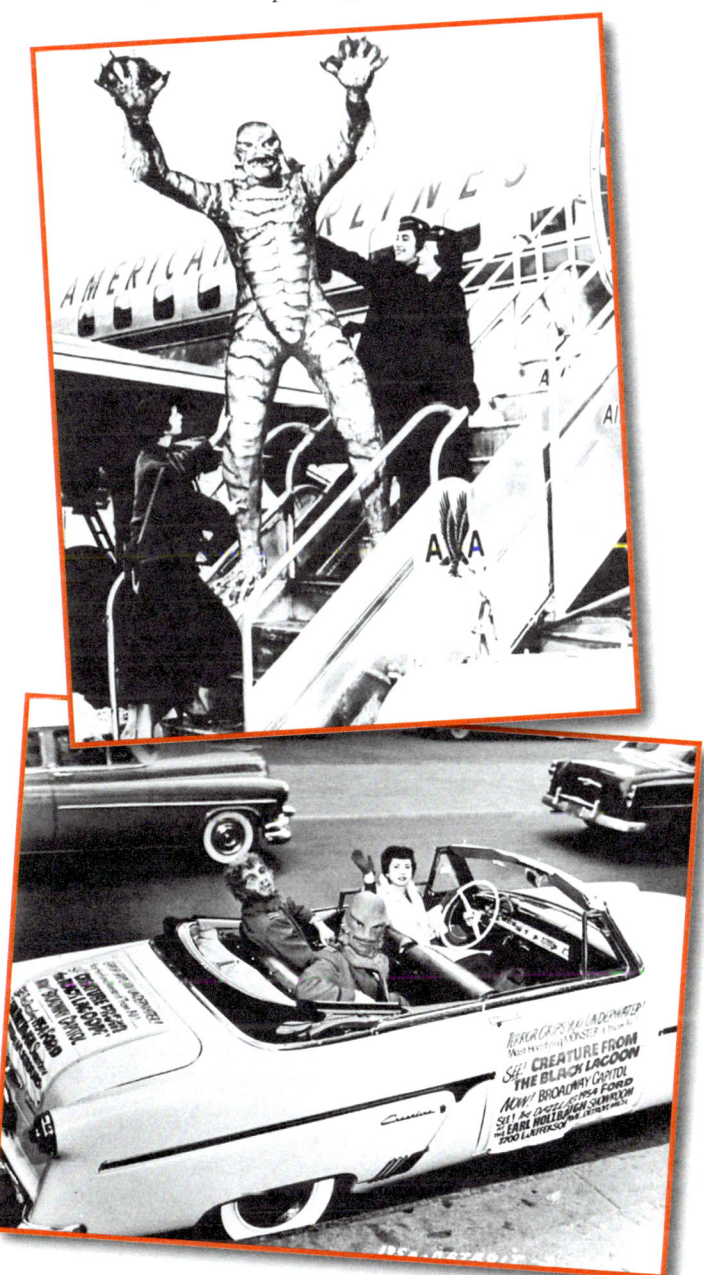

Detroit was the scene of much silliness at the time of Black Lagoon's *opening: The Gill Man (a cardboard cutout, anyway) is helped off a plane by stewardesses, and a coat- and scarf-wearing Creature gets a VIP ride alongside Mr. Hyde (from the then-newish* Abbott and Costello Meet Dr. Jekyll and Mr. Hyde*). Stunts like these helped the movie do good "wicket business," as* Variety *liked to call it.*

supporting short was specifically identified as the Three Stooges comedy *Spooks!* (1953), likewise in 3-D.

Within the sample of around 900 movie theaters across the U.S. during this period, 15 percent of all screenings of *Black Lagoon* were double-billed with *Project M-7*,[91] making this the closest thing to a "regular co-feature" for the movie. This double bill was attested in almost every state and throughout that entire [February to September] period.

Black Lagoon had many other co-features throughout 1954, with Kiss determining that (after *Project M-7*) it was most often paired with Rock Hudson's *Taza, Son of Cochise* (also in 3-D), Audie Murphy's *Ride Clear of Diablo*, Vera Ralston's *Jubilee Trail*, Robert Stack's *The Iron Glove*, Red Skelton's *The Great Diamond Robbery* and, for a double-dose of sci-fi, Peter Graves' *Killers from Space*.

Kiss' long list of *Black Lagoon* co-features continues with *Border River* (Joel McCrea), *Drums Across the River* (Audie Murphy again), *The Fighting Lawman* (Wayne Morris), *Geraldine* (Mala Powers), *The Golden Idol* (Johnny "Bomba the Jungle Boy" Sheffield), *Highway Dragnet* (Richard Conte), *Hot News* (Stanley Clements), *The Last Posse* (Broderick Crawford), *The Long, Long Trailer* (Lucille Ball), *Man in the Attic* (Jack Palance as Jack the Ripper), *The Naked Jungle* (Eleanor Parker), *Outlaw Territory* (Macdonald Carey), *Playgirl* (Shelley Winters), *Private Eyes* (The Bowery Boys), *Racing Blood* (Bill Williams), *Rails Into Laramie* (John Payne), *Riding Shotgun* (Randolph Scott), *Saskatchewan* (Alan Ladd), *Siege at Red River* (Van Johnson), *Spaceways* (Howard Duff), *The Steel Lady* (Rod Cameron), *Tennessee Champ* (Shelley Winters), *Three Young Texans* (Jeffrey Hunter), *Undercover Agent* (Dermot Walsh), *Wicked Woman* (Beverly Michaels) and the older pictures *Yankee Buccaneer* (1952), *Silver City* (1951), *Rachel and the Stranger* (1948)—even Laurel and Hardy's *Sons of the Desert* (1933)!

Kiss adds,

> In terms of the movie's "first run" in cinemas, I made my cut-off point the end of September 1954, the simple reason being that there were only a handful of first-run screenings during that month, with October yielding more or less nothing at all. By the end of September, the movie had penetrated even into the most remote rural communities in Tennessee and Kansas, and effectively had nowhere left to open as a new release. So, the September 1954 cut-off point more or less asserted itself.

On the DVD audio commentary for *The Creature Walks Among Us*, Bob Burns said that he was a teenager in 1954 when he first saw *Black Lagoon*, back in the days when you could sit in a theater and watch a movie run "four or five" times if you wanted: "I did it for all four or five runs! The 3-D in it was amazing. The stuff they shot in Florida—the Creature looked like he was actually floating [in the air in the theater auditorium] in front of you. It was really something." As Dennis Saleh wrote in his book *Science Fiction Gold: Film Classics of the 50s*, "The darkened theater and shadowy waters of the Black Lagoon would join in mid-air, there where the creature swirled suspended above the audience."

Another testimony to the quality of the 3-D in *Black Lagoon*: In the days before his two Best Visual Effects Oscar wins, Robert Skotak was an uncredited member of the *Jaws 3-D* (1983) visual effects team and, prior to beginning work on the shark movie, he and other effects artists screened 3-D prints of both *Black Lagoon* and *It Came from Outer Space*. "It was a humbling experience for a new generation of 'hot-shot' effects guys who somehow thought all the stuff done way-back-when must've been really primitive," he told me. "After seeing both *It Came* and *Black Lagoon* in the original, two-projector polarized 3-D, a great silence fell over these guys, 'cause this so-called 'primitive stuff' looked far better than the 'new' technology of 1982."

At the end of 1954, Ernest B. Wehmeyer of Universal's Production Budget Department signed a Summary of Production Budget which showed that *Creature from the Black Lagoon* had run up total direct charges of $463,700. After studio overhead was tacked on, the cost of the movie came to $613,243.

Fabulist Jack Arnold told at least one interviewer that *Black Lagoon* saved Universal from bankruptcy. While the movie was certainly a moneymaker, it was not nearly in *that* class. At the beginning of 1955, *Variety* ran its list of 1954 movies that made $1,000,000 or more at the domestic (U.S. and Canada) box office, and Paramount's *White Christmas* headed the 124-title lineup with an estimated $12,000,000. In the sci-fi and horror category, the top money-earner was Warners' *Them!* with $2,200,000, followed by the same studio's tri-dimensional *Phantom of the Rue Morgue* with $1,450,000. Batting cleanup monster-wise was *Black Lagoon* with its $1,300,000 domestic take, down near the bottom of the list in a tie with Lana Turner's *Flame and the Flesh*, Rosemary Clooney's *Red Garters*, Vera Ralston's *Jubilee Trail et al. Black Lagoon* wasn't even *Universal's* biggest grosser of the year, having been blown out of the (lagoon) water by the biopic *The Glenn Miller Story* ($7,000,000) and the distaff melodrama *Magnificent Obsession* ($5,000,000). Other Universal movies that outdid *Black Lagoon*'s $1.3 million were *Saskatchewan*, *Francis Joins the Wacs*, *The Black Shield of Falworth*, *Walking My Baby Back Home*, *Ma and Pa Kettle at Home*, *Johnny Dark* and *War Arrow*.

By the end of 1954, *Collier's* magazine was reporting that *Black Lagoon* "has racked up a gross of $3,000,000 to date, better than many a high-budget picture." (That $3,000,000 figure must include foreign grosses. Or perhaps Universal just made it up and spoonfed it to *Collier's*.) In that same article it's revealed that the Gill Man costume cost $12,000, and Bud Westmore was calling him "our bread-and-butter monster" because of his (the Gill Man's) proven appeal. Ten months earlier, talking to interviewer Bob Thomas, Westmore had disparagingly said of the Gill Man, "We sort of fell down on that one."

Harry Essex told me, "Universal wanted the same success [that it had had with *It Came from Outer Space*], and it turned out to be even more successful than *It Came from Outer Space*! They didn't anticipate it—Ray Bradbury wasn't involved this time—but it broke through, it just played forever and it's playing now. I don't know why it should have been that successful, but to this day it's kind of a cult picture."

Julie Adams told *Psychotronic* interviewer Dennis Daniel: "I think one of the reasons films like *King Kong* and *Creature from the Black Lagoon* survive is there's a kind of poetry in the monster; a poignancy in his longing for love, for something different. For something beyond his scope in life." In an interview on the website The Atlantic, she carried the thought further: "I did feel that [Kay Lawrence] had a kind of understanding of the human part of the Creature. A sense that this was not just some misstep of nature, that there was something poignant, there was something moving, there were human qualities within this Creature."

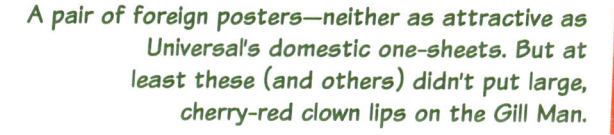

A pair of foreign posters—neither as attractive as Universal's domestic one-sheets. But at least these (and others) didn't put large, cherry-red clown lips on the Gill Man.

"The Creature scared people, but there was also a sort of sweetness about him," she told me:

> In the real classics, there always is that feeling of compassion for the monster. I think maybe it touches something in ourselves, maybe the darker parts of ourselves, that long to be loved and think they really *can't* ever be loved. It strikes a chord within us. That's what *Creature from the Black Lagoon* did.

The Critics' Corner

Los Angeles Examiner: The underwater scenes are fantastic and the direction smartly paced.

••••••••••••••••••••••

Los Angeles Times: Beside [*Creature from the Black Lagoon*], Bela Lugosi's [old horror movies] are as tame as a seed catalogue.[92]

••••••••••••••••••••••

Photoplay: Short on science, the picture's long enough on excitement, strongly recalling the hit *Beast from 20,000 Fathoms*.

••••••••••••••••••••••

Los Angeles Daily News: As the action unreels with the speed of an anchor being hoisted, Miss Adams changes bathing suits several times, walks woodenly and persistently into danger, and screams so often and so loud that little babes in the audience grew pale.

••••••••••••••••••••••

Oakland [California] *Tribune*: While the creature may give some of the small fry and the more timid chills of fright, he impressed us as a fairly mild character, not at all up to [Universal's] past creations such as Dracula or the Wolf Man.… On the whole, *Creature from the Black Lagoon* is more amusing than frightening. Although it must be added, that Jack Arnold's direction exploits every possible situation for maximum suspense…

••••••••••••••••••••••

Cue: [I]t ain't funny, McGee. On the contrary, it's pretty scary, and *Creature from the Black Lagoon* is a first-rate thriller chiller of its sci-fi type. The dark dank Amazonian jungle setting, the 152 underwater scenes and sequences, the eerie horror of the war between the would-be captors and their fishy ancestor—these pack plenty of excitement, all the more because they're in 3-D.

••••••••••••••••••••••

Variety: Monsters from out of space have been getting a film ride of late in science fiction offerings, but in this 3-D hackle-raiser Universal reverts to the prehistoric. It's horror guaranteed to spook the chiller fan and amuse others. Excellent exploitation possibilities.… The 3-D lensing adds to the eerie effects of the underwater footage, as well as to the monster's several appearances on land. The below-water scraps between skin divers and the prehistoric thing are thrilling and will pop goose pimples on the susceptible fan, as will the closeup scenes of the scaly, gilled creature. Jack Arnold's direction has done a first-rate job of developing chills and suspense…

••••••••••••••••••••••

Oakland [California] *Tribune*: The gill man proves an admirable underwater swimmer, whose technique may well be envied by the less capable among us.

••••••••••••••••••••••

Hollywood Reporter: [T]oo much time is wasted on underwater shots which are neither novel or dramatic enough to hold interest for the entire footage. Pruning here would help.

••••••••••••••••••••••

Fairbanks [Alaska] *Daily News Miner*: Terrifying science fiction combines with phenomenal underwater photography to make [*Black Lagoon*] a remarkable excursion into excitement.… [It's] a new screen experience and one of the most thrilling that you have ever enjoyed. It will scare you, but you may be sure that it will entertain you.

••••••••••••••••••••••

St. Petersburg [Florida] *Times*: "GILL MAN TERRIFIES AUDIENCE HERE; TOPS *FRANKENSTEIN*" … The Gill Man [is] more frightening than Frankenstein or Dracula …The picture is more fiction than science but it has a gripping quality that holds the audience. It is made in two mediums, 3-D and standard and, of course, would be far more exciting in 3-D, especially when the Gill Man walks toward the audience or when a bat comes screeching out of a cave past [Richard] Carlson's face.

Marginalia
By Tom Weaver

- At least one version of the script, Essex's revised second draft screenplay, begins with a description of a shot of "Cosmic Dust (Nebulae)" revolving in outer space and advises the reader to see the December 8, 1952, issue of *Life* for an artist's concept. The issue was the magazine's historic "The Earth Is Born" edition and the artist was Chesley Bonestell. The caption for the specified image begins, "The solar system is born out of a rotating cloud of gas and dust."
- The unexpected hazards of making a monster suit: Ricou Browning recalls that, once the various

pieces of the Gill Man suit were made, the plan was to glue them, jigsaw puzzle-style, to a white leotard *with him in it.* "The first piece they were gonna put on, was on the chest," he told me.

They put the glue on the leotard and they put the piece on. Jack Kevan said, "It'll take a little while for that to dry, and then we'll put the others on." Well, as it started drying, I said, "Jack, this thing is *burning* me." He said, "It's just the glue getting a little warm." I said [*more firmly*], "Jack, this thing *is burning me.*" And then finally I said, "I'm taking this off one way or the other!" They grabbed the chest piece and peeled it off and got the leotard off of me, and sure enough, I had blisters on my chest. As a consequence of that, they built a mold of my body and then they put the leotard on *that*, and then they glued the pieces onto the leotard on the mold.

Today (2014) Browning still has a scar from that burn.

◆ Newt Perry's daughter Delee tells me that when Universal was considering shooting part of *Black Lagoon* in Florida, they consulted with her dad because of his history of working with Hollywood moviemakers on Florida locations:

He'd helped with Tarzan movies, with *The Yearling* [1946], *Distant Drums* [1951], a lot of movies that had wild settings—they needed his experience and his contacts. When Universal came up with the idea of doing this Creature movie, Daddy suggested Wakulla Springs and the Creature people found it to be a *wonderful* setting, with the natural woods and the clear water.

They also asked him if he would like to play the part of the Creature. Well, at that time he was very involved with his other projects, and he figured out that there just wasn't enough time for him to also be in the Creature movie, so he had to turn them down.

An offer extended for Newton Perry to play the Gill Man? I emailed and asked Ricou Browning if this sounded like something that had actually happened and Browning, ever the diplomat, wrote me back, "Don't know fer sure ... but I don't think so." Ginger Stanley sounded even more dubious: "Not to my knowledge. I don't think so, 'cause Newt was quite heavy. He was short and heavy. I don't think he would have been what they were looking for in a Creature."

◆ Who in the blue hell is Frank Acuna? Never once have I conducted an interview, or read an interview, in which *Black Lagoon* veterans mention him, but Universal "Production Service Memos" in the weeks leading up to Day One of shooting call for him to be repeatedly paid for "Gill Man costumes," "remodeling of Gill Man costumes," etc. Clayton Moore wrote in his autobiography *I Was That Masked Man* that his first Lone Ranger costume was made by Acuna, whom he called "an independent costumer." When some of the late Mr. Acuna's paperwork was sold on eBay, photos of the documents were posted; on his letterhead he called himself a tailor, and the seller touted him as a "costumer designer for the stars." He appears to have been Liberace's costume designer for some years. What could an independent contractor like Acuna have done, Creature costume-wise, that they couldn't have done themselves at Universal City? We may never know. But he made good money *doin'* it.

◆ One wonders if Nestor Paiva would have been given the opportunity to play *Black Lagoon*'s boat captain if the role had remained as prominent as it was in Maurice Zimm's treatment, which made a comedic-romantic duo out of the captain and the spinsterish Winnie. (In the Zimm draft, the captain is also something of a coward, in moments of crisis spouting Mantan Moreland-esque lines like "I forgot to stay home!") Casting-related paperwork dated May 22, 1953, lists a number of other actors under consideration for the part, all of them higher on the Hollywood food chain than Paiva: Leo Carrillo, Alfonso Bedoya, George Tobias, Mikhail Rasumny and even past Oscar nominees Akim Tamiroff and Thomas Gomez.

◆ In the finished film, Reed sees marine biology as a stepping stone to space travel, but in the Zimm treatment, Reed sees the sea as an *alternative* to it: While observing "weird, awesome, nightmarish creatures" in the ocean depths, he tells Kay, "Maybe I'll finally be able to make people realize that they don't have to look to outer space for other worlds to explore."

◆ In the 1940 Universal horror-adventure *The Mummy's Hand*, the expedition into the Egyptian desert is accompanied by a character named Dr. Petrie, that surname chosen perhaps because there was then a famous real-life Egyptologist-archaeologist named Flinders Petrie; for audience members who'd heard of him, this little detail subtly gave the movie a touch of verisimilitude. And *Black Lagoon*'s expedition is accompanied by Whit Bissell as Dr. Edwin Thompson, *that* name chosen perhaps because there was a famous real-life archaeologist named Edward Thompson, known for his south-of-the-border excavations. Coincidence?

◆ Ricou Browning said that, during Wakulla production, never once did he set out to scare anybody with his Gill Man suit—but he still remembered the time he *did*: One day while working on the barge, he suddenly needed to go ashore and use a rest room. "I swam underwater—sometimes it was easier to swim underwater in that suit than it was to swim on the surface," he told me. With only his head showing (no Gill Man head), he frog-kicked his way to shore, emerged from the water—and then saw a woman and a little girl standing nearby. And the girl saw the body of his Creature suit. Ricou recalls, "She started screaming and running and the mother went after her, and I went after *both* of them, trying to say, 'Hey, hey, it's okay, it's okay!' But me saying, 'It's okay!' didn't do a thing [*laughs*]. They took off, and that's the last I saw of 'em!"

- The idea of having Mark Williams, during his last dive, consider murdering Reed survived all the way into the final screenplay: Underwater, as Reed struggles to get the cable around the tree barricade, Williams stands watch; and in a closeup we were to see his eyes "fixed on Reed's back—a target for his harpoon. He fingers the weapon—almost as though he'd bring it into play."

More from that final screenplay: By the end of Reed's next dive, he has successfully hooked the cable around the tree and given the Gill Man a good shot of rotenone; the Gill Man falls back and frantically flails, "as a man does in chasing off a swarm of insects." But then there was to have been a moment of *Jaws*-like suspense as Reed anxiously tries to swim back to the *Rita* before the rotenone-clouded water clears and the Gill Man can come after him again. Reed reaches the ladder and cries out "Quick—!" for Maia and Lucas to grab his hands and pull him up. The Gill Man sees Reed's feet still dangling in the water and swims in, *just* missing him.

- As in a lot of monster movies, the deaths in *Black Lagoon* occur in reverse order of the actors' billing: First the uncredited Perry Lopez and Rodd Redwing, then eighth-billed Henry Escalante, seventh-billed Bernie Gozier and finally, third-billed Richard Denning.
- Three of Reed's lines aren't in the script and sound dubbed-in so I'd bet you a microphone they were added in post-production:
  1. On the deck of the *Rita*, after Kay has been abducted by the Creature, Reed says, "Lucas, get to the beach entrance!"
  2. In the grotto, when the Gill Man approaches the embracing Reed and Kay, Reed barks, "Get back, Kay! Get back!"
  3. Moments later, after the Creature has been on the receiving end of several slugs from Lucas and Maia's rifles, Reed says, "No, no more, let him go."

Not only do they sound post-dubbed but in all cases, we hear the lines when we can't see Reed's lips: in the first, because he's looking down to put on a diving belt, in the second because his back is to the camera, and in the third because the Creature gets between him and the camera. The line "Lucas, get to the beach entrance!" provides a motivation for Lucas and Maia's otherwise inexplicable appearance in the grotto a few minutes later.

- Alongside Ben Chapman's yarn about the makeup department creating a large Gill Man ding dong, add this one to the files of "Bullshit ... or not?":

The Internet Movie Database's list of *Black Lagoon* crew members includes Jack N. Young as one of the movie's uncredited stuntmen. Nowhere in the Universal production paperwork I've seen does his name appear, so I did some Internet snooping, found his email address and wrote to ask where to find him in the movie. His email reply came *tout suite* and, according to Young, he's the Creature in the underwater ballet! He elaborated:

> After the picture wrapped, there were some scenes that didn't work, or for whatever reason wanted some reshoots. They hired me since I had been a frogman in World War II and was very good underwater. I worked only two days on the studio back lot in a tank. I did the backward swimming with Julie Adams' stuntgirl on top and a couple other scenes swimming amongst the weeds. I was surprised they gave me a credit. [Author's note: They didn't.]
>
> They built me a ten-minute air tank (very small) in the Gill Man suit hump behind my neck. The camera guys had regular tanks. I could work a couple minutes, hold my breath for a little while which gave them the chance to shoot a lot without coming to the surface.
>
> Thanks for writing. Hope this satisfies your questions. Good luck with your book.

To paraphrase Criswell: "My friends, you have seen this sworn testimony. *Can you prove that it didn't happen?*"

To directly quote Ricou Browning, "Don't know where these people come from!"

Another old gent who may be hitting the rotenone is Charles "Chuck" Willcox, who under various names appeared in a few movies (*The True Story of Jesse James*, *Rockabilly Baby*, *I Was a Teenage Werewolf* [all 1957], *Speed Crazy* [1959] *et al.*)—and in 2012 told Charles Greenwald of the weekly California newspaper *The Santa Ynew Valley Journal* that he played the title role in *Creature from the Black Lagoon*. According to the anonymously written Willcox bio on IMDb, "[T]he Creature was supposed to be played by Ricou Browning. Browning experienced problems adjusting to the suit underwater. So a stuntman with underwater scuba experience (Chuck Willcox) was hastily hired to finish filming. Part of the deal was that Willcox could not take credit for the film." The Solvang, California, resident also maintains that he went through his Gill Man paces in the waters of nearby Zaca Lake in Santa Barbara County. This book's research associate Robert J. Kiss scoured the Internet and presented me with his findings:

> Two overviews of filmmaking at Zaca Lake published in 1990 and 1995 make no mention of *Creature from the Black Lagoon*. Rather, the Zaca Lake–*Black Lagoon* connection appears to assert itself—in print, at least—only beginning in 2004, when Chuck Willcox appeared in person at the Zaca Lake resort on the occasion of *Black Lagoon*'s 50th anniversary. Since then, the assertion has made its way into several newspaper articles and at least two local history books, in addition to being reiterated in publicity materials for the Zaca Lake Retreat. During 2004 and 2005, Willcox was engaged more broadly in securing himself some extra public fanfare and affirming to the local community that he "had achieved some prominence as stuntman for famous Hollywood actors" while seeking (successfully) to have his Santa Ynez Valley residence declared a place of historic merit, with his career as a stuntman contributing to the building's history.

To quote Ricou Browning: "Another one!"

◆ Trivia question for diehard fans: In *Creature from the Black Lagoon*, does any character ever call him the Gill Man or the Creature? He's called "it," "he," "him," a "thing," "a human being that can live underwater," "a merman," "a demon," "a man-fish," "some monster" and "that fellow down there"—and, yes, the Creature and the Gill Man. Dr. Thompson twice calls him a Gill Man, and Reed says, "I've got a hunch this … [*groping for the right word*] this *creature* remembers the past and *more*...."

◆ When one *Black Lagoon*-playing theater came up with the idea to have a man dressed as a half-fish, half-human prowl the streets, Harman W. Nichols, a United Press staff correspondent, applied for the job in order to get a story for his syndicated column. Carrying a Washington byline, the column laid out the situation: "The newspaper ads said that the RKO–Keith movie parlor was looking for a man to run about town acting like a monster. Good pay, the ads said."

He then described what ensued:

> Don Ewing, a talented makeup man around town, took one look at my beak and sort of beamed.
>
> "I don't think we're going to need much makeup here," he said. "At least for the man part of the monster." … Ewing told me to shed my shirt. And then he got out the grease buckets and all sorts of weird looking paints.
>
> I don't think I'll ever go into the movies on an all-out scale. It was hot in the makeup room, and a lot hotter under that load of goo. Not only that, the makeup fellow plastered stuff on my face for something over two hours. Over half a pound of putty went onto my snout, which was big enough in the first place.
>
> The putty kept falling off, so Ewing finally glued it on. Getting it off later was something else. He also put some stickum on a set of phony sideburns.
>
> The rest of the re-build on the face was done sort of splashwise. A dash of blue, which clashes with a few splatters of green.
>
> This unsightly mess was topped with a bonnet that looked something like half a coconut shell, only not quite so pretty.
>
> On came a pair of green pants, with tail attached and a purple shirt, which for some reason Ewing fitted backward on me.

Nichols then posed for some pictures with a pretty model "[sitting] on my lap in front of a typewriter acting like a news lady.… It took another half an hour to scrub all that goo off. All in a day's work, but I don't recommend it."

◆ Quite pleased with *Black Lagoon*'s box office reception, Universal ran a full-page ad in the March 3, 1954, *Variety,* dominated by artwork of the Gill Man carrying Kay and the headline "Not Since *Frankenstein* Has Horror Paid Off Like This!" Below was a list of theaters where the chiller had done record business—for example, the Broadway-Capitol in Detroit ("Doubled the gross of any previous U-I picture"), the Century Theatre in Grand Rapids ("Set all-time house record") and the Capitol Theatre in Kalamazoo, the Franklin Theatre in Saginaw and the Strand Theatre in Flint ("Set all-time U-I house record"). Also named were movie houses where *Creature* had topped the studio's recent hits *Bend of the River* and *The Mississippi Gambler* (1953).

◆ So, okay, *Creature* was a moneymaker—but was it a Moneymaker with a capital M? No, not by a far piece. It made a tidy profit, for what it was and what it cost, but in those days, a gen-yoo-wine *hit*-hit was a movie that grossed north of $10,000,000 domestically. On the next rung down, *waaay* down, there were films like, say, *The Caine Mutiny* (1954) which brought in $8,700,000. To get to a total of $8,700,000 (the domestic gross of a second-tier hit like *Caine Mutiny*), you'd have to combine the domestic grosses of *all three* Gill Man movies … and then add the domestic gross of *This Island Earth … and Tarantula … and The Mole People … and Curucu, Beast of the Amazon … and The Incredible Shrinking Man.* At that point you'd be close but you still wouldn't be at $8,700,000.

◆ *Creature from the Black Lagoon* was the cover story in the May 1954 issue of *Mechanix Illustrated*, the Harvey B. Jones story inside brimming with what sounds like spoonfed studio hype (the cost of the designing, modeling and experimentation Gill Man suit ran to $18,000, 32 different head models were made, etc.).

- ◆ The Gill Man also made the cover of the August 1954 issue of the magazine *The Skin Diver*; inside, a two-page article revealed that part of the secret of *Black Lagoon*'s financial success was ... well, the magazine *The Skin Diver*:

What [Universal] may never know is just why the Gill Man was so popular with moviegoers. They may look towards the healthy growth in popularity of our sport and the *Skin Diver* magazine, for a telling example. Maybe it's just the attraction of a good yarn involving skin divers and underwater adventure that made the picture so appealing. Monsters have come and monsters have gone on the screen, but when one appears that tries, even in science fiction, to allegedly resemble a pre–skin diver hereditary missing link, then Hollywood has found favor among the countless thousands of new and veteran devotees to our sport. "Viva la Gill Man!" says the studio, and let the people come back for seconds. The Gill Man is apparently here to stay.

- ◆ *Creature from the Black Lagoon* is repeatedly referenced in Billy Wilder's *The Seven Year Itch* (1955), the Marilyn Monroe–starring adaptation of Broadway's long-running sex comedy. Second-billed Tommy [*sic*] Ewell reprises his stage role as a Manhattan publishing firm's associate editor who sends his wife and son out into the country on a summer vacation; he returns to his midtown brownstone apartment determined *not* to live it up while they're gone, despite his Walter Mitty–ish "dream bubbles" (daydreams seen on-screen) in which he's a great lover, irresistible to women. But he meets and instantly falls for luscious upstairs neighbor Marilyn, a TV commercial actress, and makes a few maladroit passes. She brushes them off lightly but over-imaginative Ewell frets about the situation he's put himself in, and has irrational daydreams in which she's telling the world he attacked her. ("He was frothing at the mouth—just like *the Creature from the Black Lagoon*!" she says directly into the camera in two dream bubbles.) After Ewell invites Monroe to dinner and "an air-conditioned movie," the next thing we see is a theater marquee advertising *The* [*sic*] *Creature from the Black Lagoon*, topped by a towering cut-out of the Gill Man carrying Kay. The camera pans down (we now see *Black Lagoon* promotional material on display at street level) to an exiting crowd, mostly Screen Actors Guild extras but also including Monroe in her iconic white halter dress and Ewell:

MONROE: Didn't you just love the picture? *I* did. But I just felt so sorry for the Creature. At the end.
EWELL: *Sorry* for the Creature? [*shrug*] What did you want, him to marry the girl?
MONROE [*stopping in her tracks*]: He *was* kind of scary-looking. But he wasn't really *all* bad. I think he just craved a little affection. You know? A sense of being loved and needed and wanted.
EWELL [*nods*]: That's a very interesting point of view! [*Laughs.*]

It's fun to hear an analysis of the Gill Man character coming out of Marilyn Monroe's mouth ... and fun*ny* to realize that this dumb bunny's take on the Creature, designed to get audience laughs in 1955, is identical to the straight-faced analysis of generations of *Creature from the Black Lagoon* fans to come!

When the scene was about to be shot in Manhattan, the 20th Century–Fox publicity boys let it be known in advance when and where Marilyn would be doing it, so thousands of fans lined the opposite side of the street for a shoot that went from two a.m. until nearly dawn. "The *Creature* theater" was the Trans-Lux 52nd Street on Lexington Avenue.[93] In the scene, after Monroe and Ewell discuss the Creature, a gust of air comes up from a sidewalk subway grate and lifts Marilyn's skirt; onlookers got more than they hoped for

The Outer Limits' "Tourist Attraction" script called for an army of froggy prehistoric critters, but the show's producers could only afford to pay Project Unlimited enough for these three full-body suits. Producer Joseph Stefano called the episode "the closest we ever came to those kinds of schlocky sci-fi movies that overran the '50s."

1. Creature from the Black Lagoon (1954)

when her bare legs and white panties were revealed, again and again in 15 or more takes. "Higher! Higher!" the spectators chanted. One *un*smiling face in the crowd was that of Marilyn's husband of nine months, baseball great Joe DiMaggio; the Yankee Clipper took a dim view of the proceedings. As the American Film Institute website summarizes the situation:

> Modern sources frequently assert that the shooting of the sequence contributed to the demise of Monroe's short-lived, troubled marriage.... During the filming of the "skirt blowing" sequence, DiMaggio allegedly became infuriated by the huge crowd's opportunity to ogle his wife's legs, as her skirt was blown up much higher than it does in the completed picture. DiMaggio and Monroe reportedly fought after the location filming was completed; two weeks later, Monroe filed for divorce.

Even though *The Seven Year Itch* was one of Fox's top grossers of the year, its *Creature from the Black Lagoon* plugs couldn't do that movie much good box office-wise, because by the time *Seven Year Itch* came out, *Black Lagoon* was long-gone from theater screens. In fact, *Seven Year Itch* took so long to open that by June 1955 when it did, *Revenge of the Creature* was playing and *The Creature Walks Among Us* was already in the works!

◆ Harry Essex wrote both of Richard Carlson's best-remembered sci-fis, *It Came from Outer Space* and *Black Lagoon*, and they almost shared a third credit: In October 1954, the actor was signed to star in writer-director Essex's sci-fi indie *The Dune Roller*. Two years later *The Dune Roller* was again announced, this time with Thelma Schnee scripting, Carlson directing and starring, and production in Haiti planned. It was finally made as *The Cremators* (1972), with Essex writing, directing and co-producing, and no Carlson in sight.

◆ The ABC-TV series *The Outer Limits* tipped its hat to *Creature from the Black Lagoon* with its December 23, 1963, episode "Tourist Attraction," scripted by Dean Riesner of *Coogan's Bluff*–*Dirty Harry*–*The Enforcer* fame. Here the "Mark Williams character" is the protagonist: John Dexter (played by "Special Guest Star" Ralph Meeker) is a roughhewn, globetrotting big-businessman testing underwater research gear off the coast of a Panamerican country, and the "David Reed equivalent" is the marine biologist (Jerry Douglas) in his employ, who is occasionally rudely *reminded* that he is an employee. In Davy Jones' locker, Dexter finds a man-sized, frog-like creature, and from here, the story goes off in new (non–*Creature*) directions. But for the first half, it's *Creature from the Black Lagoon* that is

Night Gallery's "Pickman's Model" ghoul (played by Robert Prohaska) had Gill Man arms and legs. For their work, its designers Leonard Engelman and John Chambers, plus makeup department head Nick Marcellino, received an "Outstanding Achievement in Makeup" Emmy nomination.

"controlling transmission": Two American men (one like Williams, the other more like Reed) on the south-of-the-border sea floor, hunting a 300 million-year-old fish-monster of local legend, gives off unmistakable *Creature* vibes. There are even snatches of music that are *Creature*-y, and the "fish locator" gizmos on the men's boat make you think of the *Creature Walks* Fishscope.

◆ Both Chris Mueller, Jr., and Ben Chapman told Bob Burns that, right after *Black Lagoon*, there was talk at Universal of featuring a Gill Woman in the sequel. According to Mueller, the Gill Woman would have worn the prototype Creature head, or something *like* it. Although that prototype head was supposed to be a Gill *Man*, the head eventually seen in the movie looked *so* fearsome that the prototype appeared almost feminine by comparison. Burns also directs our attention to the 1954 *Collier's* magazine article on the Universal monster makers and its photo of Westmore and Co. making a plaster of Paris mold of a pretty starlet's body: "That's probably the gal who was going to be 'the Bride of the Creature.'"

- If you wish you could have seen a Mrs. Gill Man, look no further than "Lindemann's Catch," a Rod Serling–scripted 1972 episode of the Universal teleseries *Night Gallery*. Set in a turn-of-the-20th-century New England fishing village, it stars Stuart Whitman as a misanthropic captain who finds in one of his nets a beautiful mermaid (Anabel Garth). By the end, she's not so beautiful, sporting a Creature-like head with bulging golden eyes, pink lips and long parted-in-the-middle hair.

"Lindemann's Catch" was the third *Night Gallery* episode in the space of six weeks with creatures partly resembling *the* Creature. Three weeks before it, in December 1971, came "The Painted Mirror" with Zsa Zsa Gabor as a meanie thrift shop owner climactically stalked by a monster (we see only its Gill Man hands). Two weeks before *that* was the occult-flavored "Pickman's Model" (1971), based on H.P. Lovecraft's story. Bradford Dillman stars as a half-mad artist whose wrong-side-of-the-tracks house in 1890s Boston has a subterranean entrance to tunnels where an eldritch race of loathsome creatures dwells; he paints their portraits. The one that makes a climactic appearance was energetically portrayed by twentysomething stuntman Robert Prohaska, son of veteran monkey and monster player Janos Prohaska. In 1974, Prohaska *pere et fils* (and dozens of other Hollywood-ites) died in the industry's worst plane crash. A majorly frightening note: Bob Burns came "this-close" to being on that doomed plane.

- TV's *Voyage to the Bottom of the Sea* also featured an episode with some *Creature from the Black Lagoon* echoes, its third-season "Thing from Inner Space." Wearing a dashy neckerchief, guest star Hugh Marlowe plays TV star Bainbridge Wells, host of the series *Science on the Move*; as the episode begins, he and his camera-and-sound crew are standing on the shoreline of Murro Atoll, 800 miles west of Chile, Wells talking into the camera about the legend of a Murro Lagoon sea monster. With an electronic device that produces ultrasonic sound, he says he'll try to lure it—and he does, the roaring, rubber-spike-covered beast (Dawson Palmer) making a *tout suite* appearance out of the water. Actually, this opener isn't as reminiscent of *Black Lagoon* the Movie as it is of the Maurice Zimm treatment which commences with Lyman Reed making a televised bathysphere descent, Reed hoping this achievement will enable him to raise money for a South American expedition. Wells, too, does what *he* does not for science but for money—for himself. Once Wells convinces Admiral Nelson (Richard Basehart) to take the *Seaview* on a monster-hunting expedition, we get *Creature*-y scenes of Wells becoming Mark Williams-like in his determination, the monster tranquilized and captured in a lagoon beach scene, being put into a *Seaview* specimen tank (and busting out of same), etc. Teleplay writer William Welch was responsible for dozens of *Voyage* episodes and not a lot of 'em were what you'd call overloaded with originality.

- For decades, Bob Burns, his wife Kathy and their friends built sets and staged

One of the celebs who caught Bob Burns' 1982 Halloween show "The Creature" was the original movie's still-stunning (at 56) star Julie Adams. Between performances she posed on the cave set with Bill Malone, who made and wore the outfit in the show.

1. Creature from the Black Lagoon (1954)

elaborate Halloween shows in the front yard and driveway of the Burnses' Burbank home, several of them based on movie favorites (*Forbidden Planet, The Exorcist, Alien*, etc.). In 1982 it was *Creature from the Black Lagoon*'s turn: On an enclosed cave set, a "paleontologist" took 25 or 30 people at a time on a spooky "scientific tour" capped by a startlingly sudden appearance by the Gill Man (the Burnses' pal Bill Malone, in a suit of his own creation). Made by visual effects artist Mike Minor, an eight-foot-long sign hung near the cave entrance read:

Bob Burns and Friends'
Halloween Extravaganza '82
The Creature
Dedicated with Love to Chris Mueller, Jr.

One night Julie Adams arrived unannounced to see the show. The whole story of the Burnses' Creature show, and all their other Halloween shows, is told in the final chapter of Bob's 2013 book *Bob Burns' Monster Kid Memories*.

- *Creature from the Black Lagoon—The Musical*, a live stage show loosely based on the 1954 movie, began playing at a theater in the Universal Studios Hollywood theme park in July 2009; Julie Adams attended the musical comedy's premiere performance. The information above comes from Wikipedia—admittedly not much of a source but that's okay, since from all reports this wasn't much of a show. It played to lots of empty seats for a couple of months before sinking from sight, probably not a performance too soon.
- In October 2013, the Motion Picture Academy celebrated Universal Pictures' 100th anniversary by playing several of the studio's classic horrors at the Samuel Goldwyn Theatre on Wilshire in Beverly Hills. The October 16 double-bill of *The Invisible Man* (1933) and *Black Lagoon* was attended by Julie Adams, who was interviewed on stage, and David J. Schow, the latter subsequently emailing me:

Last night's screening was weirdly revelatory. It was a digital screening in polarized 3-D (not a print). The big-screen clarity gave over-familiar shots a depth and weight that allowed me to notice things I had never noticed before:

Like a thread hanging from the *Rita*'s canopy…

Like a fly crawling on the edge of the *Rita* rowboat when the Creature makes his first grab for Kay's leg…

"This is the planet Earth…." But what's that in the shot? Why, it's a power cord or mount frame or something angular, hanging onto the frame at the lower left, previously obscured by contrast, now revealed by 3-D (it's kin to the visible mirror in the beginning of *It Came from Outer Space*).

I've always thought the Creature's first full appearance—rocketing up out of the weeds to the familiar musical sting—appeared weirdly truncated, as though it was half of a longer shot, possibly one seen later in the movie. Never before now did I notice that the Creature is visible (his whole body) lurking in the prior shot, right behind diver Williams, just for a split second. You can step-frame through the DVD … and there he is!

Also, when the divers surface to re-board the *Rita* the first time, you can see the net hanging underwater beyond them, and it appears that it has already got a huge hole in it (before the Creature rips it up).

The fossil claw projecting out from the screen from the rock face got applause; it looked that good.

The Creature's first "land grab" (the claw scraping the bank) was the first place I noticed the freshened sound mix, as you could hear the claws raking through the sand. (Now I can hear it on the older DVD too.) Some of the music cues seem remixed (at least, different sections of the orchestra have more presence). During the attachments of the cable around the tree barricade, both above and below water, the background chugging of the *Rita*'s engine is much more noticeable.

They even finessed out the visible wires in the "bat shot" and the shot where the Creature grabs and lifts Reed.

The Music of *Creature from the Black Lagoon*
By David Schecter

The Universal Music Factory

In the 1940s and 1950s, the majority of Hollywood film scores were created through relatively simple means: Either one of the studios' contract composers or an independent composer would be enlisted to write an original background music score. The process was similar to hiring an actor to star in a motion picture. Three examples in the science fiction–horror genre include Dimitri Tiomkin's *The Thing from*

Irving Gertz and Herman Stein, reunited in 1996 after 30 years (courtesy Monstrous Movie Music).

Another World (1951), David Buttolph's *The Beast from 20,000 Fathoms* (1953) and Bronislau Kaper's *Them!* (1954), with each composer receiving a screen credit in the movie they scored.

However, some of the smaller studios like Columbia and Universal devised other ways of fashioning film scores. Although Universal occasionally sported original scores written by a single composer, including Frank Skinner's *The World in His Arms* and Hans J. Salter's *Bend of the River* (both 1952), the studio also created underscores using more unconventional means, such as having more than one composer write the music. In 1953, Universal's *It Came from Outer Space* featured one of these musical conglomerations, the original score being composed fairly equally by Irving Gertz, Henry Mancini and Herman Stein. And over the next three years, Universal took even more irregular routes in manufacturing the scores for *Creature from the Black Lagoon*, *Revenge of the Creature* and *The Creature Walks Among Us*.

More often than not during this era, Universal's music scores received shorter shrift than those created by other production companies, as a portion of the scores often contained music written for the studio's prior motion pictures. Although there was often some newly written material to help freshen up these concoctions, at other times Universal's scores consisted of only previously written compositions. This practice of re-using and adapting older cues (individual pieces of music) was nothing new for the studio, with its Flash Gordon serials being prime examples. Occasionally, some of the actual older recordings were re-used in the new soundtracks, but because the Musicians Union frowned upon this practice, almost every one of these jerry-rigged scores was re-recorded with Universal's contract orchestra, which managed to help create a more unified sounding musical whole.

During the 1940s and early 1950s, music from the same Universal pictures was repeatedly "tracked" (re-used) in subsequent studio productions. The source movies supplying this music included both well-known and mostly forgotten films like *Son of Frankenstein* (1939), *Arizona Cyclone*, *The Wolf Man* (1941), *The Ghost of Frankenstein*, *Sherlock Holmes and the Voice of Terror*, *Who Done It?* (1942), *The Invisible Man Returns*, *Enter Arsene Lupin* (1944), *Pillow of Death*, *House of Dracula* (1945), *The Killers* (1946), *Buck Privates Come Home*, *I'll Be Yours*, *The Web* (1947), *Up in Central Park*, *You Gotta Stay Happy*, *Letter from an Unknown Woman*, *Abbott and Costello Meet Frankenstein*, *Family Honeymoon*, *Feudin', Fussin' and A-Fightin'*, *For the Love of Mary*, *River Lady*, *The Saxon Charm* (1948), *The Fighting O'Flynn* (1949), *Curtain Call at Cactus Creek*, *South Sea Sinner*, *Wyoming Mail*, *Harvey* (1950) and many others. The music was written by composers like Daniele Amfitheatrof, Johnny Green, Karl Hajos, William Lava, Milton Rosen, Miklos Rozsa, Hans J. Salter, Paul Sawtell, Frank Skinner, Walter Scharf, Edward Ward and Eric Zeisl.

The same cues from these films were often dragged out again and again for re-use. This was probably due more to familiarity than laziness, as the composers who assembled the compiled scores knew which cues had worked previously and would likely work again in new contexts. The music manuscripts from Universal's earlier movies were kept in bound conductor's books that contained shorthand versions of the bulkier full orchestral scores, and they were catalogued by film title in the studio's music library. These abbreviated scores didn't include all the notes that the musicians would play, but they allowed the conductor to lead the orchestra without having to flip pages every few seconds, which would have been both noisy and likely to lead to performance errors.

In addition to the conductor's books, Universal's music library also contained individual cues in folders catalogued under titles like "chase," "dramatic," "fight," "light and lively," "pretty," "suspense," etc. There was even a category named "descriptive," but descriptive of *what*, it didn't specify. The folders contained some of the most-frequently used cues that the studio's soundtrack compilers depended

1. Creature from the Black Lagoon (1954)

upon over the years. Need some music for a romantic scene? Just reach into the "pretty" folder and pull out a love theme!

The music Universal chose to re-use had less to do with the type of film the score was originally written for or the composer who wrote it, and more to do with whether a particular cue would fit with the new scene it was being considered for. Frank Skinner's brilliant background music for *Abbott and Costello Meet Frankenstein* was re-used in subsequent Abbott and Costello "Meet the Monster" movies, but the music's excellence wasn't as important as the fact that many of the cues worked equally well in the team's later monster-comedy features. On the other hand, Milton Rosen and Arthur Lange's superb score for Abbott and Costello's *The Time of Their Lives* (1946) wasn't re-used very much simply because the style of that singular musical creation didn't lend itself to future Abbott and Costello vehicles or many other productions.

Music from many a forgotten film was endlessly recycled because it was able to serve as generic action, mystery, or horror music, while music from more famous movies was often overlooked because its flavor didn't match the needs of newer pictures, or if it was too closely associated with the film it was originally written for. But not always. Even as famous a motif as Herman Stein's monster theme for *Creature from the Black Lagoon* was occasionally re-used in non Creature settings, but at least this was handled with relative restraint.

Although tracking older music into new productions might not sound like a very creative enterprise, it was both a musical challenge and an exacting technical job. After a composer selected the particular library cues that would be re-used, the music often needed to be reworked in terms of composition, tempo, dynamics and orchestration. The composer would decide which measures to use from each library cue, and then he'd "stitch" the disparate sections together, occasionally adding one or two newly composed measures so one piece would flow into the next, as the contiguous cues were often written by different composers in different tempos, keys, etc.

After the composer sketched out a blueprint of the musical amalgamation, a studio copyist would write out new conductor's scores to be used at the recording session. The orchestra members' parts would either be written from scratch or, if only slight adjustments were made to the earlier pieces, the older parts might be marked up so the music could be performed in the new, altered fashion. But regardless of any changes, the finished "construction" usually retained a record of the various cue titles, composers and music publishers associated with the original sources. This made sense considering these were rearrangements of previously written music rather than brand-new compositions.

The continual re-use of the same library cues over time contributed to a staleness in many of Universal's scores, to where moviegoers who normally didn't notice film music recognized certain pieces when the music's presence wasn't supposed to be so noticeable. This tended to lessen the dramatic impact those scenes might have had with music specifically written for them.

These hash-like scores would occasionally be spiced up with an original Main Title and a few other newly composed cues, with the latest pieces often sharing a similar musical theme for a particular character or event that wasn't a part of any of the earlier movies' scores. But by the late 1940s, some of the studio's library cues had been called into service so frequently it's hard to believe the written scores hadn't disintegrated due to overuse, despite being printed on extremely heavy-duty stock.

Universal's penchant for re-using music wasn't different from what some other studios were doing at the time, only Universal did it with more frequency than the others. Columbia might have come close—but Columbia didn't have a music staff like Universal did, so they probably could be forgiven for some of their borrowing. Regardless of a movie's genre or budget, it wasn't always easy finding a totally original score in a Universal motion picture, so given the studio's propensity to re-use music nearly every chance it got, audiences should be grateful Universal didn't fire all their in-house composers and freelancers and score every movie entirely from library cues.

In the 1940s Universal employed a host of musical directors (aka music supervisors) such as Edgar Fairchild,

Joseph Gershenson, left, and Henry Mancini (courtesy Henry Mancini Estate).

Charles Previn, Hans J. Salter, Paul Sawtell, Milton Schwarzwald, Frank Skinner, Edward Ward and others, but by the start of the '50s there was only one: Joseph Gershenson. The studio's music library had also been slightly freshened up, with cues from more recent melodramas, westerns, swashbucklers and other genres being added to the older pieces. Composers Salter and Skinner, who had been writing much of the new music for Universal's '40s pictures, were now joined by newcomers Stein and Mancini, as well as by freelancers Gertz, Lava, Heinz Roemheld and others. And although Salter and Skinner would still get sole or joint music credits on many of the pictures they scored, for the most part, the only music credit to appear on many of Universal's films from 1949 until 1969 would be Gershenson's for music supervisor.

The Russian-born Gershenson began his show business career in 1920 conducting pit orchestras in movie theaters to accompany silent films. His earliest work for Universal was as an associate producer, executive producer or producer on films such as *Dark Streets of Cairo* (1940), *House of Dracula* (1945) and *Little Giant* (1946), sometimes under the pseudonym Joseph G. Sanford. In the late 1950s he resumed this aspect of his career, producing *Step Down to Terror, Monster on the Campus* (1958), *Curse of the Undead* (1959) and *The Leech Woman* (1960). Despite moviegoers associating his name with Universal's music, Gershenson was not a film composer. He ran the studio's music department, being an excellent administrator, and as a conductor he had a good sense of timing and a solid understanding of drama.

Gershenson was also an excellent judge of talent, giving aspiring composers like Stein and Mancini the opportunities they deserved, as well as assembling a team of staff and freelance writers who were used in different groupings to score many of the studio's pictures. Gershenson would sometimes move a composer off one picture and onto another with seemingly little regard to logic, but the composers were talented enough to know how to merge their skills with those of their co-writers, enabling them to create musical tapestries that seldom sounded as disjointed as might have been expected. While it's easy to blame Gershenson for allowing too many movies to depend upon the re-use of older music, the studio had very tight budgets in every aspect of production. It's doubtful that the music budgets would have allowed all of Universal's pictures to have original scores, which would have required hiring extra freelancers to compose the rest of the music.

The studio's film music was usually orchestrated by the gifted David Tamkin (and occasionally by Charles Maxwell), and it was then conducted by Gershenson leading Universal's contract orchestra on Stage 10. All of those factors further coalesced these individual compositions into what seemed—without paying too much attention—to be the works of a single author. In later years Gershenson would claim that he auditioned composers' themes to decide which were the best for a picture, but that didn't happen. The composers were extremely talented musicians and craftsmen whose compositional and dramatic instincts allowed them to function without outside guidance or assistance. They knew how to work together to create the best possible scores, whether from writing original material or by weaving together the underscore from original and pre-existing pieces. However, because Gershenson usually received the sole music credit on Universal's motion pictures, that created the false impression that he was some sort of compositional genius—perhaps second only to Beethoven. In fact, he didn't write a note of film music, although he was credited with writing lyrics for the occasional film song.

After a picture was scored and the music was recorded on the movie's soundtrack, cue sheets were prepared. These were legal-music documents containing an accounting of every cue heard in the film. The cue sheets contained information about who wrote each composition, the music publishing companies that owned them, and the cues' duration and type (instrumental background, a song performed on camera or in the background, etc.). Regardless of whether the music was newly composed for the picture or was a re-use of an earlier composition, it would appear on the cue sheet. But these documents occasionally contained a bit of fiction. Sometimes, cues that were credited as being newly written were not entirely new, as the composers—either under a time-crunch or finding their Muse on temporary vacation—would borrow from pieces they had written for previous movies. Occasionally, they would adapt the works of other composers without any mention of this appearing on the cue sheets. However, most of these mistakes should probably not be attributed to the composers, as the errors of notation were more likely made by the music department employee who created the cue sheets.

Because of these oversights, a composer who adapted somebody else's pre-existing piece was sometimes wrongly credited with being the cue's author, or else his name was added as a co-writer of the original composition. This created the false impression that the composers collaborated on individual cues, which almost never happened. Other times, adaptations or re-uses were given new names, further obscuring a composition's origins. And when subsequent films borrowed from these secondary uses, the new cue names and/or composers sometimes replaced the original, correct information. Over the passage of time, cue sheets often contained more than their share of inaccurate data, to where it's often difficult ascertaining the exact source of a particular cue or musical theme. These altered credits directly affected who received royalties for this music, because performing rights societies pay composers and publishers based upon cue sheet information. In later years, even composers like Gertz,

Mancini and Stein sometimes couldn't remember which of them came up with a particular theme that others adapted for other uses in the same and subsequent pictures.

There didn't seem to be much logic behind why one movie was blessed with an original score and another wasn't. Occasionally, an outside composer like Miklos Rozsa would be brought in to score a film like *Kiss the Blood Off My Hands*, *The Naked City* (1948) and *A Time to Love and a Time to Die* (1958), but these were relatively rare occurrences. Many of the studio's more prestigious films of the 1940s and 1950s that were given the royal music treatment had their scores supplied by Universal stalwarts Salter or Skinner, including *The Prince Who Was a Thief* (1951) and *The Man from the Alamo* (1953).

But a larger budget didn't necessarily mean that a movie would receive an original score, as a number of the studio's more expensive pictures used more library music than some of their cheaper productions. One reason for this might have been because the higher-budgeted films spent most of their money on more famous actors and directors, not to mention pricier costumes and sets, so there wasn't extra music lying around to pay for new music. The difference between the music budgets of large and small pictures was frighteningly insignificant.

On the other side of the musical coin, some of Universal's lower-budgeted programmers—while often providing good excuses to trot out the same tired library cues—would sometimes have nearly original or completely original scores in them. The throwaway *The Mole People* (1956), which boasts a marvelously evocative pseudo-ethnic score by Roemheld and Salter, with some additional choice moments by Stein, would seem to be one of the last pictures to deserve such auditory enhancement. And *Abbott and Costello Meet the Keystone Kops* and *Abbott and Costello Meet the Mummy*, both made in 1955, long after the comedy duo's financial and artistic peak, featured a combined 100+ minutes of original compositions and only 11 seconds of tracked music. Yet these two pictures followed the team's *Abbott and Costello Meet the Invisible Man* (1951), *Lost in Alaska* (1952), *Abbott and Costello Go to Mars* and *Abbott and Costello Meet Dr. Jekyll and Mr. Hyde* (1953), all of which contained a wealth of re-used cues.

A film's budget was probably less important in influencing whether a new score would be written for a particular motion picture than the production schedule at the time. As some of Universal's composers were on contract, they were always working on some movie—as opposed to just sitting around doing nothing—so the studio kept them very busy. Three days on this picture, five days on that one, with composers being taken off one project and moved onto another as deadlines dictated. More important films like *The Lawless Breed* and *Creature from the Black Lagoon*—which you'd think would deserve original scores—probably contained so much borrowed music because Universal's composers were also working on a number of other productions at the same time.

Around the time Gershenson took over, some of Universal's composers began receiving music publishing rights for their new compositions. This meant that although Universal had the right to use the music synchronously in their motion pictures, the studio's publishing arm didn't own all the rights they had in the past. This change was important because it meant that companies other than Universal now had a larger financial interest in having certain music used. Now some of the composers would receive both writers' and publishers' shares of royalty income when the films played on television, or in overseas venues, or if the music was released on record or played on the radio. Why this happened is beyond the scope of this book, but it directly or indirectly influenced why certain cues were used in many of Universal's motion pictures, especially throughout the 1950s. Because in Hollywood, financial considerations always trump artistic ones.

While it's commonly believed that composers and other creative artists have almost no business sense, most Hollywood composers were smart enough to know that they needed good business advisors. Although writing music was important to them, so was making a living, and if the composers themselves weren't shrewd enough businessmen, the savvy ones hired managers, agents, accountants and attorneys to help them get work, make good deals, maximize their income and protect their assets from all the crooks infesting Tinseltown. Unfortunately, their managers, agents, accountants and attorneys sometimes turned out to be among the most dishonest people they would ever encounter.

The business aspect of motion picture music should not be underestimated when thinking about a composer's career. Whether it was inviting the right people to parties, saying the right things to the powers-that-be, or realizing that sometimes it was best to not take credit or ownership for writing something, successful composers needed to know more than just how to create music. Because certain things that could financially benefit a composer in the short term might work against him in the long run. Such as when your music director wanted to "steal" some of your money, but in return for thinning your wallet he would also make sure you continued to get work. All of these factors were just as important to a composer's career as his ability to write memorable melodies. There was a lot of ghost-writing and other backroom deal-making going on in the industry for purely monetary reasons, so one has to be careful when looking at cue sheets, contracts, film credits and other legal documents purporting to state who wrote what music. Because truth is often stranger than copyright registrations!

This short detour into the business aspect of Universal's film music is not to imply that any studio's music department was more or less honest or dishonest than any other. Nor does the importance of business matters mean that the compositions churned out by Universal's movie factory were anything less than superb, because their output rivaled that of more musically renowned studios like Warner Brothers, 20th Century–Fox and MGM. Although Universal didn't have any composers as famous as Bernard Herrmann, Max Steiner, Alfred Newman, Victor Young and others of their illustrious ilk, and its smaller orchestra couldn't provide the same orchestral density that some of the larger studio orchestras could with a dozen or more extra musicians, Universal's "team" was every bit as capable and creative as the other studios' music departments. Whether it was for a glossy Rock Hudson soap opera, a Rory Calhoun Western or a pulp science fiction thriller with rubber-faced monsters, Universal consistently produced high-quality scores regardless of the value of the movies they were written for. Their musical creations often elevated the films to a higher level, and other times they were the best thing in the pictures.

Music from the Black Lagoon

It Came from Outer Space, the science fiction film Universal-International released the year before *Creature from the Black Lagoon*, received grand musical treatment. Its brilliant, modernistic original score was divided fairly equally among freelance composer Irving Gertz and staff composers Henry Mancini and Herman Stein, none of whom received screen credit. One reason *It Came from Outer Space* received new music was because it was a much more important production than previous 1950s horror-science fiction movies, whose scores were either completely or partly tracked (*The Strange Door, The Black Castle, Abbott and Costello Meet the Invisible Man, Abbott and Costello Go to Mars, Abbott and Costello Meet Dr. Jekyll and Mr. Hyde*). Perhaps a more important rationale was that *It Came from Outer Space* was Universal's first serious science fiction venture in ages, not to mention its first invaders-from-space film. That meant there was nothing fresh or appropriate in their music library to use in many of the movie's scenes. But it's to Universal's credit that they stayed away from tracked music in certain romantic, action and atmospheric sequences, which could have been scored via library cues. Although to be accurate, the picture does contain a two-second excerpt of a pop song heard over a radio, that being Mancini's "Jitterbug Routine," originally composed for the Ann Blyth comedy *Sally and Saint Anne* (1952).

Unfortunately, *Creature from the Black Lagoon* was not given the same musical reverence as its science fiction predecessor, with only about two-thirds of the Gill Man score being original, while the remaining third contained library tracks. This mix of new and old was the same approach taken by many other Universal movies of the period, including *The Duel at Silver Creek, Has Anybody Seen My Gal, Here Come the Nelsons, Horizons West, Just Across the Street, Lost in Alaska, Son of Ali Baba* and *Yankee Buccaneer*, all from 1952.

Creature from the Black Lagoon's score did contain something only hinted at in *It Came from Outer Space*, that being an unforgettable monster motif that would resonate with moviegoers. Herman Stein's *Ooooo-wooooo-ooooo-wooooo* Theremin theme for the Xenomorphs worked well in *It Came from Outer Space*, but it didn't permeate into the audience's memory. That's because the aliens weren't seen very frequently, and therefore their theme wasn't repeated too much. In addition, the motif was orchestrated in many different ways, and while that is appropriate for film scoring, it prevented listeners from being hammered endlessly by the same exact version of the theme until it became a permanent part of their memories. However, for *Black Lagoon*, Stein fashioned the most memorable monster motif heard in decades, with its *BAH-BAH-BAHHH!* almost always being played on strident high brass. The movie relied so heavily upon the three-note Creature theme that the Gill Man soon became inseparable from his motif forevermore, and the connection between monster and musical signature wouldn't be equaled until John Williams' score for *Jaws*.

Although Universal's scores sometimes offered an uncomfortable mix of old and new cues, quite a bit of creative editing and rewriting went into *Black Lagoon*'s music. Some of the older pieces were flavored with newly written additions, including the incorporation of the monster's theme. The tracked cues were not the brief snippets they often were in other movies, but for the most part were substantial excerpts of the earlier cues. And perhaps more than usual, much of the previously written material was substantially reworked to closely match the new picture's visuals. The result of all this musical chicanery was an integration of past and present that was so well-done that many people have assumed the entire score was written specifically for the Gill Man movie. Repeated viewings of the film have only further cemented the association between the images and the music synched to it, so that when you watch any of the movies that supplied cues to *Creature from the Black Lagoon*, you have a hard time accepting the music in those pre–Creature contexts.

Par for the course, the only music credit in *Black Lagoon* went to Joseph Gershenson as musical director, that single credit belying the complexity of one of the more varied scores in 1950s sci-fi-horror. This lack of a composer's credit is probably the main reason the music is seldom mentioned alongside the monster genre's accepted classics like Akira Ifukube's *Gojira* (1954), Max Steiner's *King Kong* and Bronislau Kaper's *Them!* Because those composers were credited in their pictures, it made their works eminently easier for film critics and others to write and rhapsodize about. The lack of a composer screen credit was something faced by those who toiled in other Universal departments, including makeup and special effects, as this was during an era when opening title credit sequences only lasted for about 75 seconds, as opposed to today, when they seem to take up half the picture's running time. While the practice of short shrifting music credits occurred at other studios, Universal's composers were affected the most because their studio used multiple composers or older music more often than anywhere else.

While some film music aficionados realize that Gershenson didn't write the *Black Lagoon* score, many are wrongly convinced that Hans J. Salter was solely responsible for its creation. The first recording of *Creature from the Black Lagoon* music was on the 1959 "Themes from Horror Movies" record album (Coral Records CRL 57240), which featured Dick Jacobs conducting his minuscule orchestra through cheesy arrangements of mostly Universal sci-fi–horror film music of the 1940s and 1950s with varying degrees of disappointment. The album's only *Black Lagoon* cue, "The Monster Attacks" (actual title: "Monster Attacks, Part 1"), correctly credited Salter as the composer, but the record failed to mention the other composers who worked on the film. When the Varese Sarabande label reissued the recording on LP (1978) and CD (1993), both under the title "Themes from Classic Science Fiction, Fantasy and Horror Films," the liner notes failed to mention the other composers who worked on the picture.

Further perpetuating the inaccuracy was a 1980 record album containing only Salter's original *Creature from the Black Lagoon* music tracks, followed by a 1994 CD of that same music on the Intrada label. Again, these releases didn't mention that Salter was only one of a number of composers whose music was in the picture, which should have been apparent considering his cues represented only a narrow spectrum of the thematic material heard in the film's score. On the other hand, producer William Alland claimed that "the genius who did the music on my films was Hank Mancini," although he probably stated this because he enjoyed being associated with Mancini, who was more famous than all of Universal's other composers combined. In 2002, this writer's Monstrous Movie Music CD label recorded almost all the *Creature from the Black Lagoon* music that had never before been released, as well as a few pieces that had previously been issued.

Of the 44 cues listed on *Creature from the Black Lagoon*'s cue sheets, 29 were written specifically for the picture, with the remainder being composed for prior Universal movies. Of the newly composed music, Salter wrote 12 cues, Mancini wrote 10 and Stein wrote seven, although Stein also composed some of the main thematic material that was reworked by Salter and Mancini. Of the 15 tracked cues, six were written by Milton Rosen, four by Stein, two by Mancini, two by Salter, and one by Robert Emmett Dolan. There are actually only 36 different compositions in the film, with eight of the 44 being used more than once.

The films contributing library music to *Creature from the Black Lagoon* include *City Beneath the Sea* (1953) and *Mr. Peabody and the Mermaid*, both water-themed pictures and predictable choices for appropriate-sounding music. Perhaps less obvious music sources are the Westerns *The Redhead from Wyoming* (1953) and *Ride Clear of Diablo* (1954), as well as the crime drama *The Glass Web* (1953) and the exotic adventure *East of Sumatra* (1953). Although *Black Lagoon* is a monster movie, only four pre-existing cues came from horror films, two from *It Came from Outer Space*, one from *The Ghost of Frankenstein* and one from *The Wolf Man*. These last two horror pieces were written by Salter in the early 1940s, but even a lot of Salter's "new" Creature music borrowed liberally from his previous scores, including exact lifts from *The Golden Horde*, *Thunder on the Hill*, *Tomahawk* (1951), *Bend of the River* (1952) and *The Great Sioux Uprising* (1953). It isn't known why his music relied on these older sources so much, but as Mancini's and Stein's also did to a lesser extent, it's likely that a rapidly approaching deadline forced the composers to reach into their back catalogues and quickly grab something that allowed them to finish the job on time.

Music is very important to *Creature from the Black Lagoon* and its two sequels because science fiction, fantasy and horror films benefit from musical accompaniment. Music helps suspend the audience's pronounced disbelief, as it has the ability to draw you into the drama despite implausible plots or visuals. But even among Universal's science fiction productions of the '50s, musical accompaniment played an amplified role in all three Gill Man movies. While underscore covers less than half the running time of *It Came from Outer Space*, *The Monolith Monsters* and *Tarantula*, background music is heard in 63 percent of *Creature from the Black Lagoon*, 72 percent of *Revenge of the Creature* and 66 percent of *The Creature Walks Among Us*. Almost every underwater shot in *Black Lagoon* is musically enhanced, which should be a cinematic law because most aquatic scenes are slow-moving, and without music they can be ponderously dull. Because of the lack of dialogue and sound effects in *Black Lagoon*'s underwater sequences, the music is usually prominent in the audio mix, which helps make these scenes as engaging as the dry ones, something few water-themed pictures have accomplished.

Despite the borrowing of older music sources, the movie's soundtrack has an immediate freshness and appropriateness, mainly because the first 18-plus minutes of the film contain only newly written underscore. The different composers' cues are distributed fairly evenly throughout the entire picture until Salter's music dominates the climax. This "scrambled egg" approach manages to lend a kind of haphazard uniformity to the musical proceedings, and the ubiquitous use of the Creature theme further ties everything together. Stein's Creature–advancing theme is also used quite a bit by Salter and occasionally by Mancini, but other than those themes, the three composers often went in their own directions, and their different styles are quite evident.

The orchestrations for the new music and also much of the earlier music were by David Tamkin, which helps to further coalesce the disparate elements into a musical whole. All of the old and new music in *Creature from the Black Lagoon* was recorded by the studio's orchestra in an eight-hour session under Gershenson's baton on December 23, 1953. Universal's contract orchestra of about three dozen instrumentalists would vary slightly from film to film, but it mainly consisted of two flutes (also playing alto flute and piccolo), one oboe/English horn, one bassoon, four clarinets (some doubling bass clarinet), two French horns, three trumpets, three trombones, one keyboard (piano, celesta, organ), one harp, 10 violins, two violas, four cellos, one bass and percussion. The make-up of a typical classical or studio orchestra's string section usually has more violas than cellos, but Universal frequently reversed the balance, probably because cellos have a more powerful sound, which would give more weight to this part of the orchestra. Tuba player Jack Barsby was added to the orchestra for all three Creature scores to add some extra *oomph* to the low brass.

Herman Stein was responsible for writing some of the main thematic material for the picture, just as he had done on *It Came from Outer Space*. Gershenson trusted the 38-year-old composer a lot, as Stein was often chosen to write Universal's Main Titles, which Stein described as being "naked," with no dialogue or sound effects for the music to hide behind. Because of that, the composer considered these opening musical statements to be the scariest pieces he had to write for the movies. Some of Stein's Main Title work can be heard in *Horizons West* (1952), *The Glass Web* (1953), *Johnny Dark* (1954), *A Day of Fury*, *The Great Man* (1956), *Quantez* (1957), *The Lady Takes a Flyer* (1958) and *No Name on the Bullet* (1959), and his music would figure in ten of the studio's 1950s science fiction Main Titles, including *Black Lagoon*, *It Came from Outer Space*, *This Island Earth*, *Tarantula* and *The Land Unknown*.

Universal's collaborative scores often contained a wider variety of thematic material than those scores written by a single composer, especially considering the severe time constraints these projects were usually under. While Mancini and others have stated that Universal's "team efforts" featured various composers adapting each other's themes throughout a picture, this was the exception more than the rule, occurring most notably when the composers were told to base their cues on a song, such as when *The Incredible Shrinking Man*'s score was written by Gertz, Salter and Stein, but the main theme was a song written by Earl E. Lawrence and Foster Carling. And there were non-song instances when there was more borrowing than normal, a prime example being when Gertz, Lava, Lou Maury and Stanley Wilson took consistent advantage of a seven-note ethnic-sounding snake theme for *Cult of the Cobra* (1955).

However, for many Universal movies, one composer's motifs seldom bore thematic resemblance to what the others created, and this is understandable given that composers would prefer to write their own music than adapt somebody else's. While Gertz, Stein and Mancini used some of the same themes in *It Came from Outer Space*, a number of their cues were unique to each composer. Gertz and Lava employed extremely different thematic material in the cues each wrote for *The Deadly Mantis*, while *The Land Unknown*'s collaborative score by Roemheld, Salter, Stein and Mancini didn't even seem to have any themes anyone could have adapted even if they'd wanted to.

Universal's composers were already somewhat typecast even by the early 1950s, probably due to Gershenson or Rosen assigning specific kinds of scenes to particular writers. Mancini was being asked to score more than his share of "lighter" cues, some serving as instrumental source music. These compositions were heard in the movies over a radio or TV, or as background music in a restaurant or nightclub. Salter was scoring a lot of monster and action sequences in Universal's sci-fi pictures, and Stein created many of the main themes and Main Titles. There were certainly numerous exceptions to these unwritten rules, as each composer could and did write every imaginable type of cue, but over time you can see certain composers' outputs skewed in particular directions. Stein always regretted that he was seldom allowed to write a "tune" that had the potential of becoming a hit song, something his melodic gifts were certainly suited for. But even Mancini, who received more song assignments than most of the other staff composers, didn't get much publicity or many record releases for his film tunes, as there seemed to be a major disconnect between Universal's songwriters and the music publishing companies' promotional machines. Universal depended upon a few songwriters when they needed a tune for a picture, but they were seldom the composers who wrote the bulk of their orchestral film music.

The most noticeable aspect of *Black Lagoon*'s score is Stein's three-note Creature theme, which is memorable for two reasons. First, it's often played on flutter-tongued brass (mostly trumpets), an approach taken by other monster themes, including *It Came from Beneath the Sea*, *This Island Earth* (1955), *The Beast of Hollow Mountain* (1956) and *The*

1. Creature from the Black Lagoon (1954)

Alligator People (1959). The last note of the theme is actually a three-note, half-step cluster chord, which basically means it contains a dissonance contributing to the sound's beastliness. Secondly, and most important, the theme serves as a very repetitive leitmotif (an identifying musical theme), because almost every time you see the Gill Man, or glimpse any part of his body, or even his wet footprints, you hear his theme. The motif blasts forth approximately 130 times in the movie, which averages out to one *BAH-BAH-BAHHH!* every 23 seconds. The blaring theme is incredibly effective when the Creature during stretches when the Creature is infrequently seen; when he appears more regularly, the motif loses some of its effectiveness. It eventually serves as more of a strident sound effect than a musical theme, especially since it was not adapted into many other forms beyond the initial creation. The instrumental expansion of the motif would have to wait for the picture's two sequels.

Universal's composers didn't like using this primitive leitmotif style of scoring, a practice that was common back in the 1930s, because by the mid-50s it was considered passé to musically mimic something already visible on-screen. This approach was pejoratively known as Mickey-Mousing, as it was almost always used in cartoons, where a character's climb up a ladder would be matched by the music playing higher and higher. Given Gershenson's generally solid musical instincts, one would assume that producer William Alland or somebody else on the production side wanted to hear *BAH-BAH-BAHHH!* every time the Creature was seen. It was probably felt that a musical signature would help cement the beast's "star status," with this connection between the Gill Man and the score already being hinted at in the screenplay, which refers to "strange music" when the Creature is glimpsed.

With this dictate from above, the composers had to try to write the kind of music they felt the picture needed, while at the same time incorporating the thematic intrusion whenever the Creature or one of his body parts was seen. Universal probably had no idea how much the motif would help fashion the Creature's celebrity status, but along with his unique aquatic style and superbly designed rubber suit, the music helped forge a singular cinematic creation. Due to the theme's close association with the Gill Man, Stein's motif wasn't re-used in too many other films. However, it does appear in very limited fashion in *The Monolith Monsters*, *Posse from Hell* (1961), the all-tracked *Let's Kill Uncle* (1966) and a few other select places, not the least of which is *The*

Herman Stein's BAH-BAH-BAHHH! Creature theme (© 1954 Gilead Music Co.).

As pointed out in the 1954 *Collier's* magazine article "Monsters Made to Order," "[T]here's more to a really good ghoul than meets the uninformed eye. The creature of horror must be scary, but he must also inspire a certain reluctant sympathy, even affection."

Thing That Couldn't Die (1958), which re-used 29 pieces of music that were written for the first and third Creature movies.

There are many outstanding musical moments in *Black Lagoon*, courtesy of both the newly composed and the tracked sources. Herman Stein's "Main Title" opens the film with a powerful brassy fanfare that plays during the Universal-International logo, promising horrors beyond anyone's wildest belief. Unlike Alfred Newman's 20th Century–Fox fanfare, Max Steiner's fanfare for Warner Brothers or even Jimmy McHugh's Universal Pictures fanfare heard during the 1930s and '40s—all of which appeared in hundreds of movies—many of Universal's 1950s films featured an individual fanfare written to play during the logo of one particular film. This approach helped get each various adventure off in its own new direction rather than remind the audience of previous Universal motion pictures they had seen. So powerful was *Black Lagoon*'s opening that a slightly faster version of Stein's fanfare began the two sequels, and *Tarantula* also appropriated it, conducted at an even faster tempo.

After the fanfare, the remainder of Stein's "Main Title" introduces his three-note Creature theme playing on various instruments, followed by Hammond organ supplying an ominous melody while being accompanied by furtively trilling clarinets and strings. All of this serves to add a sense of the unknown to the proceedings. Stein requested that the organist play "screwy," which probably meant a setting with high partials (pure tones that are part of a complex tone). He used a similar effect in his later Main Titles for *The Mole People* and *The Land Unknown*, as well as in his atmospheric *This Island Earth* cue "From Unit #16," heard near the beginning of that film when a strange package is delivered to the research laboratory.

Born in Philadelphia, Pennsylvania, on August 19, 1915, Stein taught himself orchestration by studying scores at the local library. He was working professionally by the age of 15, and was soon arranging for radio programs and jazz orchestras, including work during the 1930s and '40s for Count Basie, Blanche Calloway, Red Norvo and others. He moved to Los Angeles in 1948 and studied composition with the esteemed Mario Castelnuovo-Tedesco, but after one lesson, Mario realized he had nothing to teach his newest pupil, so the two instead became lifelong friends. In 1950 Stein sent a record to Joseph Gershenson at Universal containing the composer's first movie score, written for an industrial film about the banking industry. Gershenson hired him immediately as an arranger, and Stein became a staff composer the following year. His first arranging job for Universal was for *The Strange Door*, where he adapted "March of the Priests" (from Mozart's opera *The Magic Flute*) for chamber orchestra; it's heard during the movie's wedding scene. Stein's first composing job for the studio was *Here Come the Nelsons*.

Along with Henry Mancini, Stein's jazz-influenced, muscular style of American writing would help define the sound of Universal in the 1950s and science fiction music in particular, as he composed memorable themes for many of the studio's horror films of this era. Stein's writing graced close to 200 films and shorts, among them *Horizons West* (1952), *All I Desire, Tumbleweed, It Came from Outer Space* (1953), *Dawn at Socorro, Naked Alibi* (1954), *Destry, Tarantula, Abbott and Costello Meet the Keystone Kops, The Far Country, This Island Earth* (1955), *The Unguarded Moment, Francis in the Haunted House, I've Lived Before, The Great Man* (1956), *The Lady Takes a Flyer* (1958) and *The Intruder* (1962). He also wrote music for commercials and television, including *Daniel Boone, Lost in Space, Voyage to the Bottom*

Herman Stein in 1996 (courtesy Monstrous Movie Music).

1. Creature from the Black Lagoon (1954)

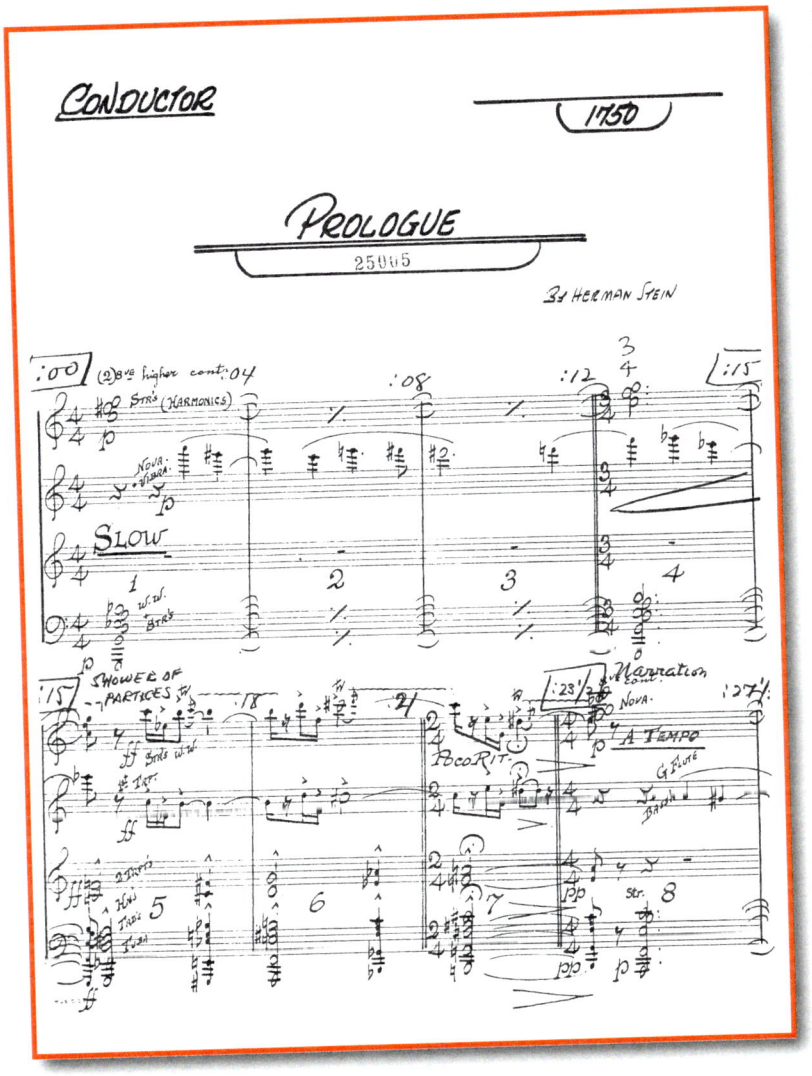

Conductor's score of Herman Stein's "Prologue" from Black Lagoon (© 1954 Gilead Music Co.).

winds and trumpet, while Hammond organ (sometimes notated as "Hammy" on the written scores) highlights the cooling of the Earth and strings portray the restless sea.

As life forms, the strings warm, and alto flute and bassoon effectively accompany the footprints of a primitive amphibian on the beach. The tones of an alto flute evoke a sense of mystery; this instrument was called on time and again in the movies to create a similar atmosphere. Requiring more air than a regular flute, the alto flute has a breathiness that contributes to the strangeness of its sound. When the camera moves in on a fossilized claw protruding from a Devonian limestone deposit, a variation of the Creature theme plays, ending on a portentous trill. It isn't important that the fossil juts from the rocks in a position so conspicuous that paleontologists wouldn't run across anything like this in 10,000 years—the point is, it looks great in 3-D!

"The Webbed Hand," also written by Stein, begins after Dr. Maia tells his native guides to wait in camp so he can get help from his institute in digging out the rest of the skeleton. Low strings highlight a disturbance in the water, and when the Creature's hand appears by the river bank, the "official version" of the Creature theme is heard for the first time on flutter-tongued brass, just in case the audience didn't notice the scaly, clawed appendage. Groaning brass plays the Creature-advancing theme until the hand vanishes from sight, this motif being used throughout the film to connote the Gill Man's movement. This cue and the soon-to-be-heard, thematically related Stein piece "That Hand Again" help affix the Creature to his musical motifs.

Henry Mancini's "The Diver" displays the composer's lyrical skills, adding an evocative background as Kay Lawrence pulls on the Morajo Bay barge's depth marker. When the scene cuts underwater, woodwinds, harp, celesta, vibraphone and strings add musical color to the shots of marine life. The ensemble ascends, informing the viewer that ichthyologist David Reed is swimming to the surface off-camera, and then clarinets halt the ascent while he waits to adjust to the pressure change. This lovely cue was re-used five times as a leitmotif for a talisman in *The Thing That Couldn't Die*, which *still* isn't reason enough to watch that dreadful film about a severed head residing in a box. For a short biography on Henry Mancini, see the music chapter on *The Creature Walks Among Us*.

Mancini's brief "Marine Life" offers a hypnotic riff on

of the Sea and *Wagon Train*. The composer passed away at his Los Angeles home on March 15, 2007, after finally receiving some recognition for the years he spent in relative obscurity due to his lack of receiving a screen credit on many of his motion pictures.

Stein's "Prologue" was mostly obscured in *Black Lagoon* by narration and noisy explosions, but the musical mood changes heard amidst the clatter still manage to splendidly augment the visuals that set the tale in motion. As the narration summarizes the story of life on Earth in less than two minutes, the music lends some credibility to a science lesson that would have been laughed out of any junior high school biology class. The cue uses ethereal sounds from Hammond organ, vibraphone and string harmonics to accompany an image of the Earth forming from a nebula of cosmic dust. As explosions send three-dimensional ejecta toward the viewer, variations of the Creature theme sound on wood-flutes and clarinets as Kay gazes at the Instituto's tank of sharks. This is the kind of scene where a library cue could have easily been used, but thankfully wasn't. In this sequence we learn that practical, money-conscious Mark Williams doesn't belong within 200 miles of a scientific institute when he asks if the fossilized

Herman Stein's Creature-advancing theme (© 1954 Gilead Music Co.).

webbed claw might possibly belong to Pleistocene Man. Yes, Mark, but only if Pleistocene Man celebrated Halloween and this was part of his prehistoric costume.

Herman Stein's "That Hand Again" reprises the Creature horror music introduced in "The Webbed Hand," the composition playing when the Gill Man kills the two native guides. It's not known which piece was written first, as composers don't necessarily score their scenes in film order. Instead, they often work on them in whatever order they choose, or in the order the sequences are completed by the filmmakers. "That Hand Again" uses groaning brass to play the Creature-advancing theme while Stein's Creature theme blares forth 11 times in this 1:35-long cue.

"Almost Caught" is Hans J. Salter's first cue in *Black Lagoon*. Salter scored his scenes fairly close to the visuals, and as this film sequence moves from image to image, the music follows its every twist and turn. The composition begins with a dissolve to a bloodied, gnarled hand, with the unsettling image of the destroyed campsite painted by flute, oboe and clarinets. The tempo picks up as the scientists run toward the tent, with a percussive blast from gong and timpani as they eye the devastation. When Kay wanders near the water's edge and the Creature's claw reaches for her leg, *BAH-BAH-BAHHH!* cries out three times, and turbulent low brass and woodwinds bellow as the Creature swims away without his catch of the day. Salter scored *Black Lagoon* in a way that was reminiscent of how he wrote music for his 1940s horror films, and this approach worked because the Gill Man picture was essentially a dressed-up '40s monster movie.

Salter was born in Vienna, Austria, on January 14, 1896, got his education from the Vienna Academy of Music, and studied composition with Alban Berg, Franz Schreiker and others. He was music director of the State Opera in Berlin before being hired to compose music at UFA studios. Salter emigrated to America in 1937 and was soon under contract at Universal, where he worked for nearly 30 years, arranging, composing, conducting and serving as musical director. He also composed for other studios and for television, and was nominated for a number of Academy Awards, including *Christmas Holiday* (1944) and *This Love of Ours* (1945). Some of his other film music was written for *Black Friday* (1940), *The Wolf Man* (1941), *The Ghost of Frankenstein* (1942), two versions of *The Spoilers* (1942 and 1955), *His Butler's Sister* (1943), *Scarlet Street* (1945), *Magnificent Doll* (1946), *Frenchie* (1950), *The Prince Who Was a Thief*, *You Never Can Tell* (1951), *Black Horse Canyon* (1954), *The Mole People* (1956), *The Man in the Net* (1959), *If a Man*

Hans J. Salter's pencil sketch for "Almost Caught" from *Black Lagoon* (© 1954 Salter Publishing Co., courtesy AFHU).

Answers (1962), *Beau Geste* (1966) and the television shows *Dick Powell Presents, Maya* and *Wichita Town*. Salter died in Studio City, California, on July 23, 1994, at the age of 98, fortunately living long enough to finally hear new recordings of his music released on CD.

Mancini's "Digger's Failure" begins with a playful clarinet motif as Lucas relaxes while the others work. Purposeful woodwinds, tremolo strings, and then French horn trace the expedition's failure to find additional fossils. Mancini opened this cue with a humorous touch, even though the previous sequence showed the carnage of the Creature's first killings. It's possible that the composer might have felt the lighter musical moment provided a needed break for a film with almost no comic relief, this serious approach thankfully being shared by all of Universal's sci-fi thrillers. While the entire film would usually be screened once for the team of composers, each composer would then focus only on the particular sequences assigned to him. Because Mancini couldn't be expected to remember every frame outside of the scenes he was working on, it's also possible that he just didn't recall the prior scene of destruction and how the humorous touch might seem a bit odd following right after it.

When the *Rita* heads down an Amazon tributary, Mancini's beautiful "Unknown River" augments the exotic surroundings. The cue also supplies appropriate background music for the romance between Reed and Kay, with French horns playing the melody while woodwinds provide accompaniment. When the scene cuts from the *Rita* to a shot of Reed accidentally startling Kay on deck, you can both see and hear a film edit, which occurred because the sequence originally contained a shadowy shot of the Creature swimming alongside the boat. But no matter how shadowy that image might have been, it required the addition of the Creature theme, so when the shot was later removed from the film, the music had to be removed as well. "Unknown River" was then edited rather than rewritten and re-recorded, as the music budget wouldn't have allowed an extra recording session to fine-tune the cue. A portion of "Unknown River" originated in the cue "Doctor's Diagnosis," a Mancini-composed piece from the Western *The Great Sioux Uprising*, where it complements a budding romance between Jonathan (Jeff Chandler) and Joan (Faith Domergue).

When the *Rita* approaches the Black Lagoon, a 59-second excerpt from Robert Emmett Dolan's gorgeous "Tale of the Mermaid" was chosen to musically illustrate this sequence. Written for the 1948 romantic-comedy *Mr. Peabody and the Mermaid*, it was composed for a scene where Mr. Peabody (William Powell) explains to a psychologist how he was fishing off a Caribbean island and snagged the mermaid Lenore (Ann Blyth, wearing a tail). The original cue was 74 measures long but only 17 of them were used in *Black Lagoon*, with flutes, celesta, and tremolo strings creating a magical mood that provides one last moment of beauty and tranquility before the monster action soon to follow. Because Universal had produced few aquatic-themed movies, in retrospect it seems obvious that part of *Mr. Peabody and the Mermaid*'s score would be appropriated for the monster movie, but not too much of it given that the romantic comedy was much lighter fare. In one sense, *Mr. Peabody and the Mermaid* is oddly similar to *Creature from the Black Lagoon*. While the mermaid film is about a half-fish in love with a man, *Black Lagoon* is about a half-fish in love with a woman. The main difference being claws.

Universal's 1953 adventure *City Beneath the Sea* is an enjoyable escapist yarn about romance and undersea treasure-

Hans Salter

In the documentary Back to the Black Lagoon *(2000), Julie Adams said that Carlson "had a wonderful kind of sophistication about him, that I thought worked very well in these [sci-fi] pictures because, when you put Richard Carlson there and he believes in what's going on, it gives it a great ring of truth because you think, 'Wow. It must be true!'"*

hunting off the coast of Kingston, Jamaica. It tells the tale of fun-loving, girl-chasing deep-sea divers Brad (Robert Ryan) and Tony (Anthony Quinn), trying to retrieve $1,000,000 in gold bullion from a ship that went down near a sunken city. The film's title, shots of the underwater city, and an earthquake resulted in the movie sometimes being touted and reviewed as a "science fiction thriller," even though the only speculative aspect of the picture is how Mala Powers managed to fit into her skintight bathing suit.

City Beneath the Sea plays a prominent role in the Creature's musical legacy, with the film's cues appearing 5 times in *Black Lagoon* and 12 times in *Revenge of the Creature*. *City Beneath the Sea*'s sci-fi perception might have been solidified by the prominent use of Novachord in some of its underwater sequences, as the instrument imparts an otherworldly gloss to the drama. The Novachord was a polyphonic synthesizer invented in 1939 by Laurens Hammond, who also created the Hammond organ. The 72-key instrument (pianos normally have 88) had long been used by Hollywood to help bolster the meager string sections of studio orchestras, but by the 1940s and 1950s Novachords were being used to create spooky or out-of-the-ordinary atmospheres. Both the Novachord and Hammond organ contributed mightily to many of Universal's horror and science fiction soundtracks.

Because a lot of *City Beneath the Sea* cues were written for marine sequences, the music was ideal for inclusion in the first two Creature movies. When *City Beneath the Sea*'s music was re-recorded for *Black Lagoon*, the Hammond organ took over where the Novachord had been previously used. The otherworldly luster created by the keyboard in these cues also helped this music mesh with some of the newly composed *Black Lagoon* pieces that also featured unearthly organ sounds.

City Beneath the Sea's score was a mostly original, collaborative work a few notches above Universal's usual high standards. Rosen and Stein wrote some of the sterling dramatic cues, with Mancini contributing to the score's lighter moments and jazzy pieces. Mancini also wrote part of the "Main Title," and despite a lovely opening reminiscent of his "End Title" from *It Came from Outer Space*, it is surprisingly and disappointingly one of the film's weaker musical moments. This is because Universal employed too many chefs in the musical kitchen, basing part of the "Main Title" on "Time for Love," a song composed by Frederick Herbert and Arnold Hughes. This section did not mesh with Mancini's composition, resulting in a very disjointed opening musical statement. "Time for Love" was probably woven throughout *City Beneath the Sea* because Universal was hoping for a hit song, with the same songwriting team also contributing other tunes to the picture. Adding to *City Beneath the Sea*'s musical concoction was "Damballa," a drum-and-chanting voodoo piece written by Le Roi Antoine, who appears in the movie as a calypso singer.

City Beneath the Sea's last two reels feature the least satisfying part of the score—an affliction suffered by many Universal pictures, as the music department often managed to throw a bunch of old cues into the latter parts of their movies, even when almost everything before that was original. *City Beneath the Sea*'s musical climax was a slapped-together affair of Frank Skinner and Hans Salter tracked cues from *The Web* (1947), *The Raging Tide* (1951), *The Raiders* and *Bend of the River* (1952). An impending deadline might have been responsible, but budgetary constraints might have also been behind the re-used music, because if the studio's contract writers were already too busy, freelance composers would have been needed to supply additional original music. Especially considering $660 of the music budget had already been spent on 12 voodoo singers, and $250 was needed for a voice double for "Mama Mary."

Even with the extras, the *City Beneath the Sea* music budget was a mere $17,700 out of the movie's total budget of $709,280, that 2.5 percent portion illustrating how trifling music was considered in films of the era. While *City Beneath the Sea*'s "musical direction" credit again went to Joseph Gershenson, not so typical was Hal Belfer's credit for "Musical Numbers." Belfer was a dance director whose job often entailed teaching non-dancers how to move without falling on their faces. When a dance director receives a music credit while the actual film composers don't, that speaks volumes about how unimportant film music was deemed in Hollywood.

Excerpts from Milton Rosen's *City Beneath the Sea* cue "Salvage of the Lady Luck" are heard three times in *Black Lagoon*, always covering underwater action, which isn't surprising considering the cue was originally written for a scene that takes place almost entirely under the ocean. In *City Beneath the Sea*, the four-minute piece begins when Brad descends from the deck of the *American Beauty* after the sunken ship *Lady Luck* has been dynamited. The cue ends after he opens a strongbox containing gold, and a basket for transporting the loot is lowered to the ocean floor. Among the composition's many highlights is a six-note motif played on woodwinds, marimba and Novachord, creating what Rosen referred to as a "Theremin effect."

Only certain parts of the 108-measure "Salvage of the Lady Luck" were used in the Creature films, with just over two minutes dusted off for the *Black Lagoon* sequence when Aqualunged Reed and Williams leave the *Rita* to swim for rock samples. After the movie cuts briefly back to the boat, a second excerpt of the piece plays underwater, ending just before the Creature reaches out for the divers. Tracked cues were often adapted for their new uses by altering the tempo and making minor orchestration and composition changes, but few modifications were made to help "Salvage of the Lady Luck" fit the action in these *Black Lagoon* scenes. Therefore, while the piece more than adequately covers the visuals, the cue's various musical moods often play against the images being shown. "Salvage of the Lady Luck" can also be heard in *Abbott and Costello Go to Mars* when Bud and Lou land the spaceship in New Orleans. Here, the Novachord provides the necessary alien ambience to help convince the comedy team that they're on the Red Planet. A very brief excerpt of the cue again serves that same general purpose when two escaped convicts spot the rocket and think Martians have landed.

Born in Yonkers, New York, on August 2, 1906, Milton Sonnett Rosen attended Damrosch's Institute of Musical Art, and he had two of his early concert works performed, at Carnegie Hall and by the Boston Symphony Orchestra under Arthur Fiedler. After working as a violinist, composer, arranger and conductor for radio and theaters, in 1939 he became a composer and conductor for Universal. From 1950 through 1973 he was assistant to the head of the studio's music department, occasionally taking on the role of musical director, and he conducted many of the studio's shorts. He supervised, arranged, composed and conducted for over 300 features, shorts and television commercials, contributing songs or scores to pictures including *Enter Arsene Lupin* (1944), *Sudan* (1945), *The Spider Woman Strikes Back*, *Tangier*, *The Time of Their Lives* (1946), *Slave Girl*, *Pirates of Monterey* (1947), *The Challenge* (1948), *Target Unknown* (1951), *Lost in Alaska* (1952) and *Ride Clear of Diablo* (1954). He passed away on December 28, 1994, in Kailua, Hawaii.

Mancini's 18-second-long "Duke's Little Helper" covers the forgettable scene where simple-minded boat captain Lucas asks Dr. Maia, "What these rocks tell you anyway?" and the otherwise intelligent scientist actually tries to explain the uranium lead dating test to him. The cue's real purpose is to innocuously break up two uses of "Salvage of the Lady Luck," as that action cue would have interfered with the inconsequential dialogue. The quiet "Duke's Little Helper" employs clarinet and tremolo strings to accomplish its task of staying in the background. For more about this piece that was written for the 1953 adventure *East of Sumatra*, see the music chapter on *Revenge of the Creature*.

"Brad Rescues Tony" is another Milt Rosen cue written for *City Beneath the Sea*, and it plays for just under two minutes in *Black Lagoon* when Reed and Williams dive for rock samples. Mancini added the Creature theme when the Gill Man reaches out for a diver, as well as another brassy insert, probably because Rosen didn't work on the *Creature* score. In *City Beneath the Sea*, the piece highlights a scene where Tony is trapped undersea and Brad attempts to save him, the composition bearing some thematic similarity to "Salvage of the Lady Luck."

Kay's waterlogged ballet with the Gill Man is not only *Black Lagoon*'s most famous setpiece, it's also the score's musical centerpiece. While the striking visuals and sexual imagery definitely help make the sequence so memorable, the music provides almost all the dramatic impetus for this mostly dialogue-free episode. Herman Stein's "Kay and the Monster, Part 1" begins the sequence, and when Kay enters the water wearing a form-fitting, puberty-inducing white bathing suit, Stein's glorious writing takes over with flutes, clarinets and swirling harp emphasizing her enjoyment. As she does the backstroke, orchestra bells and vibraphone add a sparkle to her aquatics. Although "Kay and the Monster,

Milton Rosen in his Universal office in the 1950s (courtesy Monstrous Movie Music).

sounds one final time just before Kay climbs safely onboard the *Rita*, intensifying that last moment when we fear he will reach out and pull her under. One or both of the "Kay and the Monster" pieces would find later use in *Revenge of the Creature*, as well as in Universal's shorts *Against the Stream*, *Blue Coast* and *Hot Reels*.

Stein composed "Tony Visits Port Royale, Part 1," yet another *City Beneath the Sea* cue, this one written for the scene when Tony leaves the *Volga Boatman* and dives toward the sunken city. The rhythmic cue's melody is played by English horn and French horns, then later picked up by trumpet, flute and oboe, with cymbal and brass highlighting Tony spotting the ship. While the two-part cue was over five minutes long in *City Beneath the Sea*, only the first part was re-used in *Black Lagoon*. It was presented without much alteration, being heard when Reed and Williams, armed with camera and speargun respectively, swim toward the audience for 3-D purposes. The cue was probably included in *Black Lagoon* because the music's propulsive quality suggests a strong sense of motion lacking in the slow-moving visuals. Unfortunately, the music is mixed at such a low volume that pretty much the only audible sound is bubbles. This might be the film's least involving sequence, due to both the absence of prominent underscore as well as the fact that it's Creature-less for most of its duration.

When the Gill Man's hand slides up a rock and he lunges for the divers, that 9-second cue with the Creature theme is a Mancini composition titled "Monster Speared." It's basically connective material to link "Tony Visits Port Royale, Part 1" with a partial reappearance of Stein's "That Hand Again," and it's unknown why "Monster Speared" received its own cue title, as other insertions of the Creature theme into tracked cues were not considered compositions deserving their own cue names.

Black Lagoon's fifth reel contains a lot of tracked music, both from other movies as well as from within *Black Lagoon* itself. Besides the previously mentioned cues, there is also a second use of Rosen's "Brad Rescues Tony, Part 2" and Mancini's "Monster Gets Mark, Part 1." About a minute of this latter cue plays when Reed and Williams swim after the Creature in order to photograph him. Mancini's complete "Monster Gets Mark, Part 1" was actually composed for *Creature*'s eighth reel, proving that the picture wasn't scored

Part 1" is credited with being an original cue, the first 18 measures—including the abovementioned section—derived from another *City Beneath the Sea* cue, Stein's playfully romantic "A Whale of a Catch." In that film, the piece underscores a scene where Terry (Mala Powers) pulls Brad's fishing line so he'll think he's hooked a big one. Stein's new writing for "Kay and the Monster, Part 1" begins when the Gill Man is glimpsed, whereupon the composer's lower, darker music takes over, with the Creature-advancing theme sounding low on groaning clarinets, bass clarinets, bassoon, organ and string bass.

Stein's "Kay and the Monster, Part 2" segues from the previous cue when the scene cuts back underwater, the music continuing the threatening mood. After a menacing gong, low instruments play the Creature theme as the Gill Man swims around Kay's kicking legs, with brass crescendos and trilling woodwinds and strings accenting the three times the Creature reaches out to touch her. When Kay submerges and the Creature retreats from sight, rhythmic low instruments remind us that she is still not safe. After Kay surfaces, the music calms, and as she swims toward the *Rita* with the Creature in pursuit, the orchestra plays a powerful reprise of the Creature-advancing theme. The Creature theme

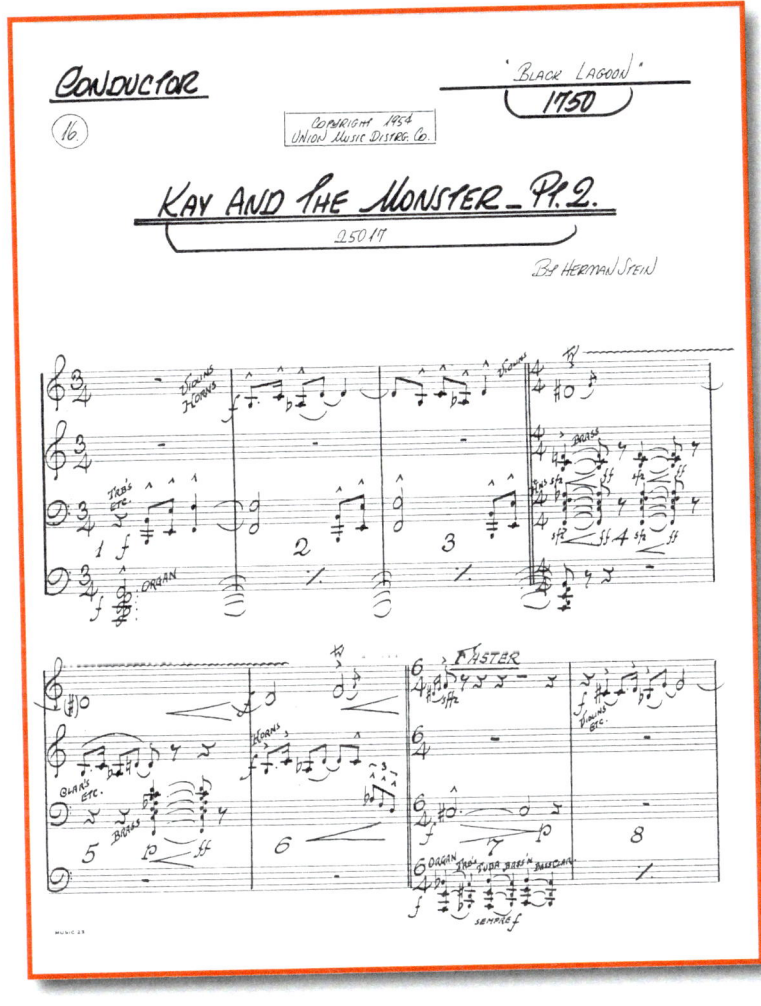

1. Creature from the Black Lagoon (1954)

an unearthly atmosphere, and dissonant notes on harp and vibraphone add to the sense of uneasiness. When Kay tosses a cigarette in the water, three versions of the Creature theme sound as the Gill Man watches from below. Although "Henry's Trap" fits this scene very well, it was written for the engrossing 1953 crime melodrama *The Glass Web*. *Black Lagoon* used only 9 of Rosen's 31 original measures, with one of the movie's composers adding the newly written measures containing the Creature themes. For more about this cue, see the *Revenge of the Creature* music chapter.

Black Lagoon's sixth reel begins with a lengthy (2:21) excerpt from Rosen's atmospheric "Clay Meets a Badman." The cue plays as Reed and Williams row out to drop rotenone sacks to sink deeper into the lagoon. Marimba, bassoon, harp and cellos descend with the rotenone, and vibraphone and marimba help beat out the slow wait for something to happen. Audie Murphy Westerns were a Universal staple in the 1950s, and just as Murphy's *The Duel at Silver Creek* (1952) and *Drums Across the River* (1954) provided music for *Tarantula* and *Monster on the Campus* respectively, *Ride Clear of Diablo* donated "Clay Meets a Badman" to both *Black Lagoon* and *Revenge*. Rosen's cue was originally written for a scene where Clay O'Mara (Murphy) waits in a saloon for Whitey Kincaid (Dan Duryea), and the music's ability to convey the passage of time was why it was chosen to illustrate similar scenes in the first two Creature pictures. The composition was restructured for its *Black Lagoon* use, which is why the music fits the new scene so snugly.

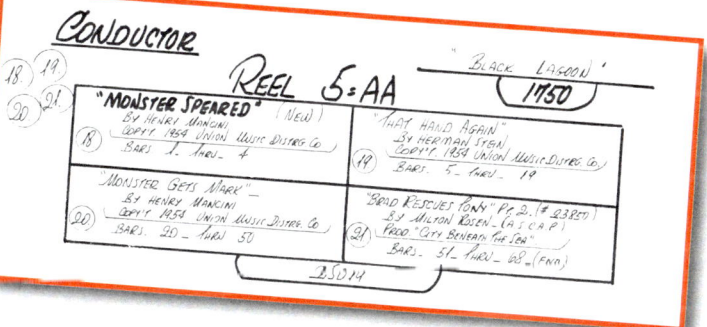

Conductor's score of Herman Stein's "Kay and the Monster, Part 2" from Black Lagoon (© 1954 Gilead Music Co.).

in sequence, as the whole composition would have been written first, with the excerpt later deriving from it.

Most of Hans Salter's *Black Lagoon* contributions occur in the second half of the film. His music runs the gamut from evocatively atmospheric to healthy doses of shock, but his contributions are definitely weighted toward the latter because so many of his sequences feature the beast, and therefore they include prominent use of Stein's Creature theme. "The Monster Strikes Back," which plays when the Gill Man kills Chico on deck, sounds just like its title implies, making use of the theme and other aggressive brass. The scene also contains a rare shot of the Creature being seen without his theme being heard, this extraordinary event occurring when he walks past a porthole.

"Henry's Trap," a Milt Rosen cue, augments the scene where rotenone is dispersed on the water's surface to try to knock out the Creature. Harmonic tremolo strings create

Conductor's score showing old and new cues combined for use in Creature from the Black Lagoon (courtesy Monstrous Movie Music).

Ride Clear of Diablo features a typical Universal mixed-bag score, combining original cues (15 by Stein, 7 by Rosen) with tracked cues aplenty dating back to Edward Ward's music from *Men of Texas* (1942). The soundtrack also interweaves the Frederick Herbert–Arnold Hughes song "Wanted" throughout the drama.

Salter's three-part "Monster Attacks" sequence in *Black Lagoon* encompasses nearly six minutes of music, beginning when the Creature unsuccessfully tries to climb aboard the *Rita*, and ending when the drugged Gill Man is captured. While the crew keeps watch, "Monster Attacks, Part 1" starts on pastoral English horn, the lovely melody soon being taken over by clarinet. Marimba and strings remain quietly in the background, but provide a subtle clue that the mood is about to change. When the beast's head rises from the water, the Creature theme takes over, with trilling strings and woodwinds helping to shatter the tranquility. The music quiets somewhat as the Gill Man vanishes, but when he reappears, the Creature-advancing theme calls out as the orchestral onslaught begins, with cluttered brass, gong and Hammond organ generating musical dissonance to match the visual threat.

"Monster Attacks, Part 2" plays when Reed and Williams swim after the Gill Man, with fast string writing being replaced at various times by alto flute, oboe and clarinet, all serving as the calm before the next storm. Muted brass and bass clarinet darken the mood slightly, and as Reed emerges in the Creature's grotto, woodwinds and vibraphone produce an apprehensive atmosphere. When Williams joins him and they see the Creature's fresh footprints, the Creature-advancing theme accentuates this, a nice touch because it hints at the Creature's movement despite the static print. Then, in another curious omission, there's a glimpse of the Creature walking away without his theme sounding. Whether any of the composers had their pay docked for this unacceptable oversight isn't known.

The Creature theme blares out to begin Salter's "Monster Attacks, Part 3," heard when the Gill Man gulps air before spotting his love interest sitting on the beach by the water. As he pursues the woman of his wet dreams, both the Creature theme and the Creature-advancing theme take over, a cymbal roll adding to the cacophony. Full-orchestral writing covers the sequence when he lifts Kay and tries to carry her off, helping to keep the dramatic level high despite Julie Adams almost needing to roll into the Creature's arms so he can pick her up. A wide assortment of woodwinds plays melodic phrases as the Gill Man is netted and caged on the boat. An excerpt from "Monster Attacks, Part 3" is reprised in the following reel when the Creature mauls

First trumpet part for Hans J. Salter's "The Monster Strikes Back" from *Black Lagoon* (© 1954 Salter Publishing Co., courtesy AFHU).

Dr. Thompson. This and other secondary uses of new music within the picture further imply that there was inadequate time to properly score *Creature From the Black Lagoon*.

Henry Mancini's evocative "Monster Caught" uses bass clarinet and piano arpeggios (where the notes of a chord are played in succession rather than simultaneously) to enhance the mysteriousness of the night as Dr. Thompson keeps watch over the caged Creature. When the Gill Man is glimpsed, the Creature theme plays on woodwinds, a welcome change from the more common, boisterous trumpet version, this rendition helping to reveal emotions in the captured beast besides rage. A glimpse of Kay elicits a lovely variation of the theme on harp, this being a rare instance of the motif playing during an image of someone other than the Creature—Mancini's clever way of linking the man-fish to the object of his scaly desires.

Universal re-used "Monster Caught" in quite a few movies, with one of the more bizarre instances being Jack Arnold's 1956 drama *Outside the Law*. However, once you get used to it in this very different context, it serves its atmospheric purpose well the few times it's heard in the picture. The cue was also taken out of storage for the 1956 Jock Mahoney Western *Showdown at Abilene*, and it plays an important role in *The Monolith Monsters*. In that movie it's heard in the laboratory when Dave (Grant Williams) realizes that salt might halt the growth of the cosmic crystals. Although Mancini is credited with writing an original composition called "Solution" for this sequence, the first 45 seconds are, in fact, "Monster Caught." It isn't until Dave puts salt water on the rock that Mancini's new writing for *The Monolith Monsters* takes over. This is one of an endless number of examples that illustrates how music written for a particular scene can work equally well in a completely different type of scene in another picture.

Right after "Monster Caught" is heard in *Black Lagoon*, there are some curious instances of tracking, the first being a :23 excerpt from Stein's "The Thing Follows." This music sounds when the Creature eyes his wooden cage while Dr. Thompson begins to fall asleep, which is no doubt what *you'd* do if you were supposed to keep watch over an inhuman killer from the dawn of time. The cue was written for the previous year's *It Came from Outer Space*, covering the scene where John Putnam (Richard Carlson) and Ellen Fields (Barbara Rush) barely avoid driving into a Xenomorph who's jaywalking across the desert road. Part of "The Thing Follows" used in *Black Lagoon* wasn't even heard in *It Came from Outer Space*, as that particular section was removed from the earlier picture when Putnam shines a spotlight on a three-dimensionally threatening Joshua tree. The music for that startling moment was not heard until it accompanied the *Black Lagoon* shot when Kay awakens the sleeping Dr. Thompson. "The Thing Follows" made further appearances in the all-tracked films *Running Wild* (1955) and *Monster on the Campus*.

The next contiguous cue in *Black Lagoon* is a :21 reprise of Mancini's "Monster Caught," heard when Kay and Dr. Thompson begin conversing. Then, right after a bird cries, a second, longer re-use of "The Thing Follows" retains the tension as the Creature tests the strength of his cage. When the Gill Man bursts from his enclosure, a :33 reprise of Salter's "Monster Attacks, Part 3" sounds, somewhat buried in the audio mix as the beast is set on fire and dives into the water.

Mancini's "Minyora's Plan" plays after Lucas pulls a colossal knife on Williams and then starts up the *Rita* and heads for the lagoon egress, with vibraphone, harp and bass marimba beating time as the anxious crew heads toward a Creature-built barricade. "Minyora's Plan" was composed for the previous year's *East of Sumatra*, where it enhances a nighttime scene when sexy Minyora (Suzan Ball) secretly visits he-man Duke (Jeff Chandler). This cue had much life after *East of Sumatra*, including appearances in *Drums Across the River* (1954), *Running Wild* (1955), *Six Black Horses* (1962), *Kitten with a Whip* (1964) and *Gunpoint* (1966). Some of the music in the full-length "Minyora's Plan" that wasn't heard in *Black Lagoon* was called into service to provide subdued tension for *The Thing That Couldn't Die*. It's heard in that decapitation flick when Boyd (James Anderson) sneaks into the bedroom of Aunt Flavia (Peggy Converse) to steal a key to the room containing a chest with a disembodied Head (Head).

All five of the cues in *Black Lagoon*'s seventh reel (from the first "The Thing Follows" through "Minyora's Plan") were tracked from earlier sources. And only :33 of the 3:04 of music in the entire reel was fast action music, with the rest being slow and sparsely orchestrated, meaning that it didn't require a lot of notes. Although it wouldn't have taken more than a day for a single composer to write completely new music for the entire reel, this part of the film included some of the last scenes that were shot, and the looming deadline precluded the possibility of anything new being composed and orchestrated. It's a safe bet that *Black Lagoon*'s entire score needed to be created rather quickly, but because it was such an important movie for Universal, they were aware they still needed a healthy dose of new music to go along with the older material.

Unfortunately, the entire sequence when the winch is attached to the log barricade until the Creature rips off the cable is not scored, and this includes underwater shots of the Gill Man, which are noticeably silent. Also without musical accompaniment is the subsequent fistfight between Reed and Williams, and as a result, the entire four-minute span is one of the least dramatic parts of the motion picture.

Two of Mancini's finest *Black Lagoon* compositions are "Monster Gets Mark, Part 1" and "Monster Gets Mark, Part 2," which play during the lengthy sequence when Reed tries to hook the winch cable to the log barricade while Williams fends off the Gill Man, the second cue ending after Williams' lifeless body floats to the surface. During part one, tremolo strings and uncertain woodwind sounds presage Reed's descent into the water, but fortunately the music remains at a substantial volume even when he's underwater and the bubbly sound effects get louder. The second part of the cue begins shortly after the Creature yanks the spear from his abdomen and swims toward Williams. Mancini uses a wealth of devices and orchestral colors to enhance the energetic compositions, including piano, snare drum, tympani, cymbal, xylophone and vibraphone, even occasionally offering some slight variations on the Creature theme. If you watch the underwater action with the sound turned off, you'll realize that a huge proportion of the dramatic impact is due to the composer's splendid contributions. In one instance when Williams chases the Creature downward, the powerful music maintains the excitement despite some less-than-thrilling visuals, including an image of the Creature doing a backstroke more befitting a lazy Sunday afternoon at the lagoon.

Although "Monster Gets Mark, Part 2" sounds like it was composed specifically for *Black Lagoon*, eight bars originated in "Hot Fight," Mancini's climactic cue from *East of Sumatra*, heard when torch-wielding Duke and Kiang fight with knives the size of canoe oars. Some of these same "Hot Fight" measures were also used in *Tarantula* after the giant arachnid finishes off the mutated Prof. Deemer. In *Black Lagoon*, the "Hot Fight" excerpt plays when speargun-armed Reed swims rapidly toward Williams and the Gill Man, who are battling in the water's sediment. Both parts of "Monster Gets Mark" had subsequent lives themselves, including an appearance in *Showdown at Abilene*. And in another Audie Murphy Western, *Posse from Hell*—whose soundtrack was patched together from 86 tracked cues—"Monster Gets Mark, Part 1" can be briefly heard. The clue to recognizing it in that picture is to listen for the Creature theme in the middle of the lonesome prairie.

Mancini's writing for the "Monster Gets Mark" sequence shows that even at this early stage of his film music career, his dramatic instincts were already fully developed. In his later, more famous years, the composer would downplay some of the work he did during this part of his life, probably because the projects weren't always as serious or mainstream as some of his later, more illustrious jobs—not to mention that because he was only one part of a writing team, he was seldom credited on his Universal movies. But some of Mancini's most striking dramatic compositions were done during his mostly anonymous years as a Universal staff composer. Mancini did re-record both of these *Creature from the Black Lagoon* pieces on his 1990 album "Mancini in Surround," albeit at a more leisurely pace and in re-orchestrated fashion. He also conducted the works at the Hollywood Bowl and elsewhere during his 1991 concert tour, so he was aware at this later point in his life that his early work had both an audience and merit strictly as music.[94]

Eight of the last nine *Black Lagoon* cues were composed by Salter, many written in his furious monster-mode idiom. But although the cue sheets list much of this music as being original, quite a bit derived from Stein's themes, and it was also peppered with guest appearances from previously written Salter cues dating back to the early 1940s. Although Salter had every right to be all monstered-out after scoring so many horror films in the 1940s, he was still able to come up with a lot of new material for later 1950s horror films *The Mole People*, *The Incredible Shrinking Man* and *The Land Unknown*. Therefore, his self-borrowing in *Black Lagoon*'s last reel was probably due to time constraints rather than any lack of creativity on the composer's part.

"Monster Aboard" is heard when the Creature's claw reaches through the *Rita* porthole for the bandaged Dr. Thompson, who's having one of the worst boat trips in history. The beginning of Salter's cue makes substantial use of material Stein wrote for "The Webbed Hand" and "That Hand Again."

Salter's "Doping the Monster" is a two-part composition separated by a brief occurrence of tracked music, and although each part of "Doping the Monster" has the same name, they are not the exact same pieces. The first version plays as Reed begins wrapping the cable around the log, with mostly quiet woodwinds and strings supporting the subdued action. "The Monster's Trial" supplies the tracked measures, covering the action as the Creature swims toward Reed, who sends the beast reeling with a pressurized blast of rotenone from an air tank. This was an excerpt of a cue from Salter's *The Ghost of Frankenstein*, a film that supplied tracked music to a plethora of pictures including *The Mummy's Tomb* (1942), *Son of Dracula* (1943) and *The Black Castle* (1952).

The second "Doping the Monster" plays when the Gill Man continues his attack and is sprayed by another cloud of rotenone; the cue ends after Reed climbs safely on board the *Rita*. Salter employs furious action music during some fairly static scenes of Reed fixing the cable to the log in order to keep the excitement level heightened. This incarnation of "Doping the Monster" duplicates some material heard in the first version, but it also appropriates 33 measures from Salter's 1952 adventure score for *Against All Flags*, where it was titled "Rescue, Part 2." It's used in that pirate film during the climactic swordfight between Errol Flynn and Anthony Quinn.

Salter obviously liked this particular fight music a lot, because it also turned up in "Cochise Fights Neegam" and "Geronimo Vanquished," two cues from his score for the 1952 Jeff Chandler Western *Battle at Apache Pass*. The different cue titles show how inexact the science of tracing film music's origins can be. In the mostly tracked 1952 swashbuckler *Yankee Buccaneer*, also starring Chandler, the same music reappears, again under the same title "Geronimo Vanquished." Still other musical lives of this cue occurred in a pair of Boris Karloff movies, *The Strange Door* and *The Black Castle*, being heard in the former film when Voltan (Karloff) almost knifes Denis de Beaulieu (Richard Stapley).

1. Creature from the Black Lagoon (1954)

In both of the Karloff-related appearances, the piece was titled "Attempted Murder," which is what the composition was named in Salter's score for 1951's *Thunder on the Hill*. This Douglas Sirk–directed thriller features a beauteous 23-year-old Ann Blyth, and the climactic cue accompanies the maniacal Dr. Jeffries (Robert Douglas) attacking Sister Mary (Claudette Colbert) in the bell tower. *Thunder on the Hill* provided a number of cues to other Universal movies of the 1950s, but "Attempted Murder" stands out in terms of the frequency with which it was re-used. Whether or not this particular music had even earlier incarnations predating *Thunder on the Hill* isn't known, but it wouldn't be surprising to discover that Salter composed the piece as an infant and he later based his high school alma mater on it.

Salter's next *Black Lagoon* cue is "Kay's Last Peril," which begins when the Gill Man climbs on deck after the log is cleared away, the piece ending after the Creature abducts Kay and takes her to his grotto. The composition is similar to some of Salter's other writing in the film, using Stein's motifs throughout much of its duration. A mere 21 seconds of Salter's tracked "Mob Psychology" immediately follows when Reed surfaces in the Creature's grotto and calls out to Kay. Although the cue is credited to *The Ghost of Frankenstein*, the music had already appeared in the previous year's *The Wolf Man*. Why Salter couldn't write entirely new music for this short, quiet sequence isn't known, unless this reel was scored near the end of the production deadline and the music would have needed to be conducted and recorded while the ink on the scores was still wet. But one would think Salter at least could have borrowed from within the picture, using some similar music he had already composed for *Black Lagoon*.

There are two versions of "Kay's Last Peril" listed on the film's cue sheets, but these are different compositions masquerading under the same title, the duplication possibly being due to a temporary lack of creativity by Universal's cue-namer or some last-minute alterations. The second rendition plays when Reed searches for Kay in the mist-enshrouded grotto and is attacked by a motorized bat on a string. Obviously, even in the atomic 1950s, Universal still had outdated props they wanted to get some extra mileage from, and Salter's music sounds like it belongs in a '40s Mummy or Frankenstein movie. And although "Kay's Last Peril" is credited as being newly written for *Black Lagoon*, it includes part of "Bull Throws Man," a cue that Salter wrote for *Untamed*

Conductor's score of Hans J. Salter's "Attempted Murder" from *Thunder on the Hill* (© 1951 Salter Publishing Co., courtesy AFHU).

Frontier (1952), heard in that Western when Shelley Winters operates on an injured worker. In Salter's 1951 score for *Tomahawk*, this same music occurs in the cue "Operation Arrowhead," covering a similar medical scene when Van Heflin removes an Indian arrowhead from an old man.

Salter's "End Title" bursts forth during *Black Lagoon*'s climactic sequence when the Gill Man rises from the Jacuzzi in his grotto and finds Reed and Kay snuggling when they should be high-tailing it out of there. The cue begins with a direct lift from "Monster Attacks, Part 3," written for an earlier *Black Lagoon* scene, and then Salter combines more of his own music with some of Stein's themes as the Creature advances on his prey. When a hail of bullets forces the beast to drop Reed, the monster turns on his attackers accompanied by 43 seconds of rousing music. And even though the Gill Man is stumbling like a drunken sailor, this thrilling musical passage sustains the excitement until the

Conductor's score of Hans J. Salter's "Miner's Fight" from *Bend of the River* (© 1952 Salter Publishing Co., courtesy AFHU).

wounded Creature disappears into the water, never to be seen again (until the following year). Although *Black Lagoon*'s cue sheets designate the "End Title" as being a new composition, this particular music is an uncredited re-use of a piece Salter composed for the James Stewart Western *Bend of the River*.

Bend of the River's score was written by Salter with very minor assistance from Frank Skinner, and the 37 measures used in *Black Lagoon* come from the 112-bar cue "Miner's Fight," which plays near *Bend of the River*'s climax when Stewart dukes it out with Arthur Kennedy in a covered wagon in a turbulent river. Kennedy loses the battle and disappears into the water, a fate similar to that suffered by the Gill Man, which might have been why Salter considered re-using that cue in the first place. A slower version of the same music is heard earlier in *Bend of the River* during the cue "Fight for Supplies, Part 1." Like many Universal cues, the roots and branches of the studio's music could be very long and twisted, and "Fight for Supplies, Part 1" was also re-used when evil Capt. Meade drowns in the ocean during the climax of *City Beneath the Sea*, a film that donated its own set of cues to *Creature from the Black Lagoon*.

Moviegoers often associate the music they hear with the visuals they're synched with, but if you close your eyes when watching this part of *Black Lagoon*, you'll realize that Salter's creation is not "monster music," but rather just solid generic action music. It's as suitable for a Western, adventure or swashbuckler as it is to a horror picture, and that's why "Miner's Fight" was re-used by Universal in so many movies. In *Yankee Buccaneer*, a slowed-down version of the cue augments a battle between a knife-wielding diver and what looks like a huge, plush, toothless shark. In fact, the music is so exciting it almost puts teeth in its mouth. But *Bend of the River*'s score was not just used for watery battles, as it was one of the most popular sources in the studio's music library. It donated cues to many subsequent films, including *Horizons West*, *Yankee Buccaneer*, *Lost in Alaska* (1952), *Column South*, *Gunsmoke*, *The Great Sioux Uprising*, *The Redhead from Wyoming* (1953), *Ride Clear of Diablo*, *Dawn at Socorro*, *Drums Across the River* (1954), *Outside the Law* (1956), *Taggart* (1964) and *Gunpoint* (1966).

Salter claimed that the Westerns he saw as a teenager in Vienna movie theaters helped him to later score Westerns in Hollywood. While this was no doubt partially accurate, Salter's Western music usually sounded more like his adventure music, his horror music or his crime music than it sounded like other composers' Western music. And this is true of most film composers, as their own styles are generally more significant than the genres they happen to be writing for. A fight was a fight to Salter, whether the adversary wore a black cowboy hat, wielded a sword, or had gills and claws.

As confusing as the multiple lives that some of Universal's music had, the studio took similar advantage of all their other assets. *Bend of the River* starred the Creature's first two love interests, Julie Adams and Lori Nelson. Perhaps if there had been a third Gill Man sequel, the Creature might have battled it out on the frontier with Audie Murphy riding Francis the Talking Mule?

Following the *Bend of the River* excerpt in *Black Lagoon*, Salter's "End Title" adds some original music, with descending low brass and woodwinds playing alongside the beast's tragic descent to his sequel-laden doom. After a hug between Reed and Kay is warmed by strings, the Gill Man sinks into the inky black depths to the accompaniment of two inversions of the Creature theme. The piece concludes with a happy-ending fanfare originally written for the 1951 Genghis Khan picture *The Golden Horde*, which includes Salter's three-note signature tag—the composer's personal statement that he liked the music he wrote for a particular picture. However, because the tag was tracked into *Black Lagoon* from *The Golden Horde*, we'll never know whether the tag's inclusion meant that Salter still liked his music from *The Golden Horde*, whether he liked the original music he wrote for *Black Lagoon*, whether he liked *all* the old movie scores he pillaged for re-use in *Black Lagoon*, or whether he liked every drop of old and new music he contributed to the Gill Man movie.

Herman Stein's "End Cast" closes *Creature from the Black Lagoon* on a bright note, which isn't surprising, since it was originally written to end the breezy Maureen O'Hara western *The Redhead from Wyoming*. This motion picture featured 7 new cues by Stein, a short piece by Rosen, and a plethora of tracked cues, most from westerns. Stein obviously had little time to score *The Redhead from Wyoming*, as he copied the film's "End Cast" from its "End Title," and part of the "End Title" had already been copied from Stein's "Fireside Chat" from *The Duel at Silver Creek*. The composers who put together the tracked sections of scores used a lot of ingenuity in compiling the various cues. An example of this occurs in the climax of *Running Wild*, where two excerpts from *Redhead*'s "End Title" were sandwiched around a passage from *The Duel at Silver Creek*'s "Fireside Chat," the thematic similarities between the pieces helping one cue flow seamlessly into the next.

Salter's music for *Black Lagoon* lived on, and not just in the two Creature sequels and other Universal pictures. Salter, either acting on his own or in tandem with somebody at Universal, licensed out recordings of some of his original music tracks for use in a host of independent movies, few of them memorable. These were probably unauthorized uses, as the cues were renamed and assigned to new publishing companies. The result was that horror movie fans were often perplexed when they recognized some of the Gill Man's music in these productions. In the atrocious *Dracula vs. Frankenstein* (1971), Salter and Mancini's Creature music plays in scenes featuring the greasepaint vampire and the cauliflower-head monster, as do both composers' tracks from *This Island Earth*. The equally abysmal *Women of the Prehistoric Planet* (1966) uses Salter's *Black Lagoon* tracks to highlight a giant lizard, a deadly snake, a menacing volcano and even more horrifying images such as prehistoric men wearing fashion furs. The picture also contains a healthy dose of Salter's tracks from *This Island Earth* and *The Incredible Shrinking Man*, Leith Stevens' *Destination Moon* (1950) cues, and other music that deserved a far better fate. Salter's "Mob Psychology," which was re-used in *Black Lagoon*, is heard in *First Spaceship on Venus* (1962), sharing company with music from *This Island Earth*. But perhaps the ultimate indignity to the Creature's music occurred when some of Salter's *Black Lagoon* tracks appeared in the U.S. version of Toho's *King Kong vs. Godzilla* (1963) which, although it was meant to be satirical, still managed to be an insult to both monsters.

Analysis
By Steve Kronenberg

Creature from the Black Lagoon is the watershed film of Universal's 1950s catalogue. It is the studio's first true horror film of the decade, the first to be filmed in 3-D (*It Came from Outer Space* belongs more to the science fiction genre) and the first to employ a full, head-to-toe monster suit to depict its title character, inspiring countless imitations that varied wildly in budget and quality.

But *Black Lagoon*'s greatest impact was cultural: The film unveiled a memorable monster that was immediately and forever associated with the 1950s. More importantly, the Creature became a horror icon even before the film was brought to television, joining the ranks of the great Golden Age monsters Dracula, the Frankenstein Monster, the Mummy, the Wolf Man and—the monster the Creature most resembles—King Kong.

> It's the idea of my picture. The Beast was a tough guy too. He could lick the world. But when he saw Beauty, she got him. He went soft. He forgot his wisdom and the little fellas licked him.—Carl Denham (Robert Armstrong) in *King Kong*

Like Kong, the Creature is not a product of mad science or myth, but a biological aberration and prehistoric holdover. The Creature rules his dark underwater domain in the Amazon the way Kong was master of the misty Skull Island—

and neither of them takes kindly to strangers invading their space. Most of all, the Creature "apes" Kong's humanoid characteristics: Both are captivated and victimized by the desire for a beautiful woman, and both die amidst great audience sympathy. Indeed, producer William Alland specifically intended *Black Lagoon* to be an aquatic remake of *Kong*.

Aside from its tremendous importance to the horror genre, *Black Lagoon* is, in and of itself, a superb film. Reams of pages have been written about its flawlessly designed and executed monster suit. The film also boasts a fine cast of '50s genre stalwarts, and an imposing female presence in Julie Adams. But the real stars of *Black Lagoon* are its cinematographers William E. Snyder, who handled the topside photography, and the great Charles "Scotty" Welbourne, who shot and co-directed the film's memorable underwater scenes.

The opening scene sets the film's tone: We see a series of explosions framing a lecture on the Earth's beginning and the process of evolution. We are then treated us to a beautiful shot of the ocean and an adjoining beach—and an ominous shot of large webbed footprints leading from the water.

It's "Scotty" Welbourne's water imagery that dominates *Black Lagoon*. His moody, mystic style that gives the movie its panache as a horror film. His murky underwater photography makes the Creature's underwater kingdom as dark and ominous as *Dracula*'s Borgo Pass or *Kong*'s Skull Island. Initially, Welbourne, Snyder (and director Jack Arnold) "tease" us with mere hints of the Creature's presence: a footprint here, a shot of the Creature's slimy, webbed extremity there. But the first full shot of the merman is a joy to behold: In the depths of the lagoon, we get a startling closeup of the Creature lunging *upward* and past the camera! Welbourne's aptitude for mood and lighting is also exemplified by a fine medium shot of the Creature seen through a patch of seaweed, which filigrees the monster's face and further distorts his grotesque features.

And it's Welbourne who deserves full credit for the justly celebrated scene in which the Creature sees and tracks Kay as she swims through the water. He turns a standard "monster pursuing the girl" scene into a surreal and sexual water ballet. Welbourne's camera tracks with the Creature as he swims parallel to Kay beneath the water, contrasting her figure and form with the Creature's unnatural body as they move in unison. Welbourne also captures the scene's aesthetic beauty: Ricou Browning's Creature and Adams' underwater double, Ginger Stanley, swim and play off each other marvelously. And as Welbourne gives us a closeup of the Creature plucking at Kay's foot, the ballet's sexuality becomes even more explicit: Welbourne has presented us with the first example of underwater foreplay in horror film history! (Indeed, the scene resembles Kong's "foreplay" with Fay Wray both on the ceremonial altar and on Skull Mountain.) As Kay swims back to the boat, Welbourne follows the Creature's graceful yet ominous movements through the water in pursuit of his new love.

Welbourne tempers the beauty and grace of the scene with the appropriate mood: His camera captures the sheer isolation and darkness of the water, creating a classically scary and atmospheric scenario. The water ballet is *Black Lagoon*'s

The amorous amphibian (Ben Chapman) with Kay (Julie Adams) in his worshipful sights. Douglas Brode in his book The Films of the Fifties *writes that, like King Kong, the Creature is "the unchallenged god of a lost world suddenly made vulnerable by his weakness for the beauty he has never before experienced."*

most famous and celebrated scene, and rightly so: Welbourne brilliantly blends beauty, grace, form and subtle lighting with the darkness and mood that we expect and appreciate from any horror film. (In *The Horror Show* [CBS-TV, 1979], a Richard Schickel–scripted retrospective on the history of horror movies, host-narrator Anthony Perkins calls this scene "Beauty and the Beast, retold in modern terms.")

Welbourne's aptitude for mood, light and shadow is prominent throughout the film. After Williams harpoons the Creature, Welbourne provides a magnificent, atmospheric long shot of the Creature swimming down, down to the entrance to its grotto in the depths of the Lagoon—a shot that also conveys the vastness of the Creature's underwater kingdom.

Yet this scene is merely a prelude for Welbourne's most unsettling underwater shot: the Creature seizing Williams and pulling him down to his death. Welbourne isolates the Creature and his struggling, hapless prey and follows their *every move* as the monster swims ever deeper. Welbourne's camera captures the furious, inhuman side of the Creature, while concentrating on Williams' claustrophobic peril: He is helplessly locked in the Creature's embrace and pulled to the darkest depths. Welbourne's remarkable penchant for contrasting lighting highlights the shot: As the Creature drags Williams ever deeper, Welbourne gradually and delicately dims the lighting, illuminating the murky grayness of the water with scattered shafts of light, creating a surreal tone as well as a sense of depth. In fact, it is the lighting that marks the sheer eeriness of this particular scene. The scene is, arguably, the most haunting and unnerving series of shots in any 1950s horror film.

Welbourne also shines in a similarly beautiful, although less startling underwater shot of the Creature, with the abducted Kay under his arm, taking her down to his underwater grotto. The scene is magnificently lit, an eerie *danse macabre*, as the Creature silently carries his still, unconscious "bride" to his bizarre, miasmic digs.

Welbourne's stunning underwater achievements are *Black Lagoon*'s highlights. But Snyder's topside photography succeeds in providing some subtle and not-so-subtle jolts. Snyder is especially adept at closeups and point of view shots. In the several "teaser" shots that precede our full view of the Creature, Snyder delivers eerie, ominous closeups of the Creature's scaly hand appearing on a bank of the Amazon and nearly grabbing an unknowing Kay. The best of these "teaser" shots has Snyder's camera segueing from Dr. Maia's discovery of the fossilized Creature hand to the *real* thing sliding up from the water and then down! Snyder also provides a menacing closeup of the Creature's legs as he shuffles along the deck of the boat.

Snyder gives us a memorably moody long shot in the night scene of the Creature standing near the shore as Reed (aboard the *Rita*) shines a searchlight onto him. Toward the end, we get fine medium shots of the Creature climbing onto the *Rita*, balanced with shifts to Kay, then to the Creature as he closes in. Much of the credit for this collage should go to the brilliance of editor Ted J. Kent, whose superb work graces such Golden Age masterpieces as *Frankenstein* (1931), *Bride of Frankenstein* (1935) and *The Invisible Man* (1933).

Particularly eerie is Snyder's closeup of the Creature after he is caught and caged on the boat, his distorted features and wide eyes made more grotesque by the water in which he is immersed. Snyder's lighting in this scene gives the Creature's face an unsettling glow, reminiscent of the way Karl Freund and Charles Stumar lit Boris Karloff's visage in *The Mummy* (1932). As the Creature tries to escape its cage, Snyder's camera tightly focuses on the monster's wide eyes and gasping mouth, augmenting the scene's nightmarish quality. And as the Creature breaks out of its cage, Snyder and editor Kent furiously shift from the monster to his mate, as Kay and Dr. Thompson casually converse on deck. Kent's editing work allows the tension to build as he blends Snyder's shots of the ready-to-make-his-move Creature with Kay and Thompson's oblivious socializing. Later, Snyder and Kent also combine to deliver another of the film's subtly suspenseful scenes: Snyder's camera focuses on the Creature's hand reaching through a porthole to menace a bandaged and bedridden Thompson, as Thompson mutely tries to alert everyone to the impending attack. *Black Lagoon* is a technical and artistic triumph, largely due to the haunting and imaginative camerawork of Snyder and Welbourne, and Kent's lean, fast and furious editing.

The final scenes in the Creature's caves and grotto contain the film's most atmospheric touches: subtle lighting, craggy, twisted sets, and a pervasive mist reminiscent of the most haunting Golden Age landscapes. A particular highlight is the way Snyder lights the water in the flooded grotto so that it reflects off the rocks, creating a surreal sense of distortion that adds to the spookery. Once the grotto scene is set, he then delivers a medium shot of the Creature rising from a shallow pool of mist-shrouded water—an homage both to the Golden Age Gothics, and to the scene in *King Kong* in which the man-eating serpent ascends from the foggy, hellish marshland to attack Denham and his crew. Welbourne's camera consistently conveys and plays upon our fear of the unknown and what lies just below the surface of placid waters. His technique was not lost on the makers of *Jaws* and its sequels and innumerable rip-offs. (In fact, Steven Spielberg has repeatedly cited *Black Lagoon*'s influence on the making of his famous shark attack film.)

Black Lagoon's sound effects and music cannot be underestimated. The film's thunderous, ominous music score immediately commands audience attention. It was composed by three cinema stalwarts: Hans J. Salter (who created the memorable, haunting scores for Universal's Silver Age Classics *Son of Frankenstein* [1939], *The Wolf Man* [1941], *The Ghost of Frankenstein* [1942] *et al.*), Herman Stein and a young Henry Mancini. The score is pervaded by Stein's now-famous, crescendoing three-note Creature theme—which was used in the two sequels and which indelibly identifies the Creature with his audience. Salter, Stein and Mancini also furnish atmospheric music throughout the film's many eerie underwater scenes—and the Gill Man's three-note theme is used to heighten the suspense whenever the monster, or one of his webbed extremities, appears on screen.

Black Lagoon's eeriness is equally dependent on sound effects. Especially prevalent are sinister jungle sounds: splashing waves, high-pitched bird calls and those throaty, unnerving Creature growls. The sound effects contribute much to the film's sense of suspense, the tense interludes between Creature scenes and the fear of the unknown that pervades *Black Lagoon*: an unmistakable influence on the way sound effects heightened underwater terror in countless *Black Lagoon* rip-offs and, later, in *Jaws*.

Though *Black Lagoon*'s greatness is marked by its technicians, the film is enhanced by the natural, believable acting of its solid cast. Richard Carlson, so stoic and natural in *It Came from Outer Space*, reprises the role of the serious scientific academic in his portrayal of David Reed. Reed gives us the Creature's evolutionary origins, providing us with the biologic linchpin of the monster's existence. Reed, like Carlson's John Putnam in *It Came from Outer Space*, is determined to solve the film's scientific mystery: What is this Creature, where did it come from and what are its human antecedents? Carlson's Reed is *Black Lagoon*'s scientific conscience—another echo of his performance in *It Came from Outer Space*. It's Reed who fights to preserve the Creature and prevent its exploitation (or destruction) at the hands of Richard Denning's greedy Mark Williams. Of course, the film implies that Reed and Williams are romantic rivals, vying for the affections of Julie Adams's Kay Lawrence. But the antagonism turns professional as each man has different designs on the Creature. This clash between Denning's flamboyant showman and Carlson's academician is, according to co-scripter Arthur Ross, the dramatic core of the film. In an interview with Tom Weaver, Ross stated that the animus between Carlson and Denning was

> in essence, the two different attitudes toward nature—the aggressive person feels nature is something that you use and exploit, take advantage of, turn to your own needs regardless of the consequences, and the enlightened scientist says, "You try to extrapolate as much as you can from what is natural in our world without really attacking or exploiting it." Those were the essential dominating dramatic points that were made in *Creature from the Black Lagoon*.

In addition, both actors convey this tension superbly. Williams' speech about capturing the Creature embodies his character's avarice: As he sits in the rowboat with harpoon gun at the ready, eyes darting and lips pursing, he exclaims, "We must have the *proof*!" On the other hand, Reed is both a model of reserve and academic passion as he begs Williams to leave the Creature alone: "We didn't come here to fight monsters! We're not equipped for it!" In another scene, Reed chides Williams for harpooning the Creature: "Why did you shoot? You weren't attacked!" Carlson's calm, measured style counters Denning's greed and also provides the crucial sympathetic link between the Creature and the audience. Like his Putnam in *It Came from Outer Space*, Carlson's Reed is bent on protecting and preserving the alien in his midst. Yet, as Reed slowly realizes he must *indeed* fight a monster, his enthusiasm surfaces. Note Carlson's zeal as he develops his idea to stun the Creature with a spray gun full of rotenone. Reed finally develops into the film's stalwart but reluctant hero as he drives off the attacking Creature with the rotenone and, later, enters the Creature's grotto to rescue Kay.

Adams also shines as the beautiful heroine, Kay Lawrence. She exudes a natural, relaxed quality, augmented by a sense of solidity and strength. She also seems to have more savvy than the average '50s horror heroine—even displaying some biological knowledge to offset Carlson's expertise. Adams carries herself with delicacy and poise, a lost art among today's leading ladies.

Veteran B stalwart Nestor Paiva adds some welcome "local color" to the film as Lucas, captain of the *Rita*. His genial, grizzled style, marked by a half-smoked (half-chewed?) cigar firmly implanted in his mouth, offsets the tension between Carlson and Denning. Paiva is especially adept at countering Denning's pretensions. When Denning angrily confronts Paiva and orders him to remain in the Black Lagoon after repeated attacks by the Creature, Paiva whips out a knife, puts the point under Denning's chin and ominously grins, "You weesh to say something, meester? Huh?" Audiences in 1954 probably cheered at this scene.

Finally, the two uncredited actors who play the Gill Man, Ricou Browning and Ben Chapman, are essential to the movie's iconography. Browning's wonderful balletic swimming makes this monster a thing of beauty, grace and yes, style. Indeed, the Creature's humanity—and the audience's sympathy—are invoked by the "water ballet" sequence with Adams and her double Ginger Stanley. This sense of sympathy is accentuated by Chapman, who conveys the Creature on land as somewhat clumsy, lumbering and lovesick.

And Chapman's act of gasping for air while in the Creature suit is scientifically sound—but also augments the sense of pity we feel for him. Indeed, the film's final scene, with Chapman gasping for air as he staggers toward the water after being shot, is one of the most pathetic and touching images of 1950s horror. Again *King Kong* is invoked—both the scene in which Kong is stunned by a gas bomb and struggles for consciousness, and the sad finale atop the Empire State Building.

Much has been written about Milicent Patrick's brilliant and influential design for the Creature's suit. But Browning and Chapman brought the suit to life, and gave us a monster both beautiful and terrifying to behold. At the same time, both men underscored the Creature's endearing pathos as a misfit and victim of man's inhumanity—a quality inherent in our greatest movie monsters. As director Jack Arnold said in a *Cinefantastique* interview, "I set out to make the Creature a very sympathetic character. He's violent because he's provoked into violence. Inherent in the character is the statement that all of us have violence within, and if provoked, are capable of any bizarre retaliation. If let alone, and understood, that's when we overcome the primeval urges that we all are cursed with."

From the memorable design of its monster to its brilliant underwater photography, *Creature from the Black Lagoon* is a triumph of film technology. It also served as inspiration for two sequels and innumerable imitators: *The Monster of Piedras Blancas* (1959), *Destination Inner Space* (1966) and *Humanoids from the Deep* (1980) immediately come to mind. And dare we say Paul Blaisdell and his ingenious 1950s monster creations for American International Pictures might have been lost without *Black Lagoon*'s inspiration. But the film ultimately stands as an example of how a moderate budget can still yield high adventure, a tight, no-nonsense storyline, and serious, believable performances from a carefully assembled cast. Audiences in 1954 heartily agreed—so much so that another cycle of Universal's sequelitis was born.

> It is made very clear at the end of *Creature from the Black Lagoon* that the gill-man is probably, but not necessarily, deceased. You can already see ahead to "Son of the Creature."—from *Black Lagoon*'s *New York Herald Tribune* review

REVENGE OF THE CREATURE

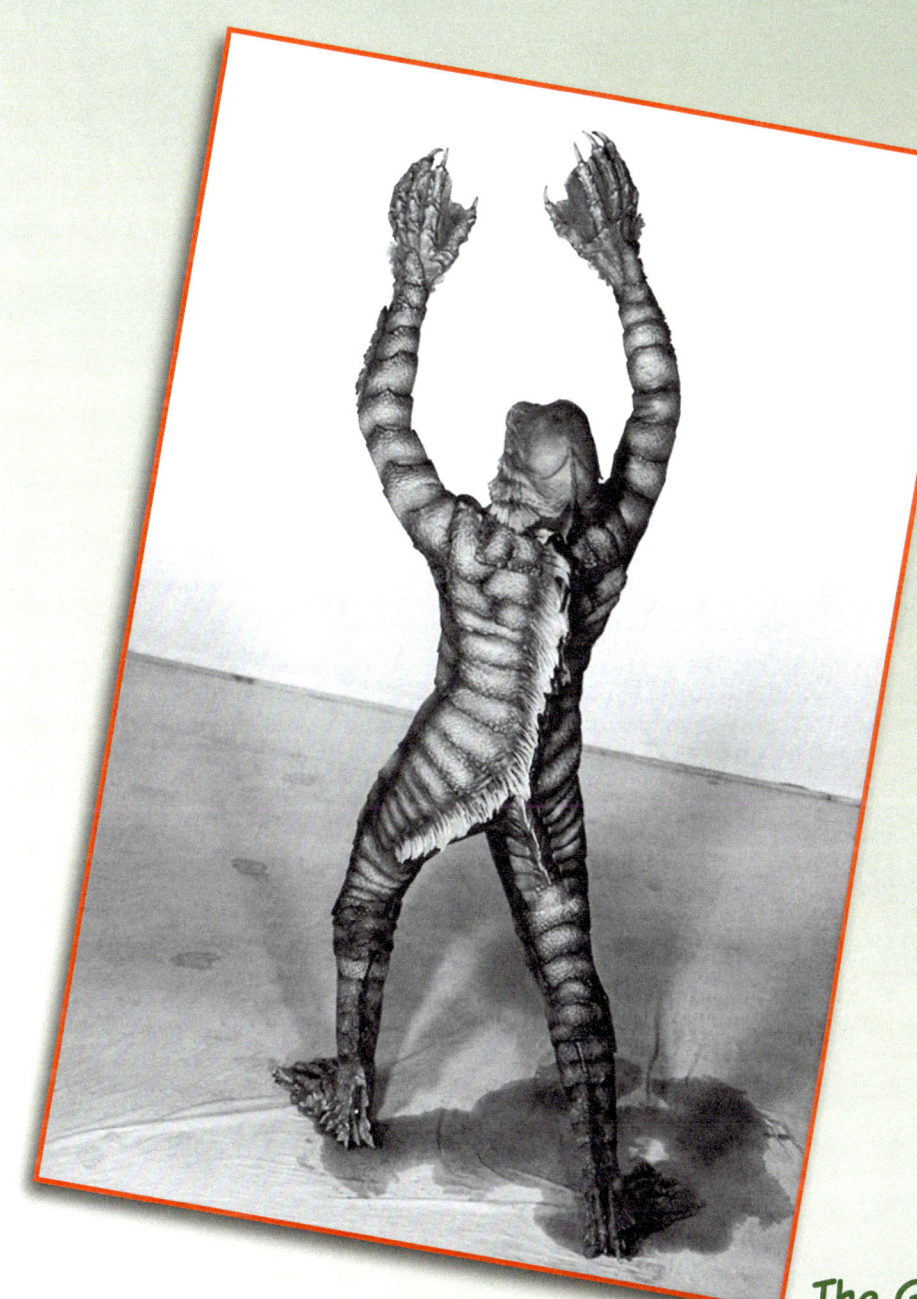

2

The Gill Man's back!

Revenge of the Creature Full Credit Information

CREDITS: Produced by William Alland; Directed by Jack Arnold; Screenplay: Martin Berkeley; Story: William Alland; Photography: Charles S. Welbourne [aka "Scotty" Welbourne]; Editor: Paul Weatherwax; Art Directors: Alexander Golitzen and Alfred Sweeney; Set Decorators: Russell A. Gausman and Julia Heron; Sound: Leslie I. Carey and Jack Bolger; Music Supervisor: Joseph Gershenson; Gowns: Jay A. Morley, Jr.; Makeup: Bud Westmore; Hair Stylist: Joan St. Oegger; Assistant Director: Fred Frank; **Uncredited:** Original Music: William Lava, Herman Stein and Henry Mancini; Tracked Music: Hans J. Salter, Herman Stein, Henry Mancini, Milton Rosen, Frank Skinner, Nick Nuzzi, Milton Rosen, Everett Carter, Don Raye, Gene de Paul and Pat Johnson; Unit Production Managers: Russ Haverick and Edward Dodds; Second Assistant Director: Dolph Zimmer; Script Clerks: Dixie McCoy and Hughes (Dorothy Hughes?); Assistant Cameramen: Walter Bluemel and Mellatt/Melott? (Mark Marlatt?); Camera Operator: L. Ward (Lloyd Ward?); Extra Camera: Ted Saizis and Blache (Irwin Blache?); Extra Assistant Cameraman: Vincent Saizis; Process Crew Cameraman: Stine (Clifford Stine?); Still Photographers: Glenn Kirkpatrick and Sherman Clark; Camera Mechanic: F. McConihay; Sound Editors: Al Kennedy and Ben Hendricks; Key Grip: Jack Flesher; Grips: E. Jones (Ed Jones?) and S. Vanzanten/Van Zanten?; Gaffer: T. Bellah (Tex Bellah?); Best Boy: L. Hopton (Lyman Hopton?); Electrician: H. Honn; Generator Operator: H. Spear; First Prop Man: Solly Martino; Prop Shop Man: D. Wolz; Wardrobe Man: M. Tierney (Michael Tierney?); Wardrobe Woman: M. Bunch (Martha Bunch?); Hair Stylist: Lillian Burkhart; Body Makeup Woman: B. Craven (Beverly Cravens?); Cashier: M. Epstein; Propmaker: Frank Brendel; First Aid Men: R.A. Guyer and Jerry Parker; Technician: Ledge Haddow; Assistant Prop Man: Bud Laraby; Sound Recordist: Donald Cunliffe; Mike Man: F. Wilkinson (Frank H. Wilkinson?); Cable Man: Moran (Harry Moran?); Publicist: Robert Sill; Coordinator: Ray Gockel; Safety Divers: Charles McNabb and Shirley Woolery; Stand-in for John Agar: Joe Walls; Stand-in for Lori Nelson: Barbara Jones; Photo Double for Lori Nelson: Edna Ryan; Stand-in: Paul Mathews; Florida Extras Casting: Maude Hecht and Charlotte Kaye; Dog Provider: Henry East; **September 28 Added Scenes:** Director: Joseph Pevney; Writer: *probably* Richard Alan Simmons; Photography: Glassberg (Irving Glassberg?); Art Director: Smith (Robert E. Smith?); Set Dresser: Austin (John Austin?); Editor: Paul Weatherwax; Camera Operator: Dodds (William Dodds?); Assistant Cameramen: Walter Bluemel, Williams (Walter Williams?); Unit Manager: Dodds (Edward Dodds?); Assistant Director: G. McLean (Gordon McLean?); Second Assistant Director: J. Cunningham (Jack Cunningham?); Script Clerk: Hughes (Dorothy Hughes?); First Grip: Brown (Everett Brown?); Second Grip: Jones (Ed Jones?); Gaffer: Kurland (Norton Kurland?); Best Boy: Harris; First Prop Man: Solly Martino; Assistant Prop Man: Gunstrom (Harry Grundstrum?); Makeup: F. Prehoda (Frank Prehoda?); Mixer: Jowett (Corson Jowett?); Sound Recorder: Swartz (James Swartz?); Mike Man: Gorback (Frank Gorback?); Cable Man: Perry; **Per Tom Hennesy:** Creature Costume: Jack Kevan, Tom Case and Beau Hickman; 82 minutes.

CAST: John Agar (*Prof. Clete Ferguson*), Lori Nelson (*Helen Dobson*), John Bromfield (*Joe Hayes*), Nestor Paiva (*Lucas*), Grandon Rhodes (*Jackson Foster*), Dave Willock (*Lou Gibson*), Robert B. Williams (*George Johnson*), Charles R. Cane (*Captain of Police*), Flippy the "Educated" Porpoise (*Himself*); **Uncredited:** Tom Hennesy (*The Gill Man/Oceanarium Diver*), Ricou Browning (*The Gill Man/Laboratory Assistant*), Robert Nelson (*Dr. McCuller*), Diane De Laire (*Miss Abbott*), Clint Eastwood (*Jennings*), Betty Jane Howarth (*Screaming Oceanarium Onlooker*), Don C. Harvey (*Mac—Group Leader*), Robert Wehling (*Joe—Searchlight Operator*), Sydney Mason (*Police Radio Announcer*), Jack Gargan (*Police Launch Skipper*), Charles Victor (*Police Launch Helmsman*), Ned Le Fevre (*Radio Newscaster*), Brett Halsey (*Pete*), Robert Hoy (*Charlie*), Charles Gibb, Mike Doyle (*Cops on Beach*), Bill Baldwin (*Voice of Police Dispatcher*), Ken Peters (*WNTV Announcer*), Wallace Mussallem (*Rita II Crew Member*), James Fisher (*Radio Announcer-Interviewer on Receiving Tank Promenade*), Jere Beery, Sr. (*Photographer on Receiving Tank Promenade*), Steve Wehking (*Reporter on Receiving Tank Promenade*), Gloria Selph (*Ocean Harbor Patron*), Richard O. Watson (*Ocean Harbor Patron Who Knocks Over the Creature Standee*), John Carcaba, Mildred Baskin, Mary Blackmer (*Running Patrons at Ocean Harbor*), Sally Baskin (*Running Child at Ocean Harbor*), Judeena Blackmer (*Running-and-Falling Child at Ocean Harbor*), Julian Fant, Pat Powers (*Smoochers in Convertible*), Bill Young (*Policeman Who Interrupts Smoochers*), Loretta Agar (*Screaming Woman on Boat*), Don House, Maria Gardner (*Bits*), Robert Lee Tinney (*John Agar's Double*), Ginger Stanley (*Lori Nelson's Double*); **Per Universal publicity blurbs:** Jack Brandon, Harry Neill (*Photographers*), Faye Weathersby, Melissa Butcher (*Girls on Beach*); **Per Universal Weekly Layoff Reports:** Clint Eastwood, David Janssen, Race Gentry, John Saxon, William Reynolds (*Voices*); **Per Tom Hennesy:** John Lamb (*Diver*); **In footage that may not have made the final cut:** John Lamb (*The Gill Man*).

Production History
By Tom Weaver

KAY: Do you suppose [the Creature] remembers Mark's attack and—and seeks *revenge*?
MARK: I welcome it!—dialogue from *Creature from the Black Lagoon*

In *Creature from the Black Lagoon*, the Gill Man did get a measure of payback against the humans who arrived uninvited in his edenic Black Lagoon and disrupted his solitary but satisfactory existence. And that was just a warm-up…

> Since *Creature from the Black Lagoon* will probably be a $2,000,000 grosser, Universal-International has already started Martin Berkeley on a script for a follow-up feature and re-engaged director Jack Arnold, who made the other film, besides assigning William Alland to produce. Studio feels it has another Frankenstein monster, Dracula, Wolf Man potential in the new horror manifestation.

So wrote Edwin Schallert, drama editor of *The Los Angeles Times*, in his April 15, 1954, column—but the idea that the web-footed wonder was sequel-worthy had occurred to producer Alland long before the successful 1954 release of *Creature from the Black Lagoon*. In fact, long before the *production* of *Creature from the Black Lagoon*. In fact, before the first word of the first *Creature from the Black Lagoon* screenplay had been written!

By December 1952, when the ink was still wet on Maurice Zimm's *Black Lagoon* treatment, Alland had already decided that one of the things that had to change was Zimm's ending in which the Gill Man is devoured by piranha. Alland foresaw the advisability of keeping the frog-like fellow alive, or at least leaving his fate in doubt, in order to have the freedom to let him continue into sequels.

On February 25, 1954, around the time of *Black Lagoon*'s first playdates, the hiring of Berkeley as sequel-writer was discussed at the meeting of Universal's Operating Committee. According to the minutes, "We have an agreement employing him to write a treatment of not less than 40 pages on 'Black Lagoon Sequel.' Treatment is to be delivered within 4 weeks from February 24, 1954, and compensation will be payable at the rate of ⅓ upon execution of agreement, ⅓ at the end of two weeks and ⅓ upon delivery of treatment." Berkeley earned his money early: His treatment is dated March 19. Location shooting at Marineland, Florida's, Marine Studios, "The World's First Oceanarium," was obviously already under consideration, because that's where much of this treatment (and his eventual script, and the eventual movie) is set. Apparently Berkeley, or *some*one connected with the project, even researched the layout of the place, because in the treatment a scene description of a plane's ar-

The Hollywood Reporter's Jack Moffitt sagely pointed out in his Revenge of the Creature *review, "Movie heroes survive by clean living, but movie monsters can only prolong their lives by making money." Make money* Creature from the Black Lagoon *did, paving the way for* Revenge.

rival at Marineland is followed by the note that a river "wide enough for the landing of a plane, is at the back door of Marineland, some 200 feet away."[1]

Berkeley was born on August 21, 1904, in a rough part of "The Borough of Churches," Brooklyn, New York. According to an article on the writer in a 1938 *New York Journal-American*, it was a neighborhood where he saw "gangsterdom and hoodlumism" at first hand (Al Capone was born ten blocks from the Berkeley family's residence in the Grand Street section), and already by 1938, four of the boys with whom Berkeley went to school had "'burned' for murder." By the time he was in his early twenties, he was acting on Broadway; by his early thirties, he had written a pair of Broadway plays, both short-lived. One of them, 1938's *Roosty*, was the basis for the movie *The Penalty* (1941) starring Edward Arnold and Lionel Barrymore. In 1943, that crime drama was "disapproved for all export" by the Los Angeles Board of Review of the Office of Censorship because it was "lawless throughout, with killings, juvenile delinquency, and other undesirable features." By that time, 1943, Berkeley was laboring in the B-movie vineyards as a screenwriter himself. Soon he was also writing for TV.

Life around the Berkeley household changed in April 1951 when screenwriter Richard Collins told the House Un-American Activities Committee that Berkeley was a former Communist.[2] And indeed he was, Berkeley himself told HUAC in September; he said he was active in the party from 1937 to 1943 but had "consistently fought" the Communists from '43 until the present time. According to Berkeley, he was testifying despite three anonymous threats of bodily harm to him and his family (received via phone at his Pacoima home) if he should name names not previously mentioned to the committee. But "name names" he did, those of more than 100 persons, many prominent on Broadway or in Hollywood, whom he said he had known positively as party members. Afterwards, Berkeley's TV- and movie-writing career resumed; his big-screen fortes were Westerns and sci-fi (*Revenge of the Creature*, *Tarantula* [1955], *The Deadly Mantis* [1957], all three Alland productions), while his strong suits on TV were Westerns and anthology series. Robert M. Fresco, co-writer of *Tarantula*, told me:

> Martin Berkeley—Marty Berkowitz. He was another person who was on the Universal payroll to keep them looking good in the eyes of the John Waynes and Adolphe Menjous and the Ward Bonds. Marty Berkeley finked on all the Screen Writers Guild guys. He was a dirty word to most people. He was a big Brooklyn kid trying to be English. Tattersalls and tweeds, tweeds that had enough hair so you had to comb 'em every two days. Bespoke shoes. Suits from Savile Row. Think of Rex Harrison as Henry Higgins. A really horsy English gentleman—he played the part perfectly, you would have thought that he was born in Buckinghamshire instead of Brooklyn [*laughs*]. And he had one of the most beautiful automobiles. Parked in the parking lot next to my old Ford, he had a Jaguar sedan, as big as the old Bentleys. I went to his home once, and he had a picture of Hitler over the john and he had an American flag next to his desk, just in case anybody questioned.

According to an August 2012 *Huffington Post* (website) story by Marcus Baram, Ray Bradbury was the subject of an FBI investigation in the 1960s because of alleged Communist leanings—and the finger had been pointed at him by guess-who. The story continued:

> Bradbury's suspected activity was reported to the bureau by screenwriter Martin Berkeley, who claimed that science fiction writers were prone to being Communists and that the genre was uniquely capable of indoctrinating readers in Communist ideologies. "He noted that some of Bradbury's stories have been definitely slanted against the United States and its capitalistic form of government," according to the file.
>
> A popular writer like Bradbury was positioned to "spread poison" about U.S. political institutions, Berkeley told the FBI. "Informant stated that the general aim of these science fiction writers is to frighten the people into a state of paralysis or psychological incompetence bordering on hysteria which would make it very possible to conduct a Third World War … which the American people would seriously believe could not be won since their morale had been seriously destroyed."

Berkeley's May 6, 1979, passing in Florida wasn't mentioned by *Variety* or by any other show biz source that I could locate. Fast-forward to 1999 and the publication of film historian Thomas Doherty's "The Price of Kazan's 'Crime,'" a newspaper article on director Elia Kazan—who had his own well-documented "history" with HUAC. The piece was read by Berkeley's son William D. Berkeley of Newton, Massachusetts, who shared some thoughts in the Letters to the Editor section of *The Boston Globe*:

> My father, Martin Berkeley, a good commercial screenwriter unencumbered with Kazan's enormous creative talents, did have in common with the better-known director an infamous history of naming names before the House Un-American Activities Committee. In fact, he named more of his fellow filmmakers than any other "friendly witness" of that unfortunate time.
>
> It would be a mistake for anyone to think that those who chose to respond to the paranoia of McCarthyism by cooperating with HUAC and other Red-baiting agencies did so solely to save their own careers.
>
> My father's brief flirtation with the Communists took place in the 1930s. He himself was named in the early 1950s. During my late teens, our household included a seemingly permanent visitor—the FBI agent assigned to both guard my father and elicit more information from him.
>
> I'm certain that saving his own skin was at least part of

the motivation my father had for informing on his friends. But we also have to remember that the Russian Communists who captured the minds and hearts of American intellectuals in the 1930s and helped the United States win the war in the 1940s began to be seen in the 1950s for the totalitarians they were.

During his declining years, my father's own personal politics reflected the schizophrenia of those difficult times. He was an extreme pro–labor liberal on domestic affairs and a virulent anti–Communist on international issues. I am convinced that a large part of his naming names was a genuine feeling of patriotism, however misguided that may seem with the wisdom hindsight affords.

The final irony is that it has been the "friendly witnesses" like Kazan and my father who have attracted the wrath of contemporary liberal intellectuals. Where is the criticism of the movie moguls of that time who enforced the HUAC blacklists? Management, once again, misbehaves with impunity while labor suffers the consequences.

Just days before Berkeley turned in his treatment for the *Black Lagoon* sequel, Universal execs received good news about the ticket sales of the first film: As encapsulated in a New York–datelined *Hollywood Reporter* item of March 18:

> Universal-International's new record-breaking horror film, which opened at the Paramount and Fenway theaters in Boston on Tuesday to launch more than 100 dates in the New England territory, rolled up more than $5000 for one of the biggest opening days in the history of the two theaters.
> The picture also opened at the Paramount Theatre in Atlanta last Thursday, launching a territorial saturation opening in that area, and set a new first-week U-I record of $14,500, topping by almost $4000 any previous U-I film to play the house.
> *Creature from the Black Lagoon* is scheduled to have 22 territorial saturation playoffs during the next few weeks, utilizing coordinated promotional television, radio and newspapers.

Universal and director Jack Arnold had an approximately two-year association in which he megged their *Girls in the Night, It Came from Outer Space, The Glass Web* (all 1953) and *Black Lagoon*; but then, according to a March 9, 1954, *Variety* story, they parted company. The night before the *Variety* story ran, a studio spokesman said that there were no negotiations on with Arnold for any future services, but "a possibility exists he may be asked back to direct other scientifiction pix." In April he was invited to do just that: direct the movie then being called "*Black Lagoon* Sequel."

At about that same time, "Scotty" Welbourne, photographer (and, some would say, director) of *Black Lagoon*'s Wakulla Springs location footage, received from Universal general production manager Gilbert Kurland a letter asking if he would be available to shoot the sequel. In a May 4 reply, Welbourne said he was quite sure he would be free to do so. Evidently in a chatty mood, Welbourne lingered at his typewriter a while longer, adding,

> Stopped for a quick swim with Ricky [Ricou Browning] while passing through Wakulla Springs and discovered that the underwater growth (similar to seaweed) that we used to such an advantage in *Black Lagoon* is entirely gone, leaving it with quite a bare look. However the eelgrass and tree logs are very much the same. Just thought I would mention this in case you are writing your script around this type of terrain.

He continued by mentioning that he had recently written, directed and photographed a four-reel color adventure story about a couple of deep sea divers and a girl stowaway; and then went on: "Most of the Florida gang used on *Black Lagoon* and the Disney show [1954's *20000 Leagues Under the Sea*] have become a little difficult. So in shooting my own picture with my own money I have had to devise ways and means of cutting corners and still obtain the same result. If any of the knowledge I have gained can be of any advantage to you I will be glad to do anything I can."

Kurland next reached out to the Creature himself, Ricou Browning—but not to offer him the opportunity to reprise his role. In a May 13 letter to Browning (then residing at 401 Roosevelt Drive in Tallahassee) he wrote,

> At this time we are planning to make a sequel of [*sic*] the picture *Creature from the Black Lagoon* starting about the 15th of June at St. Augustine, Florida. We are going to use a man who is six foot six tall [*sic*] and weighs about 220 pounds, as, in this picture, the creature has more work above water and it is necessary for him to appear larger.[3]
> I am writing you to see if you might be interested in working with us at St. Augustine helping with the creature and doing odd and end jobs [*sic*] underwater. Therefore, if you are interested, write me by return mail giving me your telephone number and I will discuss what I have in mind more fully with you at that time.
> Trusting you are enjoying good health.
> Sincerely yours,
> Gilbert Kurland

In 2013 I showed a copy of this letter to Browning, who said he has no memory of ever receiving it. He distinctly remembered that the movie was already in production at Marine Studios when he was telephoned and offered the Creature role; we'll get to that story in a bit.

By this point, the spring of 1954, the original *Creature from the Black Lagoon* was part of a group of movies that were making Hollywood history: According to a New York–bylined May 3, 1954, article in *Variety*,

> A record $4,935,000 in foreign and domestic billings were grabbed by Universal in the wind-up week of ... sales drives which ended May 1.
> This is the highest number of billings for Universal and is believed to be the highest single-week billings in film industry history.

Eye-yi-yi! The heads made for Revenge's *topside and water Creatures were new and rather different sculpts, with eyes that look like tanning bed goggles, not at all organic. Here the Gill Man appears to be highly offended that most fans have never liked his new look.*

Results were accomplished primarily by U's "Golden Dozen," topped by *The Glenn Miller Story*.... Other pictures included *Yankee Pasha, Creature from the Black Lagoon, Saskatchewan* and *Rails Into Laramie*.

On May 11, Kurland reported to the Operating Committee that he had "engaged one man and lined up a second to portray the Gill Man" in the sequel, and that their full-body costumes were currently being designed and built. Presumably the two unnamed men were the two men who *had* the jobs at the start of shooting, diver John Lamb and stuntman Tom Hennesy.[4] A bit later in *Revenge*'s production history, a memo indicated that $300 a week would be the salary of both Lamb ("Gill Man #1"), scheduled to work from May 5 to August 2, and Hennesy ("Gill Man #2"), working from June 5 to August 2.

"I was called out to Universal for an interview with the producer, Bill Alland," Hennesy said in our 1994 interview:

> I had a *couple* of interviews with him—I had to wear a swimsuit and so forth, so that he could determine how I would look in the Creature suit. I was hired on the basis of those interviews, apparently, and on the basis of my experience as a stuntman and actor. I then started to work [on the Creature costume] with the fellows in the makeup department, like Bud Westmore, who I knew very well. Bud and Jack Kevan and Tom Case and Beau Hickman were the ones who I worked with, mostly.

According to Bob Burns, the Gill Man suits for this movie were made very differently than the *Black Lagoon* suits: Full-body casts, front and back, were made of Hennesy and Lamb, from the neck clear down to the ankles. Using the resultant molds, front-and-back Gill Man suit halves were created and put together. Burns said, "Doing it that way was a lot easier and a lot faster than doing it piecemeal, which was how they did it for the first movie. *That* took forever." A *Creature Walks* photo of this new procedure in progress can be found in that movie's chapter.

On May 17 or 18 (sources differ), Alland, Arnold and unit production manager Edward Dodds departed for Florida to scout locations. Within days, they had completed arrangements with representatives of Marine Studios, located on the ocean shore in north Flagler County, and received a promise of cooperation in shooting the new Creature movie there. (In *Revenge*, the seaquarium where the story takes place is called Ocean Harbor.) At that time, this deep-sea zoo was one of the state's top tourist destinations, drawing as many as 500,000 visitors annually.

Throughout the 1950s, Marineland[5] was *home* to Sally Baskin, the daughter of Tom and Mildred Baskin who operated Marine Studios' motel, the Marine Village Court, which was a few hundred feet south of Marine Studios on Ocean Boulevard. The Marine Village Court was the Universal troupe's headquarters during their Marineland shooting. "I was the only child raised at Marineland—I was there from 1947 until 1960," said Sally, who was 12 years old when the Gill Man came a-calling.

"Marine Studios was begun by several men," Sally told me:

> There was Cornelius Vanderbilt Whitney, there was his cousin W. Douglas Burden, there was Ilya Tolstoy [grandson of novelist Leo Tolstoy] and there was Sherman Pratt.[6] What had happened was, they'd been in the jungles of somewhere-or-other and visited a friend who was making a wildlife movie, and this person had built a compound and kept the animals in it while he filmed 'em. Whitney and the others wondered, "Would this work with marine animals?"

From the 1999 book *Reel Nature—America's Romance with Wildlife on Film* we get a few more details: Gregg Mitman wrote that the impetus for "holding sea life in captivity to make its filming feasible" was Merian C. Cooper's film

2. Revenge of the Creature (1955)

A seagull's-eye view of Marine Studios (the seagull is flying south):
 1. Porpoise Stadium, where Flippy the "Educated" Porpoise performed.
 2. The rectangular oceanarium for sharks, barracuda, a Gill Man, etc.
 3. The small receiving tank where Joe "walks" the unconscious Gill Man.
 4. The round oceanarium for dolphins.
 5. The Dolphin Restaurant. To the right is Marine Studios' parking lot.
 6. The Marine Village Court where *Revenge* cast and crew stayed. To the left of it is the part of the beach where the John Agar–Lori Nelson love scene was filmed, and where the cast and crew's after-hours beach parties took place.

Chang (1927), photographed in the Thailand jungles and featuring an elephant stampede "shot within a stockade large enough not to impede the animals' actual movements and behaviors, yet small enough to allow camera operators to take action shots with relative ease. [Burden and Tolstoy] decided that a similar approach could be used to obtain underwater action shots of marine life."

The marine mammal park's founders' search for a practical location led them to the Sunshine State, as Cornelius Vanderbilt "Sonny" Whitney wrote in his 1977 memoir *High Peaks*:

> Florida, with the Gulf Stream offshore and a good year-round climate, seemed to us the best place to start exploration.... Ilya Tolstoy was dispatched to locate a site. I started, in the summer of 1936, catching large sharks off Montauk Point in the eastern tip of Long Island [New York], penning them up and studying their behavior to see whether they would survive in captivity. Douglas Burden worked with the Museum of Natural History to devise a type of harpoon with syringe and drug which could tranquilize any large creature from the sea long enough to transport it to shore and then to the projected giant oceanariums we visualized. By late summer Tolstoy returned with the great news that he had found a practical site for the type of operation we envisioned [near St. Augustine], at a spot where the inland waterways came within several hundred yards of the Atlantic Ocean.... [F]ish caught in the sea or inland waterways could be transported by boat with minimum delay to the site...
>
> The problems, however, were: a one-lane sand road from St. Augustine south, no great centers of population nearby, the site was presently flooded with brackish sea water, no telephone service, and no supply of fresh or drinkable water.

Once a few of these challenges were met, there were a variety of new ones involved in the actual building of the place, which began in May 1937. Sally Baskin continued,

> They ran into a lot of problems, including an engineering problem: They had to build tanks that would be able to hold a large capacity of water, which meant that the walls were going to be too thick for people to see through the glass portholes. So they developed a webbing system of steel rods and so on; that way, the walls didn't have to be as thick and they could put the portholes in. They also had to come up with a certain cement and a certain paint that would withstand the saltwater, and a filtration system where they could bring the water out of the ocean and get the seaweed and sand out. This must sound like a pretty big task, but they did it all within one year, which was amazing. All these engineers and workers were brought in and they put Marine Studios together.

Marine Studios was originally conceived as a way to provide a "window to the ocean" and constructed so that movie companies and still photographers could go into enclosed corridors, running at different elevations around each oceanarium's perimeter, and shoot underwater locales by aiming their cameras through any one of the corridors' 200 tempered glass portholes. (According to Burden, the portholes were arranged so that "each observer can sit comfortably in relative darkness [as if] in a motion picture theater, looking out into a brilliant world of the undersea.") Construction was finished at a cost of $500,000 and on June 23, 1938, it opened to the general public. On the day of the ribbon-cutting ceremony, the narrow A1A highway became a proverbial parking lot in both directions, as Baskin describes: "Thirty thousand people came! The cars were lined up all the way to Crescent Beach, about ten miles north. They were bumper to bumper, Model Ts, Model As and whatever else kind of cars they had! Once the owners realized they were 'onto' something here, they built a restaurant and also a motel which looked like a castle out of Disneyworld. It even had a tower room, which was the honeymoon suite."

Marineland quickly became Florida's most successful and popular tourist attraction; according to a 1939 *Life* magazine article, it drew more than 200,000 visitors its first year. Cheryl Messinger and Terran McGinnis wrote in their 2011 book *Marineland*, "Its special allure attracted a seemingly nonstop stream of scientists, writers, artists, celebrities and members of the media. For the first time, showmanship was added to the display of marine life, thanks to daring deep-sea divers and friendly sailor-clad dolphin trainers."

For a fun look at Marine Studios in its early days, catch the nine-minute color short *Marine Circus* (1939), which occasionally runs as filler on Turner Classic Movies. This "Pete Smith Specialty" begins with exterior shots of the vacation center, sunny blue skies smiling down upon it, before showing us the fish-eat-fish world below the surface of its oceanaria. With the musical accompaniment of the Strauss waltz "Roses from the South" we see sharks, dolphins, a half-ton manatee, a 500-pound giant grouper and a super-sized turtle named Grumpy, the latter becoming quite a pest to a hardhat diver who descends at feeding time with a basket of fish.[7] Narrating in his usual talking-out-of-the-side-of-his-mouth style, Smith is both humorous *and* highly informative. More on *Marine Circus* later in this chapter.

After Marine Studios had been in operation for a few years, "World War II came along and it had to be closed down due to the fact that it was right there on the coast," said Baskin:

> With German ships going up and down the Atlantic, it was a good target! They let the different animals and fish go, they drained the tanks and the Coast Guard took it over, along with the motel and the restaurant.[8]
>
> After World War II ended and Marine Studios was re-opened, some men from there came into St. Augustine to see my uncle who was the owner-manager of the Castle Warden Hotel, which is now a Ripley's Believe It or Not museum. My uncle's name was Norton Baskin and he was married to Marjorie Kinnan Rawlings, who wrote *The Yearling* [the Pulitzer Prize–winning 1938 novel]. The men asked him if he would consider coming down and being the manager of the restaurant and the motel. Once he looked into it, he said, "This is a little bit more than I want to tackle," so he suggested they contact his brother—my dad—Tom Baskin and my mom Mildred, who were then managing a little Ocala motel. When my parents were interviewed about running the motel, they told the men, "We have a three-year-old daughter," and the men said, "Oh, *that's* no problem. We'll find her a bed and a dresser!" At Marineland, I had the run of the beach and I had the run (to a point) of Marine Studios, so any time anything was happening, I was there in the middle of it! Our motel was technically the only big motel between St. Augustine Beach and south to Flagler Beach so, if there was anything going on at Marineland, movies, documentaries, *any*thing, the moviemakers stayed at the motel. Of course, that's what happened with *Revenge of the Creature*: They came in and they took over most of the rooms at the motel.

In one of those rooms was an actor who would become a top leading man of the 1950s sci-fi-monster boom; *Revenge of the Creature* was his sci-fi debut *and* his Universal debut. All but one of the movies he made as a Universal contractee were SF, ultimately prompting him to tell a studio exec that he'd like to play in normal pictures. And when the exec said he couldn't promise that would ever happen, the actor promptly "walked"!

Marry me before I go overseas and get killed!

In a car parked between a drugstore and an old ladies' home, 24-year-old John Agar used that line to propose to his 16-year-old girlfriend, actress Shirley Temple. According to her 1988 autobiography *Child Star*, Temple had met "Sergeant Jack," a "gangling Air Corps recruit," at a party and soon began going out with him. While dating Agar, she also had a *second* boyfriend, with the idea that, *this* way, neither relationship could get serious. But she failed to stick with that plan, as her lamp of love shone too bright for handsome, uniformed, brass-buttoned Agar. He wangled a 15-day pass to get married while the child bride-to-be coped with 36,900 letters commenting on the upcoming nuptials—some of them quite critical of the example she was setting for other teenagers. Tap dancer Bill "Bojangles" Robinson, who shared the screen with Temple in four of her early films (and became a loyal friend), was playing an engagement in New York and therefore unable to attend the wedding, but he did take the time to write and send Agar a cautionary missive: "You ever hurt this girl, I'll come and cut you!"

At the September 1945 wedding, wrote Temple, "benign expressions wreathed the faces of our 500 guests, some of whom I recognized." But just a few days later, her romantic world caved in: At a candlelit dinner party at the home of actor Robert Benchley, Agar danced and locked lips with a starlet-type as Temple looked on (and other guests watched *her* for her reaction). Later that night, driving home, Agar said, "Always wanted to marry a long-legged model. Not someone like you." The Agars would live most of their married life in Shirley's former "playhouse," a cottage on the Temple family grounds just 50 yards from the home of Shirley's parents; it had been built to house her collection of dolls, by 1945 nearly 2000, sent to her by fans and "dressed after the fashion of about every nationality on Earth" (*Variety*).

Once he got out of the service, Agar did a lot of hanging around the house … and golfing … and drinking … and flirting in public. The director of the Temple movie *Honeymoon* (1947) ordered him off the set for being a distraction. Just as gossip columnists were starting to jab at this jobless tail on the kite of a famous wife, Shirley's boss, producer David O. Selznick, decided that Agar was ready for the movies. Signed by Selznick at $150 a week, Agar made his debut as a cavalry lieutenant in director John Ford's *Fort Apache* (1948), a Western starring John Wayne as a cavalry captain, Henry Fonda as the ambitious new fort commander and Temple (also on loanout from Selznick, and pregnant in real life) as Fonda's daughter who falls in love with Agar. *Fort Apache* was one of the top grossers of the year but the second Temple-Agar film, RKO's turn-of-the-century comedy *Adventure in Baltimore* (1949) starring Robert Young, reportedly lost $785,000.[9] In the interim, their daughter Linda Susan was born, but not without the usual drama: One night when Temple (in the final stages of pregnancy) was sleeping, Agar drunkenly brought home a similarly sloshed redhead and they barged into her bedroom. ("Get up! Let's have a party.") And on the night that Temple realized she was about to give birth, she couldn't wake him and had to drive herself to the hospital.[10]

A regular eye- and ear-witness to all of this dysfunction at the junction was the couple's rotund cook. Fed up with Agar's treatment of Temple,

John Agar was 24 when he married actress Shirley Temple (pictured), 28 when they divorced and—D-U-I-yi-yil—30 when prison doors first slammed on him. In the decades since, and to this day, AGAR is the answer to "Mr. Shirley Temple" in countless crossword puzzles.

she spent one long night brooding and drinking out of Agar's bottle. Then, come the dawn's early light, she armed herself with a butcher knife and, hissing "You dog!," proceeded to chase Agar around the living room! Fresh out of places to run, the "dog" was cowering between the aquarium and the baby grand piano when Temple stepped in and cooled things down. Temple then of course had to dispense with the cook's services, but "I might better have fired him and kept her," she wrote in *Child Star*. "Good cooks were hard to find." She added,

> Compulsively gregarious, lacking in self-esteem, zigzagging between loving husband and insensitive wastrel—his case would be meat and potatoes for a psychologist. But despite everything, I loved him, and desperately wanted him to love me.

According to Temple, Agar simultaneously marked their third wedding anniversary, and marked *her*, with a blow that spun her around and landed her on their bedroom floor. The end of the trail for the tumultuous marriage was the door of the Los Angeles County Courthouse where on December 5, 1949, a divorce was granted. Agar's lawyer told the judge that, whenever difficulties arose during their days as man and wife, "Mr. Agar acted at all times as a gentleman."

A fannish fondness for Agar probably makes the average Monster Kid want to reject some of the foregoing stories spun by Temple in her book. (And a reader does get the impression she *is* out to belittle him: She never once calls him by his professional name, just Sergeant Jack and Jack Agar, Jr.) But Agar's pattern of subsequent behavior—demonstrated not behind closed bedroom doors but in public, and documented in newspapers, court records, etc.—give her yarns the ring of truth. For a few years following the Temple-Agar breakup, he continued to play supporting parts in movies from major studios, but then America started reading more about his drunk driving arrests and convictions than about his movie and TV career. He began playing the leads in minor indies, and also made a good showing in the early Schenck-Koch production *Shield for Murder* (1954) as an LAPD detective who learns that a brother cop (Edmond O'Brien) is guilty of robbery and murder. According to the Hollywood trade papers, Schenck-Koch wanted to put Agar under a term pact,[11] but then the actor got an offer from Universal and signed a one-year contract that commenced on June 1, 1954.

The 33-year-old actor was quickly assigned to the new 3-D Gill Man movie, and the first time he stepped in front of a Universal camera was probably June 12, when Jack Arnold made tri-dimensional underwater tests of Agar, second lead John Bromfield and Gill Man John Lamb in the studio tank, with "Scotty" Welbourne manning the cameras. (According to *Revenge of the Creature*'s Showman's Manual, athletic 6'2" Agar's swimming skills, both on the surface and underwater, led to him being chosen over other leading men for *The Golden Mistress* [1954] and for *Revenge*.)

Agar's character in *Revenge*, Clete Ferguson, may have been partially based on animal trainer Adolf Frohn, recruited by Marine Studios in 1949 to determine the extent to which a dolphin could be trained to obey commands. Frohn worked with a dolphin named Flippy[12] and achieved amazing results—so amazing that when a fully trained Flippy was unveiled to the press in 1951, he became an overnight star via magazine and newspaper coverage plus TV and newsreel exposure. Surely the man responsible, Frohn, also enjoyed a little of that celebrity spotlight. We'll

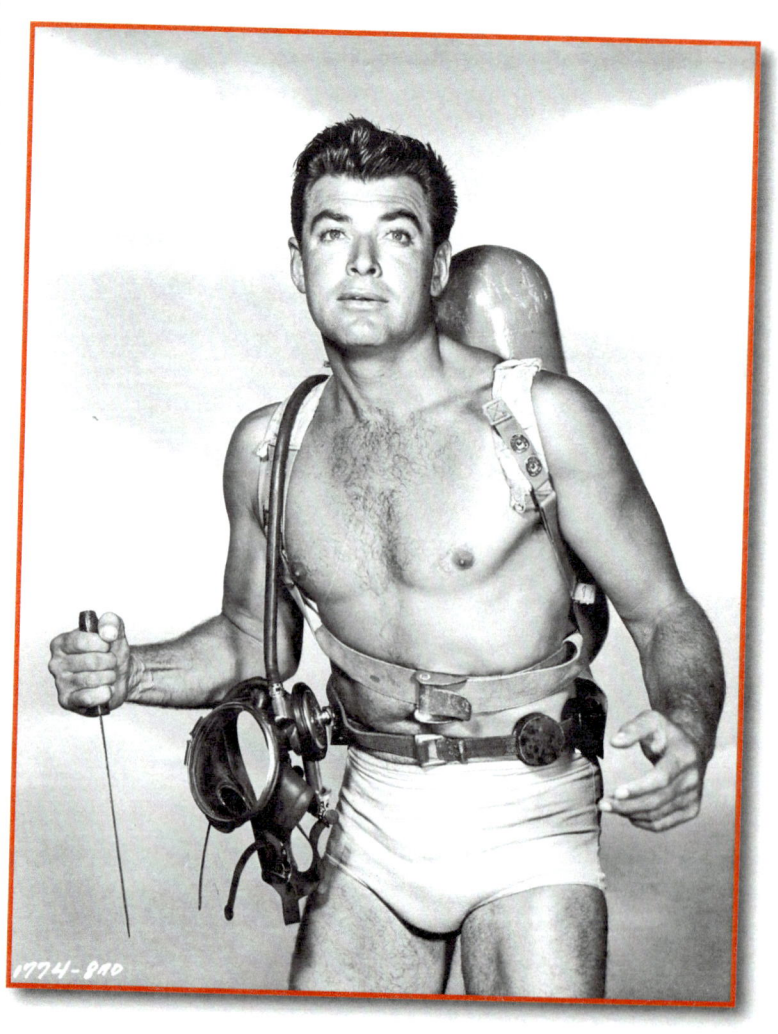

John Bromfield is ready for whatever comes at him, out of the Black Lagoon or elsewhere.

never know for sure if the character of Clete, an animal behavioralist training a Gill Man at a sea zoo, was inspired by the real-life animal behavioralist who famously trained Flippy at that same sea zoo, but to me it seems like a real possibility. Especially once I came across an article about Flippy in a 1952 issue of *Natural History* magazine. It begins,

> Discussing the accomplishments of Flippy, the trained porpoise under observation at Marine Studios, Marineland, Florida, someone commented:
> "If Flippy gets any smarter, he'll be talking."
> To which Adolf Frohn, Flippy's trainer, replied, "He does talk, but we aren't smart enough to understand him."

*Some*one involved in the writing of *Revenge of the Creature* had to have read up on Flippy and/or Frohn and found this quote, either in *Natural History* or elsewhere, because how else do we explain this dialogue exchange in the *Revenge* scene set at the Flippy exhibition?:

> HELEN (Lori Nelson): If Flippy gets any smarter, he'll start talking.
> CLETE (Agar): *He* talks all right. *We're* just not smart enough to understand him.

A line from a *Popular Mechanics* article on Flippy may also have been paraphrased for *Revenge*: In 1952, the magazine's Richard F. Dempewolff wrote, "Flippy is proving that porpoises have a brain development so advanced that it may compare with that of the dog and the chimpanzee." In the *Revenge* scene mentioned above, Clete continues, "A porpoise has a very large and well-developed brain. In fact, his intelligence lies somewhere between a chimpanzee and a dog."

Revenge was Agar's first Universal assignment under his new contract, and was Lori Nelson's *last* under *hers*. (In order for her to be in the picture,

On Universal's Stage 16 on the afternoon of June 2, 1954, Jack Arnold directed Allison Hayes (pictured) and Lori Nelson in black-and-white tests for a movie the Daily Production Report called "Sequel to Creature from Black Lagoon." We ass-u-me this means that Hayes, then a Universal contractee, was in the running for the role of Helen.

Lori Nelson was just out of her teens when she made Revenge; seven years Julie Adams' junior, she seemed like she could be the little sister of Adams' Kay Lawrence from the first Gill Man movie. Three years earlier (1951), Nelson *did* play Adams' kid sister in her debut film *Bend of the River*.

her term had to be extended via a holdover clause.) When Alland first ideated a *King Kong*–based man-fish movie back in 1952 and wrote his story treatment "The Sea Monster," he called for a blonde (as in *Kong*, with Fay Wray in blonde wig as Ann Darrow); now, with champagne blonde Nelson, he got one. Since *Black Lagoon* may have given audiences the impression that the Creature's tastes ran to brunettes (Julie Adams as Kay), *Revenge* viewers are prepped for the eventual appearance of a fair-haired leading lady (Nelson as Helen) by two lines of dialogue: When Robert B. Williams' character Johnson, sweltering aboard the *Rita II*, says he'd like a tall cold beer, John Bromfield's Joe Hayes jokes, "Or a short warm blonde." Minutes later, when Robert Nelson's Dr. McCuller barges into the animal psychology department babbling about a great new scientific discovery, Agar's Clete quips, "Whatcha got, Mac? Someone unearth a natural blonde?"

John Bromfield, who made his movie debut hunting whales in *Harpoon* (1948), hunts a much smaller but more dangerous aquatic specimen in his *Revenge* role as Joe Hayes. A freelancer, he was paid $750 a week for the two-week assignment. Agar, Nelson and Bromfield did their hair, makeup and wardrobe tests on Stage 9 on June 17; it was only one of several wardrobe test days for Nelson, who had just finished her work in the Audie Murphy Western *Destry* (1955). Welbourne was again behind the camera on the 17th, working with a crew absorbed from the tests for the upcoming Western *Man Without a Star* (1955).

At first the role of oceanarium manager George Johnson was assigned to Harvey Stephens, an oldtimer

On the eve of leaving on a 1954 European vacation, William Alland (right) got a nice send-off from several U-I colleagues, and was presented with a piece of artwork spoofing his monstrous movie achievements

with stage and screen appearances dating back decades; he'd just wrapped up a five-year run in Broadway's *South Pacific*. Ultimately that small role went to an even *older*-timer with a similar list of stage and movie credits: Grandon Rhodes was cast on July 12 and flown to Florida the next day. The career of Olan Soule began in a tent show and moved to the stage and to radio before his first day on a movie soundstage; Soule was slated to play Ocean Harbor press agent Gibson before the role was reassigned to Dave Willock.[13] By switching to Willock, the studio also saved a few bucks: Soule's price was $750 a week, and replacement Willock got only $600 a week.

In my Alland interview, he minimized his contribution to *Revenge of the Creature*—and it's true that he had a lot less input here than he did on *Black Lagoon*. He admitted that he made the Gill Man sequels reluctantly, at a time when he was producing four movies a year and "had [other] things on his mind."[14] Regarding *Revenge*, he told me,

> I don't remember being there [Marineland] for that; as a matter of fact, if I went at all, I went maybe once. Jack Arnold was directing, and I had enough confidence in him that he would do whatever the script said and that would be it.
>
> I blew that thing [*Revenge*] through my nose. Had I really wanted to do a good job, I would have done an entirely different sort of thing there.... I pretty much left both those films [*Revenge* and *The Creature Walks Among Us*] up to their directors: "Here's the script. Shoot it."

Alland had a lot more to do with *Revenge* than he remembered: The basic plot was his idea and he received a story credit[15]; he was part of the group that went to Florida to scout locations and to make arrangements with Marine Studios; and during the scriptwriting phase he consulted for several hours with Dr. Joseph A. Gengerelli, a UCLA professor of psychology. But the result of the consultation, a scene found in an early draft of the script, never made it to the screen. In that draft, Clete's first scene finds him running a rat through a testing maze; the rat has a miniature short wave radio receiver on its back, the receiver base sewed into the skin. Affixed to the base is a crystal detector with a spiral antenna and a silver mount connected by a short wire to a sharpened silver electrode which enters the brain. (This experiment was actually conducted by Gengerelli at UCLA; see the November 28, 1949, issue of *Life* magazine for details.) As the rat goes through the maze, avoiding all detours, it becomes obvious that it's being prompted by the chuckling Clete through the use of short wave.

Universal did get a start on arranging to feature a lab rats scene in the movie: In a June 9 memo, the studio's director of public relations William Gordon wrote to Alland that he'd had a phone conversation with psychologist Loh Tseng Tsai of Tulane University:

> I have arranged for us to receive from him in New York a 16mm film which covers the bulk of his experiments with rats. This will be air shipped to us so that you can quickly determine which if any of these experiments you would like to have him prepare for inclusion in your production. In this way, he can prepare the rats and the necessary apparatus for the specific film to be shot.
>
> ... A most important consideration from his standpoint is that his work be represented in a proper and dignified manner. I assured him that the purpose of the scene is to establish our leading man as a top-flight animal psychologist, and we know of no better way to dramatize this.
>
> The question as to whether or not credit shall be given to him in dialogue will be determined later.

Universal offered the good doctor $2500 plus transportation for himself and his equipment but he held out for more. As he wrote Universal,

> In view of [the] fact that six more weeks of continuous training in addition to my previous four years of work are necessary to provide you with top performance of my animals for your film, I am compelled to ask a minimum of $7500 plus air transportation and hotel accommodations. I am sure you can easily double the audience of your film by including this unique experiment of tremendous and worldwide human interest.

Perhaps Dr. Loh aimed too high and priced himself out of a job; or maybe a June 29 letter to Gordon from Dr. W.A. Young, Western Regional Director of the Humane Society, queered the deal. Having read the script, Dr. Young made it clear that the action in the animal experimentation scene "should be simulation. I am sure there are people who would be quite squeamish about such action if the actual experiment was shown." For whatever reason, this scene that Alland apparently wanted *was* dropped (which was all to the good, in the opinion of this quite squeamish animal lover).

I've talked with many people who knew Alland in the 1950s but perhaps only one from even earlier days: Actor Arthur Anderson, who as a 14-year-old in 1937 first worked with Orson Welles and later became a member of Welles' Mercury Theatre. On the subject of fellow Mercury Player Alland, he told me,

> Besides playing small parts in Orson's plays *Julius Caesar* and *The Shoemaker's Holiday*, Bill Alland was also a valuable all-around assistant to Orson on the *Mercury Theatre on the Air*, Orson's radio program. There had been a well-known Russian theater director named [Yevgeny] Vakhtangov, and for some reason Orson used to refer to Alland as Vakhtangov. During afternoon rehearsals, Studio One [at CBS] would echo with Orson's [*Anderson shouts:*] "*Vakhtangov, bring me my pineapple juice!*"

Alland was Orson's all-around assistant, always available

to bring pineapple juice or to do whatever Orson told him to do. I had no conversations with Alland, he was too busy doing things for Orson [*laughs*]! Alland and I really had nothing in common, but I had nothing against him, and I can remember observing him, that's all. [Welles' personal assistant] Bill Herz referred to Alland as Orson's toady. I just looked up "toady" in the dictionary, and a toady is a person who will do anything you want in the hope of gaining your favor. I can't say that about Alland from personal experience, but that's what everybody says about him. But when Orson later brought him to Hollywood to cast him in *Citizen Kane* [1941], that was William Alland's opportunity to make contacts, which he obviously did, and that's how he was able to make a greater success, completely independent of Orson Welles. So being yelled at turned out to be something ultimately useful: He got his start with Orson, and he got the idea for *Creature from the Black Lagoon* at one of Orson's parties. Obviously it was to his advantage to be a toady!

In the 2008 film *Me and Orson Welles*, set during the Mercury Theatre days, Zac Efron stars as a 17-year-old wannabe actor (a character based on Arthur Anderson) and, deep in the supporting cast, English actor Iain McKee plays Alland, repeatedly commanded by Welles (Christian McKay), "Vakhtangov, my pineapple juice!"

Amidst all the pre-production activity on the new Gill Man movie, the vital matter of its title was also being considered. For rather a long time, it was internally called "*Black Lagoon* Sequel," "*Creature* Sequel," "Sequel to *Black Lagoon*," "Sequel to *Creature from the Black Lagoon*" and *Return of the Creature from the Black Lagoon* as the titling can was endlessly kicked down the road. On June 4, publicity man Archie Herzoff wrote in a memo to members of his staff,

> A new title is being sought for our forthcoming sequel to *Creature from the Black Lagoon*. Inasmuch as the picture is scheduled to go into production shortly, the studio would like to resolve the question of a title as quickly as possible. The problem with a new title is that while it is of extreme importance to capitalize on the identification benefits of the previous picture, the new title must also convey the feeling that the sequel is completely new, and not a reissue of the first picture.

On June 22 a memo revealed that the movie would be called *Return of the Creature*; that title hung on throughout production, but fell by the wayside soon after.

Several drafts of Berkeley's script have passed through my hands but most of them were undated. This prevents me from presenting (as I did in the *Black Lagoon* chapter) a chronological series of script synopses showing the plot's evolution from treatment to final draft. So instead, I'll mention some of the differences between the various scripts and the finished film at appropriate points in this chapter, and in the section titled "Other Script-to-Screen Changes."

Synopsis

It is dank and fetid in the rotting jungle that borders the mysterious Lagoon. CAMERA PANS SLOWLY but reveals no sign of life and there is no sound of any living thing. It is as though death had the Lagoon in its fist.
—part of the opening paragraph of Martin Berkeley's The Return of the Creature screenplay

The credits appear on-screen and it's *deja "view"* all over again: They're typographically identical to the titles seen in *Creature from the Black Lagoon*, again they appear against a moving background of outer space gas clouds, and the Herman Stein–composed "Main Title" from *Black Lagoon* is played. Even *Black Lagoon* shots of the Amazon, its footage of Lucas (Nestor Paiva) at the wheel house and the crocodile on the log are reused—all in just the first few seconds!

Putt-putt-putting its way along the torrid Upper Amazon is the *Rita II*, captained by Lucas and carrying two passengers, husky he-man Joe Hayes (John Bromfield) and middle-aged George Johnson (Robert B. Williams). Employees of Ocean Harbor, a Florida oceanarium, they have come to capture the Gill Man and bring him back alive, for scientific study and public exhibition. When Joe catches sight of a crocodile[16] and mistakes it for the man-fish, Lucas reacts with amusement: "You think maybe that eez eet? Ho ho, *no*! The thing you are looking for can break that in two, pfffft!" That night, after dinner in a below-decks cabin, a grimfaced Lucas reminds Joe and Johnson of the score at the end of the previous year's humans vs. Gill Man slugfest: "In the end, five persons were dead. The Gill Man—still dere!"

Creature from the Black Lagoon is almost up to the 25-minute mark before our first good look at the Gill Man but in *Revenge* we get Creature action right out of the box. Just short of the eight-minute mark, during a shot of a large bird (perhaps a white stork) perched on a floating log, he surges up out of the water to grab it; seconds later, in an underwater shot, he swims toward camera and pokes his head above the surface to watch as more two-legged snakes (aboard the *Rita*

2. Revenge of the Creature (1955)

II) enter his primordial Garden of Eden. Joe dons old-fashioned "John Brown" diving equipment (large round metal helmet, canvas suit, air hose connected to a pump on the boat) and goes underwater to seal off the lagoon entrance with a net; he and Johnson talk back and forth via an intercom. No doubt remembering the last time he had "guests," an unprovoked Gill Man attacks the submerged Joe from behind. Joe's attempts to escape the Creature's clutches fail, but the men on the boat are able to drive the monster away with rifle fire. (Filmed but not used: a shot of the Gill Man taking a bullet to the shoulder.) Joe, bleeding inside his slashed suit, is hauled back aboard the boat.

Joe (his arm in a sling) and Johnson decide to take the easy way out and kayo the Gill Man by doing some "dynamite fishing" (a.k.a. "blast fishing," a real-life, usually illegal practice). Multiple metal cans of explosives dot the lagoon surface as, using a plunger, Johnson detonates them all simultaneously. Fish float to the surface, then a lifeless-looking Gill Man. We next see a telephoto of that image, in the hand of a TV newscaster who tells his audience that the Creature, still numbed by the dynamite blast, is in the process of being flown to Ocean Harbor. The scene switches to a university setting as Prof. Clete Ferguson (John Agar), director of the Department of Animal Psychology, hears from his assistant Dr. McCuller (Robert Nelson) about the capture of the Gill Man. McCuller excitedly urges Clete to get in on the Ocean Harbor action, and Clete rushes off to arrange a leave of absence.

The Gill Man arrives at Ocean Harbor aboard the seaquarium's *Porpoise III*. Joe tells park manager Foster (Grandon Rhodes) and

In Revenge, *we see this establishing shot of a building preceding the scene in Clete Ferguson's Animal Psychology lab. In real life, then ...*

... and now ... the building is the University of Southern California's Edward L. Doheny, Jr., Memorial Library, where an ocean of Universal production paperwork is stored and where much of the research for this book was done (courtesy Lucy Chase Williams).

press agent Lou (Dave Willock) that their newly arrived "big attraction" is still comatose and may not pull through. A stretcher hoist is used to get the man-fish from the boat to Ocean Harbor's shallow "receiving tank" (also known as "the flume"); the top deck of the tank is aswarm with reporters, still photographers and newsreel cameramen watching the procedure. Joe glides the face-down Gill Man back and forth across the surface in hopes that the water moving past his gills will revive him.[17] It's America's most disastrous rollout (pre–Obamacare): The Gill Man remains comatose and the watching crowd grows bored and quiet. At one point the Gill Man says to himself, "'Fraid I gotta change my name to Creature of the Edinboro Park Kiddie Pool!" Okay, that's only in the *Mystery Science Theater* version.

A radio announcer (James Fisher) with a portable mike describes the (in)action and gets a quick interview with Helen Dobson, a Belmont University science major visiting Ocean Harbor to gather material for her master's thesis on ichthyology. (The May 5, 1954, first draft screenplay upgrades her to *Dr.* Helen Dobson of Belmont University, Texas.) After about two hours of being "walked" by Joe, the Creature wakes up ornery, roaring and attacking attendants until being netted and roped. Joe is again in charge of operations when the Gill Man, still struggling against the net and ropes, is moved by divers from the receiving tank through an underwater gateway to the park's enormous oceanarium. On the bottom, a long chain runs from a ring in a steel plate to a manacle that is snapped closed around the monster's left ankle before the net is removed.

> They dared to bring him back alive from his haunts deep in the jungles of the Amazon. They dared to put him on display with the other denizens of the deep while thousands came to marvel and wonder!
> —*Revenge of the Creature* trailer narration

There's excitement in the salt air on the day that Ocean Harbor officially debuts its newest attraction, the Gill Man; the circus-type music heard in different parts of the "Creature Opening Day" scene helps create a bit of a Ringling Brothers–Gargantua the Gorilla atmosphere.[18] Helen is part of the horde of gaping patrons scrutinizing the Gill Man from corridors on the dry side of the oceanarium's large sub-waterline portholes. As though he has the ability to tell "Lori Nelson—Movie Star" from $10-a-day Florida extras, the man-fish is soon spending a lot of time giving her the glad eye. Also attracted to Helen are both Clete and Joe.

To test the Gill Man's capacity to learn, Clete and Helen begin a regular routine of donning skin diver gear and descending into the tank. The first time, Helen brings a metal basket full of food, puts it down in front of the Gill Man and, as he approaches, sternly says "Stop!" into her throat microphone; via an underwater amplifier, she can be loudly heard. As the uncomprehending Gill Man opens the cage, Clete pokes him with an electrified bull prod. To avoid further tastes of the bull prod, the Gill Man quickly learns that "Stop!" means stop, and does just that. Working together brings on romance for Clete and Helen.

One day in the oceanarium, when Helen gets too close, her scaly-armored admirer grabs her. Clete comes to her rescue with the bull prod but quickly finds himself disarmed and engaged in a life-and-death struggle. (The Gill Man tears off Clete's diving mask and air supply to give himself the upper claw, just as he did when fighting Mark Williams in *Black Lagoon*.) Helen's shouts of "Stop!" get the now-conditioned Creature to release Clete, who swims to safety with Helen. The Creature proceeds to run amok (well, to *swim* amok), breaking the chain on his ankle manacle. When he tries to climb out of the oceanarium, Joe pushes him back in with a boat hook. But in the process, Joe loses his balance and topples into the water, where the Creature throttles him and pounds his head face-first on the tank bottom. This officially begins the "Revenge" phase of the movie. He then spectacularly springs from the oceanarium bottom to the top of the wall. Scores of screaming spectators flee as the Gill Man grapples with an attendant on the promenade and then, bellowing with rage, walks out on his show biz career. He ambles through the park, out an exit, overturns a parked car, then makes his way down the beach and into the Atlantic. Standing on the promenade over the body of the fished-out Joe, Clete shakes his head to signify to Helen that he's a goner.

Several days after the Gill Man's escape, he makes a dead-of-night appearance from out of the river near the Star Motel where Helen has a room. From outside, the aqueous ogre watches through a screen door as she undresses and goes into the bathroom to take a shower. When the Gill Man enters the living room, Helen's snarling German Shepherd Chris takes a flying leap at him. Clete, also staying at the motel, hears Chris' dying howl and hurries to the scene. The Gill Man is gone, and Helen (just stepping out of the

With a nurse shark in the foreground, the Gill Man (Ricou Browning) and Helen (Lori Nelson) give each other the once-over. The glass in Marine Studios' viewing windows withstood pressures of 1800 pounds per square inch.

shower) heard nothing. The Gill Man spies on them behind a patch of palmetto, the dead dog at his feet.

When Clete and Helen decide to go on a leisurely cruise to Jacksonville aboard the *Porpoise III*, the Gill Man shows up at the wharf at departure time and begins to trail the boat up the river. The lovers dance to slow music and kiss on deck,[19] and then when the boat develops motor trouble that necessitates a stop, they go for a swim. This leads to a reprise of another scene from *Black Lagoon*, "the underwater ballet," with the Gill Man spying on them, playfully touching her foot and even swimming directly below the unsuspecting couple. At one point, Clete and Helen are underwater when they go into a tight embrace and kiss and sink to the shallow river's bottom; as the camera tilts down with them, it reveals that the Gill Man is standing just feet away, watching. After Clete and Helen go back aboard the boat, the monster tries to climb a rope hanging from the transom. When the motor starts and the boat lurches forward, he falls back into the water.

That night in Jacksonville, Clete and Helen dance at a river's-edge Southbank restaurant, "The Lobster House," and make honeyed conversation about love, Clete even quoting from 17th-century poet Sir John Suckling's "I Prithee Send Me Back My Heart"(!). Again the Gill Man inexplicably materializes, as though he's got "H-E-L-E-N" punched into his GPS. Jazz musicians are performing a hot number when he enters and lets out a bellow; *New York Times* reviewer Howard H. Thompson called the monster's "roaring invasion of a hot jam session, scattering 'cats' all over the place," the funniest scene in the picture. The Gill Man grabs Helen and dives into the river with her. Search operations begin immediately but, even with an unconscious girl tucked under one arm, the Gill Man manages to elude them. (*Harrison's Reports*: "Miss Nelson evidently has nine lives, for although she falls into the clutches of the creature and is dragged under water several times, she comes up alive.") From their moving car, two young men (Brett Halsey and Robert Hoy) see a motionless Helen lying on a moonlit beach; they pull over and rush to her side. The Creature, who had waded off-shore for a breath of fresh water, resents their intrusion and ragdolls the Good Samaritans.

Once the men's bodies are found, a cavalry of cops and civil defense men converge on the area. Men with a mobile searchlight find on the beach the unconscious Helen, again unattended as the Gill Man has had to make another brief return to the water. When he reappears in time to prevent her rescue, one searcher fires his Very pistol. Helen awakens and begins screaming as the Gill Man (dripping wet and therefore looking like he's peeing on her) picks her up and carries her away. Arriving with reinforcements, Clete repeatedly shouts "Stop!" into a loudspeaker as the Gill Man wades into the river. At last the amphibious man obediently comes to a halt and, turning to face his pursuers, sets Helen down (in the script's words) "as though she were a delicate Dresden doll." Tension fills the air as Helen inches away from the Gill Man toward Clete—and as soon as she's clear of the monster's claws, the many gathered policemen open fire. Bellowing, he turns and dives into the water as the fusillade continues. An underwater shot of the man-beast stock-still and sinking into the darkness caps the movie.

Bios from the *Black Lagoon*
By Tom Weaver

John Agar as Prof. Clete Ferguson

> I have to confess that John Agar was never one of my favorites. He always seemed ... well, a little goofy. The awkward stiff smile looked forced.—"They Did Science! —Dr. Paul Armstrong's Handy Guide to '50s Sci-Fi Heroes" by Larry Blamire, *Video Watchdog* #120

Truth be told, he sometimes *did* appear a bit goofy, especially when playing men of medicine or science in his sci-fis. But for a lot of adultolescent Monster Kids, John Agar's many drive-in monster movies, combined with his white-haired geniality at latter-day SF conventions and autograph shows, made him "tops in our book." Okay, maybe he *was* a goof ... but he was *our* goof!

John George Agar, Jr., was born in Chicago in 1921, the oldest of four children of a local meat packer. The profits of the Agar Meat Packing and Provisions Co. were enough that John grew up in an affluent atmosphere, but had to earn his own spending money ($3 a week) by rising at 4:30 a.m. and helping to herd pigs into the slaughterhouse. After the 1935 death of his dad,[20] Agar was sent to the Pawling School in Dutchess County, New York. He went into the Army in 1942 and was a 22-year-old sergeant when he met teenage actress Shirley Temple.

Their wedding at L.A.'s Wilshire Methodist Church more closely resembled an old-fashioned Hollywood premiere: Almost five hours before the ceremony, fans began to congregate on the sidewalk in front of the church. Soon more than 5000 people lined the street, held back by sawhorses and ropes as four dozen city, studio and military policemen attempted to maintain order. Robert M. Fresco, a decade later the writer of Agar's *Tarantula*, was at this time a teenager living near Wilshire, and he recalled for me that Temple's Army sergeant brother helped with the "crowd control" (i.e., pushing people around). On the Agars' wedding night, the Associated Press phoned Temple's mother and told her that Temple had been killed in an auto crash off a hilly Westwood road into a deep, rocky canyon. The following day, the AP apologized for its mistaken identification of the accident corpse.

Producer David O. Selznick offered Agar a screen test and, if he "passed" that, a course of dramatic instruction for

2. Revenge of the Creature (1955)

which Agar would be paid $150 a week.[21] "I had been making $83 a week as a buck sergeant," Agar told Lester and Irene David, authors of the book *The Shirley Temple Story*. "It seemed like taking money under false pretenses, but he wanted me and I accepted." At one point in 1946, there was a report that Jennifer Jones, Temple and Agar might star in a new screen version of *Little Women* but instead the rookie actor debuted (with special "And Introducing" billing) in the first film in director John Ford's "Cavalry Trilogy," *Fort Apache* with John Wayne, Henry Fonda and Temple. *New York Herald Tribune* reviewer Howard Barnes wrote that Temple and Agar "quite fail to make the love story more than passably credible and engaging." Sans Temple, Agar was soon ensconced in the he-man casts of two more John Wayne features, the Cavalry Trilogy's *She Wore a Yellow Ribbon* (1949) and the World War II actioner *Sands of Iwo Jima* (1949)—the latter earning "The Duke" an Oscar nomination.

Love's lily wilted and Temple won a December 1949 divorce on a charge of extreme mental cruelty; the actress had testified that Agar drank to excess, romanced other women and even drove her to thoughts of suicide. He was ordered to pay $100 a month support for their 22-month-old daughter Linda Susan. As of the last time I asked Agar about his first marriage, he hadn't spoken to Temple since the divorce, nor seen Linda Susan since she was six.

Agar continued to land acting jobs and to land in jail on drunk driving charges. At one trial, a deputy city attorney admonished the all-woman jury, "I know how women are about movie stars. You're not going to let this man off just because he's a nice-looking fellow, are you? You're not going to tell yourselves, 'Gee, I can't do that to him'?" In April 1951, he made his vaudeville debut at the Olympic Theatre in Miami, with *Variety*'s Lary complimenting him on his "pleasant, self-effacing personality" and a baritone singing voice which was "a cut above some of the screen lads." Later that month, he was back in his Windy City home town, appearing at the Oriental and getting a strong reception.

In May 1951, Agar and 28-year-old movie extra Loretta Barnett Combs went to Las Vegas to get hitched. The couple appeared before County Clerk Helen Scott Reed and asked for a marriage license, but Reed refused because it was obvious that Agar was pie-eyed. Agar denied it and pleaded for 30 minutes; Reed said that if he drank some black coffee and ran around the courthouse until he sobered up, she would grant him the license. Some time later that day, a clear-headed Agar got the license, and he and Combs said their "I do"s in the courtroom of a district judge.

Another courtroom appearance later that year was very different: In August, Agar was branded a "potential killer" by a judge who sentenced him to five months in jail for his drunk driving offenses. The judge recommended that Agar be sent to the city's prison farm where he could get "exercise, fresh air and possibly assist in the work there." A model prisoner, Agar had his term reduced to two months by the judge and was a free man by the end of October. He soon violated his probation by starting to drink again: His January 1952 return to the bottle resulted in a January 1953 return to the jug. (In the one-year interim, he did summer stock and starred in the indie feature *Man of Conflict* for

John Agar's wife Loretta stands by her man in July 1951 as he goes to court to face two drunk driving charges. She was with him at the time of one of his arrests (courtesy Photofest).

John Agar and his mustache checked out of the Crossbar Hotel (aka the Los Angeles County Jail) in May 1953 after he served 100 days of a 120-day DUI sentence. At that point, he was looking ahead to still another court appearance, for drunk driving and driving with a suspended license (courtesy Photofest).

[Makelim's lawyer] said, "Are you sure you want to sign this?" I didn't hesitate to sign it. I am willing to bet $250,000 that John will never take a drink again.... John isn't a drinking boy. I could have done the same thing he did and paid a $10 fine, but I'm not tall and handsome and I wasn't married to America's sweetheart, so he got four months in jail.

In Agar's book *On the Good Ship Hollywood*, the actor said that he began drinking heavily while doing his early movies with John Wayne and other actors who'd spend their nights and weekends lapping up lakes of liquor, and admitted that he began pulling producer-director Hal R. Makelim; more on him in a moment.) Agar told Lester and Irene David:

There were 75 other prisoners—rapists, arsonists and gunmen—in a cellblock built to house 36. I slept on a mattress placed on a stone floor. Those were dark days, the worst of my life. Two things kept me going then. Without them, I'm damn sure I would have slipped lower and lower, and eventually been destroyed. One was my wife Loretta. Loretta has been at my side ever since we were married in 1951.[22] My second source of strength was, and still is, God.

While Agar was in jail the second time, Makelim put up his bond, paid his lawyer's fees and put him under contract so that the actor would have a job when he came out. After Agar's release, producer-director-actor Hugo Haas wanted to borrow him for his upcoming production *Bait* (1954) but, knowing his rep, wrote a contract that if Agar didn't show up for work, or if he held up the picture, Makelim would have to fork over any losses on the $250,000 movie. "My attorney said he had never seen such a contract," Makelim told a United Press Hollywood correspondent:

At Marine Studios, John Agar poses with six-year-old Jere Beery, Jr. The Florida boy's father and sister had bits in the movie and he too was supposed to appear, but he blew it (courtesy Jere Beery, Jr.).

the cork even more in the wake of his split from Temple. He took full responsibility for his drinking but allowed himself one paragraph to "vent":

> I would like to say (and I know I sound vindictive and whining, but I do not mean to) that had I been a huge star like a Barrymore or an Errol Flynn or a Spencer Tracy, my drinking probably would have been covered up. After all, those guys would just trash entire bars and hotel rooms and really hurt people, but the studios would come along behind them and mop it all up, clean it all up, pay people off, make all the repairs and keep it all a secret, because those guys were big moneymakers for the studios, and so it was a wise investment for their little "escapades" to be made to disappear. I wasn't a big enough star for them to bail me out, so they didn't, and I lost my [Selznick] contract. I wasn't worth keeping. Life for me was a mess, and I was making that happen. I myself. Ironically, later on, I heard that Mr. Selznick was drinking heavily himself, so it was bitterly amusing to me that he dropped my contract and took away my livelihood when he had the same problem himself.

There will be more on the life and times of John Agar in this book's companion volume *Universal Terrors—The 1950s*.

Lori Nelson as Helen Dobson

Revenge of the Creature is filled with scenes of violence but apparently they didn't faze India's censors in 1955, because the 31 feet (approximately 20 seconds) they ordered cut from the movie weren't the least bit violent. What they found objectionable … was Lori Nelson. From a scene of the actress in her "bathing costume," 13 feet was cut; from a scene in which she wears a low-cut bodice, 18 feet was cut; and then *Revenge of the Creature* was acceptable for exhibition in Mother India. The curvy, whistle-provoking Lori had come a long ways since her first meetings (in 1950) with Universal casting people and the signing of her contract: She was then just 16 and, with studio-provided braces on her teeth, she finished high school in Universal's little red schoolhouse!

The Creature's second crush, "only child" Dixie Kay Nelson was born in Santa Fe, New Mexico; on her dad's side, her great-great uncle was General John J. Pershing, leader of World War I's American Expeditionary Forces. At two and a half, the blue-eyed moppet danced in a home town show. Later voted Santa Fe's most talented and beautiful child, she toured the state billed as Santa Fe's Shirley Temple. When she was still a tyke, the family moved to Hollywood where she worked as a photographic model (children's clothes), appeared in USO shows at veterans' hospitals, acted in little theater productions, etc. She had her first shot at a movie job when she tested for the role of Cassandra Tower in Warners' *Kings Row* (1942); she lost out because she looked too young. (Later in her career, a publicist, or *some*body, embellished this early incident, falsely claiming that she won the part but then had to bow out because of a serious blood infection and rheumatic fever.) Her parents allowed her to continue to model and act right through her teenage years as long as it didn't interfere with her schoolwork.

The Nelson family's neighbors knew of Dixie Kay's ambitions and introduced her to producer Arthur Landau, self-proclaimed discoverer of Jean Harlow, who expressed interest in casting her as Harlow in a movie account of the platinum bombshell's life and times. This went nowhere. The same neighbors brought her to the attention of agent Milo Frank, who saw possibilities in her, but Mom didn't

Four- or five-year-old Dixie Kay Nelson dressed for a dancing lesson. She still has the shoes, which are now bronzed.

want Dixie Kay making the studio rounds for interviews and screen tests instead of having a normal high school life. Finally the mother agreed to allow Frank to take her on a Saturday to MGM, to meet one of the casting people—but on the big day, they learned that the casting man had suffered an attack of appendicitis. Undeterred, Frank instead took her to Universal where a casting exec showed interest. After Universal dramatic coach Sophie Rosenstein tutored Nelson for several weekends, an audition resulted in a seven-year contract, signed on her 17th birthday.

Universal wanted to bill their newest, youngest contract player as Dorothy Nelson but she didn't care for that, and the front office allowed her to submit a list of names more to her liking. They selected one of the names she suggested, Loree (her mother's name), and she became Lori Nelson. A $75-a-week contractee, she film-debuted in what would be her best Universal picture, director Anthony Mann's *Bend of the River* (1952), the Technicolor tale of a wagon train of Missouri farmers seeking to form a settlement in Oregon (where much of the movie was shot). Julie Adams and Lori played the daughters of settler Jay C. Flippen, Julie clinching at the fadeout with star James Stewart and Lori with a pre-stardom Rock Hudson. Next she played the oldest of the 15 Kettle children in two Ma and Pa Kettle comedies, *Ma and Pa Kettle at the Fair* (released in 1952) and *Ma and Pa Kettle at Waikiki* (not released until more than three years later, in 1955).[23] The Ma and Pa Kettle movies were money magnets for Universal, not one of them making less than $2,000,000 domestically (U.S. and Canada) until *Waikiki*—and even *Waikiki* at $1.5 million, more than any of the Creature movies made domestically, was no slouch.

Lori and Tab Hunter were named 1952's most promising new stars once the votes were counted in *Photoplay*'s "Choose Your Star" poll, and then role-wise things briefly improved when she got a good part in the heart-tugging period piece *All I Desire* (1953): Under Douglas Sirk's direction she played a headstrong small-town gal whose mother (Barbara Stanwyck) is returning to her family after years of estrangement. "Miss Nelson, given her first real opportunity, proves she is a good actress as well as a looker," wrote a *Hollywood Reporter* reviewer.[24] Mostly, however, she continued to play thankless roles in the company's bread-and-butter pictures.

For a long spell, Nelson was on loanout to RKO for the deep-sea diving adventure *Underwater!* (1955), returning to Universal to find that some shuffling-of-personnel had gone on in her absence: "When I came back," she told me, "I knew practically no one and practically no one knew me!" She left after two more pictures, *Destry* and *Revenge of the Creature*. She approached the latter warily: In July 1998, as part of a FANEX panel of oldie sci-fi stars, she told an audience:

> Along toward the end, all of a sudden Universal decided they wanted to put me in *Revenge of the Creature*. I thought, "Gee whiz, I don't want to really *do* that, but I guess I *have* to because I'm under contract and they can tell me what to do if they want to, and I can't say no to anything."

In 1956 she told interviewer Bob Thomas that the split with Universal was her idea "because I knew I was getting nowhere playing the girlfriend of Tony Curtis and Audie Murphy." Three years later she recalled her unrewarding Universal assignments in a *Variety* interview:

> Unfortunately, the pictures Universal-International makes are not those which the industry likes, and if the industry doesn't like them it doesn't help your career. I know my craft. I'm attractive. I have something to offer. But this doesn't seem to mean a thing. People

After Universal, Lori Nelson started occasionally playing more "grown-up" and glamorous roles than she had on the San Fernando Valley lot.

say, "She's been around a long time." It's kind of tragic. Where do you go from here?

Nelson had her first freelancing role in *I Died a Thousand Times* (1955), Warners' remake of their 1941 Humphrey Bogart starrer *High Sierra*, with Nelson in the old Joan Leslie role of a shy, clubfooted teenager. After another Warners picture, *Sincerely Yours* (1955) with Liberace, she began going the low-budget route with the Western *Mohawk* (1956), her second sci-fi foray *Day the World Ended* (1956) and the dragstrip drama *Hot Rod Girl* (1956) with Lori in the title role. She was Dean Martin's girl in the Martin and Lewis movie *Pardners* (1956), a fun-filled remake of Bing Crosby's *Rhythm on the Range* (1936): "It was the next-to-the-last movie Dean Martin and Jerry Lewis did together, so they were not having a great deal to do with each other at that point," she told me. "But it was still a lot of fun, a lot of foolishness going on behind the scenes, and the craziness of the two of them." She finished up her early movie career with a pair of 1957 Schenck-Koch productions, *Outlaw's Son*, a Western–juvenile delinquent combo with Ben Cooper,[25] and *Untamed Youth*. In the latter, Lori (in black wig) and platinum powerhouse Mamie Van Doren star as sisters arrested for vagrancy and sentenced to 30 days of cotton pickin' alongside other juveniles of both sexes. Rock'n'roll and other forms of mayhem ensue.

There was also lots of TV work for Lori, even the movie-length special *The Pied Piper of Hamelin* (1957) with Van Johnson in the title role and Lori wearing a black pigtailed wig as Mara, daughter of the Hamelin mayor (Claude Rains). She then had her own series *How to Marry a Millionaire*, co-starring with Merry Anders and Barbara Eden as sexy New York bachelorettes looking to trap wealthy husbands; Lori reprised the character played by Betty Grable in the 1953 movie that inspired the series. Nelson wearied of the day-to-day rut of a TV series; also, despite her top billing, she found herself third in everything, with Eden getting the most footage and Anders having all the sharpest lines. Her discontent mounted when her bosses insisted that the three go without pay on their personal appearance tours. After 39 episodes, Nelson and the series' owners were irreconcilable, so Lori's character Greta was written out of the show (she was said

In one of her first movies after Universal, Day the World Ended (1956), Lori Nelson became the object of the affection of yet another monster (Paul Blaisdell). The movie's producer Alex Gordon cast Nelson and Richard Denning in the leads because of their Creature connections.

to have married and moved away) and Lisa Gaye came in as the third girl. "Everybody thought I was crazy to give up security in such an insecure business," Nelson told *TV Guide*:

> But I'm the sort of actress who rebels at doing the same thing week in and week out. My forte is dramatic acting ... I believe that nine-tenths of the people in this business feel

just the way I do. Particularly in series. A series is a grind. And if the part's just fluff and nonsense, a girl's likely to get lost in the shuffle. I'm tired of people coming up to me and saying, "Oh, aren't you one of those three cute girls in *How to Marry a Millionaire*?" Then they ask, "Which one?"

She said in another of her way-back-when interviews that, in her eight years in the business, she'd played just three parts she was proud of: *All I Desire*, *I Died a Thousand Times* and a *Climax!* TV episode. Away from the studios, she was still living at home with her parents on Bellaire Avenue in North Hollywood.

Around the same time as a 1960 interview in which the never-been-married beauty said she'd never wed an actor ("I don't like actors"), there was romance and a little-publicized engagement to Burt Reynolds, then at the beginning of his career. Six months after Reynolds' manic depressive behavior resulted in a breakup, Nelson married Johnny Mann of the Johnny Mann Singers. Daughter Lori Susan was born the following year (1962), and then Jennifer Lee three years later. After a series of separations and reconciliations, Nelson and Mann untied the marital knot in 1971, and Lori took on the task of raising her two daughters alone. In 1979 she began acting again on little theater stages; she was Miss Lucy, acid-tongued mistress of a Southern political boss, in the Gene Dynarski Theatre's production of *Sweet Bird of Youth*. ("Lori Nelson proves again what a magnificent performer she is by tackling the role of Miss Lucy, a complete career turnaround."—*Hollywood Studio Magazine*.) Then the acting was crowded out of her life by her duties as owner of Lori Facials and Cosmetics, a business operating out of a beauty shop near her home.

Amongst Los Angeles women there was a tear gas fad in the early 1980s(!) and the LAPD's Detective Sgt. Joe Reiner made extra money nights and weekends teaching women when and how to employ spray cans of tear gas upon assailants. One evening he was teaching a class of about 30 women in a private house, "and ten minutes 'in,' there was a knock on the door," Reiner told me. "Somebody opened the door, and in walked the most beautiful woman I had ever seen in my entire life. And just so gracious! It was Lori. She was dressed completely in white, with a white coat on. It was as if she'd stepped out of an old *Photoplay* magazine [*laughs*]!" This was the beginning of two years in which she and Reiner platonically palled around together. "As a guy," Reiner continued,

> I was *dying* to take her out. But I thought I didn't have the slightest hope of ever dating her, and I never asked her for a date. Finally one day I just looked at her and I said, "You wouldn't go out on a *date* with me, would you?" and she said, "No." I said, "Well, I didn't think so."
>
> She said, "*But* … if you ask me in the right way … I'll accept." That started the whole thing going. Our lives were

A very chic Lori Nelson as she appeared in the stage production Who Was That Lady I Saw You With?, *directed by Werner Klemperer and starring Joey Bishop and Harvey Korman.*

opposite: She was a glamorous woman, a beautiful Hollywood actress, and I was a police officer, a detective, and we were completely opposite. Then one day, we were talking, just sitting there talking, and suddenly she said, "Why don't we get married?" And I said, "Well … yeah, why *don't* we?"

Nelson not only popped the question, she made their wedding rings, which they wear to this day (2013 was their 30th anniversary). For a while, she kept busy buying and selling antiques. There were even a few final movie roles: In 1994 she had a small part in the TV movie *Secret Sins of the Father* with Beau Bridges (who also directed) and his father Lloyd Bridges, and in 1998 she appeared in director Fred Olen Ray's family-friendly *Mom, Can I Keep Her?*, about a kid followed home from school by a gorilla which he now wants to keep. Ray had met her at the 1998 FANEX in Hunt Valley, Maryland, and thought it would be cool to have her make a one-scene cameo.

In more recent years Nelson guested at a number of

autograph shows, where the average fan coming to her table was mainly interested in Guess Who. "I played opposite Rock Hudson, Tony Curtis, Jimmy Stewart, Dean Martin and Audie Murphy," she told me, "but who's the leading man *everybody* wants to ask me about? The Gill Man! ... It's so funny, Universal had to twist my arm a little to be in a monster movie. But if I knew then how popular they would remain, I would have twisted *their* arm to be in a couple more!"

John Bromfield as Joe Hayes

> John Bromfield, God love him, was certainly not an actor. A good-looking, wonderful person, but I really don't think he was much of an actor.
>
> —Beverly Garland

After appearing in nine Universal movies plus RKO's Underwater! *(1955), Lori Nelson wasn't keen on doing* Revenge of the Creature: *"You generally started [a movie career] with something like that—you didn't want to build up to it!" she told me. She's since made peace with her large-lipped lover boy. At top she's pictured with Cortlandt Hull's "Witch's Dungeon" Gill Man figure at a New Jersey Chiller Theatre expo, and on bottom with husband Joe Reiner, who accompanies her on her convention gigs.*

Wellll, maybe that's true. But John Bromfield *was* a rugged outdoorsman and a deep sea angler; in his first movie he hand-harpooned a couple of whales, one of them a 68-ton humpback. All of which sounds a good bit more fun, adventurous and rewarding than the rather ordinary feat of being an okay actor.

Bromfield (real name: Farron McClain Brumfield) was born in South Bend, Indiana. (His much-older cousin, Pulitzer Prize–winning novelist Louis Bromfield, had an uncredited hand in the writing of the 1931 *Dracula*.) The family moved to Venice, California, when Farron was still small. Always athletically inclined, he later excelled at football, boxing, etc., then began earning his living on tuna clippers. After Navy service, he returned to his job as a commercial fisherman. One day while mending his nets on the Santa Monica beach, he was approached by brothers who offered him a part in their upcoming fishing film *Harpoon*. "I thought they were putting me on," Bromfield wrote to author Everett Aaker in 1993. "But when I showed my father their cards, he encouraged me to make an appointment with them." The movie was shot in Alaska, on the actual locale associated with the story, between May and September 1947.[26] By the time *Harpoon* premiered late in 1948, the idea of acting had the fisherman well hooked and he was already playing supporting parts for Paramount producer Hal B. Wallis (starting with 1948's *Sorry, Wrong Number*).

He was next in Wallis' *Rope of Sand* (1949) which featured *Casablanca* alumni Paul Henreid, Claude Rains and Peter Lorre plus Bromfield's second wife (as of November 1948), curvy French beauty Corinne Calvet. Calvet's dishy 1983 autobiography *Has Corinne Been a Good Girl?* makes theirs sound like the stereotypically unhealthy, wackadoodle Hollywood marriage. They met in a hospital (she was recuperating from a Sunset Blvd. auto smash-up, he was there twice a day visiting his ailing mother) and there was an immediate attraction. Bromfield was very definite that he was not the marrying kind, but when the U.S. government refused to extend Calvet's visa, Bromfield instantly stepped up to the plate and married her so that, automatically, she could stay in the country. It was a passionate union but Calvet was troubled by "the gulf in education, taste, sensibility and values" that separated them. Then there was the night that Wallis made a move on her. When she resisted, he told her that Bromfield had married her on his (Wallis') say-so: The producer wanted her to stay in Hollywood and do *Rope of Sand*, and Bromfield had acceded to his boss' request with the expectation that this would advance his career.

After Wallis dropped Bromfield and the actor couldn't find work, 20th Century–Fox production chief Darryl F. Zanuck invited Calvet to his office and, "with his erect penis standing proudly out of his unzipped pants," told her he'd make Bromfield a leading man if she'd come with him to Palm Springs "for a weekend of sunny sex play." All that night, Calvet debated with herself whether to tell Bromfield what had happened. Finally she woke her husband and laid out the sordid tale:

When I finished saying that I was willing to do it with his consent he looked at me in total disgust. "You bitch. You could have done it without telling me." Grabbing his pillow he pretended to go back to sleep.

But they remained married, with Corinne appearing in big pictures (*On the Riviera*, a couple of John Fords, more) while the guy Hollywood thought of as Mr. Calvet eked out a living as part of the Palookaville casts of the Bowery Boys'

John Bromfield (1922–2005) is seen with wife Corinne Calvet at a Hollywood Park horse race. He unsuccessfully tested for the role of Samson in *Samson and Delilah* (1949); when producer Hal B. Wallis saw the test, he signed Bromfield to a $250-a-week contract. Calvet wondered if Wallis did it just to get the Burt Lancaster–like Bromfield off the market: Wallis had Lancaster under contract (courtesy Photofest).

Hold That Line (1952), a *Racket Squad* episode *et al*. Calvet told interviewer Earl Wilson she married Bromfield because of his tendency to be "a gentle brute": "Women need a good spanking from time to time…. Johnny has spanked me a few times. He's always masterful in his spanking and I behave better after."

Despite all the ups and downs, and some extracurricular bedroom activity on both sides, Bromfield was still busted up when he walked in on Calvet in bed with actor John

Fontaine (aka Jeffrey Stone): "With the anguished sound of a wounded animal he ran back into the living room," Calvet wrote. "I had never before seen a man cry the way I saw my husband crying now." In divorce court, Calvet testified that Bromfield told her to take up sports as a means of working off her desire to become a mother.

Going to Florida for *Revenge of the Creature* was "like a vacation" for Bromfield, who spent some of his spare time surf-fishing and caught a lot of striper bass. He recalled *Revenge* as a fun experience which included barbecues on the beach and singing around a big bonfire. He then forged ahead with yet more junky movies, including *Frontier Gambler* (1956), a low-budget ripoff of the film noir classic *Laura* (1944) with Bromfield in the equivalent of the Dana Andrews role, and *Manfish* (1956), a made-in-Jamaica adventure-melodrama whose Edgar Allan Poe–inspired finale has Bromfield as the equivalent of Poe's old man with the hideous heart(!). When Bromfield signed to make *Curucu, Beast of the Amazon* (1956) in Brazil, he brought along his girlfriend Larri Thomas, a movie and TV dancer,[27] and in the movie she played the small part of (what else?) a dancer. Bromfield and Thomas wed during the location trek—but the marriage ceremony couldn't take place in Brazil because the country didn't recognize divorces. So they got married aboard the steamship S.S. *Argentina* in international waters off the Brazilian coast. Thomas told me, "There was a nice American minister on board, and he and his wife were given a few shekels to [perform the ceremony], and that was it."

Bromfield became quite the busy actor when Desi Arnaz and Lucille Ball signed him to star in the syndicated series *The Sheriff of Cochise*, a *Highway Patrol*–like "modern Western" set in Cochise County, Arizona. Bromfield had the title role of Sheriff Frank Morgan, with his deputy played by the show's creator, actor-songwriter Stan Jones. The highly rated series was on the air two years when Bromfield's character was promoted to marshal and the show's title was changed to *U.S. Marshal* because of his new rank. He described the show in a 1959 interview as a seven-days-a-week job (he studied his scripts on weekends, made publicity tours, traveled on behalf of the Red Cross and the National Safety Council, etc.). He said he could continue to maintain that grueling schedule for another two years: "I figure sure, you kill yourself, but by then you will have a pretty good income, and you can pick and choose what you want to do next." What he did next, after the show's run ended, was visit Japan, where *U.S. Marshal* (and he) had a large following. He was immediately put to work in a movie inspired by his show, *Marshal Morgan and the Tokyo Police*, with Bromfield as an FBI agent on the trail of an international narcotics ring; it also featured his *U.S. Marshal* co-star James Griffith.[28] This was reportedly the first time an American had headlined a Nipponese picture.

By this time, his marriage to Larri Thomas had ended in divorce. When I asked her why it went kaput, she said loudly, "*I'd love to know*! 'Cause he was the nicest guy, very handsome, very sweet, he did not beat me … I don't know. I can't tell you, I wish I could. We remained friends, and when I married [dancer] Bruce Hoy and had children, two girls, John brought my children Christmas presents in a big station wagon that said **JOHN BROMFIELD—SHERIFF OF COCHISE**, bless his heart." I showed her a letter from Bromfield to Aaker in which the actor wrote, "My third wife Lari [*sic*] Thomas was a dancer, a true gypsy who loved dancing more than she loved me and so that didn't work." Larri's reaction: "I don't like the sound of that at all…" and, after a pause, "*That's* interesting to know…." And, of course: "You would think after six years of marriage John would at least give me the second 'r' in my name!"

John Bromfield and Larri Thomas first locked eyes during the making of Easy to Love *(1953) and found each other … well, easy to love. At the end of 1955 they were married at sea, off the coast of Brazil.*

After about 1960, most of the new credits on Bromfield's show biz résumé were sports films on fishing and hunting, with Bromfield involved behind the scenes. He did a lot of fishing and hunting himself (natch) and, with his final wife, dancer-singer Mary Ellen Tillotson, also traveled the country in a motor home. In the early 1990s Bromfield and the missus relocated from Southern California to Lake Havasu City, Arizona. He retired in 2003 and coped with health issues, including Alzheimer's and Parkinson's. The 83-year-old Bromfield was in Palm Desert, California, seeking medical treatment when the bell tolled for him in September 2005.

Nestor Paiva as Lucas

Easy-to-please Creature fans might derive a few moments of amusement from the Columbia programmer *Flame of Stamboul* (1951), an espionage yarn with *Black Lagoon*'s Richard Denning and Nestor Paiva as intelligence officers on the trail of mercenary spies in Turkey. And Paiva fans will get a chuckle out of the scene where the fez-wearing, heavily accented Paiva unexpectedly drops the accent and, now sounding like the All-American Guy Next Door, starts talking to Denning about his family and where he's from: "Fresno, California!" It's obviously a line provided by Paiva himself, as that was the actor's real-life birthplace!

With a solid physique, big bald head and the ability to adopt an array of foreign dialects, Paiva (1905–66) was nicely cut out for the villainous roles he played throughout his 30-year movie career. According to Geoffrey L. Gomes' *Classic Images* article "Nestor Caetano Paiva: A Portuguese American in Hollywood," the actor's father Francisco, a Portuguese immigrant, was a teenager when he came to the U.S. in 1881, finding employment in California as a sheepherder and eventually owning his own flocks. In 1891, on a return visit to his native country, he wooed and wed Marianna, a girl from his village. In Portugal, they had two children, and then more in America, where Francisco was now working as a Fresno grocer. Many of the Paivas' children died while still babies, including a Nestor who preceded "our" Nestor. (Gomes writes, "Of 12 children born between 1892 and 1908, half did not survive infancy—stark testimony to the high infant-mortality rate of the period.")

In school, "our" Nestor was an athlete and also acted in some high school shows. Plans to become a teacher led him first to the University of San Francisco and then the University of California at Berkeley, where he played football and taught swimming in the phys ed department. The aspiration to teach went by the wayside once he began participating in college stage productions; his first was *Antigone* in which he played a 90-year-old man. After graduation he worked with stock companies in the San Francisco area and on radio. He came to Hollywood in 1934 and soon found himself under heavy makeup playing the role of the villainous Squire Cribbs in the Theatre Mart's parodic production of *The Drunkard*, a 19th-century temperance play. The producers had expected *The Drunkard* to run for perhaps one season but it became an institution, the Show That Would Not Die, perhaps partly because it invited audience participation (attendees would cheer, boo and sing along with the song "There Is a Tavern in the Town"). Paiva's dastardly character was on the receiving end of audience hisses for 11 years; the play went on for many more after his departure, closing in 1959 after almost 9500 performances. (Watch a recreation of *The Drunkard* in 1934's *The Old Fashioned Way* with W.C. Fields, one of the Theatre Mart production's biggest fans. It features some of the Theatre Mart players.)

In April 1937 Paiva made an inauspicious movie bow,

In a 30-year movie-TV career, character actor Nestor Paiva got to play an extensive assortment of types—including a South Pacific island's cannibal chief in the 1943 musical comedy Rhythm of the Islands *(courtesy Photofest).*

2. Revenge of the Creature (1955)

unbilled as a Civilian Conservation Corps camp captain in Monogram's *Blazing Barriers*. Most of his early film roles came with no screen credit, but movie audiences got used to seeing that scowling face in A-pictures and B flicks. Some of his bigger roles were in serials, most notably the wartime chapterplays *King of the Mounties* (1942, as the Italian enemy agent Count Baroni) and *Don Winslow of the Coast Guard* (1943, as the Scorpion). On-screen in these serials Paiva wreaked havoc on Dubya Dubya 2 America but off-screen he helped build B-17s at Lockheed Aircraft, served as an air raid warden (as did his wife Maxine) and worked with the USO. Most readers of this book already know he was one of the gangsters in Abbott and Costello's *Hold That Ghost* (1941), prowling around the "haunted" roadhouse covered by a sheer sheet to masquerade as a ghost. *Hold That Ghost* was his "Universal Horrors" debut, and also Richard Carlson's; and while Carlson was third-billed and Paiva uncredited, it's the sheet-clad Paiva who (sorta) plays the title role! Then in 1949, he was one of the obnoxious nightclub drunks who riles up the giant gorilla in *Mighty Joe Young* (1949). Paiva's son Joe told *Filmfax*'s John J.J. Johnson,

> One time, [my dad] was driving down Ventura Blvd. and a cop pulled him over. The officer actually thought my dad was a wanted criminal and took him down to the police station. My dad played so many heavies and villains that this officer was sure he'd arrested a Public Enemy Number One. My dad wasn't overly upset about it. He called us from the station and said, "Hey, I've got a great story for you when I get home."

By the 1950s Paiva was playing a slightly higher percentage of Nice Guy roles, among them the understanding dad of young Jim Thorpe (Billy Gray) in the early scenes of *Jim Thorpe—All-American* (1951). He became a bit of a fixture in Universal's sci-fi movies, starting in *Black Lagoon* and continuing in *Revenge of the Creature*, again playing boat captain Lucas. You may feel a touch of *déjà vu* watching Paiva's first *Revenge* scene: a grinning, cigar-smoking Lucas blowing the boat's whistle and laughing as an alarmed crocodile leaps off a log into the water. Well, you *should* get that seen-it-before feeling, because it's footage taken from *Creature from the Black Lagoon*. On *Revenge*, the editorial department found it necessary to reuse that *Black Lagoon* shot of Paiva (approximately 20 feet), prompting the studio to get the necessary clearances from him and the Screen Actors Guild. (In the *Mystery Science Theater* version of *Revenge*, this shot is now accompanied by Popeye-ish "kuk-kuk-kuk-kuk!" laughter.) The actor was also featured in Universal's *Tarantula* (1955) and *The Mole People* (1956).

Paiva was capable of the most vile deeds on-screen but (again according to Gomes' *Classic Images* article) in real life he was a devoted family man who taught Sunday school and served on the church board. When he realized that playing a substantial role in the Western *Comanche* (1956) would keep him from home longer than he'd like, he brought the family to Mexico *with* him, and his kids even got to appear as pioneer children slain by Indians.

In the 1960s Paiva did most of his work on TV, even doing voices for Hanna-Barbera's animated action series *Jonny Quest* (instantly recognizable, the actor provides *three* characters' voices in the premiere episode "The Mystery of the Lizard Men"). What movie roles there *were*, were often sci-fi or horror: the saloon owner in *Jesse James Meets Frankenstein's Daughter* (1966), the monstrous-looking Chairman, barking out orders in Martian (with English subtitles) in *The Three Stooges in Orbit* (1962), etc. In *The Madmen of Mandoras* (1963), Paiva plays the full-of-surprises Mandoras police chief and takes part in the explosive climactic scene—which is scored with the Gill Man's *BAH-BAH-BAHHH!* theme, as though that music followed Paiva around from movie to movie!

Badman's Territory, one of RKO's biggest moneymakers in 1946, featured many of the Old West's best-known bandits as characters in its story of a "land beyond the law" bordering the Oklahoma Territory. Many of the baddies (the James Brothers, the Daltons, Belle Starr, et al.) are likable but not Nestor Paiva's scheming Sam Bass (courtesy Photofest).

By 1965 Paiva was battling stomach cancer; at least one of the Hollywood trade papers reported the news of his major surgery at the Sherman Oaks Community Hospital, where he was expected to be confined for two weeks. He subsequently struggled to work while suffering from the disease, and did get in several more movie and TV licks. His last two movies were both for William Castle, *Let's Kill Uncle* (1966) and *The Spirit Is Willing* (1967), the latter featuring Paiva at the beginning of the funny pre-credits sequence.

On July 27, 1966, a *Hollywood Reporter* item revealed that Paiva had celebrated his 30th year as an actor with his signing for a featured role in the upcoming *The Caper of the Golden Bulls* (1967). He didn't make it into the picture, nor live to see the aforementioned Castle movies: Paiva died in hospital on Friday, September 9, 1966. The 61-year-old actor's services were held the following Monday afternoon at Church of the Hills, Forest Lawn.

Flippy the "Educated" Porpoise as Himself

It was estimated that the antics of Marine Studios' Flippy the "Educated" Porpoise entertained roughly a million persons. A *Revenge of the Creature* bit player and interviewee of mine, Julian Fant, got to see Flippy early in his show biz career. *How* early? *So* early that Flippy was still *un*educated! Fant told me,

> While in high school, a couple of friends and I would ride our bikes from our houses, about six miles across the causeway, into what they called Vilano Beach. Back in the sand dunes, there was a saltwater lagoon which came in off the Inland Waterway. It had a tidal flow in and out, it was five or six feet deep, but pretty wide.
>
> We had been swimming there occasionally for quite a while, and all of a sudden, one day when we went there, we saw that a chain link fence enclosure, a big rectangular deal, had been built around it. We couldn't figure out what it was for. Then the next time we went, a guy in a pith helmet was standing in the enclosure with a bucket and a baton. We saw him throw the baton out across the lagoon, and a big wave went after it, and retrieved it, and brought it back to him. And when he gave the retriever some fish out of the bucket, we realized it was a porpoise. What we were seeing was the first Marine Studios porpoise being trained: The man's name was Adolf Frohn, an animal behaviorist, and Marine Studios had hired him to train this porpoise, which must have been Flippy.

It was Marine Studios co-founder and "big fish" W. Douglas Burden[29] who wondered if a dolphin (…porpoise … what*ever*) could be trained to do tricks, and in 1949 a secret experiment began. Forty-five-year-old Frohn was a fourth-generation circus trainer who, according to the Messinger-McGinnis book *Marineland*, "had performed in his father's trained sea lion act at the age of 12, worked with world-renowned animal trainer Frank Buck, and was working for Ringling Bros. and Barnum & Bailey Circus at the time." This was Frohn's first attempt with a water-dwelling mammal. "Frankly, when I first undertook the training I had no confidence at all in what I could accomplish," Frohn later admitted. "I had worked with many animals and birds but, previous to this, had never seen a porpoise."

The other half of the experiment was Flippy ("Sonny"

A fun publicity photograph of John Agar and Lori Nelson serving as jumpmasters for Marine Studios' premier performer Flippy, six and a half feet and 200 pounds of "Educated" Porpoise. Construction of Marine Studios' Porpoise Stadium was completed in early 1954 and it formally opened to the public in April, shortly before the Revenge crew's arrival.

Whitney's *wife du jour* came up with the name). A two-year-old, he had been captured in a nearby inlet by means of a net that blocked his escape. Frohn had requested a young female because he'd learned from experience that females of any species could be trained more quickly, but reluctantly accepted the male.

According to a *Natural History* magazine article by Marine Studios publicity director John Dillin, the first step in animal training is to teach the critter its source of food, so Flippy was promptly made aware that Frohn was "the fishman." At first, the fish snacks were thrown into Flippy's tank, but at the end of just one week Flippy was taking food from Frohn's hand. Achievement came fast as Frohn won the mammal's confidence. The *Natural History* article continues, "From this point in the progressive training program, Mr. Frohn has jealously guarded his secrets of just how he has accomplished the final results. It is clear, however, that infinite patience was a prime requisite."

In late February 1951, Marine Studios announced to the press their year-and-a-half-long experiment, and the outcome that had exceeded all expectations. Thousands of newspapers carried the story of the world's only educated porpoise; there was also newsreel and TV coverage. Marine Studios maintained that the experiment had been conducted purely in the interest of science, but now Flippy (and the built-in grin that Nature gave him) was a heart-warming sensation, and so thoughts turned to making him the star of his own *exhibition* (Marine Studios didn't want to use the word "show").

Revenge of the Creature provides a filmed record of his … ahem … *exhibition*. As seen in the movie, Flippy would jump up to ring a bell suspended high above the water's surface; retrieve a dumbbell; hoist a "porpoise pennant"; turn over and over on the surface of the water; catch and bring back a football; and jump through a suspended hoop.[30] In 1953, perhaps partly thanks to the fact that Flippy had clicked (get it?) with the public, Marine Studios attendance increased to 700,000 visitors at two bucks a head.[31]

Frohn left in 1955 to train dolphins for the then-new Miami Seaquarium, the first thorn (competitor) in Marine Studios' blubber. According to Mitman's *Reel Nature*, Frohn's replacement was Keller Breland, a man hired

> to devise a new set of training techniques that utilized science rather than the craft knowledge of circus animal trainers for its dolphin show…. In a matter of two short months, Breland's assistant, André Cowan, a Marine Studios maintenance department worker, had [Flippy's understudy] Algae performing a stunning set of feats that far sur-

Like his fellow mammal Clint Eastwood, Flippy made his on-camera feature film debut in *Revenge of the Creature*.

passed Flippy's talents. Algae waved his tail to the audience, leaped high in the air to catch a football, tossed a basketball through a hoop five and a half feet above the water, and made a high jump to take the rubber tip off a pole suspended about 16 feet above the water. It had taken Frohn six months simply to get a dolphin to ring a bell.

Grief, which forever stalks the world, paused at Marine Studios in the summer of 1955: Almost exactly a year after his performance for Universal's cameras, Flippy quit eating on July 31. (Despite a lack of concrete evidence, I suspect that a contributing factor may have been Algae's Eve Harrington–like rise to Porpoise Stadium stardom.) On August 2, his lifeless body was found in his … ahem … private quarters. "Trick Porpoise Death Mystery" was the title of at least one of the newspaper articles announcing his passing. Flippy was eight years old, the prime of porpoise life, and the cause of his death was unknown.[32]

Tom Hennesy as the Creature

Hennesy was the ultimate man's man. He was one of the most incredibly strong, wealthy, tough, opinionated guys you'd ever know. He was what mountain men want to be!
—Gary Lockwood, 2013

In latter-day interviews, *Black Lagoon*'s Ben Chapman never complained much about the rigors of wearing the Land Gill Man suit, but *Revenge of the Creature*'s Tom Hennesy made it sound like the ugly ordeal it *had* to have been. "It was terribly uncomfortable and very restrictive," he said in our 1994 interview:

> The vision was terrible, you had no peripheral vision, there were just little holes in the center of each [Creature] eye and you'd try to line up your own eyes. It was difficult to move, it was difficult even to *breathe*—you had to breathe through the mouth. And [Florida] was incredibly hot and humid. I probably weighed about 225 pounds when I went down to Florida, and about 200 when I came back to Hollywood. I also developed kidney stones later on, and I was told that more than likely the reason was that [in Florida] I was in the area of the highest incidence of kidney stones in the country; there's something about the minerals in the water. Plus, the *constriction* [of the tight-fitting Gill Man suit]; you couldn't relieve yourself whenever nature called, they only took the suit off you once a day, at noon. There was *no way* of getting out of the thing except to have two or three people help you, and it took a considerable amount of time.... Everything you did in that thing was probably three times as difficult as it would be for someone else who wasn't restricted like that.

All things considered, *Revenge of the Creature* sounds like it was a lousy experience for Hennesy: For the "privilege" of working his tail off in that suit, he endured hot Florida weather, was gnawed by no-see-ums, received meager wages (comparatively), was denied a screen credit, and got a going-away present of long-lasting health problems.[33] He said in our interview that if he'd been offered the Gill Man role in *The Creature Walks Among Us*, he wouldn't have taken it; and I bet that if he could have turned back the clock and relived the day he was offered the *Revenge* job, he wouldn't have taken *that* either.

Born and raised in La Cañada, California, Hennesy played a lot of college football throughout the 1940s, and was on the USC team in the 1943 and '44 Rose Bowl games. During that time he got his first part-time movie work, as an extra, bit player and stuntman. He also enrolled in the Naval ROTC (Reserve Officers' Training Corps, not *Revenge of the Creature*) and spent three wartime years in the Navy. Once he was discharged, he worked as a police officer and a forest ranger-game warden on Catalina Island.

Universal's new rubber-suited webfoot: college footballer-turned-stuntman Tom Hennesy, who found the job "very difficult, very exhausting—one of the toughest things that I've done." His other genre jobs included Abbott and Costello's *Jack and the Beanstalk* (1952), doubling Buddy Baer as the Giant, and an episode of Boris Karloff's *Thriller*.

2. Revenge of the Creature (1955) 171

> Tom Hennesy, the "Gill Man" ... is an accredited school teacher, now teaching Natalie Wood at WB!
> —Army Archerd in his *Daily Variety* column, May 6, 1955

After a return to college, Hennesy became a general secondary and elementary teacher in virtually all the Hollywood film and TV studios, with the long list of his students including Paul Anka, Annette Funicello, Tommy Rettig and Tim Considine. On *Rebel Without a Cause* (1955) he was tutor, welfare worker and on-set guardian to Natalie Wood, a smoking, swearing, hot-to-trot 16-year-old handful of trouble, and was in charge of young Sal Mineo as well. Wood later told *Look* magazine that she and Mineo "would tell him that we had arranged interviews for [him for] an acting job ... we made up the interviews to get rid of him." Hennesy, interviewed by Suzanne Finstad for her book *Natasha—A Biography of Natalie Wood*, said that Wood flirted with him at the commissary and when he took her to dinner during a night shoot: "She'd kind of play games like that, but I told her to knock it off—I didn't want any kind of suspicion of anything like that."[34]

On the side Hennesy continued to do stunt work and to play small movie and TV roles—Westerns, mostly. At 6'5" he was the right size for monster roles, but after the Gill Man the only one he played was on Universal's *Thriller* TV series: In the dripping-with-atmosphere "The Return of Andrew Bentley" (1961), he was The Familiar, a faceless demon doing the evil bidding of a sorcerer's ghost (Reggie Nalder). A blurry "ripple effect" makes The Familiar hard to see even in closeups and (a real missed opportunity) nothing is done to make it obvious how tall he is.

Tall-in-the-saddle John Wayne liked having lots of same-sized, equally formidable actors and stuntmen in his movies, and Hennesy became something of a semi-regular. On *The Alamo* (1960) Wayne asked him to beef up weight-wise and, with help from the movie's caterer, he did; Hennesy packed on 50-plus pounds (which, unfortunately, he then carried for many years). Over time, Hennesy had become a friend to Wayne, a visitor to his home, sailed with him on many occasions, etc. In fact, schoolteacher Hennesy tutored Wayne's teenage son Patrick on the set of *Mister Roberts* (1955) and Wayne's eight-year-old Ethan on *Big Jake* (1971). It appears that Hennesy may have shared some of Wayne's concerns about our country's future: Gary Lockwood, star of *2001: A Space Odyssey* (1968), told me that Hennesy

In *The Comancheros* (1961), John Wayne went fist to fist with Tom Hennesy's Gordo, a man-mountain henchman comically impervious to chairs smashed over his head. Hennesy was uncredited in the film, as were *Creature Walks'* Leigh Snowden, Gregg Palmer and stuntman Chuck Roberson, the last man to play the Gill Man (at the tail end of *Creature Walks* production).

was "pretty far right" in his politics and that the hippie movement got Hennesy to thinking there might be an attempt at a revolution in the offing. Hennesy revealed to Lockwood that, if that day came, he was prepared, with a .50-caliber machine-gun and plenty of shells buried on his property!

The movie affording viewers the best look at Hennesy might be *Big Jake*, in which the title character (John Wayne) moseys into a saloon full of oil drillers, asks who's the orneriest, is directed to the king-sized, bearded Mr. Sweet (Hennesy)—and breaks a pool cue over his head! (Don't ask why, it's a long story.) The blow has no effect other than to anger Mr. Sweet who, in a one-sided fight complete with "funny music," repeatedly belts and floors Big Jake. In the roadshow production *The Alamo* he's one of Davy Crockett's (Wayne) Tennesseans, the coonskin-capped, one-eyed Bull, and in a San Antonio de Bexar cantina, he and Davy play "a game the boys play back in Tennessee": Bull hits Davy with his best punch, but Davy remains standing. "*Ohhh nnno!*" Bull cries out in a huge Todd-AO-screen-filling closeup, as it's now Davy's turn to try to knock Bull off his feet. Davy's southpaw punch sends Bull crashing backward, the 39th time (out of 39) Bull has lost this "game" to Davy. Hennesy also gets comically clobbered in Wayne's *McLintock!* (1963) and *The War Wagon* (1967); in the former he was part of the mud pit melee, in the latter he was the bartender ("We don't *serve* Indians!") in the saloon brawl.

There was exciting action in Hennesy's private life in 1978 when the devastating Agoura-Malibu Firestorm came knocking on the door of his beachfront home in Malibu, wildfire capital of the world. Lockwood, a neighbor, was out kayaking when he first saw its smoke; accompanied by his brother, he rushed over to Hennesy's and found him hosing down his all-wood house. Lockwood continued,

> Hennesy had planted a big huge bamboo grove in a little arroyo. It hadn't rained in some time, and the fire came raging down and got into his bamboo, and now the fire started coming up to his property. My brother was up on the roof, wetting things down, and I was trying to help Hennesy release his horses onto the beach and do whatever else I could. After a period of time, running around and everything, Tom was getting kind of crazy, he was beginning to realize everything was gonna go and he was getting a little meshugganah in the head. I was trying to calm him down a little bit when the smoke became incredible. I began to see smoke coming out of Hennesy's chimney, which meant that the inside of the house was on fire. So I told my brother to jump off the roof.
>
> At that point, one of the weirdest things happened: I began to hear gunshots. Remember I told you that that crazy Hennesy had somehow commandeered a .50-caliber machine-gun and some shells, and he had 'em buried in the ground, gettin' ready for the revolution? Apparently the shells caught fire, because they were going off! Well, .50-caliber machine-gun bullets are not exactly what I want to dodge! I said, "Tom, you gotta get *out* of here." He was a pretty big man, you couldn't force him to do *any*thing, but we got his car keys and got him in his car and said, "Drive away." By then, you couldn't see, there was so much black smoke coming from the mountains—it was blanking out the sun. Smoke inhalation was now the enemy. Driving out of there in my own car, I couldn't see because it was so dark, and I damn near ran into a Ferrari that was parked in the PCH turning lane.

How hot *was* the firestorm?: According to Joan Didion's 1979 book *The White Album*, "temperatures [got] up to 2500 degrees Fahrenheit. Horses caught fire and were shot on the beach, birds exploded in the air. Houses did not explode but imploded, as in a nuclear strike." The Hennesy home, built on one of the nicest pieces of land in all of Malibu, was destroyed, along with 229 others. Hennesy rebuilt on the same spot.

The rather full life of Tom Hennesy additionally included working with emotionally disturbed juvenile offenders and acting as the head of the Huntington Beach oil production company which his father had helped to found in the 1920s. When it was sold in 1991, he semi-retired. In 1999, the *Los Angeles Times* listed Hennesy's Malibu home for $7.5 million: "The property, three lots on 2.4 acres, has a six-bedroom, seven-bath bluff-top house with a road that leads almost to the water." By then he was dealing with a host of health woes: arthritis, hip and knee joint instability, muscle degeneration, etc.

In September 2003, *Revenge of the Creature* was one of the movies featured in the ten-day World 3-D Film Expo at Hollywood's Egyptian Theater, with Hennesy and Lori Nelson in attendance to do a pre-show Q&A. "Hennesy sort of looked like a mountain man," attendee Bob Burns recalled for me. "He had long hair and a beard. He was very crippled up and walked with two crutches, very slowly." (During the eternity it took Hennesy to get to the front of the auditorium, moderator Mike Schlesinger broke the tension by joking to the audience, "He's more used to being in water!") Burns added that Hennesy was friendly but "not at all like Ben Chapman. Hennesy being more of a stunt guy, he wasn't used to talking about the films that he was in—especially with a large crowd. I kinda got the feeling that he didn't really want to be there. He didn't seem like he cared for the publicity like Ben did."

Burns described Hennesy as "crippled up" at that 2003 appearance; Hennesy described him*self* as crippled up a decade earlier, in an interview with John Wayne fan Tim Lilley (printed in Lilley's 2010 book *Campfire Conversations Complete*):

I haven't been involved in film work in recent times. I'm kind of crippled up. All the years that I banged myself around, did running saddle falls, horse falls and everything, without the benefit of pads half the time, playing Indians with no pads, that sort of thing … I just knocked the hell out of myself, but I thought I was invincible. Turns out I wasn't. Also, I played football for years, and I was also a boxer. So, the whole thing together kind of piled up on me.… Stuntwork. I would never recommend it to any kids of mine.

The last time I phoned Hennesy was in 2010 and he told me he was about to have surgery in connection with some long-ago stunt injuries, plus some injuries he'd incurred trying to save his house from that 1978 fire. I intended to press him for some more Creature and career memories for this book and then I diddled too long and missed out on the opportunity: Thomas Daniel Hennesy died at age 87 on May 23, 2011.

Production

> The skeery *Black Lagoon* gets itself a sequel with John Agar and Lori Nelson in the top roles. It will be called *Return of the Creature*.
>
> Universal-International made so much money with the original science fiction tale its sequel goes before the camera within two weeks…
>
> The same team which made *The Black Lagoon*, Director Jack Arnold and Producer William Alland, head for Florida where all the locations will be filmed.
> — "Louella Parsons in Hollywood," June 9, 1954

In 1953, the first unit and second unit scenes of *Creature from the Black Lagoon* had been shot simultaneously, Jack Arnold working on the former at Universal and James Havens and "Scotty" Welbourne handling the latter in Florida. On *Revenge*, Arnold was the director of both units. The second unit work came first: Arnold and members of the key crew departed on the morning of June 18 for St. Augustine to confirm all the location arrangements. The schedule called for pre-production shooting to begin on June 25 and continue for ten days without sound, lights or cast.

In Dana M. Reemes' book *Directed by Jack Arnold*, interviewee Arnold talked about location-scouting Marine Studios and being shown the oceanarium filled with sharks, barracuda, etc. He asked the Marine Studios people to divide the oceanarium with a net, with all the dangerous sea creatures on one side and the area where they'd be shooting on the other. "I knew [the actors would] take one look in the tank and refuse to get in," Arnold told Reemes.

> So the Marineland people promised me they'd arrange for a net. I returned some while later with the production company to get ready to shoot—there was no net! I said, "Where's the net?" They said I didn't need a net because the fish were too well-fed to bother the actors. So I had a little problem. How the hell was I going to get my actors to go in there? Now as it happened, I had this really nutty cameraman on that picture who didn't mind swimming around in there with the sharks. He talked me into going into the tank with him to show everybody how safe it was. So I put on a diving mask and scuba tanks and jumped in with my eyes closed. After a few moments I slowly opened one eye and about a yard away there was this goddamn shark at least 12 feet long looking straight at me. I didn't know what the hell to do so I just froze. It moved slowly toward me and brushed against me as it passed. Its skin felt awful, like sandpaper. After the shark moved off I came up and said, "Nothing to it, fellas!" The joke is that by the third day everyone was actually kicking the sharks out of the way.

Ricou Browning confirms that that was no net: "We had no choice: The sharks were there and *we* were there," he told me. "And we had to shoot!" I asked Browning why they

WANTED
BY
Universal International Picture Co.
Movie Extras
For Feature Film Being Made in Vicinity of St. Augustine
ALL AGES 5-50 Years
COME FOR INTERVIEW
TO
CIVIC CENTER
7:30 P.M. Thursday and Friday Nights

Many St. Augustine residents first learned that Hollywood was coming to town on June 23, 1954, when this notice appeared in the local newspaper, the St. Augustine Record.

didn't shoot in the safer (no sharks!) dolphin oceanarium, and he said that that tank was much shallower, and it featured crowd-pleasing dolphin shows which Marine Studios would not have cancelled.

In the days leading up to the scheduled start of production, the balance of Arnold's second unit crew arrived in Florida, and shooting began right on schedule on June 25. According to that day's production report, and those of June 26 and June 28, John Lamb and Ricou Browning were both present bright and early on each of three days. The paperwork doesn't specifically say what they *did* on June 25 and 26, just that both of 'em were *there*. Memorize that tidbit of info, because we'll be returning to it.

Right away the troupe ran into hard luck: As they tried to get some of their first underwater shots in the oceanarium, they twice had to contend with a camera in need of repair, plus park personnel who, in order to feed the fish, regularly made the moviemakers leave the oceanarium.[35] Many of the crew members had arrived by 7:30 a.m. that June 25 but there was no filming until over eight hours later, at 3:35 p.m. They didn't expose much footage that day, just part of the scene where the bound-in-a-net Gill Man is brought into the oceanarium by divers and chained to the floor. (The 30-foot chain and shackle were made of aluminum.)

Who played the Creature on that first day (and on the second and on the start of the third)? Lamb was hired to play the monster underwater, and at Universal a Creature suit was made for him; but as many fans already know, his "performance" failed to impress director Arnold, who then had Browning assume the role. But Lamb had to have played the Gill Man at *some* early stage of production, in order for Arnold to *be* unimpressed—yes? On Day Three of second unit work (June 28), the Daily Production Report includes the notation "LAMB COULD NOT DO SCENE—PUT RICKY [RICOU BROWNING] INTO SUIT," which *to me* indicates that in all Gill Man footage shot prior to that Day Three notation, Lamb is in the suit. But Browning flatly insists, "I did *all* the underwater scenes"—and Tom Hennesy told me in 1994 that in the scenes featuring the bound-in-a-net Gill Man (shot on Days One and Two), the Gill Man was Browning.

Yes, this is all very complicated and confusing, and I promise we'll get past it as quickly as possible.

Day Two, a Saturday, went a lot better than the first, with a crew call of 7:30, a first shot at 9:08, and the only problems minor ones (repairs to the camera and to the Gill Man suit). The morning was spent in the receiving tank getting underwater shots of the kayoed Gill Man being "walked" by Joe; reviving and swimming around; and fighting with Joe. In the afternoon, after work moved back to the oceanarium, there were retakes of the shots of three

St. Augustine photographer Jere Beery, Sr., worked as an extra in *Revenge*, playing one of the photographers on the receiving tank promenade; so as long as he was there with a camera anyway, he took a series of photographs, including this one of Joe (John Bromfield) battling the Gill Man (Tom Hennesy) (courtesy Jere Beery, Jr.).

divers bringing the netted-up Gill Man to the bottom of the oceanarium and securing the anklet chain, plus shots of the net being removed and the Gill Man doing his first bit of oceanarium swimming. As mentioned above, *according to the Daily Production Reports* the Gill Man casting switch (from Lamb to Browning) wasn't made until Monday, so it should still be Lamb on Saturday. But Hennesy, who played one of the three divers, told me,

> I remember the sequence where Ricou played the Creature in a cargo net, being transported into the Marine Studios oceanarium. They had an air hose in there for him so that he could get air when needed; they incorporated it into the scene in such a way that it looked like a line. John Lamb, myself and one or two underwater attendants [played the men who] introduced the Creature into the oceanarium.[36]

And Ricou Browning recalls *being* the Gill Man in that scene, in an email to me adding the detail, "In long shots it was a dummy Creature, in close shots it was me."

Monday, June 28 began comically, although surely no one there at the time was amused: First thing in the a.m., a loaded camera went down into the oceanarium and a shot was lined up … and then the camera had to be brought up and *re*loaded, because it was accidentally running throughout that entire process! Lamb *was* in the Gill Man suit that morning, the production paperwork unmistakably says it was him: In the first shot of the day, a bit after 9:30, he swam around in the oceanarium, trying to convey anger. And at 10:30, script supervisor Dixie McCoy made the abovementioned Production Report notation "LAMB COULD NOT DO SCENE—PUT RICKY INTO SUIT." Elsewhere on that report, someone else (different handwriting) wrote, "50 minute delay due to John Lamb being unable to do required underwater swimming—necessitating changing to Ricou Browning."

Now you know how the surviving production paperwork … very sloppily handwritten, some of it indecipherable, with many misspellings, … describes the initial shooting of Gill Man scenes on Friday, June 25, Saturday, June 26, and the morning of Monday, June 28. According to the paperwork, Lamb and Browning were both there on those three days (but the paperwork does *not* say what they did on the first two days); Day Three began with Lamb floundering in the Gill Man suit and Browning replacing him.

Browning has an unshakable memory of playing the Gill Man right from *the very first moment* he stepped foot on the Marineland location—not only in the net scene but also being "walked" in the flume. He told me,

> I got a call from Jack Arnold asking me, "How would you like to work on a new Creature film?" I said sure and asked, "You want me to come to L.A. and get fitted for the costume?" He said, "No, we are already at Marine Studios in Florida and we need you to come down and work as the Creature. Can you get down here as soon as possible?" I said, "Okay, I can leave tonight," and I did—I drove down to Marine Studios. Once I arrived, Jack Kevan started cutting the John Lamb suits down to fit me so that I could begin to work immediately.[37]

The Gill Man became a full-fledged member of the Universal Monster blueblood club when the sequel Revenge of the Creature *made him a franchise monster; many fans consider him the last classic monster to rise from the Universal cauldron. In this photograph, Ricou Browning goes from Gill Man to milkman, tending to the needs of 19-month-old Ricou Jr.*

There's a natural inclination to place more trust in original production paperwork than on someone's (Browning's) memory of 60-year-old events … but when he's as emphatic as Ricou is, and when Hennesy backs him up (saying that it was Ricou as the Creature in a scene shot on Day One and/or Day Two), that "trust" in the paperwork begins to waver. There has to be a simple explanation that would make both the production paperwork *and* Ricou's memory correct, but probably too many years have passed to figure out what it is.

"John Lamb was a 'water man,' and they had hired him to do part of the [Creature swimming scenes]," Hennesy told me. "They did makeup tests and built a suit for John; he spent quite a bit of time in the [makeup department] before he went to Florida. But he ended up doing very little. I guess they shot a couple of things with John as the Creature, and the director became disenchanted with the way that John looked in the water; he said he looked like a man in a suit! So, unfortunately for John, they decided to terminate his employment [as the Creature]."

Sally Baskin remembers being told at the time that "the Hollywood stuntman" (Lamb) had to be replaced by Browning. Keep in mind that these are second-hand stories relayed to me by someone who was 12 when *she* heard them: Sally told me, "[Lamb] was there playing the Gill Man, but then the next thing I knew, it was Ricou Browning. I asked why, and they said that the first guy finally said, 'I can't *do* this!' The suit made him real nervous, claustrophobic, and he didn't like the sharks and other big fish all around."

Is John Lamb seen in the movie, even in a single shot, as the Creature? I don't know.

While Lamb did remain with the unit, from that morning on, only Browning played the Gill Man in underwater shots. But the switch created an annoying distraction: Browning's suits in *Black Lagoon*, made specifically for him, were form-fitting, whereas the Lamb suits that he had to wear in *Revenge* were big on him. Ricou said they were cut down a little, in order to make them fit better, but apparently there wasn't much they could do about the too-big head. Consequently, as the submerged Browning did his between-takes breathing, air would collect inside it—and, as cameras rolled, it seeped out through the foam rubber top via a stream of bubbles.

"Just before I'd do a shot, I'd push down on the top of my head, trying to get some of the air out," Browning told me. "But that head was so much bigger than the original [*Black Lagoon*] head, so much looser on me, that it held a lot more air." Equally unfortunate: The Creature heads worn in this movie by Browning *and* Hennesy have eyes that look like tanning bed goggles. Also, because the Marine Studios tank was filled with saltwater that made Browning's Gill Man suit more buoyant, he had to have more weights strapped to his body in order to be able to stay below the surface.

With Ricou in the Lamb suit, Monday's shooting resumed with the scene of Joe bringing the Gill Man a mesh cage full of fish, and the Gill Man sitting on the bottom-of-the-oceanarium anchor eating them. In the afternoon, $200-a-week underwater swimmers Ginger Stanley and Robert Lee Tinney joined the underwater cast of players: Stanley played Helen and Tinney played Clete in the scene where they begin to teach the Gill Man the meaning of "Stop!"[38] Stanley shares her memories of the making of *Revenge* in the interview in Chapter 6, "Creature Conversations."

Browning recalls another order of business he tried to take care of, early in the shooting of the sequel:

> I called Universal in California—I can't remember just who I talked to, it might've been the producer—and I told him that I'd like to get credit for playing the underwater Creature in the new film. Universal said that they couldn't do that; however, they would give me a great deal of publicity that would help me get future jobs. They *did* follow through with this and sent me a lot of clippings, stories about me playing the Creature. I believe that I asked for $600 a week which they gave me with no argument.

Florida rain, a regular nuisance for the *Black Lagoon* second unit during their Wakulla shooting, became a problem for the *Revenge* troupe for the first time that day: It clouded up at 3:25 and began raining ten minutes later, and it was still raining when they called it quits at 4:25. It didn't pay to get out of bed on the 29th, a day when practically nothing got on film because of heavy overcast skies, Marine Studios' regular fish-feedings, multiple camera jams, director Arnold needing to meet with the oceanarium manager, etc.

The next day (June 30) there was a different location, Silver Springs,[39] approximately 85 miles southwest of Marineland, but the same headaches (camera trouble, poor light, etc.). On this, the first of three days of Silver Springs production, the camera went underwater for a Gill Man's-eye view of swimming lovers Clete and Helen (Tinney and Stanley) taking their *Porpoise III* dip, hardhat diver Joe's descent into the Black Lagoon, part of the Black Lagoon fight between the Gill Man and Joe, and a shot of the Gill Man swimming as "bullets" strike the surface and course downward. That last bit of footage was used in both the Black Lagoon scene when it's Johnson firing, and in the Florida beach finale when it's the police firing.[40] A forgotten prop at Silver Springs: the Ocean Harbor manacle for the Gill Man's left ankle. He should be wearing it as he trails the *Porpoise III,* as he swims under Clete and Helen, and as he swims away from the rifle-firing policemen, but in all of those second-half-of-the-movie underwater scenes, his leg is bare.[41]

On July 1 at Silver Springs, the moviemakers again alternated between shooting underwater scenes of the Gill Man fighting Joe, and the Gill Man voyeuristically watching Clete and Helen. Browning told me he can't remember who doubled for John Bromfield as Joe in their fight scene: "He was just a hardhat diver who I think they hired out of Jacksonville. I have no idea who he was." The July 1 production paperwork doesn't mention the participation of an additional local diver, and *does* say that John Lamb and Browning's safety diver Charles McNabb *were* there; but Browning said that Joe's double was neither of them.

Around midday, the glass on the blimp of the under-

Ricou Browning with Revenge director Jack Arnold. When the Creature helmet was on him, the black makeup made it impossible to see, inside the Creature's mouth, the skin around Browning's mouth.

water camera broke and the camera flooded, ruining all the film inside. Welbourne drove to Palatka, almost 50 miles north, to fetch his own camera and he returned with it a little after two o'clock. Shooting resumed around three but then ended for the day at 3:35 when a thunderstorm came in. At this point, the production was a bit over budget and a day behind schedule. Welbourne's mobile underwater camera was again used on July 2, the company's last day in Silver Springs, as they concentrated on finishing the Clete–Helen–Gill Man scene. They wrapped things up at 2:40, loaded their trucks and got back to Marineland at just past six.

Between light conditions, rain, camera malfunctions and other problems, it isn't surprising that the company was beginning to fall behind—but there *may* also have been another reason. During production, the movie's publicist Robert Sill wrote to Universal's assistant publicity director Jack Diamond, "For reasons which I'll tell you when I return, the [Marine Studios] people were very cool and scarcely cooperative during the first couple of weeks the company was here. That, as well as the weather, had something to do with the company's falling behind schedule. Relations have improved very much in the past few days, so the work is proceeding much more smoothly now." The tense situation is even referenced in a Universal publicity release (probably also written by Sill) which may or may not have been distributed:

> [The *Revenge of the Creature* troupe] encountered a very cool and standoffish, if not downright hostile, attitude when they first came to Marineland. This proved something of a handicap at first to their production work, for the cooperation they received was grudging at best. All of this had changed to warm friendship and superlative cooperation before they left, and it was accomplished by the Hollywood folks' taking no apparent notice of the original hostility and acting themselves as simple, friendly souls who took it for granted that their friendship would be reciprocated—as it eventually was.

Regarding Sill's claims, Browning said, "This guy was dead wrong. They were *very* cooperative." Gloria Selph, widow of Marine Studios' aquarist Carl Selph,[42] recalled, "I saw nothing nor did I hear anything other than lots of fun for all involved," and Marine Studios guide-announcer Mike Gannon chimed in: "[The *Revenge* people] got complete cooperation from us and there was *never* any tension."[43] And if all these people are mistaken (which I'm sure they're *not*) and there *was* some early Marine Studios antagonism toward the moviemakers, the opportunity to shoot at the park was worth the hassle; the remarkable setting of exotic oceanaria and milling crowds makes *Revenge of the Creature* a one of a kind '50s monster movie. "What is probably the most unusual aquarium in the world makes a nice, picturesque background indeed," *The New York Times*' Howard H. Thompson wrote in his otherwise ornery *Revenge* review.[44]

Back at Marine Studios, the troupe put in a long, productive day on Saturday, July 3, getting lots of underwater oceanarium footage of Clete and Helen working with the Gill Man. Following the Fourth of July, they made up for Saturday's success with a lousy day on Monday, July 5: The scene of the Gill Man dragging Joe to the oceanarium bottom was all they had "in the can" by ten o'clock, when the light got bad and *stayed* bad. When a rainstorm set in at 3:30, they called it a day. By now they were two days behind schedule and $5000 over budget. July 6 got off to a bad start light-wise, but once things improved they got back into the oceanarium and shot more Clete–Helen–Gill Man byplay plus the monster's fight with Clete.

Universal cranked out a number of press items about Agar and Nelson doing their own aqualung diving in the oceanarium scenes. And in the 1980s, as I did my first interviews with them during my wet-behind-the-ears days, they talked about the experience and I swallowed it hook, line and sinker; the yarns they spun appeared in my magazine articles and earliest books. But Agar and Nelson

I was sitting there and I felt something tug on my foot. I looked down and, glory, it was a big turtle, and he had taken a big hunk out of the heel of the Creature's foot and he was swimming off with it. Luckily, he didn't get *me*, he got the foam rubber, and he was trying to eat it. I realized that this was my last pair of flippers—I wore the other ones out, 'cause the way you swim and hit things, you tear 'em up pretty much. That was the last pair, so I got out of the chain, swam up fast as I could and I was yelling to Jack Kevan, but he couldn't understand me. So I finally swam over there and he finally understood me: "The turtle's got the heel of the foot!" so everybody dove in the water and they went after the turtle [*laughs*]! They did get the piece back, and then I had to come out and they had to rinse it in fresh water and glue it back on.

In a publicity blurb about this incident, Universal said that the turtle was 350 pounds. (Ricou: "I don't think it was quite that big but I couldn't swear to it one way or the other.") Agar told me that Browning was nipped at by big sea turtles (plural) while director Arnold kept "turtle" singular and made it sound like Browning's suit was constantly having chunks bitten out of it; but Browning's memory is one turtle, one bite incident.[45]

Arnold liked to tell latter-day interviewers that he donned scuba gear and supervised the Creature movies' underwater scenes but that was certainly untrue in the case of *Black Lagoon*; Arnold was home in California when those underwater scenes were shot in Wakulla Springs. And Browning has no first-hand memory of the director underwater on *Revenge*:

Above water, Arnold and the rest of us would go over whatever scene was going to be shot next, talk about it, and then we'd go down and *do* it; or if we *didn't* do it, we'd come back up and talk again. If, once I was already underwater, they needed to give me some new instruction to do something simple, they would write it on a slate and show it to me: "Swim left to right," "Now swim right to left," "Pretend you're eating a fish," whatever it was. With no facemask on, my vision was poor, so they had to put the slate right up next to me and write in big letters, for me to be able to read it.

As far as Jack Arnold going underwater, I'm not sure. I was so busy doing my job, I wasn't positive who-all was underwater. But I would guess he didn't only because, if he did, I'm sure they would have shot a whole lot of publicity shots, and I've never seen any such photos.

Ginger Stanley also has no memory of Arnold getting wet:

"My, what big lies you have, Grandma!" For years, Lori Nelson and John Agar merrily told *Revenge* fans of the fun they had scuba-diving in the Marine Studios oceanarium during production. We were being harmlessly fooled: Underwater, Helen and Clete were played by no one but doubles Robert Lee Tinney and Ginger Stanley, pictured.

didn't do any underwater oceanarium acting; in fact, they were still in California, 2400 miles away, when Robert Lee Tinney and Ginger Stanley played Clete and Helen in all those scenes. (Perhaps at some point after they arrived in Florida, Agar and Nelson did swim in the oceanarium, either for fun or for still photography publicity purposes or both, and years later they remembered doing more oceanarium work in the movie than they really did.)

Browning recalled a loggerhead turtle giving him some trouble:

I had gone in the [oceanarium] and I was sitting down on a big anchor. They had the chain around my ankle in that scene, but I could get out of it any time I wanted. Anyway,

2. Revenge of the Creature (1955) 179

I don't really remember being next to him in a suit underwater, ever. I think of him being right up on the deck: He was always right there as we were going down into the water and as we were coming out. So I believe he did his directing from up on that deck. And if he had to see what we were doing underwater, he could go and watch us through those viewing windows that ran around those tanks.

Shooting on July 7 went well, other than the fact that a member of Ricou's safety team, his sister Shirley Woolery, "became ill from water infection from tank," according to the Production Report. One of the scenes shot that day: Clete and Joe attaching wires to the Gill Man (doped and unconscious on the bottom of the oceanarium) in order to measure his brain's electrical impulses.[46] Thursday, July 8, was the twelfth and last day of second unit work (which was supposed to take only ten days). The morning began with irritation and a lost hour as Flippy the "Educated" Porpoise refused to perform for the moviemakers who had set up cameras at his pool. Retreating in defeat, the filmmakers moved to the area near the Marine Studios box office—where, unlike Flippy, residents of St. Augustine were ready, willing and *eager* to perform.

"A movie studio coming to *our* area to make a movie? *Sure*, there was a feeling of excitement!" said John Carcaba, a University of Florida student when he played one of the panicky-looking Marine Studios evacuees during the Creature-on-the-loose scene. He told me, "St. Augustine's a small town, and you gotta remember, the movie industry hadn't come there yet.[47] So yes, there was excitement. Everybody was like, 'Hey! Somethin' new!,' and a few of my buddies were doin' it, so I decided, 'This sounds exciting. Let's have *at* it!' It was a novel experience for us." Sally Baskin said with a laugh, "When they put the call out that they needed extras, they came a-running!"

According to Universal publicity, during the moviemakers' several weeks at Marineland, they used 300 extras, all townsfolk of St. Augustine, the sleepy Florida city of approximately 14,000 located 18 miles away. Many of them were members of the St. Augustine Little Theater ... not surprising, since the extras casting was done by Maude Hecht and Charlotte Kaye, the Little Theater's leading lights.

"It was like the circus coming to town!" Judeena Blackmer excitedly recalled for me; she was five and a half when she played the child who trips and falls in the path of the Gill Man. "When the *Revenge* people arrived and made it known that they needed extras, it was a big deal for the people there, and I think everybody in St. Augustine showed up [*laughs*]! I'm *serious*! I know all my mom's friends went, and all their kids went. I wish you could talk to my mom,

Ocean Harbor's Gill Man standee is a blown-up shot of Ben Chapman as the Creature from the first movie, not the rather different-looking Creature seen in this *one. The pretty lady posing with it is probably Maria Gardner, a leading St. Augustine Little Theater player.*

she's gone, but she always told of the story of how, when the Creature escaped from the oceanarium and everybody ran, the people literally mowed down one of the chain link fences. When they ran, *they ran* [*laughs*]!"

Working for the first time with the St. Augustine locals, Arnold and Co. got the shot where the camera focuses on a life-sized cutout of the Gill Man, then pulls back to show a pretty girl getting her picture taken standing next to it. On the left is the box office, which is doing a brisk business. The movie camera then pans right to follow the girl and her photographer and, beyond them, we see the oceanarium.

The filmmakers then got the adrenaline of the extras going by getting various shots of folks fleeing the wrath of the Gill Man. Seventy-three people earned $10 a head that day, before rain put an end to all activity in the mid-afternoon. In one memorable moment, especially for fans seeing a tri-dimensional print, a pair of young men vault over a railing near the box office, the second one bumping the Creature cutout which topples toward the camera. Julian Fant, a 23-year-old St. Augustinian when *Revenge* was made, told me,

> A lot of my classmates were in the panic scene and, watching the movie, I can recognize a number of those kids. One of them was a neighbor who grew up with me from boyhood, by the name of Dick Watson. He later became involved with the University of Florida football team—he was quite an athlete—and then after he graduated, he became a circuit judge in St. Augustine for quite a few years. *He* was the kid who jumped over the rail near the Marine Studios front entrance and knocked over the cutout of the Creature.

Watson died in 2011, a few years after the courthouse complex on Lewis Speedway in St. Augustine was named the Richard O. Watson Judicial Center in honor of the well-respected senior jurist.

Extra Gloria Selph told me that even though there was no sound equipment there, "everybody—*everybody* who was running and waving their arms and acting like terrified people—we all *screamed*. Rewatching the movie the other day, I did not see my son, a little boy at that time, running beside me, but he did and he had a wonderful time yelling, 'cause he had to be so quiet other times!"

In addition to all the locals who played small parts or worked as extras, there were more who pitched in behind the scenes—like Sally Baskin's mom Mildred, wife and assistant of the manager of the Marine Village Court. Sally told me, "Whenever there were clothes that the movie people needed washed right away, an emergency situation, my mother would say, '*I'll* wash 'em up,' and she did, and she would hang 'em out by the beach and get 'em dry. My mother ended up washing a *lot* of clothes for them!"

Like many Hollywood movies, *Revenge* was planned with the precision of troop movements: Overlapping with the completion of the second unit work was the arrival from California of cast members plus behind-the-scenes folks (makeup, wardrobe, sound, electricians, etc.) whose services hadn't been needed during all the no-actors, no-lights, no-sound shooting done to date. In order to get to Florida, on at least two nights, groups of them had a midnight meeting with a bus at Universal's "B" gate; the bus delivered them to Los Angeles International Airport for a 1:20 a.m. American Airlines flight to Atlanta, where they then boarded a second plane bound for Jacksonville. Stars John Agar and Lori Nelson were aboard one of those red-eye flights, but beforehand they received preferential treatment: Rather than waiting for a bus at the Universal gate, they were met at their homes by a chauffeured car and brought to LAX. Nelson was picked at 5044 Bellaire Avenue, North Hollywood, at 11:45 p.m. and rode to the 249 West Spaulding,

Sally Baskin's dad Tom managed the Marine Village Court and her mom Mildred (pictured with an unidentified Revenge crew member) was his assistant. "Of course, Mom pretty much ran the place," Sally said with a laugh. "That's a daughter talking!" (courtesy Sally Baskin).

Beverly Hills, home of Agar, and together they proceeded to the airport.

The *Revenge* troupe's sleeping accommodations (61 beds) were provided by the Marine Village Court. Sally Baskin thought that having all these movie people at the motel managed by her parents was "pretty neat":

> I was then 12 years old, and of course when I found out that John Agar had been married to Shirley Temple, he had stars in his crown. John Bromfield was flexing the muscles constantly and walking around in his little Speedo, and I wasn't too impressed by that. But Lori Nelson—I fell in love with her. She was *so* nice, *so* sweet. And everybody else, too, they were very kind to me.

Just eight years little Sally's senior, Nelson came onto the movie unaware of Jack Arnold's reputation as one of Universal's resident wolves—and not just when the autumn moon was bright. Nelson told me that, while settling into her motel room, she was surprised to find that the connecting door to the adjoining room was unlocked. One phone call to the front desk later, she had her explanation: The next room was Arnold's, and the married, twice-her-age director had instructed motel staffers to unlock it. Move, countermove: Nelson locked the door herself, then asked her hairdresser Lillian Burkhart to double-up with her, "tossing cold water on Jack Arnold's little plan," as Lori put it. Arnold, undeterred, persisted in visiting the women's room, offering neck and foot massages; Lori and Lillian would let him stick around and chat, but massages were a no-no.[48] At Nelson's request, Burkhart stuck by her side so tightly that Tom Hennesy assumed they were mother and daughter ("Lori's mother was there constantly!" Hennesy said with a laugh in our interview), and Sally Baskin came to the conclusion that the joined-at-the-hip Burkhart was Nelson's "personal helper and companion." Because of Lori and Lillian's constant togetherness, Arnold finally had to give up. When I asked Nelson if I could use this anecdote in print, she said that since Arnold never worried about his reputation while he was alive, *she*

One day during the making of *Revenge*, a woman makeup artist told 12-year-old Sally Baskin, "This is your makeup day. I'm going to make you up." Sally recalls, "And, oh, they glamorized me! My makeup and hair were done as we sat out on a little patio. Lori Nelson was sitting there too, giving her opinion and making me think I was *sooo* important. My life was a bathing suit or shirt-and-shorts, I didn't go the glamour route, so it was kind of fun!" The result is pictured (courtesy Sally Baskin).

Lori Nelson and two unidentified women, both members of the *Revenge* crew. Presumably one of them is her hairdresser Lillian Burkhart, who stuck to Lori like glue to protect her from director Jack Arnold (courtesy Sally Baskin).

wasn't going to worry about his reputation while he was dead.

"He was a dreadful man, a goddamn terrible sexual harasser," William Alland told me in 1995:

> Well, you know, sexual harassment only became in the last few years something that people *do* something about. Today Jack would be arrested, he was sick in the head that way. At Universal, the secretaries always came from the secretarial pool, and when Jack worked for me, we'd give him an office with a secretary. Jesus, they had one hell of a job getting secretaries for him, nobody wanted to work for him. So many secretaries complained about his behavior, you wouldn't believe it. Awful! I *think* the studio finally stopped supplying him with secretaries. Secretaries just *blanched* at the idea of having to go to work for him. Just a terrible man.

Prior to Susan Hart's days of AIP stardom, she had a brush with the pervy picturemaker when she was hired to play a bit in Bob Hope's *A Global Affair* (1964). On a locker room set at MGM, she and fellow bit player Brenda Benet rehearsed a scene in which they exchanged a few lines while taking off their sweaters, as called for in the script—and then director Arnold announced that in the take, they were to remove their sweaters and then also their blouses (i.e., strip right down to their undergarments). Stunned, Hart whispered to Benet, "I'm not going to do this," and got back a "Neither am I!" Hart told Arnold that this wasn't in the script or mentioned when she got the part, and that she'd have to call her agent. "It was a lecherous move," Hart told me. "I was angry and insulted. And when we balked, he was not happy." Over the phone, Hart's agent Fred Briskin told her not to do it, which she didn't; Benet refused also.[49]

By this time, the mid–1960s, Arnold was working mostly in TV, directing *and* producing, with *Gilligan's Island* and *Mr. Terrific* among the series to his credit (or *dis*credit—you make the call!). Decades after *Mr. Terrific*'s short run, the blood pressure of its star Stephen Strimpell still would soar at the mention of Arnold's name. In a 2002 letter he raged to me about what he called "Jack's satyriasis":

> Once, at a script conference, I advised him that he should go to a whorehouse every day before shooting and get it off since his behavior was reprehensible, and, furthermore, reflected on me since my name was all over the thing [the *Mr. Terrific* series]. The advice was clearly not taken, and a silence fell o'er the room like an Old Testament plague.
>
> There was one time when a young actress actually brought her grandmother with her onto the *Mr. Terrific* set to protect her from the incarnation of sexual depravity (Jack Arnold, lest you missed it and how could you?). And the honorable producer of *Gilligan's Island* and horror films put the moves on the grandmother! I saw him pull the top of her blouse away and look down at her breasts. As is the case in situations so appalling, we were all speechless. And there was more.

Ginger Stanley, Lori's underwater double on *Revenge*, told me that Arnold's reputation as a wolf preceded him to Marine Studios, "and I think Lori *was* afraid of him. But," she added, "he could not have been nicer to me. He talked to me almost like a father figure, very nice, very complimentary, never made a pass. I didn't see him make any passes at Lori, but then again, Lori and I were rarely in the same place at the same time: If I was there, then she was not, because I was her double! All I can say is that he was exceedingly nice to me." John Agar, star of *Revenge* and Arnold's *Tarantula* (1955), also never saw that side of the director and liked him very much. In 1986 (while Arnold was still alive), Agar said in our first interview, "I've always had nothing but great respect for Jack Arnold.... So far as I was concerned, he was a very knowledgeable director and he gave his all trying to make 'em the best that he could. Jack is a great guy. I don't think Universal was too kind to Jack, I think he should have been given a lot more opportunities."

On July 9, the words "Start of Principal Photography" were written across the front of the Daily Production Report. And on Day One of first unit production, Florida weather being what it is, they had to play everything by ear: At 8:45 a.m. when they were ready to shoot outdoors, the sky *wasn't* ready (insufficient light), so they moved to a porthole corridor and shot the first scene of Clete and Helen (now played by Agar and Nelson) watching the Gill Man through portholes. Nelson told me on the *Revenge of the Creature* DVD audio commentary,

> One of the most impressive and most exciting things about being down in Marineland, Florida, was watching Ricou Browning do all of those underwater scenes. I was *so* impressed with him. I think I was more impressed with him than anything else about the movie.... It was just fantastic, the way he did it. And he was so *graceful* in that big, heavy, cumbersome suit. He *really* moved like a fish.

Her companion in commentary Bob Burns concurred: "I'm still fascinated by the way that he could move in the suit. From wearing [gorilla] suits, I know how constrictive they can be, and he just made it look so effortless—totally. It was just amazing."

Even the scene of Agar and Nelson in the oceanarium corridor—an *interior*—was affected by the weather: As the actors rehearsed, a bad storm broke out and the oceanarium water became so dark that little could be seen through the portholes! A change in the camera setup enabled Arnold to shoot closeups of the two actors delivering their dialogue with the viewing window less prominently featured. The rain stopped at 12:20 but the heavy storm clouds lingered and continued to put a crimp in the activities. In the mid-afternoon the cameras went back into the oceanarium for inside-looking-out panning shots of the faces of gawkers

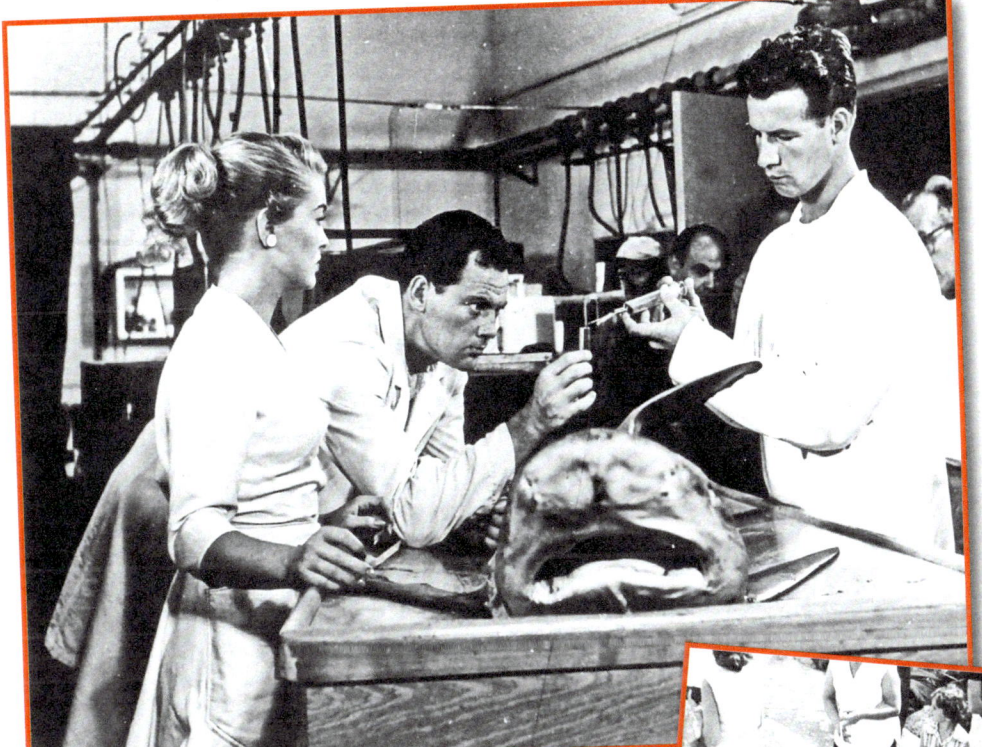

For the lab scene, Ricou Browning shed his foam rubber epidermis to play a lab-smocked assistant, using a hypodermic needle to draw blood from a dead shark.

pearance here. This was one of just three interiors shot in Florida, the other locations being the porthole corridor and Jacksonville's Lobster House. After lunch, all equipment was moved back to the porthole corridor and more of that Clete–Helen scene was shot. At the day's end, rather than simply dismissing the corridor's many extras, the moviemakers instructed them to *run* out—footage that could eventually be added to the Gill Man's Ocean Harbor rampage scene.

A day of rest (Sunday, July 11) and then back in the oceanarium on Monday for shots of the Gill Man looking out a porthole (including Agar and Nelson) at the portholes. Since the light conditions had been extremely poor all day and might be just as bad the *next* day, Arnold and a few crew members adjourned to Marine Studios' research lab (read all about its establishment and purpose in Gregg Mitman's book *Reel Nature*) and discussed the possibility of having to spend July 10 shooting in there.

Sure enough, there was no sun in that part of the Sunshine State on Saturday, July 10, so into the lab Agar, Nelson and the crew went, getting lots of shots of Agar putting a crab in a small fish tank and putting drops in a beaker, Nelson using a microscope and handling test tubes, etc. (Some of these shots aren't in the movie.) Browning even makes a cameo ap-

Tom Hennesy gets set to take his stretcher hoist ride from the truck to the receiving tank—and wonders whether he'll get there in one piece (courtesy Jere Beery, Jr.).

hole at Helen; and then back to the corridor for shots of Helen looking *in* the porthole at the Gill Man. Here for the first of *three* times in *Revenge*, Arnold fell back on his tried-and-true hand-on-the-shoulder trick: Nelson is at the porthole, tensely staring through the tempered glass into the face of Browning's Gill Man inches away, when Agar suddenly reaches in and touches her. But surprise-wise it's a complete bust, because Agar's stationary shadow is clearly visible on the wall beside her throughout the buildup.

Newly arrived in Florida, actors Grandon Rhodes, Dave Willock and Robert B. Williams did their first work on July 13 as scenes in and around the Marine Studios receiving tank were shot: the stretcher bearing the Gill Man (Hennesy) descending into the tank, Joe "walking" the Gill Man, and onlooker Helen being interviewed by a microphone-wielding radio announcer (played by James Fisher, in real life a radio announcer on WFOY, the oldest radio station in St. Augustine). Hennesy remembered the stretcher hoist well in our interview:

> When they first brought the Creature into the small receiving tank, I did that part of it.... [T]he operator of the hoist said that it was very ancient and rickety and noisy, and he said that he hoped that it worked better than it did the last time. When asked what he meant by that, he said that they had been hoisting a shark or a porpoise into the tank and the thing unwound and collapsed, and the fish was dropped onto the pavement below, and killed, evidently.

According to Universal paperwork, it was decided early in *Revenge*'s planning that for the scene of the Gill Man arriving at Ocean Harbor, "we will use the identical methods employed at Marine Studios for the transference and handling of large fish, since they are colorful and extremely visual." And Sally Baskin confirms that they did just that:

> The Gill Man arrives on the boat *Porpoise III*, which was an actual Marine Studios boat that would go out and capture porpoise, dolphin, shark, whatever [which would then be kept in a "live well" inside the boat]. The boat would come in to the dock, just as you see in the movie, and they would take the porpoise, dolphin, shark, whatever, out through the side hatchway and onto that canvas stretcher and bring it to the receiving tank—the whole procedure you see in the movie. Then the sharks had to be walked, to get their gill systems working. The dolphins would be walked, too, but it was pretty much to calm them down. Smaller fish—barracudas and all—would be put directly into the oceanarium, but the sharks and dolphins had to be walked before they could be let loose.[50]

On the promenade watching the "walking" of the Creature are dozens of St. Augustine locals-cum-movie extras, some of them well-known in the community. The reporter standing behind Helen, taking notes as she's interviewed, was played by Steve Wehking, who with his wife Bonnie ran the concession stand on the St. Augustine Beach Pier, local kids' favorite summer hangout. Moments later, the camera-carrying man who says that Joe has been walking the Gill Man "about two hours" is Jere Beery, Sr., one of

Fishin' Accomplished: The captured Gill Man (Hennesy) arrives at Ocean Harbor. The PA announcer calls this action "the Creature's official entry into the 20th century."

the city's commercial photographers.[51] At the time, Beery was the only professional shutterbug taking pictures of tourists enjoying the city's famous horse and carriage rides. He also owned and operated a photographic studio on Aviles Street. His son Jere Beery, Jr., told me,

> At the time [the summer of 1954], I was six years old and my dad and mom and my sister Patsy and I were starring in a production of *The Great Big Doorstep* at the St. Augustine Little Theater on Artillery Lane. Evidently one of Universal's scouts, or *some*body, came to the theater and saw the acting ability of my family and told Daddy, "Get your family together and come down and interview for some parts." The part that he interviewed for was that of a reporter-photographer. And it just so happens that my dad *was* a professional photographer, and he had his own equipment; *that* was kind of a bonus for them, they didn't have to provide him with props. My sister Patsy was hired to play in another scene.

The Beery family was then living near the St. Augustine Lighthouse, in what was once the lighthouse keeper's building; the Coast Guard had recently put this duplex up for rent. The Beerys occupied half of it for $35 a month, "and I grew up, from that point on, with a lighthouse in my backyard, not more than 75 or 80 feet away," Jere Jr. told me.[52] Jere Jr. was up for the *Revenge* role of a child who, fleeing the Gill Man at Ocean Harbor, trips and falls onto a cargo net and then cowers as the Gill Man looms above him. He auditioned for the job at home:

> I can't tell you if it was the director, assistant director, producer or *who* it was, but some guy came and auditioned me on the floor of our kitchen: I laid down on the floor and my dad pretended like he was the Creature and I acted scared and cried and all that. And I got the part. When we got to Marineland where my scene was going to be shot, they wanted to do some rehearsals right on the spot where the scene was going to be shot—they had the cargo net on the ground there and everything. But the rehearsals weren't *with* the monster or my father, they were with some guy who was, like, the assistant director or some prop man or gaffer playing the part of the monster. He struck me as funny, and I started laughin', and when you're six years old and you get to gigglin', you can't quit it. Every time I would lie down on the ground and this assistant director (or whoever he was) would pretend like he was the Creature, I would crack up!
> They tried it three or four times and I was getting no better, and evidently it wasn't a comedy [*laughs*], so I was "out." That's how I shot myself in the foot. At the time, I was not that disappointed about losing out on the part. I was just there for the fun of it. I got to be at Marine Studios all day long—didn't have to have a ticket [*laughs*]—and I got to see everything that was goin' on and I got to hang out in "the actors' area" with John Agar and Lori Nelson and John Bromfield, because at that particular time, *briefly*, I was "an actor"! It wasn't until years later that I realized the magnitude of my blunder. If I hadn't started giggling, it would have been a Beery family hat trick, three of us in one picture.[53]

Jere Jr.'s website tells the story of his family's brushes with show biz and features marvelous photos his dad took in and around the flume on that memorable July 13, including some with the Creature in action. (Google "Jere Beery" "Revenge of the Creature" to find it.) Actually, Beery Sr. took a lot more pics than the handful that exist now: For several days on the *Revenge* set he photographed everything that was happening, using up perhaps as many as 23 rolls of 120 black-and-white film. But some time in the late 1950s, a basement water pipe broke and all of his stored photos and negatives were destroyed. Jere Jr. had nine *Revenge* photos upstairs in his room because he'd recently taken them to school for Show and Tell, so they're the nine survivors.

Jere Jr. has one more colorful memory of his time on the *Revenge* set:

> One other thing that's stayed with me is that, there at Marine Studios that day there was a small trailer, and inside the trailer there were maybe a dozen or more Creature suits, different colors and different sizes—evidently Ricou Browning was shorter than Tom Hennesy. They were all basically the same color but some were lighter, some were darker. I wish that my dad had gotten a picture of *that*, because that's really a behind-the-scenes type sight that a lot of fans would have enjoyed. That stuck in my mind to the extent that I've *never* forgotten: There I was, six years old, standing at the trailer door and lookin' at like a dozen monsters hanging up in a trailer. I'll *never* forget that!

It's hard not to notice that Tom Hennesy's Land Creature has a lot more pep in his step throughout *Revenge* than Ben Chapman's did in *Black Lagoon* (plus a habit of lashing out with his arms in a swatting-at-flies sort of way). Perhaps the change to a step-lively Gill Man was necessitated by the Ocean Harbor escape scene. In *Black Lagoon*, the Gill Man walked at a dawdling pace that, in the land speed record books, earned him a spot between the Frankenstein Monster and the Mummy; if the Gill Man had tried to escape from Ocean Harbor at that rate, the screaming, panicking crowds would have looked ridiculous. In fact, Ocean Harbor might have had to stay open late waiting for him to get to the egress!

On July 14 the receiving tank battle between the Gill Man and his captors was filmed. Except for a few mid-afternoon minutes spent waiting for the light to improve, the weather apparently cooperated, making it a good day for the still-behind-schedule, still-over-budget production. But it wasn't a good day for the beleaguered Gill Man Tom Hennesy, who told me:

I was fighting at least three people there, Bromfield and two local Florida stuntmen. It was very difficult, and I had to fight to keep from being drowned. They weren't accomplished Hollywood stuntmen, *any* of 'em, so I had a hell of a fight with all three of them. I got frustrated, 'cause these guys were choking me, and if they had gotten me underwater, they would have held me down and drowned me! I could tell immediately that this was no game—maybe these guys thought I *was* a creature! Maybe they thought they were fighting for *their* lives, but I felt that I was fighting for *mine*. So I finally said, "The heck with it," it was do or die, so I did what I had to do, and it became a knock-down, drag-out brawl!

In 2003 Hennesy told this anecdote to the World 3-D Film Expo audience, this time specifying that Bromfield was *not* one of the guys fighting as though Hennesy was an actual monster. He now classified the others as local musclemen rather than stuntmen and, perhaps playing to the audience, came up with an even better punchline:

I finally got so exasperated with these guys … I picked up one guy and threw him into the wall [*audience laughter*]. I was told that he got three fractured ribs out of it [*audience gasps and groans*]. And the rest of 'em kinda backed off a little bit [*audience laughter*].

Even though a good bit of what Hennesy did in the movie as "Gill Man #2" would seem to fall into the category of stunt work, he got only $300 a week. That's less than half of what John Bromfield got per week, three-tenths of what Nestor Paiva got per week, half of what Dave Willock got per week. Even some of the Floridian butchers, bakers and candlestick makers recruited to play tiny one-day roles for $70 paychecks made more in a day than Hennesy did! He told me,

They were very cheap with me, they didn't want to pay any stunt adjustments, they just wanted to pay the contract-agreed price, which is not normal practice for stunt work. The whole portrayal of the Creature was not just an acting job, it was a *stunt* job, a *difficult* stunt job. In order to be fair, they should have made adjustments for a number of things. I asked for some adjustments on various occasions and was refused, and they acted as though I'd be terminated if I asked again.

When Hennesy related the story about the receiving tank attendants getting carried away, he could have been talking about his fight with them on this date, July 14, or the fight he had on July 23 when he returned to the tank for over an hour to do many fight retakes. Worst case scenario: He was talking about *both* fights!

The men contending with Hennesy in the receiving tank apparently took the Creature seriously, and so did Universal: In a July 15 letter sent from Florida to the studio's assistant publicity director Jack Diamond, *Revenge* publicist Robert Sill wrote that production manager Russ Haverick was in Jacksonville making hotel arrangements for the unit's upcoming stay there, and the press agent for the hotel had come up with a publicity gimmick: "It's simple enough—have the Gill Man photographed registering at the hotel—and there's no doubt that at least the local papers would go for it. There's even a chance that the wire services would use it." Sill continued,

I told Russ, however, that this was just the sort of gag that I had been instructed not to stage, explaining that we wanted to do nothing that would lessen the Creature's horror impact. Having already virtually assured the [Jacksonville hotel press agent] that we'd go for the stunt, Russ asked me to do what he does on all questions of policy in

Joe (John Bromfield) looks like he's getting tough with the Gill Man (Tom Hennesy), but no Creatures were harmed during the making of this movie: The Universal prop shop made boat hooks out of balsa and rubber, with rubber tips. The script called for the Creature to recognize and remember Joe from encounter to encounter and develop a deep hatred; the movie doesn't get this idea across.

his own job, which is to check with my superior at the studio."

Diamond wrote back to Sill: "You are right in policy matter on Creature Jacksonville hotel registration stunt, which is exactly what we seek to avoid even though it is pushover publicity opportunity. As discussed here at highest levels, we wish to publicize Creature in scariest possible manner and not poke fun at."

On July 15, Hennesy's Creature was back in the oceanarium, struggling to climb out past a boat hook–wielding Joe, and pulling Joe into the water. The accent remained on action on July 16 with more takes of the abovementioned battle, plus the memorable down-shot of Browning's Gill Man rocketing head-first out of the tank toward the tri-dimensional camera. Browning told me that, in preparation for that shot, "they put a strap around my waist that also went over my shoulders, and the straps all came together in a big ring at the back of my neck. Once that was all secure, I got into the Creature suit. They hooked a cable into that ring, and then they had the cable go up into a pulley. Then they had men with ropes that were tied to the cable, and they all just yanked it, and yanked me right outta there!" He recalled being jerked up too high on the first attempt, and everything going well on the second. The book *Directed by Jack Arnold* includes storyboard artwork of this scene, and it shows the Creature standing on the oceanarium bottom on one end of a seesaw; Browning said no such contraption was used.

On the morning of July 17, the company got a shot of Agar and Nelson lowering a loudspeaker into the oceanarium ("Testing, one, two, three, four!"). They then moved to Porpoise Stadium for footage of Agar, Nelson and Bromfield in the audience of a Flippy performance. They were joined there by the newest member of the cast, a six-year-old male German Shepherd playing Chris, Helen's "one true love and favorite boyfriend."[54] After lunch, operations moved to the Marineland wharf and the scene of the *Porpoise III* arriving with its Creature cargo. As noted earlier, the *Porpoise III* was the actual "collection boat" or "catch boat" on which Marine Studios' specimen hunters went out to sea to get new recruits for exhibition at the marine mammal park. The body of water in the wharf scenes is a lagoon off of the Intracoastal Waterway.

Perhaps because the filmmakers were now behind schedule and $12,500 over budget, Florida shooting became seven days a week. The first Sunday of work (July 18) began back in Porpoise Stadium with Flippy again failing to do his tricks for the cameras.[55] Thinking on their feet, the filmmakers moved their equipment to the beach near the Marine Village Court in preparation for the shooting of Clete and Helen's love scene, then returned to Flippy's tank, set up a camera and filmed part of the "Educated" Porpoise's regular 9:30 performance (Flippy jumping through the suspended paper hoop). They then headed *back* to the beach and shot the romantic scene with Agar, Nelson and Chris the dog.[56] The dog ruined nearly a dozen takes so you wonder who Jack Arnold was more eager to strangle, the dog or Flippy. Then it was back to Porpoise Stadium to photograph *two* more regularly scheduled Flippy performances. An unhappy Arnold had to burn up a lot of film photographing most or all of the Flippy shows newsreel-style because he didn't know what Flippy would do next or when he'd do it: Arnold went through over 6680 feet of raw stock that day, 2460 of it wasted.

Also unhappy that day was little Sally Baskin, who was sorely disappointed at what did and didn't happen during the filming of Agar and Nelson's beach scene:

> When I was told they were going to do a kissing scene, boy, being 12 years old, I wanted to check *into* that! There was a rock wall, to hold back the sand dunes, and I sat up on that, and I watched as about 20 people stood all around [Agar and Nelson] lying on a towel. The dresser was trying to make sure that her bathing suit was just right and that his shorts were just right, and a makeup person was making sure their hair was just right, and I was thinkin', "When are they gonna get to this kissing scene?" Well, then they rolled the cameras, and I thought, "What kind of people want to kiss while there's 20 people watchin' 'em?" To me, kissing was a very loving thing! Well, John and Lori got through the scene and they got up and walked separate ways, and I thought, "Huh? What's *this* about?" [*Laughs.*] It was not anything like what I expected!

Agar and Nelson, the only two actors to work that Sunday, got the next two days off as the rest of the *Revenge* company trekked to Palatka, Florida, to shoot the topside parts of the Black Lagoon opener. On Monday they traveled to the location from 6 a.m. to 7:15, spent 45 minutes loading their belongings onto a barge, and then at eight o'clock they proceeded several miles up Rice Creek, a St. Johns River tributary. Repeating his Lucas role from *Black Lagoon*, Nestor Paiva joined the cast that morning, sharing scenes with Bromfield and Robert B. Williams as Ocean Harbor's Creature hunters. Shot this first day at Palatka were the action scenes: the *Rita II* arriving and dropping anchor; Joe descending the ladder into the water; Johnson, Lucas and the two native crew members on deck trying to save the underwater Joe from the Creature.

Cast and crew got back to Marineland at 6:40 p.m. The next day (Tuesday, July 20), the second half of the Palatka shooting was done. Universal publicity mentions that these Black Lagoon scenes were shot under a fierce sun and in stifling atmosphere, and this time, it was no flack's fabrication: At 9:15 a.m., Wallace Mussallem, a Florida local playing one of Lucas' native crewmen, fell unconscious as a result of the steamy, jungle-like heat. At another point in the day, script clerk Dixie McCoy became the second casualty of the subtropical climate. Browning added a detail *not* supplied by the publicity department: Not only was Rice Creek hot and the air thick with humidity, but they were shooting about a mile from a paper mill, and the stench was overpowering! "The paper mill, just down the way, discharged their waste water [chemicals, etc.] in Rice Creek," he ruefully recalled. Presumably the mill in question was the Hudson Pulp & Paper Corp. mill, which began operations in Palatka in 1947. It's now a Georgia-Pacific mill, annually producing over a half-million tons of paper products.

Sally Baskin didn't accompany the troupe to Rice Creek but she saw them when they returned:

> They were transported back and forth by bus, and I'd be around when they returned to Marineland and I can remember how bad they smelled. Rice Creek was very smelly, very odorous, very slimy, and when they would come out of the water there, they'd have slime coming off of their suits and off of their bodies. When they got back to Marineland, the first place they headed was to the beach. Nobody went straight to their rooms, they went straight to the beach and jumped into the ocean, clothes and all, trying to get that smell off of 'em. There's no other smell like a paper mill!

Browning told me that swimming in Rice Creek was "as bad as swimming in your toilet."

On that second day of Rice Creek shooting, the blast that (storyline-wise) concusses the Gill Man was set off a little before three, sending water sky-high. You'll notice that, after the detonation, the cans that supposedly contained the explosives drop from the sky and bob around undamaged; that's because no explosives were used. According to Browning, the moviemakers somehow created the large upheaval of water with a great "eruption of air," as he calls it. "I don't know exactly how they set the charge, but it wasn't dynamite or anything like that." The fish on the surface in the next scene were dead fish that had been bought and brought to the location. "Some would float and some wouldn't," Browning continued, "so air was pumped into the ones that wouldn't, to make them stay on the surface."

Also shot that day was the unforgettable moment where the Gill Man snatches the bird off the log. Browning said that the bird was the tame pet of a friend. "We didn't harm it," he told me. "I set it there on the log and went under, came up, grabbed it, pulled it down, then came back up with it and let it go."

Lori Nelson didn't have to go on that dreadful-sounding Palatka excursion, but Florida shooting was no day in the park for her either. "Oh, boy, I'll tell ya, [Florida is] hot," she said on the *Revenge* audio commentary. "It's *hot* and *humid* and *almost* unbearable. And we were there for quite some time! We

Robert B. Williams, John Bromfield, Nestor Paiva and, in wig and hat, Florida local Wallace Mussallem (1923–2008) as a Rita II crew member. Wallace's younger brother Edward Mussallem, former mayor of St. Augustine, laughingly told me, "Wallace went out on location to do the movie, it was hot-hot weather, he passed out, and he got paid all of $20! When the movie came out, we all went to see him in it. Well, if you blinked your eyes, you'd have missed him!"

were there for several weeks.… It was so humid that our shoes mildewed in the closet. And the bugs were pretty bad."

There *were* compensations and they included, according to Baskin, "a bonfire on the beach just about every night, and swimming, and everything else. After each day's work was over, they [the moviemakers] would be 'in their cups' [drunk] and get into their afternoon parties."

"We all got kind of carried away on that picture," Agar told me. "We started having water gun fights and, gosh, it got to the point where one guy got up on top of a cottage with a bucket of water and poured it all over a bunch of people! … We just had a heck of a good time."

"We had a water fight and a big one," Browning recalled, "but it was only for one night. I think we started around sunset and it lasted until about 10, 10:30 at night. We would fill balloons with water. We chased each other around the motel and tossed the balloons until they broke on the wall or on their bodies, and it was a lot of fun. Everybody participated and it was a pretty wet night. I believed it ended when we went down to the beach, built a fire and had a few *more* drinks and a few more laughs. But not enough drinks that we were unable to go to work the next morning."

July 21 was a never-to-be-forgotten day for many St. Augustinians as Arnold and Co. resumed shooting at Marineland with more shots of the stampede that follows the Gill Man's escape. Seventy-five extras got $10 each for joining in this mass exodus. First they shot, twice, the vignette where a mother and her little girl are trying to outpace the Gill Man, the latter falling onto a cargo net while the mother obliviously continues on alone. Five-year-old Judeena Blackmer—a relative of stage and movie actor Sidney Blackmer—played the girl, having replaced giggler Jere Beery, Jr., in the role. (Judeena and Jere were classmates; Jere told me, "She was the first girl I ever had a crush on. She was absolutely adorable.") Judeena vividly recalled for me that in a rehearsal,

> the monster was going to come around the corner of a building, and I was supposed to see him and scream and run. Then when he came around the corner, the guy was in the rubber suit but he didn't have the head on. Well, that was *not* scary, and I guess I was not very good at fakin' an "I'm scared" scream. We did it a couple of times, and I just wasn't afraid. But I'll never forget, they did a take, and he came around the corner, *and he had the head on*. It scared the absolute *stew* out of me! I ran, and I was supposed to fall on top of the net. I ran … and I ran … [*Laughs.*] I did not fall, I just *ran*, it scared me so bad![57] So then we did it again, and that's the one little split-second that I was in the picture. By the way, I recently learned that Clint Eastwood is also in that movie, in a small part. *He* got "discovered," and I didn't [*laughs*]! And I think I was cuter than *he* was!

The woman playing the mother in the scene was paid $70 rather than the $10 that the other extras got. She was *not* Judeena's mother—although Judeena's mother Mary *was* part of the frenzied-looking crowd. As Judeena puts it, "Yeah, she was there—with everybody *else* in St. Augustine!" Judeena watches for her mom every time she sees the movie but has never been able to spot her in the panoramic shots of running extras. She adds, "My kids, they watch the movie and their attitude is, 'Oh, come *on. That's* not scary.' And I say, 'Yeah, but it was back *then*.'" In his *Revenge* review, Al

Wiped out from the heat of the suit and exertion, Ricou Browning rests his head on an inner tube and grabs 40 winks. This shot is from either *Revenge of the Creature* or *Creature Walks* (courtesy State Archives of Florida).

While escaping from Ocean Harbor, the Creature (Tom Hennesy) looms over a little girl (Judeena Blackmer) who has tripped and fallen. After Judeena grew up and became a mother, one of her kids looked at this photograph and asked, "What's the Creature doin' coming out from behind a shower curtain?"

Ricketts of *Pacific Stars and Stripes* pointed out that when the Gill Man "gallantly" bypassed the mother and child, he proved "beyond a doubt that chivalry was in bloom in the days of dinosaurs and pterodactyls."

In this escape scene, John Carcaba was one of the young men putting daylight between himself and the Gill Man. He told me, "Working in *Revenge of the Creature* goes back a few years but I still look back on it fondly. It was a very interesting experience. And I'll add as a side note that, when I moved to my present home, I began gettin' rid of a whole bunch of stuff, and I found my Universal Studios metal badge that I pinned on every day when we were on the set. That identified you as part of 'the cast.' We were supposed to turn the badges back in, I think, but I never did."

After shooting Judeena's scene, the filmmakers moved their cameras back to the top deck of the oceanarium and photographed Gill Man Tom Hennesy clambering out over the wall, with hysteria breaking out all about him. Watch in the distant background, on the right, as Agar dives into the oceanarium[58] and into a situation that he admits "could have been a little disastrous." Agar told me,

> There's one part of the main tank that had a kind of rock formation just below the surface. During the scene where the Creature escapes—grabs Johnny Bromfield, pulls him in the water and kills him—I was standing at the far end of the tank. *Why* I did this I will never know [*laughs*], but I dove back into the tank at that point, not realizing how close to the surface of the water those rocks were. If I hadn't flattened my dive at the last second, I would've hit it flush. This is just speculation, but if I had hit there hard and maybe gotten a bloody nose or something, it might have been a different kind of story, according to what I've heard about sharks and the way they smell blood out in water.

More escape scene footage was shot in the afternoon. In order for Gill Man Hennesy to flip the Pontiac sedan, cables ran from the vehicle to a tow truck which pulled it over. (It was Hennesy's memory that a tow truck was used, and there *is* a tow truck on the July 21 production report's "Special Equipment" list. But onlooker Sally Baskin remembers men on the beach pulling the cables on the car, which she described as "stripped until all it *was* was a shell.") Many extras formed a large off-camera audience as the action was shot twice: once with the camera shooting up from the beach at the car and Creature with Marine Studios in the background, the other time shooting the car and Creature with the Atlantic Ocean in the background. *Both* times, Hennesy was a bit concerned: "It was a dangerous thing for people working around there," he said in our interview, "because if a cable had broken and whipped back, it could have killed *every*one." (In an early script, it's not an empty car but a stalled car filled with sightseers that gets overturned.)

The camera-on-the-beach take was used even though the rolling car very noticeably clips the camera, making it pan to the left a bit—and thereby giving us a glimpse, in the distant background, of a building marked Marine Studios Biological Station, which is where interior lab scenes featuring Agar, Nelson and Browning were shot several days earlier. This shot, plus another shot where a sabal palm partially hides a Marine Studios sign on a building wall (approximately 30:50 on the DVD), are the only two "plugs" that Marine Studios gets in *Revenge*.[59] Otherwise, all Marine Studios signs were avoided by Universal's cameras, or perhaps removed, and Ocean Harbor signs substituted: We see the words "Ocean Harbor" on a wall when the Gill Man is arriving via stretcher hoist, and in two spots on a billboard during Flippy's performance. Ocean Harbor is also written atop Flippy's suspended paper hoop. In ad-

2. Revenge of the Creature (1955)

On the Marineland wharf, a crew member waves a flag, presumably to signal the Porpoise III *crew to bring in the boat for the opening shot of the "Creature arrives at Ocean Harbor" scene. This photograph was taken by Sally Baskin's father Tom Baskin, manager of the Marine Village Court.*

dition, John Bromfield's Joe Hayes, many attendants and the *Porpoise III* sailor have Ocean Harbor on their shirtfronts.

On the morning of Thursday, July 22, Agar and Nelson bid farewell to Marineland ... on film, anyway. That was the day they went to the wharf and shot the scene of Clete and Helen leaving on the *Porpoise III*, with Johnson (played by Robert B. Williams) on hand to see them off. (Johnson's palms-up throwaway line "Sorry about everything that happened!" is all the memorial that their recently deceased mutual friend Joe Hayes gets; story-wise, Joe really *does* get kicked to the curb.) Then the filmmakers proceeded in boats up the St. Johns River to shoot Clete and Helen's romantic cruise. Ricou Browning and Tom Hennesy came along on the excursion but neither worked on camera until after 6 p.m. when one of them was in the shot where the Gill Man reaches out of the water for the boat's dangling stern rope, and has it pulled from his hand when the boat begins moving. Browning guesses that it was Hennesy because he doesn't remember doing it himself.

The last day of Marine Studios photography, Friday, July 23, began late because the company planned to shoot night-for-night scenes well past the witching hour. The first stop was the receiving tank, to shoot retakes of the fight (the Gill Man vs. Joe and the Ocean Harbor attendants). There was a crew call for one p.m. but because of poor light and off-and-on rain, nothing was shot until 3:20—and even then, they were shooting in the rain. This was the last scene, and the last day on the movie, for actors Bromfield and Williams.

A few minutes were then spent trying to get a closeup shot of an Ocean Harbor announcer (no doubt played by a local) describing some action, probably Flippy-related. After 22 minutes, script clerk Dixie McCoy wrote in her notes "ACTOR COULD NOT DO IT" and they moved their equipment to the motel location. After dinner and some rehearsals, they shot the night scene of Clete and Helen looking for Helen's dog, unaware that the Gill Man has killed it and is watching them from hiding. Eleven days earlier in the shooting, in a porthole corridor scene, director Arnold pulled the old "hand on the shoulder" gag out of his bag of fright tricks and had Clete scare Helen; at the motel, Helen returns the favor, unexpectedly coming up behind Clete during their search for the dog. Agar and Nelson finished the scene and were dismissed at 11:42.

At that point, on that same site (near the water's edge by the motel), more St. Augustinians joined the cast: Pat Powers and Julian Fant as lovebirds in a Ford convertible, warming up for "paradise by the dashboard light." Real-life newlywed Powers was the daughter of St. Augustine photographer Jere Beery, Sr., who had already appeared in a *Revenge* scene at the Marine Studios receiving tank. Nineteen years old, she was then working as a tour guide at Potter's Wax Museum (America's first wax museum) in downtown St. Augustine.

Fant was a radio announcer at St. Augustine's local CBS affiliate WFOY, a job he'd held since junior high school days (he was there a total of ten years). Fant told me, "At that time I was involved with the St. Augustine Little Theater, and I think it was Maude Hecht [one of the Little Theater mucky-mucks] who recommended me for the part in *Revenge*." He continued,

Earlier in the evening, while Patsy and I were being coached for our scene, my wife Millie was sitting on the dock at the end of our "lover's lane" with John Agar and Lori Nelson and some of the film crew. It grew cool and John, suave star that he was, offered to go up to the motel and get Lori's sweater, and a shirt of his for Millie. He let her keep the shirt, and she gave it to me. I wore it a few times before donating it to my high school for a fund raiser.

In the convertible scene, Arnold uses the hand-on-the-shoulder trick yet *again*: As we watch the boy (driver's seat) and girl (passenger seat) kissing, a hand enters the shot from camera left and touches the girl, who lets out a horrified cry. But it's not the Gill Man, it's a policeman (played by local cop Bill Young) who tells the kids to break it up and go home. The hand-on-shoulder gag worked well in *It Came from Outer Space* and *Creature from the Black Lagoon* but not one of the three in *Revenge* (Clete to Helen, Helen to Clete, policeman to smooching girl) is effective at all. And yet there'd be more in Arnold's sci-fi future, in *Tarantula*, *Monster on the Campus* (1958) and *The Space Children* (1958).

After shooting of the lovebirds' scene began at 11:30, "Patsy and I had to do about 13 retakes before we got it right," Fant recalls. "And her husband Clayton was present for the filming, as was my wife Millie. But Patsy seemed to enjoy the repeats [the kissing part] as much as I did! One of the takes was rejected because they detected a breath mint in my mouth [*laughs*]!" A supper break commenced at 12:45 a.m., and then at 1:15 work resumed—and so did the retakes. Fant said, "The convertible had a rather loud exhaust, and the first time we drove off, the sound was too loud, necessitating a retake. Another retake was required because I braked too soon and flashed brake lights. We were there until the wee hours of the morning." It took until 3:05 a.m. to shoot the entire scene, plus a shot of Gill Man Hennesy wading up out of the river. According to Fant, "Patsy, Bill Young and I each got $70 for the evening, and it was welcome in my case: Millie and I were married in 1951, had a son one year later, and a daughter one year after that!"[60] For Pat Powers' brother Jere Beery, Jr., watching *Revenge* today is a special experience: He told me, "To see on the screen relatives of yours that have passed away, and they look so alive and you remember 'em that way and all that ... it still moves me to see Daddy and Patsy." Pat and Clayton Powers were the stars of the amateur production *The Return of the Creature*, a 21-minute spoof of *Revenge of the Creature*, simultaneously made by several Marine Studios announcer-guides. A writeup on *The Return of the Creature* appears in Chapter 5, "Aquatic Kith and Kin," and its writer and co-director Mike Gannon is interviewed in Chapter 6, "Creature Conversations."

Most of the Universal people involved with the late-night shooting probably slept late the next day (July 24), and then at four in the afternoon, the crew and what remained of the cast (Agar, Nelson, Creatures Browning and Hennesy, Nelson's water double Ginger Stanley) made the one-hour, 45-minute hike north to Jacksonville, where the balance of the Florida shooting would take place. Again they'd be shooting night-for-night on July 25 (the second and last Sunday that the company worked), this time at Jacksonville's river's-edge Lobster House restaurant. Universal paid $250 a night to use it as a location.

The Gill Man begins to demonstrate a miraculous ability to show up everywhere Helen does, the way Droopy the police bloodhound keeps one step ahead of the Swing Swing Prison escapee in the Tex Avery cartoon Dumb-Hounded *(1943). The* Los Angeles Times *reviewer nailed it when he mentioned that the Creature trails Helen "like his terrestrial counterpart, Sam Spade." (Pictured: Lori Nelson, John Agar, Tom Hennesy.)*

Cameras rolled for the first time that night at 8:50 with an out-the-restaurant-window shot of downtown Jacksonville's skyline on the other side of the St. Johns River[61]; the camera pulls back across the dance floor to show bartenders, band members and dancers, including Agar and Nelson. Forty-one extras were used plus three bartenders. And a long night it was, as many parts of the Lobster House scene, some featuring the Gill Man, were photographed, including (between three and four a.m.) footage of the carried-away drummer and his priceless expression when he first sees the party-crashing man-fish. (In the script, the music makers are described as a small Dixieland band, their music "hot, orgiastic, passionate," with the faces of their listeners "reflecting the jungle beat." An earlier draft specifies that they're "colored musicians.") You don't need the Daily Production Report to know that the Lobster House interiors were shot out of sequence, just watch the clock over the door. When Clete and Helen exit to get a breath of air, it's 9:10; they return moments later and it's 1:10; when the Gill Man enters, it's 10:49; seconds later, as he knocks Clete aside, grabs Helen and exits, it's again 1:10.

Browning was napping on the Lobster House roof when he heard the screaming start—and these were no play-acting screams:

> They used people from the insurance building next door as extras, and these people all came with their husbands, wives, girlfriends, whatever, all dressed in formal wear.... I was sitting on top of the roof when suddenly I heard all this commotion. What had happened was, they had moved the arc lights up into the ceilings, and set off the automatic sprinkler system. The entire bunch of people were just full of water and rust—the sprinkler system probably was never used, and was full of rusty water.

It was circa 4 a.m. when the heat from the lights activated the sprinklers. The extras' all-nighter had ended with a shower of dirty water, and some of them went home with ruined clothes; there was no begrudging *any* of them their $10 paychecks. ("But they were all good sports about it," Browning told me.) The extras were dismissed at 4:10, in the midst of a 50-minute clean-up. In the one and only shot taken afterwards, a Creature-clobbered Clete fell to the restaurant floor, woozily picked himself up and ran out the door.

Mayhem was on the Lobster House menu again the following night (Monday, July 26), another long one for all concerned. Forty-eight extras worked, plus Agar, Nelson, Hennesy and (their last day of employment on the picture) Browning and Ginger Stanley. Shooting began with the scene of the Gill Man (Hennesy) carrying Helen (Stanley) toward the Lobster House railing and diving with her into the St. Johns River, with Clete (Agar) in hot pursuit. Hennesy recalled it as the scene "which almost cost me my life." He said in our interview:

> This river was a notorious river ... it had treacherous currents. I was told that they'd had several drownings at this location, and there were warning signs everywhere for people not to swim there. So there should have been more preparation and precautions taken for our scene in the water there. The only "lifeguard" or *anything* of that nature was Ricou Browning, who was there that night, standing by.
>
> The first thing Ginger and I had to do was dive off of the pier and into the water, and swim underwater to a buoy, some distance out from the pier. Ginger just had a light chiffon dress on ... but I must have had at least 30 pounds of weights on, to keep submerged in that suit. We went off the pier and made it out to the buoy. Before we could do the next shot, there was a lot of changing of camera angles and working with equipment that had to be done. We were standing in a pickup boat.... Even though I could hardly see, I remember looking around, because you always like to see what to anticipate, what might happen. I noticed a hawser line hanging down behind the stern of this pickup boat, into the water [dangerous because it could get fouled in the boat's propeller]. I called it to the attention of several people who were nearby, and Jack Arnold said, "You do *your* work and we'll do *ours*! We know what we're doing, we have men that are taking care of that." I said, "Well, I certainly hope so, because it's very, very important." "Well, you just do *your* job and we'll do ours!"

According to Hennesy, when he and Stanley got back in the water and filming resumed, the first thing that happened was that they got caught in an undertow:

> I was dragged down and came up some distance away from the buoy. I could hear yelling and screaming; Ginger Stanley had been swept away, too, and although she was a powerful swimmer, someone who made her *living* as a swimmer, she wasn't able to get back. Ricou Browning dove in and went after *her*, and had help from some other people, and they managed to get *her* back. [Author's note: Stanley's memory is that when she realized that Hennesy had released her, she swam by herself to the buoy where Browning awaited her.] But I was *gone*. I couldn't see anything—I'd come to the surface and it was pitch black, and all I could do was yell. Every time I'd come to the surface, I'd try to get some air before I went back down again. After what seemed like an eternity, I heard some voices when I came up, and I saw a skiff approaching me—a large skiff, with a couple of guys in it. So I grabbed a-hold of the bow and held on. It happened that they were there on the banks of the river with a lot of spectators, and heard me yelling, so they came out to help me. When they showed up, I think I was about to go down for the last time.

Hennesy added that he got back to the Lobster House during the company's supper break and found Arnold "partying with all of the local extra girls and people—they were eating and drinking and so forth!" He continued:

Well, one of the crew became incensed with Arnold—Arnold was totally responsible for what happened, he was in charge of the operation. So this person lit into him in no uncertain terms—he was a big, burly guy, I think he was a grip. He told Arnold that *he* should be thrown in the river—amongst other things!—and that it was unthinkable for them to do any more work that night, after damn near killing a man.

... [Arnold] demanded a great deal and didn't have much consideration—no consideration for *me*, anyway. I don't know about the rest of the actors. I think that he was *in*considerate and insensitive. He was limited [by the fact that] he only had one person to use in those Creature scenes, and he wanted to get as much done as fast as he could. So he took advantage of the situation. I've worked with a lot of directors, and he wouldn't rate too highly, from a standpoint of being considerate, in my book.

Hennesy's memory was that production shut down for the night as a result of the incident and the subsequent blow-up, but he was incorrect: "The show must go on," and it did, and with Hennesy still part of the proceedings.[62] They shot footage of Clete in the water with the gong buoy and the police boat, and then spent an hour lining up, rehearsing and trying to shoot a scene in which man-and-woman boaters (played by locals) react to the sight of the Gill Man and Helen by the buoy. The time was wasted; according to the script clerk's notes, "2 PEOPLE COULD NOT DO SCENE." With dawn approaching, they went back to the Lobster House and shot the exterior scene of Clete and Helen talking and kissing, plus a dolly shot of the Gill Man coming into a big closeup. Then the moviemakers took another stab at the man-and-woman-in-a-boat scene ... but on this go-round, the woman was Loretta Agar, John's wife, who did it at director Arnold's request. According to a Universal publicity blurb,

> Loretta worked briefly in the film studios as a dancer some ten years ago but she has never done anything that could even remotely be called acting on stage, screen or anywhere. She agreed to give it a try. She got into the cockpit of a small launch where she was to play her scene. One rehearsal and then a perfect take.

By now, it was after 5 in the morning. Agar, Nelson and Hennesy were finally dismissed while the cameras went back inside the Lobster House for shots of the jammin' musicians; and then they shot a process plate of the Jacksonville skyline. The sun had risen by the time the last of the members of the company were free to leave.

The two Creatures, Browning and Hennesy, roomed together in a Jacksonville hotel during this phase of the production, an experience Ricou still laughs about. He told Chiller Radio in 2006:

> [Hennesy] moved into the hotel before I was there, and when I arrived, I was all grubby and dirty from a day's work. I went in to take a shower and there was a caiman, which is a South American alligator, about three feet long, in the bathtub! He had purchased it and he was gonna take it home with him [as a pet]!

With the Florida shooting now complete (two days behind schedule and $20,000 over budget), cast and crew headed back to California. Aboard American Airlines Flight 907 on July 28 were Arnold, Welbourne, the Agars, Nelson, Hennesy *et al.*, with the rest of the returnees on other flights. A Universal publicity item pointed out that cast and crew had worked a month in Florida where it was sweltering hot not only by day but also at night—and then returned to California where, during some of the nighttime outdoor work, chilly cast members swathed themselves in coats, wraps and blankets as soon as the cameras stopped grinding.

The next day, on Universal's Stage 14, the Star Motel interiors were photographed. Work began with a shot of Nelson removing a stocking and combing her hair as the Gill Man (Hennesy) stands gaping outside her window. That shot, plus others with the Creature watching through the room's screen doors as Helen disrobes, reached the screen even though, in a June 1954 letter to Universal, the Production Code Administration's Joseph Breen emphatically stated that the "entire sequence of the Creature peeking through a window to watch Helen undress is not acceptable as written. In any rewrite of this material we feel it important that care be exercised to avoid any sexual emphasis that might suggest bestiality." Universal did suggest bestiality by filming and using the shots of a gaga Gill Man ogling Helen; and when *Revenge of the Creature* was ready for release, they did much *more* than just suggest it in their radio spots:

> When the Black Lagoon surrendered this monster from the dawn of time—all civilization shuddered! When a woman's beauty tempted him—a million dead years of wild desire was aroused!

And in a different radio ad:

> Be startled by the dangerous desires that enflame him ... as he seizes a beautiful woman, holding her captive for his distant Amazon lair!

Additionally, in the *Revenge of the Creature* trailer, narrator Marvin Miller proclaims in awestruck tones, "They dared to [tempt the Gill Man] with the lure of a woman's beauty, thinking that mere chains could hold in check the primeval forces that surged and roiled within this strange being from the dawn of time!"

Howard H. Thompson of *The New York Times* wrote in his May 14, 1955, *Revenge* review, "Yesterday's audience was convulsed when Gill, let's call him, spying on Miss Nelson's preparations to retire, gives a tremendous adenoidal gulp." One man's trash is another man's treasure: The *Castle* of Frankenstein reviewer who tackled Revenge called the Gill Man's gulping an example of the picture's "strong thread of period eroticism"!

Sixty-five minutes went down the drain when the moviemakers were unable to get a shot of Chris (Helen's dog) leaping at the Gill Man. Arnold and others on the set no doubt remembered that that same dog had blown nearly a dozen takes during the shooting of a beach scene several days earlier, and were probably glad to see his term of employment come to an end. The screenplay called for a medium close shot of the Gill Man snatching the leaping dog by the throat; on the motel room set that day, Hennesy did "wrestle" with a dummy dog, but the shot wasn't used.

If a Gill Man fan could travel back in time and visit the sets of Revenge of the Creature for one day, probably no one would pick Friday, July 30, because nothing but dud scenes were shot on that date. But they'd all miss out on witnessing a historic Hollywood event: the on-camera debut of Universal contractee Clint Eastwood, playing the role of a student on the movie's Animal Psychology Lab set. The 24-year-old actor arrived on Stage 16 on time for his 8:30 set call and waited while the comedy relief scenes of laboratory assistant Miss Abbott (played by Diane De Laire), Clete (Agar) and Neal the chimpanzee were shot. Of course the chimp ruined a bunch of takes, not to mention the one spoiled when his trainer showed up in the shot.

Then, before and after lunch, Eastwood (in a white lab coat) did his first movie acting[63] as Jennings, a student who announces to Clete his suspicion that a missing white mouse must have been eaten by its cage-mate, a cat—but then Jennings finds the mouse in his own lab coat pocket. Goofy music from Francis Joins the Wacs (1954) plays throughout the scene, which couldn't be un-funnier. But, silly as the scene is, it could have been worse: In the script, after Jennings expresses the opinion that the mouse has been devoured, we hear squeaking that prompts a chuckling Clete to reach into Jennings' lab coat pocket and pull out the missing mouse; "[Clete] hands it to Jennings, who, scared stiff, fumbles with it." Scrutinizing the Daily Production Report, it appears that on his first day acting in a movie, Eastwood may have blown as many takes as the chimpanzee!

According to Richard Schickel's *Clint Eastwood—A Biography*, a lot of drama surrounded Clint's casting in the movie. On the day before this scene was to be shot, producer Alland (one of Eastwood's "chief studio supporters") took him down to the set to meet Jack Arnold, and trouble ensued: Arnold felt that it was going to be a lousy scene (which it is!) and told Alland that he wouldn't shoot it.

Scriptwriter Martin Berkeley described Clete (John Agar, right) as a "tall, tweedy man with a twinkle in his eye. He is in his 30s, the sort of guy who is popular with both students and faculty. He does NOT wear glasses and he is NOT a pedant." Berkeley apparently felt that no movie could have two *men of science who weren't nerds, so he called for Clete's assistant Dr. McCuller to be "short, fat and wheezy. HE wears the thick-lensed spectacles." Actor Robert Nelson (left) doesn't fit the description.*

"They were arguing like crazy," Clint remembers. "It was nothing against me, but meanwhile I'm just standing there, this big, gawky kid getting more kind of anxious about the whole thing. Finally, Arnold says, 'Okay, I'll shoot it, but we're not gonna use it in the goddamn picture.' So I just said, 'Well, nice to meet you, Mr. Arnold.'"

But as they were leaving the stage Alland told him, "Don't worry about it, you should be there tomorrow morning." But, of course, [Eastwood] did worry: "My first scene in my first picture, and here I got a director who hates the scene and doesn't want to shoot it. You can imagine how adverse those circumstances were." They did not improve when he set to work: Clint blew his lines on the first two takes. From his position by the camera the crusty Arnold could be heard muttering, "That's great, that's just great." Oh, shit, Clint said to himself, I'm really in this over my head. But John Agar—"bless his heart"—reassured him: Don't worry about it, don't listen to him, just relax.

"So I sucked my gut in and jumped in there and did it. And afterward nobody said goodbye or anything. I left there with my confidence knocked back about three notches, because I felt if in every picture we had to go through that, that's kind of an exhausting process."

In 1954, Bronze Medal–winning Olympic athlete Floyd Simmons was a young actor training alongside Eastwood in Universal's Talent School. Quoted in Patrick McGilligan's *Clint—The Life and Legend*, he had a 180-degree-different memory of Eastwood's attitude after his day's work on *Revenge*: "I remember Clint very excited, and telling me over and over how he handled his scene. It was a cute little scene that he hoped would attract some attention. We had seen *Wings* [1927] in class, and he kept comparing it to the Gary Cooper scene where Coop had to sew a button on his jacket. That was the most memorable thing [in *Wings*] to some fans—a good-looking young guy having trouble sewing on a button."

Tom Hennesy also recalled an early encounter with Eastwood, telling me:

> I was in the casting office at Universal when I saw him for the first time. He came to the window—instead of coming through the main lobby and into casting, he came to the window—and he was complaining that the guards wouldn't let him drive his car onto the lot. He said he was a contract player and he thought he had that right and that privilege, and he was very upset. I don't want to belittle him, but I thought to myself that he was new in the business, he was "green," and that he thought that he was more important than he was! And, as I recall, they *didn't* cater to him, they told him that he'd have to park outside [*laughs*]!

Coincidentally, John Agar was the star of *three* of uncredited bit player Eastwood's first movies, *Revenge of the Creature*, *Tarantula* and the Western *Star in the Dust* (1956). "Clint was great to work with," Agar told interviewers John Brunas and Terry Pace:

> He was just starting out, and he really wanted to make a good impression.... I remember that Jack Arnold got on him one day [on *Revenge*], and Clint looked pretty upset. I kept thinking about how nervous I felt the first time I worked with Ford and he got on my case. So I went over to Clint and said, "Don't let it get to you. Just get over it, move on, and do your best." He went on and did a great job, and he and Jack got along fine from then on.

"He was shy and self-effacing," Arnold said in *Directed by Jack Arnold*. "Little did I realize he would someday be a star. When I told him I was going to put the white rat in his pocket he said softly, 'You are?' I said, 'Don't worry, it won't hurt you.'" Arnold conveniently "forgets" to mention what a hard time he gave the scared first-time movie actor. In Schickel's Eastwood book, however, the actor said that in time he did make peace with Arnold: On the set of one of the Eastwood-starring *Rawhide* TV episodes that Arnold directed, they once joked about their first encounter on *Revenge of the Creature*.

"[Universal] made a lot of cheapies in those days, a lot of B pictures," Eastwood recalled in a different interview. "I'd always play the young lieutenant or the lab technician who came in and said, 'He went that way,' or 'This happened,' or 'Doctor, here are the X-rays,' and he'd say, 'Get lost, kid,' I'd go out, and that would be the end of it." In 1979, when Eastwood got the retro treatment at London's National Film Theater, 22 of his movies were shown "starting with 1954's *Revenge of the Creature* (which contained a now-you-see-him-now-you-don't quickie by the actor)" (*Variety*).

On the afternoon of July 30, the rest of the Animal Psychology Lab scene was shot, including the entrance of Dr. McCuller (Robert Nelson), who brings Clete a copy of a newspaper featuring a story on the Creature's capture. Nelson blew a line, but apparently no one noticed or cared because the take is in the movie: He was supposed to say that Devonian critters like the Gill Man should have died out a quarter of a *billion* years ago, but instead he says "quarter of a million." What's funny about this is that, in *Creature from the Black Lagoon*, Dr. Reed says that the Devonian period (which lasted from 400 million years ago until 350 million years ago) was just *150* million years ago, an unforgivable boner coming from scientist Reed. Now in *Revenge*, Dr. McCuller is "off" by an *additional* 149,750,000 years. Funnily enough, in the whole Creature trilogy, the only character who *isn't* incorrect when he puts an approximate date on the Devonian period ("millions of centuries [ago]")—is Lucas!

After the lab sequence was done, two more mundane interior scenes were tackled, the first featuring a police radio announcer talking into a microphone. The minuscule role was played by Sydney Mason, who you'll find funny-looking in a bushy black toupee if you recognize him as the bald Dr. Matos of *Creature from the Black Lagoon*. Then longtime radio actor Ned Le Fevre played his scenes as a radio newscaster reporting on the Gill Manhunt; in his three appearances, spaced throughout the closing reels, the one thing he tells us which we wouldn't otherwise know is that Clete is Helen's fiancé. Le Fevre was heard in many of the early-day radio soap operas and was Red Skelton's announcer for some time. He was also the lead voice in the TV cartoon series *Clutch Cargo* and *Space Angel*. In 1966, he died of cancer at age 54.

July 30 was also the day that Universal's Archie Herzoff notified his staff via a memo that a *second* search for a title was being instituted, the present title *Return of the Creature* having been deemed unacceptable. Herzoff wrote, "This time—please note—the new title should *not* use the word *Return* or any other word that might suggest that this is a return of the original feature. Please forward your suggestions to me by noon Wednesday, August 4."

On Saturday, July 31, Hennesy had an 8 a.m. set call but arrived late following a car breakdown en route to the studio. Then it was right to work alongside Lori Nelson as they got into the Process Stage's pool and enacted the scene where Helen climbs onto the clanging gong buoy and then is pulled back into the water by the Gill Man. With footage of the nocturnal Jacksonville skyline on the process screen, this action was repeated several times before they moved on to shots of Clete swimming around, riding with cops (Jack Gargan, Charles Victor) in the police launch, etc.

The day ended with actor Brett Halsey and actor-stuntman Robert Hoy in a roadster in front of the process screen playing Pete and Charlie, young men debating the wisdom of going to college. On Monday, August 2, Halsey and Hoy completed the scene, no longer on the Process Stage but now on the back lot—in fact, on the edge of Park Lake, the body of water that "played" the Black Lagoon in the first *Creature* movie. (Park Lake shows up a third time in *The Creature Walks Among Us*, there "playing" the Florida Everglades waterway where the scientists in the dinghy search for the Gill Man.) Again it was night-for-night work with a shooting call of 8:15, with much of the initial activity involving shots of Pete and Charlie spotting Helen unconscious on the beach and rushing to her side. There was a midnight dinner, and then in the wee small hours of the night the fun started with a shot of Hennesy's Creature attacking the men, making short work of them, then picking up and carrying off Helen.[64] Between 4 and 5 a.m., they got the attention-getting shot of the Gill Man holding Charlie (Hoy) overhead and flinging him through the air into a palm tree. Hoy told me that he was wearing a harness, with piano wire running from the harness to a crane boom high above. The crane had him at a point where he was horizontally positioned right above Hennesy's head, and then Hennesy pretended to throw him and he swung away at the end of the wires. Late in his flight, Hoy must be right under the boom because he *regains* a little bit of altitude before reaching the tree, but despite this mini-blooper, it's still quite a striking moment.

Knowing that he floated upward a bit, like a rising fastball, led Hoy to categorize the stunt to me as "kind of Mickey Mouse"; he thought the scene could have been improved if it had been cut differently. He added, "We wrapped the tree with burlap. When Hennesy pushed, off I went, and I hit that tree hard! I was really bruised—I was black and blue the next day, in my chest area or in my rib area. I had *some* pads on, but we didn't have rib pads in those days." New York–born, a Marine turned Nevada cowboy turned movie actor-stuntman, Hoy stunted and/or acted in dozens of Westerns (not to mention playing a regular role during the entire 1967–71 run of TV's *High Chaparral*), and

As Helen (Lori Nelson) lies unconscious, the Gill Man (Tom Hennesy) advances on her would-be rescuers (Brett Halsey and Robert Hoy).

he had scores of film and TV credits in other genres. During his 50-odd-year Hollywood career he also worked as a stunt coordinator and second unit director and was one of the founders of the Stuntman's Association. In the penthouse suite of Northridge Hospital, in front of many of his Hollywood colleagues, gravely ill cancer victim Hoy received the Golden Boot award on January 28, 2010, and died at the hospital in the arms of his wife Kiva less than two weeks later.

"Bobby was a pretty good actor," Halsey told me, "but his problem was, he made so much money as a stuntman that he couldn't *afford* to act. Back in the days when Warner Brothers woefully underpaid their TV Western stars, Bobby turned down the lead in a series because he couldn't afford to take the pay cut!" A Universal contractee, Halsey had already seen *Creature from the Black Lagoon* ("I probably went to the premiere") and called the Gill Man costume "a *great* suit"—but he laughed that in person, the illusion of working with a monster was spoiled when Hennesy would sit down with them, drink coffee, have a cigarette, etc. He continued,

> We shot all night, and by the end I looked really bad, my face was covered with "blood" and stuff. And I just wanted to go home, I didn't want to stop and take a shower or wash up. So I figured, "To hell with it, I'll do it when I get home." But, driving home, the looks I got from other cars were really spectacular [*laughs*]. I looked like I'd just been half-beaten to death.

Again cast and crew were dismissed by morning twilight and the next couple nights would be more of the same. They assembled on the back lot on the evening of August 3 for scenes of the police captain (Charles R. Cane) and Clete at the mobilization point, addressing the searchers; group leader Mac (Don C. Harvey) and spotlight operator Joe (Robert Wehling, future scripter of 1962's *Eegah*) spotting Helen supine on the beach but also encountering the Creature; Clete, the police captain and others arriving on the scene, etc. A *Castle of Frankenstein* liked the look of these climactic scenes, calling it a "strikingly photographed floodlit climax."

The company was dismissed at 5:50 a.m. on the morning of the 4th but they were back late that afternoon, in daylight, filming Agar and Nelson swimming in Park Lake—retakes of the above-water half of the river cruise scene where Clete and Helen swim and cavort, unaware that the Creature is beneath them. When the dinner break was over and darkness had fallen, the company shot the movie's closing sequence: the Gill Man carrying Helen toward the water with Clete yelling "Stop!," multiple takes of the Gill Man putting Helen down in the water, being shot by the cops, etc. What a way for Hennesy to spend his (31st) birthday. Following a midnight dinner, parts of earlier beach scenes were also shot. The company was dismissed at 4:55 a.m.

Thursday, August 5, was the last day of principal photography and the cast was down to just Lori Nelson and Tom Hennesy. The latter arrived first for some late-afternoon Park Lake shots of the Gill Man standing in water amidst floating flowers; these were for use in the Black Lagoon scene of the Gill Man looking at the *Rita II*, but they didn't make it into the movie. There were also retakes of the scene of the knocked-out Gill Man rising to the dead-fish-covered lagoon surface; Hennesy rose face-up the first time and face-down the second. Following dinner, var-

John Agar and Lori Nelson didn't fare too well with Revenge's reviewers, but the Creature did all right: According to Variety, "If credits were to be given in order of performance values, the fellow who plays the scaly monster in the film certainly would rate top billing. Expertly made up, he's the only one who looks and acts believable." (Pictured: Nelson, Tom Hennesy.)

ious beach scenes were tackled, among them a shot of the Very pistol flare lighting up the sky. Nearly a dozen duds rocketed upward before one finally worked and they got the shot.

This bit of aggravation was followed by yet another delay when one of Hennesy's toenails somehow got torn off(!), a mishap that cost the company 25 minutes. From then until almost 11:30, more Creature, Helen and Creature-*and*-Helen beach shots were taken, and then a midnight lunch was served for those who wanted it. The picture was now finished (wellll ... sorta), two days behind schedule and approximately $22,000 over budget. When Lori Nelson was dismissed at 11:15 that night, her required services in connection with *Revenge of the Creature* were completed and her employment at Universal expired. With her 21st birthday just days away, her present from Universal was a pink slip, and not the kind you wear.

On September 2, a crew shot a number of inserts needed for the movie, among them a graph machine in operation, broadsheet newspapers with shrieking headlines about the Creature's Ocean Harbor escape, Helen's dead dog (actually a dummy dog) lying on the ground, and a woman's hand writing the Creature's physical examination report. The report, affixed to a clipboard and dated July 10, 1954 (the day the lab scene was shot), describes the Creature's skin as "ALLIGATOR SKIN—THICK PLATES" and gives their color as "GREEN TO RED TO BLACK." Other comments, perhaps made-up and nonsensical, include "MASSIVE SALLDOWN—APPEARS WELL DEVELOPED" (?), "MASSIVE EMULTI GILL PLATES" (??) and "ANIMAL-LIKE MYOPATHE" (???). An additional player joined the cast that day: In a big closeup, Universal contractee Betty Jane Howarth let rip a scream as the Ocean Harbor patron startled by the Gill Man's porpoise-like leap out of the oceanarium.

Throughout pre-production and production, the movie was alternately called *Return of the Creature from the Black Lagoon*, *Return of the Creature* and *The Return of the Creature*; I suspect that all three were "placeholders" while the publicity department tried to dream up something better. On September 7, a Universal memo advised that a title had been selected from the lists submitted by their publicists: *Revenge of the Creature*, which had been suggested by both Harry Ormiston and Herman Levy. A promised $75 prize was split three ways, between Ormiston, Levy and Bob Holt, whose submissions had included the close-enough *The Creature's Revenge* and *Vengeance of the Creature*. Among the submissions that finished out of the money:

Beware the Creature
The Black Lagoon Creature Rises Again
Bride of the Creature
Bride of the Gill Man
Captivity of the Creature
City in Terror
Comeback of the Creature from the Black Lagoon
The Creature Comes Back
The Creature from the Black Lagoon Stalks the Streets
The Creature in the Tank
The Creature Leaves the Black Lagoon
The Creature That Never Died
The Creature They Couldn't Kill!
Escape from the Black Lagoon
Gill Man at Large
Gill Man vs. Science
The Half Human Monster
New Adventures of the Creature
Passion of the Creature from the Black Lagoon
Reign of Horror
Science vs. Gill Man
Strange Creature
Struggle to the Death
The Taming of the Creature from the Black Lagoon
Terrifying Creature
Terror of the Unknown
Undersea Monster

Universal spent a lot of time coming up with a title that would cause no one to wonder if this was merely a reissue of the first *Creature* movie ... so I hope no studio representative ever saw the Cameo Theater's (Rocky Mount, North Carolina) May 8, 1955, *Sunday Telegram* newspaper ad advertising it as

The Revenge of the
CREATURE FROM BLACK LAGOON

Apparently *some*one at Universal got the idea that the beginning of *Revenge* seemed rushed, or that the movie was too short, or that it didn't quite make sense, or *some*thing, because many weeks after *Revenge* wrapped, added scenes were filmed. Screenwriter Richard Alan Simmons was assigned to the picture from September 20 to 27, so presumably everything shot on September 28 flowed from his pen (or typewriter). By now Jack Arnold had moved on to his next directing assignment, the Western *The Man from Bitter Ridge* (1955), so Joseph Pevney helmed the shooting of these additional scenes. There was an 8:30 shooting call on Stage 6 and the first order of business was the *Rita II* cabin scene with John Bromfield, Nestor Paiva and Robert B. Williams as Joe, Lucas and Johnson, respectively. After a 25-minute delay caused by the need to apply a makeup beard to Paiva (so that he'd look like he did in the exterior scenes shot in Palatka), the three cigarette-puffing actors played the scene, which runs three and a half minutes in the picture. After lunch,

John Agar came in to stand in closeup, hold two test tubes and spout a bit of scientific double-talk ("Red corpuscle content only ten percent less than human blood ... un-nucleated structure!"), a 20-something-second tag for the Ocean Harbor research lab scene. Last came the 30-something-second scene of an on-the-air TV newsman (Ken Peters) at his desk, holding up a photo of the newly captured Gill Man and describing its transport to Ocean Harbor. This extra day of shooting caused a budget revision from $502,625 to $509,000.

When I interviewed Joseph Pevney about his Universal horror film *The Strange Door* (1951), I also asked about these added *Revenge* scenes; quite understandably, a half-century after doing this unremarkable one-day chore, he had no recollection of it.[65] The addition of the cabin and TV newsman scenes (both featured in *Revenge*'s first quarter-hour) do improve the movie; without them, there'd be no recap of the events of *Black Lagoon*, no upfront mention of the Gill Man's Missing Link status, no indication why Ocean Harbor is interested in the aquatic humanoid, no reminder of his inability to exist out of water for more than a few minutes, etc. (Also, Lucas' new, solemnly delivered spiel about the "man-feesh" having an inner demon driving it through "millions of centuries" nicely sets a mood.) Realizing how much these scenes add to the movie also makes you realize how sloppy Berkeley's script is, and how anxious he was to get to the action: In his final screenplay, we get our first Gill Man sighting (seizing the bird on the log) in the second paragraph of page one, his underwater fight with Joe on page six, and he's knocked out by the explosion on page ten. By page 14 we're already at Ocean Harbor! After the Gill Man is chained to the oceanarium floor, however, the pace gets quite slack: The whole middle of the movie is strictly dullsville, and an editor could clip out 15 minutes or more with no viewer ever knowing the difference. And the animals![66]

What Berkeley did do well was emulate *King Kong*, a movie whose plot was in Alland's mind when he first pitched *Creature from the Black Lagoon* to Universal. No doubt some, most or *all* of the *Kong*-ish scenes in Berkeley's script were there at the behest of Alland (Alland does get an on-screen "Story by" credit on *Revenge*). In both *Kong* and the original *Black Lagoon*, an expedition headed up by two men, a woman and a boat captain goes to the endmost part of the Earth and finds a Land That Time Forgot complete with monster. The beast is enthralled by the charms of the expedition's beauty, and this leads to his capture. Now forget about the final reel of *Black Lagoon* and jump ahead to *Revenge* where again the monster falls into the hands of expedition members; they transport him to the United States, where he's chained and put on display *à la* Kong for the amusement of paying audiences. Flashbulbs bring out the fury of the monster—in *King Kong* because Kong thinks the photographers are attacking Ann, in *Revenge* because the Gill Man himself doesn't like bright lights.[67] Eventually both monsters break their chains, Kong taking a wrist manacle away as a visual reminder of his captivity, the Gill Man his ankle manacle. (A back-to-back screening of *Black Lagoon* and *Revenge* really gives off "*Kong* vibes" but *Revenge* can do the job alone—if you don't mind that its equivalent of the Skull Island scenes runs a scant 12 minutes.)

The dead giveaway that *King Kong* was in *some*body's mind during the writing of *Revenge*: On-screen in *Kong* and on paper in the *Revenge* script is an identical scene of a child endangered by the rampageous monster. In the *King Kong* scene of Kong running amok in the Skull Island village, a kid sits on the ground as the giant ape, seen in deep background, stomps closer and closer. We next see the kid's mother, who realizes what's happening and, after a horror-stricken moment, springs into action. At the last instant, she snatches her kid up out of danger and Kong continues on his way. Compare that with Berkeley's script description of the moment where the Ocean Harbor kid falls in the path of the Gill Man:

> The mother screams as [her] youngster stumbles and falls directly in the path of the oncoming monster which comes closer and closer from b.g. [background]. The mother tenses stiffly for an instant, horror-stricken, then comes to life, snatches her precious one out of danger as the Gill Man continues on its way.

Then of course the Gill Man tracks down his blonde dream girl (against million-to-one odds) and abducts her, just as Kong implausibly finds and abducts Ann, and this leads to an intensification of the "monsterhunt." In one early draft of the script, the completely shameless Berkeley even (pardon the pun) apes *King Kong*'s unforgettable Empire State Building finale: After the Gill Man responds to Clete's shouted "Stop!"s and lets loose of Helen, a *helicopter* (rather than biplanes) moves in!:

> A searchlight blinks on and strikes full upon the Gill Man, which roars at the ungainly manmade machine. The copter hovers and a burst of bullets clips the water. At the same time, the riot guns start to speak. Suddenly the Gill Man dives into the surf and disappears. The copter drops lower and lower, its bullets riddling the surface. The cops run to the water's edge, blazing away.[68]

The downside to *Revenge*'s *Kong*–like finale is that *Creature from the Black Lagoon*, on a much more modest scale, had already used it (the shot-up Gill Man escapes into the water and then limply sinks out of sight); in fact, *Revenge*'s shot of the sinking Gill Man *is* from *Black Lagoon*. The way *Revenge* starts with footage from *Black Lagoon* ("A Tributary of the Upper Amazon," other shots of the jungle and wildlife, Lucas at the wheel house), then duplicates *Black Lagoon*'s ending and reuses *another* bit of old footage, is disappointing. To the diehard Monster Kid, it calls to mind the been-there-done-that way that *House of Dracula* (1945) cheats fans by recycling the fiery climax of *The Ghost of Frankenstein* (1942).[69]

By imitating *Kong* so closely, *Revenge* makes you feel even sorrier for the Gill Man than you do in *Black Lagoon*. In *Black Lagoon* his domain is invaded, he suffers from unrequited love and he gets a raw deal all around, but *Revenge* adds insult to his injuries by doing all those things to him again *and,* it piles on the indignities of an abduction, being chained up, put on display and stared at, struggling to survive in unfamiliar terrain far from the tranquil depths of his lagoon, etc.[70]

Around the same time that the added scenes were shot, various Universal contractees did some voice work on the movie, dubbing the lines of characters played by Floridians, etc. On September 27, Clint Eastwood's voice was recorded as he provided "wild lines" for *Revenge* as well as for *Chief Crazy Horse*. Other contractees doing voice-only chores on *Revenge* included William Reynolds, David Janssen, Race Gentry and John Saxon. Saxon is the voice of the *Porpoise III* sailor who takes Clete and Helen on their love cruise. I mailed a DVD of *Revenge* to William Reynolds and asked him to listen for himself, and he says he believes he's the Ocean Harbor loudspeaker announcer ("That sounds like my Armed Forces Radio voice").

On October 20, 1954, Marine Studios' W.F. Rolleston wrote Universal to remind them of their promise to provide a copy of the finished script so that the accuracy of scientific references could be checked. (And, yes, in Universal's contract with Marineland, it does actually say, "[T]he use by us of scientific expressions in the dialogue of the script of said photoplay relating to marine life shall be subject to your perusal.") Probably ruing the day that stipulation was made, the studio's Gilbert Kurland sent him a complete dialogue transcript on November 23 and, sure enough, Rolleston found something to beef about: In a December 6 letter, he complained about Flippy being called a fish (he was a mammal) and objected to the dialogue of the announcer who describes the Flippy exhibition:

> It is entirely too flippant and of a nature that you would expect to emanate from a circus barker's mouth.... Over the years we have established a reputation of presenting our exhibition to the public in a dignified manner and it is felt that this particular dialog would prove injurious to our best interest.[71] Your personnel has observed our presentation of the trained porpoise act on a number of occasions and in addition to this a tape recording was sent to your company in California of our announcer's description to the public of the trained porpoise act. Therefore, we were quite surprised to find the script unnecessarily departing so far from what actually takes place.

Meanwhile, Universal was still being haunted by the Lobster House sprinkler incident of many months prior: The supper club's owner Irving D. Glickstein persisted in trying to get the studio to compensate the extras whose clothes were damaged. In a September 8, 1954, letter, Glickstein asked that payment be expedited "as I am constantly being bothered by the claimants"; and when no moneys were forthcoming, he wrote a January 3, 1955, letter reminding Universal that an on-site promise of reimbursement to three of the extras had been made by Jack Arnold and production manager Russ Haverick: "[T]he extras did suffer a loss and are looking to the Lobster House for compensation. We in turn, turn to you and ask you to please check with your insurance company to find out the amount of the claim and send these people checks for same. We trust you will do this at once as this has been hanging fire for about six months." The extras *did* finally receive their reimbursement checks in March 1955, seven or eight months after the night of the mishap. (One of the names on Mr. Glickstein's list of aggrieved parties was Wynelle Arnette—and Universal probably had no way of knowing, in those pre–Google days, that the lady's *full* name was Wynelle Arnette *Glickstein*.)

"Irving D. Glickstein, known as 'Ducky' Glickstein, appears to have been a character indeed," my research associate Robert J. Kiss pointed out following a fast perusal of Internet records. "His name comes up in many tens of court cases over a 40-year period, usually also involving his brother Dr. Felix Glickstein, with the two consistently being represented in court by another relative, Joseph M. Glickstein!" Kiss adds that the Lobster House was one of several downtown Jacksonville buildings destroyed during a series of "suspicious and mysterious" fires in the early 1960s: "They became so commonplace that the local press didn't report about many of them in any detail. When the Waterhouse Warehouse Company (extremely close to the location of the Lobster House, by the Acosta Bridge) went up in flames on June 9, 1963, local Florida newspapers noted merely that it was 'the fifth suspicious multi-alarm fire in the past month'!" Local newspaper coverage of the Lobster House fire has so far eluded the redoubtable Mr. Kiss: "The lack of press attention is surely surprising, in view of the Lobster House's evident popularity. Even the Jacksonville Fire Museum's chronicle from 1951 to 2000 lists many of the endless cycle of mysterious early 1960s fires, but once again, there is no specific reference to the Lobster House. That there *was* a fire which burned down the Lobster House is beyond a doubt, though; the insurance company paid out $75,000, as mentioned in a series of court cases that dragged on into the late 1980s." Did the automatic sprinklers go off *that* time? The answer to that question may have gone to the grave with Irving D. "Ducky" Glickstein in 1971.

3 Area Splurge for 3-D Creature

(New York) U-I's *Revenge of the Creature*, first 3-D production to be released in nearly a year,[72] will be given three pre-release territorial saturation openings, starting with a world premiere at the Broadway Capitol Theatre, Detroit, March 29.

The picture also opens that day at the Roger Sherman Theatre, New Haven, to launch a series of New England openings, and on April 1 at the Hippodrome, Cleveland, which also will mark a series of openings in that territory.

The decision to launch *Revenge of the Creature* in 3-D, according to Charles J. Feldman, v.-p. and general sales manager, is in line with U-I's policy of making pictures "for all types of theaters, all types of screens and all types of projection."

—*The Hollywood Reporter*, March 10, 1955

"This is the type show that screams for showmanship," according to the *Revenge of the Creature* pressbook, and yet most of their exploitation ideas were straight out of squaresville: put diving equipment or a tank of tropical fish on display in your theater lobby, show the movie to Sea Scouts and Boy Scouts and encourage them to talk it up, get a local aquarium to display some 40 × 60 panels showing scenes from the movie, etc. Making *Revenge*'s 3-D sound like something special, posters called it "3-D *Horror*scope," a "*New* Thrill Wonder!" The narrator of a 60-second radio spot promised that in *Revenge,* "you'll see the fury no one can escape—when the monster they couldn't kill rages for revenge against mankind—and looses terror on the city as thousands flee in panic!"

Again the Gill Man made appearances at some of the theaters showing the movie. On March 19, 1955, just days ahead of *Revenge*'s first playdates, Archie Herzoff wrote to Herman Kass of Universal in New York,

> We will have a "Creature" costume available for exploitation purposes as requested in your wire of the 18th. The suit is in need of refurbishing and it will take Buddy Westmore's makeup department at least two days to put it in condition. You can therefore figure we won't be able to ship it to you before this coming Tuesday March 22nd.
>
> If you intend to have someone wear it, the makeup department points out that it is a two-man job to get the suit onto an individual, and while it doesn't take makeup experts to do the job, you will find that the first time it is put on someone it will take at least an hour, perhaps longer, to get the wearer dressed in it.
>
> I am going to ask Bud Westmore to write you separately with more detailed instructions as to how to put the suit on someone, if that is your intention.

That was indeed their intention; contained in a crate, the costume was shipped air freight to a theater in Detroit on March 23. I wish there was more information about the Creature's Detroit p.a. but my "go-to guy" on such matters, this book's priceless research assistant Robert J. Kiss, ran into a limestone wall:

> I wasn't able to locate *any* examples of the Creature suit being employed to promote the movie at theaters—*but* (and it's a big *but*), all the digital and microfilm collections of Detroit newspapers are missing all the papers for the week of the premiere! If these newspapers still exist, then it's likely only in their original form in a Detroit archive or library. I did find evidence of a creature coloring contest that was fairly widely used at early screenings, though!

Universal's plan was for the Creature to hit the Motor City, and then the costume was scheduled to continue on to a Cleveland theater. It probably made the rounds 'til it was in tatters. Another "no-brainer" for exhibitors was to take advantage of the only Friday the 13th of 1955, May 13, and show *Revenge* at midnight (that was done at theaters in Iowa, Texas and probably more states), or run it with *Cult of the Cobra* as a "Special Double Horror Show" (as in Michigan and probably other places). At the Olympic in Cicero, Illinois, attendees got a Faint Check—a coupon "that entitles you to return and see the double HORROR SHOW at the Olympic Theatre if you faint while watching [*Revenge* and *Cult*]."

According to an article in the Sunday, April 3, 1955, *St. Augustine Record* newspaper, the locally made *Revenge* would begin playing that day at the Matanzas Theatre on Cathedral Place. On the same page, the theater ran an ad for *Revenge* specifying that this was its "North Florida Premiere":

> SEE: YOUR FRIENDS AND
> NEIGHBORS ON OUR SCREEN—
> SEE: LOCAL—FAMILIAR SPOTS

Because so many St. Augustinians were *in* the movie, it's surprising to find that *Revenge* appears to have played for only three days at the air-conditioned Matanzas, Sunday and Tuesday in 3-D and Monday in 2-D. The Monday 2-D showings were accompanied by a nine-year-old Paramount cartoon called *Stork Crazy*. There was an ad in the *St. Augustine Record* each of the three days it ran, and a different poster in the ad each day.

Revenge's Showman's Manual offered a typically offbase synopsis that calls Creature hunter George Johnson the owner of Ocean Harbor, says the Gill Man escapes into a river (he escaped into the Atlantic Ocean)—and, interestingly, ends by noting that the Gill Man, though plugged by police bullets, succeeds at making a deep-dive getaway.[73] In that final *Revenge* shot, the Gill Man looks dead to me—just as dead as he looked in that *same* shot when it was used for the first time at the end of *Black Lagoon*. But it gave the critic for Bridgeport, Connecticut's, *Sunday Herald* the impression that "the Creature gets away, in case they want to make a sequel." The *Los Angeles Times*' *Revenge* reviewer also suspected there'd be a third Gill Man go-round, writing that the Creature "presumably still roams the waters of Florida, waiting for yet a third appearance under the title *The Creature Fights Back*."

The Release
By Robert J. Kiss

In January 1955, Universal-International announced within the trade and mainstream press its intention to premiere *Revenge of the Creature* in Detroit and then give it "a nationwide, simultaneous release," making the film available both in 3-D and flat versions; and the company appears to have stuck to this plan. Loew's Poli in New Haven, Connecticut, may have jumped the gun a little by opening the movie on March 29 rather than March 30, and its screening on that date was not specifically promoted as a "premiere." The movie opened in many tens of cities prior to its belated New York release, having even reached theaters at U.S. military bases in Japan prior to its Friday the 13th opening at the Globe in New York City on May 13. *Revenge*'s "flat" premiere took place on April 1 at the Majestic in Bridgeport, Connecticut, and "flat" bookings were common even during the earliest phases of the movie's first run.

3-D vs. Flat Screenings, March to October 1955

Erskine Johnson, in his syndicated "Hollywood Today!" column of April 23, 1955, observed, "Revival of 3-D by U-I for its *The Return of the Creature* [*sic*] is a 50 percent success. Half of the theaters booking the picture, in both wide screen and 3-D, are playing it as a depthie." This seems to be roughly accurate for the period through to April 23, when the comment was published: Within the sample up to that date, 44 percent of screenings were in 3-D.[74] However, the picture changes significantly if one looks at the entire period from March through to October 1955, with just 26 percent of screenings in 3-D within the sample of around 900 movie theaters across the U.S.

As a Stand-Alone Feature, March to October 1955

Within the sample of around 900 movie theaters across the U.S. during this period, 38 percent of all *Revenge* screenings took the form of a standalone presentation supported only by "selected shorts." This form of presentation was common in three types of location: (i) higher-rung theaters showing the movie in 3-D in large cities; (ii) theaters in small towns where single bills were generally the norm anyway, typically showing the movie "flat"; and (iii) theaters throughout the state of Texas. Overall, 43 percent of stand-alone screenings were in 3-D, although in Texas this figure rose to 84 percent. Thus, there may perhaps be more than initially meets the eye to a comment made in Frank Morriss' syndicated "Here, There and Hollywood" column of May 5, 1955: "So successful was Universal-International with *Revenge of the Creature* that it is considering several more 3-D movies. Although 3-D is dead in most quarters, it is still popular in Texas, and there are plenty of movie houses there." If Texas were excluded from the sample of around 900 movie theaters, then the overall tally of standalone *Revenge* screenings nationwide would fall to 28 percent.

Regular Co-Feature, March to October 1955

Within the sample of around 900 movie theaters across the U.S. during this period, 44 percent of all *Revenge* screenings were double-billed with *Cult of the Cobra*, meaning that this was both the movie's regular co-feature and the single most common way to see the movie during its first run. This double-bill was attested throughout the entire period from March to October 1955, and in all states other than Texas. Just 20 percent of screenings of this double-bill nationwide showed *Revenge* in 3-D.

Alphabetical List of Other Co-Features, March to October 1955

The month mentioned in each case is the earliest in which I've found the pairing attested among the sample of around 900 U.S. movie theaters. All of these double-bill pairings collectively make up only 18 percent of the total for first-run screenings of *Revenge of the Creature* within the sample, and the majority of these screenings were at lower-rung small town and neighborhood theaters. Just five percent of screenings of these double-bills na-

Outside a Cleveland theater, a pint-sized Gill Man poses with a fan. Notice how much the legs are rolled up for Stumpy's benefit.

The Creature draws a mostly black crowd, with lucky patrons getting their photograph taken beside him.

tionwide showed *Revenge of the Creature* in 3-D. *Three of the movies paired with Revenge,* namely *Destry, Ma and Pa Kettle at Waikiki* and *Underwater!,* also feature Lori Nelson.

October 1955	*Abbott and Costello Meet the Mummy*
July 1955	*The Barefoot Contessa* (Humphrey Bogart)
August 1955	*Captain Lightfoot* (Rock Hudson)
September 1955	*Deep in My Heart* (Jose Ferrer)
August 1955	*Destry* (Audie Murphy)
October 1955	*The Far Horizons* (Fred MacMurray)
July 1955	*Four Guns to the Border* (Rory Calhoun)
May 1955	*High Society* (The Bowery Boys)
May 1955	*Island in the Sky* (John Wayne)
July 1955	*Ma and Pa Kettle at Waikiki* (one theater only)
May 1955	*Meet Me at the Fair* (Dan Dailey)
June 1955	*Playgirl* (Shelley Winters)
September 1955	*Port of Hell* (Dane Clark)
June 1955	*Rage at Dawn* (Randolph Scott)
April 1955	*Rails into Laramie* (John Payne)
August 1955	*Run for Cover* (James Cagney)
August 1955	*Siege at Red River* (Van Johnson)
July 1955	*Smoke Signal* (Dana Andrews)
September 1955	*Southwest Passage* (Rod Cameron)
April 1955	*The Square Ring* (Jack Warner)
May 1955	*Underwater!* (Jane Russell)
May 1955	*You Know What Sailors Are* (Akim Tamiroff)

The Critics' Corner

There was a general attitude of disdain shown towards *Revenge of the Creature* on account of its being a sequel. Haughty A.H. Weiler of *The New York Times* gave the original *Creature* and *The Creature Walks Among Us* snotty reviews, and in the interim between them, Howard H. Thompson, his equal in ivory tower snottiness, tackled *Revenge*:

> That man is here again, Universal's "Gill Man," who made such an unmemorable debut last year in *Creature from the Black Lagoon*.... [Agar, Nelson and Bromfield] all stumble around foolishly.

Cue called *Revenge of the Creature* a "thoroughly fourth-rate juvenile thriller ... John Agar and Lori Nelson are pretty unconvincing." According to the *New York Herald Tribune*'s W.K.Z., "The dialogue is also a throwback to Devonian times, and the movie really isn't as scary as horror fans might hope. The folks must be getting soft up at Universal-International, the studio that gave us Dracula, Frankenstein and other such undesirables." Fred W. Fox of the *Los Angeles Mirror-News* provided this brickbat: "When moviegoers get a so-called mystery or horror picture from Universal City, they don't have to 'reach' for it. It's almost always spelled out in deez-doze-and-dem dialogue, and the acting is plain meat and potatoes, nothing fancy. John Agar, Lori Nelson and John Bromfield act like three sophomores from one of Universal's campus comedies from the dead days of silent pictures. They're ponderously unromantic and uninteresting." *The Hollywood Reporter* agreed with the latter assessment: "Agar, Bromfield and Miss Nelson are attractive young people, but their reading of dialogue has not progressed beyond the drama school stage."

Pacific Stars and Stripes' Al Ricketts titled his review "Gill Man Returns—Wet and Soggy":

> [Agar and Nelson] descend into the observation tank to study the critter's various likes and dislikes. The shapely Miss Nelson, in a tight-fitting bathing suit, is dangled in front of the chained he-creature like a luscious Christmas goody. And in no time at all there is very little question concerning his likes and dislikes.
>
> [After his escape] he devotes his time to window-peeping and popping-up in the weirdest places as he hatches a plan for kidnapping his lady-love.
>
> Other than the creature's ability to display emotion by flaring his scaly gills, and a playful porpoise that leaps high into the air for a dead fish, there is a noticeable lack of talent throughout the film.

Even some of the trade papers were less than impressed. *Harrison's Reports* considered it "a fair sequel" and called the storyline "rather thin." The reviewer also pointed out that it was "[u]nobjectionable for the family, except that it is hardly suitable for nervous children." The *Motion Picture Exhibitor* critic managed to squeeze out a few lines of faint praise: "Youngsters and meller fans who appreciate this type of fare should be entertained by the proceedings.... The story is fairly routine but interesting enough, and the cast, direction, and production are about average."

Several of the reviewers commented upon the camerawork,[75] among them Thompson of *The New York Times* ("[There's] some sharp nocturnal photography toward the end") and *Variety*'s Hift ("Charles S. Welbourne's lensing in many spots is distinctive and unusual"). *Variety*'s man on the aisle did complain, however, that Welbourne failed to take advantage of the deep-dimension medium:

> [Welbourne] makes surprisingly little use of possible 3-D effects. In much of footage, the 3-D effects are barely noticeable. There are a couple of spots where the depth effect is remarkable, however, and it makes one wonder why the production crew didn't bother to aim for more of the same.

The *Variety* reviewer went on:

> Considering that this is the first 3-D picture to reach the public in over a year, it's unfortunate that it's not a better

Some guy in a Creature helmet mugs for the cameras of Detroit's WXYZ-TV Channel 7, an early ABC affiliate.

one.... [The fact that the Gill Man] only roars and has no speaking lines helps since the script … is hardly on the expert side. There's an unusual volume of dialog that serves mostly to bridge the gaps between the action sequences that audiences presumably came to see. There are too few of those, but some of them are staged with sock effect, with or without 3-D. Underwater scenes involving the Gill Man, and particularly his escape from the aquarium, have been directed by Jack Arnold for shock value and they build up tension nicely.

Motion Picture Daily pointed out,

[*Revenge*] is the only 3-D entry of any studio this year, and smart showmen may capitalize on its uniqueness to revive interest in the medium. Whether the public will be receptive to 3-D again remains to be seen. [*Revenge*] uses 3-D effects sparingly, but, for example, an extra note of horror was felt when scaly hands reached out from the screen, seemingly tipping the nose of the viewer. The theater owner can decide whether these few moments of novelty justify exhibition in the 3-D medium, for Universal also will release this picture in its conventional form.

And a writer for the *Fitchburg* (Massachusetts) *Sentinel* cheerfully reviewed the *Revenge-Cult of the Cobra* twin bill:

The great legion of moviegoers who like to be scared out of their wits as part of an evening's fun will have a king-size helping of fright for their diversion [when seeing *Revenge* and *Cult*].... Although [the Gill Man's] objective is Miss Nelson personally, he manages to terrorize a whole city in the process of trying to steal her away to his watery abode where, not being a gill girl, she would only drown anyway.

When Jack Arnold was interviewed by *Photon* magazine's Mark McGee and Susan Frank, he said, "Of the three Creature films, I thought *Revenge of the Creature* was superior."

Early in 1956, *Variety* ran a list of the 107 features of 1955 that had grossed a million or more in domestic rentals (U.S. and Canada), and among these blue-chippers were five sci-fis. Towering above the others in the #4 position was Disney's *20000 Leagues Under the Sea* which had made $8,000,000, a total that earned it a spot not only on 1955's list of hits, but also on the list of the top moneymakers of all time. Continuing with the 1955 list, *It Came from Beneath the Sea* came in at #74 with $1.7 million,[76] *This Island Earth* at #75, also with $1.7 million, and *Revenge of the Creature* at #101 with $1.1 million. The fifth and final sci-fi title, *Conquest of Space*, squeaked in at #104 with $1 million.

Marginalia
By Tom Weaver

◆ Jack Kevan was one of the Creature series' hardest workers and, in a perfect world, all articles and books about these movies would be filled with Kevan quotes and anecdotes. But working with Bud "The Ego Has Landed" Westmore led to Kevan's leaving the business entirely; afterwards, getting Kevan to talk about his Hollywood experiences was like pulling teeth.

In the wake of *Black Lagoon* production he did get a pat on the back from management: In a November 16, 1953, memo, production manager Gilbert Kurland wrote, "In view of the outstanding job Jack Kevan, makeup artist, did in designing and working extremely long hours on the underwater monster for *Black Lagoon*, it has been decided to give him one weeks salary as a token of our appreciation."

Born in Pittsburgh, Kevan attended UCLA and then, at about age 20, he started doing makeup at MGM; probably his most notable job in those early years was making up main characters in *The Wizard of Oz* (1939). And probably the most laudable thing he did in his professional *life* was during World War II, when he made prosthetic appliances for wounded men throughout the Pacific. At some point, he worked for Alexander Korda at England's Shepperton Studios; he told me that he had his family with him but that, "after a year and a half or two years, I got homesick at Christmas and [we] came home." By the late '40s he was plying his trade at Universal, where his credits included *Abbott and Costello Meet Frankenstein* (1948) and ... *Meet Dr. Jekyll and Mr. Hyde* (1953), *It Came from Outer Space*, *Man of a Thousand Faces* (1957) and scores of others. In 1958 he and *Black Lagoon* dialogue director Irvin Berwick struck out on their own and made the Creature-inspired *The Monster of Piedras Blancas* (see Chapter 5, "Aquatic Kith and Kin"). He subsequently co-wrote two more movies for his producer-director pal Berwick and this appears to be his last movie-related work. When he had an opportunity to go into the cosmetics business, he jumped at it; he built a factory and plants and had 2000 distributors all over the world. He retired in 1979.

I got some of the above information from him during a 1992 phone call, when I was doing a MagicImage book on *Creature from the Black Lagoon*. I made that "interview" short and sweet because I'd been warned that he wouldn't go very far down Memory Lane for me, if he'd do it at *all*; and I did sense while I was getting him to reminisce that he was hating every minute of it. I dedicated the MagicImage book to him and to William Alland. While doing research for *this* book, I noticed that back in the Universal days when Kevan did (rarely) get his name mentioned in a publicity item or an article, they almost always got the name wrong: Jack Keevan, Jack Devan, Jack Gavin, etc. Could that have been *more* Bud Westmore deviltry? I'd like to think that Kevan was as happy in all other phases of his life as he was *un*happy about the movie years. At age 84, John E. "Jack" Kevan died in early 1997. My MagicImage *Creature* book's other dedicatee Alland followed him in death at the end of that year.

◆ I asked Ricou Browning if, in 1954 when *Revenge* was made, he was at all bummed by Universal's failure to ask him to return as the Creature right from the get-go, and he offered an indifferent shrug and told me, "I didn't know it at that time but now, having been in the motion picture business for umpteen years, I *know* this is how studios work: After you've been in a movie, they couldn't care less. They have no feelings whatsoever one way or the other. Everything's money, and whatever is convenient. That's how all studios operate."

◆ Between St. Augustine and Marineland was a public beach where one of Browning's underwater safety men, his longtime friend Charles McNabb, thought they could have some fun: He told Browning that they should borrow the Creature costume one weekend, have Browning get into it on a boat, then let him swim to shore and rise up out of the water in front of the beachgoers, just to "see what'll happen." Browning's sensible reaction: "I told Charlie, 'Well, that'd be fine, except that some idiot will think he can shoot me, and *do* it!' So, no, we didn't go through with that!"

◆ When the *Revenge* unit trekked to Silver Springs to shoot underwater scenes, at least one crew member had been there before: second assistant director Dolph Zimmer, who in 1939 assistant-directed MGM's *Tarzan Finds a Son!* on that same site. *MGM on Location*, a short about the Tarzan troupe's Silver Springs junket, features Zimmer on-camera as he supervises the shooting of a swimming scene with Johnny Sheffield as Boy. It also provides a topside look at Silver Springs (something we don't get in *Revenge*) and shows how the below-the-waterline cameramen got their shots in that era of moviemaking (1939). *MGM on Location* is one of the extras on the Warner Home Video DVD *The Tarzan Collection*.

◆ While shooting underwater at Silver Springs, the

moviemakers may not have gotten enough usable footage of the Gill Man, because in the following-the-*Porpoise III* sequence, a piece of Gill Man swimming footage from the original *Black Lagoon* is seen *three times*. The first two times we see it, he swims left to right; the third time we see it, he swims right to left because the shot's been flipped, perhaps to camouflage its recurring use. But flipping it gives viewers the impression that the Gill Man has lost his bearings and started swimming in the wrong direction!

- Freelance actor Nestor Paiva, reprising his semi-comic relief role as boat captain Lucas from the first *Creature* movie, pulled down $1000 for his one-week *Revenge* assignment (and earned every nickel of it, if the Palatka shooting was as hot and awful as everyone says it was). Paiva again got glowing reviews: John Bromfield said, "Having him with us was a real plus for the film," and the *Hollywood Reporter* reviewer wrote, "Nestor Paiva, as a blowsy South American riverman, gives the best performance in the picture."

- Blooper: In the scene where Joe is "walking" the knocked-out Gill Man in the Ocean Harbor flume, notice that in all shots where the camera is topside the Gill Man is floating face-down on the surface but in all shots where the camera is underwater, the Gill Man is well below the surface, completely submerged.

- *Revenge* was shot at Marine Studios at a time when the world-famous attraction had a free-admission policy for residents of the immediate area. This good will gesture sounds magnanimous but in actuality it cost them very little: The place had been around for years and all the locals had long ago seen all that there was to see, and therefore rarely if ever returned! But as the date of the Gill Man Gang's arrival loomed, the Marine Studios brass realized that their policy now presented them with a problem, and that they needed to avoid local publicity that mentioned the moviemakers' presence. Their very good dollars-and-cents reason was spelled out in a letter that *Revenge* publicist Robert Sill wrote to a Universal co-worker during production: Marine Studios feared that locals "would descend on the place in droves to see a movie company at work, thus cluttering up the joint with so many deadheads that paying customers would be kept out."

Actually, the local newspaper, the *St. Augustine Record*, did run two short stories on the moviemakers' activities, one on July 14 and the other on July 23, their last day at Marine Studios. The July 14 story noted that the Hollywood troupe "numbered 53 persons, seven of whom are actors.… At top strength the company numbered ten additional technicians of various trades who were engaged in Florida. These included Glenn Kirkpatrick of Winter Haven, expert underwater still photographer, and Ricou Browning, accomplished diver and underwater swimmer who was the man inside the awesome epidermis of the Creature for the underwater shots." The July 23 article repeatedly calls Universal's new movie *The Return of the Monster*, "a sequel to *The Monster from the Black Lagoon*."

- While *Revenge* was in production at Marine Studios, the family of Sally Baskin shot color home movies that give us a small taste of the spirit of silly fun that often prevailed on the set. For one thing, we see Lori Nelson, so ladylike in *Revenge,* sneak up behind Agar and slip an ice cube down the middle-back of his bathing trunks! Then Little Miss Innocent catches sight of the home movie cameraman, realizes her prank was caught on film, and busts out laughing.

- Unlike *Black Lagoon* and *The Creature Walks Among Us, Revenge of the Creature* has no human villain. But since practically every character in *Revenge*, even Helen, takes part in the Creature's capture or his cruel "shock treatment" taming or his destruction, perhaps *every*body in the picture is a villain! In the documentary *Back to the Black Lagoon* (2000), historian Paul M. Jensen opined,

I think *Revenge of the Creature* should probably be called *Revenge of the Scientists*, because there's so much about what goes on in this film where the scientists are in a sense *tormenting* this creature in captivity, in the name of science, as they go through a process of negative conditioning.

- It's a Man Man Man Man World: After you set aside the Creature's three leading ladies, the actress with the largest speaking part in the entire trilogy is *Revenge*'s Diane De Laire as the Animal Psychology Lab's Miss Abbott (a 70-second scene, talking first to the chimp and then to Clete). Running a very distant second is *Creature Walks*' Liliane Molieri with eight words: "Si, señores? Ah, Señor Grant, entre, por favor!"

Third place: *Revenge*'s Pat Powers as the girl caught necking in the convertible, with four words: "We weren't doing anything." In fourth and last place: *Revenge*'s five-year-old Judeena Blackmer with *one* word: "Mommy!" Beyond these four, the only gals seen in the series are the extras in *Revenge*. Most 1950s sci-fi-horror movies are similarly set on worlds that look to be almost completely men-only.

◆ One oft-seen *Revenge* still is a nighttime shot of the Gill Man (Hennesy) in knee-deep water holding Helen (Lori Nelson), who is screaming and pulling away from him. That image of Nelson was later turned into artwork and incorporated into the poster for *The Day of the Triffids* (1963), where now she's held tight by a branch (root?) of one of that movie's walking trees!

◆ On the January 12, 1955, episode of Steve Allen's *Tonight Show*, a Gill Man mask was featured and *Revenge of the Creature* got a plug. For some reason the movie was referred to as *Return of the Creature* even though that title had long-ago been dropped.

◆ Gill Man Tom Hennesy somehow got the idea that the Creature growls and roars we hear in *Revenge* are the noises he made on-set—and he went on to say that he'd been told that they were used again in *Creature Walks*. Actually, the same Creature roars are heard in all three movies; Bob Burns says that the sound is identical to the roar of a big pig or a boar.

◆ The *Revenge* trailer isn't quite the test of courage that *Black Lagoon*'s was, but it begins with a bang (shots of Ocean Harbor's hordes of running evacuees, and the Gill Man menacing the fallen girl), as superimpositions warn us to "PREPARE FOR A NEW EXPERIENCE" ... "IN SUSPENSE." Like the *Black Lagoon* coming attraction, it even features a new, trailer-made shot: Against a limbo background with light-reflected-off-water dancing on it, the Gill Man marches toward us and, roaring, swipes his arm three times, spelling out the superimposed words REVENGE (first swipe) OF THE (second swipe) CREATURE (third swipe).

◆ On April 7, 1955, the daily newspaper *The Cleveland Press* printed the following letter from Mrs. Rose Binkovitz of 4181 Wilmington Road:

We all admit television is a great medium of education for young children, but why let it scare them so? For the past week the Hippodrome Theater has been advertising *Revenge of the Creature* quite a few times during the day. My baby ran away from the television into the kitchen crying and the little girl keeps asking all kinds of questions why the Creature does such horrible things.

There must be a better way of advertising, besides frightening young children half to death, isn't there?

Universal publicist Clark Ramsay must have been responsible for the TV spots because Jeff Livingston, the studio's Eastern advertising manager, sent him a copy of the abovementioned newspaper page along with a note reading,

Dear Clark,
Aren't you ashamed of yourself?

◆ The final cost of *Revenge of the Creature* was tabulated in a July 7, 1955, Summary of Production Report: It had total direct charges of $420,100. Studio overhead of 26.75 percent added $112,377, bringing the total to $532,477. The original *Creature* came in at $613,243.

◆ *Revenge* was often double-billed with *Abbott and Costello Meet the Mummy* (1955), making it hard to miss noticing that stuntman Eddie Parker plays Klaris the Mummy in that comedy exactly as though he'd been told to play it like the Creature. Gone was the dragging foot and the molasses pace of the previous decade's Kharis; here the Mummy lopes along with long Gill Man–like strides and even mouth-breathes like a fish out of water. *The Hollywood Reporter*'s reviewer made sure that his readers noticed that *he* noticed, mentioning Klaris' "frog-like gasps" and calling him "a creature from the dry oasis."

◆ The Creature-Kharis Connection: Surely by coincidence, the first two Creature movies mirror the plots of the first two Kharis movies. In *The Mummy's Hand* (1940), an archaeological expedition looking for the remains of an ancient Egyptian goes to her old stomping grounds and instead encounters a live and quite dangerous mummy, a rough approximation of the events in *Creature from the Black Lagoon*. Then in *The Mummy's Tomb* (1942), the Mummy comes to America to exact revenge and a mostly new set of players must contend with the monster, now loose in our own backyards. Both Mummy movies, of course, feature final-reel scenes of Kharis toting off the girl—although he does it at the behest of a high priest, not for his own amorous ends.

On a related note: Coincidence or rip-off?:

The finale of Hammer Films' *The Mummy* (1959) appears to have been ... "inspired," let's say ... by that of *Revenge of the Creature*. In both movies, the monster has carted the girl off into the night, and the hero, the police and locals are in hot pursuit; all these folks find the monster just as he's carrying her into a body of water. Because of a spoken appeal, the monster stops wading into the water and finally, reluctantly puts the girl down. There's suspense as she begins to move away from him, but once she's in the clear, the men on the bank open up with their firearms, and the shot-up monster climactically disappears into the water. In *The Mummy*'s buildup to this climax, there's even a duplicate of a shot from *Revenge*: Christopher Lee's Kharis takes *long*, loping, Gill Man–like steps away from the camera as he carries the unconscious girl down a dark, moonlit path. It couldn't be more identical to *Revenge*'s moonlit shot of the Gill Man carrying Helen away from the camera down the beach-side path if Hammer had a Moviola and that reel of *Revenge* on their set.

◆ *Revenge of the Creature* made its second splash—a bigger one than its *theatrical* release made—when a 3-D version hit broadcast TV. In February 1982, after getting special FCC permission, New Orleans UHF indie WGNO-TV (Channel 26) became the first commercial TV station in the U.S. to play a 3-D film, namely *Revenge*. (It had already been shown in 3-D on cable TV stations elsewhere.) The showing was extensively promoted, with 127 Time-Saver convenience stores selling two-pair packages of 3-D movie glasses for 99 cents each. Raymond Foss, a Time-Saver manager, said in an Associated Press story, "[It] was the most unbelievable thing I've even seen. We just sold 500 [pairs of glasses] in less than 15 minutes." He added,

I don't know why people are going so crazy. If you could open up people's minds, you would probably find some pretty strange things.

The AP story continued:

By showtime Tuesday night [February 9], 340,000 pairs of the glasses had been sold and the chain's marketing director, Frank Artz, Jr., said Time-Saver probably could have sold 200,000 to 300,000 more had the manufacturer been able to keep up with his orders.

Artz said 40,000 more glasses were being shipped today and he hoped another 100,000 will be here by Saturday night when the Creature takes revenge again in a repeat performance.

"One man was screaming at me into the phone about how he had spent $20 in gas driving all over town [looking for glasses]," said WGNO switchboard operator Damaris Alvarado.

"I've never seen my store so crowded. I got 700 [pairs] at 12:30 p.m. (Tuesday) and they were gone before 1 p.m.," said a manager in Metairie.

... The station was caught off guard by the demand for glasses, saying its biggest feature last year, a showing of the Oscar-winning film *The Deer Hunter* [1978], drew about 120,000 viewers.

"Originally, our people said everyone at Channel 26 projected that 100,000 sets of glasses would be enough," Artz said. "But we sold those in less than four hours."

Independent New York station WPIX brought the 3-D *Revenge* to the tri-state area (New York, New Jersey, Connecticut) on Monday, July 26, 1982; it ran five days after Zacherley and Mighty Joe Young, Jr. (a guy in a gorilla suit), were the 2-D emcees of rival station WOR's 3-D broadcast of 1954's *Gorilla at Large*. Three-D-wise, *Gorilla at Large* had left many WOR viewers disappointed (and headachy!), and the next day the station found itself dealing with phone calls of complaint and a general tri-state Bronx cheer. WPIX now knew to anticipate a similar negative reaction to the 3-D in *Revenge* and attempted to head off this potential problem by circulating a letter saying that the showing of the film was "all in fun and charity, and hardly worth people getting irate over." (Burger King restaurants were selling the *Revenge* 3-D glasses, with moneys going to the Easter Seal Society.) As in New Orleans, the glasses were two-for-99 cents, with scalpers getting $5 a pair. According to the *New York Daily News*, soon hundreds of area residents could be spotted wearing them in public, "from the beaches of Fire Island to the benches of Central Park." About 2,750,000 pairs of glasses sold, which translated into $750,000 for Easter Seal services for disabled children and adults. *Revenge*'s WPIX audience was estimated at 3.7 million—28 percent of TV viewers. WOR's *Gorilla at Large* had gotten 22 percent.

◆ No Gill Man fan ever watched *Jaws 3-D* (1983) without thinking a dozen times of *Revenge of the Creature* and also, occasionally, *Creature from the Black Lagoon*. It's set in Florida at a Sea World where a ten-foot renegade great white has set up shop in the manmade lagoon. After a few killings its presence is detected, and a Mark Williams–like undersea hunter (Simon MacCorkindale) announces that he wants to kill rather than capture it. A blonde marine biologist (Bess Armstrong) holds out for catching it and then letting Sea World exhibit the only great white in captivity. You'll flash back to *Black Lagoon* and *Revenge* constantly as there's a discussion about "dynamite fishing" to catch the shark, the beast is moved via stretcher hoist and "walked" in a holding tank to get it breathing, there are friendly chattering Flippy-like dolphins, etc. In the second half, it gets more like *Gorgo* (1961). The movie's *raison d'être*: 3-D shots of floating objects (a large fish head, a man's severed arm, etc.), the camera fixated on them so ridiculously long that the excesses of 1950s 3-D movies pale by comparison. Richard Matheson, one of the several writers credited on-screen, told me he wrote a good outline and script "and if they had done it right and if it had been directed by somebody who knew how to direct, I think it would have been an excellent movie." Maybe. One last *Revenge*-related tidbit: In real life, the opening of the Florida Sea World seen in this movie put a hurtin' on Marineland attendance, a slump that lasted for decades and nearly caused Marineland to go belly-up. Speaking of *Jaws*…

◆ We all cringe at the ludicrousness of the *Revenge* Gill Man having the ability to repeatedly locate Helen, first at her motel, then at the Ocean Harbor pier, then at the Lobster House. The same sort of thing also happens, magnified to the nth power of stupid, in Universal's *Jaws: The Revenge* (1987). "*This* time … it's *personal*": A great white, apparently on a crusade to chomp every member of the late Sheriff Brody's family, finds them wherever they go, first on Amity Island and then in the Bahamas(!). The cast includes Lorraine Gary as the sheriff's widow (the shark chews her up in a dream sequence and chases her boat in the finale), Lance Guest as her marine biologist son Michael (the shark goes after him a couple times), Mitchell Anderson as her deputy sheriff son Sean (the shark kills him on his police boat), Judith Barsi as Michael's five-year-old daughter (the shark attacks the banana boat on which she is riding), "And **Michael Caine** as Hoagie." It's hard to tell because the background music is loud, but I believe that in the shark's last scene, the Gill Man roar comes out of its toothy mouth a couple times.

◆ Universal's *Back to the Future Part III* (1990) features a daylight scene set at a deserted 1955 drive-in, with Marty (Michael J. Fox) wearing Western clothes as he prepares to time-travel back to the Old West. Referring to his frilly, fruity-looking outfit, he complains to his friend "Doc" Brown (Christopher Lloyd). "Clint Eastwood never wore anything like this."

Doc asks, "Clint who?"

Marty happens to be standing next to a glass display case with side-by-side posters of *Revenge of the Creature* and *Tarantula* and says, "That's right … you haven't *heard* of him yet." One wonders how many *Back to the Future* fans in a hundred … or a hundred *thousand* … knew that *Revenge* and *Tarantula* were two of the actor's earliest movies. In the distance, on the drive-in's marquee, we can see the titles of other 1955 Universal releases: *Francis in the Navy* (also with Eastwood), *Ma and Pa Kettle at Waikiki* and *Abbott and Costello Meet the Mummy*.

◆ In 1993, *Revenge of the Creature* and *The Creature Walks Among Us* made their home video bow ($14.98 VHS tapes) in an MCA Universal batch that also included *The Ghost of Frankenstein*, *The Mummy's Tomb*, *The Mummy's Ghost* and *House of Dracula*. According to *The New York Times*, this "Little Crop of Horrors" landed on *Billboard*'s list of bestsellers of the week. But what screwball wrote the synopsis for the *Revenge* packaging? According to the screwball, the imprisoned Gill Man "begins to emerge as a hauntingly beautiful alien, and a female researcher (Lori Nelson) forms an uneasy emotional link with him, as her own doubts about career vs. motherhood parallel the Creature's feelings of alienation and confinement. Soon they are both driven to break free of their respective 'prisons' with exciting results."

From the "It could have been worse" department: A later Universal VHS release, *and* the Legacy Collection DVD, include text crediting John Agar with playing the role of the Creature!

◆ Years after finishing work on the Gill Man trilogy, Ricou Browning got a phone call from a Lobster House–like restaurant and was told that they were planning a celebration of the shooting of *Revenge of the Creature* in their area. "And he said to me, 'We'd like you to come up. Would you be interested?' I said, 'Sure! Why not?' He said, 'And you can bring the Creature suit, can't you?' I said, 'Well, I don't *have* the suit.'

- "And the restaurant guy said, 'Oh, I see…. Well, thank you anyway!'"
- *Revenge*'s kicked-to-the-curb Creature John Lamb went on to do the underwater photography for TV's *Sea Hunt* and *Voyage to the Bottom of the Sea*; wrote, produced, photographed and directed 1962's *The Mermaids of Tiburon*; and also made a slew of 1970s and '80s porno flicks, some of them in 3-D. In 2003 he planned to attend the World 3-D Film Expo's *Revenge* screening and participate in the Q&A, but pulled out at the last minute because he felt unwell. Taking Lamb's place that night on the Egyptian Theater stage was his good buddy Dan Symmes, co-organizer of the 3-D Film Expo (and Lamb's collaborator on some of his pornos), and Symmes relayed a few of the *Revenge*-related things that Lamb told *him* over the years: According to Lamb (according to Symmes), the time he did spend in the Marine Studios tank in the Gill Man suit was scary because the moviemakers put "two football-sized chunks of lead down the middle of his back [to keep Lamb and his buoyant monster costume submerged]; he couldn't see out of the mask, it was very hard to see out of it; and he was chained to the bottom so he can't go anywhere; and he's got to hope somebody's gonna stick that air hose in his mouth occasionally." (He could have laid it on even thicker by also mentioning the sharks!) It does sound like a scene out of a nightmare, a great job to be fired from, which was what happened, probably to Lamb's relief.
- The funniest moment during the abovementioned Q&A: Asked to name the scenes in which he played the Gill Man, Tom Hennesy struggled to answer, and Lori Nelson helpfully interjected that it was Hennesy as the Gill Man who "kidnapped me, and took into the water, and took me out of the water and *laid me on the beach*" (italics mine). Instantly she realized the double meaning of what she'd just said and made a funny face, and there were whoops, laughs and applause from audience members. Moderator Mike Schlesinger took the comedy ball and ran with it: "You wanna rephrase that?" [*Big laughs from audience*] "Good God, woman, there are children here!"
- In 2013, Marineland's 75th Anniversary festivities included a June 8 double-bill of *Revenge of the Creature* and *Zaat*, a 1971 low-budgeter with a Gill Man–like monster, also partially shot at the sea zoo. (When the unheard-of *Zaat* debuted on home video circa 2001, *Fangoria*'s video reviewer Dr. Cyclops said it "stinks like last month's bait…. It isn't *every* movie that can make you yearn to be watching *Octaman* instead!") *Zaat*'s 83-year-old writer-producer-director Don Barton was scheduled to speak at the Marineland screening but no-showed because he had passed away that very morning.

  There was more platinum anniversary fun at Marineland when Nellie, a bottlenose dolphin (or a porpoise … what*ever*), born there in 1953 and named after one of the joint's ticket takers, turned 60. Sixty is around 120 in human years, and it made Nellie the world's oldest dolphin (or whatever) in human care. Born in '53, Nellie very well *could* be one of the many … whatevers … seen in *Revenge of the Creature* (hence this paragraph). She's been the mascot of Jacksonville University since 1970 and received an honorary doctorate degree from Jacksonville U in May 2013. I'll bet she's the *only Creature* trilogy veteran with a doctorate degree! (Take *that*, Richard Carlson!) She died in 2014 at age 61.
- According to the website floridathemeparks.com, Marineland today "is not a theme park in the usual sense…. There are no shows to watch the animals do tricks, but rather it's a park that shows visitors how marine life learns, hunts and lives in their natural environment. [It serves] as a link between the public and the sea world, promoting awareness of the fragile marine and coastal environments and inspiring everyone to protect these precious resources." Awwww, Mom, can't we go to Wet 'n Wild in Orlando instead?!

Other Script-to-Screen Changes

- For the beginning of *Revenge*, screenwriter Berkeley envisioned an elaborate encore of *Creature from the Black Lagoon*'s "creation of the planet" prologue, this one coming *before* the opening credits rather than after. In an early screenplay, he called for the sequel to begin with a shot of a mass of huge gray clouds; in the center, small and insignificant, is a slow revolving ball: the Earth. A narrator intones:

At the start of time, the cooling Earth was enveloped by clouds which held the waters of the new planet.... Then the rains fell <u>endlessly</u>, and the waters became the sea. It was in the darkness of the ocean that the miracle of birth occurred. The first living thing. A single cell. The sun warmed the waters and life grew more complex. Jellyfish drifted across the face of the ocean. Sponges grew on rocky bottoms. The polyp built his coral reefs. The ocean teemed with living things for the sea is a home. Then at long last God created Man in His own image [*Author's note: At this moment, the shadow of a man was to move across the foreground*] and time had meaning. But deep down in the Amazon, time stopped—and <u>today</u> is <u>yesterday</u>!

Now, Berkeley continues, the camera should tilt toward a river, and swoop down as though to plunge through the huge lily pads on its surface. Lap dissolve to an underwater shot of the Gill Man:

You can hardly see him at first, he is so far away. He is a distant, unbelievable shadow. Then as he swims menacingly toward the camera, main title. During the credits, the Gill Man comes closer and closer and with the final credit its face fills the screen. Its subhuman eyes bulge into the lens. A taloned hand rips forward as though to claw the audience.

◆ The bottom-of-the-Lagoon fight between Joe and the Gill Man is quite different on-screen from what was described in an early script, where they fight without viewers getting a good look at the Gill Man. In that script, Joe goes down with the net as a pair of eyes watches him underwater and a long taloned hand grips a ledge of submerged rock; next we see the Creature's "almost human" mouth, drawn back in anger. The underwater battle is then seen from the viewpoint of the men aboard the boat. When Joe is finally hauled back aboard, there is a flash of "the cruel taloned hand" as it tries to pull him back into the water.

◆ In the final screenplay's description of this underwater fight scene, Joe lets out "a scream of terror" that is heard over the intercom by the men on the *Rita II*.

◆ The movie doesn't show us how the Gill Man is brought from the Black Lagoon to Florida, but in one early draft we're told and in another we're *shown*, and in both we get an idea how much the Gill Man hates Joe. In the draft that *tells* us how, the Creature is put in a tank (sealed with a steel grating) on the *Rita II* and, as the boat returns, Johnson uses a wireless to tell the world that they are bringing the Creature to Manaus, and then *from* Manaus they will fly to Florida with him. As he sends the message, Joe (his head bandaged) stares angrily into the tank ... and the baleful-looking Gill Man returns the stare. In the script that *shows* us how he gets to Florida, we see a plane over South American jungles, and inside it is a sealed tank similar to the one aboard the *Rita II*. Joe offers food to the Gill Man but it refuses to eat, instead shaking the tank and roaring at Joe. Perhaps these scenes were dropped in favor of the idea of having the Creature comatose from the Black Lagoon explosion until he's "walked" in the Ocean Harbor receiving tank.

◆ As the Gill Man is deposited in the Ocean Harbor flume, the radio announcer was to have delivered this passage of dialogue: "Over the years man has found countless relics of the past—bones skulls—even completely preserved specimens of the mammoth in the wastes of Siberia—kept intact by the sub-freezing cold—but, never before, has man seen the *past alive*—"

◆ In Clete Ferguson's first on-screen scene, he instantly comes across as a happy doofus, cuddling Neal the chimp, playing "straight man" to it, and making a joke out of Miss Abbott's remark that Neal is as bright as a two- or three-year-old. But in an early script draft he makes a much more serious first impression, responding to Miss Abbott's comment with, "That's not quite good enough, Miss Abbott. When we conclude these tests, we should be able to prove that he is brighter than a four-year-old child—although that is not why we're spending all this time and money. The question is—what are the special differences between ape and human intelligence."

◆ *Revenge* audiences' "Now's our chance to get some popcorn" opportunity comes in the oceanarium scene where the Gill Man is tricked into eating a doped fish so that Clete and Joe can swim down and attach wires to the unconscious merman and measure his brain's electrical impulses. In one early script, the action is a lot livelier: The Gill Man, alive and kickin', battles half a dozen attendants who, under Clete's supervision, use boat hooks and long poles to herd him into a "squeeze box"—a steel frame affair with just enough room inside to hold him. Once he is trapped inside it, various gizmos are attached so that they can take their measurements.

- At least one draft of the script included a grisly touch in the oceanarium scene where the Gill Man gets his mitts on Helen: When Clete tries to save her, "he's clawed savagely and the tank is stained with his blood." And the following scripted bit of action didn't make it from page to screen either: Helen repeatedly calls out "Stop!" and

[r]eluctantly the Gill Man obeys. He turns from Clete, stares at Helen, their eyes hold and, slowly, as though to please the girl, it releases him. Clete rises to the surface. Helen climbs swiftly out of the tank, helps him up over the edge. He sways dizzily and she takes him into her arms. As they embrace, the Gill Man looks up, watches them and, in a jealous fury, roars with frustration. It churns the water as it swims toward Helen, only to be caught up short by the length of chain around its ankle.

And in *another* scripted but un-filmed bit, the Creature's fury at the escape of Clete and Helen gets *all* the denizens of the tank in an uproar: "Porpoises leap high into the air, sharks swim in swift, angry circles. There is bedlam below."

Incidentally, there would indeed have been "bedlam below" if porpoises and/or dolphins shared an oceanarium with sharks, as Berkeley's script called for. "If dolphins and porpoises got in with the sharks, they'd kill the sharks," Sally Baskin told me. "Dolphins and porpoises are unique in that, if there's a shark and they feel endangered, or if the shark threatens their babies, they go straight for the shark's gill system. They have a very hard nose, and they will ram 'em. I've seen this happen, and it's not a pretty sight." A funny 1941 article on Marine Studios called the porpoise "the Joe Louis of this fish colony. [It is] a breath-taking sight to see one of them forget his good manners and go to work on a shark. They're faster and smarter than a shark, and they spot the shark his teeth."

- In the movie, the Gill Man climbs out of the oceanarium and is confronted by an attendant with a pike pole; the Gill Man quickly disarms him and pushes him into the water. In the script, the attendant's fate was much worse: "The Creature grabs the man's pole, shoves against it, impaling it into the fellow's body."

The idea of killing the attendant was dropped but in the montage of newspaper front pages that follows, we see the *Daily Herald* banner headline "Gill Man Kills Guards" (plural) and the story's lead paragraph: "The prehistoric monster labelled The Gill Man by Professor Clete Ferguson and his Ocean Harbor Laboratory associates, snapped his ankle chain, pulled attendant Joe Hayes into the tank and choked him to death. An attendant rushing at the monster with a pike pole was himself impaled."

- During the Creature's oceanarium escape in one script version, he's running past the Ocean Harbor box office when he comes face to face with the lifesized cutout of himself: "[The Creature] backs away, half in fright, half in wonderment, bellows angrily, leaps for the cardboard figure. The cutout topples to the ground."

- In the *Black Lagoon* scene where Kay dives off the *Rita* to take a swim, the script called for an underwater shot in which she breaks the surface and swims off-camera—and then the camera tilts down to show the Gill Man watching. Identically, the *Revenge* screenplay describes an underwater shot of Clete and Helen entering the water after a dive off the *Porpoise III* and, "[a]s their bodies go PAST CAMERA, the head of the Gill Man bobs INTO SHOT … watching."

- One script's description of the motel night scene where Clete searches for Helen's dog includes a long shot with a tree casting "a weird, crouching shadow" in Clete's path; a breeze is making a branch move. When Clete sees it, he stops dead in his tracks and stiffens with fear—then, realizing what it really is, he sighs with relief. It's a safe guess that scripter Berkeley got the idea from the night scene in *It Came from Outer Space* where Putnam (Richard Carlson) and Ellen (Barbara Rush) are scared by a Joshua tree.

- In the final draft, the climactic shooting of the Creature is different from what ended up in the movie: On paper, once Helen has rushed into Clete's arms, the Gill Man suddenly starts after her, "faster … faster, its eyes upon the girl, making incoherent, inarticulate, animal-like noises." The police captain, taking his sweet time, finally aims and shoots but the Gill Man, hit, continues to advance toward her. Only now do the other cops begin to fire—as do men on the opposite bank.

The Music of Revenge of the Creature
By David Schecter

Revenge of the Music

The Gill Man was already a celebrity by the time his sequel began production, and it was obvious that part of his star image was his *Creature from the Black Lagoon* musical theme. Not surprisingly, Herman Stein's three-note motif figures prominently in *Revenge of the Creature*, as does a lot of other music heard in the original Gill Man movie. The sequel's score borrows liberally from cues composed for the original Gill Man film as well as from older compositions that were tracked into the first Creature picture, as some of those library pieces had now become inextricably associated with the monster. However, there are a couple of notable differences between the first two Creature scores. For starters, there's a lot less original music in *Revenge of the Creature* due to all the borrowing from the first picture. Secondly, there is only limited original contributions by Stein and Henry Mancini and no new music by Hans J. Salter. Almost all the new music was written by William Lava, who was not involved in the first picture. His eight original compositions provide most of the musical highlights in the webbed sequel.

Revenge of the Creature's soundtrack contains a dizzying 72 cues, with 53 having already appeared in *Creature from the Black Lagoon*. Although there were only 44 cues in the first film, multiple uses of many of those pieces were incorporated into the sequel. Additional tracked cues came from *You Can't Cheat an Honest Man* (1939) and *Francis Joins the Wacs* (1954), as well as some songs used as source music. Another difference from *Black Lagoon*'s music is that while the first score contains only 21 cues under a minute long, *Revenge*'s score features 49 cues of that length, resulting in the sequel's score sounding much more disjointed.

Revenge of the Creature's 82-minute running time sports over 59 minutes of music, a whopping 72 percent of the film's length, even more than the 70 percent used in *The Incredible Shrinking Man*, a film that required substantial musical enhancement because there was so little dialogue in the picture. The large percentage of music in *Revenge* shows that somebody at Universal knew how important music was to a Gill Man movie. However, new music was obviously not deemed quite so important, because of the hour of music in the sequel, only about 14 minutes were original underscore. Needless to say, the movie's only music credit for this concoction was Joseph Gershenson's for music supervision.

The studio didn't re-use music because their composers couldn't think of anything new to write. On the contrary, these gifted artists would have always preferred to compose music for the films they were working on, rather than having to fiddle with somebody else's pieces that were written for previous motion pictures. Older music was re-used to save time and money, as it was quicker to have composers adjust a few measures and have the orchestra newly perform the pieces, rather than to have them write entirely new compositions, which then needed to be orchestrated and copied so the studio musicians could play their parts during the recording sessions. Given the tremendous number of movies Universal was churning out at fixed budgets, the staff composers' talents were probably being used on what were considered more important projects being made at the same time as *Revenge of the Creature*. Although Universal's composers selected which library cues would be tracked into the pictures they were working on, they weren't allowed to choose whether an assignment would require original or re-used material, as that would have been dictated by Gershenson or his assistant Milton Rosen.

Revenge of the Creature's music budget got as high as $22,800 during pre-production, but even so, it's possible that its soundtrack was a combination of newly recorded music as well as re-uses of older recordings from previous movies, as the 9½-hour joint recording session held on October 29, 1954, was for both *Revenge* and *Six Bridges to Cross*, the latter film having almost 30 minutes of new music in it. While the single session wouldn't have been long enough to record both scores in their entirety, it's possible there was another scoring session devoted to the remainder of *Six Bridges to Cross*. If so, those recording logs haven't turned up yet. If the *Revenge* score did re-use some earlier recordings, that could imply that some of the music budget was spent on other things. The musicians who played a Henry Mancini jazz cue composed for *Revenge* stayed a little longer at the session than the other orchestra players, who weren't needed for this different style of pop music.

Other than Lava's original compositions, there were only three additional pieces specifically written for *Revenge of the Creature*. Two came courtesy of Stein; these were both minor contributions, although one played a featured role. For the sequel, Stein was asked to add six measures to the middle of the "Main Title" he wrote for *Creature from the Black Lagoon*. This amended opening musical statement used the extra brassy bars to fill up the time needed to thank Florida's Marine Studios, as the sequel's credits were 17 seconds longer than the original's. This partial re-use of the previous film's "Main Title" helped re-immerse the audience in the Gill Man's world while also offering a musical hint that there would be some new surprises.

Lava's work on *Revenge of the Creature* is superb throughout, with his first cue being "Jungle Boat." Unfortunately, this composition is mixed so quietly in the film's soundtrack that it's easier to hear animal and bird cries than Lava's evocative creation. His atmospheric piece, heard after the "Main Title," is colorfully enhanced by vibraphone, harp and piano. "Jungle Boat" offers at least a fresh attempt not heard in the film's next 14 cues, all of which were re-uses of previously written music from *Black Lagoon, City Beneath the Sea, East of Sumatra* and *The Glass Web*.

William Ben Lava was born on March 18, 1911, in St. Paul, Minnesota. He started piano lessons when he was seven, but eventually quit his studies. As a youth he supposedly could play any melody after hearing it, and he soon became proficient on many instruments. Although he studied conducting with Albert Coates, he considered himself a "composer without formal musical education," and he attended Northwestern University as a journalism major. He sold stories to *Argosy* magazine and *The Literary Digest*, but when he had trouble finding enough work as an author, he got a job as an assistant to a claims agent at a railway, and then sold automobiles and bed springs. He learned to arrange music from an old friend who was an arranger for Wayne King's orchestra. Before long, Lava sold his first arrangement and was soon working for radio programs and theater engagements. Arriving in Hollywood in 1936, he arranged for musical radio shows such as *Camel Caravan* and Fred Astaire's *The Packard Hour*, with John Green.

Lava signed a contract with Republic in 1937, his first background score being for the serial *The Painted Stallion*, and three years later he signed a contract with Warner Brothers. He also scored short subjects and a lot of series television, with some of his best-known work being for *Zorro* and *F Troop*. His music can be heard in an incredible number of productions, including *Red River Range* (1938), *Adventures of Red Ryder, King of the Royal Mounted* (1940), *House of Dracula* (1945), *So You Want to Be a Salesman* (1947), *Moonrise* (1948), *Cattle Town* (1952), *Phantom from Space* (1953), *Stormy the Thoroughbred* (1954), *Smoke Signal, Abbott and Costello Meet the Keystone Kops, Cult of the Cobra, The Littlest Outlaw* (1955), *Chamber of Horrors* (1966), *Chubasco* (1967) and *Dracula vs. Frankenstein* (1971), plus a slew of Looney Tunes, Merrie Melodies, and Pink Panther cartoons. Lava is also reputed to have contributed to such landmark scores as *Destination Tokyo* (1943), *Since You Went Away* (1944) *and Saratoga Trunk* (1945). The composer passed away on February 20, 1971, in Los Angeles.

After "Jungle Boat," *Revenge of the Creature*'s first two reels contain a potpourri of older cues, with 8 written for *Creature from the Black Lagoon*. These include Stein's "Prologue" and "That Hand Again," and Mancini's "Monster Speared" and "Monster Gets Mark, Part 1," the latter composition heard when the Creature grabs the bird off the log and again when Joe battles the Gill Man at the Black Lagoon bottom. The opening reels of *Revenge* also feature six cues that were tracked into *Creature from the Black Lagoon* from other movies. These include Rosen's "Salvage of the Lady Luck," "Brad Rescues Tony, Part 2" and "Henry's Trap," and Mancini's "Duke's Little Helper." It's likely that all this familiar music was used near the opening of the picture to bring back immediate memories of the first film.

The fact that there's nobody named

William and Lee Lava (courtesy William Lava family).

2. Revenge of the Creature (1955)

Duke in *Black Lagoon* or *Revenge* should provide sufficient evidence that "Duke's Little Helper" came from an outside source. The piece was composed for *East of Sumatra*, a 1953 Budd Boetticher–directed adventure involving brawny tin miners, angry natives and romance on a Pacific island ruled by Anthony "I Can Be Whatever Ethnicity You Need" Quinn. The original 2:40-long cue enhances a scene after Duke (Jeff Chandler) makes mad passionate love to betrothed old flame Lory (Marilyn Maxwell), then gets soused on cheap liquor and smooches with luscious native girl Minyora (Suzan Ball, who plays the luscious native girl Venita in *City Beneath the Sea*, only wearing different outfits). Had this footage been part of a recruitment reel for future tin miners, many more males would have answered the digging call. *East of Sumatra*'s exotic score was co-composed by Stein, Mancini, and Irving Gertz, who all referred to the movie as *East of Sinatra*. The film also includes the song "Strange Land," written by Benjamin Sherman (Scatman) Crothers, who appears in the picture. The score contributed many cues to subsequent Universal movies, with Mancini's "Minyora's Plan" and "Hot Fight" also being tracked into *Black Lagoon*.

In the first Creature film, Rosen's cue "Henry's Trap" augmented rotenone being sprinkled on the water's surface to try to knock out the Gill Man. In *Revenge*, the composition serves a similar purpose, conveying the crew's anticipation as they wait for the Creature to appear after they detonate dynamite in the water. "Henry's Trap" was originally written for the climax of director Jack Arnold's *The Glass Web* (1953), heard when Don Newell (John Forsythe) leaves the television studio booth and faces deranged, gun-wielding Henry Hayes (Edward G. Robinson). In addition to being used in *Black Lagoon* and (twice) in *Revenge*, "Henry's Trap" was also heard in the 1954 Audie Murphy Western *Drums Across the River*, which contained 96 cues. Out of that ridiculous number of musical fragments, only 11 were original, courtesy of Stein and Mancini, with the remaining 85 being tracked or source music cues by Mancini, Rosen, Salter, Skinner, Stein, and Walter Scharf.

The Glass Web's original score was composed by Frank Skinner, Rosen and Stein, with two tracked cues added to the proceedings. When Paula (Kathleen Hughes) is shot in the movie's opening scene, Stein's "Willis Case" contains a three-note motif similar to a variation of the Creature theme that Mancini later used in *Black Lagoon*'s "Monster Gets Mark, Part 2." This resemblance isn't surprising, because in various Universal movies one can hear Stein cues that sound like Salter, Mancini cues that sound like Lava, Heinz Roemheld cues that sound like Gertz, and almost every other possible combination. This was because these composers worked in proximity and often had to adapt each other's cues, so it's to be expected that ideas originating with one composer would occasionally find their way in another's work. When Mancini did some work on *This Island Earth* (1955), he gave the Metaluna Mutant a three-note theme on flutter-tongued trumpets, an obvious variation of Stein's Creature theme. Perhaps Mancini was asked to come up with something close to the Creature motif, hoping it would transform the interstellar insect into as big a star as the Gill Man.

Revenge of the Creature's third original piece of music occurs a full 13:30 into the picture, with Stein's inconsequential five-second "Stunning Captive" being heard after the crew spots the unconscious Creature floating to the Lagoon's surface. One would think that a cue with such a compelling title would be more memorable than it is, but it's hard to watch the scene and even notice the music. It's even harder to understand why anyone felt that a new composition should be used here, as a note or two from any other previously written cue would have equally sufficed.

After the story moves to Ocean Harbor, Florida, two Frank Skinner cues from *Francis Joins the Wacs* are re-used for the laboratory scene featuring Clint Eastwood and a chimpanzee, with the ape clearly being the better actor at this early stage of Eastwood's career. The 1954 talking mule comedy starred Donald O'Connor as Peter Stirling and Julie Adams as Capt. Jane Parker. The score was by Gertz, Mancini and Skinner, and other than a few source music songs, this Francis series entry received an entirely original score. The Skinner pieces that were tracked into *Revenge* were "Psycho Nurse," a lightweight, frenetic piece written for a scene where Peter first meets daffy nurse Humpert (Zasu Pitts), and "Peter's Painting," a comedic number heard when a psychiatrist interprets Peter's artwork to gain insight into his psyche.

It's obvious why cues from *Francis Joins the Wacs* were used in the Gill Man sequel. "Psycho Nurse" was written for a laboratory scene with animals—including a chimpanzee—and the *Revenge* sequence scored with the same music also took place in a laboratory with animals—including a chimpanzee. In addition, the Francis movie had multiple sequences where characters painted pictures, and in *Revenge*, the chimpanzee is also painting a picture. As if those reasons weren't enough, the Creature sequel was released one year after *Francis Joins the Wacs*, meaning that the mule cues were obviously still fresh in the minds of those in Universal's music department.

Working against these similarities was the noticeable problem that the Francis movie—even though it was well-done—was an out-and-out comedy, and its music was too silly for the Creature picture. Lava or another composer certainly could have provided more suitable original material for *Revenge of the Creature* that would have kept the Eastwood sequence light without totally losing the mood of the horror picture, which the Francis music unfortunately does. *Francis Joins the Wacs* offers a rewarding opportunity to watch the splendid acting of Julie Adams, who made about 20 1950s Universal motion pictures and seldom gave a performance that was less than superb. It could be argued that her *Francis Joins the Wacs* character was portrayed almost as realistically as her role as Kay in *Black Lagoon*, her underplayed approach in the comedy contributing greatly to the humorous quality of her scenes.

Revenge of the Creature's third reel offers 8 cues by Mancini, Rosen, Salter and Stein that were previously used in *Black Lagoon*, but thankfully this part of the film is invigorated by the inclusion of Lava's second and third original compositions, which occur back to back. As the beast is chained to the bottom of the Ocean Harbor oceanarium, the 2:30-long "Chained" offers a number of novel orchestrations of the Creature theme that are markedly different from the flutter-tongued trumpet approach taken in *Black Lagoon*. Some of the composition and its voicings (instrumental combinations) bear a resemblance to Lava's writing in *The Deadly Mantis* (1957), which he co-scored with Irving Gertz.

Lava's "Exhibit of the Prehistoric" is heard on the Creature's opening day at Ocean Harbor, and after a playful beginning highlighting fish being fed to eager porpoises, the composition becomes moodily effective, with stopped horns, piano and vibraphone imparting an appropriate sense of mystery to shots of the Gill Man. It's a welcome relief that every image of the Creature in the sequel is not accentuated with Stein's blaring Creature theme, because the beast is seen so often that such wall-to-wall musical accompaniment would have been too much of an audio barrage. This subtler approach works well because the sequel sometimes presents a quieter and more intelligent Gill Man than what's seen in the original. The *Revenge* underscore is more subdued both in terms of containing fewer instances of the Creature theme as well as having many of them orchestrated in less-than-earsplitting ways.

Unfortunately, just when we've become spoiled on original Lava music, 14 of the next 15 cues are reprised from *Black Lagoon* and Universal's music library, including pieces written for *Ride Clear of Diablo* and *City Beneath the Sea*. The latter film supplies re-uses of Rosen's "Brad Rescues Tony, Part 2" and "Salvage of the Lady Luck" to the sequence where Clete Ferguson and Helen Dobson observe the chained Creature swimming in his tank. Shortly after this segment, almost three minutes of the same two cues are used again when Clete and Helen join the Creature in the tank.

In the midst of these tracked pieces, W.C. Fields fans should be happy to hear the "Charlie McCarthy March," used in the comedian's *You Can't Cheat an Honest Man*. In *Revenge of the Creature*, the

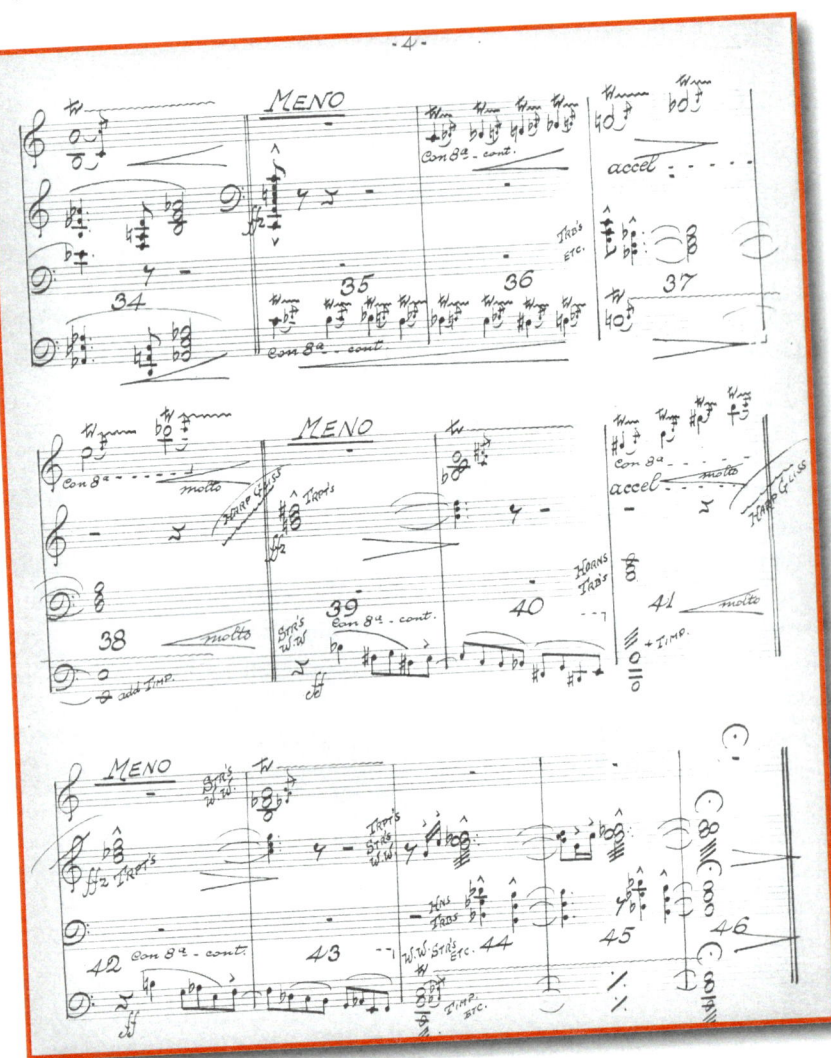

Conductor's score of William Lava's "Chained" from Revenge of the Creature (© 1955 RABB Trust Publishing/Willenora Publishing Co., courtesy William Lava family).

16-year-old circus cue serves as background music as Flippy the "Educated" Porpoise performs. Flippy fans might be disappointed to learn that the soggy mammal didn't have his own theme composed for him. The "Charlie McCarthy March" was written by Nick Nuzzi, who was the head music librarian for Universal in the 1950s, in charge of getting copies of the tracked cues to the composers when they requested them for re-use purposes. The same circus piece was used in a number of Universal pictures, including near the end of *Francis Goes to West Point* (1952), which was another Donald O'Connor–Talking Mule vehicle, this one co-starring Lori Nelson (*Revenge of the Creature*) and Gregg Palmer (*The Creature Walks Among Us*).

Songs like "Charlie McCarthy March" (as opposed to orchestral cues) were also re-used from picture to picture, often as "source music" coming over a radio or TV, or as background music heard in a nightclub or other location. Tunes used in this fashion didn't serve the same dramatic purpose as the underscore because they weren't written to precisely match or accentuate the visuals, and therefore they were sometimes chosen more for business reasons than artistic ones. The composers and the music publishers who owned the songs would benefit from their re-use, and there were song pluggers hanging around all the studios trying to get their new and old songs placed in current film productions. While motion picture studios often preferred to use songs controlled by their own publishing companies, sometimes a specific tune they didn't own was necessary for a particular plot or scene. In those cases, they'd have to license that music from the music publisher of that song, who would receive a licensing fee as well as performance royalties when that movie played on television in the future.

Milton Rosen's apprehensive "Clay Meets a Badman" makes three appearances in *Revenge of the Creature*, including one at the end of the all-tracked fourth reel, and another at the beginning of the fifth reel. This *Ride Clear of Diablo* cue had already been used in context with the native drug rotenone in *Black Lagoon*, and one of its reappearances in *Revenge* covers the scene where Clete and Joe lower the cage with the doped fish to the hungry Gill Man. As Clete waits for the drug to take effect, the composition's use of vibraphone and marimba helps create a sense of unease. This cue was appropriated for many other Universal movies, including *Drums Across the River*.

Lava's next two new *Revenge* compositions are again back to back. "Physical" augments the laboratory scene where Clete's team analyzes the Gill Man's biology, with mysterious sounds from harp, celesta and vibraphone enhancing the surprising medical results. Subtle high strings and celesta add an effective, disquieting touch at the end that nicely enhances Clete's statement that the Creature's physical make-up is just outside what would be considered human. "Romance Disturbed" highlights Clete and Helen relaxing at the beach with her dog, Chris. Strings, clarinets, harp and vibraphone provide the humorous "hit" at the end of the pretty composition when Chris shakes his wet fur on the couple. Thankfully, Lava was given the opportunity to provide an original love theme for this first romantic scene between the two characters, although it's unfortunate he couldn't use this music elsewhere in the film to provide some musical continuity. Instead, those other romantic moments were covered by tracked cues from motion pictures containing unrelated thematic material.

Compare Lava's evocative original melody in "Romance Disturbed" with the re-use of Stein's "Sand Rock," which plays a minute later in the porthole corridor as Clete and Helen discuss the danger of Helen entering the water with the Gill Man. "Sand Rock," written for *It Came from Outer Space*, works perfectly well from a dramatic standpoint in *Revenge of the Creature*. But the melody played an important role during the opening narration and closing credits of that 1953 visitors-from-space picture, and fans of Universal's science fiction films could have easily been pulled out of *Revenge of the Creature*'s dramatics, wondering, "Now, where have I heard that before?" Of course, Universal's music department obviously wasn't thinking along those lines, which is why "Sand Rock" was also drafted into service for the happy ending of Audie Murphy's *Drums Across the River*, it was again used in a romantic desert setting in *Tarantula*, and it highlighted a gorgeous ranch in the 1958 Jock Mahoney Western *Money, Women and Guns*.

The lengthy sequence when the Gill Man breaks loose from his chain, kills Joe and escapes into the Atlantic Ocean was scored with excerpts from *Black Lagoon*'s "Monster Attacks, Part 2" and "Monster Attacks, Part 3" by Salter, and "Monster Gets Mark, Part 2" by Mancini. The section of Mancini's cue that was originally written for Williams' death in the original Gill Man film similarly emphasizes Joe's death in the sequel. As this entire musical sequence is over six and a half minutes long and features very prominently in the audio mix due to the limited dialogue, it was a sorely missed opportunity for some newly composed action music.

Over eight minutes after Lava's previous *Revenge of the Creature* cue, the composer's anything-but-subtle "Newspaper Montage" is a brief, cacophonous and enjoyably outlandish newly written piece that uses Stein's Creature theme five times in clever fashion, highlighting newspaper headlines announcing the Gill Man's escape. The Everett Carter–Milton Rosen song "I Am, Are You?" plays as source music during the nocturnal motel scene when the Gill Man approaches a young couple making out in a convertible. It's not known why this particular song was chosen, but a safe guess might be that it had something to do with Rosen being Joseph Gershenson's assistant, although to be fair, Rosen was a capable composer as well.

Another Lava original, "Gillman on the Prowl" segues from "I Am, Are You?" when the Creature spots a "vacancy"

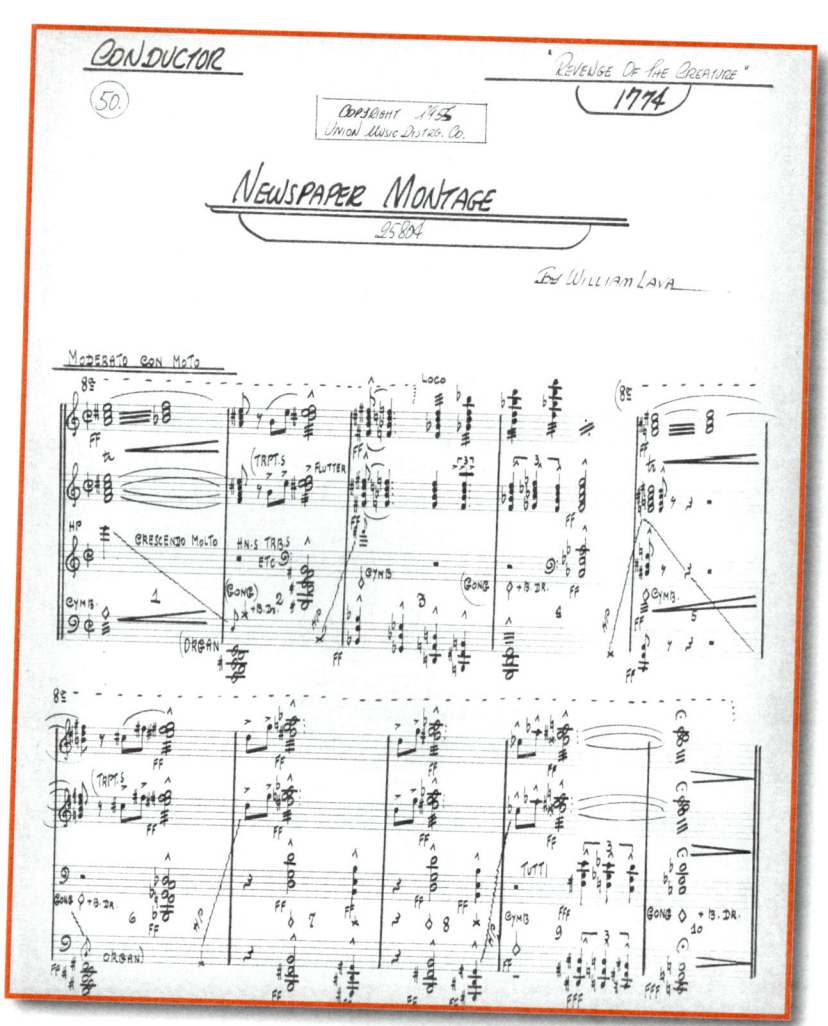

Conductor's score of William Lava's "Newspaper Montage" from *Revenge of the Creature* (© 1955 RABB Trust Publishing/Willenora Publishing Co., courtesy William Lava family).

sign at Helen's motel and decides to check in on her. Woodwinds and harp create some apprehensive atmosphere as she freshens up for bed, and although Lava accentuates the Creature theme with flutter-tongued trumpets, he does it quite different from Stein's original creation, muting the brass to maintain the scene's quiet ambiance. The theme reverts to its snarling past when the amphibious visitor is attacked by canine Chris in Helen's room.

"Where Is Chris?," Lava's last original composition in *Revenge of the Creature*, builds a suitably suspenseful atmosphere using tremolo and pizzicato strings, harp and other orchestral coloring as Clete and Helen search for her missing dog, with a gong signaling the pet's demise. Lava's music is perfectly appropriate for the visuals and allows filmgoers to remain ensconced in the drama, which is what you'd expect from original underscore. Because even when tracked film music is creatively adapted for use in other movies, subtle dramatic mismatches caused by old music being synched to new images can resonate subconsciously. An example of this occurs about a half-minute after "Where Is Chris?" when Mancini's evocatively airy "Monster Caught" plays for a mere 16 seconds, but the gentle *Black Lagoon* cue still manages to seem totally out-of-place against shots of the Gill Man swimming furiously after Clete and Helen aboard the *Porpoise III*.

Of the last 19 cues heard in *Revenge of the Creature*, 18 were either originally written for *Black Lagoon*, older pieces that were tracked into *Black Lagoon*, or songs. Mancini's "Unknown River" takes on roughly the same role it did in the first Creature movie, here providing lovely travelogue music as the *Porpoise III* begins its journey. The Everett Carter–Milton Rosen song "Nice to See You" plays as source music while Clete and Helen slow-dance on deck, but this was a pre-existing song not composed for the picture.

During the *Revenge* swimming sequence "inspired" by the one in *Black Lagoon*, the music heard when Clete and Helen are in the water is Rosen's "Salvage of the Lady Luck" from *City Beneath the Sea*, as well as two uses of Stein's "Kay and the Monster, Part 1" and one of "Kay and the Monster, Part 2." These Stein pieces were recorded with slight variations from the originals, but the attempt was obviously made to try to recreate the mood of Kay's watery dip in the first Gill Man movie. In *Revenge*, the dazzling musical opening of "Kay and the Monster, Part 1" is used to portray Clete and Helen, but if the beautiful passage is already indelibly linked in your mind to Julie Adams in her eye-catching white bathing suit, having the same music depict Clete in his swim trunks somehow seems "off." With no offense to the fetching Lori Nelson, who looks lovely in her own white swimsuit.

In the midst of the musical drudgery that covers *Revenge of the Creature*'s last act, there is one final original composition. It's heard at the nightclub by the river's edge, right after a source music excerpt from the standard "I'll Remember April," composed by Don Raye, Gene de Paul and Pat Johnson. Henry Mancini's sole new contribution to *Revenge of the Creature* is a jazz combo instrumental titled "The Gillman Stomp," the type of piece Mancini was already associated with at this early point in his film music career. The composition begins just before Clete and Helen kiss outside the club, and as they return inside, the music is heard full-blast, complete with ad libs done "Basie style." When the Creature climbs from the water and approaches the unsuspecting crowd, the Gill Man is seen without his theme being heard, a rare occurrence in the first movie and throughout much of the sequel. The source music was presumably allowed center stage here so the surprised reaction of the drummer made logical sense, as the Creature theme might have implied the beast's visibility before the percussionist actually spotted him.

Mancini's peppy number appeared in other Universal movies, including *Running Wild* (1955), where it's heard as prominent dance music for William Campbell and Kathleen Case. In the 1958 teen flick *Live Fast, Die Young* it went under the name "Teen Age Bop," having significant electric guitar added to the arrangement, and it was also used in a beach scene in the 1959 Lana Turner romance *Imitation of Life*.

"The Gillman Stomp" was one of the rare times one of Universal's regular staff composers was asked to write a prominent source music cue, as the studio usually either brushed off a standard, re-used a tune already written for a previous movie, or had one of their songwriting teams come up with something. But given that a jazz combo was performing in the scene, this sort of arrangement was right up Mancini's alley, so using him made sense. How the tune didn't catch on with a name like "The Gillman Stomp" isn't known, but the person who probably came up with the title—and who came up with many of Universal's clever cue titles—was head music editor Frederick "Herbie" Herbert (formerly Frederick Stahlberg). In addition to writing song lyrics for the studio's motion pictures (often in conjunction with composer Arnold Hughes), Herbert also spotted the pictures with the composers to determine which sequences needed music.

After the nightclub abduction sequence, *Revenge of the Creature*'s ending offers a virtual repeat of the musical finale used in *Black Lagoon*. Other than a lengthy excerpt from Mancini's "Monster Gets Mark, Part 2"—which wasn't featured in the first film's climax—the rest of the underscore contains bits and pieces of Salter's "Doping the Monster," "The Monster's Trial," "Kay's Last Peril" and "End Title," as well as Stein's "End Cast."

Salter's "End Title" fulfills the same basic purpose it did in *Black Lagoon*, although this time the excerpt from *Bend of the River* isn't included. Instead, other measures from the "End Title" are repeated, seemingly at random and with no compositional flow. Not surprisingly, Universal also didn't want to mess with the musical coda used in *Black Lagoon*, so Herman Stein's same "End Cast" (originally written for *The Redhead from Wyoming*) was re-recorded for *Revenge of the Creature*. For whatever reason, the performance of the composition in the sequel lacks the crispness heard in the first Gill Man picture. The thematically related piece used as the End Cast for *Tarantula* (1955) was derived from *The Redhead from Wyoming*'s lengthier "End Title."

As appropriate as the tracked music dominating *Revenge of the Creature* might have been, the freshness of William Lava's contributions demonstrates that a completely original score would have noticeably improved the movie while still keeping it close to its musical roots. But it's obvious that Universal wasn't interested in offering too novel a perspective on the Gill Man at this point in his career. That approach would have to wait until the final film of the Creature trilogy, still another year off.

Conductor's score of Henry Mancini's "The Gillman Stomp" from Revenge of the Creature (© 1955 Northridge Music Co., courtesy of Henry Mancini Estate).

Lava didn't receive a screen credit for *Revenge of the Creature* because Universal's policy was to omit a composing credit when more than one composer worked on the same picture, unless the main writer contributed 80 percent of the music, in which case that single composer would receive credit along with Gershenson's credit for music supervision. But there were certainly exceptions to these rules going way back, including *The Invisible Man Returns* (1940) and *Pittsburgh* (1942), both co-credited to Salter and Skinner. And in the Gershenson era, the 1956 Barbara Stanwyck film *There's Always Tomorrow* was co-credited to Stein and Roemheld. *Sign of the Pagan* (1954) and *The Rawhide Years* (1956) were both co-credited to Salter and Skinner, even though Stein wrote music for the former picture, and Eric Zeisl had some tracked music in the latter.

But regardless of stated policies, the reality was that almost every time more than one composer worked on a picture, the only music credit went to Gershenson, although this shouldn't have always been the case. One prime example is *This Island Earth*, where Stein wrote "only" about 75 percent of the score, including every original composition from reel one to most of reel eight. The 8 minutes of music in the ninth reel were scored by Mancini and Salter, with some of Salter's writing being based on Stein's themes and ideas.

In Universal's defense, the studio was a factory, cranking out pictures at a breakneck pace, and imminent scoring deadlines could be met by having a few composers writing music for the same movie, while others were adapting music from earlier pictures. This set-up allowed one composer to easily be taken off one film and moved to a more pressing assignment. However, when deadlines weren't looming, the only result of replacing one composer with another was that no composer would receive a screen credit. It would have taken Stein only half a day to compose an additional 1:30 of music so he'd have written 80 percent of *This Island Earth*'s score. Therefore, the other composers might have been asked to "help" him, or else he might have been moved to another project, solely to prevent him from getting a composer credit for this prestigious picture. As it turned out, the only person to receive a full-screen credit on *This Island Earth* besides producer William Alland and director Joseph Newman was Joseph Gershenson.

Lava's lack of a credit on *Revenge of the Creature* is much more defensible from the perspective of Universal's music department. Although he wrote over 80 percent of the original music in the motion picture, due to the wealth of tracked cues that were used, he only contributed to about 19 percent of the film's score. But given how important his music was to the movie, it's unfortunate that there couldn't have been a credit revealing his significant contribution.

Analysis
By Steve Kronenberg

The popularity, quality and impact of *Creature from the Black Lagoon* made a sequel inevitable. But *Revenge of the Creature* was also a hastily made sequel; it represents the quickest turnaround time for any Universal horror follow-up. And perhaps it's this haste which makes *Revenge* so inferior to its glorious progenitor. Coincidentally, the only other genre sequel that was just as speedily produced was 1933's *The Son of Kong*—the inferior follow-up to the classic that *Creature from the Black Lagoon* most resembled! Researcher Robert J. Kiss points out that *Revenge* followed so hard on the heels of *Black Lagoon* that the latter was still playing widely throughout Florida during June and July 1954 (when *Revenge* was being filmed there), both as a regular feature and also by way of special midnight screenings.

It's not as though *Revenge* doesn't try to be a worthy sequel. The familiar and beloved three-note *Creature* theme music opens the film and is pervasive throughout. William Alland reprises his role as producer, Jack Arnold again directs and, most importantly, Charles "Scotty" Welbourne lenses the *entire* film—both underwater and topside.

The film's beginning also resembles *Black Lagoon*. There is an evolutionary-biological prologue that serves as a build-up to the Gill Man—delivered by another returning *Creature* vet, Nestor Paiva, again playing Lucas. Lucas' opening segment is one of *Revenge*'s highlights, as he warns Joe and Johnson about the size and strength of the monster they are seeking:

> It doesn't *belong* in our world…. This beast exists because it is stronger than this thing that you call "evolution." In it is some force of life … a demon! … driving it through millions of centuries. And it does not surrender so easily to weaklings like you and me. This is the thing that you hunt for. Think on it.

Lucas then laughs ominously—a fine teaser for an audience nervously awaiting the Gill Man's appearance.

Fortunately, the audience doesn't have long to wait:

2. Revenge of the Creature (1955)

We see Ricou Browning's Creature almost immediately, accompanied by his theme music, swiping at a bird on a log on the Black Lagoon surface. Welbourne's camera then captures the Gill Man gliding gracefully through the water filigreed by sunlight—a reprise of the arresting photographic style Welbourne brought to the original *Black Lagoon*.

Indeed, whatever style *Revenge* possesses is almost entirely a function of Welbourne's camera. *Revenge* proves that Welbourne's aptitude for underwater photography is peerless. All of *Revenge*'s sub-aquatic scenes are highlighted by Welbourne's murky, spooky lighting technique. The Creature's memorable Black Lagoon attack on Joe Hayes is shot as a chaotic crazy quilt of bubbles and thrashing bodies. (Still, the excitement of the scene doesn't approach Welbourne's unsettling shot of Mark Williams being dragged to the depths of the lagoon in the original film.) After the attack on Joe, Welbourne shoots the Creature swimming off into gray and murky waters amidst furious gunfire—an example of how Welbourne can precisely capture mood and tone.

Later, in the receiving tank scene, Welbourne delivers an eerie shot of the Gill Man silently floating face down in the water, just waiting to strike as Joe attempts to revive him. Welbourne beautifully captures the heightened anticipation conveyed by this silent tableau. We continue to see Joe quietly gliding the Creature through the water; as Welbourne shoots the Creature from *below* the water, we are the first to see him regain consciousness. He then moves his limbs, stands up and roars at the curious crowd surrounding him, before the battle royal ensues. Welbourne's camera (and Arnold's direction) allow the initially subdued scene to build to a crescendo, and it represents one of *Revenge*'s most exciting segments.

After this action-packed scene, Welbourne delivers an excellent, atmospheric shot of the Creature brought to the bottom of the oceanarium in ropes and netting. Welbourne shoots the Gill Man as a squirming, thrashing prisoner of "civilization." Credit Welbourne *and* Ricou Browning for again evoking our sympathy for this monster, as we see him chained and swimming desperately.

Welbourne is equally adept at capturing the Creature's ominous qualities: We get an excellent, arresting closeup of the monster staring at Helen for the first time through a porthole of the oceanarium in which he is imprisoned. Yet, the Creature's mystery, menace—and style—are diluted by these scenes, as we watch him receiving a basket of fish food in his aquatic prison. This ferocious monster of *Creature from the Black Lagoon* almost resembles a domesticated lab rat as he eats a drugged fish and pathetically sinks to the bottom, asleep.

When the Creature finally escapes his captors and rampages through Ocean Harbor, Welbourne captures the chaos of the crowds in medium and closeup shots reminiscent of *King Kong*'s wild walk through the streets of New York. We also get a fine long shot of the Gill Man heading for the ocean after his escape, a shot which accentuates his loneliness and solitude. And as the Creature heads toward Helen's motel room, Welbourne delivers a haunting, sinister medium shot of the monster enveloped in darkness, advancing toward his new bride-to-be. This moody scene is immediately followed by an equally unnerving shot of the Creature peering at Helen through the motel window, backed by the black night landscape, again reminiscent of *Kong* peeping in at Fay Wray through the New York hotel window. As the Gill Man enters Helen's room, the action is effectively punctuated by the loud, crescendo-ing Creature

The Gill Man (Tom Hennesy) watches Helen (Lori Nelson) strip, a scene that somehow made it into the movie even though censor Joseph Breen forbade it. Breen's only other complaints were with two lines of dialogue: a "Jeez" uttered by an Ocean Harbor spectator as the Gill Man arrives via stretcher hoist, and a "Mother of God" spoken almost inaudibly by a cop as he looks at Pete and Charlie's bodies.

theme music. Helen later takes a river swim with Clete. Welbourne then sets up an abridged "water ballet" sequence, similar to the memorable scene in *Black Lagoon*, as Helen and the Gill Man swim parallel to each other in a series of shots. Welbourne's underwater photography in *Revenge* is typically beautiful but, sad to say, the surreal lighting and editing in the original *Black Lagoon* are absent here.

After the Gill Man abducts Helen, Welbourne's aptitude for atmosphere is again displayed as the Creature advances on the pair of boys who discover her unconscious on a dark, lonely stretch of beach. After dispatching them, the Creature sweeps Helen in his arms in classic 1950s style and walks with her into the darkness—a superbly moody long shot. Immediately, Welbourne delivers a disturbing closeup of the Creature dripping wet, gills pulsating, carrying Helen as both are enveloped in the darkness. Likewise, during the film's climax, we get a startling medium shot of the monster advancing toward Helen, lit by a police spotlight.

Clearly, Welbourne is responsible for whatever panache *Revenge* possesses. His penchant for crisp underwater photography and his ability to capture mood and action are all that make *Revenge* worth savoring. Unfortunately, the cast—and especially the script—do not do justice to Welbourne's work. John Agar, always a stock 1950s hero, delivered solid if uninspiring performances in several genre films. But in *Revenge*, his stolid stiffness is not helped by Martin Berkeley's second-rate script. Agar is hopelessly caught in a series of silly interludes with Lori Nelson and, at the beginning of the film, a particularly annoying scene with a chimp and a young Clint Eastwood. In addition, Agar's stock leading man is devoid of the complexity and credibility of Richard Carlson's David Reed in the 1954 original. Lori Nelson is an attractive leading lady, but possesses none of the strength and natural acting ability of Julie Adams. In addition, Berkeley's script only hints at some possible tension between Clete and Joe over Helen's affections. The kind of dynamism that existed between Reed and Williams in the original never surfaces here, robbing the film of a potentially interesting subplot. In addition, Berkeley wastes too much time "explaining" the biology of the Creature, his evolutionary origins, blood type and sleeping patterns. The script delivers plenty of boring "science" but not enough interesting "fiction."

Further, Berkeley's screenplay focuses far too much on the romantic byplay between Clete and Helen in a series of annoyingly saccharine scenes. When Agar clumsily tries to exude manly charm with the sylph-like, flirtatious Nelson, their lack of chemistry is only accentuated. Audience time is also wasted by a series of boring romantic scenes between the two lovers—obvious, time-consuming "filler" when contrasted with the supercharged action of *Black Lagoon*. And Berkeley's dialogue for these scenes is as insipid as 1950s Hollywood could get. During Clete and Helen's beach scene she muses, "Sometimes I wonder how I ever got started in all this ... science, fish, ichthyology. Where will it all lead me? As a *person*, I mean." Later, Berkeley saddles Nelson with even more banality: "[Love] makes the word go 'round, but what do we know about it? Is it a fact? Is it chemistry, electricity?" (Not that there is any to be had here!) No wonder *Revenge*'s *Time* magazine reviewer wrote, "Between screams, Lori Nelson unfortunately has enough breath left to engage John Agar in just about the limpest dialogue since the invention of talking pictures."

While the film takes too much time building the Clete-Helen romance, we see far too little of the always-delightful Nestor Paiva—a memorable player in *Creature from the Black Lagoon*. Paiva's role is almost a token cameo, though Berkeley gives him the film's funniest line: "I hope you ain't going to blow up my boat, Mr. Johnson. Like my wife, she's not much, but she's all I have!"

Berkeley is also guilty of wasted character potential. Dave Willock's Lou Gibson is the film's exploitative huckster—seemingly willing to endanger hundreds of people for the chance to cash in on the Creature's captivity. Yet, this mini–Carl Denham is given nothing to do and very little to say. John Bromfield and Robert B. Williams would have been equally interesting as exploiters—the yin to John Agar's scientific yang. Unfortunately, that tension never develops: Agar is not allowed to display any academic conscience over the Creature's plight, and Bromfield does little before the Creature kills him off.

What Berkeley *tries* to get right is the Creature's pathos—a concept which, as in *King Kong*, is underscored when the Gill Man is forcibly moved from his Amazon home to "civilization." We see this ferocious monster subdued by ropes, nets, chains and drugs—a Kong-like freak for the world to gape at. In one scene, Clete tells Helen how he plans to shock the Creature with an electric bull prod to condition his behavior. Notably, he says he "hates" to use the bull prod, but he uses it frequently all the same! Helen is the only character to express any *real* sympathy for the man-fish: "Y'know, I ... I *pity* him sometimes. He's so *alone*," she tells Clete. "The only one of his kind in the world. Well, he's like an orphan in time." This is *Revenge*'s most evocative line of dialogue—and the only one that concedes the Creature's pathos.

It almost seems as though Jack Arnold *knew* that *Revenge* could not live up to *Black Lagoon* in any meaningful way. While Welbourne acquits himself well, Arnold was left without the supremely effective cast and screenwriters of the original film. What he *did* have was a hack screen-

As if Revenge *wasn't sufficiently reminiscent of* King Kong, *there are publicity photographs of the Gill Man (Tom Hennesy) chained to the wall behind him, evoking memories of Kong's "theatrical stage debut" in the 1933 movie. In this strange shot from that photo shoot, John Bromfield is also chained!*

writer in Martin Berkeley and an uninteresting cast. Worse, our Gill Man hero, while more pathetic than ever, seems surprisingly subdued by Berkeley's script and Arnold's direction. The exotic mystery and style with which he was imbued in *Creature from the Black Lagoon* is sadly diluted here. In the Amazon River of the original, the Gill Man's environs were just as ominous and terrifying as he was. In *Revenge*, imprisonment seems to tame him: There's little menace, explicit or implicit. We may *see* more of the Creature in this sequel, but his confined, sterile surroundings rob him of his mystique. When he escapes, he is just another '50s monster on the loose: more interesting, but still not much different than the Beast from 20,000 Fathoms or Godzilla.

Still, *Revenge of the Creature* was popular enough to inspire yet a second sequel. *Revenge of the Creature* represented the last time Jack Arnold and the Gill Man would work together. Arnold would go on to bigger (*Tarantula*), smaller (*The Incredible Shrinking Man*) and *better* things.

THE CREATURE WALKS AMONG US

3

He's BAH-BAH-BACK again!

227

The Creature Walks Among Us Full Credit Information

CREDITS: Produced by William Alland; Directed by John Sherwood; Story and Screenplay: Arthur Ross; Photography: Maury Gertsman; Editor: Edward Curtiss; Art Directors: Alexander Golitzen and Robert E. Smith; Set Decorators: Russell A. Gausman and John P. Austin; Sound: Leslie I. Carey and Robert Pritchard; Music Supervisor: Joseph Gershenson; Gowns: Jay A. Morley, Jr.; Makeup: Bud Westmore; Hair Stylist: Joan St. Oegger; Assistant Director: Joseph E. Kenny; Special Photography: Clifford Stine. **Uncredited:** Music: Henry Mancini, Irving Gertz, Heinz Roemheld, Hans J. Salter and Herman Stein; Tracked Music: Henry Mancini, Hans J. Salter and Herman Stein; Piano Player: Lyman Gandee; Guitar Player: Hilmer J. "Tiny" Timbrell; Second Assistant Directors: James Welch and Wilbur Mosier; Unit Manager: Lew Leary; Script Supervisor: Adele Cannon; Dialogue Director: Leon Charles; Camera Operators: Ed Pyle and Towers (Richard Towers?); Assistant Cameramen: Lew Schwartz, Kurland, Bluemel (Walter Bluemel?), Green and Kelley; Key Grip: Russ Franks; Second Grip: Al Hall; Gaffer: Max Nippell; Best Boys: Ed Hobson and Todd (Al Todd?); First Prop Man: Julius Rosenkrantz; Assistant Prop Men: Lawrence and Murdock (Robert Murdock?); Sound Recordist: James Swartz; Mike Man: Roger Parish; Mixer: Althouse (Charles Althouse?); Cable Men: Jim Rogers, Devore (Perry Devore?), Wilson and Kyte (Robert Kyte?); Wardrobe Men: Roger J. Weinberg, Truman Eli and Jobe (Bill Jobe?); Wardrobe Woman: Rose Pryor; Makeup: Vincent Romaine, Reedall (Mark Reedall?), Dawn (Bob Dawn?) and Case (Tom Case?); Hair Stylist: Jo Sweeney; Publicist: Robert Sill; Still Photographers: William Walling and Lane (Rollie Lane?); Sound Editors: George Hoagland, Peter Berkos and Bob Bratton; Technical Advisor: Dr. N. Edward Gourson; Stand-ins: Walt Lawrence, Lloyd Dawson and Joe Walls; Coordinator: Ray Gockel; **Florida Second Unit**: Director: James C. Havens; Photography: Charles S. Welbourne [aka "Scotty" Welbourne]; Camera Operator: Irwin Blache; Assistant Cameramen: Bluemel (Walter Bluemel?) and Hugh Gibson; Unit Manager: Norman Deming; Assistant Director: George Lollier; Makeup: Reedall (Mark Reedall?), Dawn (Bob Dawn?) and McCoy (Frank McCoy?); Script Supervisor: Forrest (Bob Forrest?); Still Photographers: Paul Rubenstein and Cline; First Grip: Flesher (Jack Flesher?); Second Grip: Jones (Ed Jones?); First Prop Man: Murdock (Robert Murdock?); Prop Shop Man: Brendel (Frank Brendel?); Wardrobe Man: Tierney (Michael Tierney?); Cashier: Kohler; First Aid Man: Einel; Safety Diver: Charles McNabb; 78 minutes.

CAST: Jeff Morrow (*Dr. William Barton*), Rex Reason (*Dr. Tom Morgan*), Leigh Snowden (*Marcia Barton*), Gregg Palmer (*Jed Grant*), Maurice Manson (*Dr. Borg*), James Rawley (*Dr. Johnson*), David McMahon (*Capt. Stanley*), Paul Fierro (*Morteno*), Lillian Molieri (*Mrs. Morteno*), Larry Hudson (*State Trooper*), Frank Chase (*Steward*); **Uncredited**: Ricou Browning, Don Megowan (*The Gill Man*), Paul Stader (*Jeff Morrow's Stunt Double*), Jesse Thompson (*Jeff Morrow's Double—Convertible Scene*), Alex Sharp (*Rex Reason's Stunt Double*), Dick Wells (*Rex Reason's Underwater Double*), Shirley Deas (*Leigh Snowden's Double—Convertible Scene*), Ruth Skinner (*Leigh Snowden's Underwater Double*), Joe Walls (*Gregg Palmer's Stunt Double*), Jim Jackson (*Gregg Palmer's Underwater Double*), Joe Yrigoyen (*Maurice Manson's Stunt Double*), Ken Terrell (*James Rawley's Stunt Double*), Chuck Roberson (*Don Megowan's Stunt Double*), Joseph Gibson, Alex Bremmer (*Doubles*).

Production History
By Tom Weaver

> Hollywood's always playing a game called "I've Got a Sequel." Now it's a sequel to Revenge of the Creature, which was a sequel to Creature from the Black Lagoon.
> If this keeps up we're a cinch to be seeing a sequel to the sequel to the sequel titled "The Creature Takes a Wife."
> —Hollywood columnist Erskine Johnson, May 1955

In the third and last of the Gill Man movies, there's no 3-D, no Beauty and the Beast, no Jack Arnold and practically no Gill Man—not the A-list movie monster that audiences expected, anyway. *The Creature Walks Among Us* hits the same story notes found in *Black Lagoon* and/or *Revenge* (an expedition of scientists + girl + big game hunter invade the Creature's realm, capture him, imprison him for study, Creature escapes) and yet it's also *very* different. The designation "a 'fish out of water' story" has never been better applied.

All credit, or blame, goes to the sole writer, *Creature Walks* being the one Gill Man movie that *had* a sole writer, Arthur Ross. Part of the phalanx of screen scribes responsible for the original *Creature from the Black Lagoon*, he returned to the series and wrote *Creature Walks* because "I needed money!" he told me with a laugh.

> I had a new baby and all that. I was doing something else at the time, and Bill Alland said, "Will you do one more?" He said the studio wanted another Creature picture, but he couldn't get a story that was right. After Bill and I talked about it, I thought about it for about a day and I hit upon the idea once again of something rooted in scientific reality: that environment *or* the genes control our growth. In this case, the Creature is hunted by some scientists and caught in a fire, and his gills slough off. He is kept under medical care and attention, and he is treated properly, and he begins to respond. But as soon as the Creature begins to sense that one of the scientists is hostile to him, he begins to revert to the brute force of nature that he was originally.

Ross also appears to have derived some inspiration from recent news stories about the work of the University of Chicago's Sherwood L. Washburn (1911–2000): The associate professor of anthropology had tried to prove that man's evolutionary rise, from the point at which we were ape-like fellows walking on all fours, was not as gradual as Darwin had posited. According to Washburn, an evolutionary change in the pelvis led to the ability of ape-men to walk on two legs—and *that* was a game-changer, opening the door for lots more Good Stuff on the road to making us the new'n'improved gents we are today. (Washburn's presentation of his theories probably had a firmer foundation in anthropological lingo, but you get the drift.) According to a 1951 newspaper article on Washburn's findings,

> [i]f the funds were available, the University of Chicago laboratories would attempt to duplicate this change. By an operation, the pelvis and gluteus muscle of apes would be altered so that the animals could walk. Studies then would be made of what they could accomplish with their hands and use of tools.

(Shades of Dr. Moreau!) "Sherry" Washburn's *New York Times* obituary called him a pioneering primatologist who "won nearly every medal and prize given in his field" and a teacher whose university lectures "inspired standing ovations from his students."

Ross' 13-page treatment *The Creature of Man*, dated May 10, 1955, includes a mention of Washburn's findings: Dr. William Barton, the character played by Jeff Morrow in the eventual movie, talks about Washburn's idea to surgically shorten the pelvis of an ape "and make him the 'missing link'"; Barton proposes that the same sort of speed-up-evolution work be done on the Creature. The Creature is, after all, even closer to Man: Now retired to Florida (yet another human trait!), the Creature has

> developed a cunning through the conditioning of having been captured twice. Here is a man—not a fish. He walks upright, has lungs; metabolism; circulatory system; heart; brain position and size are that of the prehistoric man who made shelter for himself and brought man forward.

Barton feels that if he can transform the Creature into a man, that will prove that he can also transform a present-day man into a "man of the future" who can move into outer space and live free of the Earth. (Actually, this idea isn't new to the series: In *Black Lagoon*'s first reel, Dr. Reed says the study of prehistoric links between land and marine life may lead to a means for modern man to adapt to the rigors of life on other planets. Maybe Ross wrote that dialogue too.)

The notion of surgically transforming a prehistoric monster into a man as a warm-up act before surgically transforming a 20th-century man into a futuristic being is truly wonky, and seems better suited to an episode of the macabre science fiction-horror TV series *The Outer Limits*. Within the movie, Barton's hare-brained scheme is sometimes laid out in oblique terms, to the point where the casual fan tunes it out as gobbledygook. Many, probably all of *Creature Walks*' 1956 reviewers either didn't quite "get" what Barton was proposing, or didn't think it was worth trying to describe to their readers. Avoiding the issue, the *Harrison's Reports* review says that Barton seeks to catch the Creature merely "to achieve greater medical fame." *Motion Picture Exhibitor* was vague, telling its readers that Barton wishes to capture the Creature "so he can conduct experiments." *The New York Times* made no attempt to relate the idea in back of the plot, getting around it by simply calling the Barton character "a disturbed gent [who's] not quite certain whether to use a scalpel on the Creature or his fists on his wife." *Variety* critic Brog also avoided the "why"s of Dr. Barton's undertaking, but was probably alibi-ing this gap in his synopsis when he wrote that Ross' scripting is "shadowy" in detailing some of the motivations. *No one* was more amusingly perplexed than the *Los Angeles Times* critic who somehow arrived at the conclusion that Barton's ultimate goal was to put *the Gill Man* in a rocket:

> The leader of the expedition babbles wildly about sending the creature into space, to the distress of the other three, who don't seem to know why they're after the beast.

Even the *Creature Walks* pressbook's official plot synopsis steers clear of trying to explain all (or *any*) of the goals of Barton, dumbing it down to "[Barton] heads an expedition to capture the fabulous Gill Man" and letting it go at that.

"Barton is a throwback to the mad scientist of the Universal Gothics," David J. Schow wrote me. "He's *nuts*, madder than a Nazi eugenics loon, and equally dedicated to his own berserk theories which, because he is a mad scientist, don't have to make linear sense."

Ross' May 10 draft *The Creature of Man* is a blueprint for the first half of the movie and is very much like it, except for the actions and attitudes of the character of Barton's wife Marcia. It begins with a scene of a fancy Italian car speeding furiously along a Florida road, another big expensive sports car racing behind it. At a yacht landing, they come to a stop. The driver of the first car, Marcia Barton, is a reckless, "sports-minded" woman who always takes unnecessary risks. She laughs at the driver of the second car, her wealthy surgeon husband William Barton.

On the yacht, we meet members of an expedition that Barton is financing: geneticist Thomas Garvey, who has

Barton's (Jeff Morrow) mad-sounding ultimate plan was to mutate modern-day humans to the point where they can live in outer space. And he was in a hurry about it: In an early draft, he asserted, "We can free ourselves from Earth in one generation. Be free of Earth and live out there."

been working on mutated species in sea life; diver and hunter Jed Grant; and Drs. Simpson and Borg. Barton believes it is possible to mutate a species into existence—that is, by making radical changes, bring about a new species from an old rather than accept the slow, gradual process involved in waiting for nature to do the trick. For the first of many times, Garvey disagrees.

The hunt for the Gill Man begins with a visit to an Everglades fisherman whose hand was mangled in a clash with the merman. Marcia, physically fearless and an expert hunter, fills her time on the yacht by killing alligators with her rifle and by taunting her husband, who she knows will not challenge her. She seems to be attracted to Garvey and to Grant.

Near the isolated island where the Gill Man was last

3. The Creature Walks Among Us (1956)

seen, a first dive, a deep one, is to be made. Marcia accompanies Garvey, Grant and an assistant despite Garvey's warning that at great depths, first-time divers suffer from "the euphoria" and attempt to remove their scuba gear "and swim with the freedom of the sea life around them." Once below, Marcia tries to make a sexy game of tag out of it, first with Garvey (who doesn't bite) and then with Grant (who does). They do not see "the darting, watching shadow of the Gill Man" behind them. Back aboard the boat, Marcia taunts Garvey for being remote and implies that she'd like to go on more dives with Grant. Dr. Borg, who had monitored the sub-aquatic movements of the four using "a radar set and screen," tells them that something followed them.

The scientists wait for the Gill Man to make the next move, which he doesn't, so Garvey and Grant go after *him*: They dive by night with portable floodlights and a supply of rotenone, and with Marcia again in tow. They do spot the Gill Man but just then, Marcia succumbs to "the euphoria," removing her mouthpiece. Garvey has to knock her out before he can rescue her. Back on the yacht, Barton calls Marcia a fool and she calls him a coward, "[a]fraid to hunt as she hunts, live as dangerously as she does, as Jed Grant does." While trailing the Gill Man to the Everglades, Barton talks more about his reasons for forming this expedition: to create a new species and go down in medical history alongside Darwin, Lamarck, Haldane and (that name again) Washburn.

In case the Gill Man comes aboard the yacht, nets are suspended in various spots; they can be dropped on him with the pull of a level. Come aboard the yacht he does, and he battles his way out of a net. A terrified Grant picks up a deck torch and hurls it into the monster's face, enveloping his head in oil-fire. Another net drops on the burning Gill Man, but he breaks out of it and dives overboard.[1]

Barton, Garvey, Marcia, Grant and two assistants follow the Gill Man into the Everglades in a flat-bottomed boat. The man-beast attacks, toppling a huge dead tree toward them and then capsizing the boat. He picks up a log to crush his pursuers, but then collapses unconscious. The Gill Man is rushed back to the yacht; his burned gills are not working. An X-ray reveals the presence of lungs, so surgery is performed and he begins to respire. Garvey warns Barton not to play God and disturb the balance of nature. Barton boasts, "I'm not afraid of unknown things." Meanwhile, the bored Marcia is spending time diving with Grant, "and their contact underwater is far more intimate than it is aboard the ship."

Suffering from amnesia, the Gill Man awakes not with a roar or even a whimper, simply staring about the room and at the lights. "When will his memory return?" the script asks the reader. "Will it ever return? Is he now 'prehistoric man'— or only a vegetating form of life that will never regain its senses and cunning." As the yacht heads for Barton's California home, lab experiments are performed on the Gill Man. His metabolism having changed, he now eats only cooked food. Chemical components in his food mutate his external physical characteristics: Swarthy skin appears on his face, a bridge in the nose is manifest, lips are seen. To Barton, this means that a modern man can be metabolically altered in order to survive on another planet. Garvey again disagrees.

Barton and Marcia argue some more, and after he falls asleep, she goes to the Creature's cabin and tells guard Grant that she wants to get her first look at the improved model. "[The] changed facial characteristics … now are almost those of an aboriginal man. Very high cheekbones; an elongated but not disproportionate jaw. But still only seen in shadows."

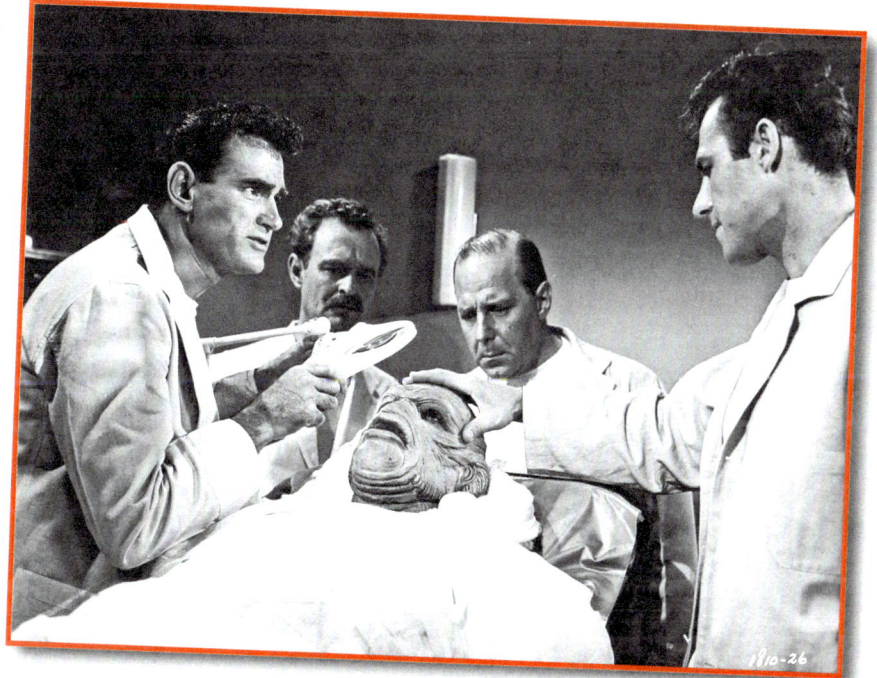

Rebel Without the Gauze: After removing his bandages, Jeff Morrow, James Rawley, Maurice Manson and Rex Reason examine the Creature (Don Megowan) that, in the tradition of mistreated, misunderstood monsters, has been tracked down, speared, burned and removed from his Everglades haven. The *Los Angeles Times* reviewer nailed it: "The four who set out to recapture the beast are enough to make the Curies turn over in their graves."

Marcia and Grant make out, unaware that they're being watched by the Creature, who also stares at the water. He comes out of his room and approaches the canoodlers until she sees him and screams. In fear, the Creature steps back, and then moves to the rail. He's hesitant to jump into the water but, as everyone aboard noisily converges on him, he takes the plunge. The Creature needs to keep coming up for air, so Garvey dons an aqualung to attempt to save him. When the Creature finally passes out, Garvey keeps him afloat while awaiting the rescue launch. There's yet more bitter arguing between Barton and Marcia, this time involving her two-timing him with Grant.

By this point, the Creature's hand- and foot-talons are gone, and there's less webbing on his hands and feet, making them look almost human. Barton exults while Garvey (sigh) *again* disagrees. Borg runs an electroencephalograph test on the Creature and there's an indication that his memory might be returning. Will the savageness of the Creature also return?

And on that cliffhanger note, this treatment ends in mid-page. But stay tuned: *Next* we examine a later, longer treatment, 43 pages compared to the initial one's 13. The events of the 13-page treatment are here stretched out to 19 pages, so we begin with some of the alterations and additions found therein:

- In the opening scene, Marcia now drives a Mercedes-Benz sports car with Barton following in a Jaguar XK-120.[2]
- When Barton arrives at the yacht landing a short time after Marcia does, he icily tells her, "You drive like a child." Mouthy Marcia's comeback line: "Fast cars were meant for children—grown-up children."
- Marcia puts out the lure for Garvey and Grant "in a way which seems more calculated to hurt her husband for some secret conflict rather than to impress Dr. Garvey and Grant."
- What could have been a key scene is included in this draft, but it didn't survive into the movie: After the first dive, Barton fiercely summons Marcia into their suite of rooms to tell her he doesn't like her friendship with "that laborer" (Grant). Marcia quickly becomes conciliatory and begs that they not argue again. It becomes clear that he has driven her half-mad by always holding her to impossible standards: the perfect wife *and* perfect companion *and* perfect hostess, *and and and*. As tears come to her eyes, she says, "[You wanted to] make me into some kind of woman—someone different than who I was. I never had a chance to know who I was." Barton comes back at her with:

Everything you know—everything you are—everything good—I taught you. You were only a pretty girl—nothing more than a pretty girl when I married you. Anonymous in a crowd. Nothing.

Barton is nothing if not consistent in his nuttiness: obsessed with transforming the Gill Man into a more-perfect man, with transforming modern man into a more-perfect man of the future, and with transforming Marcia into the perfect woman.

- After Garvey saves "euphoria" victim Marcia, they have a long talk—longer than the one in the movie—with Garvey even spouting a quote from Albert Schweitzer about "reverence for life." (Hold that thought, "reverence for life," for a page or so.) The dialogue is all quite boring, and reminiscent of the "point-counterpoint-*counter*counterpoint" sparring that Reed and Kay do in one of Ross' *Black Lagoon* drafts.
- Ross attempts to explain Barton's "create a new species" mania: "It is implicit that Dr. Barton's will to be the 'creator of strength' is in large part his inability to live with man—and with woman with a measure of happiness. Due to the rigid, unyielding 'dehumanization' of himself—he looks not at earth but at the stars; but not to the stars as a goal—but only as an escape."

And now in this 43-page treatment, the story picks up with the yacht entering the Golden Gate and being stopped by a Coast Guard cutter whose captain informs the scientists that their request for an entry permit for the Creature into the United States has been granted. But the California State Police are adamant that there be maximum security measures at the Creature's ultimate destination, the ranch of Dr. Barton.

At the ranch, located in a mountain valley 30 miles from the Bay, Barton and Garvey show the California Highway Patrol's Lt. Granik the stockade[3] which the Creature shares with some cows, sheep and chickens. The Creature is staring straight ahead as if seeing nothing. At night he listens to the sound of a nearby waterfall. The next day, the education of the Creature begins: He is shown objects as they're being named, then listens to classical music and a record of a man singing. Finally Marcia is brought out to sing to him, accompanied by Garvey on Spanish guitar. Their rendition of the Spanish folk tune "Cancion Triste" elicits from the man-fish a reaction described in the caption of the photo of Leigh Snowden and Rex Reason in this chapter's section on the music of *Creature Walks*. (These scenes are reminiscent of the education of the caveman in 1970's *Trog*.)

3. The Creature Walks Among Us (1956) 233

One night the Creature senses a presence and quickly sits up in his bunk. A mountain lion leaps the stockade fence and goes after one of the sheep. Then at last the lion senses the Creature, and leaps for his throat. The Creature raises the screaming lion over his head and slams it to the ground with brutal force. The scientists worry that he's reverting to violence, but then realize that he was actually defending the defenseless—the animals of the stockade which had become familiar to him. When Marcia notices that his hand is bleeding, she slips into the stockade with a first aid kit to tend to him (*Androcles and the Gill Man*?). Slowly and cautiously she bandages the wound as the Creature fixes his eyes on her. The scientists remove the bodies of the lion and sheep and bury them in a pit next to the stockade. None of them noticed that the gate did not lock behind them, but the Creature did.

Yet another flare-up between Barton and Marcia ends with him slapping her. The Creature sees this. Marcia takes a dip in the pool and the wolfish Grant wants to join her; she tells him to go away. Barton appears on the scene and, after Marcia has gone back inside, he takes Grant to the far end of the house, near a utility shed, and orders him to immediately leave the premises. Grant makes the deriding remark, "It could've been *any* guy, your wife'd get friendly with, Barton. She hates *you* that much"—prompting Barton to pick up a two-by-four and beat him to death. Dazed and frantic, Barton ties Grant's body to a horse and walks off with it, and the Creature secretly follows. Barton flings the body into a lake, watches it sink and then mounts the horse and gallops away.

The Creature remains at the scene and, as dawn breaks, his memory stirs: He moves to the edge of the lake, dips his hand into the water and then, looking almost triumphant, dives in. The Creature sees Grant's body get caught in the current and he follows it, into a river and then toward the waterfall. When the body snags on a dead log, the Creature finally catches up with it and hauls it out of the river. Back ashore, he examines the body and really thinks about death for the first time, and the fact that Grant was killed wantonly. The "*reverence for life*" which has growing within him, now that he's more human, compels him to carry the body back to the Barton home with the intention of putting it in the burial hole with the lion and sheep. But a worker sees him and lets out a scream. An alarm rings and everyone rushes out to see the Creature with Grant's body in his arms (and they assume that he has reverted to violence). Barton realizes what the Creature is holding and screams, "Kill him." Garvey argues with him (as always!) so Barton begins firing wildly, finally hitting the Creature with his fourth shot. The Creature drops Grant and charges at Barton, as the others pull their guns.

Screaming "Stop it!," Marcia gets between the men and the Creature and accuses her husband of killing Grant: "[Y]ou're insane. You walk and talk like a human being—but you're an insane animal! You imagine enemies—you conjure up hate like a witch!" Pulling out her gun and pointing it menacingly at the men, she orders them into the laboratory building and, from outside, locks them in. Then she and the Creature walk together into the hills, toward the water.

At the edge of the lake, the Creature (who has been warily eyeing Marcia's holstered gun) abruptly snatches it, tears it apart and throws it into the water. Marcia is frightened but, when he extends his bloody arm for her to bandage it, she tears a strip of cloth from her slip hem. The Creature

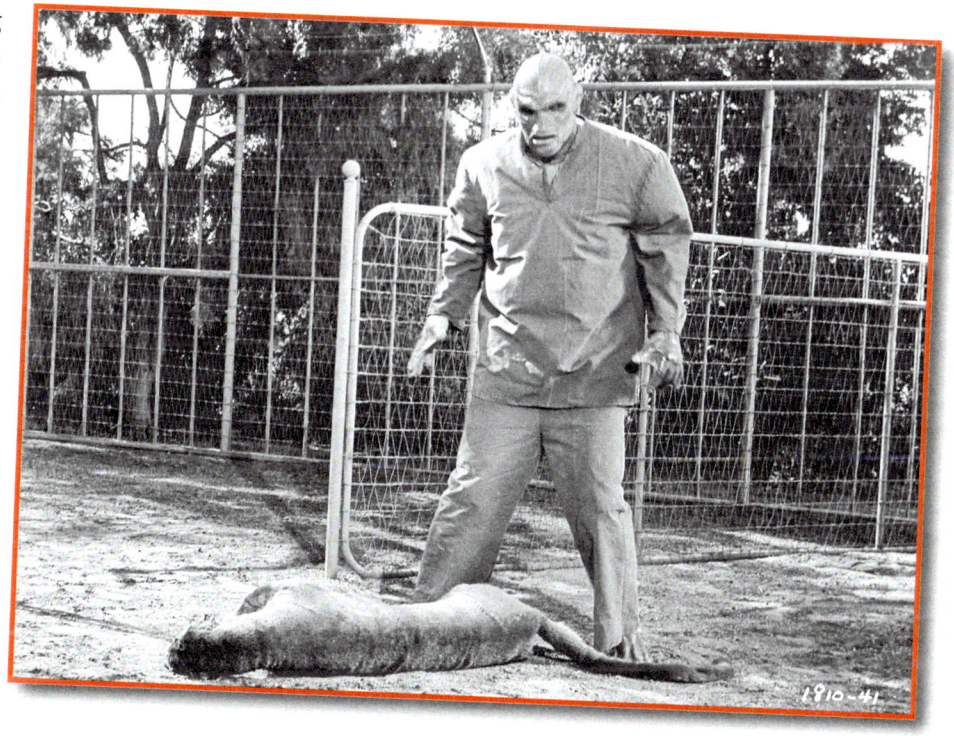

American Humane Association director W.A. Young wrote a letter to Universal expressing concern over the lion-kills-sheep and Gill Man–kills-lion scene. He advised that both the dead sheep and dead lion should be dummies, and asked that a member of his staff be allowed to observe the filming.

rips off half his sleeve to expose the wound—and Marcia is horrified to see that the heavy green "Gill Man hide" is returning. Noticing her response, he tries to cover his arm with his hand, and *that* now has the hide again too. Angered by her reaction, he shakes her to make her continue to look at him, then tears off his shirt; *more* hide. Marcia's scream infuriates the Creature, who takes out his wrath on nearby trees and plants.

Hearing car motors, the Creature sees that the scientists and some state policemen are coming. He rolls some rocks down a hill to block the road, but the men now approach on foot. Barton takes a shot at the Creature, prompting him to jump into the lake. Barton, "his distorted mind [having] returned to its animal roots," trains his gun on Marcia, but when Garvey appears, Barton pretends to have been aiming at something else. Garvey dons an aqualung and goes after the Creature. First in the lake and then the river, the two stalk each other, until the Creature goes over the waterfall.

The underwater search for the Creature resumes in the river below, but the divers can't find him because the Creature is watching them from directly under the falls, withstanding the thousands of tons of cascading water where no man can go. That night he returns upstream and then leaves the water, slipping unseen into the woods. When he arrives at the ranch house, he gets into the swimming pool. In the house are Barton, Garvey and Marcia, the latter announcing that she will leave Barton. ("[S]he has made the decision because marriage and love must be a sharing of equals.") Barton now thinks there's something between Garvey and Marcia, so when they go outside, he pulls his gun on them as they're passing the pool. With lightning speed, the Creature reaches out of the water, grabs Barton and pulls him in. When the Creature climbs out of the pool, Garvey and Marcia race back into the house, where despite the danger, yet another long discussion ensues (their certainty that Barton killed Grant, how Barton's mental condition and threats of violence toward her worsened over the years, how she tried to defy him, why he never sought help, *ad nauseam*). It's obvious that Garvey and Marcia are attracted to each other. A state police car pulls up and the officers see Barton's body in the pool.

At dusk on a windswept stretch of Bay beach, near a sign warning of riptides, a lifeguard sees a distant figure moving toward the water and shouts out to him. The figure pauses: "CLOSE SHOT shows the face—the human face and the Gill Man form of the Creature." He goes into the sea and disappears. The lifeguard reacts with puzzlement (some lifeguard!) as "the CAMERA HOLDS ON the rip currents and waves and the wide expanse of water."

Needless to say, this hideous story needed, and received, as much corrective surgery as the Gill Man before it was camera-ready. I've read a number of the interim scripts in which the plotline slowly climbed the evolutionary ladder toward acceptability; but again (as in my research on *Revenge of the Creature*) some were undated, *and,* there were other complications, making it impossible for me to present a synopsis of each script in chronological order. So here and there throughout the rest of this chapter, I'll cite the written-but-unfilmed highlights (and low-lights) of some of these other scripts.

Production-wise, the action began to pick up in the midsummer of 1955: On August 9, producer William Alland, director John Sherwood, second unit director James C. Havens and a.d. Ronnie Rondell left to scout *Creature Walks* locations in Miami, Tampa and Wakulla Springs. At that point, the plan was for second unit shooting to begin in Florida on August 22, and first unit work to commence in the studio on August 26.

"The reason I didn't direct the third Creature film was I felt that I didn't have anything more to contribute to it," Jack Arnold told interviewer David J. Schow. "I'd done two, created the first one [*sic*], and all I could do was repeat myself. By that time, I'd been promoted into A pictures, and I was doing something with Lana Turner and Jeff Chandler and [other] major stars.[4] I thought, 'Let someone else take a crack at it and see if they can add something to it.'" In *Directed by Jack Arnold*, Dana M. Reemes adds that Arnold didn't direct *Creature Walks* because "[he thought] it would be difficult for him to equal his previous efforts." Arnold said he felt this would be a good opportunity for the man he called his assistant director, John Sherwood, "to step up to director."[5] Reemes continues,

> Arnold feels that *The Creature Walks Among Us* is the weakest film of the three[6] because the two previous films had already explored every aspect of the Gill Man's personality and relationship with humans. In defense of the film, however, it may be pointed out that *Creature Walks* is in some respects a different kind of story from the other two, perhaps not to be compared to them. It is less an adventure and is more brooding and existential. The film's subtext is also somewhat different in the statement it makes about our relationship with nature and the ends of applied science.

Regardless of how Sherwood landed the gig, getting the helmsman's job on *Creature Walks* had to have been a highlight in his career, after working as an assistant director for two decades. His a.d. credits included Astaire and Rogers' *Follow the Fleet* (1936), James Cagney's Grand National productions *Great Guy* and *Something to Sing About* (1937), a number of Goldwyn pictures from the early 1940s and even *Gone with the Wind* (1939), as a second unit assistant director. Since 1946 he had been working pretty exclusively for Universal-

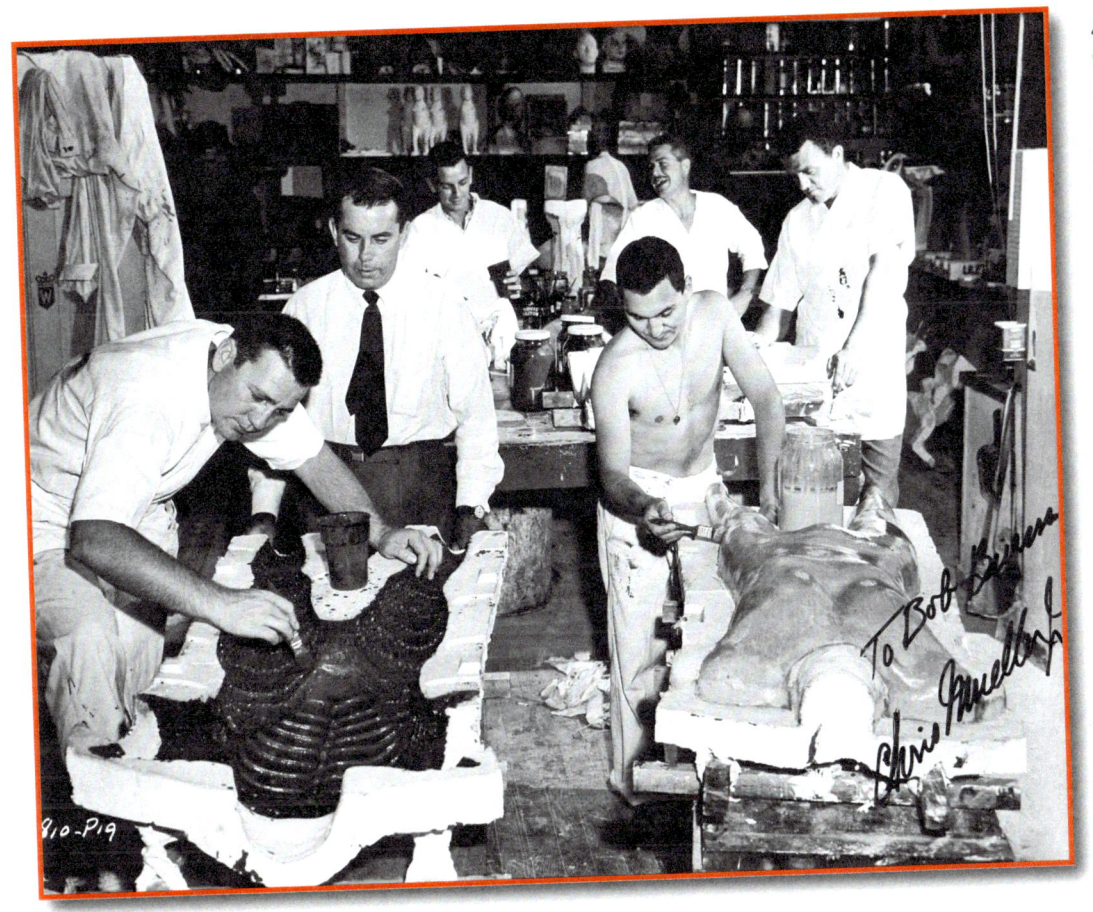

3. The Creature Walks Among Us (1956)

Another new Gill Man suit was made for Creature Walks. *The man on the left is painting the negative mold with dark green latex skin under the supervision of Bud Westmore (with necktie). We ass-u-me that Jack Kevan (in the background behind the shirtless guy) also had a hand in it but we have zero proof.*

I was a 'studio man,' so to speak, and as such, it was very difficult for me to break out."

At the August 15 Studio Operating Committee meeting, it was revealed that *Creature Walks* location shooting would take place on Florida's Gulf Coast in Fort Myers and at North Florida's Wakulla Springs, where the underwater parts of *Black Lagoon* were made. Alland and Sherwood were scheduled to be back at the studio that day, with the rest of their crew slated to return the next day upon completion of their scouting activities.

By August 17, the starring cast of the movie was tentatively set: Jeff Morrow and Rex Reason, veterans of the then-new *This Island Earth* (1955), plus Leigh Snowden, playing her first lead for the company after several supporting roles. Universal stuck with those three, but one name on an August 17 memo comes as a surprise: Pencilled in for the role of guide Jed Grant was contractee David Janssen—who'd already had a brush with the Gill Man series when he did post-production voice work on *Revenge of the Creature*. Internal studio paperwork gives the address of Morrow as 10824 Lindbrook Drive in L.A. and Reason's as 409 Winchester in Glendale. Gregg Palmer, once a studio contractee but now freelancing, got the role of Grant ("A man of great strength and fairly animal attitudes," according to the script); Palmer returned to his old Universal stomping grounds for $500 a week with a three-week guarantee. Earning the same total amount but working only *two* weeks was $750-a-week actor Maurice Manson, making his movie debut as Dr. Borg. James Rawley, formerly a commanding officer of the Far East Network of Armed Forces Radio Service, was

International. In late July 1955 he made his bow as a director on two U-I short subjects, a Miss Universe Technicolor short and a musical featurette starring Ralph Marterie, Eydie Gorme, Steve Lawrence and the Hi Los; he then moved on to his first feature, *Creature Walks*.[7] Sherwood made such an impression on producer Alland that, when I interviewed Alland in 1995 and asked why Jack Arnold didn't direct *Creature Walks*, Alland was surprised to hear that Arnold *hadn't* directed it! "I have a hunch that either Jack was not available or that he *also* was appalled at the script—although I *don't* think he would have turned it down for that reason, I think that he was most probably busy with something else," the producer told me.

> John Sherwood was an assistant director and he'd been around for years. Having him direct it was the studio's idea, not mine. By this time, I couldn't have cared less, see? And I don't know how much directing Sherwood did after that. The idea for a third Creature film wasn't mine. I never wanted to make a sequel at all.[8] And, once the decision was made to make it, the whole idea was to make it so cheap that we wouldn't lose money.

When I asked Alland if he ever protested when assigned to produce a picture he thought was a bad idea, he laughed, "I would invoke Jesus—that was about it! My problem was that

Stunner Leigh Snowden began her career by doing a sexy walk in a Jack Benny TV episode and another in Kiss Me Deadly *(1955). In her one monster movie, it's the Creature, not Snowden, who* Walks.

piped aboard to play Dr. Johnson (named Dr. Simpson in all the scripts right up to the last minute) for $600 a week for two weeks. His "Hollywood career" to date had consisted of some stage work plus a few TV appearances and uncredited movie roles.

When last we saw the Creature (*Revenge*), he was on the receiving end of police bullets on a shoreline in the Jacksonville area; in *Creature Walks* he rears his scaly head a few hundred miles south, in the tropical Everglades. Ricou Browning was enlisted to return as the underwater Gill Man but yet again the movie would have a new Land Creature, 33-year-old Don Megowan of 19220 Cantara Street, Reseda. At 6'7" he was the tallest of the topside Creatures but, like past players of the role, his paychecks were undersized (in comparison to some of the other freelance actors): $500 a week with a two-week guarantee. As pointed out in an August 15, 1955, *Daily Variety* news item, Megowan's casting marked the first time the studio had hired an actor for the Gill Man role: "In previous *Creature* pix," it continued, "part was played by a stuntman." Wellll, Browning was a college student and Ben Chapman a dancer—but, yes, neither was an actor. You'll read in all the Gill Man Lit that Browning played the un-burned, scaly Creature and then (after the fire) Megowan played the burned, clothed one, but actually both had the chance to play both.

During the era of too-tall TV heroes (Clint Walker, James Arness, et al.), finding actors who could go toe to toe with them was a cinch; the trick was to find ones who could go nose to nose with 'em. Don Megowan (1922–81) more than filled the bill—and his sturdy 6'7" frame also made him right for monster roles. Pictured: Bill Williams, Megowan, Clint Walker.

Synopsis

There are no outer space gas clouds behind the opening titles, as in the first two Gill Man movies: *Creature Walks* gives us a different background, roiling, frothy seawater (no doubt the propeller-churned spume at the stern of a boat). The on-screen credits are in the same "font," for lack of a better word, as those seen in *Creature* and *Revenge*, and we hear Herman Stein's *Creature* main title music for a third time. No other Universal monster series used a main title cue more than twice.[9]

The members of a new Creature-hunting expedition converge aboard the magnificent yacht *Vagabondia III*, moored at a private wharf on the Florida coastline near the Keys. The moneybags behind the outing, surgeon William Barton (Jeff Morrow), is "a man whose fame is not enough," according to the script's thumbnail description of the character. "[H]e seeks immortality by making a major contribution. He studies nature—to change nature. To be above it. People mean less than his ambition." With some difficulty, he's persuaded his wife Marcia (Leigh Snowden) to accompany him; the script tells us that she "seeks release from the fear of her husband who doesn't show love—but is possessively jealous of any man who even pays casual attention to her." The scientists recruited by Barton for the trip are geneticist Tom Morgan (Rex Reason), Roentgenologist-electronics expert Dr. Borg (Maurice Manson) and biochemist Dr. Johnson (James Rawley). Guiding them into the Everglades will be hunter Jed Grant (Gregg Palmer), the man whose information about the whereabouts of the Gill Man has instigated this expedition. The *Vagabondia III* sets sail.

The yacht comes complete with a fully equipped laboratory where Borg demonstrates for his colleagues "the scope"—a sonar machine he'll be using to find and track the Gill Man underwater. (Nobody in the movie calls it "the Fishscope" but the script does, and that's good enough for me.) Currently on its glowing screen is a moving cluster of white images that Borg identifies as a nearby school of barracuda. Amidst the Fishscope's noisy pinging, Grant jokes, "Takes all the kick out of fishing if you know what's right there in the water."

"On this particular trip, we'd *better* know what's in the water," Barton responds grimly.

En route to the Gill Man's new haunts, the yacht makes a stop near a fishing village and the scientists come ashore to pay a call at the simple home of Morteno (Paul Fierro), an alligator hunter. Lying in bed, his face lined by angry scars, Morteno tells his visitors that, while hunting, he shot at something in the water—and that a "devil" (the Gill Man) reared up and grabbed his gun. Morteno says he fought back with his hunting knife—"*Animal malvado*, there was plenty blood!"—but the battle left him with the torn face, a useless arm and, he demonstrates as he crosses the room to fetch the blood-stained knife, a hitch in his giddy-up.[10]

Back on the yacht, Johnson examines the Gill Man blood and determines that its red corpuscle count is halfway between the count in mammals and in marine life vertebrae: "Nature moving out of one phase into another," as Barton puts it. With a "Told ya so!" glint in his eyes, he announces that the Creature can be changed, right down to "the gene structure," and a new species brought into existence. If this is done, he insists, then work can begin on making Man physically capable of "taking the next giant step," into outer space. Morgan doesn't like the idea of bypassing nature but he, Borg and Johnson, all possessed of a scientific curiosity, agree to stay on.

While preparing to make an aqualung dive in order to test the equipment, Morgan and Grant are joined by Marcia (in white bathing suit, natch) who insists, over her husband's objections, on accompanying them. Seventeen minutes "into" the movie, we get our first glimpse of the Creature (actually, a Creature shot from *Black Lagoon*) as the merman follows and spies on the swimmers.[11] By now Marcia has descended too far and is suffering from deep-diving sickness, and the men must swim to her rescue. Morgan carries Marcia up onto the boat and into the salon. A shot of a glowering Barton, accompanied by a single discordant note of music, makes it plain he's not thinking about his wife's condition but about the fact that another man has his hands

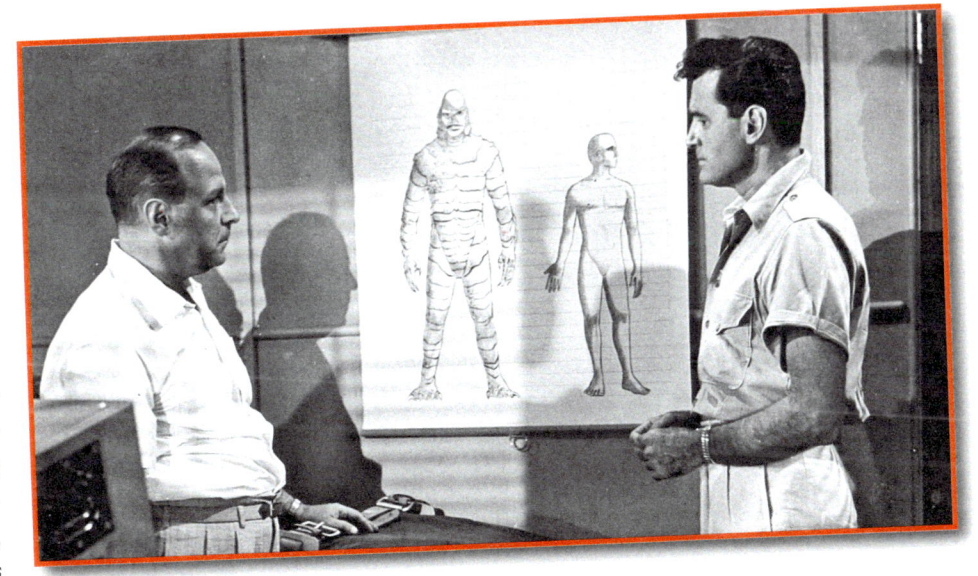

Creature Walks audiences were primed for the post-fire sight of a suddenly stocky Gill Man by this pull-down chart, which already depicts a rather bulked-up man-fish. According to a line of dialogue in another scene, the Gill Man tips the Toledos at 300 pounds. (Pictured: Manson, Morrow.)

on her. Later, in the privacy of Marcia's stateroom, he tells her, "Don't ever try to leave me. Don't ever try to make a *fool* of me." (In early versions of the script, one of Marcia's lines in this scene, delivered in a near-whisper, is, "We haven't been husband and wife—for a long time.")

At night, with the Fishscope guiding them, the yacht stays on the trail of the submerged Gill Man as he leads them into a shallow part of the river, and it begins to look as though the hunters may become the hunted. In a large dinghy, Barton, Morgan, Grant, Johnson and Borg (still manning the Fishscope) head down a dark, narrow inlet until the fellow with the fins suddenly bursts out of the water and smashes the bow-mounted searchlight.[12] After he leaps up into the boat, Grant shoots him with two tranquilizer-filled spears. The Gill Man throws a Jeep gasoline can at Grant, accidentally dousing himself in gas in the process, and Grant lobs back a lit kerosene lamp which sets the man-fish alight.[13]

Flame, set, match: The one-two punch of tranquilizer and painful burns cause the Gill Man to lose consciousness. We next see him lying motionless on a surgical table in the yacht lab, thickly bandaged from head to toe. With his gills burned, he's dying of suffocation, but X-rays reveal a perfect lung formation and Barton performs a tracheotomy.[14] The sound of the Creature's labored, wheezy breathing fills the room as the surgeon exults, "We *are* changing a sea creature into a land creature."

"We only used what nature offered," Morgan quietly demurs. Studying the result of the Creature's electroencephalograph test, Barton speculates that an hour-plus of oxygen deprivation to the brain may have caused permanent damage. When the Creature's hand and head bandages are removed, we see that the fire has burned away the outer scales to reveal a structure of human skin. Barton orders that Grant and the ship hands make a sailcloth suit for him.

There's a celebration in the salon that night, with lots of yuks, Marcia wrapped in a tight dress, Barton lapping up the liquor and, ultimately, another boring Barton-Morgan faceoff, this one involving metabolic changes, the effect of the interaction of heredity and environment, "Are the corpuscles beveled?," zzzzzzz. "We only changed the skin, doctor, not the animal," Morgan tells Barton, adding that they can bring out the best or worst in the Creature with the way they treat him.[15] The party is officially over when Barton drunkenly paws Marcia, then angrily casts her aside. It's just not Marcia's night: Some time later, Grant leaves his guard post at the Creature's cabin door and begins forcibly kissing the struggling, unwilling lady. (When it comes to Marcia, Grant is a guy "who thinks 'no' is a three-letter word," as Mike Hammer puts it in *Kiss Me Deadly*.) The Creature breaks out of his cabin, kayoes Grant, wanders out onto the stern deck and instinctively dives into the water. Rising from bed in striped silk pajamas, Morgan realizes that the Creature will use his lungs and drown, so he makes a daring hose-breathing descent to the sea floor to find and rescue him.

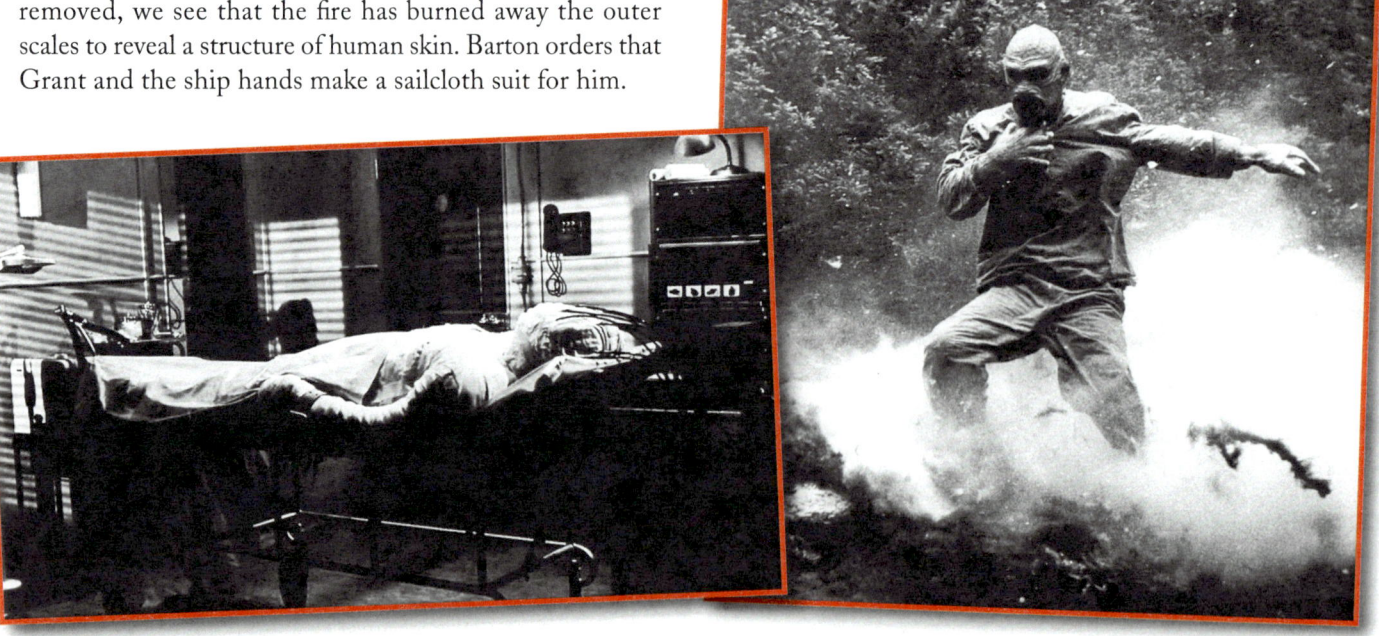

There's no comic relief in *Creature Walks* but it does have its laughable moments, such as when the doctors are examining the burned Creature, his head (including nose, mouth and gills) bandaged-wrapped tight as a vise, and Barton announces, "He isn't converting enough air into oxygen!" Ya *think?*

The mutated Creature (Ricou Browning) discovers to his dismay that he can no longer breathe underwater. Notice that, to make the 175-pound Browning look more like Don Megowan's big bull of a Creature, he is wearing shoulder pads; the Wakulla Springs water pressure makes his shirt cling to his body so tightly that they are hard to miss.

3. The Creature Walks Among Us (1956)

A stock shot of San Francisco Bay and the Oakland Bay Bridge signals that the homeward-bound yacht is nearing its destination, Barton's Sausalito home. His hilltop Barton Ranch has been made ready for the arrival of the Gill Man ("The grimmest cargo ever brought to civilization!"—trailer narrator). An electrified fence surrounds the property, the ranch hands tote rifles, and a large animal stockade has been built in front of the house. The now gill-less Gill Man is transported there in a moving van and escorted into the enclosure, where some sheep and goats are already penned. At night he looks at and listens to the water in a lake below, as eerie music conveys the idea that the water is calling to him. From a "viewing room" attached to the enclosure, Barton and Morgan watch him through a one-way mirror. Morgan believes that the Creature's aggressive tendencies have diminished because he's recently been treated with kindness. Without naming names, Barton tries to make Marcia the focus of their speculative conversation; Morgan implies that Barton sometimes makes his own reality. Throughout arid stretches of plot like this, we occasionally get a couple shots of the Creature pussyfooting around in his pen, but they don't relieve the dullness.

Marcia takes a dip in the lake but soon has unwanted company, Grant. (Grant could use a little of Clete Ferguson's electrified bullprod–"Stop!" conditioning.) A mountain lion becomes aware of the stockade's bleating animals and gets over the fence, killing a sheep. The Creature watches the horrific scene in a state of great distress, then lunges forward. The lion leaps at him but the Creature makes an impressive midair catch and brutally kills it. This is his first act of violence since the operation, but Morgan doesn't count it against him: "I think he killed the lion defending himself."

As the night wears on, Barton gets more worked-up over his delusion that Marcia is two-timing him, and finally barges into Grant's room, waking him to fire him and tell him to pack up and leave. (The pacing of the scene is helped by the fact that Grant sleeps fully dressed, right down to his shoes!) As they're walking down an exterior stairway, Grant cruelly mocks Barton until he snaps, pulls out his pistol and clubs Grant to death. This incenses the murder's one eyewitness, the Creature, who, as a *Los Angeles Times* reviewer points out, "has grasped the Golden Rule a little better than the humans." The monster's agitation gives Barton the bright idea to cover up his crime by putting Grant's body in the stockade, so it will appear that the Creature killed him.

The Creature, visibly upset by the violence, watches as Barton drags the body into the enclosure, deposits it on the ground and exits. Then the monster springs into action, mangling the gate and following Barton up to the house's second-story and inside. He moves from one darkened room to the next, bellowing and hurling heavy furniture. At one point he corners Morgan and Marcia but, perhaps remembering that Morgan saved him from drowning, spares them. (Kindness repaid *with* kindness, as Morgan had earlier predicted?) He then catches Barton out on the veranda, lifting him overhead and slamming him to the ground below. As a parting gesture, he shoves a shotgun-wielding ranch hand through the glass wall of his sentry house and topples a brick fence post before lurching off into the night.

Marcia (Leigh Snowden) and Morgan (Rex Reason) cower before the Creature (Don Megowan). The scene was to have ended with Marcia fainting and Morgan scooping her up and carrying her away, but that last bit of footage was discarded.

The next morning, in the Barton Ranch living room, Morgan, Borg and Johnson discuss the events of the night before, Morgan maintaining that the Creature has taken a step forward ("He didn't attack until he was attacked") and that Barton "killed an enemy of his own creation. The whole world was his enemy." Morgan and Marcia shake hands and eyeball one another in a way that creates the impression that they will meet again soon.

Several miles away, the Creature is on spaghetti legs as he laboriously walks to the crown of a barren hill, drawn by the sound of crashing surf. The hilltop overlooks a rocky beach pounded by large, cresting ocean waves. As the more-man-than-fish fish-man stands with gray sky as background, he is bleeding from multiple upper-body bullet holes, and his shoulders rise and fall with each labored breath. Unable to survive in water, but nevertheless drawn to it, the former master of the deep begins lumbering down the hill toward the ocean as the scene fades to black.

Bios from the *Black Lagoon*
By Tom Weaver

Jeff Morrow as Dr. William Barton

> When I was a little girl, and my parents and I would go on an outing, my mom loved to stop at the market on the way home. My dad [Jeff Morrow] and I would be sitting there, having to wait. Not my favorite thing, probably not his either. So my dad would tell me Shakespearean plays. They were also my bedtime stories, instead of fairy tales and things like that. He wouldn't do *Macbeth* or *King Lear* very often, but he would do *Twelfth Night*, *Much Ado About Nothing*, basically all the comedies. It would take him 20 minutes to tell a story.
> —Lissa Morrow, 2012

The youngest of four children of Brooklyn mortician John B. Morrow,[16] the future Jeff Morrow (real name: Irving Morrow) was a high schooler when he first became interested in drama: On their Victrola, his parents would play a record on which actor Taylor Holmes recited two poems, one of them Kipling's "Gunga Din." "[Holmes] was very good, and therefore I played and played it," Morrow told interviewers Jim and Tom Goldrup (*Feature Players: Stories Behind the Faces, Volume 2*). "I thought it was exciting and learned the dialogue quite well, but had no idea of being an actor." But one day in English class, each student had to get up and read part of a poem. Morrow said that the average kid "would read in this dreary monotone as if they were going to the gallows," so when he got up and performed quite well, his listeners were "suddenly stunned into silence.... [T]here was this tense attention from everybody in the class." The teacher noticed; the next day, Morrow was drafted to play the lead in the senior class play.

Despite a drama coach's recommendation that he try for a stage career, Morrow wanted to be a commercial illustrator, and enrolled at Brooklyn's Pratt Institute, an art college. But after Pratt, "the call of the boards" became hard to resist, and he began using his earnings as a freelance commercial illustrator to pay his way through drama school. While there, he was seen by the head of a Chester, Pennsylvania, stock company in need of a young leading man. Morrow took the job but the outfit soon went broke. Next he worked with a little stock company in Connecticut.

"My dad said there were times when all he had was peanut butter," Lissa Morrow told me. "This was during the Depression. His family wasn't broke, but possibly once he went out on his own, he didn't want to ask for help. That's why he lost his teeth—because [in his "lean years"] he didn't have enough milk and things like that. He went through the rest of his life with a lot of crowns and caps."

The short-lived Broadway play *Penal Law* (1930) may have been Morrow's Great White Way debut; later in 1930 he landed a role in *Once in a Lifetime*, which had a year-long run. His other Broadway credits included *A Midsummer Night's Dream* (1932), *Romeo and Juliet* (1934–35) with Katharine Cornell and Basil Rathbone (plus a one-year-later revival with Cornell and Maurice Evans), *The Barretts of Wimpole Street* (1935) and *St. Joan* (1936), both with Cornell, *Twelfth Night* (1940–41) with Helen Hayes and Evans, *Macbeth* (1941–42) with Evans and Judith Anderson *et al*. He also designed and painted sets for dozens of plays for Clare Tree Major's Children's Theatre.

3. The Creature Walks Among Us (1956)

Just as screen offers were starting to come Morrow's way, Uncle Sam, World War II and the Army Air Corps intervened. Three years later he returned to civilian life and to the New York stage. His new credits included 1949's *Diamond Lil* (as one of Mae West's suitors), 1950's *The Lady from the Sea* with Luise Rainer, 1951's *Billy Budd* and more. By this time, he had found a co-star for life: actress Anna Karen. Lissa told me:

> Jed Harris was then a famous New York producer, and she being a beginning actress, she was temping, working as a receptionist in Harris' office. My dad came into the office, Harris was casting a play I guess, and she met him. An actor named Paul Dubov was probably her closest friend at the time, and she told Paul afterwards, "A man came to the office, the most *beautiful* creature I've ever seen, *so* handsome. I don't even wanna *talk* to him, because somebody like that must be a playboy, a horror, a runaround…!" My dad had a couple call-backs so he came in another few times and they talked, and then he didn't get the part. Well, the day he learned he didn't get the part, as he was leaving, he asked her out. She asked, "How come you waited until now to ask me out?" and he said, "I didn't want to ask you out and have you think I was doing it because I wanted to get the part." *That* was my dad, that was the type of person he was. So they went out, and he proposed on either the first or second date! He said, "I am quite sure that I want to marry you," and she asked, "What do you mean by 'quite'?" He said, "*Completely*." They got married three months later.

Irving Morrow as he looked in 1939, when appearing on Broadway in the comedy What a Life.

By the 1950s Morrow was also acting on TV, sometimes as real-life historical figures (for instance, Blackbeard, Paul Gauguin, Abraham Lincoln and Chief Justice John Marshall). He also got his movie career off to a strong start with an excellent supporting role in the first CinemaScope feature, 20th Century–Fox's Biblical epic *The Robe* (1953).[17] Richard Burton stars as the Roman tribune who supervises the crucifixion of Christ; tenth-billed Morrow plays his surly, scar-faced subordinate officer, rolling dice in the shadow of the cross on which Christ is dying and casually asking Burton, "Your first crucifixion, isn't it?" Burton, haunted by his deed, converts to Christianity and later, in a town square, engages in a sprawling sword-fight with Morrow. Their battle, and the Burton-Morrow dialogue exchange which precedes it, are among the movie's highlights. Lissa Morrow recalls,

> He liked Burton, although my father, as far as I know, was pretty much a straight arrow. He didn't gossip about what people did, he didn't even think about it or *look*, so I think he was the only person who didn't know Burton and [co-star] Jean Simmons were having an affair. Burton liked to *have* a few [liked to drink], and he wasn't real keen on rehearsal, which my dad *was*; and because my dad had been in the theater, he had done a lot of fencing. So my dad did rehearse; Burton would kind of show up; and in the big swordfight, they had two accidents. I can't remember if my dad nicked Burton or the other way around, but one of 'em almost lost an eye—got cut over the eyebrow. And both men sliced off a bit of skin on the other's hand, basically because Burton was … I

Jeff Morrow (right) and his wife, Anna Karen (center), laboring behind the scenes on a stage production. According to a 1938 news item, Morrow was looking forward to the day "when it may be possible for him to found a permanent theater where he will have an opportunity to use to the full his knowledge of the varied departments of the stage."

Jeff Morrow and wife Anna Karen at a mid-1950s premiere. Tom Weaver asked their daughter Lissa why her dad went from "Irving Morrow" to "Jeff Morrow" at around the time he married; she said, "I think because my mother couldn't stand the name Irving!"

younger than he was. They didn't find out until he went to Europe and he had to get a passport; Universal had to verify how old he was, when he was born, and that's when they found out he was born in 1907. He always looked ten years younger than he was, and that's why he never told his age. He used to say, "Don't ever ask anybody about their age, their political persuasion or…"—he didn't say "sexual orientation" at that time, but that's what he meant. In fact, my dad and mom didn't tell *me* how old they were until I was about 20. They didn't trust me! I think Universal probably would have renewed his contract, except they suddenly found they had a *forty*-eight-year-old when they thought they had a *thirty*-eight-year-old.

Morrow cut a dashing figure as the Irish patriot and received some good notices, including the on-target *Hollywood Reporter* accolade, "Jeff Morrow, who seems at his best in parts slightly larger than life, plays Captain Thunderbolt with fine theatrical bravura." He went on to do two more movies at Universal, the boxing story *World in My Corner* (1956)[19] and finally *Creature Walks*.

Thereafter he freelanced, playing supporting roles in bigger pictures (Martin and Lewis' *Pardners* [1956], where he's very funny as a baddie, the Biblical *The Story of Ruth* [1960]) and starring in smaller ones (sci-fis, Westerns, etc.).

mean, he was *sober*, but he'd had a night's drinking and hadn't paid attention.[18] But my dad liked Burton, he thought he was a very entertaining guy and very funny.

In his first Universal picture *Tanganyika* (1954), Morrow played a renegade white man stirring up natives in 1903 East Africa; after it wrapped, the studio announced that he had been signed to a two-picture-a-year contract. He was again (after *The Robe*) imposing in Roman regalia in their top production of the year, the more-talk-than-action *Sign of the Pagan* (1954), then received top billing for the first time in *This Island Earth*. Playing 19th-century Irish rebel leader Captain Thunderbolt in Universal's *Captain Lightfoot* (1955) entailed a trip to the Emerald Isle, where the Rock Hudson-starrer was shot. This had to have been a treat for Morrow since, as Lissa recalls, "In Ireland, actors were treated like royalty in those days, and *he* was on *Captain Lightfoot*. Very wealthy people would invite the actors to dinner, 'Come to my chateau,' etc." But there was a downside, as Lissa reveals:

He didn't have a birth certificate, and when they signed him at Universal, they thought he was about ten years

The Pacific became the grave of the Gill Man— and of the Bartons, Jeff Morrow (1907–93) and Leigh Snowden (1929–82). Both had their cremains scattered off the California coast.

There was also stage work, including summer stock appearances opposite his wife and (his favorite theatrical production) the well-received Hollywood play *Tonight! Lincoln vs. Douglas* (1956) with Morrow making yet another appearance as Honest Abe. In 1958 he had his own syndicated Western series *Union Pacific*; the three-days-an-episode schedule was a hectic grind, with the actor forever fretting about knowing his lines. After a full season's worth of episodes were shot, Morrow was taken aback when the show's assistant director Erich von Stroheim, Jr., said to him, "If they renew this and we do another year, we could do this in two and a half days instead of three!"

Morrow and the missus also tried their hand at co-writing TV scripts; they sold a couple but nothing ever got produced. A lot of his spare time was devoted to following baseball: "He was a lifelong Dodger fan," said Lissa, "and he was *not* upset when they moved from Brooklyn to L.A., since that's what *he* had done! Occasionally he and I went to baseball games, occasionally football games. My mother was not interested in sports but I was. He would listen to the Dodgers on the radio almost every night they played."

There was a bit less movie-TV work for this "working actor" in the 1960s and he started turning up in odd places, like narrating the trailer for *Cape Fear* (1962). Then in the '70s, things slowed to a crawl. "As time goes on, what goes up must come down—and the 'coming down' is not easy," said Lissa.

> The offers stopped coming in. That's what happens. It was sad. But he wasn't angry or anything like that. As I'm sure other actors have told you, after you finish a job, you think you're never gonna work again. And then there's a certain point where that sorta *happens*. Going downhill was very difficult for him. After a while, he didn't know if he wanted to *go* to things [premieres and other events], because people wouldn't recognize him. So it was hard. He went back to working as a commercial illustrator in later years. Between that, and my mom working in real estate, that's how they made a living.

In a *Cinemacabre* interview magazine, the actor told George Stover about his new vocation: "I've done magazine illustrations; I've done elaborate technical illustrations for different things—organizational charts, progress charts, flowcharts and so on … I'd much rather be acting, but it pays the expenses comfortably." His last TV credit may have been the 1986 *Twilight Zone* segment "A Day in Beaumont," something of a comedic riff on his own *This Island Earth* and other SF oldies, with fellow vets John Agar, Kenneth Tobey and Warren Stevens.

My May 1987 *Starlog* magazine interview with Morrow *almost* resulted in one more movie on his résumé: It was read by writer-director John Carpenter and made him think of Morrow for a part in his *Prince of Darkness* (1987). Carpenter told interviewer Steve Swires in the December *Starlog*, "I called him up and we met for lunch. We talked about the old days. I even got him to reminisce about *Kronos* and *The Giant Claw* [both 1957], which were films I loved as a kid. Jeff and I both want to work together. It was the *Starlog* article which inspired me to contact him." In 2012 Carpenter told me that Morrow "wanted the part of the priest, Donald Pleasence's part, and we couldn't do that, so it never went anywhere." He continued, "Jeff Morrow was a kind man, generous with his time and indulgent with this super-fan when we met as professionals and I regressed into a 12-year-old boy in his presence."

By this point, however, the actor's health was not the best. Lissa reveals:

> Seventy-eight was my dad's *real* death age, in my opinion. One day while he was taking a nap, my mother … who couldn't know what this was going to cause, it wasn't her fault … she thought he looked a little gray. So she called a doctor, and the doctor said, "Take him to the hospital right now." If she hadn't, my father would have laid down and died in his sleep, with all his faculties, and had a pretty good life. Instead, his last years were … pretty awful. They put a pacemaker in him, and after that, everything went downhill. His autopsy revealed that he'd had mini-strokes, and we think they came about *after* he had the pacemaker. He started declining in 1988 or '89 but still could function, although he could not drive. Then the last three years were painful. We'd go to the Academy and Henry Darrow would come over, an actor who knew my dad pretty well, and my dad didn't know who he was. Henry was very nice; people are understanding.

Needless to say, the new normal was very difficult for Mrs. Morrow because for decades they'd done "everything" together: worked in plays, rehearsed, traveled, went to language courses, etc. Lissa says that she and her husband

> would sometimes take my dad out to dinner, because I think there were times when my mother, who went to work as a real estate agent every day, couldn't face coming home to dinner. Throughout her life, most of her evenings with my dad had been spent talking about the theater or current events or something like that, so I think it was *extremely* difficult to come home to someone who now could only repeat something 30 times to you in an evening.
>
> The pacemaker kept him alive, but when it needed a new battery, my mother's doctor told her, "If you let them do that, *his* life will be absolute horror, and yours will be equally so." A pacemaker keeps snapping-on your heart when you're ready to die, it keeps you from dying—and if the *rest* of you is falling apart, you don't want to *do* that. So she said no, and he died of natural causes, about a month after.

It was in a Canoga Park nursing home that Morrow drew his last breath, the day after Christmas 1993. Anna Karen followed him in death in 2009.

One more memory from Lissa Morrow:

My dad was probably the best person *ever* with his fans. He was absolutely wonderful. From half a dozen to a dozen people who started in his fan club became friends. He used to talk about some of them. After he died, I found that he and my mom had saved maybe 50,000 letters—they had 'em in boxes, just about *ev-er-y-thing* that anyone ever wrote them, from like 1941 on. Unfortunately some of that is chaff and not wheat, but I came across scores of long letters, all addressed to "Uncle Jeff and Aunt Anna." I'm like, "These aren't cousins of mine. What side of the family could *they* be on?" I read the letters, and they were from fans who would describe the things going on in their lives. These letters started in like 1958 and went 'til about 1990.

Mutt and Jeff: Morrow (right) in the mid-1980s, coping with this book's co-author Tom Weaver.

In one of the letters, a woman wrote in the most powerful way about how "Talking to you, Uncle Jeff, helped me through this period, and I don't think I would have made it without you and your constant comfort and support"—it went on and on, I was almost crying as I read this thing. I had the address, so I looked her up on the Internet and called her and told her who I was. She was a fan when she was 16 or 17, joined my dad's fan club, and they formed this bond; and she told me, when her husband had cancer and was dying, how my dad would call him, and how my dad would call *her*, on a regular basis, and just sort of "be there." And then after the husband died, how my dad was calling her and comforting her. Her parents were dead, so my dad's support was the thing that carried her through the grief.

That's the kind of thing he would do. And any fan who came out to California would get to meet my dad and my mom—they would have lunch, they would do *some*thing with them. When I think of other actors ... I can't imagine *any* other actor who would do this...

Rex Reason as Dr. Tom Morgan

Rex Reason was born in 1928 in Berlin, Germany, during the approximately two years that his father Rex G. Reason[20] of the General Motors Acceptance Corp. spent in Europe on business, together with his wife Jean Spencer Robinson. Sixteen months later, shortly after the family's return to the United States, a second son, Rhodes, was born in California. In the wake of his parents' divorce, the Reason boys were raised by their mother, a Christian Scientist. Her father Spencer Robinson, the first mayor of Glendale, had a stable and many horses which the brothers "rode up and down in the hills acting like cowboys and Indians," Rex told interviewers Tom and Jim Goldrup. "It got in my blood at this time, the whole feeling of acting, of being somebody."

Rex's mother was delighted when he was offered a starring role in a high school stage production of *Seventh Heaven* and she drummed his lines into him even after he fell ill and was confined to bed! (Rhodes was also in *Seventh Heaven*.) At 17 Rex enlisted in the Army and used his time in uniform trying to figure out what to do with his life. He ultimately decided on acting, spending a year and a half studying at

Rex Reason as he appeared in his first film, Storm Over Tibet (1952). Twenty-two years old, he did his scenes of "mountain-climbing" on a General Service Studios soundstage, with "snow" (corn flakes painted white and propelled by wind machines) getting stuck in his nostrils.

the Pasadena Playhouse and then working with the Ben Bard Players.

In January 1951, he made his movie bow (opposite Diana Douglas, wife of Kirk) as the star of director Andrew Marton's indie *Storm Over Tibet*. Loaded with footage of the Himalayas shot by Marton during a 1936 expedition, *Storm* told the sometimes eerie tale of a U.S. Army captain (Reason) in Tibet, about to return home after World War II, and bringing back a souvenir: the demonic-looking skull mask of the Tibetan God of Death, which he stole from a Buddhist temple. After the crash of a plane he *should* have co-piloted but didn't, he becomes convinced that its pilot suffered the fate the Death God intended for *him*.

MGM studio chief Dore Schary saw *Storm Over Tibet* and, impressed by Reason, signed him to a term contract. According to the *Hollywood Reporter*'s page-one story "21 New Faces Signed by MGM" (November 29, 1951), Metro had a systematic plan to build up one of the largest rosters of "fresh personalities" in its history; the 21 hired in the past year also included Leslie Caron, Fernando Lamas and Dawn Addams. But for Reason, the end result was uncredited, crumb-sized parts in the studio's *Scaramouche* and *The Girl in White*. His next contract signing (April 24, 1952) was at Columbia, where again he was used sparsely: He had unbilled roles in 1953's *Salome* and *China Venture* and a supporting part in *Mission Over Korea*. The latter got a scornful thumbs-down from the *New York Times*' Howard H. Thompson, but he capped his review by mentioning that "in exactly two scenes, totaling approximately three minutes, a newcomer named Rex Reason wins top acting honors" with his performance as a hard-nosed major.

Things began to break Reason's way in the summer of 1953 when he signed a long-term contract at Universal and was given a top part in the color-3-D *Taza, Son of Cochise* with Rock Hudson and Barbara Rush.[21] *Taza* begins with a dying Cochise (an unbilled Jeff Chandler) exhorting Taza (Hudson) to honor the peace that the Chiricahua have made with the white eyes. But Taza's hot-blooded younger brother Naiche (Reason with wig and brown contact lenses) has the troublemaking attitude of "I want to live like an Apache warrior—by the lance, the arrow and the knife!" The events that follow are just what you'd expect; the story can't compare with Utah's stunning outdoor scenery and big blue skies.

Reason's *Taza* role as the bloodthirsty brother set the course for most of the Universal roles that ensued. Starring Jeff Chandler and Rhonda Fleming and set in 1800, his next movie was the serio-comic *Yankee Pasha* (1954), which metamorphoses during its globetrotting 83-minute running time from Salem, Massachusetts, romantic yarn to high-seas pirate swashbuckler to Moroccan-set desert adventure! With beard and mustache, Reason comes into the story during its third phase as Omar Id-Din, aga of the Janissaries and the greatest marksman in all Islam, who buys Fleming for his harem and gets a gory comeuppance while jousting with Chandler.

No one was more surprised than Reason when *Taza* and *Yankee Pasha* reached the screen with the actor billed under the name Bart Roberts. He told me,

> Rock Hudson walked in on me one morning with a trade paper spread open in front of him, and he said, "Hi, Bart." I said, "What do you mean?" and he read to me, "'Rex Reason's name now changed to Bart Roberts.'" Well, that made me a little disturbed. So I went and talked to Ed Muhl, who was head of production at Universal, and I said, "You know, if my name were Bart Roberts, I bet you'd change it to Rex Reason!" I told him Rex Reason was a good name and he didn't argue—he said, "Fine, you can have it back."

Around the same time as *Taza*, Universal considered the actor for the role of Dr. David Reed, hero of *Creature from the Black Lagoon*. A May 22, 1953, memo lists Reason (actually, "Bart Roberts"), Gregg Palmer and Richard Long as possibilities for that starring part.

Publicists called Universal's outer space adventure *This Island Earth* Reason's first romantic lead at the studio, even though he never once gets romantic with co-star Faith Domergue. According to a 1954 *Hollywood Reporter* item, Universal was claiming that Reason was getting the same buildup they'd given some of their top stars (Jeff Chandler, Tony Curtis and Rock Hudson) but the fact was that the studio kept casting him as stinkers, in the Westerns *Smoke Signal*, *Kiss of Fire* (both 1955) and, his last Universal, *Raw Edge* (1956).[22]

In the next couple years he divided his time between features and TV, his credits in the latter medium including his own series *Man Without a Gun*, in which he played a Dakota Territory newspaper editor vanquishing crooks with printer's ink (scathing editorials) rather than lead. Episodes of this now-forgotten and hard-to-find series were shot in just *two days*, a grind that took a toll on its star. He told interviewer Mike Barnum in *Classic Images* magazine,

> I kind of enjoyed that series, but it really wore me out.... I worked and worked and worked, and then I came down with encephalitis.... The doctor told me to prepare for my funeral, but somehow I pulled through. For ten months after that, I could not work. I had to learn how to walk, lift a fork, a glass, trying to get my coordination back. The illness just took everything out of me.

Movie-wise, Reason was in Warners' *Band of Angels* (1957) with Clark Gable, but more typical of his post–Universal film fare were the five cheapies he did for indie mogul Robert L. Lippert. Lippert's troubleshooter Maury Dexter told me that he still vividly recalls the day he and Reason

Rex Reason said that he enjoyed "character roles" (as in Kiss of Fire with Jack Palance, pictured right) "because I could lose myself. To my mind, I wasn't good-looking enough to be a Rock Hudson or somebody like that."

grow up. I never went through the experiences of a normal 22-year-old—going off skiing, having fun, and getting into trouble. I was just disciplined and worked hard ... I worked, was always on time, and ... I really felt empty inside." He elaborated for me, saying that after about a dozen episodes of *The Roaring 20's*, "the enthusiasm slowed down, even though I felt quite comfortable in my role of Scott Norris the reporter":

> I realized that I did not want to live and die as an actor. Eleven years of working at breakneck speed suddenly began hitting me. I decided to bow out, to leave the business. It was not easy—acting was all that I knew—but mentally and spiritually, I knew I was entering a new phase of my life. "Fame and fortune" was not the answer to the quest in my life.

He bought his way out of his Warners contract nine months before its expiration date and prepared to leave the acting profession, incurring the wrath of his agent Henry Willson who promised to blackball him. Work-wise he couldn't figure out where to go from there; he said he did a lot of Bible-reading during these difficult days. His road to rediscovery led to a job in the real estate biz, which in turn led to romance: He told Barnum in *Classic Images* that one day when he was at work, "out from the broker's office came this little redhead with a book in her hand which she was looking at. She walked right by me, didn't even look at me. Well, though I was no longer an actor, my ego was still intact [*laughs*].... I got up and went back to the desk where she

chatted on the set of *The Miracle of the Hills* (1959) and being taken aback when the actor, talking about his future plans, said, "I think I'm joining the ministry." He didn't, but he *has* been a spiritual person all of his adult life. He told me that at 17, while in the Army, he found in a bookstore a copy of *The Infinite Way* (1947), written and self-published by Joel S. Goldsmith, a spiritual leader, mystic and founder of the Infinite Way movement. From that day on, that book has been near and dear to him; "I am *engrossed* with living the Infinite Way," he told me in 2013.

Circa January 1960 he signed a long-term contract at Warners where he was the star of another teleseries, *The Roaring 20's*, this time playing a reporter chasing crime news in Prohibition Era New York City. He guested on other Warners shows (*77 Sunset Strip*, *Bronco*, *The Alaskans*, more) and got in a few additional TV credits before calling it quits in 1963.[23] He told the Goldrups that part of the reason he decided to move outside the entertainment lane was that he'd started in movies at 22, and "from 22 on, I didn't really

Family-friendly and religious-themed, 1959's The Miracle of the Hills starred Rex Reason as the new Episcopal vicar of an 1880s coal mining town. Maury Dexter (right) remembers Rex as "a total professional and a damn good actor."

was working. She had a pile of papers on her desk and on top was a letter that began, 'The kingdom of God is within you.'"

The little redhead was Shirley Ann Hake, a divorcee with three kids. She told me that, at that point in her life, Men = Trouble, and she admits that she did blow right past Reason—but she *did* sneak a peek:

> I came out of the brokerage office and I saw this tall, good-looking guy in a white cashmere sports jacket, and he had black hair and blue eyes—*that's* unusual. But I just walked by him. I had three children to support, I had a job, sometimes I had *two* jobs, plus I was learning real estate, so it was a serious time for me and I didn't have time for [romance]. I went over to a desk and spread out my stuff, and on the desk was a letter from my dad which was very personal and inspirational. I had it sitting there 'cause I would read it often. Rex came over and he asked, "Do you mind if I sit down?" and I thought, "Look at this desk, can't you see I'm busy?"—I didn't say that, I was *thinking* that. But I said okay. So he sat down across from me and then he asked, "May I read this letter?" I thought to myself, "Boy, this guy's really nervy!" but then I thought, "The letter is gonna scare him off. This good-looking guy is gonna start reading it and then he's gonna dash out of here, because the first words in the letter are 'The kingdom of God is within you.'"

Just the opposite happened: As Reason read the letter, he thought, "Well, this is right up my alley." Once Shirley Ann found out that he was unmarried and living with his mother and his two children from a past marriage, she agreed to go a real estate–related meeting with him—and then another, and another, afterwards having coffee at a drive-in restaurant with waitresses on roller skates. It was a couple months later, when a restaurant waitress asked Reason for his autograph, that Shirley Ann first learned that he had once been an actor. In 1968, after a three-and-a-half year courtship, Shirley Ann became Mrs. Reason,[24] and *they* became the parents of a Brady Bunch-y blended family of five (his two and her three). Shirley Ann still hasn't seen all his movies but, among the ones she has seen, she's most enjoyed *Kiss of Fire* and *The Sad Horse* (1959).

Reason kept his nose to the real estate grindstone for years, then became a loan broker. He can be heard on the spoken word albums *Inspirational Recordings*, "with selected musical backgrounds, especially designed for contemplative meditation" (according to his website rexreason.com); they're individually signed and numbered by Reason. And like other sci-fi stars of the 1950s, he got a nice reception at monster movie conventions and autograph shows (for as long as he did them; he now feels he's too "gosh darn old" to attend). "I was just overwhelmed by the people's [his fans'] reaction," he told "Astounding B Monster" Marty Baumann.

This one guy came up to me. He had a funny shirt on that showed all his muscles. I asked, "Were you born with that or do you work out?" He said, "I'm here because of you, Mr. Reason. You so impressed me when I was young, I wanted to be big and strong and have a voice like yours. I'm working on the voice. I don't have that yet." Things like that are just as exciting as can be for me.

Leigh Snowden as Marcia Barton

> No one in town had ever heard of Leigh until Jack Benny asked her to go along with his television show to San Diego [in late 1954]. Benny was appearing before 20,000 sailors at the naval base there.
> Being an astute showman, he figured that you have to give sailors more than Don Wilson and Rochester so he asked Leigh to go along. Her only bit was a walk across stage—nothing else. There was no rehearsal but Leigh apparently didn't need one.
> When she ankled in, the whistles and wolf calls sounded like VJ Day. It stopped the show and marked the first time in Benny's career that a walk-on had even stolen a scene from him.
> —from "Leigh Snowden Walked Road to Stardom," an April 1956 Associated Press story

Perhaps because Leigh Snowden has less to do with the Creature in "her" Creature movie than Julie Adams and Lori Nelson do in theirs, she seems to be of less interest to fans of the Gillogy than Adams or Nelson. (Well, *that* plus the fact that Snowden passed away long before she might have been lured to the "monster" and autograph shows.) At least she has a part with a bit of depth in *Creature Walks* and gets in a couple of good innings of dramatic acting, rather than spending most of her footage (as Julie and Lori do) serving as arm candy to the leading man and then screaming at the Gill Man. Which probably suited Snowden just fine. She once said that the last thing she wanted to be was another Marilyn Monroe: "I'd rather be called a good actress."

Snowden (real name: Martha Lee Estes) was born in Memphis, Tennessee, in 1929. On the last shopping day before Christmas 1932, her father, a government employee, is presumed to have died as a result of trying to step from one Mississippi River barge to another, falling into the water unseen and unheard. The body was not found; his wife Catherine never remarried. Catherine and Martha Lee relocated to nearby Covington where, according to the *Creature Walks* pressbook, music became "an obsession" with the little girl.

As an adult, Martha Lee worked as a department store fashion model and for photographers. In the late 1940s she became the wife of Jimmy Snowden, whom she'd met when both were attending Lambuth College in Jackson, Tennessee; they had a girl and a boy. Once Jimmy enlisted in the service, he was gone most of the time. In the summer of 1952 Martha Lee sang in light operas at the Memphis Open Air Theatre in Overton Park. Eventually the marriage to Jimmy ended in divorce and she set out for the West Coast "for the purpose of taking vocal lessons with topnotch teachers" (again from the pressbook). Her mother kept the children in her home on North Maple Street in Covington when Martha Lee went out to California.

In the Golden State, she landed more modeling jobs and also parts on several TV series, most notably the above-mentioned Jack Benny episode. When she sashayed across the stage, the legions of sailors gave the curvy, sweater-clad starlet a standing ovation that rated a *Variety* headline. "When I took the first few steps on stage and heard those sailors cheering, I gave it just a little extra," she recounted. "I don't think we should ever let an audience like that down, do you?"

"It was *such* fun!" model-actress Ina Poindexter told me about Snowden's *Jack Benny* appearance. (Martha Lee and Ina became friends in childhood, when they were North Maple neighbors.) She continued, "Martha Lee looked so much like Marilyn Monroe, who was then very popular—Martha Lee was *built* very much like Marilyn. The sailors yelled and screamed, and *she* loved it, and *they* loved it."

Hollywood talent scouts were on the young beauty's trail the very next morning. Three days later, she was hired to make her film debut (with featured billing as Leigh Snowden) in the Mike Hammer crime drama *Kiss Me Deadly* (1955), in which producer-director Robert Aldrich had her do "the walk" again: Wearing a swimsuit and playing the appropriately named character Cheesecake, she makes her appearance by the outdoor swimming pool at baddie Paul Stewart's home. She approaches the camera from the far background, doing her fun-to-watch walk the whole length of the pool before exchanging lines with, and playfully caressing, one of Stewart's henchmen (plug-ugly Jack Lambert).

Home for the blue-eyed blonde at the time was an apartment at 1441 North Hayworth, overpopulated by Snowden, Ina, Barbara Stuart (Sgt. Carter's girlfriend Bunny on TV's *Gomer Pyle—USMC*) and a couple other gals. It was a two-story apartment, living room, dinette and kitchen downstairs, two large bedrooms and two baths upstairs. The place was right off of Sunset Blvd., around the corner from Schwab's Pharmacy, and naturally became a magnet for red-blooded boys, including David Janssen (who dated Snowden), James Garner (who dated Stuart), Laurence Harvey, Hugh O'Brian, etc. (Ina: "Oh, and Charlie Chaplin, Jr.—talkin' about how his daddy wouldn't give him any money!") Snowden once had a date with Frank Sinatra but according to Ina, "On the date, he called her a broad and Martha Lee, she stuck her nose up in the air and stomped her feet and turned around and left!"

In January 1955 Snowden signed a seven-year contract with Universal-International; she told United Press staff correspondent Ron Burton that her main reason for choosing U-I was the training offered by its drama school. (Burton humorously described the school as "a unique place where studio visitors who think they've walked in on love-making by employees on company time are told, 'They're just practicing.'") After the dimple-chinned beauty worked at losing her Dixie drawl, her first Universal, the sudsy *All That Heaven Allows* (1955), called for her to play it up: As the sultry Jo-Ann Frisbee (or, as Agnes Moorehead's character calls her, "that moron Jo-Ann"), she's briefly featured in two scenes, the first set at a country club where she's getting her flirt on with a tubby, wealthy gent, the second at a cocktail party celebrating her engagement to him. Snowden got Universal's usual cheesecake buildup[25] while playing some of her roles in fantasy and sci-fi pictures: *Creature Walks*; *Francis in the Navy* (1955), an un-funny movie even by *Francis* standards, where she's a Southern-accented Navy nurse; and the Bridey Murphy–inspired *I've Lived Before* (1956), as the wife of a pilot (Jock Mahoney) who may be a reincarnated World War I aviator. Universal gave her additional exposure by loaning her out to appear on a few national TV shows, including a 1955 *Lux Video Theatre* "remake" of Universal's 1952 comedy-fantasy *It Grows on Trees*. In the AP story quoted above, a Universal exec said of *Francis in the Navy* and *Creature Walks*, "These are pictures that were not up for Academy Awards, but they are important for the buildup of a potential star. They are big grossing pictures, seen by a lot of people, as were the television shows." He continued,

> It takes plenty of audience penetration to become a star. Most young actresses don't realize this. They balk at appearing in a picture with a monster, or a mule. They want to go the Academy Award route or nothing. Most of them wind up with nothing. Leigh realized this and was happy for the chance to work [in *Francis in the Navy* and *Creature Walks*].[26]

Early in 1956 a Memphis newspaper ran a photo of Snowden returning home for a visit, the caption mentioning that at U-I she was getting "a build-up as that studio's answer to Marilyn Monroe." During her Universal stint, Snowden also appeared in *The Square Jungle* (1955), *The*

3. The Creature Walks Among Us (1956)

then-20-year-old went AWOL from Fort Ord on the eve of his Army induction. He was fined $10,000 and served four and a half months of a six-month sentence at the McNeil Island federal penitentiary. "At that time, going AWOL was such a terrible thing to do," Ina recollected. "But Dick really was a nice guy. In fact, he was a *great* guy, and very talented at what he did. He's often said that they've never given the rest of the story, how he eventually did go into the service and made up for that mistake."

Universal had warned Snowden that marrying Contino would cost her her job, and it did. "Universal asked her *please* not to do it, not to marry Dick," said Ina. "I will never understand why she was so determined. If she had left Dick Contino alone, the studio would have continued to groom her. But she was in love with him and she married him. I suppose that Martha Lee really wanted a home and a family life."

"I wouldn't take anything for the training and experience I got at U-I and for the wonderful people I

Southern belles Leigh Snowden (right) and Ina Poindexter at a party given in their honor when they made a brief return from Hollywood to their native Tennessee.

Rawhide Years and *Outside the Law* (both 1956), and dated singer-accordionist Richard Joseph "Dick" Contino. ("He looked just *like* Jimmy Snowden!" Ina exclaims.) He was Italian and handsome and big-muscled from pumping his "Stomach Steinway" and—being Catholic—he was not permitted to marry a divorcee like Leigh. But after some back and forth, the two tied the knot in September 1956. In 2013, Contino told me,

> I'll tell you what kinda pushed me over the edge and made me realize, "This [the Catholic nix on divorcees] is bullshit. I love her and I'm gonna marry her!": It was when a Catholic priest told me, "What you have to do is get married civilly. This way, if it doesn't work out, you can always get your divorce and get *re*-married in the Catholic Church." To my way of thinking, that's not a valid way of approaching any kind of relationship, to have an escape route. I said, "That's *it*, I'm gettin' married." We got married at the Beverly Hills Hotel by a justice of the peace or a judge or whatever.

Unfortunately, the groom was known not only for his musical gifts but also for 1951 headlines describing how the

Leigh Snowden and her fiancé Dick Contino at a Hollywood night spot shortly after their engagement was announced.

met there," Snowden said in November 1956. By this time, she was making beautiful music with Contino, singing to his piano accompaniment in a nightclub act. Ina said, "The marriage went all right, even though I think they went bankrupt two or three times. But she was right cheerful through it all. She never did say 'Woe is me.'" (Cynthia Patrick, star of 1956's *The Mole People*, told me that Snowden *was* "sort of sorry" she left the movie business so abruptly, and often regretted it.) By now, Snowden's two kids from the first marriage were living with them; by 1963, she and Contino also had two girls and a boy of their own.

The Continos performed together at venues around the country; Dick was regularly on the receiving end of cries of "Slacker!" and "Draft dodger!" from audience members, prompting Leigh to start bringing his discharge papers to shows and confronting hecklers with them. Out-of-control boozing and gambling was Contino's solution to the stress. According to the book *Accordion Man: The Legendary Dick Contino* by Ben Bove,[27] the low point came one disastrous night when he drank and gambled away $10,000 with a visibly upset Leigh standing by.

> Finally, with his money gone and his credit exhausted, Dick turned to Leigh for solace.
> Gathering the dignity that never abandoned her, Leigh drew herself erect and stared into her husband's eyes.
> "All right, you son of a bitch," the beauty coldly said, "you've made an ass of yourself and you've lost all of our money—now are you satisfied?"
> The remark shamed Dick and he became embarrassed; he had never before heard Leigh swear.
> Slowly, he raised his eyes, expecting Leigh to continue her verbal attack. Instead, she extended her arms, understanding that Dick was battling demons that could not be exorcised in a single night.
> "Come on, Daddy," she said, "let's go home."

"Without my wife I would have gone to the bughouse a long time ago," Contino said in a 1964 interview. When I asked him to elaborate, he said:

> Innately she was very sharp about the psychological aspect of life, and she knew how to stand by me and give me support. I went through an awful lot of emotional stress: phobias, anxieties, the Army thing. She just seemed to understand and she knew how to talk to me: "Daddy"—she always called me Daddy. "Daddy, you should do *this*" and "You should do *that*...." It was extremely comforting.

"Dick Contino and his mother were so terribly close," Ina recalled. "And then he married Martha Lee, and.... Well, *you've* seen couples where one is the other's psychologist, haven't you? He seemed to *depend* on her, *so* much."

Feature-wise, Snowden went from stardom (*Creature Walks, Outside the Law, I've Lived Before*, 1957's *Hot Rod Rumble*) to an uncredited bit: In her next and last movie,

Leigh Snowden in later years, in a head shot from her final photo shoot, and chillin' during a visit to Ina Poindexter.

the 1961 John Wayne Western *The Comancheros*, she was Ada Belle, one of two prostitutes in a comic scene with Wayne and Lee Marvin. In 1966 Contino and Leigh went to Vietnam as part of an entertainment troupe (on one occasion, cowering during a terrifying day-long enemy attack) and in 1971 Leigh returned to acting when she played Maggie in a Fresno Community Theater production of *Cat on a Hot Tin Roof*—and won a local award for her performance.

The beginning of the end came in 1972 when Leigh's daughter Mary[28] noticed a black spot on her mom's back; it was melanoma. Surgery was performed and the growth removed, but the Continos were warned that a recurrence was possible. In 1981 the Continos were in Chicago when she became ill, and Northwestern Memorial Hospital doctors determined that the cancer had returned. The Continos resided in Las Vegas but Dick, wanting his wife to have the best doctors, arranged for her admission to Cedars-Sinai in North Hollywood; Contino lived in the guest house of Barbara Stuart and her actor-husband Dick Gautier while she was hospitalized. "Leigh was a beautiful woman and very sweet and unpretentious," Gautier told me. "That Jack Benny TV show walk-on was all it took to begin her career, and no surprise: She was as gorgeous as Marilyn Monroe in her prime. If not *more* so. Then [after her acting days] she was totally dedicated to Dick and her children."

In May 1982, 52-year-old Snowden died at Cedars-Sinai. She was survived by Contino, her five kids and five grandkids—one of them born the day before her death. Her passing is now more than 30 years in the past, and Contino has been remarried since 2005.[29] But he still grows emotional when he talks about her sad end:

> She went through such hell. Between age 42 and 52 she had this illness ... and then toward the end, it was very, very tough. She was in such pain with every breath. So much pain that there was a time, much as I worshipped her, I thought I'd put a pillow over her head, so she wouldn't suffer any more. She was the great, great love of my life.

Gregg Palmer as Jed Grant

> I remember one day sitting around jawing at lunch with Jim Davis and John Agar—it coulda been on *Big Jake* [1971]—and we got to talking about science fiction movies that we were in. Taking turns, we began naming them. John Agar started out with *Tarantula* [1955]. I said, "*Zombies of Mora Tau* [1957]." Then Jim Davis came up with one [perhaps *Monster from Green Hell*, 1957], and back came John Agar with *Revenge of the Creature*. I said, "*The Creature Walks Among Us*." Then Jim Davis came out with, "*Jesse James Meets Frankenstein's Daughter* [1966]," and I said, "That's it. You win!" How can you top that one? Jeez, I know Jesse had problems with the railroad in his day, but I had no idea he'd gone on to challenge a Frankenstein!
>
> —Gregg Palmer, 2013

In *Creature Walks Among Us* diving scenes, players wore the Northill Air-Lung, and the Northill Company later prepared and published magazine ads dominated by a photo of *Creature Walks* cast members (some wearing the gear) on the yacht deck with the caption

> EASIEST breathing SCUBA simplifies beneath the surface acting and camera work in *The Creature Walks Among Us*.

As payback for allowing his image to be used in the ad, Gregg Palmer received a Northill Air Lung Regulator but, no great fan of diving, he gave it to one of his brothers. In fact, the actor who played *Creature Walks'* expert diver Jed Grant got to the point where he avoided roles that involved water work:

> I did a *Sea Hunt* [TV episode] and we were five miles out, off the coast of Long Beach. A girl and I were in the water, a couple boats nearby, and five-foot swells. All of a sudden, we

In the early 1980s, Leigh Snowden and husband Dick Contino visited the Dyersburg, Tennessee, home of Ina Poindexter, who snapped this badly overexposed photograph of Leigh and then told her the picture made her look like an angel. Cancer battler Snowden responded, "Maybe it's prophetic, Ina." She died soon thereafter.

started having sharks coming around us—these blue fin five-footers. One of the fellas on the crew said, "Oh, Gregg, don't worry about it. Hit him in the nose with your tank." I said, "*What*?!" They kept circling and she got a little frightened, and I said, "Hey, get us out of here!" Well, it took a while to get us aboard, and after that session I said, "I'm not going in again with sharks around me." And I was told, "Awww, they're only five-footers, they won't hurt ya." I said, "*Forget it*." Afterwards, I told my agent, "*No more water stuff*."

Sure enough, later I got a call to do an *Assignment: Underwater* episode and I was told, "Gregg, don't worry, they're not going out in the ocean, it's shot right in the harbor." I said okay. In one scene, I had a tank on me and I was standing on the stern of some vessel, and the director didn't know how to end the scene. I said, "Why don't I step off the stern and go into the water, and I can go under, and you can film the bubbles?" He said, "Good thinking!" We did the scene, I dropped down into the water, the camera panned down and I went under the surface and I went to take a breath…

Nothing! No air. I looked up and saw this emerald-colored light and I struggled my way up and I broke surface and took the mask and mouthpiece off. I found out later, the prop man put a dummy tank on me. He didn't know I was going to step off the boat, the scene didn't originally call for that, so he gave a dummy tank that wouldn't weigh as much as an air-filled tank. Maybe he thought the dummy should have a dummy tank [*laughs*]? Again I said, "That's all!" [water-wise] and this time I meant it!

Born in 1927, Norwegian by heritage and a San Franciscan by birth, Palmer (real name: Palmer Edwin Lee) was the son of Olaf Lee, a carpenter who built houses in the Bay Area, including his own Nordhoff Street home. After Palmer served a mid-1940s hitch in the Army Air Corps, he went to school to learn to become a radio announcer and did just that, on a San Jose station. He was encouraged to try for a career in the movies and finally moved into the Hollywood area, taking odd jobs (truck driver, loading freight cars, working as a bouncer at the Palladium, etc.) while waiting for that big break, which took its time coming. His most memorable "show biz" experience during his early Tinsel Town days was doing a screen test for the role of Li'l Abner in a proposed TV production: In it, he acted opposite Marilyn Monroe, who was up for the part of Daisy Mae!

Still using his real name Palmer Lee, the brown-haired, brown-eyed actor made his movie bow in an uncredited bit as an ambulance attendant in Paramount's *My Friend Irma Goes West* (1950), a comedy with Martin and Lewis in support, and then he played a small, screen-credited part in the Martin and Lewis–starring *That's My Boy* (1951). Tired of slow progress, he was about to chuck it all and return to San Francisco when Universal offered him a seven-year contract. Seven years sounded like a long time and he had to talk himself into it, and finally signed on the dotted line. He told me,

> I enjoyed going to work at Universal, it was like goin' to school. We [he and other contract players] were all young and we'd sit around and have lunch and if we wanted to go (say for example) ride horses on the back lot, they were there for us, and we were *encouraged* to saddle up so we'd be ready in case we were assigned to a Western or whatever. It was a friendly studio. Producers would bum cigarettes off of you, or when you walked down the hallway, they'd call you in and say, "Hey, I owe you four cigarettes. Here's a pack for you," and they'd show you pictures of their family. It was a happy time.

At first the roles played by the $75-a-week contractee were small, sometimes uncredited, but then came sixth-billing, and fifth- and fourth-, and even third- in *Taza, Son of Cochise* (1954). A May 1953 Universal memo shows that he was considered for a starring role in a movie—*Creature from the Black Lagoon*—but that part ultimately went to Richard Carlson. While *Black Lagoon* was being made in the fall of '53, producer Ross Hunter's three-hankie soaper *Magnificent Obsession* was shooting elsewhere on the lot; his hair grayed with makeup, Palmer has a nice supporting part as the lawyer secretly helping wealthy sportsman Rock Hudson atone for all the grief he's caused Jane Wyman, a widow ('cause of Hudson) who's gone blind ('cause of Hudson!). By this point, Universal had changed his screen name from Palmer Lee to Gregg Palmer. About this time, a Universal secretary tipped him off that she'd heard he was next in line for a Rock Hudson–Tony Curtis–type build-up. Then instead of a big buildup, he got the boot, along with a number of other contract players, as Universal sought to cut costs.

It was as a freelancer that 28-year-old Palmer came back to Universal to do *The Creature Walks Among Us*. Regarding the movie's stars, and its Creature, he told me,

> Both Rex [Reason] and Jeff Morrow were professionals. They would stand off-camera and read the lines to you, and not let the assistant director or the dialogue director read them. I think that's a professional way to do it—I've always done it. You get more of a motivation out of looking at the person that you're doing the story with than you could with a person reading it out of a script.
>
> … Don Megowan was a very dear friend of mine. We would always kid one another about size and weight and all that sort of thing. I used to ask him, "Don, what do you weigh?" and he would say, "194 pounds." And I'd say, "No, no—with *both* feet on the scale!"

He also said that he was fascinated by the Gill Man costume and thought it'd be fun to have a beach party some night and hire a guy to come up out of the waves in that get-up. He never got to do that, but he did have the fun of watching a gal-pal's encounter with Don Megowan's Creature:

> I had a young lady in for lunch one day and we were in the makeup room and I was showing her around, and in walked Don Megowan [in the scaly Gill Man costume]. He walked up behind my lady-friend and started breathing heavily…. She turned around, shook like an $18 television set, screamed and took off!

3. The Creature Walks Among Us (1956)

there, and we'll show the trees with the big snakes and everything up in there, and—" I said, "*That's* it. That's all you had to do, was mention 'big snakes.' No, I don't think I want to be Jungle Jim."

Palmer twice received top billing, first in producer Sam Katzman's *Zombies of Mora Tau* and then in *The Rebel Set* (1959), an excellent (for its budget category) "thieves fall out" crime drama in the vein of Stanley Kubrick's *The Killing* (1956). He was the kind of actor who, at the same time that he was starring or co-starring in pictures, would also take small parts and even uncredited bits. By this time, the late 1950s, he was married to Ruth, a nurse with three children; she and Gregg were together for 42 years, until her death in 1999.

In 1961 Stuart Whitman and Palmer had a "walk ten paces, turn and fire" pistol duel in the pre-credits sequence of the John Wayne Western *The Comancheros*; Whitman was second-billed and Palmer uncredited, which should tell you who won. Palmer didn't share the screen with Wayne in this movie but they did meet, and over the next 15 years Palmer worked in five more Wayne vehicles (including The Duke's last, 1976's *The Shootist*). Wayne called

As a Universal contractee, Gregg Palmer did a host of Westerns, plus Arabian Nights–type adventures, a Francis the Talking Mule movie and other "typical Universal" fare.

Occasionally Palmer would resist accepting an acting job (a staked-out-for-execution island native in 1957's *From Hell It Came*, for example), and even turned down opportunities to try out for the roles of Tarzan and Jungle Jim:

> For Tarzan, I went out to Selznick in Culver City, nine o'clock in the morning, and kinda foggy and cold, and I said to myself, "I don't think I wanna have a loincloth on and be goin' *oooo-a-oo-a-oo* [the Tarzan yodel] on mornings like this when it's cold." So I went in and turned that down.
>
> Then I went out to Hal Roach Studios, and his son [Hal Roach, Jr.] was going to do *Jungle Jim*. I thought they'd be shooting there at the studio [in Culver City] where they made all the Laurel and Hardy shows and so on. But, no, the son said, "We're going down to the Amazon. We'll have ya in the dugout goin' down through the Amazon

In a 1990 snapshot, Gregg Palmer (middle) pals around with fans Mike Brunas (left) and Jon Weaver.

him "Grizzly," a nickname that fit: As Palmer got on in years, he grew heavier and (in some movies) hairier.

Palmer was heavy, hairy—and *horrifying*—as the ironically named Goodfellow in Wayne's *Big Jake*: Part of a murderous gang led by Richard Boone, he's first seen behind the opening credits, riding a horse that looks small under him, as the narrator describes the long-haired, bushy-bearded brute as "maybe the worst [of Boone's bunch]. An indiscriminate killer—women, children—no consequence at all," with a razor-edged machete his weapon of choice. Palmer's 13th-billed but his character is so formidable that the movie saves him for last: Goodfellow outlives all the other baddies and takes on Wayne (and Wayne's dog) in the finale, in nighttime scenes that play like something out of a horror movie. The beard and hair were all real, all his. *Big Jake* photos of Palmer in costume were seen by producers who liked what they saw and brought him to Italy to co-star as a character called "The Hurricane Kid" in a pair of comical spaghetti Westerns.

In 1989 he decided "That's a wrap" career-wise and took his Screen Actors Guild pension. Since his wife's passing he's played a lot of golf and become a familiar face at film festivals, including the 2013 Monster Bash in Mars, Pennsylvania. He also contends with a never-ending stream of autograph requests:

> I've had letters from … well, you *name* it: From France, Germany, Switzerland, Norway, Denmark and Sweden to the Orient! Where they get the photographs, I don't know, but they send 'em to me. But it's pretty hard to read their letters, because of their way of trying to form sentences and express themselves in English. I have to really study some of them, and occasionally I've had to ask family members, "Hey, can *you* figure this out?" Some of the letters I *can't* figure out—and I was a cryptographer in the service!

Don Megowan as the Creature

> Don Megowan … will have the title role in *The Creature Walks Among Us* at Universal-International. This brings him to the studio where his mother, Mrs. Robert Megowan, held down a post as film cutter for a number of years…. Young Megowan at the request of the studio is going to attempt to "humanize" the Creature. Carl Laemmle, Sr., when Megowan was a child, once predicted he would act at Universal.
>
> —columnist Edwin Schallert, August 15, 1955

"Papa Carl" Laemmle might even have been able to predict that Don Megowan would act *as a monster* at Universal, if Don was as proportionately tall as a child as he was as a grown-up.

Because his mother worked at Universal, Megowan was one of the kids who grew up on the lot (they were known as "Universal Brats"); prior to becoming an actor, he himself had a job there as a carpenter. Megowan started seeing his name in the papers as early as May 1939, when a *Los Angeles Times* story called the 16-year-old "a giant Inglewood [California] weight star" who had just set a new track-and-field discus record of 133 feet, seven inches. Four months

Don Megowan's height has been variously given as 6'5", 6'6" and 6'7"; his son Greg vouches for the latter. Greg said that Don, in his college days, was the largest football lineman in the United States.

later, the same paper listed him among a group of 23 star prep school athletes registering at USC: One of the school's new football tackles, he was described as 6'7" and 232 pounds.

During World War II Army service, Megowan won a heavyweight boxing title. In 1947 he married his sweetheart Bette and, according to his *Los Angeles Times* obituary, became "intrigued with drama." His son Greg told me that the reason his father went into the movies was as simple as wanting a good income: "Basically it was a case where, monetarily, acting was a better choice than [other jobs]. He thought about professional football but you gotta remember, they didn't *pay* anything in professional football back then. He had a unique look because of the fact that he was 6'7" and he just kinda fell into the acting, and it paid very, very well."

Megowan's movie bow may have been an unbilled bit in *The Mob* (1951), a first-rate crimebusting drama in which tough cop Broderick Crawford goes undercover to unmask a waterfront rackets boss; in a union hall scene, big bruiser Megowan gets in his face, and Crawford wisely turns tail. Then, in rapid succession, came another uncredited part in the drama *On the Loose* (1951) and a fifth-billed role as one of baddie Fred F. Sears' henchmen in the Durango Kid Western *The Kid from Amarillo* (1951).

Next there were a couple years of uncredited parts few-and-far-between, including Sir Lancelot, seated at King Arthur's Round Table in 1954's *Prince Valiant*. Edwin Schallert wrote in a July 1953 column that Megowan "is regarded as having a promising film future." In 1955 the actor was second-billed in producer Sam Katzman's *The Werewolf*, released in 1956 (and directed by Megowan's *Kid from Amarillo* castmate Fred F. Sears). There were other good roles in 1955, one of them in the Western *A Lawless Street* where he's a scar-faced, bear-like "monster of a man" who has a *Spoilers*-type barroom brawl with Marshal Randolph Scott. Every kid in America saw him opposite Fess Parker as Alamo second-in-command Col. Travis in the *Disneyland* TV series' ratings-busting "Davy Crockett at the Alamo."

Megowan worked without screen credit when he played the *Creature Walks* role of the post-fire, gill-less Gill Man. By this time the stork had brought the actor and Bette a daughter, Vikki; son Greg was born on Megowan's birthday in 1959. Greg once asked him if playing the Creature was fun and, unsurprisingly, he said no, because of the hassle of being in the costume all day. Megowan added a second monster role to his résumé in 1958 when he played the Frankenstein Monster in the TV pilot *Tales of Frankenstein* opposite Anton Diffring.[30]

There was lots of television work for Megowan in the 1950s and early '60s, much of it in Westerns that placed him against the outdoor backgrounds which a man of his size requires for proper maneuver. Tall TV cowboy stars were then all the rage—James Arness, Clint Walker, Chuck Connors, John Russell, George Montgomery, etc.—and big Don was a perfect fit opposite these man-mountain town tamers. Greg recalls,

> He was predominantly a cowboy actor, and what he enjoyed most was the Westerns. He was friends for many years with other cowboy actors, Clint Eastwood for one, and all of them used to get together and play cards and so on.
>
> The tough thing for me, growing up, was the fact that in cowboy moves, he was almost always a bad guy and so he'd always get *killed*. As a kid, I used to say to my mom, "Why do they always kill Dad…?!" She'd tell me, "It's just a role," but still I wanted to know, "Yeah, but why does he always have to *die*??"

The actor turned up at least a half-dozen times on *Cheyenne*. Series star Clint Walker felt that the episodes featuring Megowan were a cut above because Megowan handled his parts so well; he said that the *Cheyenne* casting people probably thought so, too, because that would explain his many reappearances. "I had the utmost respect for Don," Walker told me. "He was a very fine actor, had a great voice, and was an exceptionally handsome guy. *And*, he was one of the few guys I had to look *up* to. I was six-foot five and a half at that time, and Don was at least an inch and a half taller than I was. He was a pleasure to work with, very professional. He always did an excellent job."

In one *Cheyenne*, Cheyenne (Walker) and another lawman (Megowan) step outside to face an approaching lynch mob. According to Walker,

> I had a shotgun as well as wearing my Colt .45 and he had two .45s stuck in his waistband, right in the front. At one

Don Megowan watches as prop man Clarence Peet wraps his hands in mummy-like style for the actor's role in "The Face in the Tombstone Mirror," pilot episode for the Screen Gems-Hammer Films teleseries *Tales of Frankenstein*.

point in the scene, he was supposed to pull the two .45s. Trouble is, he went to cock them as he drew them out of the waistband, which was a big mistake, because they *both* went off before he got 'em out [*laughs*]! And I don't have to tell you where he got burned! He was in the hospital for about three days. I felt *so* sorry for him!

In 1962, Megowan had his own TV series, the Cameron Mitchell–starring *The Beachcomber*. Also that year, a judge granted the actor and his wife Bette separate divorce decrees. Court aids said the double decree was common in cases "where evidence is about equal," according to a newspaper account. Mrs. Megowan won custody of their two children and $250 monthly support for herself and the youngsters.

Greg makes his dad sound like something of a workaholic: In addition to acting, he managed North Hollywood apartment buildings, sold real estate and owned and operated a bar and grill (where he'd spend 14 to 16 hours a day). All of this work was done with multi–Megowatt charisma: "He had a *huge* personality, he really did," Greg attests. "Wherever he went, he 'filled up the room.' He was funny, he had a great sense of humor, and he was *very,* very smart. What always amazed me was his ability to memorize. He could read a script once and memorize all his lines. It was incredible." In his leisure time, Megowan read a lot of books and enjoyed crossword puzzles.

The actor's 1960s big-screen credits include starring roles in the stageplay-like *The Creation of the Humanoids* (1962) and a pair of foreign films, *La strada dei giganti* (1960) and *Il terrore dei mari* (1961). "But I always felt that Don never really got a chance, in features, to show the talent that he had," said Walker. "I don't know, maybe with a better agent he would have done better in features. But maybe not. Maybe he was *too* tall, maybe *that* was it. Maybe they were afraid to try to use him as a leading man in a romantic role."

He wasn't too tall for Alva Lacy May, who became the second Mrs. M. in the late 1970s and remained with him until his 1981 death. "It was nasopharynx cancer—head and neck cancer," Greg reveals. "It came on fairly quickly, he got a big lump in his throat. By the time he got diagnosed, it was too large to remove—they'd have had to take out half of his throat. They gave him six months to live and he lived for a couple of *years*. But he suffered a lot during that time, especially in the last six months. It was bad at the end." Megowan was 59 when he died at his Panorama City home. His *Los Angeles Times* obit "Film Worker's Son Grew Up to Become Big, 'Bad' and Busy" made the hard-to-forgive flub of calling him *Dan* Megowan.

"I can't say anything but good about the guy," said Clint Walker. "I *miss* him, because we got along very well. We lost a fine actor when he passed away."

In recent years, monster magazines have featured dozens of interviews with Gill Men Ricou Browning and Ben Chapman, and even Tom Hennesy got his share of coverage—but because of Megowan's early death, he received no attention of this sort. In fact, until now, next to nothing was *ever* written about his life and Hollywood career. To further rectify

La Dolce Donnie: Megowan was top-billed in just four movies, two of them made in Italy where this shot was taken.

3. The Creature Walks Among Us (1956)

For Tarzan and the Valley of Gold *(1966), a shaved-bald Don Megowan visited Mexico's Teotihuacán ruins (and other historic sites) as he played the fifth-billed role of Mr. Train, the lead heavy's badass bodyguard. (Pictured: Nancy Kovack, Megowan.)*

this situation, there's an interview with his daughter Vikki Megowan in this book's "Creature Conversations" chapter.

Production

Under the direction of James C. Havens, the *Creature Walks Among Us* second unit began work on the morning of August 24, 1955: They left their Fort Myers, Florida, motel at seven a.m., loaded equipment onto a boat at a nearby dock and headed upriver—to photograph color background plates not for *Creature Walks* but for Universal's *Congo Crossing* (1956), an extra duty with which they'd been tasked. Fans of *Creature from the Black Lagoon* will recall that on that first Gill Man movie, Havens received a prominent on-screen credit as "Underwater Sequences" director—even though, according to William Alland, Havens had refused to go underwater and properly direct. On *Creature Walks* he received no screen credit, nor does a veteran of *both* previous Creature pictures, "Scotty" Welbourne, again behind the camera. The movie's Assistant Director Reports don't mention the name of the river where they shot, but their Fort Myers motel was minutes from the dock so it can only be the Caloosahatchee. (Maybe the a.d. *would* have mentioned it on every report if it was Florida's New River or the Joe River—but not the Caloosahatchee!)

Of course, this being Florida, the rains came and kept *on* coming: In the early afternoon, after they'd traveled upriver a ways, it got dark and began pouring, a combination that made shooting impossible. Apparently the light improved about an hour later and they shot some *Congo Crossing* "rain plates" in the heavy precipitation, but then all they did was sail upriver a bit farther and wait for the rain to stop, which it didn't. Throwing in the (wet) towel at 3:50, they returned to the motel.

It was on August 25 that their *Creature Walks* work commenced, the troupe driving northeast 70 minutes to the city of LaBelle and setting out on the boat from there, *down* the Caloosahatchee—and finding that they couldn't shoot because of poor light. Throughout the day, the unfavorable conditions prevented continuous filming but they did eventually get process plates for the movie's pilot house scene. From about 2:00 until 4:30 they waited for the heavy rain to lift, then wrapped things up. The filmmakers caught a break the next day, leaving again from LaBelle and going up and down the Caloosahatchee multiple times getting more pilot house scene process plates plus footage of the five-passenger dinghy en route to Morteno's fishing village, the *Vagabondia III* moving along the river at different speeds, etc.[31]

Meanwhile, at Universal, John Sherwood spent the day doing wardrobe and makeup tests of Morrow, Reason, Snowden, Manson, Rawley and Megowan. The men were done at 12:30 and Snowden at 3:30, at which time producer Alland and a small group tested the Creature suit in the waters of the lot's Pollard Lake. I don't know which Creature suit was tested or who was in it; presumably it was not Megowan, who had been dismissed at 12:30.

On Saturday morning, August 27, Florida weather was a problem until 11:35 but then things improved and shooting got underway, including more five-men-in-a-dinghy long shots for the lead-up to the scene at Morteno's. (The men were Florida locals working as $25-a-day extras.) Sunday there was more up-down-up-down the river as the troupe photographed another color plate for *Congo Crossing* plus several more *Creature Walks* plates, and the striking footage where the camera (bow-mounted in a boat) follows the Creature-hunting scientists' dinghy into the narrow, winding inlet. The moment where the camera pushes its way through a curtain of Spanish moss might have looked good in 3-D.

Monday found them on Fort Myers' Caloosahatchee-spanning Edison Bridge, named for longtime Fort Myers resident Thomas Alva Edison: Police stopped traffic so that the moviemakers could shoot plates for the opening scene of the Bartons' convertible making a high-speed crossing. Also photographed that day: the Bartons' car arriving at the yacht landing (shot at the Fort Myers Yacht Basin) and zooming across the Edison Bridge (a high panning shot taken from a ferry).

Local residents Shirley Deas and Jesse Thompson played the Bartons in those shots and others throughout the day.

On the other side of the country, Monday, August 29, was Day One as a feature film director for John Sherwood: On Universal's Stage 12, he began his first of ten days of interior yacht scenes. (Nearly the entire first hour of the 78-minute movie is set on the yacht or in its proximity.) All six of his principals worked, plus day player David McMahon,[32] who had the role of the yacht captain. The script describes him as "a typical Captain-for-hire. He knows who runs the ship—the owner." (The owner being Barton. Notice that Barton dresses like the captain, as though he can't bear to be seen as anything other than *the* alpha dog in any situation.) Appropriately, the first day of production found them shooting some of the movie's opening-reel scenes, in the yacht salon, corridor and lab; coincidentally, the Florida unit was simultaneously shooting the movie's *very* first scene.

Toward the end of the afternoon, Maurice Manson as Dr. Borg did his "big scene" explaining the operation and purpose of his Fishscope. *Creature Walks* was the first Hollywood feature for Manson, whose list of credits already included Broadway plays dating back to the early 1930s. He had just been part of the national company of *Tea and Sympathy* with Deborah Kerr, which happened to close on the West Coast; this presented him with the opportunity to give movie work a whirl. Although a newcomer to Hollywood soundstages, he was already friendly with a couple of his *Creature Walks* cohorts: Jeff Morrow, with whom he'd done summer stock ("I knew him very well and he was a great guy," Manson told me), and William Alland, whom he'd encountered on the night in the late '30s when he (Manson) auditioned for a part in the Mercury Theatre's upcoming production *Five Kings*:

> Oh, I had an interview with Orson Welles that's unforgettable! In the days of the old Mercury Theatre, Bill Alland was stage manager of most of the shows, and that's when I first met him. He was rehearsing the company at the National

The yacht we see in Creature Walks *was actually named the* Vagabondia III *and it was nothing if not luxe: Chartered from its owner and master George Hampton, it was a diesel yacht, 96 or 102 feet long (sources differ), whose home port was Miami. Some of the* Creature Walks *shots of it are striking, especially the day-for-night ones with exterior and interior lights aglow.*

Theatre, and Welles came in about 11:00 at night with two bottles of hooch in a package and a friend, and they went upstairs to his office in the mezzanine. I waited all night to see him, and finally at five o'clock in the morning I said to Bill, "You know, I've been here since ten-thirty last night, and it's five o'clock in the morning…!" He went up and then he came back and said, "All right, Orson'll hear you read."

So I went up and Orson's stinko, and so was his pal. *Five Kings* was sort of a Hungarian goulash of various scenes from Shakespearean historical plays; Orson said, "You read Pissel." Pissel is one of the clowns, and he has a line every 15 or 16 speeches. It's a very difficult thing to read, because there's no connection—[it's just] an exclamation here and there. Orson read the other parts, and he started *roaring* with laughter—"Oh, you're the funniest Shakespearean clown I ever *heard*!" And I wondered what the hell was funny about it, you know? He said, "We'll call you," and I went home—and I didn't hear from him. So *I* called Jeannie Rosenthal, the woman who did the lighting for the company—my interview with Orson had been set up through her. I said, "Jeannie, what gives? I read for Orson and he said he'd call me." She said, "Well, let me follow through." Then she called me back and she said, "Maurice, I'm terribly sorry I have to tell you this, but Orson says he doesn't remember ever having *heard* you!"[33]

Returning to the subject of Alland, Manson added, "Bill was worthy of much better things than that picture [*Creature Walks*]. He never got out of that science fiction [genre] and that's too bad, because the guy had a great background. He was a great guy who should have had much more of a reward for his ability."

On August 30, Sherwood resumed working on the "explaining the Fishscope" scene and tackled some lab scenes, including the one where Borg *et al.* watch divers Morgan, Marcia and Grant on the Fishscope. The only excitement was behind the camera, when gaffer Max Nippell burned his hand on a lamp and went to the studio hospital. On Florida's Lower Suncoast, Havens & Co. headed downriver, presumably all the way out into the Gulf of Mexico, because some of that day's *Vagabondia* footage has a water horizon. They again did some of their filming from a ferry, getting shots of Creature-rescuer Morgan's feet-first jump from the yacht, the men's arrival at Morteno's fishing village, etc. At this point, the second unit was a day behind schedule.

August 31, the first day of a terrible heat wave, was Don Megowan's first day on the picture: He reported to Universal's Stage 12 to do work that a dummy could have done, lie bandage-wrapped and motionless on the yacht lab's operating table as his "doctors" give him oxygen, etc. No film rolled through the camera until 10:40 a.m.: A 65-minute "story and medical term discussion" with the studio doctor N. Edward Gourson began the day, followed by another 35-minute delay for rehearsals, bringing in more medical equipment for the operation scene, and adding extra bandages to the Creature. In Florida they again spent time getting shots that wouldn't make it into the movie (sailors on a dock freeing the yacht's mooring lines, the yacht pulling away from the dock); then the troupe's equipment was loaded *onto* the yacht and they proceeded upriver to get yet *more* color *Congo Crossing* plates, footage of divers Morgan, Marcia and Grant descending the yacht ladder, Morgan and Grant on the surface helping euphoria victim Marcia *after* the dive, etc. On this last day of Fort Myers shooting, an afternoon squall and lack of light caused an hours-long delay.

At Universal, September 1 was spent on the salon set, with Morgan carrying "raptures of the deep" sufferer Marcia into the room and placing her on the couch, plus the conversations that ensue. This time it was the Sherwood troupe shooting footage destined for the dustbin: When Morgan and Marcia are alone, they talk about Marcia's proclivity for taking chances, and Morgan says, "I take *calculated* risks for a purpose. But what are *you* trying to prove?" In the final script, we find more dialogue, and a bit of action, at this point:

> MARCIA: I don't know…. Except that when you're alone all the time—well, anything's better than—
> MORGAN: But you're not alone.
> MARCIA: Of course. I'm married … and wives are never lonely—(her eyes fill with tears).
>
> Morgan's eyes assume a wary look. It isn't the prude but the cynic speaking when he says:
>
> MORGAN: Being kind to lonely wives is not my specialty, Mrs. Barton.
>
> Before the last words are out of his mouth, Marcia has slapped him hard, and without a pause she tears into him.

The tearing-into-him part *is* in the movie, but the above-mentioned dialogue exchange and slap were deleted after filming; in the movie as it exists, Marcia gets sore at Morgan over his line "I take *calculated* risks for a purpose. But what are *you* trying to prove?" One dialogue change was made before the scene was shot: In the script, Marcia tells Morgan that, ten years ago, she was 16 when Barton married her. In the movie, the age is "upped" to 17.[34] The steward who ends their conversation by entering to set the dinner table is day player Frank Chase, actor-son of Oscar-nominated Western screenwriter Borden Chase and the brother of dancer Barrie Chase. A few years later, Frank's performance as Charlie, the bespectacled, slow-witted deputy sheriff, became one of the many joys of *Attack of the 50 Foot Woman* (1958).

An unusual entry on the September 1 Production Report's list of Special Equipment was "Air Conditioning"—an item needed that day, and for many more to come. On Heat Wave Day 2, it was 110 degrees in Los Angeles, the hottest on record for that date, with "southeast winds straight from the desert floor [blowing] the heat at 10 to 12 MPH clips, like an electric fan blowing from a furnace" (*Los Angeles Times*). In Santa Monica, people were being treated for burns to the soles of their feet, and cars stalled by gasoline vapor lock were holding up traffic on all freeways.

Havens' Florida unit spent the first of September making the almost 400-mile trek from Fort Myers northwest to Wakulla Springs. Unspoiled and scenic, the place was just as it was when Universal made the original *Creature from the Black Lagoon* there in 1953 … and practically as it was in 1853. (Ricou Browning: "I think Wakulla is just like it was when the Indians were around.") A good bit of the next day was spent making preparations for shooting and testing some male and female locals for jobs as Morgan, Marcia and Grant's underwater doubles.

Reminisce is a nostalgia magazine whose articles look back on the 1930s through the early '70s; to the delight of Gill Man fans, its July–August 2002 issue featured a two-page article by James Jackson, Jr., of Miami Shores, Florida, who recalled landing the job of Palmer's double. According to Jackson, he heard on the radio that auditions for a movie would take place at Wakulla, 20 miles from his home, and decided to give it a shot. On the first morning of tryouts, over a dozen men were excused before the remaining gents were asked about their scuba diving experience; Jackson lied that he *had* dived with an air tank. "I knew using the lung was dangerous," he wrote,

> and watched as others suited up and went in the water one by one. Then it was my turn to put on the lung, along with weight belt, knife, fake radio, fathom meter and gun for underwater use.
>
> Each time I surfaced for instructions from the director, it was harder to breathe and stay afloat. I reached the point where I couldn't get enough air from the lung and shot to the surface.
>
> When the director rowed out and anxiously asked what had happened, I said I had misjudged my buoyancy because of all the equipment I was carrying.
>
> Despite this, my swim partner during tryouts, Dick Wells, and I were hired at $200 a week as underwater doubles for actors Rex Reason and Gregg Palmer!

(More on Jackson's adventures later.) If Havens intended to shoot anything on September 2, cloud formations in the morning and rain in the afternoon put a crimp in those plans. The company did manage to shoot plates for background use in the *Vagabondia* stern deck scenes before and after the Morgan-Marcia-Grant dive.

It was 108 degrees in L.A. that day, the third straight day of 100-degree-plus temperatures, and meteorologists were predicting that the area would continue to broil over the coming Labor Day weekend. You could fry an egg on the sidewalk, if you didn't mind wasting a commodity that might soon be in short supply: A bulldozer

Jim Jackson, pictured here with Browning, wrote in a 2002 issue of Reminisce *magazine, "When the film came out, I was thrilled to see myself on screen, even though it was only ten minutes and you couldn't see my face because of the mask and mouthpiece…. The experience remains vibrant in my memory."*

3. The Creature Walks Among Us (1956)   261

A great up-from-the-bottom shot of the Creature Walks moviemakers in Wakulla Springs: camera operator "Scotty" Welbourne in a metal basket hanging from a large rubber raft, an unidentified diver and, on the surface, presumably James C. Havens en route to the inner tube "perch" from which he second-unit-directed.

only "exciting" thing filmed on September 2 was the shot where, to the scientists' horror, the Creature breaks his leather wrist straps. (It's an amusingly incongruous sight to see four doctors checking on a "patient"—all with sidearms and cartridge belts at the ready in case he stirs!) The late afternoon was spent photographing more lab scenes involving the Fishscope (Borg: "He's following us at the same distance again!," Johnson: "He's following us at the same distance again!").

Part of a 45-minute delay in the start of shooting the next morning (Saturday, September 3) was putting Creature hands on Megowan and bandaging them so that, in the first shot of the morning, Morrow and Reason could *un*-bandage them. Wrapped up mummy-like and covered with a sheet, Megowan *had* to be suffering despite the air conditioning: The blistering Southland heat wave was lingering, with at least 12 people now dead. Also committed to film that day was the moment where the scientists pull off the Creature's head bandages to get their first look at his new face, and Barton and Morgan study it through a magnifying glass. Scripter Arthur Ross told me that Universal offered no objection to the way he completely changed the look of one of their major-league monsters: "No, because they knew my contribution to the first one [*Creature from the Black Lagoon*]. There wasn't *any* opposition to it, absolutely none. It was a new kind of science fiction." I also asked if, while writing this story of a surgeon making a primitive beast more man-like, H.G. Wells' *The Island of Doctor Moreau* ever crossed his mind and provided inspiration. "Yeah, maybe some," he admitted. "But in this one [*Creature Walks*]," he continued,

operator spent the day burying a mountain of dead-from-the-heat chickens in a series of cuts at Orange County's Huntington Beach dump. This kind of thing was happening all over. There was to be a pig, rabbit, turkey, chinchilla, steer *and human* death toll too.

For Megowan's sake, let's hope the Stage 12 air conditioning was set on "HIGH" as he lay *wrapped in bandages* on the Creature's Cabin set, strapped to a table and with electroencephalograph wires attached to his head.[35] The

> the Creature was caught in a fire, and the scientists didn't have too much choice. The gills were a superficial body

armor, and in the fire, he loses this semi-detached epidermic quality of a gilled body. It is on that basis that the scientist believes that he can bring out what is more human in the Creature. And he succeeds—up to a certain point.... The main thing that played a part in it was, "What kind of different thing can you do with the Creature?" And I didn't want to go back to jungle settings and the rest of it; I wanted to put him in a different environment than the one he had. This thing was half-fish and half-man, and we'd seen how the half-*fish* operates; how does the half-*man* operate? That's why he was taken out of water.

On this same day, September 3, the second unit filmmakers were also working with the "more human" Creature. On Ricou Browning's first day on the movie, he played Creature Version 2.0 underwater: descending through Wakulla's limpid water to the bottom, frantically gasping for "air," battling with Morgan (double Dick Wells) and being carried up to the surface by Morgan.

Jim Jackson (doubling Gregg Palmer as Grant) and Ruth Skinner (doubling Leigh Snowden as Marcia) also got on-camera, making a descent alongside Wells. The day had gotten off to an iffy start because of unfavorable weather conditions, and there was an afternoon delay of 20 minutes because of a fogged camera lens.

Doubles Jim Jackson, Ruth Skinner and Dick Wells descend into Wakulla Springs. In these underwater scenes you can tell which one is supposed to be Morgan because he's got one air tank and which one is supposed to be Grant because he's got two. You can tell which one is supposed to be Marcia ... period

Browning Saved from Drowning: We get an on-camera demonstration of hose-breathing when the no-gills Gill Man (Browning) is rescued by Morgan (Dick Wells). The scene is slightly spoiled by the fact that a lot of the air is fizzing out of the porous top of the full-head mask, making it look like a fish tank air-stone bubbler.

As neat as *Black Lagoon*'s underwater scenes look, the ones in *Creature Walks* are better, even though both were shot at Wakulla. "When we shot *Black Lagoon*, the Wakulla water was not as clear as it was when we did *The Creature Walks Among Us*," Browning told me. "There was a lot of rain in the months before we shot *Black Lagoon* and the water from the surrounding swamp areas drained into the spring, causing it to be darker." *Creature Walks* viewers don't know where the yacht *is* when the rescue-the-Creature scene takes place, whether in the Gulf of Mexico or the Caribbean or the Panama Canal or the Pacific, but even a chicken of the sea like me knows that none of those places have Wakulla's Evian–clear water. That said, the need to suspend disbelief is a small price to pay for the marvelous *Creature Walks* shots where the water seems to have disappeared and the swimmers appear to be "flying."

First and second units didn't work on Labor Day, Monday, September 5; in the L.A. area, a lot of 9-to-5 folks

3. The Creature Walks Among Us (1956)

Dick Wells had developed ear trouble and was treated by a Tallahassee doctor. Jim Jackson's *Reminisce* article provides a funny detail about Wells' participation: In order to match the look of Rex Reason, carbon paper was rubbed on Wells' balding head so that he would appear to have all his hair!

Ricou Browning amidst the eelgrass of Wakulla Springs. Syndicated Hollywood reporter James Bacon devoted an August 1955 column to him, humorously writing that Browning's Gill Man is set apart from the human members of his movies' casts by "huge web feet, big scales over most of his body, and a face even a mother octopus couldn't learn to love."

Ricou Browning worked for weeks on each of the first two Creature movies but just five days on Creature Walks. The safety diver giving him a drink of air in this shot is probably Charles McNabb.

Having spent the three-day Labor Day weekend practicing diving and equalizing pressure, Jackson was beginning to feel confident. But, in the water at Wakulla, a bit of his courage slipped away as they prepared to shoot "the scene I had been dreading—the 'deep one.'" In his *Reminisce* article, he continued,

> I approached the sandy bottom headfirst, more quickly than expected, and kicked hard with my fins to change direction. Sand began to swirl, which the director had warned would cloud the water and prevent filming.
>
> I quit kicking and tried to use a hand to swim but my feet began to sink in the sandy ooze. The other double came over, gently lifted me and I kicked my way to the surface.
>
> I felt relieved when I returned to the raft, until the director started yelling: "If you want to see yourself in this picture, you'd better get on the ball!"

probably wouldn't have worked even if it *wasn't* a holiday, as the Heat Wave from Hell continued to disrupt, and *take*, lives. There were now 27 dead, and the high temperature was considered a factor in *200* other deaths. To *some*one in a no-doubt air-conditioned Universal office, the heat wave was nothing more than an excuse to get a goofy publicity shot spoofing the calamitous event: starlets in shorts (Dani Crayne, Myrna Hansen, Jane Howard (aka Betty Jane Howarth), Karen Kadler, Lili Kardell, Gia Scala and *Creature Walks*' Leigh Snowden) strolling through a blizzard of artificial snow.

On both coasts, the two *Creature Walks* units were back to the grind on Tuesday. At Wakulla they did more of the sub-aquatic scene of Morgan fighting and then rescuing the smooth-skinned Creature; here and there throughout the day, they also got shots for the earlier Morgan–Marcia–Grant dive scene. The Daily Production Report reveals that

Thousands of miles from Wakulla's chilly waters, it was still hot as blazes at Universal, where Sherwood shot the salon party scene ("Change metabolism and maybeeee … maybe eliminate drunk drivers!") that devolves into another tedious Barton-Morgan debate, plus the subsequent scene of a bombed Barton raving and grabbing at Marcia. Last shot of the day: The latch on the Creature's cabin door doing an almost complete 360 as, from within, he twists it until it snaps apart and goes flying; then the door opens, letting viewers see for the first time the monster in his crudely stitched-together canvas shirt and trousers. (You'd think that losing a thick layer of scales would make the Creature look thinner but instead he now looks thickset.) Megowan had arrived on the set at one o'clock but several "takes" of that door-opening shot, photographed around 6 p.m., was all he did on-camera that day.

On September 7, the filming of the scene resumed with Grant preparing to make his middle-of-the-night move on Marcia. In the late morning, some of the set walls were taken out and new ones moved in, in order to let viewers see the *other* side (formerly the "hard camera" side) of the salon. Once that was done, the camera again rolled, capturing the scene of the heavy-breathing Creature[36] interrupting Grant's make-out session with a swiping forearm blow that sends him sprawling. (Palmer, doing his own stunt, knocks a louvered door off its top hinge and takes out a table and lamp as he falls.) After lunch, more bits and pieces of the scene were shot, plus parts of other, more mundane sequences: Marcia playing the piano in the salon until distracted by horn dog Grant, and Marcia and Barton quarreling in her stateroom.[37] Local newspapers that day carried the bad news that the record-smashing temperatures had brought the number of heat deaths to 81. September 7 was the eighth straight day of triple-digit temps, with 11 people collapsing in the street just in the central area of L.A. It's a wonder Don Megowan didn't collapse: According to a mid–September *Variety* item, he turned out to be allergic to his rubber Gill Man costume and "must wear added cotton gloves and sox—in this heat!"

In the Florida Panhandle, the day began with real-life drama: Overnight, thieves had stolen three aqualung tanks and three main picture tanks used by the actors. The local sheriff recovered two of the tanks from kids in Tallahassee, but the rest were still missing. The moviemakers were able to start shooting at 9:30, and later that morning got a shot of Browning swimming in "the classic" Gill Man costume. After lunch, unfavorable light caused a 45-minute delay, which according to the Production Report was spent "photographing stills of Dodge trucks and sedan"(!).

The smug and lecherous Grant (Gregg Palmer) gets forceful with Marcia (Leigh Snowden), intending to "make time" with her ...

... and instead gets his clock cleaned by the Creature (Don Megowan). Megowan clobbered Palmer twice and both takes were printed; one ended up in the movie, the other in the trailer.

More "dive scene" shots were taken in what remained of the afternoon. The next day, September 8, Ruth Skinner as Marcia did underwater loops and spins and other maneuvers to show that she was suffering from the "raptures of the deep," and Wells' Morgan came to her rescue. Camera operator Welbourne outdid himself shooting Marcia's narcosis scene, getting lots of bubbles between the girl and his camera, letting the camera rise past her like a rising bubble, even spinning counter-clockwise while shooting down at Marcia spinning clockwise. It's as though the cameraman got a touch of the raptures himself. Adding to the sensation of weird dreaminess is Henry Mancini's music cue "Stalking the Creature, Part 3," which is fully discussed later in this chapter, in David Schechter's section on the music of *Creature Walks*.

On Stage 12 at Universal City, scenes set on the stern of the yacht was filmed that morning, including the one where Morgan and Grant are preparing to dive and Marcia unexpectedly appears on deck in her white swimsuit and insists on joining them. One draft of the script called for her to wear a two-piece bathing suit here, prompting a disapproving nudge from the Production Code lads: "Marcia's 'two-piece bathing suit' should not be what is known as a Bikini." Next came the wharf scene where Barton and Marcia come aboard and meet Morgan, Grant and Dr. Borg; it was begun in the late afternoon and finished the next morning (September 9). To help give the false impression that it was shot outdoors, there was a wind machine on the set. Watch all of pipe-smoker Dr. Borg's exhalations quickly blow away, as though by a stiff breeze.[38]

September 9 work continued with the scene of rifle-wielding Marcia firing over the stern deck rail ("Shark! Got two of 'em. They were after a school of porpoise!"). The script called for a stock shot of sharks swimming in the open sea and then, after Marcia begins shooting, a stock shot of thrashing sharks. That prompted another letter to the studio, this one from the American Humane Association's director, W.A. Young: "I trust that this stock footage will be cut to avoid any unnecessary ugliness concerning the killing of these sharks." Universal ended up using no shark footage at all. The last of the stern scenes were finished by day's end, plus the radio shack scene of Barton using the ship-to-shore ("Sausalito ... *Sau-sal-i-to*, California..."). Outside, it was less than hellishly hot for the first time in a week and a half, sea breezes snapping the worst and longest heat wave in Southland history. The ten-day spell had caused millions of dollars of crop and livestock losses, and 103 people were dead. The worst was over but it remained unpleasantly hot *all* throughout the shooting, as actor Manson told me:

> I'll never forget that the picture was shot during that heat wave, and the poor Creature wore a rubber suit. The guy was about 6'5" and the damn rubber suit, there was no way to ventilate it. It had a zipper down the back, and whenever they opened that zipper, the perspiration just *flooded* out! But he had to be given a bit of air every once in a while—it was *torture*!

On the other side of the country, it was the second unit's last day as they filmed the remainder of the needed underwater shots: Marcia in the throes of deep-diving sickness, her rescue by Morgan, the watchful Creature hiding alongside a large rock ledge, etc. Around 4:45 they got a just-below-the-surface shot of a nozzle entering the water and expelling a cloud of rotenone (milk), and it was officially a wrap. At 8:55 the following morning (Saturday the 10th), the Californians were aboard a Los Angeles–bound plane taking off from Tallahassee Airport.

At Universal that Saturday, the first (and now only) unit made a move, too: Their ten days of yacht scenes finished, they adjourned to the Dabney House, built on the Universal backlot's Airplane Hill for their expensive Civil War drama *Tap Roots* (1948) and named for the Mississippi family (the Dabneys) at the center of that movie's *Gone with the Wind*–like

In King Kong, when Ann does her shipboard screen test, Carl Denham calls her white gown her "Beauty and Beast costume." The Gill Man series had its own Beauty and Beast costume, the one-piece white bathing suit worn by all three heroines including Creature Walks' Leigh Snowden (pictured here with Rex Reason, James Rawley and Jeff Morrow).

By fibbing that he was an experienced diver, Jim Jackson got the $200-a-week job of playing Grant (the Gregg Palmer character) underwater at Wakulla.

sounds the way we hear our*selves* when underwater sucking air through, say, a snorkel; in *our* element, *he* sounds like *we* would in *his*. Limo passengers Barton, Morgan, Marcia and Borg watch as the submissive Creature perp-walks into his new pad, a bars-and-chicken-wire stockade. What could have been a "nothing" scene becomes a highlight of the picture through the use of music, camera angles and sound effects and the sad and unexpected spectacle of America's favorite amphibious man, the Creature, reduced to zombie-like passivity.[39] Work wrapped in the afternoon after the filming of the scene of Barton and Morgan, in the stockade viewing room, having their umpteenth verbal jousting match, this one about biology vs. psychology, giving kindness, *getting* kindness, the law of the jungle vs. murder, etc. At least we're spared more choruses of "the jungle or the stars." First-time feature director Sherwood's movie was now a half-day ahead of schedule but $3000 over-budget.

Part of the morning of Monday, September 12, was spent shooting the day-for-night scene where the scientists react to the Creature's killing of the lion; a nice boom shot shows Barton and Morgan running along the house's second-floor veranda, the camera pulling back and descending to ground level as they hotfoot it down the exterior stairway.

plot. In the mid–1950s the house got a heavy workout sci-fi–wise, turning up as Exeter's Georgia mansion in *This Island Earth*, as Prof. Deemer's desert home in *Tarantula* and here in *Creature Walks* as the Barton Ranch.

With six sheep and two goats now joining the cast, Sherwood shot the effective, no-dialogue scene of the Creature's arrival at his "new home": A rental truck driven by Grant (with Johnson riding shotgun) is followed by a Chrysler Imperial limousine onto the property through its guarded gateway. In a high long shot, both vehicles pull up in front of the house (with matted-in lake background), where Grant opens the truck's rear doors. The Creature slowly materializes out of the muslin-lined blackness, walking slowly down a ramp and impassively taking in his new surroundings. Notice that the Creature is oiled up, perhaps with glycerin, in this scene and others, probably to prevent his rubber mask from looking like what it *is*, rubber. The oil makes his skin look "more like lizard skin … a natural, shiny look about it," the grand old man of monster movie fandom, Bob Burns, said on the *Creature Walks* DVD audio commentary. "That's the trouble with all foam rubber, it *does* have a very dull look to it, if it doesn't have anything *on* it."

It's a clever touch that when we hear the Creature's breathing, especially in this truck scene, this fish out of water

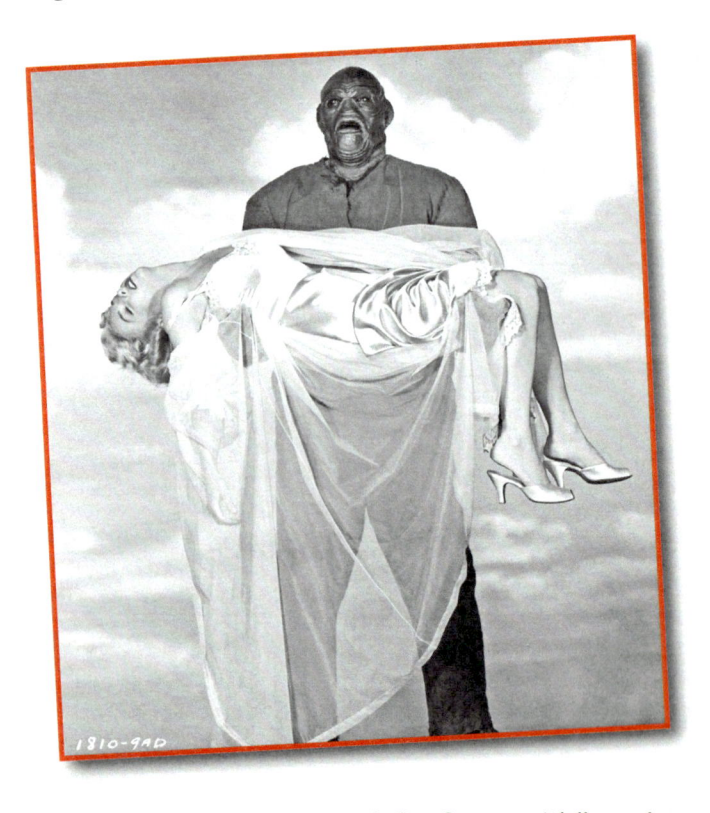

Twice burned, thrice shy? The Creature Walks script may have dispensed with the ritual of Blacky LaGoon getting grabby over the girl, but this Creature of habit was his old "bad boy" self in a few publicity photographs. (Pictured: Don Megowan, Leigh Snowden.)

3. The Creature Walks Among Us (1956) 267

Hurrying toward the stockade to take her place in the scene, Leigh Snowden slipped and spoiled a take, costing the production 22 feet of film.[40]

After lunch, they photographed more footage for use in the Creature's ranch arrival scene; a shot of the Creature standing over the dead lion (with the dead sheep in the background); a shot of Marcia sitting on the veranda railing, playing a guitar; and a shot of the caged Creature raising his head, looking for the source of the music. Twice in the movie, the monster confronts Marcia but he never lays a webbed finger on her. Has he sworn off women? (If so, who could blame him, after his "epic fail" attempts to set up light lagoon-keeping with Kay and Helen?) *So un*beguiled is he that it's almost like he's been neutered by his scientist-captors, on top of everything else. The Beauty and the Beast component that helped "make" the first two movies is conspicuous by its absence in *Creature Walks*, and perhaps not surprisingly, with Ross as solo scripter; he didn't see a great deal of value in that plot element in the *first* Creature movie! Before he came aboard *Black Lagoon* as writer, "Beauty and the Beast" *was* a big part of the story; and then again after he left; but with Ross calling the story shots alone on *Creature Walks*, the Creature clings to his stag status. Sorry, Marcia, but as the kids say today, "He's just not that *into* you."

"Leigh Snowden was that phenomenon known as the Studio Starlet," Maurice Manson told me. "[Hollywood studios] used to have these starlets who they used to promote. Not too vigorously [*laughs*], but the starlets were always there to be decorative! Her job in *Creature Walks Among Us* was to wear as little clothes as possible and to be there for the Creature to menace. That was her sole purpose in the picture!"

September 12 wrapped with the shooting of the scene in which Barton angrily barges into Grant's room and gives him his immediate eviction notice. The 13th would have been a dull day to visit the moviemakers on Stage 19, with little of interest being shot for most of the hours following the 7:48 a.m. crew call: Morgan and Marcia talking on the veranda; the final-reel living room scene with the scientists, Marcia and the state trooper (played by ham-and-egger Larry Hudson, a 1961 suicide); and another Barton-Marcia squabble, this one in her room ("You've become a ... cheap little ... *tramp!*" "Only to *you*, Bill ... only to *you*..."). On the Marcia's Room set, Snowden's sexy shadow-on-the-drape moment (as she dons her bathing suit) was the last thing filmed that afternoon; in the movie, we see that shot just before Barton enters. At least one version of the script made the goings-on a bit more provocative, prompting a scolding from the censors' office: "Scene 385 showing Marcia changing into a bathing suit with her husband 'watching' seems

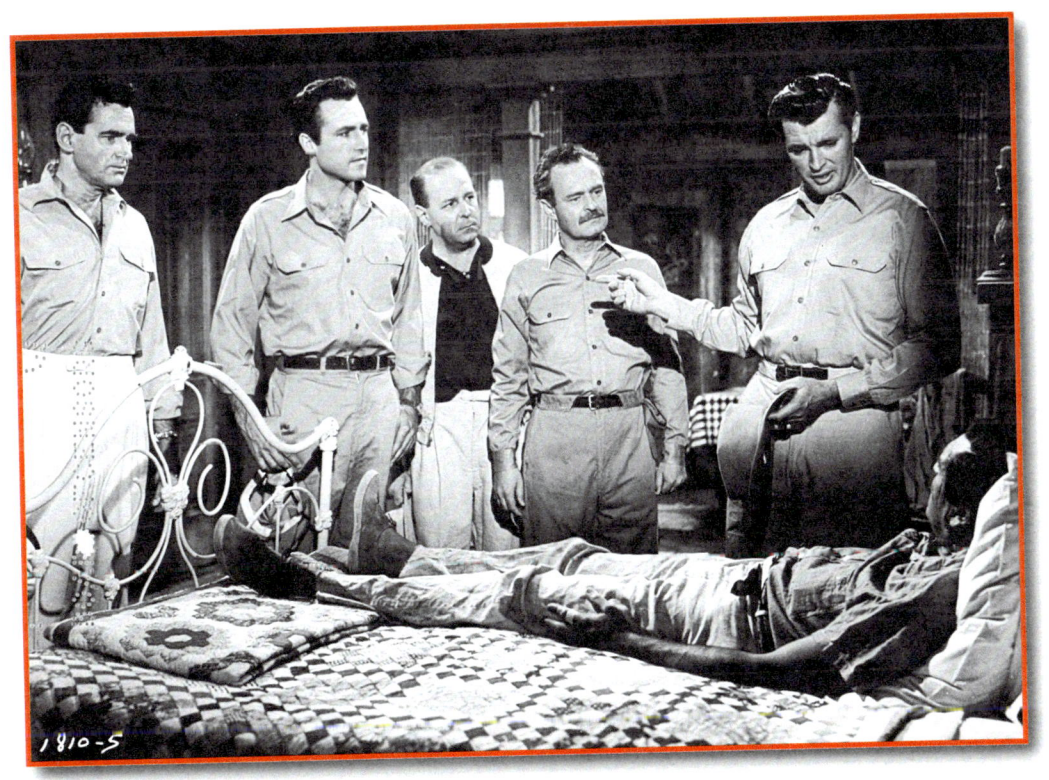

Barton (Jeff Morrow, left) and the other Gill Man hunters (Rex Reason, Maurice Manson, James Rawley and Gregg Palmer) pay a visit to the fishing village home of Morteno (Paul Fierro, abed), victim of the Creature. At the end of the scene, as Morteno is limping across the room, notice (in the background) that Barton compassionately slips some money into the hands of Morteno's wife.

overly suggestive and completely unacceptable on account of the nudity inherent in the scene."

The Morteno house scene was September 14's first order of business. After lunch, cast and crew converged on the Process Stage and got shots of the scientists and Grant in the dinghy, for use in the scene where they go from the yacht to the landing near Morteno's fishing village.[41] Next they filmed the scientists and Grant in the dinghy at the start of their Everglades Creature hunt. Notice that even in the middle of the night in a dinghy in an Everglades inlet, Barton can't be without his captain's hat, the visual reminder that he's the big Kahuna (and another indication that his mental rudder is slightly askew). The early part of that sequence was shot that afternoon (turning on the Fishscope, testing the rotenone gun, etc.); "the good stuff" wouldn't come until later.[42]

Pollard Lake, a manmade body of water on the studio back lot, was seen in numerous movies, including some "Universal Horrors": Monster–hunting villagers are seen in Pollard Lake rowboats in the 1931 *Frankenstein*, and the mud-caked Princess Ananka (Virginia Christine) bathes in its waters in *The Mummy's Curse* (1944), to name just two. Add *Creature Walks Among Us* to the list of movies utilizing it: On August 26, a Creature suit was tested there for producer Alland, and now on the morning of September 15 Leigh Snowden took a dip in Upper Pollard Lake. In the late morning she was joined in the water by Gregg Palmer as the obnoxiously persistent Grant.

After lunch, work began on the Creature's ranch house rampage. Upper Veranda and Barton's Room sets, built and furnished on Stage 19, were now *un*-built and *un*-furnished by Don Megowan: He tore down an overhead porch light fixture amidst a shower of sparks, smashed breakaway French doors, and then flipped a dresser over a nearby table. Next that table and a divan went flying. Two cameras covered the doors-dresser-table-divan action, the "A" camera getting this furniture-rearrangement in long shots and the "B" camera in medium closeups.[43] The furniture was of course on wires, giving Megowan an assist in the up-up-and-away department. On-screen the entire house-wrecking scene has no music, adding intensity to the Creature's grim trackdown of Barton. The absence of music also gives viewers the chance to really hear the Creature's Darth Vader–like breathing—not to mention his "bellowing like a wounded walrus," as the *New York Times* reviewer put it.

The Creature was still in a foul mood the next morning, making a door-damaging end run into Marcia's Stage 19 room and upending her mirrored dressing table. Next he tore through the dressing room drapes and terrorized Morgan and the screaming Marcia.

"It's *clobberin'* time!": Two more breakaway French doors later, Morrow's Barton felt the Creature's wrath as he is pitched to the veranda floor, then seized and hoisted overhead. No stuntman took Morrow's place (or Megowan's, for that matter) for the lifting-overhead scene. Morrow told me:

A kinder, gentler Gill Man? In Black Lagoon *he killed five, in* Revenge *three, but in* Creature Walks *just one: his ruthless tormentor Dr. Barton. In this shot, the Creature (Don Megowan) is about to read Barton (Jeff Morrow) his Veranda rights.*

> They had me on a wire that led up to a pulley on the ceiling. When Don Megowan reached down and grabbed me, they pulled me up with the wire as he lifted me. Needless to say, he did not throw me over; he raised me up to the ceiling and then they stopped—thank goodness!—and put a dummy up there in my place.[44]

Morrow made it sound like they shot his part of the scene on the Dabney House veranda but it was done on the soundstage replica. A few nights later, back at the Dabney House, Megowan would fling the Barton dummy earthward. Cut together in the finished movie, the two shots unfortunately feature a hard-to-miss blooper: The Creature lifts Barton and prepares to throw him over the rail, which is topped with a shelf and four big flower pots; but in the next shot, when he throws Barton, the shelf and flower pots have vanished.[45]

Morrow was back on Stage 19's Ranch interior sets the next morning (Saturday, September 17), tiptoeing around from upper hallway room to room in the hide'n'seek scenes

3. The Creature Walks Among Us (1956)

tember 19, back to the Dabney House for the final day of principal photography (all night-for-night). There's another well-done down-the-stairs boom shot as Grant goads Barton ("What's botherin' ya, Doc? Your wife?") to the breaking point—the breaking of Grant's *head*, as Barton pistol-whips him. According to the shot description in the Daily Production Report, Barton treated Grant like a King (*Rodney* King), hitting him several times and then a few *more* times for good luck even after he was lying still on the ground. But in the film's final cut, Barton delivers just one blow to an on-camera Grant, a second blow to an off-camera Grant and then a third that we only hear.

For the shots of Barton lugging Grant's body into the Creature's cage, veteran stuntman Paul Stader replaced Morrow and stand-in Joe Walls took

Dr. Barton (Jeff Morrow) must have played hooky the day his medical school taught the Hippocratic oath; "Do no harm" was the last thing on his mind. In the Creature Walks finale, the Creature (Don Megowan) gives Barton his comeuppance…and then his comedownance!

that lead up to his fatal run-in with the Creature. Rex Reason played the scene where Morgan, hearing gunshots, gets out of bed. The two actors and the crew then moved to Stage 12, where they were joined by Gregg Palmer and David McMahon on the yacht pilot house set for the stalking-the-Gill Man scene. Again a wind machine was used to carry away Palmer's cigarette smoke and give the false impression of actual filming-on-a-boat.[46]

The day ended with a silent shot of Morrow and Snowden in a convertible in front of the process screen, part of the opening scene where she's lead-footing across the bridge to the yacht landing. Before the shot could be taken, it was necessary for crew members to make it possible for Snowden to turn the wheel of the stationary car in order to fit the action on the plate.

A day of rest and then on the evening of Monday, Sep-

Barton (Jeff Morrow) goes off the dial in fury and kills Grant (Gregg Palmer) with three blows, one of them on-camera—the filmmakers doing the scene that way in defiance of Production Code enforcer Geoffrey M. Shurlock, who had written them: "The action showing Barton pistol-whipping Grant is considered excessively brutal. One crack with the pistol should be sufficient and should be indicated out of frame, by suggestion."

over for Palmer. (These shots, and all the rest of the night's shots, were silent.) Don Megowan's Creature tore through a breakaway stockade gate while Barton (played by either Morrow or Stader, probably Stader) repeatedly fired his gun as he backed up and fell over a hedge. Again the action was covered by two cameras, as was the subsequent shot of the stair-climbing Creature breaking the railing. Camera "A"'s shooting-up shot was used in the movie, Camera "B"'s shooting-down shot was used in the trailer. Jeff Morrow was dismissed at 2:50 a.m. once this was in the can.

A few minutes later, the Creature slung Barton (actually a dummy) down off the second floor porch. As mentioned above, the Gill Man getting his meat hooks on Barton is a feel-good moment in the movie because Barton's been such a stinker to his wife and to the Creature (not to mention the murder of Grant). It might have been a fright film "first" in 1956 when audiences found themselves *rooting* for a monster on a destructive tear.

A long shot of the Creature descending the staircase and walking down the drive past Barton's body was cut short for the movie so that the corpse would go unseen. Again a second camera came into play as the Creature charged after the rifle-firing, backwards-running ranch hand, shoving him through a windowed wall of the sentry house. The guard had to have been played by Stader, the only stuntman still there at that hour (now almost 4 a.m.). There were two cameras again for the Creature's toppling of the brick pillar with the electric switchbox, one inside and the other outside the gate; the shot taken by the latter camera was used in the movie. Sparks fly as the pillar falls, with the firecracker-ish sound effects a carryover from a lab scene in an old Frankenstein movie. A high long shot (taken from the porch) of the Creature disappearing into the brush was the last shot of the night; the company was dismissed from the Dabney House location at 4:50 a.m. on the morning of September 20. Principal photography had finished with a bang.

There was, however, more to be done, including two key scenes. This post-production work began with a 6:30 p.m. crew call that very same day (September 20). Park Lake, seen as the Black Lagoon in *Creature from the Black Lagoon* and used in the beach finale of *Revenge of the Creature*, was now visited by the *Creature Walks* company for the shooting of the scene of the men in the dinghy searching the Everglades inlet for the Gill Man. A quintet of $70-a-day stuntmen played the Creature hunters: Paul Stader again doubling Morrow, Joe Walls again doubling Palmer, Alex Sharp doubling Reason, Joe Yrigoyen doubling Manson and Ken Terrell doubling Rawley. The only other player there was Don Megowan, donning the scaly latex costume of the pre-fire Gill Man. Eight gallons of coffee were prepared for the long and probably cold night of work.

With the five stunt doubles in the boat, Sherwood shot a series of silent long shots. From 8:40 until almost half past ten, the boat was photographed with Grant at the spotlight, Barton steering with Johnson beside him, Borg at the Fishscope and Morgan in the stern with the rotenone gun. A little before midnight, a second camera was added for the shot of the Creature, standing amidships with two spears in him, being on the receiving end of a lit torch thrown by Grant. (The flames that engulf the monster would later be added optically.[47]) After the Creature drops into the water to douse the "flames," Morgan grabs an extinguisher and starts spraying the small fire on the dinghy floor. *That* fire was real and intentional.

After a one-hour midnight lunch, a wire was rigged to the boat so that the bow could be raised, supposedly by the Creature. On that night's list of Special Equipment is a Lorain crane, so the wire must have run from the bow to the crane's overhead arm. At about 2 a.m., in a low

The Creature (Don Megowan), concluding his home improvement kick, adds a second egress to the Barton Ranch. The very solid- and heavy-looking pillar falls amidst many sparks and much smoke, a worthy topper for a great monster-runs-riot scene.

3. The Creature Walks Among Us (1956)

Yes, the Creature Walks *Florida Everglades waterway does look a lot like the Black Lagoon from the first Gill Man movie: The same Universal back lot lake was used in both. In the dinghy are stuntmen Alex Sharp, Joe Yrigoyen, Paul Stader, Ken Terrell and Joe Walls.*

shot, the now-burned Creature came out of the water and "pushed" the bow of the boat up out of camera range. A bit later, with two cameras rolling, he did it again, Camera "A" getting a full shot and Camera "B" a medium. The wire broke on the first attempt, but on the second the dinghy's passengers were ejected, some of them none too convincingly, into the drink. A bit after 4 a.m., two cameras got the shot of the Creature attempting to lift a log, but then collapsing and slumping over it. In footage shot but not used, the boat was brought over and the Creature loaded into it. Megowan and the stuntmen were dismissed at 4:20 but it was necessary for some crew members to linger until past 5 a.m., shooting background plates that would be needed when cast members Morrow, Reason *et al.* enacted other parts of this scene on the Process Stage.

Wednesday was a well-earned day off for Megowan, Sherwood and his crew but on Thursday, September 22, they reconvened for a day of silent shots. The first stop was the back lot's Brown Hill, where they waited a while for better light, didn't get it and decided to shoot anyway. Aside from getting the Creature shots we see in the movie's finale,[48] they photographed a never-to-be-used long pan shot of the monster climbing a road to the top of the hill and a long shot of the Creature coming up the slope and into the foreground.

(You *do* feel for the Creature when you see him atop the hill, obviously in a world of hurt. Maybe it's the fact that you see the actor's eyes and he uses them to convey that he's got nothing left in the tank.)

"I'm ready for my closeup": A behind-the-scenes shot of Don Megowan as the new and improved(?) Creature, "More terrifying than ever in human form!" (radio spot line).

A bit before noon, crew and actor moved back to the stockade at the Dabney House, getting shots of the imprisoned Creature looking through the fence in the direction of the lake, reacting to the sound of the mountain lion, etc.

The lion then made his entrance, doing most or all of its scenes on the end of a wire that was painted to make it less visible. There was lots of wasted film as the lion kept heading off in wrong directions, but eventually they got all the needed footage. Creature Megowan also "battled" a dummy lion and quickly "crushed" and slammed it to the ground. One of the amusing, "only in Hollywood" items on that day's Special Equipment list: "1 Fork Lift for Lion."

On Saturday, September 24, when shooting took place on the Process Stage, one last name was added to the list of Gill Men portrayers: stuntman-actor Chuck Roberson, John Wayne's stunt double from 1949 (*The Fighting Kentuckian*) until "The Duke" came to the end of his movie trail in 1976 with *The Shootist*. At 6'3" Roberson was the runt of the litter of Land Creatures (Ben Chapman and Tom Hennesy were both 6'5", Don Megowan 6'7") but of course a difference of a couple inches would be impossible to notice; and making it "more impossible" to notice is the fact that in all of Roberson's *Creature Walks* footage he's either in water or sharing the screen with actors who are sitting down.

The morning and early afternoon were spent getting shots of Morrow, Reason, Palmer, Manson and Rawley (in a dinghy in the Process Stage pool) for the scene where they're following the Gill Man. Then it was Roberson's turn: He's seen as the Gill Man in the shot where he bursts up out of the water and into the glare of Grant's bow-mounted spotlight, and in the shot where he smashes the spotlight and sends Grant toppling backward.[49] That evening, as footage of the wave-battered ocean beach played on the process screen, Megowan (in his "burned Creature" get-up) was photographed standing in front of it in profile, shoulders rising and falling with each breath. This footage was shot at 6:19 and he was dismissed at 6:20(!). It was the last shot of the day on Megowan's last day on the movie.

"Don Megowan was a very dear friend of mine," Gregg Palmer told me. He continued,

> Don and I played brothers on an episode of *Gunsmoke* ["Phoebe Strunk"], there was a shootout at Dodge City and Don was hit. "Ma" [Virginia Gregg] told me, "Go git your brother," and I had to go out into the street, grab Don Megowan, pick him up, put him over my shoulder and carry him off. Well, when I draped him over my shoulder, his head was dragging and his feet were dragging, and it was a full day's work to make that ten steps off-camera with Don Megowan! My vertebrae are *still* achin'!

September 26 and 27 were spent on the Process Stage finishing the dinghy scene. Just before lunch on September 26, they shot footage that ultimately was not used: Grant in the dinghy bow in foreground and, in the stern in the background, the Gill Man (Roberson) knocking over a torch and, angered by the light of the Fishscope shining in his face, reaching for the machine. Getting this shot led to a bit of real-life excitement, as the fire from the fallen torch forced Rex Reason to bail out of the boat. The Production Report says that he "got leg and foot caught between Borg [Maurice Manson] and boat," whatever that means. In our 1989 interview, Reason better described the incident: "There was a little lantern on board which fell over and started a fire. I jumped out, but there was a little piece of metal on the side of the boat that ripped open my left ankle." He added that he still carries a scar from that mishap.[50]

In one shot, Gill Man Roberson jumped backwards off the dinghy stern into the water. In the movie, that footage is seen in reverse so that he appears to spring *up* out of the water and make a gold medal–worthy stuck landing aboard the dinghy. In order to be "shot" with the first of the two spears, the Gill Man was rigged with a wire; the spear would run down the wire to the point of attachment to the Gill Man suit. Getting it to work the first time took "forever" (from 4:38 p.m. 'til a quarter past 6) as one thing after another went amiss: In one take, the Gill Man stood waiting too long for the spear; in the next two, the wire broke; then he lost his balance and spoiled the shot; then the spear didn't stick; then the wire broke again. In the last shot of the day, the Gill

On the final few days of production, the Gill Man was "Bad Chuck" Roberson (1919–88). He was nicknamed "Bad Chuck" by director John Ford, who used stuntmen Roberson and Chuck Hayward on many movies. To differentiate them, Ford called Hayward "Good Chuck" and Roberson—a drinker, fighter and womanizer—"Bad Chuck" (courtesy Photofest).

3. The Creature Walks Among Us (1956)

The dinghy action scene originally had even more *action: In footage that was not used, the Gill Man (Chuck Roberson) took a few steps toward the bow, knocked over a kerosene lamp, pushed Borg aside and threw the Fishscope overboard. Because that footage was scrapped, in the finished film the Gill Man abruptly goes from the stern to amidships, and the Fishscope inexplicably vanishes.*

Man "took" the second spear as he prepared to lift the gas can.

On Tuesday cast and crew reunited on the Process Stage and things picked up right where they left off, with a full shot of Gill Man Roberson again taking a "gasoline" shower as he hurls the can, Grant lofting the torch and the Gill Man doing his "I'm on fire!" bit (even though he wasn't) and then going overboard. More bits'n'pieces of this scene's action-ful finale were shot throughout the day. By seven that evening, only Morrow, Reason and Roberson were still there cast-wise, getting the shot where Barton and Grant wade over to the kayoed Gill Man (slumped over the log) and examine him. "Bring the boat," Morrow called out to no one (Palmer, Manson and Rawley had been dismissed almost an hour earlier), and then he and Reason rolled the Creature over onto his back and began dragging him out of the shot.[51]

At 7:10 p.m., this fifth day of post-production came to an end. There were still 36 inserts and stock shots needed, but otherwise, the movie was finished. First-time feature director Sherwood had come in on schedule and on budget—although it's worth a quick mention that since the 78-minute *Creature Walks* has close to 20 minutes of second unit footage, stock shots, etc., it was as though he had directed a one-hour movie. (This was also true of Jack Arnold on *Black Lagoon*.) Universal was obviously satisfied with the job he had done because four weeks to the day later he began his second movie as director, *Raw Edge* (1956), a Technicolor Western with Rory Calhoun, Yvonne DeCarlo and an offbeat and lurid plot: In the 1842 Oregon territory, there's 1000 men to every woman, and the law specifies that any unattached woman belongs to the first man to claim her. (For instance, Mara Corday is an Indian girl whose husband has been found guilty of a crime he didn't commit and sentenced to hang; and with the just-dropped body still swingin', Mara is set upon by a horde of horny cowboys!) *Creature Walks* star Rex Reason had a supporting part as a gentleman gambler who turns out to be no gentleman.

Several months later, Sherwood was in Lone Pine directing his third movie, *The Monolith Monsters* (1957). After this, however, he went back to assistant-directing, his new credits including the excellent Audie Murphy Western *No Name on the Bullet* (1959), directed by Arnold. In March 1959 Sherwood was in New York directing second-unit scenes for the Rock Hudson–Doris Day comedy *Pillow Talk* when he took ill with pneumonia and died in Harlem's Hospital for Joint Diseases. A *Hollywood Reporter* item about his passing said that he directed "about ten features" when he actually directed three. His April 1 obit in *Variety* was even more of an April Fool's, the show biz bible calling him "a director for Universal for 25 years [and] principal director of numerous feature films." He died at age 52, 53 or circa 56, depending on where you read about him.

On September 28, the day after *The Creature Walks Among Us* wrapped, Jeff Livingston, Universal's Eastern (445 Park Avenue, NYC) advertising manager, wrote to tell publicist Clark Ramsay that he didn't think much of the title: "It sounds as if the monster was just ambling around, making trouble." He suggested lots of others, including one he particularly liked, *The Creature Stalks a City*, "which is provoking and, at the same time, lends itself to the King Kong type of ads with cars and buildings being pushed around." Other suggestions in that same letter: *The Creature's Jungle, The Creature Against the Sky, The Roaring Creature, The Creature Turns, The Creature's Secret, Creature at the Crossroads, Fifty Fathoms Under the Creature, The Creature and the Mermaid, The Creature Rises in the Everglades, The Creature, Dead or Alive!, The Creature Has Two Faces, The Creature's Master Mind* and *Creature from the Roaring Everglades*. On October 4, Universal's Eastern publicity manager Philip Gerard piped up on behalf of *The Creature Stalks the City*, calling it an excellent title and amusing himself with the alliterative comment, "[I]t has the feeling of a King Kong Kind of Kinescope." But *The Creature Walks Among Us* the title would remain.

Scripter Arthur Ross assured me that Universal had no qualms about letting him alter the Creature's appearance, but it seems as though the publicity department lads had qualms a-plenty: On the posters, we don't see Ross' new Creature but the old one. "Science Baits the Trap with a Woman's Beauty!" read one ad line, making a promise the movie wouldn't keep. "TERROR Runs Rampant on the City Streets!" and artwork of a group of panic-stricken people also violate the public trust as the Creature never gets within bellowing distance of any city ... or town ... or hamlet. The publicity mavens were also being economical with the truth with their artwork of the Gill Man straddling the Golden Gate Bridge. On one lobby card, there's a small piece of cartoon art (the Creature pushing over a section of electrified fence) where he looks like the love child of the Gill Man and Bela Lugosi's *The Phantom Creeps* robot.

Inside the pressbook, a castlist gives the names and character names of the six top-billed players plus, surprisingly,

Creature .... DON MEGOWAN and
RICOU BROWNING

This is the only one of the three movies whose pressbook reveals the names of the Creature players. What's funny about this, "Land Creature"–wise, is that Tom Hennesy probably would have liked getting official credit, and Ben Chapman would have *loved* it—and yet the only actor to get it is Don Megowan, who probably *hated* it! His daughter Vikki told me, "He downplayed all his sci-fi movies because he did not want to be stereotyped as just a sci-fi actor. Quite honestly, back in those days he really didn't want it widely publicized that he played the Creature, for fear it would hurt his opportunities for other roles."

Exhibitors reading the pressbook were also made aware that two different 16mm "Shock TV Trailers," one 60 seconds, the other 20 seconds, were available for free from Eastern advertising manager Livingston. Apparently the trailers were scary stuff back in the day; on March 16, 1956, Livingston wrote to publicist Ramsay:

> Just to let you know that you and Bob Faber have not lost your horrible touch.
> Station WEWS in Cleveland will only show *The Creature Walks Among Us* TV trailer after 9 p.m. Station KYW in Cleveland will not show the minute spots but only the 20-second ones. Station WSPD in Toledo is debating whether or not they will accept the spots at all.
> I'll keep you advised of further developments.
> Kind regards.

On the Creature Walks poster art, the Creature's multi-million-year evolutionary leap is indicated only by a pair of high-water pants with rope belt.

Leigh Snowden was described in the press as "a well-scrubbed, ladylike blonde with a figure that could give Marilyn Monroe an anxiety complex." Here she poses with a man who enjoys his job, Creature Walks co-star Rex Reason.

At no cost to Universal, one unusual publicity item was concocted by their San Francisco field representative Mike Vogel: a four-page herald in which the *Creature Walks* events are written up in tabloid style, as though they were true-life stories that had inspired this new movie. Theaters playing *Creature Walks* were solicited by the printer to order copies. The "newspaper" was called the *State-Clarion* and the headline accompanying the cover photo of the post-fire Creature read "Monster or Man? Human or Beast?" In the grand yellow-journalism tradition, a page-one story was titled "Love-Slave Wife Calls Mate Killer." One "scoop" within the paper was a story *by* Marcia Barton, "'Tried to Fight Him Off,' Sobs Gal; Asks Fair Play," which read in part:

> I eagerly accept the *State-Clarion* invitation to reply to the charges I am much to blame for the deaths of Jed Grant and my husband William Barton.
>
> The truth is, that Barton tried to make a love-slave out of me. He would go into the most awful rages if I as much as looked at another man. He killed Grant.
>
> I was never in love with Jed Grant. I turned to him only for the companionship I could not get from my husband. I was happy to find anyone to make me forget, if only for a brief moment, the shuddery shadow-world I lived in under the vicious influence of a crazy scientist and his sinister "love-laboratory."
>
> … All I can say now, is that before anyone passes judgment, they should go and see *The Creature Walks Among Us*. I am willing to rest my reputation and honesty on what the picture reveals.

It was as though the Gods of Weather frowned upon the idea of a third Gill Man feature: Clouds and rain had hampered *Creature Walks*' Florida second unit (as they did all three movies' Florida units), a killer heat wave put a hurting on its first unit team at Universal; and when the night of the *Creature Walks* preview loomed, disaster struck again: On January 25, 1956, rainstorms began sweeping over California, sending rivers out of their banks. In the Southland, rain and gusty winds caused flooding that forced many from their homes, prompted shopkeepers to sandbag entryways, and caused mudslides that blocked Coldwater Canyon and Laurel Canyon. On the 26th, the area was again relentlessly pounded, with hundreds of women and children being rescued from their flooded homes by men in trucks and boats. Roads turned to rivers, forcing the abandonment of automobiles. "Water reached nearly to the rooftops of houses in the Palms area, near Manning and Motor Aves.," reported the *Los Angeles Times*.

On the night of the 26th, during the third heaviest 24-hour rainfall in Southern California history, L.A.'s State Theatre hosted the *Creature Walks* preview, running it after a regular showing of the Glenn Ford–Donna Reed drama *Ransom!* (1956). Preview Comment Cards were handed out to the few who'd braved the elements to attend. The question

The role of Barton's tormented "trophy wife" was a stretch for Leigh Snowden, who in real life "could dance, could sing, and had an outgoing personality," according to her friend Ina Poindexter. "Leigh was really very talented, multi-talented, and she was funny. We loved being around her."

"WHICH SCENES, IF ANY, DID YOU DISLIKE?" elicited the answers "About jealousy," "House scenes," "The factual scenes and the mushy scenes," "The final scenes" and (there's a wiseguy in every crowd) "Most."

WERE ALL THE STORY POINTS CLEAR TO YOU?

No, the reasons for the changes [in the Creature] were not made clear enough.
    No, poor script. In fact, some lines ridiculous.
    What story?
    Story?

DID THE PICTURE HOLD YOUR INTEREST THROUGHOUT? IF NOT, WHERE DID IT FAIL TO HOLD YOU?

Where it deviated from adventure to psychology.
    The end.
    From the beginning to the end.
    Have to admit it—best comedy of the year.

At Universal at the next morning's Studio Operating Committee, a Mr. Batliner said that too few cards were turned in, "probably because of the adverse weather conditions" (ya *think*?), to draw any conclusions about how the movie would be greeted by audiences. According to Batliner, the Universal employees at the preview remarked that it was well-received and sustained the interest of the folks who *were* there. Down the line a bit, Preview Comment Cards mailed to the studio by other attendees included these remarks:

> Best comedy in years. All it lacked was Abbott and Costello and Liberace.
> Good for children.
> Color would have helped—at least I wouldn't have felt as though I were out $1.00.
> It is a poor way to present the subject of genetics.
> A good try.

Harrison's Reports thought that *Creature Walks*' thrills and chills were on a par with its predecessors: "It is all far-fetched, of course, but [the story makes] for a series of horrific situations that are sure to excite those who go for this type of entertainment." Funnily enough, *Harrison's* called *Creature Walks* "Adult fare" while Jack Moffitt's *Hollywood Reporter* review was titled "U-I's Newest in *Creature* Series Good Kiddie B.O." *Motion Picture Exhibitor* called it a "suitable addition to others in the series.... The story holds attention and the acting, direction and production are okay." J.P. of the *New York Herald Tribune* described the Gill Man as "the target of a mad (MAD, you hear!) scientist who wishes to speed up evolution" and wasn't much impressed by the goings-on: "Only in the dreary nether world of the sea does the picture come to life."

New York Times wiseguy A.H. Weiler gave *Creature from the Black Lagoon* a fairly negative review in 1954 and now he was back to belittle this follow-up, again more interested in trying to be funny than in writing sensibly:

> Although the cause of the common cold is still baffling mere medicos, leaders of Universal's school for advanced science fiction seem to be having no trouble at all. True, they have ignored simple sniffles. But two years ago they dredged up "a creature from the black lagoon" ... that proved to be more improbable and funnier than a running nose.... [H]e showed up again yesterday at the Globe as *The Creature Walks Among Us*. Perhaps it would be best if they tackled the ordinary cold, after all.

Weiler ended the review with "Chances are he'll be back." S.A. Desick of the *Los Angeles Examiner* said that the Creature was "still a serviceable monster as monsters go, but he scares the wits out of the script. The story that is jerry-built around him is a tiresome one of jealousy and mayhem." In a years-later review, a *Castle of Frankenstein* scribe wrote, "If you doubt [Jack] Arnold's contribution to this series, just watch—or try to—the 3rd, non–Arnold Creature epic, *The Creature Walks Among Us*."

And then there are these quotable notables:

••••••••••••••••••••••

I didn't particularly like [*Creature Walks*], I thought it was the weakest of the three.—Jack Arnold

••••••••••••••••••••••

If I had known that *Creature Walks* would be shown on television and been around [after its theatrical run], I wouldn't have done it ... I did the film feeling it was just a job, but I really hadn't anticipated the possibility of it getting on television—there weren't too many movies of that type on television at the time, and I thought of it as a picture I'd be able to simply put behind me. I personally thought it was kind of corny.... It was a comedown after *This Island Earth* and *Kiss of Fire*, a downer.—Rex Reason

••••••••••••••••••••••

The Creature Walks Among Us, I thought, sucked.—Ricou Browning

••••••••••••••••••••••

The dumbest [Gill Man movie] was *The Creature Walks Among Us*, which was terrible. Burning his gills off, and putting him in a suit...!—Ben Chapman

••••••••••••••••••••••

Universal insisted on [two *Creature*] sequels, both of which I am ashamed of. I wish to disassociate myself with the other two films as much as possible [*laughs*]! But the studio wanted to mine that thing as much as possible so I blew those two pictures through my nose and didn't want to hear any more about 'em!—William Alland

••••••••••••••••••••••

I have a copy of the *Creature* Legacy Collection [DVDs] and I watched *Creature Walks* ... and I don't think that came off as well as the first two. I think that they went too far when they tried to humanize him. Nobody wanted to see that happen to him; I thought that this was a degrading thing to do to the magnificent Creature. The first two were kinda somewhat "believable," the way they disturbed him in his habitat, but by the time they got to the third one, they missed the boat! I was kinda happy I hadn't done that one.—Ginger Stanley

••••••••••••••••••••••

One dissenting voice among the moviemakers: scripter Arthur Ross, who told me, "It turned out to be, surprisingly, not too bad a movie."

According to "H'wood on New Scientifiction Kick," a December 9, 1955, *Daily Variety* article on the resurgence

3. The Creature Walks Among Us (1956)

of sci-fi movies after a brief lull, "[Universal] may put a fourth *Creature* into work." The prospect of an additional Creature stanza was also mentioned in the *Creature Walks* pressbook, the article telling readers that if *Creature Walks* has the same success as its two predecessors, "it's quite likely that U-I will produce a fourth [Gill Man] feature."

Early Playdates
By Robert J. Kiss

The American Film Institute lists the general release of *The Creature Walks Among Us* as April 1956, specifically mentioning an April 26 New York opening. *Creature Walks* did open in New York City on April 26, but the movie had reached theaters across much of the U.S. prior to this. Even the AFI's approximate general release date of "April 1956" ought really to be shifted back to "March 1956."

The official premiere took place at the Joy Theater in New Orleans on the evening of March 6, 1956. The previous two pictures in the series had reportedly "gone over big" at the theater, and a deal to open *Creature Walks* there had been reached well in advance, with the Joy advertising the forthcoming premiere from February 24 onwards. The movie then played continuously throughout the day as a standalone feature at the theater on March 7 and March 8. This constituted a one-off showing in the state of Louisiana, where the film was otherwise not seen until April. A similar situation existed for the state of Mississippi, where *Creature Walks* played at a lone theater, the Ritz in Laurel, from March 15 to 17, prior to opening statewide in April.

The movie began playing more widely on March 21, when it opened on a double-bill with *The Price of Fear*[52] at ten Los Angeles theaters; by the end of the month, it had opened throughout California. As with the previous two Creature features, it was also seen early in the state of Michigan, for example opening at the State in Benton Harbor, the Lyric in Ludington and the Michigan Theatre in Traverse City on March 25. The movie was furthermore released to theaters throughout Ohio between March 28 and April 1, before then opening across vast swaths of the nation, from Alaska to Texas and from Oregon to Massachusetts, during the first two weeks of April. On April 13 it was also put to limited use as a Friday the 13th midnight show.

In this instance, the New York opening date must be understood specifically as referring to the film's opening in New York City; it had reached theaters elsewhere in New York State earlier in the month, for example opening in Binghamton during the first week of April and in Albany during the second week of the month.

In *Boxoffice Magazine* (January 26, 1957), exhibitor I. Roche of Vernon, Florida's, Vernon Theatre advised other movie theater impresarios, "If not played too close together, the Creature will pull a fair crowd, mostly colored patrons. Would do well on Friday–Saturday if terms were lowered a mite so it could be double-featured."

As a Standalone Feature, March to September 1956

Within the sample of around 900 movie theaters across the U.S. during this period, 24 percent of all *Creature Walks* screenings took the form of a standalone presentation supported only by "selected shorts." This form of presentation was common in two types of location: (i) theaters in small

A cool collectible, this Creature Walks pop-up pops up and up to the point where, compared to the guy he's holding, the Gill Man looks about 15 feet tall!

I've found the pairing attested among the sample of around 900 U.S. movie theaters. Collectively making up 29 percent of the total for first-run screenings of *Creature Walks*, this was far from an uncommon way to see the movie, in particular at lower-rung small town and neighborhood theaters. Nevertheless, the choice of co-billed feature could vary widely, and even the title that was most commonly paired with *Creature Walks* on the list below, the Western *Backlash*, accounted individually for just four percent of screenings nationwide.

Bold signifies a more substantial number of playdates for the double bill in question

April 1956 *Backlash* (Richard Widmark)
June 1956 *Bad Day at Black Rock* (Spencer Tracy)
September 1956 *The Birds and the Bees* (George Gobel)
June 1956 *Blackjack Ketchum, Desperado* (Howard Duff)
August 1956 *The Bowery Boys Meet the Monsters*
July 1956 *Comanche* (Dana Andrews)
September 1956 *Congo Crossing* (Virginia Mayo)
September 1956 *Dawn at Socorro* (Rory Calhoun)
May 1956 *A Day of Fury* (Dale Robertson)
June 1956 *Day the World Ended* (Richard Denning)
September 1956 *Fire Maidens from Outer Space* (Anthony Dexter)
July 1956 *It's a Dog's Life* (Jeff Richards)
May 1956 *Jaguar* (Sabu)
June 1956 *The Kettles in the Ozarks* (Marjorie Main)
August 1956 *The Last Command* (Sterling Hayden)
June 1956 *The Last Hunt* (Robert Taylor)
June 1956 *Miracle in the Rain* (Jane Wyman)
May 1956 *The Naked Street* (Farley Granger)
June 1956 **Northwest Passage** (Spencer Tracy)
September 1956 *Pardners* (Martin and Lewis—and Jeff Morrow)
August 1956 *Pete Kelly's Blues* (Jack Webb)
August 1956 *Postmark for Danger* (Terry Moore)
July 1956 **The Rawhide Years** (Tony Curtis—and Leigh Snowden in a small part as a riverboat passenger)
June 1956 *Rock Around the Clock* (Bill Haley)
April 1956 **Running Wild** (Mamie Van Doren)
September 1956 *Scared Stiff* (Martin and Lewis)
August 1956 *The Searchers* (John Wayne)
August 1956 *Shack Out on 101* (Terry Moore)
May 1956 **Star in the Dust** (John Agar)

towns where single bills were generally the norm anyway; and (ii) at the majority of theaters within Texas. *Revenge of the Creature* had likewise received special treatment as a standalone feature in Texas, and if Texas were excluded from the sample of around 900 movie theaters, then the overall tally of standalone screenings of *Creature Walks* nationwide would fall to 18 percent. Although the "selected shorts" accompanying the feature were seldom named in advertising, the titles of two Universal-International Musical Featurettes, *Mambo Madness* and *Cool and Groovy*, do appear with some frequency in newspaper ads.

Regular Co-Feature, March to September 1956

Within the sample of around 900 U.S. movie theaters during this period, 45 percent of all *Creature Walks* screenings were double-billed with *The Price of Fear*, meaning that this was both the movie's "regular co-feature" and the single most common way to see the movie during its first run. This double bill was attested nationwide throughout the entire period from March to September 1956.

Other Co-Features, March to September 1956

The other co-features are arranged alphabetically below; the month mentioned in each case is the earliest in which

3. The Creature Walks Among Us (1956)

July 1956 *The Swan* (Grace Kelly)
May 1956 *Three Bad Sisters* (Marla English)
September 1956 *The Treasure of Pancho Villa* (Rory Calhoun)
May 1956 *Tribute to a Bad Man* (James Cagney)
May 1956 *The Trouble with Harry* (Edmund Gwenn)
August 1956 *Tumbleweed* (Audie Murphy)
June 1956 *The Warriors* (Errol Flynn)
June 1956 *World Without End* (Hugh Marlowe)

Triple Bills, March to September 1956

The titles are arranged alphabetically below; the month mentioned in each case is the earliest in which I've found the triple-bill attested among the sample of around 900 movie theaters across the U.S. These three different triple bills collectively make up just two percent of the total for first-run screenings of *The Creature Walks Among Us*, and this was evidently a fairly uncommon way of first getting to experience the movie.

August 1956 *Backlash* (Richard Widmark) and *The Kettles in the Ozarks* (Marjorie Main)
August 1956 *Gentlemen Prefer Blondes* (Jane Russell) and *The Rawhide Years* (Tony Curtis)
September 1956 *Johnny O'Clock* (Dick Powell) and *Tall Man Riding* (Randolph Scott)

Domestically, Creature from the Black Lagoon reaped $1,300,000, Revenge $200,000 less than that. Creature Walks (its Italian poster pictured) didn't even rise to the seven-digit level. Universal, probably figuring that a third sequel would make even less than Creature Walks, gave the Creature his walking papers.

Marginalia
By Tom Weaver

♦ *The Creature Walks Among Us* was William Alland's last sci-fi for Universal before he started cutting corners and placing a heavy reliance on stock footage—an understandable reaction to the fact that Columbia's stock footage-filled creature feature *It Came from Beneath the Sea* (1955) had made a better domestic showing than most or all of his sci-fis, the Creature pictures included. According to an April 19, 1956, Summary of Production Report, *Creature Walks* had total direct costs of $397,100; a 27.25 percent charge for studio overhead raised its cost $108,210, to a grand total of $505,310. *Black Lagoon*'s final cost was $613,243 and *Revenge* $532,477. As Ricou Browning told me, "They spent less money on each Creature picture, so they got worse."

♦ The Morgan–Marcia–Grant diving scene includes shots of the Gill Man taken from *Black Lagoon*. You can tell the old *Black Lagoon* footage from the new *Creature Walks* shots (a) by the fact that in the new shots, he has the *Revenge of the Creature* Tanning Bed Goggle eyes and (b) by how much brighter and clearer the new footage is. Underwater Gill Man shots that looked just

The Creature Smokes Among Us—and poses for a picture with two unidentified men and producer William Alland, right.

terrific in *Black Lagoon* here look almost unacceptably dark juxtaposed with the crystal-clear, more picturesque *Creature Walks* footage. As Ricou Browning recounted earlier in this chapter, Wakulla's waters were very muddy for *Black Lagoon* and perfectly transparent for *Creature Walks*.

◆ Part of the U-I sci-fi formula was for every movie to have two male leads forever butting heads out of mistrust or dislike or both: Putnam and the sheriff in *It Came from Outer Space*, Reed and Williams in *Black Lagoon*, Exeter and Meacham in *This Island Earth* and then, after a one-movie break (*Revenge of the Creature*), Hastings and Deemer in *Tarantula*. Again in *Creature Walks* the leads can agree on nothing, Barton arch and roguish and with a crazy gleam in his eyes, and Morgan with the noble brow. But we the viewers don't know or care what the heck Barton and Morgan are talking about ("We can change the blood texture—build up the red corpuscle count—then the gene structure *has* to be affected!" "I didn't know you wanted *that* kind of an experiment!" and other exchanges of that sort). They go on and on like a couple of magpies, neither ever budges, and Morgan with his too-tight halo and priestly, superior manner becomes almost as off-putting as Barton. Their clashes aren't part of the entertainment but more like the price we pay to see the Creature a third time. These two colossal bores were the last of Universal's Squabbling Sci-Fi Leads.

◆ Blooper! Atop Dr. Borg's Fishscope screen is a DEPTH IN FEET indicator and, in the scene where Morgan, Marcia and Grant dive, we can watch it go from about 50 feet to about 200 as they descend. But moments later, as Borg examines the image blip representing the Gill Man, the Fishscope is filmed in an even tighter closeup and we can see that the DEPTH IN FEET arrow is back to zero again.

◆ *Creature Walks* star Morrow was visited on the set by wife Anna and their young daughter Lissa. Erskine Johnson wrote in his syndicated column that other *Creature Walks* cast members also brought *their* kids that day, and at one point—please let this *not* be true—Morrow suggested to the other mamas and papas, "Maybe we should call ourselves the Parent-Creatures Association."

◆ The big difference between the first two Gill Man movies and the third is that there's really no "Beauty and the Beast" component to *Creature Walks*, but here's another dissimilarity: *Creature Walks* has zero comedy relief. *Black Lagoon* and *Revenge* featured Nestor Paiva as the amusing Lucas, and *Revenge* additionally had Dave Willock as Lou getting in a few comedy licks, Clint Eastwood playing the fool, and some cute stuff with Neal the chimp and Flippy the "Educated" Porpoise. *Creature Walks* is cheerless from stem to stern.

◆ James Rawley, who plays Dr. Johnson, comes up in *Hollywood Monster: A Walk Down Elm Street with the Man of Your Dreams*, the 2009 autobiography of actor Robert "Freddy Krueger" Englund. Englund writes that he took as many drama classes as possible during junior high and high school, and adds, "I did well enough that a couple of my teachers told me I qualified to be a teacher's assistant for credits, including a wonderful high school teacher, the character actor James Rawley, who played the mad scientist in the 1956 creepy cult classic *The Creature Walks*

3. The Creature Walks Among Us (1956)

Among Us. (Considering my future in horror, it was ironic that I became the mad scientist's assistant. Hey, where's my hunchback?)" Rawley played *Creature Walks'* starring role as the mad scientist? In your *dreams*, Freddy!

Rawley was the husband of Hawaiian-born Mamo Clark, best remembered as Fletcher Christian's (Clark Gable) Tahitian bride in *Mutiny on the Bounty* (1935). Her handful of additional credits include the Republic serial *Robinson Crusoe of Clipper Island* (1936), *The Hurricane* (1937) and *One Million B.C.* (1940). In the latter's volcanic eruption scene, it's Clark's cave girl character who gets steamrollered by flowing lava in an unforgettable shot. Their 45-year marriage ended with her death from cancer in 1986.

◆ One script draft's Gill Man–on-fire and Gill Man–burned scene descriptions caught the eye of censor Geoffrey M. Shurlock, who advised Universal, "The action showing the Creature's entire head enveloped in searing flames, staggering, bumping, etc., seems excessively gruesome, and great care should be exercised in photographing same." He also asked that the moviemakers "[k]indly avoid excessive gruesomeness when photographing the Creature's 'face burned almost black from fire.'"

◆ In an early script draft, Arthur Ross described a post-fire Creature wardrobe of tight, long-sleeved, high-neck sweatshirt and something like dungarees. In a different draft the writer called for a sweatshirt with tight waist, neck and arms plus the sort of diving pants worn by underwater demolition men.

◆ Ricou Browning got no on-screen credit for the three Gill Man movies, but he did get publicity through them, including a widely published syndicated article by James Bacon. The August 1955 piece is highly complimentary, calling Ricou "undoubtedly one of the world's best underwater swimmers" and crediting the series' success to the character he played:

The casts all have been different in the three pictures, a fact which convinces the studio that the creature himself is the box office attraction. The first two in the series were made for around $700,000 and each grossed four millions around the world. This town is peopled with Oscar winners who would like to have that kind of box office return.

◆ The *Boxoffice* magazine column "The Exhibitor Has His Say" often makes for fun reading. On the subject of *Creature Walks*, D.W. Trisko of the Runge Theatre in Runge, Texas, said that the Gill Man movie did draw patrons "despite the fact U-I pulled it on us about a month previous and ruined the main draw, as the Mexican trade had mostly left by the time we got it." Paul Ricketts of the Star Drive-In in Ness City, Kansas, griped, "Hope this is the last of the Creature series. They have just about run out of material."

◆ *Creature Walks* director Sherwood *assistant-*directed at Universal for about eight years before advancing up the ladder, and his *Creature Walks* d.p. Maury Gertsman (1907–99) traveled a quite-similar path: For perhaps eight years he was a Universal camera operator in the run-up to becoming a full-fledged cinematographer. At the hind end of the 1940s horror cycle, he shot *The Jungle Captive* (1945), *House of Horrors*, *The Brute Man* (both 1946) *et al.*, and then when U-I came along and the joint got an infusion of class, he found himself lensing much more substantial

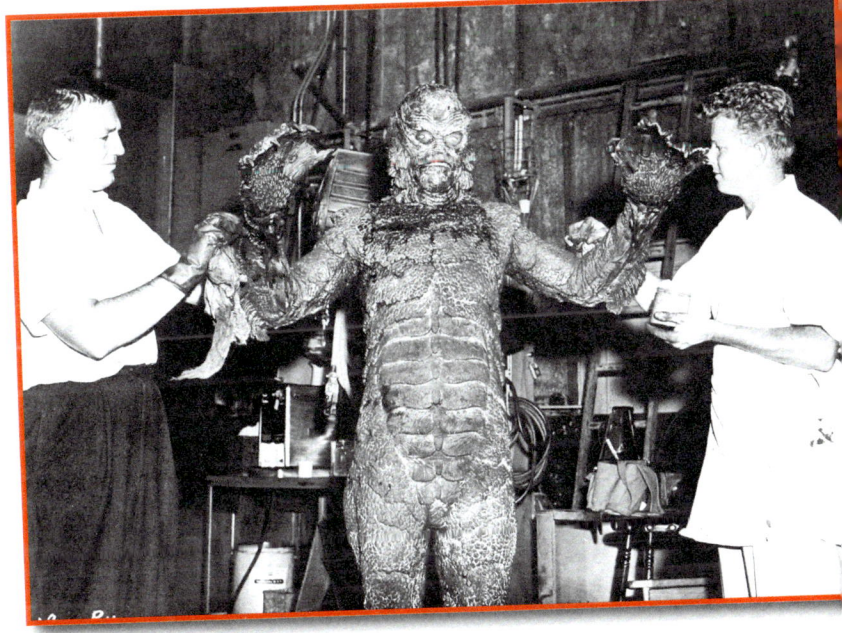

By the time Creature Walks *got to Australian audiences, censors had deleted the shot of the monster throwing Barton off the porch and also had reduced the number of closeups of the burned Creature's head and face. In this photograph, makeup men apply a mix of black paint and charcoal to the Gill Man (Chuck Roberson) to give him that burned look.*

pictures, including their huge 1955 hit *To Hell and Back*. (With domestic rentals of $6,000,000, it was Universal's *only* moneymaker of that magnitude that year.) After Universal, Gertsman shot other horror pictures—*How to Make a Monster* (1958), *Invisible Invaders* and *The Four Skulls of Jonathan Drake* (1959)—and a mountain of Lucille Ball TV episodes.

- The Creature's only two victims in *Creature Walks* are the mountain lion and Barton, both lifted overhead and then fatally slung to the ground. Apparently screenwriter Ross thought this was about the only way the monster could kill: In one of his *Black Lagoon* drafts, two of the Gill Man's three victims are picked up and slammed onto the boat deck with crushing force.

- The *Creature Walks* trailer editor wanted to include a monster-and-the-girl moment, but without one in the movie, he had to "manufacture" it: In the trailer, a yacht salon two-shot of Marcia on the couch and the Creature standing over her is followed by a closeup of the Creature, who then quickly bends down and disappears off camera, creating the impression he's excitedly reaching for her. But the latter is actually a shot of the Creature inside the ranch house, reaching down to flip a table.

- Domestically, *Creature Walks* didn't crack the $1,000,000 mark as the first two Gill Man movies had done: On *Variety*'s beginning-of-1957 list of the "Top Money Films" of 1956, *Guys and Dolls* and *The King and I* led the pack with $9,000,000 and $8,500,000 respectively and, a looong ways down, even past *The Lieutenant Wore Skirts* with Tom Ewell and *The Birds and the Bees* with George Gobel, we finally get to the year's top sci-fi, MGM's *Forbidden Planet*, with a domestic take of $1,600,000. It was distantly followed by Sam Katzman's *Earth vs. the Flying Saucers* with $1,250,000, Allied Artists' *Invasion of the Body Snatchers* with $1,200,000 and Universal's *Tarantula*, actually a late 1955 release, with $1,100,000.

  Universal had 16 movies on the 109-movie list, the biggest being the World War II saga *Away All Boats*, the soaper *All That Heaven Allows* and the biographical *The Benny Goodman Story*. Other Universals higher on *Variety*'s list than *Tarantula*: *Backlash*, *Never Say Goodbye*, *Pillars of the Sky*, *Walk the Proud Land*, *The Second Greatest Sex*, *The Spoilers* and *The Toy Tiger*. Even entries in the studio's long-in-the-tooth Ma and Pa Kettle and Talking Mule series, *The Kettles in the Ozarks* and *Francis in the Haunted House*, did better "wicket business" than Universal's sci-fi flicks of '56. If *Creature Walks* had performed as well as (say) *The Kettles in the Ozarks*, perhaps there *would* have been a fourth Creature installment. But it didn't, and Universal dropped the curtain on the Gill Man.

- In "Bilko's Vampire," an October 1958 episode of the CBS sitcom *The Phil Silvers Show*, we learn that one of Sgt. Bilko's (Silvers) buddies, Sgt. Rupert Ritzik (Joe E. Ross), is a horror movie addict who religiously watches the oldies on TV's nightly *Shriek Theater* (a takeoff on *Shock Theater*). The crazy situation escalates to the point where Bilko travels to Hollywood with Rupert, hoping to pass him off as a real vampire and make him filmdom's next Dracula! Name-dropped in the episode are Bela Lugosi and *The Mummy's Hand*, but funnier for Gill Man fans is a scene set in Rupert's home, where he refers to his nagging wife (sulking in an adjoining bedroom) as the Creature from the Other Room. And when Bilko and Rupert invade the Hollywood producers' office, look on the wall for framed photos of Don Megowan in *Creature Walks*!

- The Castle Films editor who whittled *Creature Walks* down to one-tenth of its original running time dispensed with Marcia almost entirely. The only time she's seen is in background (for about two seconds) in a veranda shot of Morgan watching the Gill Man stomping away from the toppled Barton Ranch fence.

- An episode of TV's *The Outer Limits* features a scientist who, like Dr. Barton, seeks to put evolution on the fast track: Set in a Welsh coal mining town, "The Sixth Finger" (1963) stars Edward Mulhare as a professor whose lab equipment can transform a modern man into a "man of the future," a man Mulhare expects will rise above the animal passions that lead to violence. Miner David McCallum agrees to sit in Mulhare's "isolation booth"–like chamber and be sent soaring into our biological future; like Barton, Mulhare's scientist messes with the genes to accelerate the mechanism of evolution. As the episode proceeds, McCallum hurtles through more evolutionary changes and looks more frighteningly weird each time we see him, and

3. The Creature Walks Among Us (1956)

there's anticipatory excitement as we wonder how he'll look next. After the Creature's operation in *Creature Walks*, he identically continues to evolve on his own, according to Barton ("His features, his skin—they're more like a human's every day!"), but to me he looks the same when his bandages are removed on the yacht as he does walking toward the ocean at the fadeout.

◆ The Creature was seen in Technicolor in Universal's 1981 telemovie *The Munsters' Revenge*. The kooky plot involved crooks (including Sid Caesar as the excitable Dr. Diablo) whose wax museum Chamber of Horrors figures (Herman Munster, Grandpa, the Gill Man, a werewolf, etc.) are actually robots that are sent out to commit crimes. The police think the *real* Herman and Grandpa are involved, and hilarity ensues (*not*). Amidst all the other automatons, the Gill Man Robot does a wind-up toy-like walk from place to place in a few scenes.

◆ This book isn't going to attempt to cover all the movies that ripped off the Gill Man story-wise or that feature Gill Man–like monsters—but one of the exceptions we'll make is writer-producer-director Greg Nicotero's *The United Monster Talent Agency* (2010), an eight-minute B&W spoof that depicts, newsreel-style, activity at a Hollywood firm that provides actual monsters to moviemakers. Just some of the featured creatures are Dracula, Frankenstein, the Wolf Man, the Mummy, the Thing, the Invisible Man, the Hideous Sun Demon, the Jaws shark and, natch, the Gill Man.

United Monster was something that special effects makeup artist Nicotero wanted to make for a long time. He told me,

We prepped it in five weeks and shot the entire short over a three-day period, two days at KNB [his special effects studio] and one day on location. For me it was one of the most freeing experiences I had ever had ... not only the chance to recreate every one of my favorite creatures, but then to [also include] movies I loved in the '70s like *Jaws* and *Dawn of the Dead*. This was probably the last project at KNB where the entire shop had a hand in the show, building, designing or playing various parts. Carey Jones, our shop supervisor, had done an amazing job in suit work on *Predators* [2010] and I really wanted him to play the Creature. David Schow, who plays the cameraman in that scene, said to me, "This is the closest to actually being able to go back in time and stand on set watching them shoot *Creature from the Black Lagoon*." That was the biggest compliment I ever got.

Uncredited in the cast of *The United Monster Talent Agency* is one of this book's staunchest contributors David J. Schow, who plays the cameraman filming the climactic grotto scene from *Creature from the Black Lagoon*. Inside the Gill Man costume is special effects makeup artist Carey Jones. The scene was shot inside the KNB EFX Group workshop on March 5, 2010 (photograph by Howard Berger).

◆ Several of the Gill Man series' principals had in their futures another *Creature*-related or *Creature*-like credit, some actually made, some not:
  • Jack Kevan produced, co-wrote and created the creature costume for 1959's *The Monster of Piedras Blancas* (see Chapter 5, "Aquatic Kith and Kin").
  • Ricou Browning again donned an underwater monster suit in a 1965 episode of TV's *Flipper*.[53]
  • In 1971, Harry Essex wrote and directed the junky *Black Lagoon* ripoff *Octaman*.
  • Director Jack Arnold was lined up to direct a 1980s remake of *Black Lagoon* (see Chapter 8).
  • And in the 1980s, producer William Alland cooked up the idea for a sequel, but never got past the writing stage. He told me,

After I heard that [Universal] had talked to Jack Arnold about doing a remake, I said to myself, "Jesus Christ, you can't do *that* one over again. What *could* you do?" I came up with the idea that they should do a sequel instead of a remake. Since the Creature that I had originally envisioned was so romantic, I thought he should have a family—a mate, and one or two little ones. In my story, they're all removed from the Black Lagoon and secretly transported to a lake on the big estate of a very wealthy family in the United States. They can communicate with the family, and a whole relationship develops. Unfortunately, some baddies *do* find out about 'em and try to catch 'em—they capture one or both of the children, and the mother and the father go after them and kill the baddies. Now they're wanted.

I wrote it all out, but I never pursued it or talked to anybody about it. You're the first person I've ever brought it up to. I'm not even sure that this idea would have been appreciated, but I thought they could do something very charming with it. I could visualize the mother, the father and the two little ones swimming around together [*laughs*].

◆ Clint Eastwood and Henry Mancini were able to look back on their Creature Days as stepping stones to super-stardom in their respective fields, and Ricou Browning didn't do so bad either: In a long career that started in a Black Lagoon, he has second-unit-directed, *directed*-directed, written, produced and done plenty more on movie sets wet or dry. Résumé highlights include supervising the underwater photography of an ocean of *Sea Hunt* episodes, second-unit-directing the underwater scenes in the James Bond adventures *Thunderball* (1965) and *Never Say Never Again* (1983), creating the character of Flipper (the movie-TV dolphin) and serving as vice-president, then president of Ivan Tors Studios. After directing and co-writing (with his brother-in-law Jack Cowden) the *Flipper*-like feature film *Salty* (1973), about some kids and their friendly sea lion, he began to find out how inescapable the Gill Man had become. As Cowden told an interviewer in 1983,

When we created *Salty*, [Ricou and I] went to promote the film everywhere. We went 3300 miles … and along the way we'd stop at elementary schools and give the kids a free show with the sea lion. But it would startle us every time we told them Ricou had been the Creature from the Black Lagoon. These kids would go crazy. They'd all seen it on television. They loved it.

Browning has also regularly "re-connected" with other *Black Lagoon* people and places on later projects. To name just a few, he did the underwater sequences for writer Richard Carlson's *Island of the Lost* (1967) and director Jack Arnold's *Hello Down There* (1969), returned to Wakulla Springs as a second unit director on *Joe Panther* (1976) and directed John Agar in the way-out action-exploitation flick *Mr. No Legs* (1979). "*Mr. No Legs* was a fun show to work on," he told me. "We shot it in 16mm and they then blew it up to 35mm. The actors were great to work with. The movie was shot for $80,000. We ran out of money before it was finished so we just made the car chase longer. They still owe me 3000 bucks."

Decades after donning Gill Man garb and haunting Wakulla and Silver Springs, Ricou Browning now resides in retirement some 400 miles downstate in Southwest Ranches, on the eastern edge of the Everglades—where, in Creature Walks, the Gill Man had also retired. Browning is a true son of Florida, a lifelong resident of the state (courtesy Cortlandt "The Witch's Dungeon" Hull).

As of 2013, Browning is married for the second time (the first marriage ended in divorce) and the father of four; he has 11 grandkids (including one who passed away) and three great-grandkids. He lives a leather briefcase's throw away from Alligator Alley.

◆ Wakulla Springs, still hidden in thousands of acres of Spanish moss-draped Florida woodlands, is now protected by Florida law, and not because

Black Lagoon and *Creature Walks* were partly shot there ... but we can tell ourselves that might be part of the reason. The state purchased the area in October 1985 and it's now called the Edward Ball Wakulla Springs State Park. Gill Maniacs interested in visiting the spot Where It All Began can even stay at the Wakulla Springs Lodge, just as the moviemakers did in 1953 (*Black Lagoon*) and perhaps also in 1955 (*Creature Walks*). The lodge is on the National Register of Historic Places and is designated as a National Natural Landmark ... again, not cuzza the Creature but ... *maybe*. At Wakulla, according to the lodge's website, you'll be "surrounded by nature, including canopies of oak, hickory and beech trees, the natural spring and Florida wildlife." Like the unspoiled land around it, the lodge too is just as it was in the 1950s, and even the 1940s and '30s; the only changes have been for comfort and safety. There have never been televisions in the guest rooms. Riverboat and glass bottom boat tours, 365 days a year weather permitting, offer visitors a chance to see alligators, wading birds, manatees and other creatures acclimated to the boats' presence. Athletic Creature fans (if there *are* such things) can swim and snorkel in the spring.

Other Script-to-Screen Changes

- When Grant and the scientists arrive by dinghy at the fishing village, the script calls for the houses we see to be whitewashed and clean—all except Morteno's, which is run-down and dirty, presumably to show that Morteno has been unemployed and broke since his gory Creature encounter.
- In the final screenplay, the Creature is still in rough shape after the tracheotomy, so an adrenalin injection is prepared and the hypodermic needle handed to Morgan. Aware of the need for speed, Barton takes the hypo from Morgan, replacing the short needle with a very long one as he exclaims that there's "no time for arterial injection" and shoots its contents directly into the bandaged Creature's heart. On August 31, the third day of first unit production, this injection scene *was* shot, but then not used in the movie.
- Regarding the Gill Man's lungs: The stage was set for this plot development two movies earlier, in the *Black Lagoon* scene where Reed uses the *Rita* bunkroom as a darkroom. As the Gill Man is scientifically discussed for the first time ever, Kay reminds her colleagues of the existence of the Kamongo, an air-breathing fish from the Devonian age "which still exists today, right here in the Amazon." A *Creature Walks* scene in which one of the scientists mentions the Kamongo-Creature parallels (a fish with lungs, Devonian ancestry, Amazon stomping grounds) might have been kinda neat.
- In one early draft, Arthur Ross thusly describes the Creature face that the scientists see when they remove the bandages: "[It] is similar to the contours of the first Gill Man head in makeup dept. High cheek bones, almost bridgeless nose—a long, thin-lined mouth—deeper, almost breeding eyes. The skin is swarthy."

  This is the final screenplay's description of the Creature's new face:

  It is like a death mask. No longer scaled—but swarthy in texture. Eyes deep set, unblinking over a forehead without eyebrows.... High, tartar-like cheekbones. Sunken cheeks. A thin line of mouth almost lipless. A bridgeless nose. Here is a face, stony and fierce—but immobile. But a near-human face—not a creature. Here is skin—however swarthy in color—but smooth and clearly defined.

  Critiquing the *Creature Walks* laserdisc for *Films in Review*, Roy Frumkes wrote that the post-surgery Creature "bears more than a passing resemblance to Marlon Brando in *Apocalypse Now*."
- In the final screenplay's description of the action-filled finale, Barton has just dropped Grant's body to the ground in the stockade when the Creature assumes a half-crouched position, roaring. Barton fires his gun at him. The Creature, again roaring, lunges at him. Barton runs out, slamming the gate and throwing the bolt, but loses his balance, falls and drops his gun. As he rushes to the upper porch, he's still got "frame the Creature for murder" on his mind: When Morgan appears, Barton indicates the Gill Man and yells, "Shoot him! He killed Grant! Kill him!"

  The death of Barton changed from draft to draft:
- In one version of *The Creature of Man*, the Creature hides in the swimming pool and, when

- an unsuspecting Barton passes, pulls him in and kills him.
- In another version, the Creature wrecks the Barton house room by room as Barton hides on the roof. But the monster, hearing Barton's footsteps overhead, smashes his way through the beams and shingles and gets up onto the roof. Barton climbs down and leaps into the pool, thinking the Creature won't follow. He's wrong: The Creature walks unafraid into the water, kills Barton and lets the body float to the surface.
- Yet another draft has the Creature hearing Barton on the roof, pulling down a beam to create an aperture, and joining him on the housetop. The monster traps Barton, lifts him overhead and throws him to the ground below.
- *The Creature of Man* concluded with the work-shy lifeguard content to watch the Creature vanish into the sea. A July 1955 draft of the script is instead set at a wharf at sunrise, as two small children exit a house carrying toys. Confronted by the Creature, they gasp in surprise. The Creature, his arm bleeding from one of Barton's bullets, merely looks at them, and then peers out at the water. The children, too frightened to move, are puzzled by his human-but-not-quite look. The Creature walks to the end of the pier and then pauses, "rigid, silhouetted against the breaking day." The children finally run back into their house, and a moment later their young fisherman father comes out carrying a grappling hook. When he looks toward the pier, we (the audience) see what he sees: There's no one in sight. Next, in a down-angle shot *from* the pier, we see big, heavy ripples indicating that something has just pierced the surface of the water from above. "The camera holds on the surface as the ripples spread and fade and the water becomes almost still…."

The Music of *The Creature Walks Among Us*
By David Schecter

The Music Wafts Among Us

As with its two predecessors, the final film of the Gillogy also relied on a lot on music to weave its tale, with over 51 minutes of underscore in *The Creature Walks Among Us*. With 66 percent of the movie's running time containing music, that's an even higher percentage than the first Creature picture, which is surprising considering much less action takes place underwater in this sequel, where music filled a prominent role in the two earlier films. In the case of this series entry, the third time was the charm, because unlike *Creature from the Black Lagoon* and *Revenge of the Creature* which both re-used a lot of music written for earlier films, a whopping 90 percent of the music in *Creature Walks* was composed specifically for the picture. Only 7 of the film's 35 cues came from pre-existing sources, and in all but a single instance they derived from one of the earlier Gill Man movies.

More important than the amount of music in a film is the quality of it, and for *The Creature Walks Among Us*, the team of Henry Mancini, Irving Gertz and Heinz Roemheld, with minor assistance from Hans J. Salter, provided stellar background music as good as any science fiction score of the era. The movie offered Mancini a rare opportunity to compose a considerable amount of music for one film, and he came up with some of his best writing up to this point in his career. His 32 minutes of music includes 29 being specifically written for *Creature Walks*. As usual, the assemblage of composers meant that Joseph Gershenson's name was the only music credit in the picture. Gershenson conducted the score on January 20, 1956, in a 7½-hour session that added a tuba to the studio's usual orchestral make-up, an instrumental addition that also occurred in the first two Creature films and was used to provide more power to the brass. As was usual for Universal (and which occurred in all three Gill Man movies), there were more cellos (four) than violas (two), which added some extra muscle to the small string section.

Herman Stein, who was involved in so many of Universal's sci-fi–horror movies of the 1950s, got a short break from scoring a monster movie, with his only contributions to *Creature Walks* being a tracked excerpt from *Black Lagoon*'s "That Hand Again" and a shortened version of *Revenge*'s

3. The Creature Walks Among Us (1956)   287

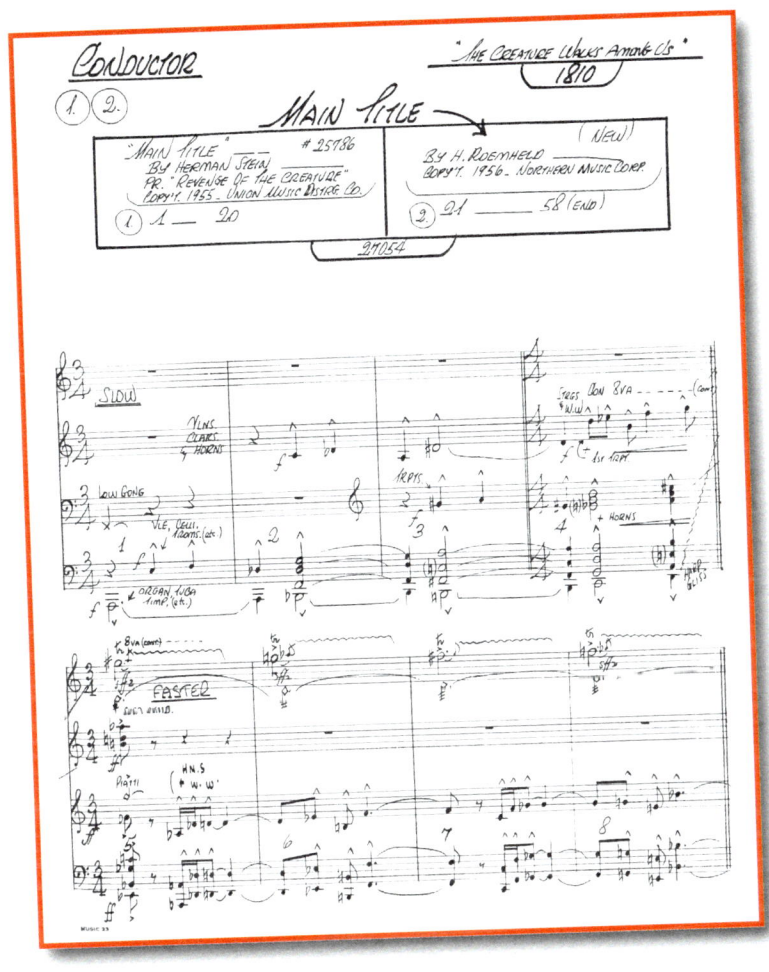

Conductor's score of "Main Title" from *The Creature Walks Among Us*, by Herman Stein and Heinz Roemheld (©1956 Gilead Music Co./USI A Music Publishing).

"Main Title." This abridged "Main Title" begins the second sequel, and it's a shame that a totally fresh opening musical statement wasn't offered, seeing as the film contained so much new underscore and offered a completely different take on the Creature's story. Universal apparently wanted everyone to know from the start that even though the Gill Man would be strolling around in clothes rather than swimming in his lagoon, this was still a Creature film. The movie's opening music was not the most brilliantly conceived in cinematic history. Not only was Stein's "Main Title" performed at what sounds like a rushed tempo, but as the credits end, a Roemheld cue (also named "Main Title") covers the rapid action when Marcia and Dr. Barton drive to the boat. This music offers an odd reprise of part of Stein's "Main Title" that already played 35 seconds earlier.

This was Roemheld's first of four 1950s monster movies, and his horror scoring pedigree went all the way back to the 1930s with *The Invisible Man* (1933), *The Black Cat* (1934) and *Dracula's Daughter* (1936). Heinz Eric Roemheld (pro- nounced **Rame** held) was born on May 1, 1901, in Milwaukee, Wisconsin. He started playing piano at age four, soloed on piano at the Majestic Vaudeville Theater House when he was 12, and graduated from the Wisconsin College of Music at 19. He went to Berlin to study music in 1921, and the following year he debuted as guest pianist with the Berlin Philharmonic Orchestra. In 1925, while performing on piano and conducting the orchestra for the silent *The Phantom of the Opera*, he was noticed by the head of Universal Pictures, Carl Laemmle, a member of the audience. Laemmle hired Roemheld to manage Universal's theaters in Washington, D.C., and later in Berlin.

When the rise of Nazism drove Roemheld back to the States, he joined Universal as a composer and music director; he later worked for Paramount and Warner Brothers, and then became a freelancer in the mid–1940s. He won the Academy Award for *Yankee Doodle Dandy* (1942), and in 1952 he wrote the standard "Ruby" for *Ruby Gentry*. He retired in 1964 to focus on classical compositions, frequently conducting them with the Milwaukee Symphony Orchestra. His concert works include piano preludes, sonatinas and string quartets. Roemheld composed, arranged or conducted music for more than 400 films, a few of which are *The White Hell of Pitz Palu* (1929), *All Quiet on the Western Front* (1930), *Sh! The Octopus* (1937), *You Can't Get Away with Murder* (1939), *Gentleman Jim* (1942), *Shine on Harvest Moon*, *Janie* (1944), *It Had to Be You* (1947), *The Lady from Shanghai*, *The Fuller Brush Man* (1948), *The Mole People* (1956), *The Land Unknown* and *The Monster That Challenged the World* (1957). He passed away on February 11, 1985.

Despite the large amount of music in *The Creature*

Heinz Roemheld (courtesy Heinz Roemheld family).

Walks Among Us, there's a total absence of underscore for over 5 minutes after the "Main Title," a prominent gap in a horror film of this type, especially when you're trying to build the proper atmosphere for the story. Salter only contributed one brief cue to the picture, the 1:25-long "The Small House," heard when the motorboat heads to the home of the injured Morteno. Serving primarily as travelogue music, it is undeniably well-written, but why Salter wasn't allowed to spend the day in bed rather than having to write this single cue is a mystery. Perhaps he had to be removed from some other picture at the same time so he wouldn't receive a screen credit on that assignment? "The Small House" got some extra mileage when it was tracked into Universal's 1958 short *Down the Magdalena*.

Only Mancini-composed music is heard between 8:50 and 31:41 of *Creature Walks*, and if you have enough free time to just close your eyes and focus on the 15:27 of music he contributed to this section, you'll understand what a major contribution he made to the movie. "Into the Deep, Part 1" begins delicately on vibraphone, harp, marimba and alto flute, with bass clarinet descending in anticipation of the divers going underwater. This dazzling composition features endless harp glissandi, vivid runs on flutes and oboe, and glittering celesta that provides beautiful aural accompaniment to the underwater sequence. When the movie occasionally cuts back to the boat's Fishscope set-up, vibraphone and clarinet paint a more anticipatory tone befitting the search for the Gill Man.

"Into the Deep, Part 1" also plays during a shark sequence near the beginning of William Castle's 1966 thriller *Let's Kill Uncle*. This movie also uses some of Stein's Creature theme during another shark scene near the end of the picture, although it's impossible to guess what cue it came from due to the excerpt's brevity. *Let's Kill Uncle* contains one of Universal's more bizarre scores, being entirely patched together from 84 tracked cues courtesy of Gertz, Lava, Mancini, Roemheld, Salter, Skinner, Stein, Stanley Wilson and even a bit of Hugo Friedhofer's music from *This Earth Is Mine* (1959).[54]

Mancini's "Into the Deep, Part 2" is very different in flavor from the first part of the cue, the composition beginning with the Creature theme as the Gill Man reaches out for the divers. Ominous piano and alternating pizzicato (plucked) and arco (bowed) strings provide the jagged rhythm while muted trumpets raise the danger level. Just before the divers decide to descend further, strings and clarinet play while French horns and trombones slowly but insistently augment the Creature's pursuit. Mancini's marvelous writing in this sequence would be adapted and re-used by the composer near the climax of *The Monolith Monsters*, heard when the dam is being prepared with dynamite.

"Stalking the Creature, Part 3" combines the tones of Mancini's two previous parts of the cue, starting when the Creature's image vanishes from the sonar screen. Quick woodwind phrases telegraph the possibility that something might be wrong, but Mancini deliberately misleads us about what's happening when upward and downward flute runs play amidst sweeping strings to augment Marcia's underwater ballet. After a repeat of some of the pursuit music used in the previous cue, Marcia swims in a dreamlike state thanks to Mancini's expressive string and harp writing. Exceedingly beautiful French horn and cello alerts us to the danger that Marcia is experiencing raptures of the deep. While she continues swimming in a trance, the orchestra builds in intensity as Morgan approaches her.

"Stalking the Creature, Part 4" should be familiar to those who own the 1959 Dick Jacobs album "Themes from Horror Movies" (reissued as "Themes from Classic Science Fiction, Fantasy and Horror Films"), although that lethargic version seems to be missing 90 percent of the strings, as well as many other important instruments that brought this superb cue to life in the picture. Despite these omissions, it comes across as one of the better renditions on that album, probably because it was a slow piece to begin with and it didn't require the full orchestra that the recording budget couldn't afford. In *Creature Walks*, the cue begins when Morgan drops his harpoon, Mancini providing downward notes to accentuate this action. As the doctor swims toward the surface carrying Marcia's motionless body, woodwind runs, with punctuations from harp and vibraphone, manage to create an ambiguous mood that perfectly fits the scene, not telegraphing whether or not she's still alive. When Marcia regains consciousness, clarinets and bassoon continue slowly, preventing the mood from becoming too joyous.

Creature Walks' lengthy underwater ballet offers a welcome variation on the swimming sequences in the two prior Gill Man movies. It not only presents a different take on a beautiful woman in aquatic danger, but it also offers something original from a musical standpoint instead of yet again dredging up Herman Stein's "Kay and the Monster" cues, most of which would have been totally inappropriate for this unique sequence. Although Mancini's *Creature Walks* cues include a few minor adaptations of some of Stein's Creature material, they are almost entirely in the character of Mancini's personal style. His Creature themes manage to offer more variability than what the composers were permitted to use in the first Gill Man picture, with Mancini's approach being more in keeping with the leeway William Lava had when he tackled the theme in *Revenge of the Creature*.

Mancini's "Poor Rich Wife," heard during a conversation between Morgan and Marcia, offers a glimpse at the lighter, jazz-based style many people associate with the composer, primarily because Mancini's many record album releases concentrated on this particular area of his prodigious output. His quiet, understated "Who's Stalking Who, Part 1" is heard when the *Vagabondia III* is in nighttime pursuit of the Creature. Mancini wisely stays away from the dialogue-heavy sections, instead using his music for dramatic punctuation during the non-talking sequences, with piano, harp and clarinet featured throughout. After the yacht reaches the end of the line and the scientists trail the Gill Man via dinghy, "Who's Stalking Who, Part 2" contains a quieter version of Mancini's pursuit theme, more suitable for this smaller marine vehicle. Mancini's *Creature Walks* music is replete with compositional devices and instrumental voicings he would use in future Universal films, as well as during his more renowned years when his name was among the most recognized in a movie's credits.

Born in Cleveland, Ohio, on April 16, 1924, and raised in West Aliquippa, Pennsylvania, Mancini studied at New York's Juilliard School of Music. After World War II, he

Henry Mancini backstage at the Hollywood Bowl, 1991 (courtesy Monstrous Movie Music).

was hired as a pianist-arranger for Tex Beneke's Glenn Miller Orchestra, and he studied in Hollywood with Ernst Krenek and Mario Castelnuovo Tedesco. Mancini wrote music for clubs and radio shows, including work for Bob Crosby, Buddy Rich and David Rose. In 1952 he was hired by Universal-International, and for the next seven years he wrote at least partial scores for over 100 of the studio's films, among them *The Golden Blade, Walking My Baby Back Home* (1953), *Border River, Creature from the Black Lagoon* (1954), *So This Is Paris* (1955), *Man Afraid, The Tattered Dress* (1957), *Touch of Evil, Damn Citizen, Flood Tide* (1958) and *The Great Impostor* (1961). Mancini then went on to compose a long line of classic film scores, including *Breakfast at Tiffany's* (1961), *Experiment in Terror, Hatari!* (1962) and *The Pink Panther* (1963), and he wrote for the popular television series *Newhart, Peter Gunn* and *Remington Steele*. Just a few of his famous songs are "Days of Wine and Roses," "Dear Heart" and "Moon River." Mancini won many Grammy Awards and Academy Awards, and released numerous popular records. He wrote a book on orchestration entitled *Sounds and Scores* and an autobiography, *Did They Mention the Music?*, in which he shares some of his memories of Universal. He was a much-loved member of the Hollywood community, and was often eager to help and give his time to others. He passed away on June 14, 1994, while still actively composing excellent film music and recording some of it for posterity.

Irving Gertz wrote just under 12 minutes of music for *The Creature Walks Among Us*, his first cue being "To Catch a Creature, Part 1." The piece segues directly from Mancini's previous piece, beginning when the lighted dinghy approaches. Strings, woodwinds and brass are colored by vibraphone and harp, with the music building and receding depending upon the dictates of the sequence. One almost forgets the trip starts out so uneventfully, as the wealth of ominous and atmospheric touches adds drama where almost none is occurring. Gertz uses a traveling motif throughout this cue to accentuate the journey, and he re-used parts of this composition in the following year's *The Monolith Monsters*. The passage is heard just under five minutes into that rocky horror picture, right before a dissolve to a long shot of the town of San Angelo. The same music is used again in *Monolith Monsters* when Dave (Grant Williams) drives to the Simpsons' destroyed house, and once more when Dave and Prof. Flanders (Trevor Bardette) drive up Old San Angelo Road during the day to investigate the meteorite site. This last cue, named "Meteor Secrets," contains a brassy variation of the three-note Creature theme that's heard when their car stops, this being a holdover from the music Gertz originally wrote for *Creature Walks*.

As one might surmise, Gertz's "To Catch a Creature, Part 2" in *Creature Walks* follows "To Catch a Creature, Part 1." It begins during a quick dissolve on the boat, building slowly until the Creature bursts from the water. One notable section occurs when the men realize that the Gill Man is coming right at them, with this particular material also being re-used by Gertz in *The Monolith Monsters*. It's heard during the mineral movie's "Prologue" when narrator Paul Frees describes the meteorite bombardment of the Earth by stating, "In every moment of every day they come…." The cue's origin explains why the Creature theme occurs three times as the meteorite explodes, although why the musical references to the Gill Man weren't deleted when the cue was rewritten for *Monolith Monsters* should probably be chalked up either to laziness or a rapidly approaching deadline.

Unfortunately, Gertz's outstanding "To Catch a Creature, Part 2" was butchered in *Creature Walks*, with the final 1:10 not being used in the movie. After the Creature ejects the men from the boat, near-silence greets this incredible event, resulting in the almost immediate and total dissipation of the suspense that was building during the entire sequence. This is especially notable when the men stand in the water and stare at the Gill Man, where the uncomfortable silence makes it almost seem like they're sharing a steam bath.

Freelancer Gertz had already done much work for Columbia and independent production companies before he was called upon by Joseph Gershenson whenever Gertz's unique talents were required at Universal. Born in Providence, Rhode Island, on May 19, 1915, he studied with Wassili Leps at the Providence College of Music, and upon arriving in California before World War II, he began work in Columbia's music department. After serving in the war in the U.S. Army Signal Corps, he began composing for films for Columbia, during which time he studied with both Mario Castelnuovo-Tedesco and Ernst Toch. Gertz served as composer and music director for many independent features during the 1940s and 1950s, with some of his work at Universal being for *Abbott and Costello Meet the Mummy, Cult of the Cobra, Smoke Signal, To Hell and Back* (1955), *Four Girls in Town, The Deadly Mantis, The Incredible Shrinking Man, Istanbul* (1957), *Wild Heritage* (1958), *Hell Bent for Leather* (1960), *Bullet for a Badman, He Rides Tall* (1964) and *Fluffy* (1965). In 1960 he was hired by 20th Century–Fox, where he worked as a composer and music director for over 12 years. A few of his other pictures include *Last of the Redmen* (1947), *Jungle Goddess* (1948), *The Bandits of Corsica* (1953), *Overland Pacific* (1954), *The First Traveling Saleslady* (1956), *Hell on Devil's Island* (1957), *The Alligator People* (1959) and *The Wizard of Baghdad* (1960), and some of his TV work was done for *Daniel Boone, The Invaders, Land of the Giants, Peyton Place* and *Voyage to the Bottom of the Sea*. After his film career ended, he concentrated on writing concert works. He was a sweet, gentle, funny and erudite man, and his contributions to the art of film scoring were exceptional. He passed away in Los Angeles on November 14, 2008, at the age of 93.

When "Marcia Noodles" on the piano aboard

Irving Gertz at home (courtesy Monstrous Movie Music).

In the movie, Morgan (Rex Reason) listens as Marcia (Leigh Snowden) idly strums a guitar. In the early treatment The Creature of Man, *these two put on a performance (he playing a hushed, muted Spanish guitar, she singing) for the benefit of the Creature, who turns toward them, watching and listening: "No movement but that—a quiet, almost stealthy movement. All the more oblique because the sadness of it is as much the loneliness of the woman singing it as the 'being' it is directed to."*

the *Vagabondia III*, she isn't really "noodling," she's making believe she's playing a solo piano composition that had been written by Mancini. And when she fiddles with her guitar later in the film, this is another Mancini piece entitled "Luring the Creature." It's hoped that these revelations don't dishearten Leigh Snowden fans into thinking that the lovely actress wasn't talented, because in real life she sang and played piano. She was also an excellent judge of musical talent, as she married Dick Contino the same year *The Creature Walks Among Us* was released. Contino was one of the most famous accordion players of his generation, as well as a singer, a session player on many film scores and an occasional actor, as in *Daddy-O* (1958) and *The Beat Generation* (1959).

The piano solo Marcia is supposedly playing was recorded in less than a half-hour after the regular January 20, 1956, recording session for the orchestra ended, with about $12 in extra pocket change going to Universal's contract pianist Lyman Gandee. Gandee was known as a practical joker when he worked in Kay Kyser's band, and he can be seen on piano in the 1940 musical-horror-comedy *You'll Find Out*. Marcia's guitar solo was recorded in a three-hour session on January 18, 1956, two days before the orchestra's recording session. The guitarist was Hilmer J. "Tiny" Timbrell, who received $48.21 for his work, which was part of the film's nearly $23,000 music budget. A Canadian-born musician who appeared as a band member in a number of late 1940s and early 1950s movies, Timbrell was a much-requested Hollywood musician, and in addition to doing a lot of film work, he played on recording sessions for Rosemary Clooney, Bing Crosby, Doris Day, Ricky Nelson and Marty Robbins. Some of his most-listened-to performances were his rhythm guitar accompaniment for Elvis Presley during the *Loving You* soundtrack sessions, and he also worked on other Elvis sessions, including the films *G. I. Blues* (1960), *Blue Hawaii* (1961), *Kid Galahad* (1962), *Viva Las Vegas* (1964) and *Easy Come, Easy Go* (1967).

Heinz Roemheld's second *Creature Walks* cue is "Mutation Accomplished." The composer wrote a total of 4:31 of music for the picture, spread over four pieces, with this cue beginning when the bandaged Creature breaks free of his operating table straps. Creepy Novachord, tremolo strings and low instruments carry the portentous composition until it ends with some energetic music that nicely augments shots of the boat moving through the water.

Mancini's moody and deliberate "The Thing Awakens" is an excellent piece heard when the Creature's bandages are removed, highlighted by low strings, subtle piano and woodwinds. The moment that the Gill Man's head is viewed, a spooky rendition of the Creature theme plays on Novachord, and glissandoing harp accentuates his altered appearance. Tinkling piano effects, harp, vibraphone and Novachord add to the eerie situation as the Creature surveys his onlookers in this memorable musical sequence.

An unexpected omission of music occurs during the scientists' drinking party following the operation. This was a prime opportunity for Universal to include a source music cue (published by Universal's Northern Music Corporation) in the background, but for some reason the scene was allowed to play without music. While such a use of music wouldn't have helped or hurt the sequence, it's still surprising that none was used.

In "Perfect Wife?" Mancini offers a style that is quite different from what's already been heard in the movie. It's more conventional, in line with the type of music he would provide for some of his later, glossier films, but it fits the mood of this scene very well. After an inebriated Dr. Barton tries to romance an unwilling Marcia, she wakes up to the

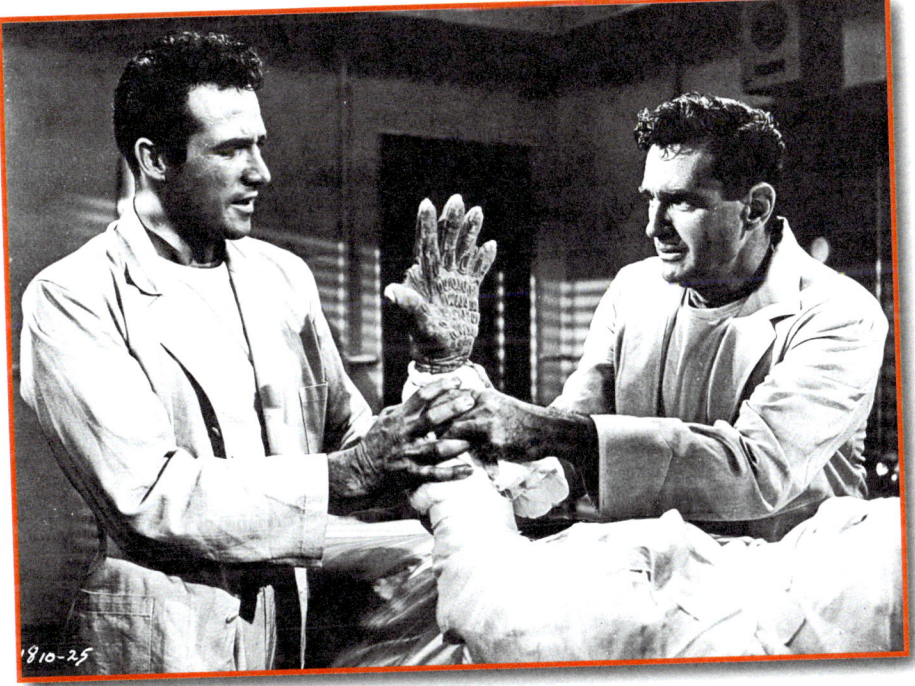

According to Creature Walks' *one-minute radio spot, the movie's scientists "dare the dangerous experiment that could create a new being ... even though it would make the Creature more fearsome with a human mind ... more powerful with human emotions!"*

strains of a lovely solo piano melody, which sex-crazed Jed Grant can obviously also hear, as he promptly seeks her out. Had somebody put lyrics to this beautiful piece of music, it might have been a hit, and as the melody was used a few times in *Creature Walks*, it's possible that someone was thinking along those lines at one time.[55]

After a fight between Marcia and Jed disturbs the Gill Man and he dives into the water, some short original Mancini compositions (all titled "Something Fishy") connect tracked *Black Lagoon* cues, including Stein's "That Hand Again," Salter's "The Monster Strikes Back" and Mancini's "Monster Gets Mark, Part 1" and "Monster Gets Mark, Part 2." The watery scenes are somewhat reminiscent of the visuals that the Creature music was originally written for in the first movie, which makes the tracked music somewhat palatable. Still, this intrusion of pre-existing music should have been avoided in what is otherwise a nearly perfect score.

As the Gill-less Gill Man is brought back to the surface, Mancini's "Hungry Leopard" from the Van Heflin–Ruth Roman adventure *Tanganyika* (1954) adds to the tracked proceedings. This is the only library cue in *Creature Walks* not to come from one of the earlier Creature movies, which is both odd and yet also perfectly in keeping with Universal's musical history. *Tanganyika* features an original score by Mancini, Salter, Stein and Lava, and it's a solid work, one that supplied a wealth of library cues to subsequent Universal motion pictures, most commonly Mancini's two-part "Hungry Leopard" and Stein's "Merrion Killed" and "Children Lost." In *Tanganyika*, "Children Lost" covers a scene where Andy, a young boy, swims above a herd of hippos. Stein's writing is vaguely reminiscent of some of the swimming sequence music he wrote for *Black Lagoon*, even though the hippos look nothing like the Gill Man and Andy looks even less like Julie Adams.

After the now-terrestrial Creature is introduced to his stockade prison in *Creature Walks*, there's a poignant moment when he looks out at the water, thanks to Mancini's low-key "Behind Bars" offering a musical effect on harp, vibraphone and Novachord that flawlessly captures the link between the Gill Man and his former liquid environment. This is a superb example of the power of underscore to relate information that can't be expressed otherwise, because without the music, viewers might have seen the Creature, then the water, but simply not made the connection.

The first part of Marcia's "Adventurous Dip" in the lake was composed by Mancini, with Roemheld supplying the last 20 seconds when the mountain lion arrives. Mancini's contribution begins as Morgan and Marcia wind up their talk about her husband, with alto flute carrying the memorable melody heard earlier in "Perfect Wife?" Solo clarinet lends a steamy undertone as Marcia dons her bathing suit behind a curtain, with English horn adding a sense of resignation as she walks out on her spouse. When she approaches the water, the love theme returns, this time on alto sax, with the light-jazz approach adding to the sexual tension between Marcia, Jed and possibly the Creature. This cue was also used in *Outside the Law* along with "Perfect Wife?" Because the two pieces shared the same melody, they worked

Conductor's score of Henry Mancini's "Hungry Leopard" from *Tanganyika* (© 1954 Northridge Music Co., courtesy Henry Mancini Estate).

3. The Creature Walks Among Us (1956)

At the Barton Ranch, "Creech" (Don Megowan) is caged by his captors (Rex Reason, James Rawley, Maurice Manson, Jeff Morrow, extras playing ranch hands). Films in Review's Roy Frumkes, covering the movie's laserdisc release, wrote that it was "moving and sincere, with some astonishing pantomime coming from under all that latex. And the third act is beautifully staged and impressively primal. It just might be a little horror noir gem."

as well together in the crime picture as they did in *Creature Walks Among Us*.

Roemheld's addendum to "Adventurous Dip," as well as his "The End of the Lion," are of a completely different nature than Mancini's contribution, befitting the vicious feline intruder. The music features flutter-tongued brass and flute, along with harp and drum rolls to describe the brutal action, the flute adding a welcome instrumental touch to the tried-and-true fluttering brass that so often depicts such monstrous movie moments.

Irving Gertz handles the *Creature Walks* climax, with "Murder by Night" covering the scene leading up to Barton killing Jed. The cue was written in typical Gertz style, with the music moving in one direction, then another, quickly changing moods from light to dark and back again. Woodwinds predominate, as they do in many of the composer's

During Arthur Ross' stint as scripter for Creature from the Black Lagoon, he had the Gill Man fight and mangle a jaguar. The scene never made it to the screen, but Ross resuscitated the idea in Creature Walks with the one-sided Creature vs. mountain lion match.

works, with strings and muted brass adding significant touches throughout. As somebody once told the composer, "It's impossible to hum your music." That might be true, but humming isn't a prerequisite for great dramatic underscore, and Gertz was brilliant at writing such music.

When the Gill Man witnesses the murder in "The Avenging Creature," the older Creature theme plays a larger role, with the music building steadily until the clawed prisoner breaks from his cage. After the Gill Man escapes, the soundtrack goes from frenzied onslaught to total silence when the Creature enters the house, but not because Gertz couldn't think of anything to write, or because he lost his pencil, or because the musicians took a cigarette break in the middle of the recording session. On the contrary, Gertz wrote some powerful action music for this sequence, but over 30 measures were not used in the film's soundtrack until the Creature catches up with Barton and throws him to his death, where it sounds suspiciously like somebody turned up the volume on their stereo. The cue ends on the quiet side except for a brief orchestral outburst as the Creature fends off an armed ranch hand before knocking down the electrified fence post and escaping. It's a shame that some of Gertz's best work was removed from the picture, because the silence during these emasculated scenes is indeed deafening. And why this happened to Gertz's contributions but not to any of the other composers' music is puzzling.

You can hear some of "The Avenging Creature" in the opening of *The Midnight Story* (1957). That Tony Curtis crime movie's score is under 27 minutes long, and it features 16 original Salter cues, as well as one by Skinner near the picture's end, which might have been included to prevent Salter from receiving a composer's credit. The film also contains a few old compositions by Mancini and Stein, as well as a most unusual opening. The movie begins with an original "Main Title" fanfare by Salter, followed by Gertz's "The Avenging Creature," then there's another short Salter piece called "Main Title" that leads to a re-use of Stein's "Main Title" from *The Glass Web*. Whoever pieced together this score certainly took a bewildering approach, including using part of Stein's "Main Title" from *Backlash* (1956) a few minutes later in the body of the film. Maybe somebody held a contest to see how many snippets of "Main Title" cues could be crammed into the opening of one motion picture.

Gertz's *Creature Walks* "End Title" begins when the surviving scientists discuss the outcome of their experiment. The composition is a mostly subdued piece designed to quietly underscore the dialogue-laden wrap-up. The bittersweet music hints that there might be romance ahead for Marcia and Morgan, but not right now given the recent tragic events. A dissolve to the shore leads to a powerful rendition of the Creature theme as the Gill Man looks out at the crashing waves. A strong orchestral surge with prominent harp and Novachord follows, and Gertz uses dissonances and instrumental clashes to musically symbolize the dilemma the land-living Creature is now facing with the ocean before him. As the film doesn't have a clear-cut resolution, Gertz cleverly chose musical devices to emphasize the same conclusion.

Mancini's "End Cast" offers a full orchestral variation of the piano piece heard in "Perfect Wife?" which might have been one last attempt to see if the tune might have "song" potential. And even though it unfortunately didn't, the cue effectively closes the musical door on this (so far) final chapter in the Creature's cinematic history. Not to mention it was a much better choice than re-using Stein's "End Cast" from *The Redhead from Wyoming* one final time.

Analysis
By Steve Kronenberg

The Creature Walks Among Us: Even the film's first-person title is provocative. One year before Herman Cohen and AIP cooked up *I Was a Teenage Werewolf* (1957), the Creature walked among "us": We—the audience and fans—are included in the horror. And "horror" is the operative word here. Though *The Creature Walks Among Us* is not in the same league as the 1954 original, it is a far better sequel than *Revenge of the Creature*. And if *Creature from the Black Lagoon* resembled a high adventure film, and *Revenge* was merely another monster-on-the-loose fest, *Creature Walks* is, of the three, the closest to a pure horror film. Its Gothic roots are reinforced by Jeff Morrow's evil scientist and the Creature's own Frankensteinian transformation. In addition, *Creature Walks* may be the first of Universal's 1950s horrors to portray its monster as an existential anti-hero—despite fans' assertions that 1957's *The Incredible Shrinking Man* was the first existentially themed genre piece.

Among *Creature Walks*' many assets is its solid cast, a group of players far superior in every way to *Revenge*'s stock performers and dull characters. The cast of *Creature Walks* is led by Jeff Morrow as the obsessed Dr. William Barton. Morrow initially portrays Barton as a serious albeit zealous professional, and his expressive, eager eyes superbly convey his enthusiasm for his Creature "capture and conversion" project. Throughout most of the film, Morrow is subdued, yet betrays just enough fervor beneath the surface to convince us that his Barton is no rational academic. When Capt. Stanley (David McMahon) tells Morrow the crew is ready to set sail after the Creature, Morrow's sly and sinister smile belies his anxiety and eagerness: "All right, captain. Get underway!" (Remember that Morrow honed that zealous quality playing another obsessed scientist in *This Island Earth*.)

Morrow's occasional, wild-eyed obsession in transforming the Creature makes a fine contrast to Rex Reason's stolid, compassionate academic—the educated, rational scholar who wants to study, not tamper with, the Gill Man: "We can learn from nature, help nature ... but we can't bypass nature!" This tension is obviously reminiscent of the clash between Reed and Williams in the original. Yet, Morrow modulates his zeal with a quiet determination. Throughout much of the film, he adopts a determined, almost granite facial expression which exemplifies his quiet obsession with the Creature. Note how intently Barton stares at the Fishscope as Morgan, Marcia and Grant descend in their scuba gear to explore the Creature's environs. And as the reckless Marcia is rescued by Morgan, Barton's face becomes a mask of subtle anger. In addition, Morrow is quite convincing in his subdued, jealousy-fueled threats to his on-screen wife. (Eventually, Morrow's jealous rages over Leigh Snowden dilute the power of his otherwise excellent performance.)

But Morrow is most delightful when his Dr. Barton resembles the obsessed mad doctors of Gothic horror. Note his wild-eyed delight as he discusses the Creature's transformation: "We *are* changing a sea creature into a land creature!" Morrow's Barton is no less passionate—and no less egocentric—than Henry Frankenstein, Henry Jekyll or Dr. Moreau. In fact, his desire to tamper with the creature's natural anatomy seems lifted directly from 1933's *Island of Lost Souls*! Yet, Morrow's Barton is also capable of pathos and insecurity. He drunkenly complains to Marcia: "The jungle or the stars. Can't they see I want to *catch* a star?" In this scene, the vulnerable and self-doubting Barton resembles yet another Golden Age mad doctor: Boris Karloff's Janos Rukh in *The Invisible Ray* (1936).

Morrow's modulated, believable, and textured performance as a subtly mad doctor highlights *Creature Walks Among Us* and augments its status as a real horror film. And Morrow does an excellent job of showing us Barton's many sides: cruelty, jealousy, insecurity, scientific obsession. He also serves as the contrasting force to Rex Reason's conscience-stricken Dr. Tom Morgan, thereby making the Creature's pathos an essential theme of the film.

Reason also delivers a surprisingly versatile performance as the leading man–hero, Dr. Morgan. He has the deep, masculine voice and commanding demeanor of most 1950s male leads, but he is more relaxed and natural than John Agar was in *Revenge*. His polite, affable interactions with the beautiful Leigh Snowden do not seem forced or flirtatious, as Agar's did with Lori Nelson. He also displays a surprisingly tender and sensitive side with Snowden, who is routinely victimized by Morrow's cruelty and jealous streak.

Reason also does a fine job portraying the film's scientific conscience, as did Richard Carlson in *Creature from the Black Lagoon*. His character is bent on capturing the Gill Man alive and unharmed—unlike Barton, who is determined to experiment on the Creature. In one scene, Morgan tells Gregg Palmer's cruel, smarmy Jed Grant: "Remember, the object is to capture him, not kill him. As much as you're tempted, try not to hit a vital area." Reason convincingly utters these lines, treating Palmer's Grant with appropriate condescension. Later, when the transformed Creature dives into the ocean with his burned gills, Morgan becomes distraught: "He'll die in the water! He'll use his lungs and he'll drown!" Morgan's fear for the Creature's life is downright touching—and he proves himself a versatile and believably sturdy hero by diving in and rescuing the hapless Gill Man.

Simultaneously, Reason conveys due respect for the Creature's right to live as one of nature's biological wonders. After the Gill Man is burned and rescued, he marvels at the fact that the Creature has lungs beneath his burned tissue—conveying the fixed, wide-eyed wonder of a Henry Frankenstein! Later in the film, his affinity, even *affection* for the Creature continues to develop. As the Gill Man lies on an operating table, we see Morgan quietly put his hand on this monster as he tells Barton: "He remembers fear. When he's afraid, he'll attack anything animal or human." In fact, it is Reason's Dr. Morgan who gives the audience a summation of the Creature's psyche—something which was barely explored in the original film and never even touched on in *Revenge*: He explains that the Creature lives in "terrible fear" because he views all men as his enemies. At the film's end, after the Creature has killed off Barton, Morgan with sympathy and sensitivity conveys an understanding of the Creature's persona: "The Creature moved a step forward. He didn't attack until he was attacked. He killed the real enemy." Rarely, if ever, has any 1950s horror film gone to such lengths to analyze the monster portrayed on screen—or to convey the notion that our real monsters often wear human faces. Far from the stock 1950s hero portrayed by John Agar in *Revenge*, Reason, like Richard Carlson, delivers a multi-faceted, sensitive performance that reaches beneath the veneer of good looks and deep voice.

Likewise, the beautiful Leigh Snowden delivers an interesting, layered performance as Marcia. Initially, Snowden seems to assume a femme fatale demeanor: Her provocative curves are on full display in a tight bathing suit, accompanied by an independent, fiery attitude that contrasts sharply with both Julie Adams in the original and (especially) Lori Nelson in *Revenge*. When the sleazy, amorous Grant asks Marcia, "Is that all you do is talk?" Marcia quickly pushes him away and retorts: "No, I like to *swim* too!"

As the film progresses, we see Snowden's Marcia as affable, dignified and tender, the victim of her obsessed and selfish husband. Snowden's natural ability to project warmth is especially conveyed in her scenes with Reason, who returns Snowden's sensitivity in kind. They do have chemistry and their scenes are far less trite and forced than those between Agar and Nelson in *Revenge*. And Snowden's Marcia, like Reason's Morgan, even projects sympathy for the Creature. As Marcia longingly eyes the ocean, she tell Morgan, "I can understand why the Creature never wanted to leave the water." The romantic "rectangle" between Barton, Morgan, Marcia and Grant may be filler, but the conflict is much better written and acted than it is in *Revenge*.

Creature Walks Among Us is most interesting in its approach to the Creature himself. This monster who, in prior films, was alternately graceful, lovesick and pathetic, here undergoes a startling transformation that defines not only the film, but the Gill Man character itself. Ricou Browning's sea-based Creature is only briefly seen. To be sure, Browning's Creature displays all the grace and style of his previous Gill Man incarnations. And in one poignant scene, there's a feeling of pathos as the burned Creature (Chuck Roberson) tries to lift a fallen tree and helplessly collapses.

Yet, it's Don Megowan as the hulking, surgically transformed Creature who carries the day in *Creature Walks Among Us*. Fans and writers have routinely and unfairly dismissed Megowan's Creature as an ugly, hulking brute—almost a perversion of Browning's stylish and lithe sea monster. But beneath the Creature mask and costume, Megowan uses his eyes and body language to deliver a surprisingly wide range of emotions.

Our first view of Megowan's transformed Creature (when his head bandages are removed) is one of the film's most memorable moments. The facial scales, burned away by fire, are replaced by a smoother, semi-human flesh that results in an even uglier, more monstrous appearance—perhaps because he looks so strikingly different from Browning's leaner, fish-like visage. But it is when the Creature opens his eyes and gazes malevolently at Barton and Morgan that we realize the menace inherent in this newly awakened Gill Man. Megowan's eyes alone tell us that the Creature is decidedly unhappy as an air-breathing "land Creature." When the Creature is moved to a stockade inhabited by sheep and goats, we note Megowan's eyes and tilt of his head as he curiously regards his new, docile neighbors. Megowan is seen walking the cage, examining his new environment with wonder and curiosity. And note how longingly Megowan gazes at the ocean through the fencing that separates him from his natural home. Megowan's genuine ability to convey hurt and pathos with his eyes makes his Creature even more pathetic than the previous portrayals by Browning, Ben Chapman and Tom Hennesy.

Yet, Megowan just as easily shifts from pathos to anger. Note the rage conveyed by

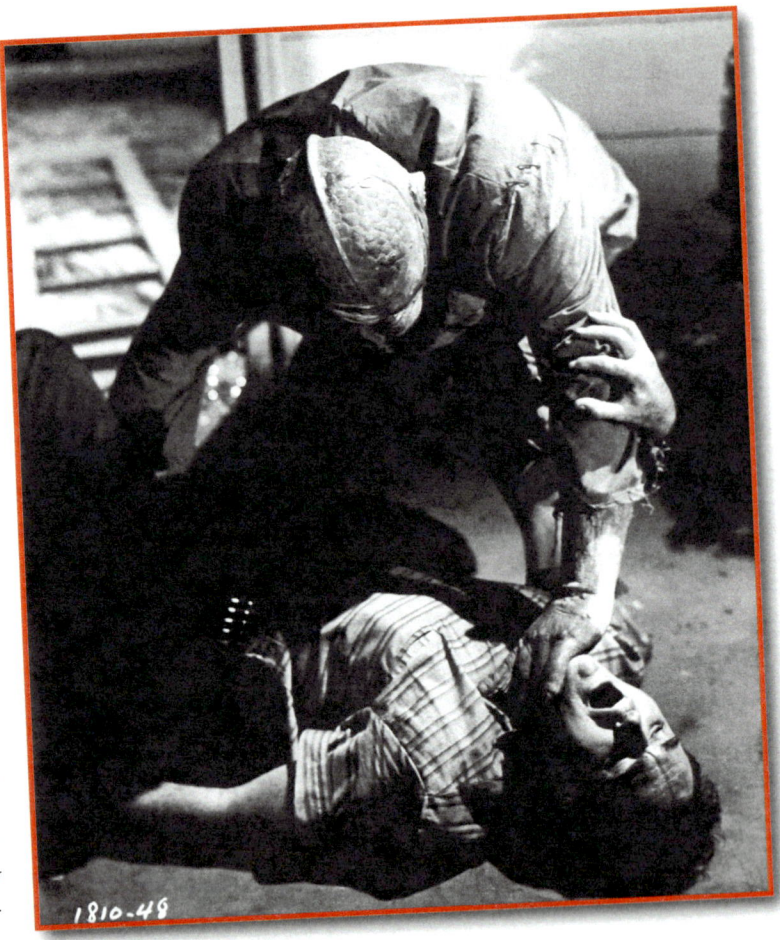

According to Hollywood columnist Erskine Johnson: "After a fight scene with the undersea monster in The Creature Walks Among Us, *Jeff Morrow wailed, 'Why can't I be in a picture titled* Marilyn Monroe Walks Among Us?'" *Pictured: Don Megowan (as the Creature) and Morrow.*

his eyes, face and body as he spies the mountain lion clawing one of the sheep that share his cage. Indeed, Megowan displays disarming fury as he viciously kills the big cat. And Megowan effectively blends anger with confusion as he witnesses Barton's murder of Grant—before his Creature goes on his own rampage and destroys Barton himself.

It is pointless to compare Boris Karloff's performance as the Frankenstein Monster with Don Megowan's Creature. Yet, Megowan's ability to convey pathos, menace, anger and childlike curiosity is wholly reminiscent of Karloff's Monster. (As mentioned above, Megowan actually played the Monster opposite Anton Diffring's Baron Frankenstein in *Tales of Frankenstein*.) Megowan's performance is the "heart and soul" of *Creature Walks Among Us* and is perhaps the one 1950s monster portrayal that truly echoes the work of a Golden Age icon. His unfairly maligned Creature is most worthy of tribute.

The solid *Creature Walks* cast is ably abetted by the film's technicians, particularly underwater d.p. "Scotty" Welbourne. He treats us to some atmospheric and murky underwater photography in the initial scenes of Browning's aquatic Gill Man. We also get a fine overhead view of Marcia performing an abridged water ballet through a cloud of bubbles. Welbourne then delivers a dark, moody long shot of Marcia, Morgan and Grant swimming through the depths with Browning's Creature gliding parallel to them. Welbourne creates a spooky, chilling tableau as he blends the darkness of the water with the rock and algae beneath the surface of the river.

Maury Gertsman's land-based camerawork, especially his penchant for closeups of the Creature, is equally effective. He delivers an evocative medium shot of Megowan's Gill Man swathed in bandages from top to bottom, again reminiscent of Karloff's Monster. And before the bandages are removed, we get a genuinely eerie shot of the Creature's inhuman, uncomprehending eyes through the bandages. This closeup emphasizes the unsettling contrast between the pure white gauze of the bandages and the Creature's burned, scaly skin. Then there are two equally disarming shots: one of the Creature's burned hand and then an even more startling view of the bandaged head with only the eyes and mouth showing. It is a bizarre, unsettling scene—perhaps because we are unaccus-

As Dennis Saleh points out in *Science Fiction Gold*, the Gill Man has been "merchandised like a celebrity screen idol: on posters, paperbacks, pencil erasers, figurines, lunch boxes, belt buckles, bars of soap, and best of all, beach towels." This cool conglomeration is a small part of the collection of David J. Schow.

tomed to seeing our favorite 1950s monster bandaged and strapped to an operating table! During the shipboard scene in which Megowan's Creature runs amok, Gertsman delivers a memorably subtle shot: The camera focuses on a door latch slowly twisting and turning—then an ominous shot of the Creature's smooth, misshapen, webbed hand reaching out to pull open the door.

Throughout the film, Gertsman ably blends darkness and light, exemplified by the scene in which Megowan's Creature walks out of the pitch-black back of a moving truck into daylight. And watch for the Welbourne-photographed scene in which Morgan dives into the water to save the Creature from drowning. He shows the Creature and his rescuer in a series of long shots, blending the dark water with shafts of light, just as he did in the 1954 original.

No scene better captures the existential angst of *Creature Walks* than the final shot of Megowan's Creature preparing for his lonely and lethal walk into the ocean. Gertsman focuses on Megowan's glistening, distorted face as he longingly gazes into the waters that beckon him. No matter that the ocean is obviously back-projected: Gertsman beautifully captures the poignancy and pathos of the Creature's last gasp at freedom, and his final passage into the water. The solitude of Megowan's Creature is permanently etched by this memorable shot. It is almost as if both previous Creature films were preludes to this scene—a final rite of passage from water to land, to water again. In *Creature Walks*, Gertsman's camera is an essential tool in capturing and appreciating the Creature's Frankensteinian persona.

Creature Walks also benefits from the kind of tight, fast pacing that graced the 1954 original—a function of John Sherwood's direction and Arthur Ross's script. In fact, *Creature Walks* opens with Morgan and Marcia racing to his laboratory-equipped yacht. Sherwood and Ross also allow for a well-timed prelude to the Creature's first appearance, as Barton and Morgan discuss the Gill Man's biology and the means to change him into an air-breathing animal. Sherwood's sense of pacing is fully realized in the Creature's first attack scene. The Gill Man silently stalks Barton's yacht by night as we anxiously await the assault to come. When it does come, Barton, Morgan, Grant *et al.* are in a dinghy and the Creature suddenly arises from the water, jumps up on the boat and is set afire by Grant. Sherwood superbly sets up the attack. Sherwood proves equally adept at staging and directing the closing action scenes with the Creature loose in the Barton home. This time it's the Creature hunting for Barton; his orgy of destruction through the house is not accompanied by music, so we hear only the Gill Man's heavy breathing and bellowing, and Marcia's screams.

Sherwood and Ross also contribute to the superb final scene, with Megowan's weary Creature eyeing the ocean and walking towards certain death. It is Ross' script that posits the idea of the Creature finally returning home, in peace, rather than dying in a hail of bullets. No Universal monster ever received such a fitting and poignant end.

The Creature Walks Among Us is marked by its believable script and performances, its Golden Age echoes of mad science, and its focus on the Creature's psychological—as well as biological—makeup. The film is not only a superior sequel, but one of Universal's best horror offerings of the 1950s.

The three-movie adventure that began at a riverside geological camp on the Amazon in Northern Brazil, ends on an ocean-view Marin County, California, hillside: The Creature (Don Megowan) is about to stagger to his doom in the closing moments of *The Creature Walks Among Us*.

PART TWO

THE OFFICIAL GILL MAN GUIDE TO THE SUNSHINE STATE

By Tom Weaver

Be the envy of ... well, surely no one of any consequence .... by being the first to go on a Creature excursion, hitting all the Florida spots where the three movies were filmed:

1. Wakulla Springs in what is now Edward Ball Wakulla Springs State Park. Shot there for *Creature from the Black Lagoon*: the underwater parts of the scene of Dr. Reed coming up from the bottom of Morajo Bay; the underwater parts of the Black Lagoon scenes; and topside river and jungle footage. Shot underwater there for *The Creature Walks Among Us*: the scene of the three divers and the Gill Man, plus the scene of Morgan rescuing the burned Creature after his escape from Barton's yacht.
2. Jacksonville, site of the Lobster House restaurant on the edge of the St. Johns River (marked) seen in *Revenge*. Also shot on the St. Johns River: topside parts of the scene of Clete and Helen aboard the *Porpoise III* and going for their swim.
3. Rice Creek in Palatka, where the topside exterior parts of *Revenge*'s Black Lagoon scenes were shot.
4. Marineland, home of Marine Studios (now Marineland of Florida) where *Revenge*'s Ocean Harbor scenes were filmed, plus the scene of the Gill Man walking into the Atlantic Ocean (also marked).
5. Silver Springs in Ocala, where the underwater parts of *Revenge*'s Black Lagoon section were photographed; also, the underwater half of the Florida-set scene where the Gill Man follows Clete and Helen during their *Porpoise III* cruise and swim.
6. (Fort Myers) and 7. (La Belle): On the Caloosahatchee River between these two cities, most of *Creature Walks*' topside footage of Dr. Barton's yacht was shot. Also seen in the movie are Fort Myers' Edison Bridge and Fort Myers Yacht Basin. It's safe to assume that when we see the yacht against a sea horizon, the yacht is in the Gulf of Mexico (marked). In a Caloosahatchee inlet, footage of the Creature hunters in their dinghy was shot.

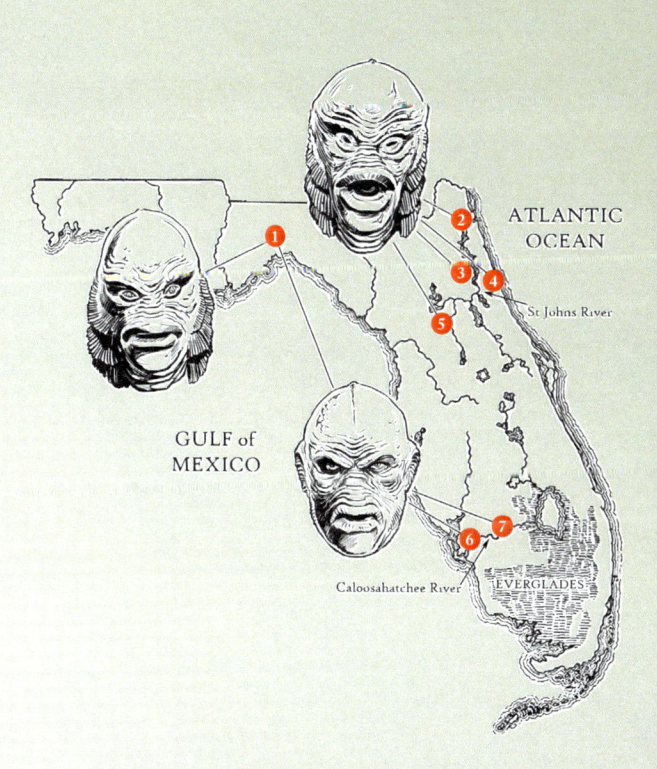

Map by Mary Runser and Kerry Gammill

AQUATIC KITH AND KIN 5

By Tom Weaver

Many writers have attempted to compile complete lists of the large- and small-screen rip-offs of the story of *Creature from the Black Lagoon* and/or the look of the Gill Man. They never make for very compelling reading, so what follows is highly selective—just four titles. My criterion: movies that would not have been made if there hadn't been a Creature series.

The Return of the Creature
(A Galaxy Interglobal Production, 1954)

CREDITS: Co-Directed by M. [Mike] Gannon, C. [Clayton] Powers; Stunts: Jody Graber; **Uncredited**: Screenplay: Mike Gannon; Photography: Mike Gannon; 21 minutes.

CAST: Ed Doyle (*The Creature*), Clayton Powers (*Dr. Clete Ferguson*), Pat Powers (*Helen Dobson*), John Gonzales (*Hernando*), Mike Gannon (*Dr. Dobson*); **Uncredited:** W.F. Rolleston (*Sam Backlash*), Carl Selph (*Dr. Fortescue*).

If you've never heard of *The Return of the Creature*, don't worry, you're in excellent company (nearly the entire population of the Earth, 7.1 billion and growing by the minute). The first time *I* heard of it was in the 1990s when I was at USC's Cinema-Television Library, going through original Universal press releases for *Revenge of the Creature*. There amidst the musty mounds of paperwork was a one-page 1954 item devoted to *Return*, probably written by *Revenge*'s publicist Robert Sill, who had accompanied the Universal troupe to Florida. In this press release (read it below), the writer refers to *Revenge of the Creature* as *The Return of the Creature* because the latter *was* the title of the second Gill Man movie throughout production:

Cast and crew of Universal-International's *The Return of the Creature* attended the world premiere of a new motion picture at Marineland, Fla.

The premiere was a pretty informal affair, the picture being projected on a screen put up in a big, dank room underneath the bleacher seats along the porpoise tank at the Marineland oceanarium. Aside from the early comers, who found a few work benches on which to sit, it was a standing room only occasion.

By what was more than a coincidence, the title of the picture that was premiered was also *The Return of the Creature*, but U-I will not sue for infringement, inasmuch as the production was a non-profit venture that will never be seen in any theatre. That's for sure, because no theatres show 8mm film.

Made strictly as a gag, the picture is a satirical version of the U-I production, written, produced, photographed and acted by the four announcers at the oceanarium, with some help in the acting department from other oceanarium personnel. In fact, two of the victims of the Creature in this version were W.F. Rolleston, vice-president and general manager of Marine Studios, Inc., which owns and operates the oceanarium, and his assistant, Carl Selph.

This version differs radically from the U-I picture, and from any other horror film ever filmed in Hollywood, in that the Creature gets the girl, and she goes with [him] willingly. And, instead of being kept in the big tank at the oceanarium, this Creature makes his home in the bathtub at the home of one of the characters.

Chiefly involved in the production were the four announcers, Clayton Powers, Ed Doyle, Mike Gannon and John Gonzales. The girl was played by Mrs. Powers. The picture was finished and screened on the last day of the U-I troupe's stay at Marineland.

Publicists being what they are, I wasn't sure at the time if any such 8mm spoof ever really existed, but it sure didn't sound like a story that anybody would bother to make up. Years later, I found proof that the press release was legit: Jere Beery, Jr., brother of the spoof's late star Pat Powers, created a website and on it he included his memories of seeing *The Return of the Creature*. Several of the things Beery wrote about it eventually turned out to be incorrect, but that's perfectly understandable as he hadn't seen it since he was a kid, a half-century earlier. The fact that he, the brother of the star, didn't have a copy or any idea how to find one made me aware that the chances of *my* unearthing one in the 2000s were slim to none. But the fact of this Creature curio's existence remained lodged in the back of my brain and, while doing *Revenge of the Creature* interviews for this book, I tried to remember to mention it to everyone who might possibly have seen it. For a while it was an exercise in frustration because every interviewee who *had* seen it (including Ricou Browning) made some variation on this comment: "Yes I saw it, and I'd love to see it again. It was *so* funny!"

Monster movie fans of my acquaintance occasionally scratch their heads and/or rib me about my willingness to go beyond the stars, writers, producers and directors of genre movies and talk to (say) stuntmen, extras, production assistants, casting people, etc.; but when I'm trying to document the making of a movie, I'll take my anecdotes where I can find 'em. And sure enough, talking to Floridians who had worked as extras in *Revenge of the Creature* yielded a lot of fun information. What some of my colleagues don't know is that when you ask a guy who worked on 200 shows to talk about *one* of them, he's maybe good for five minutes of chatter before the Memory Well runs dry; but if you ask a person who in his or her entire life was involved on only *one* movie, that person will remember *everything* and talk all day. A couple of *Revenge*'s Floridian extras had more and better stories than its stars and producer had given me, which made me want to try and locate more of them. One day I found myself chatting on the phone with a former Marine Studios employee named David Redman who had seen the spoof *The Return of the Creature* many times back in the day. And it was Redman who gave me the leads that eventually helped me to find the man who made the movie (and, hallelujah, still had a copy): one of the Marine Studios announcers mentioned in the press release above, Mike Gannon.

Gannon was 27 years old in the summer of 1954 when Universal came to Florida to make *Revenge of the Creature*. He told me,

> My summer job in college was that of announcer-slash-guide at Marine Studios, as Marineland was known in those days. "The world's first and only oceanarium"—that's the way we advertised it. This was my fourth summer working there, which was a perfect job for me. My home

Announcer-guides Mike Gannon (left) and Ed Doyle in their Marine Studios uniforms in 1954. Doyle played the Gill Man in Gannon's *The Return of the Creature*.

5. Aquatic Kith and Kin (*The Return of the Creature*)

was in St. Augustine, less than 20 miles away. It was nice outdoor work and very pleasant and a chance to meet people from all over the country.

That summer of '54, I remember being told, along with the other two guide-announcers Ed Doyle and Clayton Powers, that we were going to have visitors from Hollywood, that a crew was coming in to make a motion picture [*Revenge*]. Then this very large crew arrived, and while it didn't take over the place, its presence was certainly obvious for about three and a half weeks. At first they were in the exhibition area, around the two huge tanks, one of which contained porpoises, the other of which contained other marine specimens such as sharks and barracudas and sawfish and so on. We were told to pay them no attention, to go about our business as usual. We did of course, out of human interest, follow the filming as best we could. Ed, Clayton and myself, being in the entertainment business ourselves in a way, watched as much as we could, between our own duties, and got to know some of the film people fairly well, on a first-name basis. Everybody was very polite and we got along famously.

At a point when I think they were six days away from completing their work at Marine Studios, Ed, Clayton and I were invited to come to the wrap party they'd be having on their last day there. That evening, I got a wild idea that it would be fun to film our own picture under the same title, a satire of their film, and show it at the wrap party. Overnight I wrote a script, and then we started assigning duties.

The opening shot of Gannon's movie parodies the name Universal-International: A canvas chair, like the ones used by movie directors, has A GALAXY-INTERGLOBAL PRODUCTION written on the back rest. On the soundtrack is theremin music, *à la It Came from Outer Space* (1953). Now, in a pre-credits sequence set in a lab, we see a white-coated doctor (Gannon with glasses and made-up to look older) who rises and greets us with "Hello, I'm Dr. Dobson"—Dobson being the surname of Lori Nelson's *Revenge* character. "You are the people who wanted to hear about the Creature.... You can understand, I think, why I hesitate to talk about all this. It isn't very pleasant. I lost a lot of good friends. I lost my own daughter." He holds up a fossilized finger joint which he says was discovered in a coquina rock formation along a nearby lagoon:

> [We determined] that this joint had been lost several hundred million years ago ... or, to be more precise, two times ten to the eight years ago ... by a Gill Man, a prehistoric monster, which was still living. But what you want to hear is the story of what happened when the Creature came back ... incredible! But I'll tell you what I know. It all began in the lagoon outside our laboratory. That is where we first learned of ... the return of the Creature!

Mussorgsky's "Night on Bald Mountain" begins playing and we see a title card on which THE RETURN OF THE CREATURE is written. When water trickles down the card, the painted letters start running. On sheets of paper lying on what looks like a desktop, the cast members' names are written in stenciled letters: Ed Doyle as the Creature, Clayton Powers, Pat Powers, John Gonzales, Mike Gannon "AND A CAST OF THOUSANDS." The co-directors are "M. Gannon and C. Powers." A pair of male hands moves these sheets of paper around so that we can read them one at a time; the hands now tear them up, crumple them, pile them up and play with the pieces.

As Dobson narrates, we see a fellow fishing in a lagoon; he recoils in horror when he catches the Creature by the seat of his pants. (Although obviously a cloth costume, the monster's get-up is pretty neat, and comes complete with dorsal fin as well as fins on the backs of the arms and legs.) The Creature angrily charges up out of the water but then, says narrator Dobson, "it stopped dead—paralyzed—stunned by a sight it had not seen in two million years." We cut to a shot of pretty Helen Dobson (Pat Powers) in a one-piece bathing suit, stretching and basking in the sun. A man (Clayton Powers, Pat's real-life husband) walks up to her.

> HELEN: Clete! I mean, Dr. Ferguson! How wonderful to see you again! Down for some more research?
> CLETE: Yes. Your father, the fabulous Dr. Dobson, invited me down for another summer's tussle with hermit crabs and blood smears.

(Clete Ferguson and Helen Dobson were the character names of John Agar and Lori Nelson in *Revenge*.) Clete is about to try to get romantic when Helen finally notices the Creature watching them from the water's edge, still paralyzed in a hands-up pose. In tight closeup she does a lot of terrified silent-movie–style gaping, and Clete comes out with a stilted "Great Scott, it's the Gill Man!" Clete shouts for Dr. Dobson and his helper Hernando, telling them to bring a rope, while Helen continues to eyeball the Creature and says to herself, "There's something *about* him...." Clete and Hernando carefully approach the Creature and tangle the rope around him. "By Heaven, I've *got* him!" Clete exults.

Dr. Dobson's first thought is to put the Creature in the facility's flume but Clete resists the idea: Clete says that within 12 hours of putting him in the flume, "there'll be a million crackpot scientists, movie people, sensation seekers all over the place." (I love the dig at movie people in a spoof made to be shown to movie people!) Instead, Clete announces, he wants to take the Creature to his apartment. Like a police prisoner, the loosely trussed-up monster is loaded into the back seat of a car and driven away.

At the apartment, Clete and Helen stand in front of a closed door talking about the Gill Man, and Helen again dreamily says to herself, "There's something *about* him...." We get the impression he's in the room behind them. When the door swings open by itself, we see that it's a bathroom and the drugged and unconscious Gill Man has been stuffed into the bathtub. In the living room, Clete tells an off-camera Hernando to "go in the tub and 'walk' him around a bit more" (à la Joe Hayes "walking" the Gill Man in *Revenge*). In the next shot we see young, handsome, mustached Hernando sitting in a chair wearing a Joe Hayes–type canvas diving suit, a towel around his neck like an oldtime movie star's scarf, sipping a drink. He stands, tosses the empty glass over his shoulder and says in suave matinee idol-style, "Danger is my business!"

Clete tells Helen that capturing the Gill Man means that he'll be famous. Then, a brainstorm: "I'm going to *train* him. I'm going to *civilize* him!" Helen's response: a dreamy "There's something *about* him…." In the bathtub, we see the Gill Man coming around, lazily stretching, then contentedly crossing his hands across his belly and going back to sleep.

Clete teaches the Creature the alphabet, to read and to write; as narrator Dr. Dobson tells us, "Finally [the Creature] was playing chess—and Dr. Ferguson was losing." The Creature tosses Clete's captured chessmen aside as Clete gives the camera a long Oliver Hardy–esque look of exasperated disbelief. Clete tells Helen that he talked with the Creature about the strange way he stood paralyzed on the edge of the lagoon, and that the Creature admitted that it was the sight of Helen that froze him in his tracks. Helen looks almost orgasmic as we hear her in voiceover: "I *knew* there was something about him!" Clete is jealous but knows that he "must go on—for science!"

> CLETE: The Creature has absorbed almost everything of our culture. And he's ready now, I think, to experience the crowning achievement of modern civilization.
> HELEN (staring into the camera): You don't mean…
> CLETE (staring wild-eyed into the camera): Yes. Television!

Special guests at Clete's apartment on the night of the TV experiment include Dr. Fortescue (Carl Selph) and Sam Backlash (W.F. Rolleston) of the Sea Zoo. The three of them, and a number of other guests, crowd into the bathroom (the Creature's back in the tub) and turn out the lights; the screen is black as we hear a TV announcer's voice: "This is WNBC Television. Remember, keep the home fires burning with furniture from Macy's." We hear the Creature start to growl, and then the screams of the guests. When the lights come back on, everyone is frantically running out of the bathroom. Side by side, Dr. Fortescue and Sam Backlash get wedged in the doorway and the Creature clobbers them from behind.

The Creature goes outside and starts stomping around the neighborhood, scaring some kids playing in an alley, and then scales a fire escape to the top of a building. Clete, gun in hand, follows the Creature, and Helen follows Clete. Atop the building, the Creature manhandles Clete, lifts him overhead and throws him down into the alley. The Creature is coming down the fire escape when he encounters Helen and they lovingly embrace. They both look down at Clete's broken body, Helen smiling approvingly, and then embrace again. Clete, shirt torn, bruised and bleeding from the mouth, crawls around the alley in an endless death scene.

Fade to black.

The wrap-up returns us to the lagoon. Dr. Dobson is saying goodbye to the Creature and Helen as they prepare to go off together. The Creature shakes the hand of Dr. Dobson, who tells him to take care of her. And as the Creature and Helen move toward the water, Hernando also shakes Dr. Dobson's hand and follows the Creature and Helen. "Goodbye, Hernando," says Dobson, hanging his head and shaking it sadly. "I know that you just want to go along too. You're that type of guy … I can't figure it." Lest there be any doubt that the Creature, Helen and Hernando are a three-way in the making, Hernando looks into the camera, shrugs his shoulders in a devil-may-care way and tells us, "There's something *about* him." He takes a last swig from a liquor bottle, throws it over his shoulder and walks into the lagoon behind the Creature and Helen. The three swim away into what narrator Dr. Dobson calls "the eternal night of the sea."

Recalling the making of this cockamamie comedy, Gannon said that it was shot silent on black-and-white 8mm; after the developed film was in their hands, the cast members re-assembled to record the dialogue, sound effects,

"There's something about him," Helen (Pat Powers) muses as she casts an admiring eye upon the newly captured Gill Man (Ed Doyle). Powers (February 7, 1935–November 18, 1997) also made an uncredited appearance in Revenge of the Creature *and was the only player seen in both movies.*

etc., on audio tape. As musical background we hear several needle-drops from the aforementioned "Night on Bald Mountain" over the credits and as the fisherman reels in the Creature; then needle-drops from the "Cloudburst" movement of Ferde Grofé's "Grand Canyon Suite" throughout most of the movie's midsection, right up through the Gill Man's rooftop fight with Clete; a nice romantic portion of Khachaturian's Violin Concerto's 2nd movement as Helen and the Creature embrace; and Jean Sibelius' "Finlandia" as the dying Clete crawls down the alley. The lagoon's-edge finale has music that sounds modern (1950s), a bit like parts of Les Baxter's "The Passions" and complete with Bas Sheva–style chanting. At the wrap party, Gannon showed his movie on an adjustable speed 8mm projector and played the tape, occasionally speeding up or slowing the rate of projection to keep picture and sound in sync.

At around the halfway mark in *Return*, Clete mentions his plan to train and civilize the Creature and, interestingly enough, the balance of Gannon's movie is less like *Revenge of the Creature* than *The Creature Walks Among Us*—which was still almost a year away from being written! Clete at this point is becoming a bit unhinged and suffering from jealousy, just like *Creature Walks*' Dr. Barton. Also like Dr. Barton, Clete wants to make the Creature more human. In Gannon's movie he does this by teaching him to read and to play chess; in one of *Creature Walks*' earliest drafts, the scientists try to educate the Creature by showing him objects as they're being named, and playing classical music for him. Toward the end of both movies, the Creature briefly reverts to savagery, in *Return* because he's exposed to television, in *Creature Walks* because he witnessed an act of violence. And in both movies, the Creature makes the scientist responsible pay with his life: In *Return*, Clete is gorilla-pressed overhead and flung down from the top of a building, in *Creature Walks*, Dr. Barton is gorilla-pressed and flung down from the second-story veranda of his ranch house.

According to Gannon, two of *Return of the Creature*'s biggest fans were Marine Studios co-founder Cornelius Vanderbilt "Sonny" Whitney and his wife Marylou. "When they got a chance to see the film, they fell in love with it," he told me. "They had a print made and showed it at their various estates in Saratoga and in Manhattan and Palm Beach, and in their home in Majorca, Spain. It became quite an item among the 'glitterati' of the decade that followed!"

As mentioned above, it was David Redman who provided me with the clues that enabled me to find Gannon. Redman went to work in Marine Studios' marketing department in 1957 and also knew the Whitneys well. According to Redman, it was not so much Cornelius but mostly his decades-younger new wife who fell under the spell of Gannon's movie:

> When the Whitneys were at Marine Studios for whatever reason, Marylou would always want to show that film. Marylou being a socialite, a variety of people came down to Marine Studios as guests of the Whitneys and she'd always want them to see it. So it was mainly Marylou. "Sonny" really didn't show that much interest in the spoof, but Marylou did. Most of the time it was a small group. In the Dolphin Restaurant [spitting-distance south of Marine Studios] we had a private dining room and Marylou would want it set up in there. It was a chore showing it because there was the 8mm projector and film and then also a tape recorder and the audio tape with the music and dialogue. Everything had to be coordinated between the audio and the video, everything synced just right. Marylou loved it and I can't *tell* you how many times I showed it over the years.

I wrote to Mrs. Whitney about *The Return of the Creature* in 2013 but I might as well have cast the letter into "the eternal night of the sea"; she never responded. Nor did Clint Eastwood, to whom I wrote concerning *Revenge of the Creature*. Because my middle name is Fairness, I'm compelled to add that I'm sure both of these august public figures have assistants who make sure their bosses never see unimportant requests and crank letters. Mine certainly fit both criteria!

The humor and some of the acting in *The Return of the Creature* predates by decades the humor and acting in modern spoofs of monster oldies, especially Larry Blamire's *The Lost Skeleton of Cadavra* (2001)—which made Blamire the perfect choice to review *Return* in a 2013 issue of *Monster Bash* magazine:

> We tend to think, rather egocentrically I suppose, of '50s sci-fi-horror movie spoofs as a phenomenon of recent years (okay, *I* do), starting perhaps with *Mant!* (the film-within-a-film in director Joe Dante's *Matinee* [1993]). How startling and wonderful to find one made in the very midst of The Decade itself. Even more wonderful to find *this thing is actually good*. And by a first-timer. We're talking clever, smart, and quite funny. [*Blamire quotes some of* Return*'s absurd dialogue, then continues:*] This stuff kills me. Lines like this have the sharp edge of satire, mixed with absurdity (my favorite dish), and I'm sitting there amazed at the self-awareness of it all. Perhaps I shouldn't be. But it just seems so *savvy*.

In February 2013 I told Ron Adams, headman of Pennsylvania's Monster Bash conventions, that I'd like to show my DVD copy of *The Return of the Creature* at the next Bash (July 19–21 at the Four Points Pittsburgh North in Mars, Pennsylvania), and he happily took me up on it. He scheduled it for Friday night, July 19, and I hoped for a good turn-out. I needn't have worried: When it came time to show *Return*, there were butts in every one of the room's chairs, people standing against walls, people sitting on the floor and at least one chap lying on the floor. I shoulda taken a picture. *Now* it was time for me to hope that the reaction to the movie would also be good, so that I could honestly tell Mike Gannon that his movie had been well-received.

During the pre-credits sequence, when Dr. Dobson mentioned the fossilized finger joint found in a rock formation, there were a couple chuckles—probably hardcore fans remembering that the discovery of a fossil in a rock formation was *Creature from the Black Lagoon*'s tee-off point. There was a bigger laugh when Dr. Dobson babbled about "two times ten to the eight years ago." And the laughs (small, medium and large) continued throughout: the tearing-up of the opening credits papers, the Creature ogling Helen, Clete's announcement that he's taking the Creature home to his apartment, the Chinese fire drill–type ordeal of loading the Creature into the car, Hernando's "Danger is my business!," Clete's facial gyrations, Helen's repetition of "There's something *about* him," Hernando's "There's something *about* him" and a dozen other spots. When it ended, there was great applause and some guy twice yelling "Bravo!" at the top of his lungs. It was my pleasure to call Mike Gannon when I got home from the Bash and tell him that, 59 years *to the day* after he'd made *The Return of the Creature*, it had just had its first public exhibition, and that this "world premiere" showing was well-attended and a great hit.

Now it occurs to me: I should have made up Universal-style Preview Comment Cards for all the members of the audience, and passed them along to Gannon!

The rest of my interview with Gannon, providing much more information about the making of *The Return of the Creature*, appears in "Creature Conversations."

Curucu, Beast of the Amazon
(Universal, 1956)

CREDITS: Jewell Enterprises; Associate Producer: Edward B. Barison; Produced by Richard Kay and Harry Rybnick; Directed by Curt Siodmak; Screenplay: Curt Siodmak; Photography: Rudolf Icsey (Color); Film Editor: Terry Morse; Music: Raoul Kraushaar; 76 minutes.

CAST: John Bromfield (*Rock Dean*), Beverly Garland (*Dr. Andrea Romar*), Tom Payne (*Tupanico*), Harvey Chalk (*Father Flaviano*), Larri Thomas (*Vivian*), Wilson Viana (*Tico*).

With a title like *Curucu, Beast of the Amazon*, could a monster movie made in the immediate wake of the success of *Black Lagoon* and *Revenge* be anything *but* an attempt to cut into the Gill Man pie? Especially with John Bromfield, one of the stars of the newer Gill Man movie, in the top role?

In late 1955, Universal Horrors alumnus Curt Siodmak trekked to Brazil to direct *Curucu* [sic][1] for R-K Productions, the "R-K" designating producers Richard Kay and Harry Rybnick. The stars were Bromfield and Beverly Garland, the latter accepting the job partly because a trip to Brazil would get her away from Richard Garland, the actor she had just divorced; his boozy, bitter post-split behavior was becoming alarming.[2] Say what you want about this truly lousy movie but it has a leg-up on the Creature series in one significant way: At least this tale of an Amazonian monster was shot—sometimes quite picturesquely—on and around the Amazon.

In the very first scene, Curucu is skulking in shrubbery near a sandy

John Bromfield went to Florida to appear in Revenge of the Creature's *Brazilian Black Lagoon scenes, but had to make the actual trek to Brazil for* Curucu, Beast of the Amazon. *In this* Curucu *shot, he and co-star Beverly Garland eyeball some shrunken heads.*

5. Aquatic Kith and Kin (Curucu, Beast of the Amazon)

beach, watching a native woman fill a jug with water. He looks like a guy in a brightly colored papier-mâché Halloween costume; the head is bird-like, except for the tusks. (This is not the go-to movie for good-looking monster outfits.) As the unsuspecting woman comes toward him, the beast appears out of hiding and uses his Gill Man–type claws to make her his fifth victim. Chain-smoking plantation foreman and all-around he-man Rock Dean (Bromfield) later visits the scene, along with a police captain and a native named Tupanico (Tom Payne), and examines the beast's tracks in the sand:

> TUPANICO: A beast with claws like that of a giant bird.
> CAPTAIN: A crocodile, perhaps?
> TUPANICO: A crocodile is no bird.

(This is also not the go-to movie for good dialogue.) According to local legend, Curucu punishes Indians who have deserted their ancestral jungle homes, so now all the Indians who have done so, and taken jobs on plantations along the Amazon, are hot-footing it back to their original nests. To try and put a stop to the killings, Rock must venture into no-white-man's-land, to the falls of Curucu where these monsters are said to live. Andrea Romar (Garland), a cancer researcher, muscles in on the expedition; she needs to visit headhunter country because the mysterious process they use to shrink heads might also shrink cancer tissue. Much sexist dialogue and stock footage ensue, along with some knockout scenery and a few genuinely gruesome highlights. Ultimately the monster turns out to be a fake: Tupanico in a monster costume, dedicated to an insane plan to get his people to forsake the white man's world.

Bromfield's girlfriend, TV and movie dancer Larri Thomas,[3] accompanied him on his *Curucu* jaunt to Brazil and the two married during production. She told me, "John worked out this deal—he was always good at working out deals—where my fare to Rio would be paid by the movie company, and I in turn would do a little dance in the movie, and we would get married down there. It was weird, because John and I had our honeymoon, and then we went to São Paolo where the studio was and we shot, and *then* we got married. So we had our honeymoon in Rio before the wedding, because of the movie schedule!" When I told her that Garland complained in interviews about the hotel and the jungle, she laughed,

What jungle is *nice*? And no hotel, that a movie company is paying for, is going to be four-star! It *was* a nasty hotel. The "shower," it was just water coming *drip drip* out of the bathroom ceiling! The entire time I was there, I didn't get sick because I lived on bananas and Coca-Cola. I ate or drank nothing else and so I did not get ill. I'm sure everybody else had the turista.

My funniest recollection involves Beverly—I always called her my maid of honor even though she was not at the wedding due to motion picture scheduling. We were on this cute little boat going up the Amazon River, and they were shooting on the boat. I wasn't involved, I just was there as Mrs. Bromfield. The assistant director kept warning them that the tide was going out, but they had a couple more shots to do. Well, they did not listen to the assistant director, the tide continued to go out, and all of a sudden the boat was sitting on a mud lump in the middle of the river and the water was *gone*.

Well, Beverly and I stripped down to our undies and *walked* through this mucky mud, from the boat to the shoreline. We *had* to do it; were we going to sit on a dry-docked boat in the middle of the mud? It was *scary*—that place was loaded with piranhas! The mud was gray and very icky. And

John Bromfield and Beverly Garland with what we presume is the actual Curucu mask. "The monster turns out to be pretty much of a dud," said reviewer S.A. Desick of the Los Angeles Examiner.

psychologically, we were just crawling with bugs—I don't know that we actually *were*. But we started to giggle, and we got across the Amazon in our underwear, and we couldn't wait to get a shower *drip drip drip*. That was the funniest experience, walking across the Amazon River with Beverly Garland.

Made aware of Siodmak's movie, Universal perhaps felt that Gill Man fans might go to see it expecting another Creature feature, so they broke from their customary policy of producing all of their own program by acquiring it, making the title *Curucu, Beast of the Amazon* and reaping the rewards themselves. The Legion of Decency gave *Curucu* a "B" rating, and purity squads overseas weren't too pleased with it either. By the time the cutters got through with it in British territories, you could have shown it to a toddler; here are just *some* of the censor's dictates:

> [R]emove the closeups of the monster attacking the woman near a river and remove also the sounds of her screams…. Remove the shot of Jose's lacerated body lying in jungle and the sound of his screams…. Remove whole incident of snake fighting small animal. Remove shot of monster's claw appearing in flap of tent, closeup of Andrea's horrified face, the sound of her scream, and reduce the scene to barest minimum…. Remove shot of dead native's arm, reduced to a skeleton by piranha. Remove all but one of Andrea's screams as she is held by snake, and reduce shots of her in its coils. Remove incident of shrunken head at end of film.

Even we here in the United States didn't get to see the whole movie: It was issued a Certificate of Approval only after part of a shot was cut. In the original version, in a scene near the end, Bromfield and Garland sit on a cot in a tent, embracing and kissing—and then Bromfield pushes her down onto the cot into a supine position. That last bit had to be removed.

Hollywood Reporter reviewer James Powers halfway liked *Curucu* and saluted Siodmak for "sensibly [taking] plenty of advantage" of the authentic backgrounds, but most of the original reviews I've seen have been uncomplimentary. What might be the nastiest ran in the *Los Angeles Mirror-News*:

> Some of the most monstrous acting that's ever been exhibited is that in *Curucu, Beast of the Amazon*, but it doesn't stop there. The story and direction are also monstrous. Until I saw this movie yesterday, it was my belief that Hollywood Actor John Ireland was secure in his thespian niche. But John Bromfield of *Curucu* has finally matched Ireland. Ungallantly, my nomination must also include Beverly Garland…

The Monster of Piedras Blancas
(Filmservice Distributing, 1959)

CREDITS: A Vanwick Production; Produced by Jack Kevan; Directed by Irvin Berwick; Screenplay: H. Haile Chace; Photography: Philip Lathrop; Editor: George Gittens; 71 minutes.

CAST: Les Tremayne (*Dr. Sam Jorgenson*), Jeanne Carmen (*Lucy Sturges*), Don Sullivan (*Fred*), Forrest Lewis (*George*), John Harmon (*Sturges*), Frank Arvidson (*Kochek*), Pete Dunn (*Eddie/The Monster of Piedras Blancas*).

If the Gill Man *had* to be ripped off, well, who better to do it than some of the folks who made the Gill Man movies in the first place? That's basically what happened when the indie *The Monster of Piedras Blancas* was produced by Jack Kevan and directed by Irvin Berwick (*Black Lagoon*'s dialogue coach), with Joe Lapis (*Black Lagoon* sound recordist), James V. Swartz (*Creature Walks* sound recordist) and Luanna Sherman (*Black Lagoon* script clerk) holding down the same jobs here as before. *Piedras Blancas* d.p. Philip Lathrop, a future two-time Oscar nominee, may have double-dipped as well: Universal's last-name-only lists of *Black Lagoon* production personnel includes a camera operator named Lathrop.

Berwick and Kevan formed a company to make a program of six moderate budget features; according to a February 1957 *Hollywood Reporter* item, they were calling themselves K-B Productions and headquartered at General Service Studios. At that time, they were planning to kick off with a sci-fi, *They Came to Destroy the Earth*, scripted by Robert M. Fresco (*Tarantula, The Monolith Monsters*) and Paul de Sainte Colombe, and slated to star John Agar. By the time the company's cameras first rolled in March 1958, it had been renamed VanWick Productions (Van from Kevan, Wick from Berwick) and the lead-off movie was now *The Monster of Piedras Blancas*, written by another Universal dialogue coach, H. Haile Chace.

A California coastal community is the scene of tragedy when a rowboat drifts toward shore with the beheaded bodies of two fishermen-brothers aboard. The local constable (Forrest Lewis) thinks the boat was caught in a squall and the men were decapitated when it was smashed against the rocks. (I'm trying to picture rocks that can cut off the heads

5. Aquatic Kith and Kin (*The Monster of Piedras Blancas*)

of rowboat passengers while the passengers are in the boat—and without damaging the boat!) Their bodies appear to have been drained of blood. A grocery store owner, the gossipy, foreign-accented Kochek (Frank Arvidson), blames the gory deaths on the Monster of Piedras Blancas, a local legend for the past 30 years. Every time anybody gets mangled in this movie, their bodies are stashed in Kochek's store's ice room, perhaps explaining why the place always seems to be light on customers.

Lighthouse keeper Sturges (John Harmon), a bike-riding, cantankerous coot, obviously knows a lot more than he's telling about these deaths. His beautiful daughter Lucy (Jeanne Carmen) is the girlfriend of boyish wannabe ichthyologist Fred (Don Sullivan); Lucy and Fred have a beach picnic that day, followed by a romantic *From Here to Eternity* interlude in the surf. That night, after Fred drops Lucy off near the lighthouse, she goes skinny-dipping, and the arm of a monstrous *some*thing messes with her cast-off clothes. We later see the monster's shadow as he prowls the empty midnight streets, waddles into Kochek's place and confronts the horrified storeowner.

The next morning, the fishermen-brothers' double-header funeral (double-*be*header funeral?) is interrupted by the arrival of a gimpy, hollering kid (Irv Berwick's young son Wayne) who just discovered Kochek's headless body. A large fish scale found in the store is examined by Fred and amiable local sawbones Jorgenson (Les Tremayne), who determine that it came from a "diplovertubron," a prehistoric amphibious reptile thought to be extinct. "But this is *living tissue*," Jorgenson stresses. The Monster's next victims are a little girl and café worker Eddie (Pete Dunn); we get a partial shot of the Monster as he strolls out of Kochek's store carrying Eddie's cut-off head. At the lighthouse, Sturges comes clean with Lucy: Years ago, after the death of his wife (Lucy's mother), he became aware that the Monster was living in a cliffside cave, accessible only at low tide. The lonely, unhappy man began leaving meat scraps for the Monster and to feel protective toward him.

That night, the Monster breaks into the lighthouse and accosts Lucy, who screams and faints. To save his daughter, Sturges lures the Monster to the top of the lighthouse tower, but his plan goes awry when the Monster gets his claw-fingered hands on him and throws him to his death (*à la* Dr. Barton in *Creature Walks*). Fred, Jorgenson, the constable and other townsmen have arrived by now, and Fred rushes upstairs to confront the Monster. Lucy turns on the lighthouse light, which blinds the Monster, and Fred rifle-butts him so that he tumbles over the railing and cartwheels through the air to his destruction below.

Any Baby Boomer Monster Kid who saw *Piedras Blancas* for the first time as a tyke should be forgiven if, at that age, he found it scarier than the Creature movies. With his Gill Man–like body, Mole People hands, Metaluna Mutant feet and ugly kisser, he's much more frightening in appearance than the Creature; and the Creature never cut off heads, drank blood or killed a little girl. Also, this marine monster wasn't in the Amazon or Ocean Harbor or a mad scientist's private stockade, he was in a small town just like the one most of us grew up in (the movie was made on practical locations) and he was battled by guy- (and girl-) next-door types. Shooting on location gives the proceedings the same neat atmospherics as *The Werewolf* (1956) and *Giant from the Unknown* (1958): In the minor roles it has recog-

Jack Kevan's great Monster of Piedras Blancas outfit didn't get much screen time: Not until 65 minutes "into" this 70-something-minute movie do we get our first look at that ugly kisser.

nizable-as-real-people people playing real people rather than Hollywood actors and extras, there are brand-name grocery items in Kochek's store, and other touches of realism not often found in major-studio productions. Plus, the whole movie has a rugged, desolate, cold'n'windy feeling that backlot-made movies just can't deliver.

Kevan built the Monster suit and stuntman Pete Dunn

played him. This bowlegged cousin to the Creature is described as a mutation of the reptilian family, nearly seven feet tall. In moments of stress he lets rip with what sounds like an Indian war whoop; and like the Creature he seems to have a soft spot for the gentler sex, carrying off Lucy rather than decapitating her. As in *Black Lagoon*, suspense is built by only giving us partial glimpses of him (and his shadow); we're not permitted a full shot until six minutes from the end, as he carries the unconscious Lucy out of the lighthouse. But back in the day, probably every kid who saw the movie considered the Monster cool enough that the wait was worth it. The plot gimmick of a broken-off scale providing the tip-off that a prehistoric creature is on the loose is right out of *Black Lagoon* (the Gill Man's toenail found in the *Rita* net). There's even a hand-on-the-shoulder moment (the constable comes up behind Fred on the beach) but the moviemakers kinda blew it.

Writer Ted Newsom's excellent "making of" story on *Monster of Piedras Blancas* appeared in *Filmfax* magazine, with interviewee Berwick revealing that he and Kevan raised production funds by going from person to person on the Universal lot: "It was a collection of very small investments, $1000 here, a thousand there, maybe a few people invested $1500 or $2000.[4] I budgeted the film at—I hate to say this, because you'll laugh, it's so little—$30,000." According to Newsom's article, things were so slow at Universal at the time that the studio was all in favor of a project that would provide paychecks (not Universal's) for some of their employees. The Valley lot even supplied Kevan and Berwick with a couple of limos and a studio bus.

The town scenes were shot in seaside Cayucos, where the fun of watching Hollywood moviemakers doing a monster movie drew, at one point, 500 onlookers, according to a local paper. The lighthouse at Point Conception, about a hundred miles from Cayucos, is now on the National Register of Historic Places. Wayne Berwick, who played the kid who disrupts the funeral, limped because of a real-life bout with polio. He told Newsom that stuntman Pete Dunn could wear the Monster suit for only about ten minutes at a time because it was so hot. In the scene where the Monster carries the severed head of Eddie, what we're seeing is Pete Dunn as the Monster carrying a prop Pete Dunn head.

In January 1959 *The Hollywood Reporter* announced that a new national distributor for action exploitation movies, First National Distributing Corp., would have as its initial releases *The Monster of Piedras Blancas* and *Okefenokee*, the latter a tale of "Raw Passions in the Hell Swamps!" (ad line). When *Piedras Blancas* played in Pasadena on April 22 of that year, advertised as a premiere, the distributor listed on-screen was Filmservice Distributing Corp., which I guess is the same organization, just re-named in the interim. *Okefenokee* accompanied *Piedras Blancas* in Pasadena and throughout its first run. *Piedras Blancas* was enough of a moneymaker that Kevan and Berwick went on to make two more, *The Seventh Commandment* (1961), with *Piedras Blancas* cast alumni John Harmon, Frank Arvidson and Wayne Berwick, and *The Street Is My Beat* (1966) with Harmon. At one point Wayne Berwick, Newsom, brothers Robert and Dennis Skotak *et al.* wanted to do a *Piedras Blancas* sequel, but by that time the rights were owned by National Telefilm Associates, who wouldn't allow it.[5]

According to Wayne Berwick, for a long stretch *Piedras Blancas* was publicly played in Cayucos every year, on the Fourth of July and Halloween. In a *Scary Monsters* magazine article, Jeanne Carmen's son Brandon James wrote that his mom was invited to a 2002 showing at the Cayucos Veterans Hall; together they made the trip to Cayucos in order to attend. There was an all-California World Series baseball game that night so James feared that no one would show up for the movie, but when they got to Veterans Hall, "we

In the opening reel castlist, "The Monster of Piedras Blancas" gets special "AND" billing, as though he was a real-life critter. The movie was shot in six 16-hour days.

both froze. There were about 500 people waiting in line outside this little building in this little town. Then the fire department and the police showed up and said there were too many people to let into the building. It wasn't safe." In order for everybody to see it, the promoter arranged that the movie would be shown a second time later that evening. After both screenings, there were question-and-answer sessions in which Carmen and local residents who had worked on the movie reminisced about the experience.

The Piedras Blancas monster head plus his Mole People hands and Metaluna Mutant feet were all worn in the 1965 *Flipper* TV episode "Flipper's Monster" by … Ricou Browning (see the *Creature Walks Among Us* chapter's endnote 53).

Octaman
(A Filmers Guild Production 1971)

CREDITS: Produced by Michael Kraike; Directed by Harry Essex; Screenplay: Harry Essex; Photography: Robert Caramico (Color); Editor: Robert Freeman; 79 minutes.

CAST: Pier Angeli (*Susanna*), Kerwin Mathews (*Dr. Rick Torres*), Jeff Morrow (*Dr. John Willard*), David Essex (*The Indian*), Read Morgan (*Octaman*).

In 1971, *Black Lagoon* co-writer Harry Essex wrote and directed the amateur night-level indie *Octaman* with Pier Angeli and Kerwin Mathews. It's a "disguised remake" of *Black Lagoon* in that the original movie's archaeological expedition is now an ecological expedition, its members travel not by water (the *Rita*) but by land (in a motor home), and the monster is a cross between a man and an octopus. But beyond this inadequate camouflage, *Octaman* is pretty much a carbon copy of *Black Lagoon*; it starts with narration about "the beginning of time" (and footage of a whipped-up "primordial" sea) and climaxes with the pumped-full-of-lead title monster limping back into the water to die. In between, practically every key scene in *Black Lagoon* has a clumsy clone *somewhere* in *Octaman*.

The narrator of the pre-credits sequence talks about atomic radiation's "hideous fruit." Now we see Octaman (Read Morgan), who does indeed look hideously fruity behind the opening credits as he stands mincing against an all-black background. (The shot brings to mind the dancing-girls-on-black seen during the closing credits of AIP Beach Party movies.) It's obviously a man in a "octopus-man" costume, his arms and legs inside four of the eight tentacles, and the other tentacles flopping around empty. A fixed part of the construction of the face is a wide-open mouth ringed with pointy teeth. The way the movie just can't *wait* to show us the monster—in the first 30-something seconds—makes you think of a Monster Kid Home Movie made by a pre-teen immaturely impatient to get "the good stuff" (the monster) on-screen.

Dr. Rick Torres (Mathews) is encamped near a primitive Latin American fishing community, checking atomic contamination levels in fish eaten by the locals, when his associate Mort finds and shows him what looks like a freakishly mutated baby octopus. (Well, actually it looks like a 99¢ octopus toy that no kid would want for *one* cent.) Classifying it as a mutant, Rick brings it to the International Ecological Institute for examination by Dr. Willard (Jeff Morrow of *The Creature Walks Among Us* slumming his way through this one scene). Not only is Willard unimpressed, but he gives Rick the bad news that the institute can no longer afford to support his field studies. Meanwhile, back at Rick's camp, a native who has found a second Octababy is attacked and killed in a tent by Octaman, who then retrieves his Octababy. (We never do see an Octamom. Or even *the* Octomom.)

Cigar-sucking ex-carnival man Johnny Caruso agrees to bankroll Rick's search for the Octaman (Caruso will make it a circus attraction), and soon he, Rick, Rick's fiancée Susan (Angeli), Mort, wrangler Steve and a young native (played by Essex's son David) are setting out in a motor home to find the legendary man-fish's lair. The motor home goes long distances at a good clip but the Octaman, who walks at the speed of a guy pushing a Rolls-Royce uphill, is always creeping around nearby every time they stop. (Octaman sees multiple images of whatever he looks at, like the monster's-eye views in the 1958 *The Fly*.)

There's more action (of a sort) before the men are able to tranquilize the monster and ensnare it in a net. Caruso wants to leave with their catch immediately but Rick insists that they must first make a study of its natural habitat. Equivalently, in *Black Lagoon*, Reed and Williams stand near the tank of the captured Gill Man, Williams wanting to start back home and Reed insisting, "We've got to make a study of that grotto!" By now every *Black Lagoon* fan unfortunate enough to be watching has realized that *Octaman* is practically a scene-by-scene retelling, so of course we next see Susan and Mort (the Dr. Thompson counterpart, right down to the nearly ever-present pipe) chatting as the Octaman revives and escapes; and when our heroes decide to vamoose, they find the road blocked by a tree felled by the Octaman. On and on the movie goes, at this point feeling like it's been playing for hours. There's an interlude in a cave and a scene of the Octaman abducting the girl, before the monster is riddled with bullets—even one point-blank fired by Susan, who up 'til now has been acting as though she had some sort of sympathetic psychic connection with him. Grievously injured, the Octaman wades into a lake and disappears.

Essex told me that he made *Octaman* because "it was a chance for me to direct and to become co-producer" and "to do some kind of a takeoff on the science fiction junk [that was then] around…. But [it] came a-cropper; it didn't turn out the way I wanted it to, there just wasn't enough money for the thing. You can't do these things for ten dollars, you just can't." He said that *Octaman* cost $250,000; I bet the real cost *was* closer to ten dollars than $250,000. Five thousand went to top-billed Pier Angeli, 39-year-old Italian-born veteran of major Hollywood movies of the 1950s; *Octaman* was made during a June heat wave and she visibly suffered. "She was very sick," Essex told *Starlog* interviewer Pat Jankiewicz. "One minute she would be laughing, then have spasms. She was all mixed up. She … felt doing this was a step down." (Ya *think*?) Angeli died from a drug overdose later in the year; we might know if it was accidental or intentional if one of the first people on the scene, her actress friend Norma Eberhardt (from 1958's *The Return of Dracula*), hadn't immediately flushed all the remaining pills down the toilet. *Octaman* stands as Angeli's cinematic tombstone.

Kerwin Mathews told *Starlog*'s Steve Swires that he did the movie because he was "really *desperate* for money by that point. I believed in the actor's philosophy that activity breeds activity. I thought that as long as I kept working, more work would appear. But *Octaman* turned out to be the *worst* professional experience I had ever had…. I was only paid about $2000 for the whole film. It made me *sick* to my stomach."

Essex must have written *Octaman* with a *Black Lagoon* script at his elbow, as scenes from the older movie are constantly being copied. Even moments not worth duplicating are duplicated; for instance, during the conversation at the Ecological Institute, there are insert shots of fish in an aquarium, just as there are during *Black Lagoon*'s Instituto de Biología Marítima scene. The *Rita* is supplanted by the motor home; whereas the *Rita*'s whistle is sounded to scare a crocodile into leaping into the water, the motor home's horn is sounded to scare a (stock footage) jungle cat into a run. As a *Castle of Frankenstein* reviewer sarcastically quipped in the magazine's *Octaman* review, "[T]he original Gill Man formula was so successful that [Essex] wanted to prove it could also bomb out." Production-wise the movie is quite crude; the constant alternation of day and night shots, and the higgledy-piggledy editing, give it an Ed Wood flavor. Interestingly, if *any* of this is interesting, Essex employs a few touches that were originally scripted for *Black Lagoon* and then *not used*: The Octaman can be warded off by the light of a flashlight, and sometimes when he's near, there's a strange sort of "music" that Susan actually hears.

For years most of the reference books have called *Octaman* a 1971 release but researcher extra-

The Octaman costume and its creators, Rick Baker and Doug Beswick. Baker, 20 years old here, went on to win the first-ever Best Makeup Oscar in 1982, and several more since. The Octaman actor's arms are in the top tentacles, and the four lower tentacles are attached to them by thin fishing line. When the actor moved his arms, the tentacles below would also move.

ordinaire Robert J. Kiss says that, aside from some 1972–73 trade screenings, he could locate no evidence that it *ever* played theatrically—not in the United States, at least. Says Kiss,

> Michael Weldon refers to it as having gone straight to TV in his original *Psychotronic Encyclopedia of Film*, and I couldn't turn up a scrap of information in either the trades or mainstream press to contradict this. There are no lobby cards or 8 × 10s for the title, and the supposed one-sheet poster seems to have been more by way of a trade handout by the production company. I checked the MPAA database, and it was never submitted for a rating. Therefore the actual "U.S. release date" for *Octaman* may well be November 24, 1973, when it made its television debut. Outside the U.S., the movie played theatrically in West Germany in 1976 and went straight to video in the U.K. in 1980. But nothing that I could find predates its 1973 U.S. TV debut.

Louis B. Mayer, and perhaps also Leo the Lion, must be turning over in their graves: The current TV version of this theatrically unreleasable mess of a knockoff movie now begins and ends with the familiar logo of MGM, the Tiffany's of Hollywood studios.

Around the same time as *Octaman*, writer-director Essex laid another egg, *The Cremators* (1972), about a giant fire-engulfed meteorite, landing on Earth and rolling around some remote area in search of its many tiny missing pieces. Blame the author of the source story "Dune Roller" for the way-out premise but Essex's adaptation and direction make things far worse; to paraphrase Roger Ebert, *The Cremators* does not improve on the sight of a blank screen viewed for the same length of time. Its low points are the several scenes where the fireball (which can think, has moods, etc.) stalks people in the wilderness; we viewers regularly get fireball's-eye views of its unsuspecting human prey and we can't help but marvel that they are unable to see a sun-like, two-storey fireball a few feet away in the dead of night. Appallingly, next to this incomprehensible, amateurish snoozefest, *Octaman* actually starts to look halfway decent.

After *The Cremators*, Essex's directing career came to an unlamented end. Essex dearly wished to be remembered as a significant writer of sci-fi movies, accumulating thousands of frequent liar miles talking to interviewers about his input on *It Came from Outer Space* (1953) and *Black Lagoon*; but the proof of who-actually-wrote-what is out there to refute his every claim, and *Octaman* and *The Cremators* are out there to show the kind of work Essex did when flying solo rather than merely fine-tuning the nearly finished work of others (Ray Bradbury on *It Came*, various writers on *Black Lagoon*). Kansas City, Missouri, SF fan and entrepreneur Wade Williams recalled for me his brush with Essex:

> I had great hopes in the early 1980s of making a theatrical feature version of the television series *Space Patrol*, a childhood favorite. I had just purchased all rights to the teleseries from the estate of Helen Moser, wife of the late producer Mike Moser. I formed a corporation to sell stock and raise investment capital. It was going to be shot in Kansas City.

The two dark spots between Octaman's forehead veins are eyeholes for the actor inside. Now in the collection of Bob Burns, the head is all that's left of the costume.

> Several of us put together a script, but I felt that a known, talented and professional writer in the genre should be hired to rewrite, doctor up, or make whatever changes needed to make it the best possible screenplay considering the limitations of the budget, my limited experience, and the subject matter. I wanted people who were "names" in the genre to be attached to the project. One of my favorite films was *It Came from Outer Space* and Harry Essex and Ray Bradbury were the screenwriters. For some reason I thought Essex was the more important of the two [moviewise] because of his work on *Creature from the Black Lagoon* and other films. I associated Bradbury with novels.
>
> Scot Holton, a good friend and an excellent writer-researcher on the subject of science fiction films, introduced me to Essex. Harry met me in a dingy apartment which he explained was his office. He said he was familiar with the teleseries, shot me some ideas and said in a condescending way (like "The Great Oz" speaking to Dorothy and her friends in *The Wizard of Oz*), "Scripts cost a hundred thousand." I explained that that was a third of my budget for this film, that I already *had* a script, and that I was looking for a script doctor. I had budgeted $7500 for the job. He looked disappointed and a little tired, but then agreed to read the script and contact me later.
>
> No sooner had the plane touched down in Kansas City, I

received a call from Harry telling me the script was shit and to throw it away. However, since he liked me and had formed a good opinion of me, he said that maybe for $7500 under the table, and without the use of his name, he could write a new screenplay. He was a senior member of the Writers Guild of America and had to be careful about doing anything without a WGA agreement in place first.

I was to send a thousand a week as he wrote. This was workable. Somewhere about the 6000-mile marker, Harry decided the script he was writing was the best thing he had ever written and now he *wanted* his name on the credits. It would be necessary for me to sign a Writers Guild agreement with him so he could get screen credit. Impressed by his background, name and salesmanship, I reluctantly signed the WGA contract.

When Harry finally delivered the completed script, it was a jumbled mess of scenes from the Ed Wood school of scriptwriting. He had delivered a "screenplay" as called for in the agreement I signed, but it was not what I wanted, expected or was promised. If the first script was "shit," this was the toilet paper.

I complained to the WGA, so mediation was set up. The mediators were all chosen by the WGA. My attorney and I came from Kansas City to L.A. and presented our rock-solid case against Essex. We lost and had to pay the WGA minimum—$20,000 to Harry for a worthless first draft script. The WGA is one-sided and is apparently there to protect no-talent members regardless of the actual deal made, or the quality of the work delivered.

Essex produced, wrote and directed the film *The Cremators* which is completely unwatchable. It was based on a short story called "Dune Roller" which in 1952 was made into one of my favorite *Tales of Tomorrow* episodes, spooky and well-acted. Only a "talent" like Essex could totally ruin it. *Octaman* and *The Cremators* are probably the worst films ever made. Had I looked at these films [prior to meeting Essex], I would not have had flushed thousands down the Essex toilet. He was a total fraud and basically a cheat. I hope I was his last client. I'm not wild about Harry!

Harry J. Essex died of a heart ailment at Cedars Sinai Medical Center in 1997. He was survived by his fiancée, son, daughter, a grandson and a granddaughter.

CREATURE CONVERSATIONS

6

By Tom Weaver

In this section, three interviewees—a swimmer, a spoofer and a daughter—remember the three Gill Men:

- Swimming stunt double Ginger Stanley (from *Creature from the Black Lagoon* and *Revenge of the Creature*) talks about her sub-aquatic stints as a mermaid and model and about her friend Ricou Browning, the underwater Gill Man of the Creature trilogy;
- Mike Gannon, writer, co-director and co-star of the 8mm short *The Return of the Creature* (1954), recalls the making of that clever spoof and its Man in a ($12) Monster Suit;
- and Vikki Megowan reminisces about her actor-dad Don Megowan, who played the post-fire, "more like a human" Creature in *The Creature Walks Among Us*.

Ginger Stanley

The Creature is at the bottom of his Amazon lagoon, half-hidden in a patch of eelgrass, staring upward, awestruck. Gracefully gliding across the surface above is the object of his intense gaze, a va-va-va-voom visitor to his secret stomping grounds: Kay, a member of the scientific expedition that has just arrived to search for prehistoric fossils. He shyly watches her from his place of concealment ... ascends to a point of closer proximity and playfully pokes at the unsuspecting girl's feet ... and then backstrokes just a few feet beneath her, continuing to take in the intoxicating sight of the female form divine.

The Gill Man has had a love-at-first-sight reaction to the Girl in the White Bathing Suit *and*, in the minds and hearts of audiences, instantly evolved from fearsome fishman to lovesick lug, a monster with whom they can identify and even empathize.

Most of *Creature from the Black Lagoon* was shot on the Universal lot but for its sub-surface scenes, the studio decided to take advantage of the see-through waters of Florida's Wakulla Springs and dispatched a second unit crew there. Among the Sunshine State locals hired to work as doubles for the movie's stars were Ricou Browning as the Gill Man and blonde 21-year-old Ginger Stanley, standing in for Julie Adams as Kay. Stanley is on-camera for two and a half minutes, if *that*, but *what* a two and a half minutes: The creepy but captivating "underwater ballet" in which she plays Beauty to Browning's Beast elevates *Black Lagoon* from "just another monster movie" to latter-day classic in the Universal Monsters pantheon.

In October 1953 when she appeared in *Black Lagoon*, Stanley was already well-acquainted with the world beneath the water from teenage years spent playing a mermaid at Central Florida's Weeki Wachee Springs. In this interview, she dredges up memories of her mermaid days and her sometimes dangerous encounters with the monstrous merman of the movies.

For you to have been such an excellent swimmer in the '50s and made your living at it, I'm guessing that you first got involved with water and water sports as a kid.

A glamorous Ginger Stanley head shot from around the time she made her sci-fi movie splash as Julie Adams' swimming double in Creature from the Black Lagoon.

Yes, but only for pleasure. I was never on a swim team or anything like that; in fact, I'm not even sure that the places I lived, which were small, even had school swim teams at the time. I basically did it for fun, but I was in the water a lot. When I was young, I lived in a small town, Walhalla, South Carolina, in the foothills of the Blue Ridge Mountains. The city swimming pool was just a short distance away from my house, as well as a state park that had a large, beautiful lake where everybody went to swim. I learned to swim there in that lake and in the pool, mostly in the pool. My best friend's father taught me. Then when I was in high school we moved to Sebring, Florida. That whole town is built around a big lake, Lake Jackson, and our home happened to be half a block from its shores. I would go down there almost daily and swim in that lake, especially in the summer. Sometimes with my friends, sometimes alone, just because it was close by and it was fun and I happened to want to do it at that moment. My school was also just a short distance from Lake Jackson, and since there was no swimming pool at the school, for physical education class we walked down to the lake, taking our swimsuits and towels. We went back to our last period drenched, but nobody cared!

How did you get your "show biz break"?

One weekend when I was a high school senior at Sebring, I was attending a dance at University of Florida and I met a young lady, Sara Jo Miller, from Ocala. We became friends and started to write to each other. She was working as a secretary that summer for Bill Chappell, who was in charge of the Ocala Jaycees, and they wanted someone to enter a beauty contest the Jaycees would sponsor. She called me and said, "They aren't happy with anyone in Ocala. Would you be willing to represent us at the beauty contest?" So I came to Leesburg and did that, and at the contest I was approached by Newt Perry, who was known for his underwater abilities. He was an excellent underwater swimmer, he was an underwater instructor for the Navy SEALS, and at that beauty contest he was recruiting performers for the underwater shows he put on Weeki Wachee Springs. He said, "I'm looking for swimmers who don't look like swimmers, to portray mermaids." He wanted girls with long, flowing hair and graceful movements. Grace was required more than athletic ability, although it took great athletic ability to do these things.

Newt's shows were new—at that time they'd only been in operation two and a half, maybe three years at the most. No one had done underwater shows before, and they were possible only because of a special hose-breathing technique that Newt had developed. Otherwise the performers couldn't stay under for 45 minutes, which was how long the shows lasted.

How much preparation and training did you have to go through, in order to perform in his shows?

A *lot*. He asked me if I would come over to Weeki Wachee Springs to see an underwater show, see what the girls did, which was what *I* would be doing if I decided to work there. I saw one of the shows, he talked about it and how it was done, and the fact that each girl had to swim three shows a day. They were under for 45 minutes at a time, which is quite a bit of underwater time each day. Then we went inside his office and talked about what would be required of me, and what my training would be. He said, "We will put you up in the Mermaid Villas behind the Springs, where we put our trainees, and we will teach you all of the techniques. First you will learn things on land, like your ballet routines; you will learn surface swimming; and we will be sure that you're proficient in *every*thing before we ever put you underwater. You must also make 100 percent on a written exam about safety underwater." You had to know *all* of that before you could be in the shows. Once you had passed, and you were familiar with all of the hazards of performing underwater, then if you made

6. Creature Conversations (Ginger Stanley)

100 percent on the exam, you could be enlisted to be in their underwater shows. He said, "At that point, if you decide to stay, you go through a training period of like six weeks, and *if you can do it*, we will sign you to a contract and you'll become one of the mermaids." So that's how I got involved. I thought it was going to be maybe a summer job at the best, but it turned into a career.

The Mermaid Villas you mentioned—what were they like?

They were little cabins, like the ones you'd stay in when you went to camp. Kind of rustic. Little wooden structures that I'm sure were put up pretty fast. There were several of them, some a little larger than others. Ricou Browning's sister Shirley and her husband Dick and their daughter stayed in one of them, like their home.

Was Shirley a mermaid?

Yes she was, and Dick was an announcer—but every now and then, if they needed him, he was capable of swimming a show too. Everybody who worked around there had experience in the water, because they might have to go in and set up some props or things like that. Even if they were groundskeepers—"springskeepers" [*laughs*]—they had to be proficient at going underwater and doing these things. At the Mermaid Villas, my roommate was Florence Gothberg, who came from Auburn. When we first met, we decided we liked each other and became roommates right away. We became very close friends, and I introduced her to Charlie McNabb, who she later married.

He worked as a safety diver on all three of the Creature movies.

That's right. I was in their wedding, and later on, she and Charlie were in mine! Then, some time afterwards, the whole family was in a car and they were hit by a drunken driver. Charlie and their oldest son survived, but Florence and the younger son, who were on the side of the car that was hit, died. Very sad. She was my best friend.

When did you start working in the shows?

In 1950, and I stayed two and a half years. While I was there, so was Ricou Browning, and that was where I first met him. Newt had found Ricou as a swimmer up in Tallahassee, when Ricou was attending Florida State University. Newt recruited Ricou to come down and help him to establish the underwater shows at Weeki Wachee. These springs were about 12 miles up from the Gulf of Mexico, right outside of Brooksville. Until Newt came along, people used the springs as a dumping ground. They would take old refrigerators and anything else they wanted to throw away, and thoughtlessly drop 'em in the springs [*laughs*]! So that's what Ricou had to clear out, refrigerators, lawnmowers, old cars, tires, a small wrecked boat and other junk. He worked underwater, and this stuff was pulled up by construction workers working topside. Ricou also helped Newt to design the underwater shows.

At Weeki Wachee, we were taught how to use the underwater hose and how to maintain a certain level in the water simply by the amount of air we kept in our lungs. If you kept just a little bit of air, you would stay right at a depth of (say) 25 feet, you would not go up or down. If you found yourself taking too deep a breath from the hose, you'd have to let out a few bubbles, exhale a little bit, so that you wouldn't rise to the surface. We pretty soon figured out how to regulate this amount so well that we hardly knew we were doing it. It was like second nature, like breathing.

Who was your trainer? Newt Perry?

No, Newt couldn't train everybody. He just chose the people and hired them. I was trained by one of the mermaids who had been there a while. She was among the very first ones, her name was Patsy Boyette.

Ginger Stanley on the dock at Weeki Wachee, where she got her show business start as one of entrepreneur Newt Perry's "mermaids."

There was a long article in *The New York Times* just the other day, the whole history of the Weeki Wachee mermaid shows, and it said that in the early days, the mermaids were mostly local high school students and waitresses who weren't paid: "they worked in exchange for meals, free swimsuits and glory."

By the time I got there, they were havin' five shows a day, and we get gettin' paid. I couldn't have been there if we weren't gettin' paid; I would not have been interested in ever doing anything for free like that. I don't remember how much I got paid. It wasn't a *lot*, but it wasn't a *little* either. It was probably more than I would have been paid for working as a secretary or something like that.

And once you were underwater, your audience was where?

There was a theater built along the banks of the spring, and as the members of the audience walked in, they went down an incline. It was a pretty large theater, not very far under the water, made of metal, heavy, so that it would stay down, and curved slightly to match the curvature of the shoreline. In it there were bleachers, maybe five rows, and you could get 150 or 200 people in there. In the front of the Underwater Theater [today called the Newton Perry Underwater Theater], there were thick glass panes so the people could see out into this beautiful, clear spring, which went down to 127 feet. They could see all the way down. People were amazed by how clear the water was, they just couldn't imagine water that clear. The spring was *gorgeous*, completely unspoiled, as you can imagine back then in Florida.

I wonder if it's still that nice today.

When *we* were there, there was nothing *but* Weeki Wachee Springs and the Underwater Theater. There was not even a motel. I mentioned to you my friend Florence Gothberg; her father Ed Gothberg decided there was a need for a motel, so he retired from his air conditioning business in Birmingham, Alabama, came down to Weeki Wachee and built a motel across the street. The first building that went on there, was to build what was called the Mermaid Motel at the time. It has been remodeled several times and is still there, along with many *other* motels nowadays; a little town has grown up nearby, Spring Hill, Florida. There are many fast food restaurants and all sorts of things at the intersection of Highway 19 and Highway 50, which is where Weeki Wachee Springs is. It's now all built-up from Brooksville, all the way down 19 past the springs, all kinds of commercial buildings. Which is a shame, because it has polluted the springs. Ground water seeps down and gets into the underwater flow. The Weeki Wachee Springs water isn't as clear as it used to be … there's now a lot of eelgrass … slimy-looking green stuff along the banks … things that were never there before.

Your Weeki Wachee show: Would you describe it to me?

There were usually three mermaids performing at a time. The other two girls and I would wade into the water from the bank, we would swim out to where we knew our "stage" was underneath us,

On a hot Silver Springs day, Ginger Stanley tests with her toes and decides to do her fishing down in the water (photographs by Bruce Mozert).

and we would do a surface dive: bend at the waist and swim down, like you do from the surface of a swimming pool if you want to get to the bottom. The stage was 25 feet down, a metal enclosure that we entered through the bottom. Once we ducked up inside it, from our waists down we were standing in water and from our waists up it was air. There was a large air compressor up on the bank, and hoses ran down to the stage. Inside the stage there were valves that we controlled by hand just like you would a water faucet. We could turn up the air or turn it down at will. The stage was maybe a hundred feet from the windows of the Underwater Theater.

After standing there inside the stage for a moment, we would turn on an "air curtain": We turned a valve and bubbles of compressed air would rise up out of holes in a perforated hose that extended across the bottom-front exterior of the stage. The bubbles created a beautiful air curtain that of course came from the bottom rather than the top, which is where curtains usually come from. It completely concealed us back in that stage, so we could do whatever we wanted in there while the air curtain was on. One at a time we would duck out of the stage and perform in front of the air curtain these beautiful ballet routines. They were pretty to look at but we had to hold our breath quite a long time while we were performing them—one to two minutes.

Each of us was assigned a different routine, and each of us would perform it in front of the air curtain. There were no lights underwater, just natural light. After the three ballet routines, we would turn off the air curtain and take our air hoses. Each air hose had a nozzle we could turn up or down, giving us as much compressed air as we needed … different people liked different amounts. The three of us would swim with our hoses over to within a few feet of the Underwater Theater windows. At that point, we would feed the fish very hard dough balls. The fish somehow knew that we were coming—I guess they could hear the music from the theater, and these gorgeous fish would gather and eat out of our hands. Then we would remove our masks so that people could have a great photo opportunity, 'cause we looked pretty. We smiled and looked perfectly natural down there with all these fish around us.

After that, we would swim to old tree limbs that were embedded into the bank of the spring and we would sit there. We had underwater a bunch of small carbonated drinks, Grapettes, and we had to drink the whole six ounces. Using a very large bottle opener that was weighted and tied to a limb, each of us would open a bottle and drink the blue beverage. How we did that was, we would take air into our mouths from the hose, and then we'd put

Ginger Stanley at Silver Springs with a glass bottom boat in the background (photograph by Bruce Mozert).

the bottle up to our lips and we'd blow that air into the bottle. That air would displace the liquid which would then go into our mouths and then we would swallow. Soon the Grapette bottle was filled with air and *we* were filled with the Grapette [*laughs*].

After you'd finished the Grapette, you'd put your thumb over the opening in the bottle, to show the audience it was empty; and then you moved your thumb and the audience would see bubbles rising from the bottle as it filled with water. Back then, people thought that everything we did underwater was somehow a trick, because nobody was used to seeing *any*thing done underwater; it was the very beginning of the scuba era. And certainly no one had ever seen anybody free-swimming out there, just holding a little air hose to breathe from every now and then! Because they assumed that everything we were doing was a trick, we did everything that we could do to make our underwater actions exaggerated, to reinforce that yes we *were* doing the things we appeared to be doing. For instance, the fact that we truly did drink that Grapette underwater!

We would also eat: We were provided with firm things like carrots and apples, so that they wouldn't disintegrate and get messy. *Sometimes* bananas, but they weren't as good [*laughs*]! Apples and carrots were good; because of the color, they would "show." We could take a bite, chew it up and swallow it before we took another breath of air. Water was not mixed with the food because you could form an air pocket in your mouth, the same as the air pocket inside the stage. Where air *is*, the water can't *go*. People didn't understand, they thought, "Oh, how soggy and horrible *that* must be!" *No*, it tastes just like it tastes on land! You would take a bite, chew it up and swallow it, and convey to the audience "That was good!" with sign language—rub your tummy or whatever.

After that, we would all go out once again and perform what they called "The Underwater Elevator": We showed people how we were able to maintain our depth in the water simply by maintaining the amount of air in our lungs. If you took a deep breath of air from the hose and held it, of course you'd shoot straight to the surface, which we weren't allowed to do because then it wouldn't be an underwater show any more [*laughs*]! We had to remain down at least 15 feet and more at all times, and we did this by controlling the amount of air in our lungs. You would take maybe a half-breath of air if you wanted to stay right at eye level with the people in the audience, or a deep breath and you would *shoot* up and then you would exhale quickly and sink like a rock [*laughs*]—go down down down, *so* fast! We'd get *way* down and then take a breath of air and come back up. The audience finally understood how we could maintain a depth of, like, 15 to 25 feet most of the time, right in front of them, without it varying very much, by exhaling little bubbles of air here and there.

At one point in the show, one of the three girls had to do what they called a deep dive. This was to demonstrate not only how deep you could go in the water but, at the end of it, how long you could hold your breath coming *out* of this deep dive. One of us would swim down to around 120 feet beneath the surface, near the opening to a cavern they called "The Mouth." Billions of gallons of clear water rush out of that underwater cavern, very, very swift, and you had to go down slightly off-center of it; if you were in the current, it would push you up to the top.

You would swim down to it and wrap your legs tightly around a pipe that had been embedded there. Holding onto that pipe was the only way you could stay down, because the water was surging up so strongly past your body there. Of course by this time you were winded, so you would sit there and take a *lot* of deep breaths of air in order to get your breath back. You would breathe until you were comfortable, and then when you were ready, you would give the hose three pulls. That signal let the remaining two girls in the stage know that you were ready to have them pull the air hose away from you. That was supposed to be exciting and a surprise—the people in the audience couldn't imagine you being left down there with no air! You would wait a little bit and then once the bubbles were cleared, you would smile and swim over close to the stage, all the time holding your breath; do some ballet routines *vvvvery slowwwly*, and when you were almost out of air you would get right in front of the stage, wave goodbye, and duck up inside. This was a demonstration of "breath control," how long you could hold your breath. You did it for as long as you could, two minutes, three minutes, however long you felt you could hold it. It varied according to the day … according to how *you* felt sometimes too [*laughs*]. But audiences were amazed by this too, and it was very exciting.

Once you went up inside the stage, you waited a few minutes in order to be sure that, having been down there that deep, you were fully decompressed. Then you would get a deep breath of air from the stage and all three of you would duck down again and float up to the surface. Two would do what is called "the adagio pose": One swimmer would hold up another swimmer, who was in a pretty ballet pose, with an arched back and a knee bent. The one on the bottom would also have one

At Silver Springs, kooky photo shoots were sometimes used as an excuse to break up the day and get in the cool water. A table, chairs and a door create the illusion of an office as Ginger Stanley takes dictation and "Buck" Ray (middle), general manager of the Springs, greets a visitor. The guy playing the visitor was a man who came to the Springs to conduct business and found himself participating in a photo shoot! "It was funny the way we *did* things back then," Stanley laughs today (photograph by Bruce Mozert).

6. Creature Conversations (Ginger Stanley)

knee up. Two girls would go up that way, in the adagio pose, and the third would simply strike a pretty pose and go up alone. There had to be an ending to the show, and that's how it was ended.

Sounds like it was fun for everybody.

Once the audience was in the theater watching us, they thought they were in another world. And *we* thought we were in another world when we were swimming the shows. It was so pretty! The water was cold [*laughs*], but we were having fun while performing all these routines. This hadn't been done before, we were doing something completely new and something that people really enjoyed and were fascinated by.

Ginger Stanley affixes a bumper sticker to the car of a Silver Springs visitor (photograph by Bruce Mozert).

Incidentally, I mentioned doing the deep dive and wrapping my legs around that pipe in order to stay down there. Well, there was this huge catfish that stayed right at that pipe. Its head looked about as big as mine [*laughs*]! It was so huge that we girls wouldn't turn our backs on it, we always sat and faced it, because if one of its long barbs sticks into you, that hurts! So we didn't want that catfish to come over near us. He just sat there and swayed back and forth in the current, but we were really, really frightened of it. We kept telling Ricou about it: "Oh, that catfish was down there again!" So finally, one night, "miraculously," that big catfish disappeared, and was never seen again [*laughs*]! *Some*body, obviously, speared that catfish and got him out of there because we didn't want him there. It's one of the things I remember most about that deep dive, having to face that catfish until, finally, somebody did something about it. And it had to be Ricou—but he never would admit it![1]

How many shows a day were there?

At the time that I was there, five, sometimes six shows a day, depending on the crowds. Before Disneyworld, Weeki Wachee, Silver Springs and Cypress Gardens were the foremost destinations for people coming to (what they called) "the Florida attractions." Quite often we swimmers, on our time off, would take paddleboards and paddle our way down Weeki Wachee River and then come back up against the current. This was our "relaxation," if we had a moment between shows. It also kept you cool!

You wore swimsuits, not the mermaid tails that came later, correct?

That's right. Only for special occasions would we put on the tails. Our swimsuits were provided by whatever companies decided they were going to provide all the swimsuits for all of the swimmers that year. Various companies gave us swimsuits back then … Jantzen … Catalina … Gantner … Rosemarie Reid … they would provide 'em for free and they got publicity because their symbols were on the sides of the suits. We also had swim masks and swim fins; you couldn't do all these things underwater without the swim fins, they helped you propel through the water. The swim fins were provided by Voit.

In a little water pump house on the edge of the spring, each of us had a peg with our name on it, and on it we hung all of our equipment. Each of our masks and swim fins had our name on them as well. Before each show, you got your own mask and fins and flippers and put them on, and from that pump house you would swim out, go down to the stage, and perform as I have described.

In the beginning, before I got there, Ricou helped train the swimmers. By the time I got there, he was swimming in shows and he was in the Underwater Theater announcing shows. Later, I did that too, as I didn't want to be a lifeguard or ticket taker or some of the other things you had to do during the day when you weren't swimming. I decided that announcing was less boring than those other jobs [*laughs*], so I said, "I can announce the shows that I'm not swimming in," and I became an announcer as well as a swimmer.

Ginger Stanley on the handlebars of a bike pedaled by Dick Moses. Silver Springs PR director Bill Ray, photographer Bruce Mozert, Ricou Browning and Ginger would dream up these goofy scenarios and then get the needed props, go underwater and photograph them. Newspapers ran photographs like this as fast as the Springs folks could pump them out, helping to make the place one of the go-to spots for tourists visiting Florida (photograph by Bruce Mozert).

There was wildlife of all kinds around the banks of the spring. Sometimes duck eggs would sit so long there on the banks, in the hot sun, without hatching, that they would rot. One day Ricou found a rotten duck egg and, just before the show, he cracked it into my mask and put my mask back on my little peg [*laughs*]. All you did before the show was rinse it briefly, swish water through it, so you can imagine how the stench of that remained in that mask for the entire show! I thought, "Oh, I'm going to die before I finish the show!" It was so terrible. I vowed I would get even with him.

The very next day, when we went out to do our shows, I poured brown iodine in his swim fins [*laughs*], so when he put them on, the iodine went all the way up his legs, and of course it wasn't gonna come off and we had to go swim our shows. So he had to swim his show with iodine on the bottoms of his legs and his feet—and then wonder how he was gonna get it off! We laughed about that many times later.

Did you live in the Mermaid Villas the whole time you worked there?

No, just while I was training. If you chose to live there once you were working at Weeki Wachee, you could pay a small amount and stay. But once we were trained, most of us wanted to move on into town—Brooksville, the closest town, 12 miles away. They had a lot of little duplexes there, all brand new and side by side. You could get four girls together and live in a two-bedroom duplex, and we were right in town where we could grocery-shop and go to the movies and do things like that at night. Brooksville was small, but it *was* a town. Weeki Wachee wasn't *any*thing back then [*laughs*]! It was a spring in the middle of the woods!

Besides that catfish, what other potentially dangerous critters would be in the water with you at Weeki Wachee?

A moment ago I mentioned that for relaxation, we would paddleboard on Weeki Wachee River. A lot of people went down that river in this fashion, and one lady, Martha Bell Smith, the wife of Walton Hall Smith [the manager of Weeki Wachee Springs, post–Newt Perry], used to not only go down on those paddleboards, she decided she wanted to swim down that river. Not *too* far, but a ways, because she could go *with* the current and then get out at a certain place along the bank and simply walk back up to the Spring. It was her afternoon or evening swim. One day, an alligator came off the bank and attacked, and took a chunk out of her arm. She always went down alone, which was not smart, but she did it because she wasn't going very far. She got out of the water and, holding her injured arm, flagged down a passing car, and they got her to the hospital there in Brooksville. It was a terrible thing for all of us to know that that had happened. An alligator attack doesn't happen very often to a human.

Silver Springs photographer Bruce Mozert would capture different critters and then, come picture-taking time, hand Ginger Stanley these "live props" (here a turtle) (photograph by Bruce Mozert).

So you were never bothered?

Sometimes when we were doing the mermaid show, we would hear a little *tap-tap-tapping*, which was the signal that there was something dangerous in the water with us. Alligators would come up to the Springs sometimes. Usually they wouldn't be the great big ones, but the smaller ones. Many times, while swimming shows, we would look up and there would be alligator legs above us, on the surface. They usually didn't come down, but they were curious and they would be up there. We didn't want to be in there if the gators were there, but we couldn't do anything about it.

You said the signal was a *tap tap tap*. Who'd be tapping, and on what?

Whatever announcer was in the Underwater Theater announcing the show could see everything that was going on, and he would say, "Oh, wow, there's an alligator. I've got to let them know!" And he would *tap tap tap* on the glass window, usually with the edge of the microphone, and we'd hear it and realize, "Okay, we'd better beware. There's an alligator in here with us." We [the mermaids] really couldn't see a lot: We would have no mask, and with water in your eyes, it would be very blurry. Quite often we would hear that *tap tap tap* because our shows were the beginning of civilization coming to that spring. Nothin' had been there before, and the alligators had that place all to themselves!

To me, a New Yorker, the funny thing about you and Ricou is the way you consider the arrival of an alligator as "all in a day's work." I live several blocks from the Hudson River and if I heard that an alligator was in the Hudson, I'd be scared *inside my house*. But you guys just shrug 'em off, especially Ricou.

Growing up in Florida is different. There are alligators all over the place. I water-skied, and my children water-skied, knowing that there were alligators along the bank. We would ski right *past* 'em [*laughs*]. But many times we would wait to water-ski until we got out in the middle of the lake, instead of skiing from the dock or from the side, because there *weren't* any alligators out in the middle, they usually stayed along the banks. Somehow they disappear during the heat of the day, but at dusk they would come out to eat and to swim around. We would often water-ski in the summer until like seven, eight o'clock 'cause it doesn't get dark 'til late, and as we were coming in, we would see them along the bank and know that we'd been... [*laughs*]. We'd been *skiing* with them, basically! And we were there with our children. So in Florida it's sorta just "one of those things"; you *kind of* know they're there, but you ignore it.[2]

Not until Martha Bell Smith got attacked by one did I really realize how dangerous they were. And I'd bet that she got attacked by what they call a sow gator, which is the mother. They're very protective of their nests along the bank, so when it's time for the babies to be born, or if they have eggs that they're protecting, they're going to try to scare you away. I bet that's what happened to Martha Bell, she got close to the bank instead of staying out in the center, and she [the gator] swam out and grabbed her, to protect her nest.

You worked at Weeki Wachee two and a half years, you said.

Yes, and then on my day off I would go up and visit my sister Chris, who lived in Ocala. Weeki Wachee wasn't really a town, it was the boonies, and on days off I'd want to go someplace where there was a town, movies, places to shop and all of that. And what did I do once I finished shopping or going to a movie or whatever I did on my day off? I would go out to Silver Springs [*laughs*]. It was open to the public and they had a sand beach, much like an ocean beach. I would hang out at the beach, and of course when I'd get hot, I'd get in the water and swim. Bruce Mozert, the photographer at Silver Springs, was observing me on these many Saturdays as I did laps across the spring and of course I would do the same things

Wet-ty Crocker!
Ginger Stanley prepares Thanksgiving dinner on the Silver Springs floor. The "smoke" is either milk or the fog created by dry ice (photograph by Bruce Mozert).

there that I had been taught to do for the shows: I would do a surface dive and do some of these little back rolls and forward rolls and other ballet routines under the water because it was fun, it was entertaining to me. Bruce eventually asked me if I would come on my next day off and pose for underwater still pictures, which Silver Springs put on postcards and things like that. I told him, "Sure!" I didn't think about, "Wow, I shouldn't be doing this if I'm working at Weeki Wachee!" because there wasn't any clause in my contract that said I couldn't do things for other people.

That was a paying job also, correct?

That's correct. For a while I would go up on my day off and I was their weekend photographers' model, posing for pictures on land as well in the water. Eventually they said, "We could use you full-time," and took me to the p.r. director Peter Schaal, and they hired me to not only pose for pictures but answer the phone, paste news clippings about Silver Springs in a scrapbook—I was kept very busy doing a lot of things, four or five different little jobs.

The photographs would be used as postcards, or they'd be sent by the public relations and publicity department to newspapers and magazines all over the country. I also appeared in newsreels that were shot at Silver Springs. They would play in movie theaters, showing us having a Thanksgiving dinner underwater [*laughs*], or a circus underwater, or a fashion show underwater, or a beauty pageant underwater—you name it, we did it underwater. These newsreels would be shown all over the U.S., and maybe other places too. In my three and a half years at Silver Springs, I would say we did at least 27, 28 of those.

You were at Silver Springs when the Gill Man came into your life.

[*Laughs.*] That's right, I was booked to do the first 3-D underwater movie, which was *Creature from the Black Lagoon*. Ricou and I were just good buddies always, and because we had such fun swimming together, and because we knew each other so well from the underwater routines, when it was time to do *Creature from the Black Lagoon* at Wakulla Springs and they asked him if he would be the underwater Creature, he thought of me and highly recommended me as a swimming double for Julie Adams. He had gone to California for them to mold and make the Creature suit and make it correct for him, and they had to make two or three before they got it right. Then once they got it correct, they had to make a *lot* of them, because if one got torn or snagged, or was too wet to put on the next day, they had to have extras lined up. The same with me and the white swimsuit I wore in the movie, there wasn't just one of them.

Wakulla is a clear spring that people can swim in, but it's a state preserve so there could be no water shows or anything like *that* there. The people making *Creature* liked that the Wakulla water was so clear, and they thought that the scenery along its banks looked very much like the Amazon jungle. So they chose that as the place that they would do their filming.

During production, there were a lot of people around for safety purposes, as well as to supply air to Ricou if he needed it. They couldn't put an air supply in Ricou's Gill Man suit, the suit wouldn't accommodate it. And Ricou really couldn't see that well, his vision was quite blurred when he was doing these scenes. If you've ever been underwater and opened your eyes, you know what I mean. But if Ricou wore goggles under the Gill Man mask, they would fog up and then he *really* couldn't see! So Ricou actually did the whole thing with very blurred vision, and his peripheral vision wasn't great either.

The highlight of the whole movie, one of the best scenes in *any* monster movie, is when you're swimming with the Creature beneath you.

The funny part about our "Beauty and the Beast" underwater ballet sequence was that Ricou, because of his bad vision, kept bumping into me [*laughs*]! As the girl swam on the surface, the Gill Man had to be just *right* underneath her for it to look beautiful, almost like they were in unison, and the girl wasn't supposed to know that he was there. But Ricou didn't stay quite far enough beneath me! Any time we touched, they had to redo it, and so we redid it, I think, three or four times. All of a sudden, I would feel a little bump, or get swiped by his hand, and I'd think, "Oh! Ricou has run into me again!" The ballet routine with the Creature turned out beautifully and became one of the important scenes of the movie.

Also underwater were quite a few cameramen, and assistants, to move that 3-D camera around. Swimming around with that *big* 3-D camera, they had to take each scene from several angles. They'd never shoot a scene from one angle and say, "That's a take!," they had to get it from three or four angles and then determine which ones looked more interesting than the others.

Various people have told me that your "underwater director" James Havens wouldn't go underwater.

James Havens, the second unit director, did his work from the land [*laughs*]. We would all stand on the dock—me, "Scotty" Welbourne the underwater photographer, Ricou and Havens' assistant—and we'd go through all the motions of the scene, doing exactly what was to take place once we got down in the water. Havens would say what he wanted in each shot, describe it to everybody: "I want this in the shot," "You're gonna go here" or "You're gonna go there" or whatever. Havens wouldn't go underwater but he knew what he needed on film, and "Scotty" knew how to *get* it on film. Once we all knew in our minds what he wanted and once we got in the water, it was up to "Scotty" to capture it on film.

What did you do to get your hair dark like Julie Adams'?

She was brunette and I was blonde, but size-wise I matched her. They tried all kinds of rinses on my hair but they finally realized that, being in the water as much as I was, doing all this filming, rinses were not going to stay in and keep my hair dark. Finally we had to dye my blonde hair black—which kinda distressed me, but I was already there at Wakulla and making the movie, so I said [*reluctantly*], "Okaaay…" I was promised, "Oh, we'll get it blonde again before you go back to Silver Springs to work." But they could not get it light blonde again, it ended up more like a strawberry blonde. It took a while, but eventually it grew out.

I've never been in transparent spring water like that but I'd imagine that once you're underwater swimming around, you might get the feeling that you're flying.

You definitely have the feeling of being in another world, a different world, and of course you move easily because the water makes you so buoyant, especially if you're trained to control your air and breath. You feel as if you're in a magical underwater place, and you feel as if you're down there all alone, and it's *your* special place in the world, and you are not bothered by anything. Your thoughts and dreams can be whatever you want, and you can have a marvelous time. It is *so* beautiful there. People can't imagine what it's like unless they have been there, and they can't imagine the freedom you have with those air hoses, as compared to scuba gear. With all that heavy equipment, you can't move as freely. The ideal way, if you're going to be underwater, was the way we did it, which was by hose-breathing compressed air.

Another moment in *Black Lagoon* that everybody likes is when the Creature has the unconscious girl under his arm and he swims down to the underwater entrance to his grotto.

That dive was difficult, because I was supposed to be passed out, and like I've described, Ricou did not *have* air. Ricou had to swim with me under his arm, in a limp position, and so *one-handed* he had to swim all the way down, 80 feet beneath the surface, and duck under a limestone ledge.

We went down with our lungs full of surface air, a breath of air that we got just before we started. Both Ricou and I also needed to clear our ears *during* that descent. When you're going that deep, every ten feet you descend, you have to equalize the pressure on your ears, or your eardrums will burst. The way you clear your ears is, you hold your nose shut with your fingers and you blow, and that makes the air go into your Eustachian tubes and equalizes the pressure. I couldn't lift my hand up to my nose 'cause I was supposed to be unconscious, so I figured out that I could let my head roll over and lay against Ricou's shoulder, press my nose shut against his suit, and I could clear my ears. I don't know what *he* did, but it had to be something similar. You *can* clear your ears, if you are used to doing it, by opening your mouth and swallowing real hard, like you do on an airplane if you need to equalize pressure. I think Ricou did that as well as, every now and then, push *his* head over toward one of his shoulders, as his arm came up, and press his nose shut and clear his ears. Once we got under that ledge, there were two people with air hoses, waiting to give one to each of us. It was quite difficult, diving down 80 feet on one breath, and equalizing the pressure, but we did it. Then, of course, they said, "Can you do that again, so we can shoot it from a different angle?" And we thought, "Aaarrrgggghhh!" So we did it twice, and thank goodness that was *it*.

The main thing I remember is that we were so cold. It was October of a very cold winter. Tallahassee *is* Florida but it's more like South Georgia or Alabama, it's *way* up there in Florida, not like central and south Florida, so it was quite cold for much of the filming, especially for the people who were in and out of the water.

Jack Betz, the underwater double for Richard Denning, said in an interview that the Wakulla water was 49 degrees.

No way. The water at Wakulla is 72 degrees year-round. All the springs maintain a year-round temperature; some are 72, some are 74. We couldn't have *done* the movie in 49-degree water. We almost couldn't do it in 72-degree water [*laughs*], because of the time of year. In the summer when you hit it, it was like ice water. In the winter, it was okay because the air was not as hot. We were there in October, up in Tallahassee, which is just about Georgia as far as I'm concerned. We were pretty much freezing when we would come out of that water: After being in that chilly water for quite a while, we would be wet with 72-degree water; and then we would come out into air that might be 49 or 50. Maybe *that's* what Jack Betz meant to say, th the *air* was 49 degrees. I can remember wearing a wi coat on the little plane as I flew up to Tallahassee the movie. It was cold enough that we were careful *not* to do anything that would create any delays; we didn't want *any* disruptions in the filming because that would prolong our being cold! Ricou was complaining one time, "Oh, I'm freezing to death!" and he was shivering, and some guy got the idea that Ricou should have a little shot of brandy, to warm him up. But after one or two of these shots of brandy, he said, "No more! You can't do this, or I can't do my scene!" He said, "It's great for warming me up, but there has to be another way!" [*Laughs.*] I don't think he was a drinker anyway, because athletes usually aren't.

He *was* a smoker back then.

*Every*body smoked way back then.

Did you?

No, *heavens* no, I never smoked. Never smoked, never drank.

Make believe what happens in the movie, happened in real life: A monster grabs a girl off a boat and she faints and he carries her down 80 feet to his cave. Do her eardrums burst?

Yeah, they would, if she fainted and couldn't clear her ears and the monster carried her underwater that far. Unless she had *very* flexible eardrums that would clear on their own [*laughs*]! I still have to clear my ears when I just go down to the bottom of my swimming pool, which is ten feet deep. Even at ten feet, you can feel the pressure.

More than a few *Black Lagoon* fans are quite taken with the white bathing suit that Julie Adams wore, and you wore, in the movie. As a fashion expert, tell me what you thought of it at the time.

I had never seen a suit before where the breasts were built into the suit [*laughs*]. There were many layers of fabric there, it was thickly, thickly padded. I think it was done that way for a reason: So when this white bathing suit got wet, you would never *see* anything. I was not used to wearing a suit where the top was padded. Plus, it took a long time for it to dry, because it was so thick. The top stayed cold longer than the bottom, because it held all that water in! Also, they had cut it way-high on the front of the leg, just so the leg would look longer and prettier, and they cut the top down lower. I think another reason they padded it was so it would hold the shape regardless of whatever ballet move (or whatever else) you were doing. Your body changes as you move, and I think they wanted it to be perfection. And it *was*, it was a great suit. But I didn't get to keep one!

How many were there for you at Wakulla?

I had many suits, so I had a dry one each time I was out there. I'm sure there were duplicates in case one got torn or dirty or they couldn't use it any more for whatever reason. I think there were five of those suits there with me, so they would dry out in between. And they would have to wash 'em and clean 'em in between too, 'cause they would get body makeup on 'em. We had to wear body makeup because water makes your skin look so much whiter than it really is. They didn't want the flesh tones white-white underwater so I had body makeup all over me, arms, legs, face, everything. A makeup lady did it. [*Pause*] No, I believe it was a makeup *man*!

Tom Case and Mark Reedall were the makeup men at Wakulla.

I remember both of them, especially Tom. He did a lot of the making-up of me.

Any other memories of *Creature from the Black Lagoon*?

When it was about to open in our area, the Marion Theater in Ocala wanted Ricou and me to take part in the premiere. Ricou and I were outside the theater, in our street clothes,

The Creature (Ricou Browning) and his kayoed cutie (Ginger Stanley) in the lucid waters of Silver Springs on *Revenge of the Creature*.

and people talked to us, did interviews and took photos and whatever. Once the movie started playing inside, Ricou and I could go in and see it with the audience, when we wanted to. That was the first time we had seen it, and I was amazed. I thought it was *fantastic*, and more scary than you can imagine. We had never seen the whole script, we just were given each day's script for *that day's* shooting. So when we saw it, and saw it in 3-D, it was *so* impressive, we could not believe it. As the Creature swam toward you, his big hand actually came out into the audience as he was doing his underwater crawl, and when he reached up to grab my foot, it was as if I was treading water above the audience. When the hand touches my foot, you could hear the people in the theater go [*Stanley makes a horrified sound*]—they were screaming and whatever. It was very impressive, and the people in the audience were just scared to death, *really*. They'd never seen a movie in 3-D and underwater and scary like that. It was fun.

Creature from the Black Lagoon was so successful that Universal wanted to make a sequel, so later that year [1954] they had tryouts for underwater doubling jobs in *Revenge of the Creature* and I went again. I think they had me in mind for the job in *Revenge* right from the start, but still they went through what I guess they *always* go through, like a casting process, especially for something this important. Of course "Scotty" Welbourne and I had become buddies by then and, like Ricou, he knew what I could do underwater and that we worked well together and so forth. There were several people there trying out, not a lot, but several, 'cause not that many people could *do* it and were *good* at it. They had people audition, but I think in their hearts and minds they knew from the very beginning they were going to use me. They didn't let *me* know that, but… [*laughs*].

Where did they audition everybody?

I believe it was over where we were going to be doing the filming, at Marine Studios. Oh, by the way, when I auditioned for *Revenge of the Creature* I said, "If you're looking for someone to be an underwater swimming double, I don't choose to dye my hair again. I hope you will choose a blonde heroine! Then I can double for her." And Universal chose Lori Nelson, who was very blonde, and I doubled for her in *Revenge of the Creature*.

Universal knew how well the "Beauty and the Beast" scene in Black Lagoon had gone over, and tried it again in Revenge of the Creature.

That ballet routine had become one of the important scenes of that first movie so yes, *Revenge* had a scene like that as well. This time the ballet was shot at Silver Springs, with me doubling Lori Nelson and "Sonny" [Robert Lee] Tinney doubling John Agar, and Ricou as the Creature. "Sonny" Tinney had been trained up in Tallahassee along with Ricou, "Sonny" and Ricou were swimming buddies from Florida State University. The ballet in *Revenge* did not receive the attention that the ballet in the first movie did, because there wasn't as much interplay between the Creature and the girl. "Sonny" Tinney was part of the scene, doubling John Agar, and he and I did some fun-play-romantic things in the scene and even had a little kiss underwater because Agar's character and Lori Nelson's character were in love. For a good bit of the scene, the Creature was just standing off to the side, watching.

We also shot at Marine Studios, near St. Augustine. In the movie they called the place Ocean Harbor and they brought in the Creature and put him in one of the big tanks there as they tried to see if he was trainable. Doubling for Lori Nelson, I would go down into the Creature's tank, and Ricou was chained to the bottom—literally [*laughs*]! I had on scuba gear, but he of course was supposed to be the Creature so his only air supply came from people, between scenes, bringing him an air hose and then going back off-camera to the sidelines where they weren't seen. He had certain signals that he would use, putting up his hand when he needed a breath of air, things like this. A hose would be brought to him and he'd get some air, and then they would pick up the scene right where they left off.

We were in a tank with all sorts of creatures—moray eels, sharks and everything else. They reminded me that sharks are attracted to light colors, and I had on a white swimsuit [*laughs*]. Sharks are also attracted to shiny objects, and I was training the Creature with this shiny big ball on a chain [*laughs*]! I said [*nervously*], "Oh … sharks are attracted to these things…?" They said, "Don't worry, we have a lot of lifeguards around who will *be* there at a moment's notice." I said, "I certainly hope so!"

Who was telling you these things?

The Marine Studios safety people. I don't know if they did it to tease me or if they were trying to warn me, but they sure got the point across that I was gonna look like a tender morsel [*laughs*]! They would feed the sharks right before the scenes were shot, make sure they were well-fed so that none of them would be hungry. So in I went, swimming with the sharks and the manta rays and the moray eels, which were worse than the sharks. A moray eel is very ugly, has sharp teeth, and they don't care *who* they bite. I think sharks only attack humans if they're hungry or if there's a reason, but moray eels just don't want you in their territory. To me, they were more sinister!

All my *Revenge* interviewees talk about the beach parties. John Agar, who had a drinking problem—was he a crazy man at these parties?

Yeah, he was! He was absolutely professional when he was doing his scenes, but at night, when he was at these parties, yeah, he was always one of the ones in the water with his clothes on [*laughs*]. And trying to get everybody *else* to get in the water. Next day he would be handsome and sober and ready to do his work. He was one of *those*.

On *Revenge* you worked with two Gill Men, Browning underwater and Tom Hennesy topside.

Yes, and Ricou worked as a lifeguard when he wasn't needed to play the Creature. For example, when Tom Hennesy, the big man playing the Land Creature, took me under his arm and dived into the water at the Lobster House up in Jacksonville, Ricou was out at a buoy, as a lifeguard. In that scene they had to use "the tall Creature," they couldn't use the smaller man [Browning] if the Creature was supposed to be huge, 6'5" or whatever. On that picture, Ricou always did whatever they needed him to do, so ... out of the Creature suit, into the lifeguard position [*laughs*]!

That Lobster House scene was really something: Inside this building, they had *so* many lights on so that they could film the scene, and they forgot about the sprinkler system that was in the ceiling. When the lights got hot, all of a sudden the sprinkler system went on and water poured down on all these extras and the band and everybody else who was in there. They had to clear it out, reset, re-stage.

When Tom dove off the pier with me under his arm, he got into trouble. He had lead in his Creature feet, 'cause he had to walk very awkwardly, to lumber around on land. Everybody, including him I suppose, had forgotten about the lead in his feet, that he should not go in the water with that extra weight. He dived into the water with me and suddenly he realized, not only were there heavy currents, swift currents, and jellyfish all around, but he was in this heavy land suit with the weighted shoes and everything else, trying to swim with me under his arm! So he got in trouble, Tom did. He was supposed to swim with me over to a buoy but he couldn't make it, he had to let go of me, and he was floundering around fighting the currents and fighting this heavy suit that was filling with water, like a sponge filling up, and he thought, "Oh, my soul, what will I *do*?" But some people were out in their own little personal boats watching the filming, and a young couple came over and got him into their boat. I saw what was happening and I just continued swimming by myself and went on out to the buoy. Ricou was already out there on the buoy, working in his lifeguard capacity, and I hung onto the buoy.

The director Jack Arnold also had not anticipated all of the problems trying to put the Land Creature in the water for that scene, how difficult it was. And when we finally got back to the Lobster House, Jack Arnold asked Tom Hennesy if he would do it again! Arnold said, "We need to re-shoot that," and Tom said, "Not on your life!" [*Laughs.*] "You're gonna have to figure out some other way to do this somewhere else. Not here!" So they had to shoot part of the scene out at Universal Studios in California: In the movie, when the Creature and the girl dive into the water, that part was shot at the Lobster House in Jacksonville, but after that, most of the rest of what you see was shot in a pool on a stage at Universal.

*Ginger Stanley (left) was glad that she'd be underwater-doubling a blonde (*Revenge of the Creature *star Lori Nelson, right) in the second Gill Man movie, because she wasn't willing to dye her hair dark again as she had for the first film's Julie Adams.*

Hennesy told me the story of his "near-drowning" and I transcribed it, and when Ricou read it, he pretty much scoffed at it. Ricou said that in that foam rubber suit, Hennesy couldn't have gone under if he'd *tried* to.

I think that Tom got frightened, that he was stunned when he went into the water and realized, "Here I am in this suit, and there's a very swift current and there are jellyfish and ...

wow, what do I *do*?" I think he just was a bit overwhelmed with it all, shocked, and he panicked. In his interview with you, he didn't want to *say* that, I'm sure [*laughs*]. "How can I swim to the buoy with her under my arm, and in this current? I can't handle it all!" I'm sure he'd never tried swimming with someone under his arm. It takes a strong, proficient person to do that kind of swimming—which, of course, *Ricou* was. Ricou doesn't give himself credit for how difficult that Creature role was, all the way around.

Thank you for saying that, I'm going to enjoy putting that in the book. Every time anybody marvels about the very impressive things Ricou's done, he tries to brush it off and says it was just a job. It's hard to get him to "take the compliment"!

He doesn't know how expert he *was*, to have done all of the parts of his Creature role. Ricou doing his part underwater was so different than the people who did the land stuff [the guys who played the Land Creatures]. Those people just had to walk around in that suit, that's all they had to do. Ricou did all the work! Ricou *absolutely* was, to me, the only Creature. He's the only one who really lived under that water. He had to work hard, he had to hold his breath most of the time, he could hardly see. Ricou was so conscientious, he'd work 'til he dropped, and he did things underwater I've never seen others do. To my mind, he's "up there" with Johnny Weissmuller and names like that, people famous for what they could do in the water. Speaking of how modest Ricou is, I bet he was too modest to mention to you that at Weeki Wachee last summer [2012] there was a 65th anniversary "Mermaid Reunion," and he and I were inducted into the Weeki Wachee Springs Hall of Fame. Our plaques have a permanent place on the wall of the Underwater Theater. I bet Ricou didn't mention that to you.

No he didn't. Of course not.

Of course not. That's an accolade to him, and he never takes those very well. And *I'm* pleased for every one they'll *give* me [*laughs*]! Newt Perry was also inducted posthumously because, as I've been telling you, he started the shows there and developed the underwater hose-breathing and the concept of the show and everything else. His daughter Delee came up and accepted his plaque for him. We got beautiful replicas to bring home. Mine is on a stand in my bedroom.[3]

After *Revenge of the Creature*, you returned to Marine Studios, this time working in the porpoise tank.

They knew I had been over there, working on movies and things, and so they dreamed up an idea. They had porpoises who were very well-trained to fetch balls and other things, and what they had me do was go underwater where they had a Christmas tree partially decorated. Down there was a scuba tank with a long hose so I would have a method of getting my air. I stood by that partially decorated tree with a large basket on my arm, and these porpoises were trained to pick up these oversized balls, Christmas ornaments, very pretty in color, and bring them over and put them in the basket. I would then take them out and decorate the Christmas tree with them. This was filmed and included in a newsreel shown at movie theaters.

The same year as *Revenge*, you had another underwater doubling role, substituting for Esther Williams in *Jupiter's Darling* [1955].

Although Esther Williams was an excellent swimmer, she was not used to going to the depths that they wanted.

At Weeki Wachee's 65th Anniversary "Mermaid Reunion" in 2012, Ginger Stanley is flanked by Weeki Wachee park manager Toby Brewer (on right) and assistant park manager Robyn Anderson as she displays her "Mermaid" Hall of Fame plaque. In the second photograph, Brewer and Stanley watch as Ricou Browning puts his John Hancock on a *Black Lagoon* poster (photographs courtesy John Athanason).

Also, she ruptured an eardrum during filming, so they put an earplug in her ear and then they glued on this little, very plastic-y-looking artificial ear, over *her* ear, so no water could get to that perforated eardrum. It looked real once she got it on. She would go into the water just for closeups of her face, and then they would continue with me doing the swimming in the long shots.

Those *Jupiter's Darling* underwater scenes were shot both at Silver Springs and at Weeki Wachee Springs. In the movie, the barbarian Hannibal [Howard Keel] is getting ready to attack Rome and Esther Williams was a Roman woman held captive by Hannibal; but then she got away and some of Hannibal's men were chasing her. She and her horse went off a cliff into the water, and from then on, as a few of the soldiers pursue her underwater, it was all Silver Springs and Weeki Wachee. The chase proceeded through an old sunken galleon, and these scenes were quite beautiful. The deeper scenes were at Weeki Wachee because it has that deep cavern that I described earlier. And two of the soldiers chasing me underwater were Ricou Browning and his friend "Sonny" Tinney. The three of us were all working together again, right after *Revenge of the Creature*.

Esther Williams (left), star of MGM's Jupiter's Darling (1955), had Ginger Stanley (right) as one of her doubles in an exciting underwater chase sequence.

I assume MGM put that galleon in Silver Springs.

Yes, they put it there as a prop. Once it *was* there, Silver Springs *left* it there, 'cause then they could tell people who came by in the glass bottom boat, "Oh, there's the galleon where they filmed *Jupiter's Darling*!"

On that movie, did you hose-breathe again?

There was a hose there if anybody needed it, but I preferred to dive down holding my surface air. I have pictures of me trying to teach Esther Williams how to hose-breathe. She never quite got the hang of it; she didn't like the idea of it, she was used to just taking a breath and "doing her thing" until she couldn't hold her breath any more. Plus, as I mentioned earlier, she couldn't go very deep because she was used to a pool, not to the depth of these springs. One funny thing that happened: I was told every detail of the scene we were there to shoot, and what I was going to have to do: "You'll do *this*, you'll do *that*, you'll swim through the galleon," on and on. So when I went down, I did exactly what he said: I went down, I swam here, I swam there, I looked over my shoulder at the guys chasing me, I swam into the galleon, I turned around to look at the guys some more, I swam through the galleon and out the other side. I was down there *forever*, holding my breath, and when I came up, the whole crew, *all* the people making the movie were standing on the banks applauding, and they said, "We didn't mean you had to do it all on one breath!" I thought they wanted the whole thing done in one take [*laughs*], and so that's what I did! So of course I had to go back down and do a lot of it again, so they could film it from different angles.

A third Gill Man movie was shot in 1955, *The Creature Walks Among Us*, but you sat that one out.

That's right, I didn't do *Creature Walks Among Us*. They needed a double for Leigh Snowden but I was busy with another project, the time was not right and I couldn't do it for them. They were sorry and I was too, but it just didn't happen. In *Creature Walks Among Us*, the girl goes underwater with two guys and they're all wearing scuba gear. So the double was not free to do any pretty swimming, it was just a skill thing with scuba gear, and who wants to see a girl with scuba gear on [*laughs*]? I knew that double, her name was Ruth Skinner. She came to swim at Weeki Wachee after I left. I never swam shows with her.

In April 1955, you established a world's record by swimming seven miles underwater, the entire length of Silver River. Whose idea was it for you to try for that?

The publicity department at Silver Springs realized that it was something that nobody had ever thought of doing; and people were always calling from the news bureaus, always wanting to come to Silver Springs to film something, especially in the winter. The publicity department guys—I believe it was Ricou and Bill Ray—got together and decided that no one had ever attempted to see how long you

6. Creature Conversations (Ginger Stanley)

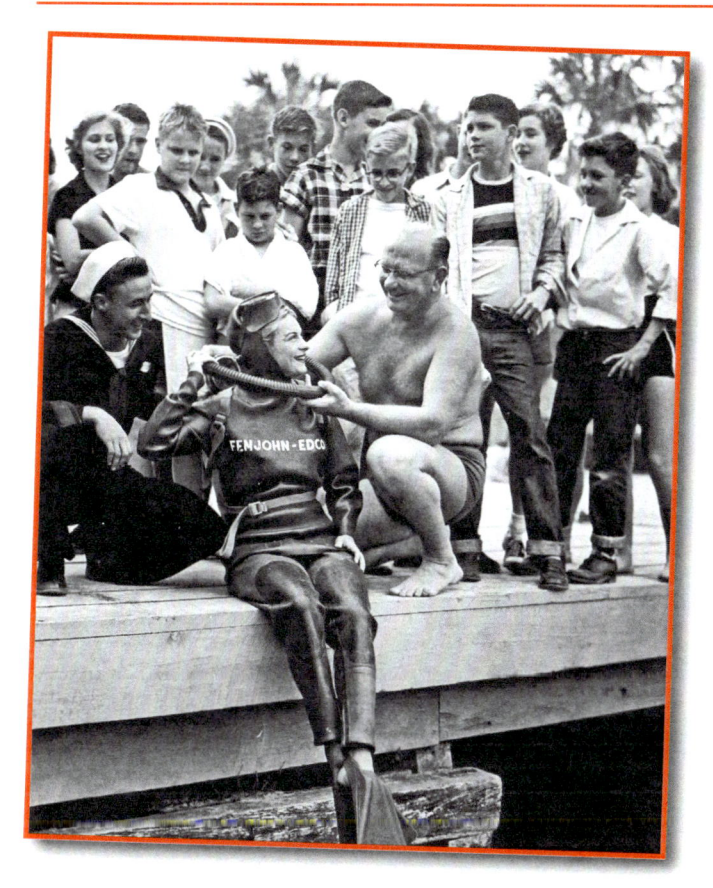

About to set a world record with a seven-mile underwater swim, Stanley is the focus of attention for a gaggle of kids and underwater cinematographer Lamar Boren (bald with glasses).

could swim or how far you could go, underwater, without surfacing. They approached me and asked if I would be willing to do this, and I said, "Well, sure." All in a day's work for me!

They contacted a Paramount News photographer who had been to Silver Springs quite a few times on other short subjects, and told him this idea, and he said, "Oh, that would be great," and he said he would come to Silver Springs and film this. As it turned out, it was a very gloomy day, it wasn't a pretty, sunny day when I was to do this. But everybody was there and you go when you're scheduled, rain or shine, and I went. I got on a wetsuit, quite different from the ones they have now, it was kind of bulky, but nevertheless a rubber exposure suit; scuba gear; the swim fins; and a facemask. I was going to start from the dock in the swimming area of Silver Springs and continue as far as I could go down Silver River, which was as clear as the Spring—I would be able to see all the way, in other words. But it ran into a darker river, a cloudy river, the Ocklawaha. The Ocklawaha was not spring water, it was murky, and as Silver River ran into it, it got too dark to see and I had to come up. In dark water you could run into tree limbs and alligators and all sorts of stuff you didn't know were there! I swam for three and a half hours.

And the newsreel photographer followed in a boat, yes?

He was on a glass bottom boat with Ricou and Bill and Bruce Mozert, the still photographer from Silver Springs. Bruce would go under the water from time to time and film part of it with his underwater camera. They had timed about how long I could go before my tank would run out of air, and they knew they had to get down there with a new tank before it ran out. While I was still swimming, Ricou would swim down to me, unbuckle the nearly empty tank, hook another one *on* me, take the mouthpiece out, put a new one in, and I'd keep *going* [*laughs*]. We did this all without me surfacing, all while I continued to move. It took four changes of air lungs, and I think at one point he also brought me down a Hershey bar or *some*thing for energy, as I could eat underwater. The water was so cold and I had been swimming for so long that I probably needed a pick-me-up. I had weights on, too, because at places the river gets rather shallow, and they wanted to be sure I did not come anywhere near the surface. If I broke surface, it wouldn't *be* an underwater record! The weights were put on me to make sure that I stayed close to the bottom of the river rather than coming on up. So I had to swim pretty hard, because I had the weights on. It was quite grueling, but it did make history; in fact, just a few years ago, one of my neighbors down the road said, "Ginger, did you realize that you were in the Guinness Book of World Records?" and I said, "Heavens no!" My seven-mile swim made the Book of Records. So I *guess* it was in there. I haven't ever looked

How much farther could you have gone if the water hadn't gotten dark?

Oh, I don't know. Probably another mile or so.

Well, you could have gone further just by turning around underwater and swimming back the way you came. That would have added to the distance.

I guess it would have. We didn't think about it. Maybe because I was tired. Maybe because I was cold. And maybe because we thought, "Oh, this is enough!" [*Laughs.*]

You also did some TV in New York.

I was on *The Garry Moore Show*, in a water-filled glass tank, showing what all I could do underwater. I was also Dick Van Dyke's underwater weathergirl when he had the CBS morning show, before going on to Hollywood. Barbara Walters was at CBS at the time and she's the one who dreamed it up: Since it was a new show, and it was going to be in competition with *The Today Show* which was already established, she said, "We need to have some

Ricou Browning helps Ginger Stanley prepare for her Silver River underwater swim.

sort of gimmick that will draw attention to our new show. Why don't we have an underwater weathergirl? I know of somebody in Florida…," because I had already been up to do *The Garry Moore Show* on CBS, and I guess Barbara remembered that I ate and drank and wrote my name on a slate underwater on Garry Moore's show.

For Dick Van Dyke's show, they built a very large tank for me and put city water in it. The city water, of course, is not nearly as clear as the water in the Florida springs—it has chlorine in it. They drew a large map of the U.S. on the side of that tank, with all of the states outlined in white. I was underwater with an air hose and a white makeup pencil, so I could write on the side of the tank. I would sit there and smile and listen, and when they said, "Snowing in the Rockies," with my white makeup pencil I would draw snowflakes over the Rockies! And when they would say, "Raining in the Northeast," I would draw raindrops! I was there for Thanksgiving Day [1955] and they had me eat a turkey leg underwater. I was the underwater weathergirl every morning for two weeks, doing it live for three different time zones. They heated the water, so I could bear being in it, but it would cool down by the third time zone. By the time I had finished my two weeks there, that hot, chlorinated water had absorbed into my blonde hair and turned it kinda green [*laughs*]. When I got home, I had to try to get that chlorine out, which was really hard!

Not long after that, you ended your "swimming career."

Yes, to get married! I was proposed to by my husband Al Hallowell, and so I left Silver Springs when I was going to be married and move to Orlando. But I told them that I would be back any time they needed me to do something underwater. I married my husband in March of 1956, and I was widowed in 1987. He died quite early; he had had two open heart surgeries. We had three daughters, Dawn in '57, Heather in '60 and Shannon in '65. I have six grandchildren now. I have five grandsons and only *one* granddaughter, and they range from age 21 down to age seven. How 'bout that [*laughs*]?

After the swimming career, though, I still worked. In 1956 and 1957 I had my own television show, *Browsing with Ginger*, what you would today call a talk show or variety show. I did two shows a week, Tuesday and Thursday afternoons, and it was on the only TV station here in Orlando, the first station built here, Channel 6, WDBO, a CBS affiliate. It was one of the first shows in town because that was the first *station* in town. It was live, so if you made a mistake it showed, and you had to say, "Oh. I'm sorry. I didn't mean to say that!" or whatever you had to say to correct it. I would do my own scripts, but never word for word, I would simply write down key words that would take me from one subject or one segment of the show into the next. I did it until I was pregnant with my first child. Back then, they didn't want you on TV if you were "showing." Now you can deliver on TV if you want to [*laughs*]! One week they had a show

Ginger Stanley went from fish to fashion, trading her comparatively short underwater career for decades of employment as a model in the Orlando area.

announcing I was leaving, and they had a little baby shower for me as the reason why I was leaving. Oh, and I'd been on Channel 6 even before I had my show: Any time there was a movie made in Central Florida and Ricou and I were involved, he and I would appear on WDBO Channel 6, 'cause they needed people to "spice the thing up." We did that for the first Creature movie, *Creature from the Black Lagoon*, and later for *Jupiter's Darling*.

Once I had my first daughter, people who had seen me on television for a year and a half started calling me and asking me if I would model their clothing for them, for charity shows and things like that. I thought, "Sure, I can do that!" and I did that for over 35 years. I was at Disney for 23 years, modeling for them: When they had big conventions there, the men would play golf and the women wanted to be entertained with fashion shows and luncheons. I did that at the Polynesian Princess and the Grand Floridian and Top of the World Disney and so on, in addition to also modeling for other people too! Sometimes I would do two or three in a day! It was something I could do while I raised my children, because usually it *was* a luncheon that was over by the time my children got out of school. Once I had done *that* for quite a while, a friend, Lisa Maile, wanted to open a school for modeling, the Lisa Maile Image Modeling and Acting, and I taught modeling there for 20 years. I taught from six to nine at night, and on Saturday mornings, so that people in high school, and ladies with jobs, could attend.

How often do you get in the water these days?

I have a backyard pool, a 20 × 40, ten-foot-deep pool. I don't go in now from October to May, when it's cold, because I had my years of doing that and I said, "Never again when the water's cold!" [*Laughs.*] About three times a week, I'll swim 100 laps, for stamina more than anything. I'd rather do that than walk.

All the stuff you learned while becoming a mermaid ... is it like riding a bicycle, do you never forget how? Do you think you could still do some of it today, at 81?

[*Pause*] I could still probably do most of it. Or *all* of it.

Even the deep dive?

Oh, yeah, I probably could. I would have no *desire* to do it [*laughs*], but I probably *could*!

Postscript: Stanley told me that mermaids still perform at Weeki Wachee—and, funnily enough, on July 5, 2013, just days after our interview in which she mentioned that fact, *The New York Times* ran the lengthy article "The Last Mermaid Show" which gave the history of the attraction and the challenges it currently faces. According to Virginia Sole-Smith's piece, Weeki Wachee Springs is now a small "city" (population: four!) and a 538-acre state park that advertises itself as "the world's only city of live mermaids." When Sole-Smith descended into the glass-fronted theater to take in a performance of "Hans Christian Andersen's 'Little Mermaid,'" the 400-seat auditorium was barely half-full, mostly seniors and toddlers. Then the curtain lifted, the show started and a "mermaid" appeared, and "for a moment, I found myself wanting to believe in mermaids," Sole-Smith wrote, "despite having met [the mermaid], standing on two legs in a locker room, just ten minutes earlier."

The attraction's heyday was in the 1960s, when it reportedly drew a half-million visitors a year, but then (pardon the pun) the bubble burst with the 1971 arrival of Disney World in Orlando. Sole-Smith wrote,

> At first, tourists would spend a day or two at Walt Disney World, then fill the rest of their week visiting other Central Florida attractions. But as Orlando's theme parks grew in number and size, vacationers stayed there. Florida's tradition of idiosyncratic, locally owned tourist attractions was displaced in much the same way as Wal-Mart replaced regional grocery stores and multiplexes put independent movie theaters out of business. Cypress Gardens closed in 2003, and Weeki Wachee was close to failure. The sidewalks were cracked; the paint peeled on plaster statues at the park's entrance; audience head counts were often in single digits.

In 2008, the Weeki Wachee city managers donated the attraction to the state of Florida. Today it's Weeki Wachee Springs State Park, "so now the mermaids are employees of the state of Florida!" Stanley says with a laugh (but yes, it's true). "They put on perhaps three shows a day; I guess that's as many times as they can fill the theater. We used to put on five or six a day." According to the *Times*, there are now 21 female and three male park performers.

Read lots more about it in the 2007 book *Weeki Wachee: City of Mermaids: A History of One of Florida's Oldest Roadside Attractions* by Lu Vickers and Sara Dionne.

Mike Gannon

During the *Revenge of the Creature* moviemakers' month-long stay at Marine Studios in Marineland, Florida (June–July 1954), one of the attraction's announcer-guides, Mike Gannon of nearby St. Augustine, had the bright idea of filming his own good-natured lampoon of their production and showing it at the *Revenge* wrap party. With the help of other announcers, he shot in black-and-white 8mm the 21-minute *The Return of the Creature* on a how-low-can-you-go budget. His fellow announcers Ed Doyle and Clayton Powers played the Gill Man and hero Clete Ferguson, respectively, and Clayton's wife Pat played the female lead.

Crudely made but very clever and laugh-out-loud

funny, *The Return of the Creature* was a hit at the wrap party *and*, 59 years later, at the July 2013 Monster Bash in Mars, Pennsylvania, where it was shown publicly for the first time and received a rousing ovation. The movie is covered in the chapter "Aquatic Kith and Kin" and here, as a supplement, Mike Gannon tells the full story of its production.

At the time when you made *The Return of the Creature*, *Creature from the Black Lagoon* was a hit in theaters across the country. Did you see it before you made your movie?

I knew of it because the *Revenge of the Creature* cast members and crew members at Marine Studios talked about it, but I had not seen it. It probably had come through St. Augustine, and I guess I hadn't been attracted to the film. I did not see that movie until late last year [2012] when it played on television. I thought it was really corny [*laughs*].

In 1954 when the *Revenge* gang came to Marine Studios, you were working there as an announcer.

A guide and announcer, yes. This was my summer job, between years at university; I had just graduated the previous June and was preparing to enter graduate school in September. In case you're not aware of the original purpose of Marine Studios: The owners, Cornelius Vanderbilt Whitney, Douglas Burden and Ilya Tolstoy, had originally planned for it to be a facility where motion pictures could be made of the marine life inhabiting the tanks. That was the reason for all the tanks' underwater portholes. So the idea of movies was always in everybody's mind, and that piece of information was part of the announcers' spiel when we gave the shows at ten, two and four around the circular tank and the rectangular tank: We mentioned that one of the original purposes of the place was to make it possible for cinematographers to get a view of these species as they lived in a semi-natural environment.

Arrangements for the *Revenge of the Creature* crew to come in had been made by the managers of Marine Studios, and I didn't know about it until they were walking around the facility and asking questions and getting acclimated to the site. Here was a film crew from Universal in Hollywood, and we of course were looking around for any familiar movie faces, stars and starlets … and we never saw anybody we recognized [*laughs*]. Over time we announcers became friends with these people. They were fascinated with what we were doing, and we were fascinated with what *they* were doing, so it was a nice mix, very friendly, and nobody got in anybody else's way.

And then you got the idea to make *Return of the Creature*. How much of the script did you write?

I wrote the whole thing, in a day and a half.[4] What we did was reverse the theme of the Hollywood movie. In their movie, the monster falls in love with the girl and he abducts her, but the police overtake them and shoot the monster, and the girl and her fiancé Clete Ferguson go off into the sunset. What we did in ours was have the *girl* fall in love with the *monster*. And then at the end, we had the monster swimming off with the girl into the sunset. We reversed the whole damn thing!

How old were you in the summer of 1954?

I was 27. I was that old but had *just* finished college, because after high school I had spent four years in radio at WIS in Columbia, South Carolina, as the sports director and the play-by-play man for the University of South Car-

While Revenge of the Creature was being shot at Marine Studios, Ed Doyle, Clayton Powers and Mike Gannon (pictured), announcer-guides at the attraction, had fun making an 8mm send-up, The Return of the Creature. To play an older man, 27-year-old Gannon put powder in his hair and wore a fake mustache.

olina Gamecocks. Then, before I went to college, I had to spend a preparatory year picking up skills that I hadn't acquired in high school; and then four years of college after that; so by the time I earned my M.A. in '55, I would be 28. But I was 27 the summer we made *The Return of the Creature*.

And you were living in St. Augustine, I assume.

Yes, in my old bedroom at home, 1 Palm Row, with my widowed mother and my youngest brother Peter. I went to work at Marine Studios each day on the company bus—it was about an 18-mile ride down the beach—and I took the bus back home in the evening.

Did you make *Return* on days off from work, or after work, or...?

Days off from work. I can't figure out how we did that: We shot the film in less than two days, and we were always together doing it, the three of us announcers, Clayton Powers, Ed Doyle and myself. How we were *all* off at the same time for that length of time, two days, I can't figure out right now from this distance in time.

How were you able to give the principal characters in *Return* the same character names as the characters in *Revenge of the Creature*?

They let me read the script. That was innocent enough—there were no secrets to give away. And we had *such* friendly relations with each other, the Marine Studios crew and the movie crew.

I'd love to know where everything was shot, starting right from the beginning: Your lab in the pre-credits sequence?

First, let me tell you that every shot in our movie had to be a one-take shot: We had no means of cutting and splicing, so everything had to be shot in sequence just as it would appear in the finished film. The camera was an 8mm camera, an Eastman Kodak. I don't know where we got it; I know it wasn't mine. We musta borrowed it from *some*body.

The first scene, in which I address the audience and tell them about the Creature, was shot in the Marine Studios lab, which was across the highway from the attraction. Marine Studios was right on the ocean, and then there was an intervening highway, Highway A1A that ran north and south alongside the attraction; then on the other side of the highway were the administration building and the lab. The lab was under the direction of a good friend of mine, a fellow who was a little older than I, but we hit it off wonderfully well because he was a very intellectual type and I was in college and interested in the same kinds of things. His name was Forrest Glen Wood ... all "woody" names, forest, glen, wood ... I used to kid him about that. And his nickname was "Woody" [*laughs*]! "Woody" and I were really close in those years, and he let us use the lab for that scene.

In your role as Dr. Dobson, you wore glasses. Were you already wearing glasses in 1954?

I did not wear glasses then. I must have borrowed them, or I may have gone down to the five-and-dime and purchased a cheap pair of frames. I thought the glasses would give me a more serious look, since I was supposed to be an ichthyologist.

After that pre-credits scene, the next thing we did was the opening credits. The idea was to spoof the kind of opening credits you'd sometimes see in Hollywood movies: the turning of pages in a book. We shot that on Aviles Street, the oldest residential street in America. It's a very narrow street without much foot traffic and *no* automobile traffic. Clayton Powers had an apartment off that street where we stored our stuff. We set up right in the middle of Aviles Street, in the sun. Clayton, who was a gifted artist and cartoonist, painted the title on a large piece of white cardboard. The paint he used was some kind of half-soluble solution, like watercolor, because watercolor will run and that was our plan. The title was painted toward the bottom of this large piece of cardboard so that somebody could squat behind it to hold it up at an angle, and I shot downward at it. Clayton's wife Pat Powers had a pitcher of water, and after I had been shooting the title for a few seconds, she started pouring the water back and forth across the top of the cardboard and it ran down over the title and the letters streamed pretty much as we planned it. This was a one-time thing, we didn't have the time to do *this* over again [*laughs*]! Then we laid out on a table pieces of paper on which Clayton had written the names of the actors and so on, and I filmed them as Clayton moved them around. When we came to the final page, Clayton did something that Hollywood never did: He picked up all the pages and tore and crumbled them into a mass [*laughs*]!

And you were the cameraman on that.

I handled the camera for the entire movie except for the scenes in which I appeared. After we did the credits, we moved straight down to Marine Studios, where there was a lagoon on the opposite side of Highway A1A from Marine Studios. All of our edge-of-the-water scenes were shot there at the lagoon. In the first lagoon scene, the fisherman who catches the Creature by the seat of his pants with a rod and reel was played by a visiting ichthyologist [*laughs*]! He was a Ph.D. doing research on some marine specimen, some fish of one kind or another, and happened to be there at the time we were making *Return of the Creature* and was laughing about the whole thing, and he said, "Boy, I'd love to be part of that." So we made him the fisherman!

As the Creature is being transported by car to Clete's apartment, we get traveling shots of a bridge and buildings.

That's the Bridge of Lions in St. Augustine. I don't remember whose car we used in that scene. Maybe it was a car we borrowed. Remember, this was a low-budget movie. Forty-eight dollars total [*laughs*]!

I also don't remember whose apartment we used as

Clete's apartment. In the scene where Clayton invites people to the apartment because he's about to show the Creature television, the two scientists who arrive to watch this experiment were played by W.F. Rolleston, the general manager of Marine Studios, and Carl Selph, who was in charge of the tanks. Apparently they took an interest in our project, a *friendly* interest. Rolleston was known as an old sourpuss to those of us who worked at Marine Studios: He never smiled, always frowning, always looking for something to criticize. Carl Selph was a more agreeable fellow. He was a very laid-back guy, very conservative in his views … and that didn't conform at *any* time with the views that Clayton and I had about life. But Carl was a decent sort and we liked him, and we liked working for him. But where Rolleston is concerned, I, in retrospect, and I'm sure at the time, I was surprised, very surprised, that he took an interest in what we were doing and even wanted to get involved. So we gave him a role in that apartment scene because he just wanted to be part of it. It was awfully good of him to do. And I think he took a lot of pleasure in it. It was a spoof, and I don't think in his entire life he'd been involved in a spoof [*laughs*]! He was such a serious guy!

And all the women in that apartment scene?

I think they were office workers from Marine Studios administration—secretaries, if I remember correctly. That's the gene pool that we called upon.

Toward the end, the Creature comes charging out of a building and starts loping down the street.

That was shot on Aviles Street. There were two things that happened there quite by accident. While we were getting ready to shoot that scene, I saw a bunch of kids, grade school kids, boys and girls, playing in the alley where we were going to film. Once we were set up, I went up to them and I said, "Hi, kids. Would you like to be in the movies?" [*Laughs.*] They all said yes. I said, "Well, I just want you to play. Then when you see a monster come around the corner into the alley, look scared and run for your lives." They all agreed. So when Ed Doyle was ready to make the turn into the alley, I told the kids, "Okay, play a game of some kind." On their own, they formed a circle and played ring around the rosie, which I guess was the most obvious thing that came to their minds; I wouldn't have known what to do myself. They hadn't yet seen the monster, so when Ed came around that corner with his arms raised threateningly in the air, the kids really *were* scared [*laughs*]—scared to death! The looks on their faces were looks of real fright! They ran down the alley and onto another street!

Then Ed went up a fire escape and onto the roof of this three-storey building, and Clayton followed. That's when the second thing that happened by accident, happened. Clayton and Ed were going to engage each other in a fight near the edge of the roof. From the alley I looked up and I thought to myself, "I don't know how to film this." This was late afternoon, and I noticed that the Western sun was showing their shadows on the side of a building on the other side of the street. And so I filmed the shadow of Ed holding the dummy [supposedly Powers' character] overhead until he dropped it off the roof, and I let the dummy fall into the shot and I followed it down into the alley. Then Clayton did his "famous" death scene where he crawls desperately while in the background we played "Finlandia," long, *aching*, sad music. Clayton had a mouthful of ketchup which he allowed to come out at certain intervals. As you see, much of it was ad libbed as we went along.

Who made the dummy?

Clayton Powers. Clayton was a true genius in many ways, and this movie would never have succeeded without him. First of all, let me say that his principal claim to fame in *my* book was the artistry with which he put together the costume of the Creature. It cost $12. He got a pair of long john underwear and sprayed on patches of dark green paint, light green paint, brown paint, giving it a mottled look. Then he put the costume on Ed and padded various parts, the arms and the legs and chest and back, with bunches of cotton so that the skin was all uneven and wild-looking. He got a pair of old automobile mechanic's gloves and put claw-like nails on the fingertips, and he sprayed the gloves to match the rest of the body. How he made the head, I've forgotten, but as you can tell from looking at the movie, it too was a work of genius. After we showed this movie at the [*Revenge*] wrap party, Clayton was praised by the man who had built the *real* Creature outfit [presumably Jack Kevan] *at a cost of $30,000*. This guy said that what Clayton had done with $12 was … magic! It not only had a fearsome look about it, but it played well to the camera. So that was high praise that Clayton fully deserved. Clayton also played Clete in the movie, and did it with an agility that is very impressive.

So the Creature suit was $12. Where'd the rest of your $48 budget go?

Part of that $48 expenditure was getting the film developed. Because we had to get a very quick turnaround, I made all kinds of inquiries in St. Augustine and Jacksonville, and *nobody* could give us a quick turnaround. But somebody gave me a tip, and I can't remember that good soul's name: "I think that the newsreel companies in New York could do that, because they *have* to develop film quickly. Maybe they would do it for you for a fee." I hit pay dirt with the first one I called "long distance," as we used to say: He said, "Yeah, we can develop your film. How much film *is* it?" I told him, and he said, "All right, we can do that for…" such-and-such an amount of money. I said, "Well, I've got to put the undeveloped film on a regular passenger airplane going to New York. Could you have somebody pick it up, develop it, and take it to an airline going to Jacksonville, Florida, the next day?" He said, "We can do that." Late one morning I took the film up to Jacksonville, to the cargo side of the airport, and it was put on a plane, and the developed film arrived late the afternoon of the next day. And when the guy in New York sent me the bill, it was very little considering what he did. It was the largest part of that $48 total, it was maybe $25 that went to that newsreel company.

And after the film came back, you did the sound.

That's right. During the interval when the film was away being developed, we practiced and rehearsed in Clayton's apartment, and after supper on the day I picked the film up in Jacksonville, we started to do the sound. We had the script, and we had to try to lip-sync and record it. Fortunately, we had a tape recorder that was pretty good in terms of sound quality. Everybody dubbed the character that he or she played. We spent most of that evening putting sound on, and then early the next morning we got up and finished the job. There were also a few sound effects that had to be worked in along the way.

Who picked the music?

Clayton is the one who picked the music, "Finlandia," "Night on Bald Mountain" and so on, and did a great job of it.

When you showed it at the wrap party, were picture and sound in sync?

We got a projector that had an adjustable speed dial so that you could increase the speed as the film passed through, or you could slow it down. I would need that, to adjust synchronization, as the motion picture played at the wrap party. I practiced *over* and *over* and *over* and *over*, until I got it down pretty damn cold.

Where was the wrap party?

The wrap party was in a big room under one of the stands. Our small screen was set up, our 8mm projector was set up, and of course the movie people had no idea what they were going to see. But when it started out with the credits for *The Return of the Creature*, they broke out in loud applause and laughter, and stayed laughing through the whole thing. They got a *huge* lift out of it, they thought that it was hilarious, and at the end they gave us a standing ovation. And the publicist there said that he wanted to borrow the film to show in Hollywood, or wherever Universal was located. We said fine, but we certainly wanted it back. I don't know what he did with it out there, if he showed it at all. Maybe they didn't have the skill to synchronize it, as I had—I warned him about that.

We showed it again at Marineland when Cornelius Vanderbilt Whitney [one of Marine Studios' owners] and his wife Marylou came down for a visit. I was very friendly over the years with them. Well, they fell in love with it and had copies made of the film and of the tape. Then she began showing it everywhere—in Kentucky, in Saratoga, in Spain—

All the places they had homes?

Yes. In Spain, they had a home in Majorca, and she played it for every guest who came. So *The*

Throughout this book, we've referred to Gannon as "Mike Gannon" because that's how he billed himself on *The Return of the Creature*. Probably we should have more respectfully called the former monsignor Dr. Michael Gannon because he's got a list of accomplishments nearly as long as the Gill Man's evolutionary chain.

Return of the Creature was an "international success" … among small groups. *Very* small groups [*laughs*]! In later years when I would see Clayton Powers, he would ask, "Do you still have a copy of our 'underground movie'?" The term "underground movie" had come into currency by that date. I don't know if ours really was an underground movie by definition, but he chuckled as he used the term to describe it.

The big question: Making the movie … was it *fun*?

It was *great* fun, knee-slapping fun with every segment that we filmed. And everything *did* go smoothly, amazingly so, considering the fact that there was no chance for a retake of any shot because we couldn't cut and splice. We were stuck with whatever we got in sequence. There were no egos involved here at all. After having done it as quickly as we did, we were all very proud of ourselves at the time we were able to show the film.

Postscript: Distinguished Service Professor Emeritus of History at the University of Florida, Dr. Michael Gannon holds graduate degrees from Catholic University in Washington, D.C., the Université de Louvain in Belgium and the University of Florida; is the author of beaucoup books (including the bestseller *Operation Drumbeat*) over the last 50 years; has written many articles and a play; was a war correspondent in Vietnam; got in the middle of a police-student conflict during his chaplain days and learned what the business end of a nightstick tastes like (for more details, Google and read the *Florida Magazine* article "A Man for All Seasons"); worked as a lecturer and a PBS talk show host; taught 16,000 University of Florida students in his 36-year teaching career; received Spain's highest academic award from the king; has a St. Augustine bridge named after him…

Oh, and he made *The Return of the Creature*, which appears on not one of the *curricula vitae* I could find on him.

Vikki Megowan

Six-foot-seven Don Megowan played the Creature in the post-fire, post-op scenes of *The Creature Walks Among Us*, and scores of other, more traditional roles in a variety of movie genres and on TV. His shoes were no doubt big but the footprint he left in the Hollywood history books is surprisingly small: Very little has been written about this giant (size-wise) of the acting profession, and he consequently became something of a man of mystery to his fans.

In this interview, an appendage to the Don Megowan bio in the *Creature Walks* chapter, his daughter Vikki sheds more light on the subject and describes the fun of having "the coolest father in the world."

Your dad's mother reportedly worked for years as a film cutter at Universal. I bet she never got an on-screen credit for cutting a movie but I'd love to try and check.

Her name was Lelia Dale Megowan, and her story is rather interesting by itself. She was born in West Virginia and when she was very young, her mother died. Lelia's father could not raise her on his own so he decided to send her by train to a family friend, Leo Pennington, in California. Her father wrote her name on a card and pinned it to her blouse, put her on the train and sent her off to this new family. Later in life she married our grandfather

Proud parents Bette and Don Megowan with daughter Vikki in the mid–1950s.

Robert Megowan. He was a baker and a heavy gambler. He became so far in debt that Grandmother went to her brother and asked him to help her find a job. This is when she obtained a job cutting negatives for a company named Pathé. She left Robert and then, through the Depression years, raised three children on her own: Doris was the oldest, Eileen next, and Dad was the youngest. Back in the '20s and '30s, this was almost unheard-of, a woman working and raising kids without any assistance. She was only 5'2" but her tenacity and strength made her look seven feet tall! Robert was 6'7", and this is where Dad and his two sisters got their height. They were all taller than six foot.

Dad lived a *very* colorful life as a child and there are some pretty good stories about him. When he was still in his younger years but close to six foot tall, he decided it would be fun to climb up on top of a large water tower close to his house. (Attached to the side of the tower was a ladder that did not go all the way to the top. Even at that young age, Dad was tall enough to make up the distance between the ladder and the top of the tower; only a tall person would be able to hoist themselves up to the top.) But then he couldn't get *down* from it, and even the firemen were stumped on how to help him! In his teen years he would jump trains to get around and traveled to many cities in and out of California. He was a rebel and a huge handful for his mother. Dad would talk about how she would punish him by sending him out to the backyard to prune a tree and find her the largest stick for a spanking. This would give her time to cool down, so Dad would spend hours working on the tree, hoping she would forget about the whole thing.

He was quite an athlete in his youth. What can you tell me about that?

I know Dad played baseball—he was the catcher. He also held the discus record at Inglewood High School. In addition, he played football as both defensive and offensive tackle. He went to the University of Southern California on a football scholarship. He allegedly was the biggest football player around at the time and was offered a pro contract after college. He was proud to be tall. He stood out in a crowd and walked with confidence, always. He made it a point to get out of the car if pulled over for a ticket. He would stand up and tower over the officer; I think he thought he could intimidate them out of giving him a ticket! Dad had a lead foot and would get caught pretty frequently.

Are you tall?

No, I take after my grandmother, I'm the runt of the family. I am 5'5", while my brother Greg is 6'4" and my mother was 5'7".

Is there a cute story that goes along with how he met your mother?

When they met, Mom was a stewardess and she did not live in California, she was here on a layover. Back then, layovers were days, not hours. She and the other stewardesses went to State Beach to sun-tan. She was lying on a towel soaking up the sun when Dad rolled over from his towel next door and asked for a cigarette. That started the courtship. Mom thought he was so handsome and for a while they had a long-distance relationship. Then Dad met her family and finally convinced her to move to California.

Do you know why and how he got into movies?

I don't know for sure. He always said that he was seen playing sports and encouraged to go into acting, but I know he took acting classes. So I am not sure how exactly that all came together.

Were his friends "movie people"? What did he do in his spare time?

He had friends of every background and walk of life. He loved people. As for spare time, he loved the pool table and playing the horses. But his favorite hobby was playing cards. He had weekly games, sometimes nightly. He played with Clint Eastwood, Clint Walker and Jack Elam along with other close friends. Incidentally, not only was his mother a film cutter way back in the day, but his cousin was the comedian Foster Brooks, and other family members were also in the television field. His sister Doris was an artist and worked for Walter Lantz, drawing Woody Woodpecker! She taught me how to draw both Woody and Bugs Bunny—she knew how to draw all the cartoon characters from the different companies.

We were very close because he was an incredible father to me. All my friends thought he was the coolest father in the world. He knew just the right things to say to keep me in line and make the right decisions. He could reason with me and get results without yelling or spanking (something that is not allowed today anyway!). He always said I was a female clone of him and our thoughts were so much the same that it was frightening. We were on the same wavelength and in the same moods at the same time.

Don Megowan as a young man, flanked by his sisters Eileen (left) and Doris. Their mama Lelia is front and center.

At times it was almost eerie. He used to say if I were older and not his daughter, we would probably be married! The trust between the two of us was incredible. I always wanted to be a parent like him, but I just could not get to that level of trust with my kids. God knows I tried! He never got riled about things, something I couldn't control with my children.

I can only remember one time when he told me *no* and that was when I was a teenager and planned on being the only girl to go camping with several teenage boys. He put his foot down on that one! But any other time I wanted to do something crazy, he would allow me to, after we talked the entire plan through. I thank him for my analytical way of thinking and down-to-earth personality.

Do you have any recollection of him talking about playing the Creature in *The Creature Walks Among Us* or the Monster in *Tales of Frankenstein* or any of his other sci-fi credits?

He downplayed all his sci-fi movies because he did not want to be stereotyped as just a sci-fi actor. Quite honestly, back in those days he really didn't want it widely publicized that he played the Creature, for fear it would hurt his opportunities for other roles. He did not want to be a sci-fi actor. As you probably have found in your research, he also did *The Creation of the Humanoids* [1962] and a couple of werewolf movies [the 1956 movie *The Werewolf* and the 1974 telemovie *Scream of the Wolf*]. That was enough for him!

In fact, he really was not a movie fan. He didn't even like to watch himself on TV or at the movies. Although I do remember going to the drive-in theater to see *Snowfire* [1958], a movie about a wild horse everyone wants to catch. He played the father of two young daughters and I cried the entire movie because they kept calling him Dad. I cried, "He is *not* your dad, he is *my* dad!" Mom and Dad left before the end because I was so upset. Today, *Snowfire* is my favorite movie that Dad did. I love horses and owned many in my younger days. They were *not* related to us but the two girls who played his daughters were named McGowan, and so were the guys who made the movie. The credits are almost comical with all the McGowans and the different spellings.[5]

I found an old newspaper article about your parents' split, and it sounds messy: "Megowan accused his wife of unjustified and unreasonable jealousy." "Mrs. Megowan charged that her husband was too friendly with French actress Denise Darcel," etc.

It takes two to tango. I think there was guilt on both sides. Mom was a very jealous woman. Dad on the other hand had women practically throwing themselves at him. I do remember Dad saying several years after the divorce that he always loved Mom and she was his first and only love until Alva [his second wife] came into his life. He made it a point to respect our mother and swore he would never say a negative thing about her to us. He kept that promise.

After the divorce, my brother Greg and I went to live with our mom, and he would pick Greg and me up religiously every Saturday or Sunday and take us back to his apartment to spend the day. He taught me how to drive his car at 12 years old! It was a yellow 1967 Bonneville and I was allowed to drive on the freeway, to the beach, wherever I wanted. He enjoyed letting me drive him back to his apartment each week. While I was still 12, he even trusted me to drive with*out* him. Back in the '60s, it was a very different time. Not much traffic, and I could pass for 16 years old.

Every Christmas, Greg and I would have Christmas breakfast with Mom and Christmas dinner with Dad and his mother and sisters and cousins. Dad was as much of a kid as us, if not *more*. I think many times the toys he got for us, really were for him. One Christmas, Dad and his family bought Greg every wind-up toy known to Man—wind-up helicopters, army trucks, soldiers, planes, etc. When Dad brought us back to Mom's house, he wound each toy up and let it loose on the kitchen floor. They covered the entire kitchen. Mom was agitated but used to Dad's playfulness.

Years after Dad passed, I was eating lunch in our lunchroom at work. Several other people were eating there also, including one lady I had seen but really didn't know. She and another lady sitting at our table were conversing, and this lady said that she once worked for Rex's Toytown in Reseda. She remembered an actor who would come in every Christmas Eve after closing and, in her words, he would "buy out the store" for his kids on Christmas morning. "His name was ... *Don*. Hmmm, what was his last name? Oh, yeah, Megowan!" I was married and my last name was different so she had no idea she was talking about my father. I immediately said, "That was my dad!" She didn't believe me until I showed her an old driver's license with my maiden name on it!

Greg told me that your dad was also an apartment building manager.

Dad managed *several* apartment buildings at one time. A man named Albert Moore was married to Dad's sister Eileen, and Uncle Albert owned and oversaw the construction of many apartment buildings. They were in different parts of North Hollywood but he had several on Arch Drive in the 4100 block in ... well, it was North Hol-

6. Creature Conversations (Vikki Megowan)

lywood back then but now the city is Studio City. My dad managed the Arch Drive apartment buildings while living in one of them. The one he lived in the longest was 4150 Arch Drive, near Ventura Blvd. That place became "party central" because many colorful people lived there: the members of the old rock band The Seeds, a couple members from Yellow Balloon, [songwriter-singer-actor] Keefe Brasselle, [*Shazam!* TV star] Michael Gray and a few others I can't remember. The parties there were out of this world. Some parts of the parties are better off kept as memories, but they would run well into the wee hours of the morning with all different band people jamming. It seemed like there were hundreds of people coming and going. They were held in the middle of the courtyard around the pool with lots of people ending up being thrown in. Dad was the manager and had to approve all parties. I don't know who originally came up with the idea of the parties but they were *all* party animals so any excuse was a good reason. One of the tenants had a refrigerator with a beer tap, and there was so much talent in the building I think some parties just happened without planning.

Also, my dad owned many exotic animals: an ocelot, monkey and most famously an Italian alligator named Juliet, who lived in one of his bathtubs at 4150. Juliet was written-about in many newspaper articles. Italian alligators are small, so Juliet was fine living in his apartment and had the full run of the place. Later, after he moved to Panorama City, he lived with a woman—rather, she lived with him—who owned a tiger!

In the 1960s he made a couple of foreign films. Did you get to go along?

I loved to tag along with Dad but was not allowed to do so until the '70s and '80s. Before the divorce, he took Mom to Italy while filming but Greg and I had to stay home with the babysitter.

I also found a 1963 news item about a serious auto accident that he was in.

This accident was scary as he almost died. Dad drove his car up a light pole. He was thrown through the windshield and "scalped" the top part of his head so that it was barely still attached. He was half in and half out of the car. Because of his size, they could not humanly remove him so they used a crane to pull him out of the car. Afterwards, he was unconscious for 36 hours. He claims he fell asleep from carbon monoxide fumes from the car, but I

Don Megowan's North Hollywood bar and grill Johnny's was once visited by B.C. (for Beautiful Cat), a tiger owned by Megowan's girlfriend(!). In this photograph, B.C. lies in a booth getting some "fluffing" and TLC from Megowan's daughter Vikki.

If you felt the need to swear at Don's bar-restaurant Megowan's Club House, you looked up the swear word in this book and used the corresponding number instead.

think he had had a drink or two also. The divorce was hard on him and he did enjoy a drink or two. That head scar was used later in a movie called *Tarzan and the Valley of Gold* [1966] where he played Mr. Train. They shaved his head for the part and emphasized the nasty scar.

Greg also mentioned that he owned a couple of restaurants. Did he do all this on-the-side stuff because the movie-TV work was slowing down?

The movie business *is* a difficult business. One moment you have more work than you can handle and the next you are unemployed. Managing the apartments provided free living and a steady income. Later he purchased a condominium and opened a bar and grill for steady income. He loved to cook and was really good at it. His first place, Johnny's, on Lankershim in North Hollywood, was started in the late '60s.

Why did he name the place Johnny's?

He took it over and the name was already on the marquee, so he kept it. Then in the mid-70s, after Johnny's, he opened a much nicer bar and grill, Megowan's Club House, on Webb in North Hollywood. He maintained that place until he passed in 1981. At Megowan's Club House, people were not allowed to swear. Dad printed up a code book with code numbers for different colorful remarks. The idea was to say, "Oh, code 371!" which would mean something like "S.O.B.!" There were even whole sentences with codes. It was actually interesting to see the people carry on entire conversations in code. Both places were always filled with regulars. His specialties that drew people in were his homemade lasagna and hamburgers. He loved people and they loved him.

A little bit ago, you mentioned his second wife Alva.

Alva Lacy May and my dad married in the late '70s. I'm not sure if she was his second cousin or even further down the bloodline; I never could figure out exactly *how* she was a cousin. But she was Dad's last true love and a beautiful person. Their wedding rings had FIRST, LAST AND ALWAYS inscribed on the inside. When he passed, Alva also put it on his gravestone. Alva outlived Dad but later breast cancer took her. Incidentally, Alva was an actress and had some small parts in a couple of movies as Alva Megowan.

Your dad also died of cancer. Was he a smoker?

Dad began smoking cigarettes at age 12. He rolled his own and became a pretty heavy smoker. When he was 48 years old, he decided to quit and did so cold turkey. He had an incredible ability to quit any addiction on his own.

I am thankful that Dad was able to walk me down the aisle for my wedding to my second and current husband Mike. Dad got to hold both my children, his grandkids. Greg was not as lucky because Dad did not see Greg get married or meet Greg's kids; in fact, he never met Greg's wife. Dad died about a month after Greg started dating the woman who became his wife (and, understandably, he did not want to meet anyone at that point of his illness). He would have been an awesome grandfather and would have added value to their upbringing in a way only he could. I married Mike on June 1, 1980, and Dad passed June 26, 1981. His throat cancer took an incredible toll on him. He went from weighing close to 300 pounds to less than 150. He wanted to die at home so his last days were spent in bed, in his own bedroom. He was always well manicured and clean: Every morning he would roll out of bed, crawl to the shower, bathe sitting on the floor and shave, then crawl back to bed. Sometimes he would ask Greg to shave him because he was exhausted from the shower. I would take a two-hour lunch break from work every day and go see him. His throat was so filled with cancer that he could not swallow food. I made protein shakes for him to drink, to try and keep his strength up. Alva was working at the bar and said he would only drink shakes or sometimes eat for me, so I made it my daily routine.

On June 26, 1981, my oldest child Michael was graduating from pre-school into grade school. It was a big affair with a cap and gown, the whole enchilada. I told Dad I would not make it for lunch that day and that I really wished he could be there for the graduation. He said, "Honey, I wish I could be there too." Greg came home from college that afternoon to find Dad in his room, not breathing, half on and half off the bed. It was a tough experience for Greg that I know he will never forget. The coroner said the time of death was around the time I would have been there for lunch. So I believe Dad *was* there to see the graduation. I also believe that the Lord works in mysterious ways, and He and Dad made sure I would be preoccupied at the time of his passing.

It was devastating that he passed at such an early age. His mother outlived him; she got to be 92 years old and outlived *two* of her three children. She was a devout Baptist who never smoked a cigarette or drank alcohol. It was almost comical when she would come to visit our house: Mom and Dad would hide all the alcohol so that our grandmother didn't know they drank! She's now buried in Inglewood Cemetery next to my dad and one of his sisters.

In the '60s and '70s, Greg and I were very popular at school and in our neighborhood: We were known as the "movie star's" kids, and people would go out of their way to tell us they had watched one of Dad's movies. One time, Greg went to a summer camp and the movie of the week was the World War II *The Devil's Brigade* [1968, with Megowan in a supporting part]. The camp director came over and asked Greg if there was any relation to the actor in the movie. Greg confirmed it was his father, and instantly became the most popular person in camp! I still get calls today from friends telling me they either saw Dad on TV recently or letting me know that one of his movies is scheduled to run.

One other thing that Greg and I are so very thankful for is the fact that there will always be a resource of pictures and movies of Dad. Our current and future families will have an opportunity that so many families don't have: being able to see our dad act, hear his voice and see his mannerisms. This is something you just can't get from a still picture, if you are fortunate enough to have a picture. My grandkids get so excited when we play a movie with Dad in it and tell them he is their great-grandfather! It also opens up conversations about *his* life, *our* lives and the many memories.

A BRIEF HISTORY OF THE BLACK LAGOON BUGLE

By David J. Schow

The Black Lagoon Bugle. What is it, or was it? Why has it been cited in academic papers and film magazines as a resource? How come nobody has ever heard of it and its biggest fans include John Landis, Joe Dante, Mick Garris, Frank Darabont, Guillermo Del Toro and other luminaries? What made Joe Bob Briggs enthusiastically endorse it? In what ways did this obscure, low-tech, private-circulation fanzine become a collector's item, all of a sudden?

Once upon a time in a world very far away from the here and now—that is, the pre–Internet, pre–DVD existence when people had heard of email but nearly no one you knew actually used it—a goofy little newsletter was born of obsession and necessity.

The obsession: the amphibious denizen of a now-classic 1954 black-and-white 3-D movie, the creation that critic Kim Newman has rightly called "the Elvis of classic monsters," variously known as the Man-Fish, the Gill Man, and the Big Green Guy: the Creature from the Black Lagoon. When most people say "creature" (small c), everyone generally knows they mean the Creature (capital c) … in short, nearly everybody's favorite monster. Even people who have never seen the films know who the Creature is. Along with Godzilla (who shares his scaly, reptilian demeanor), the Creature represents the bridge between the classic "famous monsters" and the 1950s rash of "science fictional" monster movie retrofits. Put another way, the Creature links the old school (horror films up through World War II) to the new (the atomic mutations and big bugs of the '50s by being one of the first films to be called a "science fiction horror movie." More importantly, the Creature provided the impetus for nearly every monster suit that followed in his considerably influential wake, providing a chain of title that means all those Aliens and Predators must count the Creature as an ancestor.

When viewed together, the original *Creature from the Black Lagoon* and its immediate sequel, *Revenge of the Creature* (1955), quite obviously exploit the plot-plan of another classic, 1933's immortal *King Kong*. Like Kong, the Creature is one of the few "vintage" monsters who seems to have sprung from purely cinematic, rather than literary roots, unlike Dracula or Frankenstein's beleaguered Monster.

But, *necessity*? Did the Creature really need a newsletter? Did he even actually *want* one?

For collectors, Creature memorabilia outstrips the desirability of many competitors. I can't tell you *why*. But when one collects, one sees stranger and more obscure bits and pieces—and one feels the urge to share the information. At the same time, by the early 1990s, many so-called monster magazines were flagging, failing, or morphing into new and less interesting forms. There was very little of the treehouse clubbiness of *Famous Monsters* to be found in glossier products, which tended to emulate industry trade papers or high-end celebrity gossip rags.

So, as a hobby, as an indulgence, as a cut-and-paste home-made craft, *The Black Lagoon Bugle* was born on Halloween 1991 as a one-shot one-pager for a microscopic audience who would probably find it amusing or diverting, in a greeting-card way…

… except that they didn't see it as a mere cute folly or a spasm of misplaced nostalgia. They wanted *more*.

The very first *Bugle* masthead was pulled off an illustration done on the outside of a mailing envelope by Tucson cartoonist Wolf Forrest. As evidence of its transient nature, issue #1 was not numbered. It was printed on hideous dark green paper that made it difficult to read, which was soon enough eclipsed by lighter stock—in several cases, a startling DayGlo lime. Then blue. Later aqua, teal and salmon. *Salmon*, get it?!

Like something out of the Devonian era of publishing, the 1991 Black Lagoon Bugle was a hard-to-read one-page cut-and-paste curio. Readers loved it and didn't want it to be a "one-and-done" item.

Within a mere bunch of months, actual professional artists, guys with pedigree and genre credibility, began to check in, ravenously responding to the *Bugle* as an outlet for Creature doings. The *Bugle* wasn't even aware its attraction was so strong. But thirsty acolytes surged forth like hungry zombies: Bernie Wrightson. Dave Cockrum. Steve Bissette. Gahan Wilson. Then premier illustrator Vincent Di Fate whomped up a brand-new version of the masthead, for free, without a crumb of prompting. He thought it up, did it, and sent it in all on his own. It first appeared on #5 in 1992, the first "legal-sized" issue (on legal paper instead of letter-size), and remained for the balance of the publication's run.

And *wham*—the *Bugle* was tossed into the pool and lordamercy, it began to start swimming *all on its own.*

(Not only that, but it proved to be a great repository, as well as a handy recycling bin for several *Fangoria* columns I had also written about the Big Green Guy. Plus a short story or two. An excerpt from an unpublished Steve Boyett novel, *Green*. A flag for the Rachel Ingalls novel *Mrs. Caliban*. A first-look sample of "Gills," the Creature-riffic short story you'll find in my Subterranean Press collection *Crypt Orchids*. Orts, tidbits, oddities, obscurities, stickers, stamps, collectibles, one-of-a-kinds; every Creature-related item from tangentials to tan genitals.)

It wasn't enough for people on the ever-increasing mailing list to indulge the mere passivity of reading about the L.A. subway system's Creature tiles, or see muddy, Xeroxed repros of rare or notable collectibles like the Doritos stickers or "monster money" that came out in '91. Nope—they all started *sending* stuff. Cartoons, letters, clippings, contributions galore. Sometimes, pictures that were *incredibly rare* in the real world.

Which meant more space was required. The *Bugle* jumped from a two-sided one-pager to four pages. To six pages. And in one memorable case (the March 1997 Chinese New Year issue), *eight pages*—whereupon it was discovered that an additional legal-sized page would bump the postage up a notch.

When *Black Lagoon* and *Revenge* director Jack Arnold died in March of 1992, the *Bugle* thought a eulogy was in order, and thus commenced the bitter duty of providing as much information as possible on other notable people in the Creature canon, as they passed. The *Bugle* eventually became notorious, if not famous, for its obituaries—particularly the one on Whit Bissell in 1996 (which provided more information on the man and his career in one place than any article or trade piece ever published, before or since).

Despite the darker mandates of passing time, above all the *Bugle* remained oddly fun. It was fun to cut and paste it up the "old-fashioned" way, and even more fun to hear from people who thought it was terrific fun to find a new issue in their mailbox.

Did I mention that every issue was sent out *free?* Yes, the *BLB* cost its readers not a cent, ever, even when the mailing list cleared 100 names. Eventually total strangers desired copies, which they could obtain for one U.S. buck to cover repro and postage. Otherwise, and proudly, the *BLB* never bore a price tag of any kind. The largest print run for any issue was nearly 200 copies.

Until…

7. A Brief History of *The Black Lagoon Bugle*

Then Joe Bob Briggs plugged it in his *own* newsletter *The Joe Bob Report* (formerly *We Are the Weird*) in 1993, shortly after the *Bugle* ran pictures of *Creature* star Ben Chapman reading ... well, you know.

Ricou Browning, the Creature himself, wrote to request back issues.

Vincent Di Fate quoted the *Bugle* in his doctoral thesis.

Ultimate Monster Collector Bob Burns called to say, "Come on over and shoot some *pictures*, why don'tcha?"

Creature connoisseur Bill Malone (who portrayed the Gill Man in Bob Burns' 1982 Halloween show) said, "I've got a few, you know, *photographs*."

F. Paul Wilson, author of *The Keep*, mailed in an incredibly rare Creature flip-book.

The *Bugle* pissed off *Astounding B-Monster* mastermind Marty Baumann with its "Bogus Controversy Obliteration Issue" ... but we're all pals now.

KNB EFX Group founder Greg Nicotero fell into the habit of getting something in virtually every issue. Ditto Tom Weaver, who permitted the strip-mining of assorted interviews he had done with many of the films' principals. Taylor White, founder of the world-famous Creature Features emporium in Burbank (now online, out of Sierra Madre), actually stocked the *Bugle* in his store!

And before the *Bugle* realized it, other obligations being what they were, practically a whole *decade* had rolled by ... somehow ... and abruptly readers were asking about an *online* version. This was prevented by the exigencies of copyright, and the concerted efforts of Creature fans all over the world to inaugurate sites featuring crystal-clear photos, animation, music, links and a cornucopia of images and opinions, free to everybody, with which the *Bugle* had no hope to compete, especially when it came to being timely.

The Black Lagoon Bugle was officially retired (after thanking all of its stalwarts and supporters) in 1999, with issue #22.

But, just like the most indomitable monsters, it resurged four years later with a special issue commemorating the attendance of Julie Adams at the Spring 2003 Chiller Theatre show in East Rutherford, New Jersey. That was a landmark because Ms. Adams had previously shunned most public appearances until Ben Chapman, y'know, *leaned* on her. Later that year, Julie, Ben, Ricou and Julie's swimming stunt double Ginger Stanley were all in attendance for the 50th anniversary of the original film at Creaturefest (sponsored by the Tallahassee Film Society) in Wakulla Springs, Florida—the original shooting location, in damned near the same shape as it was in 1953.

Who gave a damn? Well, consider a one-shot cut-and-paste Xeroxed fanzine, back for one more bow after a four-year absence, in competition with all the gloss and baubles offered by the Internet. The damned thing had to be reprinted *twice*. Worse, obsessed Creature fans now wanted to buy *entire runs* of the back issues, sometimes for breathtakingly high prices, especially on eBay, where a single copy once went for nearly *50 bucks* after a heated bidding war.

And that was the final roar of the *BLB* in the 21st Century.

Until ... you guessed it.

Dateline April 2010: After a seven-year absence, the *BLB* returned for a #24, prompted by two things: (1) an ongoing plagiarism controversy regarding a *Creature* book, and (2) the March 2010 filming of a short subject written and directed by *BLB* stalwart Greg Nicotero, titled *The United Monster Talent Agency*—for which Greg had KNB built an entirely

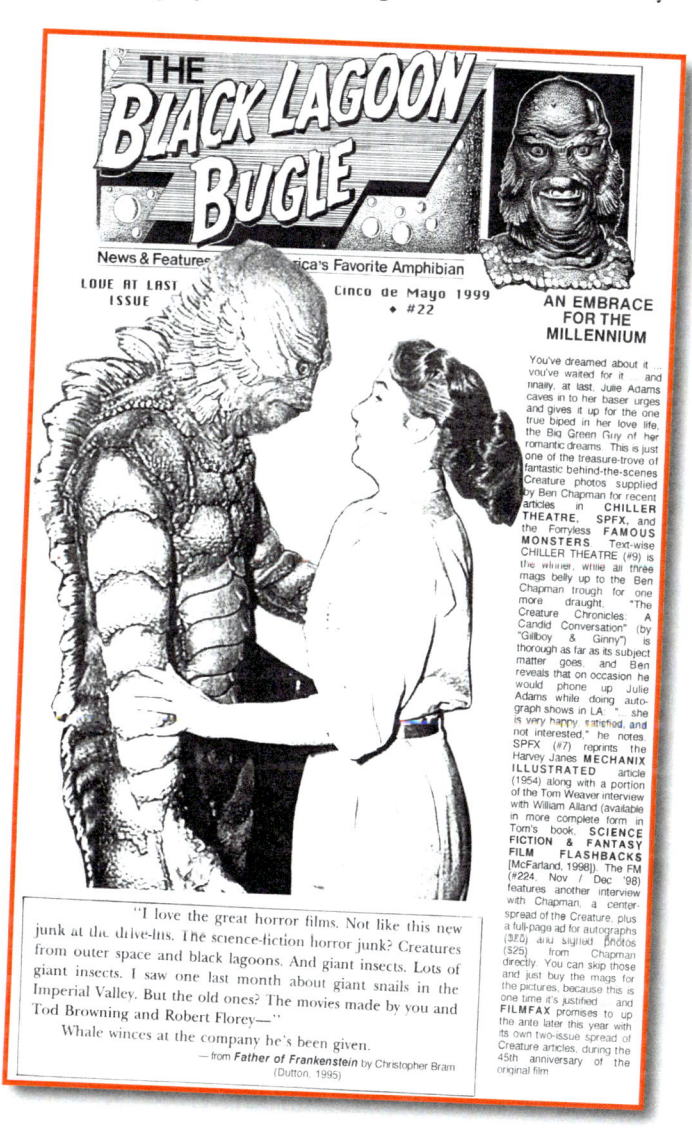

For subsequent editions of the *BLB*, the paper got bigger (legal size), the print got smaller ("Where's the magnifying glass??") and the page count grew, keeping readers up to the minute on all things Gill Man.

new, excruciatingly detailed Gill Man suit, worn by monster performer Carey Jones. In *United Monster*, Greg recreated the filming of the scene where Kay Lawrence (Cerina Vincent) is found draped over an altar-like rock in the Creature's grotto, the depth of detail even extending to matching the pattern on Kay's tied-off top. As the scene backs off to reveal the 1953 crew shooting it, that's Frank Darabont sitting in for Jack Arnold and yours truly, in '50s drag, taking the place of cinematographer William Snyder. It was like time travel. It was like a Make a Wish Foundation dream of actually being on set for the original film. It was the closest any of us will ever come to reaching back across more than half a century and touching the reality that yielded the icon.

Plus, *BLB* #24 retroactively covered the 50th anniversary Creaturefest in Wakulla Springs (2003), the limited-edition poster by Drew Struzan (2001), the newly unearthed location shots taken during the filming of *Revenge of the Creature* by Florida photographer Jere Beery (who also appears in the film), and the startling color shots released by *Life* magazine in 2008, along with the usual cartoons, drawings, digressions and weirdness native to the *BLB*.

BLB #24 debuted at the second Monsterpalooza, in Burbank, California.

Within a year, there were three Creature-related books on the drawing board: The volume you currently hold in your hands; a Julie Adams biography titled *The Lucky Southern Star: Reflections from the Black Lagoon*; and a Dreamhaven Books reprint of the 1954 "Vargo Statten" novelization of the original film.

The *BLB*'s "last roar with #24" proved that old monsters never die, and can rally for one more encore from the depths of fanzine obscurity when least expected. Old monsters, we have been taught, simply lie in wait for their next really prime scary opportunity. Currently, the *BLB* remains submerged ... but you never know.

REVENGE OF THE RETURN OF THE REMAKE OF CREATURE FROM THE BLACK LAGOON

By David J. Schow

In 1981, Universal Studios was on the verge of a renaissance as the preeminent maker of horror films. *An American Werewolf in London, Ghost Story, Conan the Barbarian, Halloween II, Psycho II, Videodrome* and remakes of *Cat People* and *The Thing* were all toplined in the first and only issue of *The Universal Studios Fantasy Newsletter*, edited by Mick Garris.[1]

That same year, John Landis had been set to produce what might have been the sci-fi–horror genre's classiest remake: a period version of Sir Arthur Conan Doyle's 1912 novel *The Lost World*. It was to be directed by Jack Arnold, master of Universal's mini-sci-fi boom of the 1950s. A thumbnail pre-production history of this 1982–84 project is available in Dana M. Reemes' 1988 book *Directed by Jack Arnold*, which also incorporates many of the storyboards prepared by Arnold and veteran production illustrator Mentor Huebner.

The Lost World fell through primarily because no executive believed that Arnold, a fellow who could maximize a budget on-camera like nobody's biz, would be incapable of working the proposed $10 million bankroll into a movie of the proposed scope. As Arnold told this writer:

> My films for Universal ranged from 700,000 to 900,000 dollars, which, in the '50s, was a lot of money. They were all under a million. We used to make 60 pictures a year at Universal. It's a hell of a lot harder to make a good film for under a million dollars nowadays than it is to make one for $15 million. As the world has seen, it's no *trick* to spend $15 million dollars, stay (on location) for a year and a half, and shoot 360 degrees on *everything*![2]

The limited foresight of the Universal bigwigs had always favored the more marketable idea of a *Creature* remake, which once again reared its scaly, batrachian head once *The Lost World* imploded. Landis was still onboard as producer with Arnold still earmarked to direct, a streamlined new Gill Man was designed by Hollywood monster maker Rick Baker, and a screenplay was commissioned from Nigel Kneale, the British television scenarist whose greatest triumph had been a TV trilogy detailing the scientific investigations of the irascible Prof. Bernard Quatermass: *The Quatermass Experiment* (1953), *Quatermass II* (1955) and *Quatermass and the Pit* (1958–59).

The signing of Kneale was unusually high-toned for a monster movie project: His work had the reputation of taking sensationalistic, lowbrow premises—alien body-snatchers, yeti, and ancient predecessors to human civilizations on Earth—and veneering them with calculatedly intelligent plotlines.[3]

Kneale's story was more or less an amalgam of bits and pieces of all three of the original *Creature* trilogy. The first 35 pages feature the penetration of the Black Lagoon by tourists. Once the Creature is stunned by infrasound waves and tranquilizer darts, he is imprisoned aboard a research ship much like the *Vagabondia III* in *The Creature Walks Among Us*. About 20 pages later he is tanked to a naval base in Long Beach, where he is "studied" (mostly tortured) by a military-corporate-religious sadist, Capt. Paul Shriver, and from here to the end the plot mostly bows to *Revenge*, including the Creature's inevitable escape into an urban area and the hijinks that ensue.

Early on, Kneale took care to introduce his favorite topic, the notion of the Creature's culture as a "lost," primitive civilization. In an underwater tunnel grotto, spunky lady shutterbug Cassie Quinn discovers "a patterning on the rock [which] can be no natural phenomena; they are too orderly. Zigzags, jagged angles cut into the rock like the decoration of some primitive people's worshipping place." We later follow the Creature into a stalactited subterrane, full of skulls:

> *Hundreds of them, ranged along the cut ledges in the rock. And thousands of bones, arranged like the contents of an orderly charnel house. But they are not human remains. These are the skulls of creatures like himself, broad-based and hugely socketed, with only rudimentary teeth. And the long bones have hands that are clawed like his own.*

The justly famous scene in which the Gill Man swims in parallel below Kay in a kind of synchronized sexual ballet is recreated on page 8 of Kneale's first revision, and by page 36, the Creature "speaks" to Cassie in "a thin, fluttering croak, identically repeated, with even intervals—'Ng … ng … ah! Ng … ng … ah!'" This helps prove that the Creature is a lot more intelligent than anyone suspects. Virile doctor-type Matt Gerrelly discovers the tale told by the Creature's blood and biopsies:

CASSIE: How human is he?
MATT: Not is. Was. They must've been land creatures, once. Like the dolphins and whales were, once. And then something, some influence, some natural catastrophe, I don't know, sent them to the water.
CASSIE: To fins and gills.
MATT: Right, they adapted. But that took time—millions of years. You see what that means? They'd have had to be the very first men!

The Creature escapes from his Fiberglas holding tank just as the research boat is hit by a Force Ten wave. He scythes through technicians and frees fish in other tanks while strategically sabotaging the ship. In response to the SOS, Shriver and his military goons appear in a big Sikorsky chopper to rescue the survivors. A tactical team puts the Creature down with gas, and by the time Cassie sees the coffin-like transport tank brought by Shriver, she realizes "they were all ready"—that is, Shriver knew about the Creature all along, and arrived prepared.

In Long Beach, the Creature is secured inside an armored observation tank and revived. Cassie and Matt are similarly "detained" and politely brutalized by Shriver, who has also captured a "first cousin" to the Creature, *Homo Horribilis*—sort of a cross between a killer walrus and a sumo wrestler, "of enormous size." According to Shriver, "They're Men of the Wrong Day. Mankind was created on the Sixth Day. These must have come too soon, the day of the creatures of the sea, and the great whales…." Being the sort of dude who gets off on training dolphins to deliver limpet mines, Shriver begins tutoring the Creature likewise, employing pain-vs.-pleasure shock treatments.

The Creature is able to communicate with Homo, and through teamwork they effect their liberation. They are spotted crossing a supermarket parking lot and frolicking in a water sprinkler. A fat guy named Harold gets wiped out when he discovers the Creature taking a rejuvenating dip in his swimming pool. (Overall, these scenes are nearly identical in form to those similarly used years later in 1997's *The Lost World: Jurassic Park*.)

Horribilis gets trapped in a pool of toxic sludge at a waste treatment plant and riddled with bullets by the fanatical Shriver. Cassie catches up with the Creature, who by now is seriously wounded and dehydrated. The Creature, remembering her, says the word "good." She and Matt transport the Creature to a "local aquarium" (originally Sea World in San Diego) where he is patched up.

Shriver barges in just as a "water rodeo" begins in the park. Calling out to the other sea critters in his croaky language, the Creature escapes. In the spirit of (then-) politically correct ecological awareness, Shriver is chomped in two by a leaping killer whale as he tries to shoot the Creature, who is then conducted by an escort of wild dolphins to the open sea.

One of the revisionists who set to work on whittling down Kneale's draft was actor-stuntman Evan Kim, who played the Bruce Lee character in *A Fistful of Yen*, the *Enter the Dragon* parody in Landis' *The Kentucky Fried Movie* (1977). Lee can also be seen co-starring with Burt Lancaster in *Go Tell the Spartans* (1978) and with Clint Eastwood in *The Dead Pool* (1988).

Further uncredited revisions—mostly on yellow pages, with additional inserts—substitute the insertion of 3-D effects shots (in a different typeface) to bias the *Creature* remake as a candidate for the brief revival enjoyed by the 3-D gimmick during the early '80s.

In the 3-D rewrite, the sole reference to the original *Creature* films occurs when Cassie nabs photos of the Creature in action. They are examined with interest by Matt and an Amazon native, Carlos:

CARLOS: It's him. The one they talk about … the fishman of the Amazon.

MATT: They caught one 30 or 40 years ago.
CASSIE: What happened to him?
MATT: Got away.

Instead of addressing the fascinating *what if*s of the Gill Man's doings since he escaped from Sausalito in 1956, we get a great deal of speculation on what he *might* be ... which is silly, since the audience already knows it's the Creature. Universal ultimately decided to place their bets on *Jaws 3-D* (1983), which itself borrowed heavily from *Revenge of the Creature*, and the remake was shelved...

Until 1992, when it was one of many projects considered by John Carpenter in the wake of *Memoirs of an Invisible Man* (1991). Multiple drafts were commissioned from Bill Phillips, who had scripted *Christine* for Carpenter in 1983. Among Phillips' other credits at the time were *Fire with Fire* (1986) and *Physical Evidence* (1989); Phillips was an Emmy nominee for writing a miniseries called *In a Child's Name*.

In Phillips' first draft, dated May 8, 1992, we encounter Pete Hazard, a cartographer whose hired plane develops a fuel leak during a tropical storm and crashes straight into the Black Lagoon. There he discovers a submerged structure with hieroglyphs visible on its exposed apex. "It looks like some kind of temple," notes the pilot, Richard, a heartbeat before he is killed by the Creature on page 8:

RICHARD: *Aaaaagh!*

The Gill Man's shadow menaces a cringing Pete (as a reprise of the first-reel scene in the 1954 film in which native guides Luis and Tomas get slaughtered), and the balance of the story takes place FIVE YEARS LATER, according to a title card. The Creature does not reappear to any significant purpose until nearly 45 pages later.

The stalwarts of this film's boat, the *El Dorado II*, are so colorless a group they are identified by *nationality*. This "We Are the World" motley crew includes a "pallid Canadian," a Frenchman, an Italian, an Amazonian Indian and a token "African-American," and most of them might just as well have VICTIM tattooed on their foreheads. We are informed that the Black Lagoon lies along the "Negro River" in Brazil, and Greenpeace is name-dropped as a way to introduce interloper Cirri Thompson—"29, pretty, with long blonde hair."[4] They discover the structure. Every single character says "It looks like some sort of temple" at least once, and soon enough they discover "a primitive wall-painting of a fish-like creature."

During this film's bow to the original film's synchro-sexual swim-along (set in a large chamber of water *inside* the temple labyrinth), we get a new description of the Gill Man:

Half-man, half-fish, he is huge, powerful. His body is plated, covered with scales, yet his skin is almost translucent, areas of green broken up with mottled colors, silvery around the gills. His hands and feet are webbed, with huge claws on each digit. And his face—a fish mouth, and inside razor-sharp rows of teeth used to rend and tear flesh. And his eyes—alive, not simply blank fish eyes, but more human—glowing with cunning, emotion, intelligence.

(The 1983 Gill Man did not have actual teeth.)

Pete Hazard, from the prologue, re-enters the story at this point, smoking hash, playing "Sympathy for the Devil" *really loud,* and casually shooting monkeys as he chugs upriver with the single-minded goal of wiping out the Creature. We are supposed to get the idea that Pete is *really bad,* and a bit obsessive about his encounter, which has left him with a long scar on his chest, though this potentially fascinating aside is not explored further. He calls the Creature the "Creature"—capital C—even though no one else has.

The Creature of the early '90s waxes more antisocial than his proposed '80s incarnation. A savage marauder with telescoping Freddy Krueger–style claws, he beheads one guy with a single blow and feeds another to a pool of piranha after imploding his skull. In the '80s drafts, the Creature only kills three people directly. The new version easily doubles the body count, not including the several people killed by *Pete!* This Creature also sweats octopus ink when consternated and, in order to stalk around on land, engages the following peculiar built-in option:

He hunches his body, contorting it, and suddenly water begins pouring out of pouches in his arms and legs. Now his skin begins subtly changing color as he starts to inflate his lungs ... his eyes undergo a transformation, the pupils taking on more detail, the flat shiny fish-lens disappearing.

(The 1992 Creature has both lungs *and* gills.)

One pointlessly elongated scene owes a huge debt to *Blowup* (1966), as the crew endlessly reviews a videotape shot by Victim #2. Cirri enhances a freeze-framed image until she is able to observe that "some kind of fish" appeared to be standing right next to the victim in the darkness. Right, lady—some kind of nine-foot-tall, bipedal *fish.*

As in the previous scripts, the Creature suffers a brief capture and shipboard imprisonment. This time, when he escapes, he steals a full-length mirror in which he admired himself during his incarceration. It's a setup for a later bit in which Pete is fooled into shooting at the Creature's *reflected image,* which in this version has to pass for a clever payoff.

Also present in this draft are monster movie flashlights which fail to work in a crisis, and a scene in which Pete gets the Creature dead-bang in his crosshairs ... and *click!*—surprise!—his rifle is *unloaded.*

The '92 version also incorporates the idea of a cavern-shrine room loaded with hundreds of Creature skeletons, "where strange primitive hieroglyphics seem to celebrate fish-men." It also ups the ante by including more pictographic wall-art "that seems to indicate some kind of man-fish king."

Ultimately everyone dies except Cirri and her "American" love-interest, Abel Gonzales. Cirri is attacked by a 45-foot anaconda and saved by the Creature, who lets them both go, presumably to bring a little peace and quiet to the Black Lagoon.

Phillips' second draft, now titled *John Carpenter's Creature from the Black Lagoon*, makes the evil Pete a poacher whose plane crashes due to the idiotic sight gag of a fuel gauge that doesn't register EMPTY until you tap it. Abel becomes a "Brazilian" who rescues Cirri from the local lawmen trying to nail her Greenpeace commando group, who are spiking trees to protect the rainforest.

Many more scenes from the 1954 film are recapitulated in this draft, dated June 29, 1992, including the scene where Kay compares the Creature to the Komongo fish: "It lived in the Devonian age, and it was a fish that breathed air.... [It] exists today. Hasn't changed in millions of years." Also copied are the scenes in which Kay pitches her smoke into the Lagoon as the Creature watches from below (in the '92 version, the butt is "biodegradable"), and the indictment of Mark Williams' abrasive opportunism: "He's also taken *credit* for a lot of important finds!" The entire sequence where the Creature boards the boat, mangles a crewman, and dives off after being set afire by a kerosene lantern, appears anew in this draft, as does the scene where the snared Creature scythes his way free of the boat net at the cost of one of his fingers, left behind.

The Creature also eats a lot more harpoons and bullets than in the previous draft. During the climax, Cirri pulls a spear out of the Gill Man (demonstrating kindness) and Abel rams a Bowie knife into the Creature's stomach (for no particular reason). The Creature lets them go anyway and sinks back into the Lagoon. "Its eyes show regret," concludes the script, though for what is not clear.

The anaconda was deleted entirely, to pop up years later in its own movie, which we'll get to.

During a brief flirtation with Jeff Bleckner, the director of Peter Benchley's *The Beast* (1996), the property was developed by Ivan Reitman in 1996 through his Northern Lights production company on the Universal lot. Four drafts were executed in rapid succession by Timothy Harris and Herschel Weingrod, who had co-written *Kindergarten Cop* (1990) and *Twins* (1988) for Reitman, as well as *Cheaper to Keep Her* (1980), *Brewster's Millions* (1985), *My Stepmother Is an Alien* (1988), *Paint It Black* (1989), *Pure Luck* (1991), *Space Jam* (1996) and the John Landis hit *Trading Places* (1983).

The only Black Lagoon in sight in the Harris-Weingrod drafts is on Pierpoint Island in Florida. It is completely blown up in the pre-credit sequence as a construction guy says, "Let's make us a beach." The explosions jostle free a football-sized egg secured deep within the coral reef. The egg hatches and a grouper is "torn to shreds" by the occupant as a title card comes up reading *The Creature from the Black Lagoon.*

FIVE YEARS LATER (yes, again) the Black Lagoon Reef Club is up and running: white sand beach, golf course, yacht marina and an upscale residential high-rise. By page four, Roger Tompkins, a resort employee, is "sucked underwater like something going down a drain" while stopping his golf cart to take a whizz on the beach.

Over the next ten pages we meet the most vanilla menu of upscale yupster fallout imaginable, led by a "perky, attractive" sales manager, who at least gets to say, "The Black Lagoon is safer than your bathtub," in this story's idea of foreshadowing. By the time the roving, subsurface Gill Man point-of-view shots ominously return, it's pretty clear that the casserole ingredients are *Jaws*, crossed with *The Poseidon Adventure*, aspiring to *Alien*.

During the reprise of the synchro-swimming scene, as the yet-to-be-seen Gill Man parallels Olympic swimmer Laura Devlin, we are informed that this Creature has a tail—"a muscled tail of a velociraptor." It also has seven fingers and a thumb, and marine biologist Alex Beck pegs it as "an early tetrapod," possibly a first cousin to a less evolved critter named *Ancanthostega*.

By page 62, most everyone has given up crying "shark" and:

> *For the first time we can see all of its head.... [T]here is nothing fish-like about it. The features are fierce, savage, but also beautiful, like a lion or an eagle. In the moonlight the Creature's finely-scaled features have the quality of beaten metal. Slowly, it emerges from the water, revealing powerfully muscled shoulders and arms, prehensile hands with gleaming razor-sharp claws. The impression is of a highly-tooled predator like Velociraptor with the heroic, almost human face of an antique Greco-Roman coin.*

Video evidence captured by a skin-diving seal named Molly also shows that the Creature has "retractable claws, like a tiger" and "rows of suckers on its palms that can adhere to any surface."

The Creature sorties onto land, where—comically—he gets stuck on top of an elevator and runs out of oxygen. He gets speared by macho Sean Hawkins, who "reels him in" as he staggers across a tennis court and a putting green. Then sprinklers pop on, reviving the Creature, who reels Sean to his own slaughter in a swimming pool, where "clouds of black ink mercifully hide the carnage."

The Creature also develops a definite letch for Laura, and Alex observes, "It's killing more than it can eat. It's behaving as if it expects to reproduce and start a family … soon." A *Sports Illustrated* swimsuit model named Tanya is impregnated to death on page 43, and Alex discovers the Creature's "male sperm" inside her corpse. Most of the resort's guests convoy out in vans just ahead of a hurricane that's due to hit, but the Creature destroys a bridge, sinking the lead van with Laura inside. Alex arrives in a one-man submersible and fires "a torpedo" at the Creature to distract it from Laura. The Creature attacks the plexi inches from Alex's faceplate, deploying "ferocious teeth which bite and twist in a lightning fast circular motion like a power drill." Alex's cohorts (from a nameless hi-tech oceanographic research boat—a match for Matt Hooper's craft in *Jaws*) drive the Creature away by lobbing dynamite into the water.

Now the bridge is out and the ferries are gone, stranding everyone on the island. Alex and Laura fall in love. The Creature tries assorted ways of getting to the people trapped inside the resort tower, killing several disposable security guys and terrorizing tenants before eating multiple shotgun blasts and losing a couple of digits to the blade of a ventilation fan. The storm knocks out the lights and phones and keeps away the Coast Guard. Alex, who knows the Creature is basically after Laura, starts calling it "loverboy" and "Casanova" under his breath.

Why Laura? Perhaps, as Alex says, "because she's the best swimmer in the whole goddamn lagoon, I guess." (The unfortunate Tanya having been killed while wearing one of Laura's bathing suits.)

The Creature single-mindedly chases Alex and Laura, killing off more peripheral characters. When Alex stuns him with the loud noise of the building's fire alarm, the Creature responds by wiping out Alex's partner with a projectile jet of ink that blinds him and burns his skin. Despite a ton of cat-and-mouse, the Creature nabs Laura and takes her to the Lagoon to mate. Laura calms the Creature down by blowing air bubbles into his face and stroking it; it's all a trick so she can spear him in the heart. His blood is "bluish." As she flees, the Creature is blown to pieces by shotgun fire. His corpse sinks beyond the reef … where another egg waits to hatch.

By 1996, Universal had offered the project to up-and-coming New Zealand director Peter Jackson, who had just completed his first feature funded by an American studio, *The Frighteners*, for producer Robert Zemeckis. Jackson remained keen to do *King Kong*, which was derailed in 1998 by the competing "big monster" remakes of *Mighty Joe Young* at Disney and *Godzilla* at TriStar. Jackson would finally realize his lavish, upmarket re-do of *Kong* in 2005, in the wake of his success with the *Lord of the Rings* trilogy.

Then Stephen Sommers came up to bat as director, having hit Universal's reboot of *The Mummy* out of the box office park in 2000. Gary Ross—the son of original *Creature* and *Creature Walks Among Us* screenwriter Arthur Ross—signed on as producer under his Larger Than Life production banner. Nominated for an Academy Award for his first produced screenplay, *Big* (1988), Gary made his directorial debut with *Pleasantville* (1998) and then directed *Seabiscuit* (2003), both of which he also wrote and produced. Sommers, whose earlier film *Deep Rising* (1998) had also dealt with an aquatic beastie, chose to port his enthusiasm into the $160 million monster mash-up *Van Helsing* (2004), which underperformed in the eyes of the studio, causing the idea of a similar *Creature* remake to go fallow again.

In 2003, prior to *Van Helsing*'s release, Universal hired Tedi Sarafian (*Terminator 3: Rise of the Machines* [2003]) to script a *Creature* remake, in anticipation of the fresh interest *Van Helsing* might bring to the rest of the studio's stable of classic movie monsters … which did not come to pass. Sommers revealed in 2004 that he had considered mixing the Creature into the wild potpourri of *Van Helsing*, telling a Zap2it.com interviewer that the first draft of *Van Helsing* had the Creature living in a moat at Frankenstein's castle. "He didn't make it into any of the other versions, and we never shot a scene with him in it," Sommers said. "It was just too much."

Under Ross' stewardship, the new *Creature* was offered to several directors, among them new-kid-on-the-block Guillermo Del Toro. Del Toro's conception of a re-thought *Creature* film was to do the whole thing "period Victorian," thereby wholly erasing the distinction between it and Doyle's original *The Lost World*, making it a straightforward homage. Not coincidentally, this inspiration rose directly from the ashes of the aborted Landis–Kneale version, and restored the Amazon jungle to a never-explored wonderland—where the Gill Man is locally worshipped as a demigod and protector of the natives. After several months of development, the project never made it to the scripting stage.[5]

Instead, by 2005, Gary Ross had committed his own determinedly modern-day take on a remake to paper.

In the prologue, a gold-mining boat plumbing the headwaters of the Amazon and crewed by a gang of drunken ethnic stereotypes is attacked by an unseen menace from below the surface. It dismembers one of them and chases two others (via POV water-level camera) in a rowboat until it catches up. One victim's scream bridges the title *Creature from the Black Lagoon* into the high-C shriek of a kabuki-painted opera singer onstage for a performance of *Madame Butterfly* in Manaus, Brazil. In attendance are John and Carrie Bradshaw. Carrie is an eco-soldier, a protector of rainforests (like Cirri in the Bill Phillips drafts); she apparently married her analyst, who was treating her for chronic fatigue syndrome. They are here because of Cassie's "drive" to see the Amazon before it is all gone (John calls it her "little experiment in self-realization"), although a young boy pegs her as a xamalkato—"like a jungle person."

They board a *carga* ("like Latin interpretation of a Mississippi riverboat") to chug up the Rio Negro, headed for a resort-style treetops lodge. As soon as they hit the Amazon, the boat's propeller fouls. The grizzled captain and his one crew member abandon John and Carrie to row away in a dinghy to get help from a village "three or four hours" away, since there's no radio. By morning, they have not returned.

Out of the fog comes the *Daedalus*, a 200-foot-long, ultramodern research vessel complete with a wine cellar and cabin Jacuzzis. Its ostensible mission is rainforest plant analysis on behalf of a huge conglomerate, Jensen Pharmaceuticals, but as onboard research scientist Walter Geller says, "We've got bigger fish...."

The *Daedalus* is co-financed by smiling-cobra capitalist Morgan Hallowell, who offers the marooned couple a lift to Iquitos. Among the crew are a bunch of one-liner subcharacters, including Don (captain), Olivier (French chef with blond dreadlocks), Andrew Simms (Australian scientist from Johns Hopkins), his lab assistant Chloe (chopped bleached hair, tats, piercings), divemaster Wayne (longhaired surfer dood), and Peter Clark (Morgan's right hand). Andrew invites the guests to stay for the long trip upriver: "You could sign a nondisclosure.... Morgan is very hush-hush about his brand new pills."

By page 37 the ship enters the Black Lagoon, so-called because the algae on the bottom makes the clear water appear black. A bizarre diamond saw mounted on the prow of the *Daedalus* shreds through a mangrove barrier to gain access. Carrie and Andrew observe the lagoon from a small dirigible. Andrew observes that the area is "an epiphyte forest"—all parasitic vines. The growth characteristics of all the local flora are aberrant and out-of-season. As Wayne dives to spear edible fish, the Creature POV reappears for the first time on page 43.

A supposedly dead fish being gutted by Olivier springs back to life in his hands, breathing as though it has lungs, its spear wound instantaneously healed over. The cut plant samples collected by Andrew begin to regenerate at incredible speed (like *Reptilicus* growing a whole new monster from an amputated leg) in the manner of human stem cells. Overnight the cut mangrove has regrown and has taken hold of the entire stern of the ship.

Morgan and Andrew argue about who owns the potential discovery. Carrie and John bicker over how she should keep taking her pills and stay out of trouble. Carrie, meanwhile, has caught Andrew's eye. Andrew ropes up into the foliage to establish a tree station. On page 59, Carrie decides to go for a swim in the lagoon, against John's strenuous objections.

The Creature POV follows her. Underwater, Carrie is ambushed by a 20-foot anaconda. She nearly drowns but suddenly "the Black Lagoon starts to go red with churning water" and the eviscerated snake floats to the surface.

Morgan mounts a stealth mission that night to stake his proprietary claim while the local Indians will go no deeper into the area, citing a "local legend." Meanwhile the dead anaconda has been coiled up (minus the head) and left outside Carrie's cabin, like an offering. The *Daedalus'* electrical power begins to flicker and stutter—the invasive, evergrowing vines have breached metal seams and begun to compromise the ship.

Crew member Ramon Esparza, hacking through the jungle with Morgan's group, gets lost and discovers a large cave containing the skeletal remains of animals. On page 70 he shines his flashlight directly into the face of the Creature:

> ... *narrow, reptilian eyes.... The head is massive, round and flared with huge armored plates that cover his gills. The jaws are enormous and powerful—less like a croc and more something that is deadly and prehistoric. As he breathes several rows of razor-sharp teeth are exposed dripping a thick viscous liquid. The Creature lifts his hands which are weirdly graceful. There are long finger-like claws with razor-sharp talons. One of them is attached to an opposable thumb. He shields himself from the beam of light and then lets out a high screeching, hissing exhale that is almost outside the range of human hearing.*

Ramon flees, slashed, and scurries up a tree. Below, the Creature just watches him. The tree is overrun with poison dart frogs, which swarm him. "Like a hundred snake bites," says Morgan, when they find Ramon's corpse.

The observation deck of the *Daedalus* has become a greenhouse and all power is shut down (kind of like your expensive BMW shutting down when the seat gets wet, due to all the microcomputers). Something has also torn up Andrew's tree station, to which Carrie suggest they all retreat since the boat has become "a floating garbage can." This irritates John further.

All the tree frog bites on Ramon's corpse have healed. But the slash marks from the Creature have not. Why? Says Walter:

> *Saliva. Whatever bit him was close enough to his own DNA that it bonded and repaired the tissue.... [L]et's say that was a spinal cord, or a failing liver. I know you don't want to talk about monsters but I'd sure be looking for whatever bit his neck.*

By bootlegging power from the batteries of a two-man submersible also on the *Daedalus*, the group is able to recover an image of the Creature from Ramon's digital camera. Wayne says,

Holy shit. Holy shit! It's that freakin' *fish*! That Jesus fish! It's the same freakin' face! *Resurrected*, dude. We speared that thing right through the heart and then it gets better! Starts *breathing*. Fu-u-uck...

By page 81, Walter calls it the Creature ... and the legend goes that it "swims like a fish and runs on the land ... so that means he has lungs and gills, because that's no aquatic mammal. He presents like a reptile." The Jesus fish, essentially, is a tadpole version of the Creature. Morgan gets excited by visions of limitless wealth and quickly organizes a five-man underwater hunt equipped with glide sleds and Tasers.

Wayne is attacked by a five-foot-long Jesus fish, which the team chases into a bioluminescent underwater cave. They Taser the prize and scoop it up in a net. As they depart, diver Mark is decapitated by the Creature (not seen except for the swipe of his claw). Diver Pablo attempts to Tase the Creature but nails Peter instead. Peter crashes his sled and dies. The Creature grabs Pablo and slits open his air gasket, holding him fast while watching him drown inside his helmet. Wayne Tases the Creature, who is left behind. As Morgan says, "We've got the little one. Let's go."

While Andrew, Carrie and Chloe continue to lark about in the repaired tree station, the body count stands at seven dead when Walter figures out a way to rig photovoltaic cells to get them solar power. John, who has spent the majority of the story moping on the boat, begins to froth at the mouth about leaving. By morning, the Jesus fish has shed its tail and escaped from Walter's lab tank.

WALTER: He's not just a baby any more.
MORGAN: So what the hell is he?
WALTER: A teenager.

The galley reeks of spoiled food. Olivier is the teen Creature's first human kill. The remaining men split into two search teams. In the galley, Wayne shoots at a scavenging spider monkey and is wounded by the ricochet. Wayne and the teen Creature tangle. Morgan shoots the teen Creature six times in the back ... but also killing Wayne with the same shots.

Up in the tree station, Carrie is surprised by the adult Creature (remember him?), who has just butchered Chloe. A tree-to-tree pursuit ensues with the Creature making like Tarzan. She is rescued by Andrew and an Indian in a dugout canoe.

The conflict now becomes stay-or-go. The *Daedalus* has a launch that can carry them a hundred miles away. Morgan wants to stay, to recapture his prize, and John doesn't want to leave because during a brief power break he was able to send out a hundred emergency emails, and wants to sit tight awaiting rescue. Morgan has Don sink the launch on purpose.

While Andrew tries to jerry-rig a safe room by securing the observation deck, Morgan and Walter dissect the teen Creature in the lab, hoping for enough power to scan DNA samples. Elsewhere on deck, Don finds a slime trail and ... his decapitated body thumps down in front of another crew member on a lower deck.

The Creature is next seen in the lab, holding the severed head of his offspring. Walter is quickly killed (in a scene reminiscent of Dr. Carrington's slapdown in *The Thing from Another World* [1951]) and the Creature devastates the lab before catching up to Morgan and crushing the life out of him in a long bear hug.

John activates Wayne's emergency beacon. But the Creature can "hear" the high frequency, and thus locates them. Walter proposes reinflating the dirigible to escape downriver, using the beacon to misdirect the Creature, who explodes onto the observation deck through a window.

John is dragged off the rising blimp by the Creature and is heard calling, still alive, so Carrie compels Andrew to go back for him. As John reaches for a dangling lanyard, he is violently pulled underwater again. Finally Carrie is able to haul him aboard the gondola, seconds before the Creature jets out of the water and grabs on, too. Andrew shoots the Creature with a flare gun and the three survivors float away.

Brett Ratner (*Rush Hour* [1998], *Rush Hour 2* [2001] and *Rush Hour 3* [2007]) was briefly attached to direct. Several actor names were bandied about, including Bill Paxton for the male lead, and 6'7" monster performer Brian Steele as the Creature. Ratner left the project to do *X-Men: The Last Stand* (2006).

Fresh off *Sahara* (2005), the next directorial candidate, Breck Eisner (son of Disney executive Michael Eisner) told *Arrow in the Head* interviewer Alex Billington that the Creature remake had to be "PG-13 scary," and that he was seeking a "dark adventure tone." Then, on November 5, 2007, the Writers Guild went on strike until February 12, 2008, and the project was scuttled again, even though Eisner had scouted in the Amazon for a month, hired a production manager, and assigned Mark "Crash" McCreery to reinvigorate the Creature's design. By mid–2008, Eisner had also taken a turn at the Ross script, noted that the Creature would be partially rendered in CGI, and that the debate had renewed over whether to shoot the movie in 3-D. By December, 2008, the remake had still not been greenlit, and by mid–2009 Eisner had turned his attention toward a remake of George Romero's *The Crazies* (2010).

Gary Ross told interviewers in 2008: "I don't think we're going to wink at the audience and make it silly in any sort of way. I think we're going to take it seriously. We're going to treat it with a certain amount of dignity. We're not approaching this in a retro-campy kind of way. It's set in

[the] present day. There are reasonable scientific underpinnings for it. It should be a really interesting journey into the jungle for both the characters and the audience. It's not a reference to what the original is."

Around this time, Robert Rodriguez (*Desperado* [1995]) announced that he would be co-producing the *Creature* remake under his Troublemaker Studios banner, in collaboration with Larger Than Life and Strike Entertainment. Simultaneously, makeup man Vincent Guastini was hired to design yet another new Gill Man.

Further heat was taken *off* the fire by the lackluster performance of Universal's reboot of *The Wolfman* (2010), directed by Joe Johnston (who had bailed from the *Mighty Joe Young* remake).

Next up: Carl Eric Rinsch, a director of TV commercials, was nominated by his mentor Ridley Scott to direct a proposed *Alien* prequel. When Scott decided to tackle the project himself, Rinsch was courted by Universal with the lure of the *Creature* remake in late 2009. By mid–2010, Rinsch had departed to do a remake of *Logan's Run*.

Strike Entertainment partner Marc Abraham told interviewer Chris Eggersten (on Bloody-Disgusting.com, October 12, 2010):

> We've gone through a bunch of different incarnations of the script and none that me and my partner were satisfied with. I think we have a really cool take on the movie now, [a] much hipper, [more] interesting version of it, and we're looking for a new writer who's after that. And, in fact, I just had breakfast and I was writing down my notes about it, about how I think it should go…. Still set in South America, really a more not-a-guy-in-a-rubber-suit…. [It's a] much more psychological transformation, [a] more literary transformation. I think it's a really interesting idea … more of an origin story, and [about] how [the transformation] happens."

With the exception of Nigel Kneale's first draft, the remake scripts are not story-driven; in their hurry to get on with the monster movie, they devolve their characters to slasher-flick cardboard, content to trade on the iconography of the original film instead of considering what qualities made the movie so archetypal. The Creature himself is particularly sold short. He frequently kills without being provoked, and next to nothing is made of his supposed "intelligence," though people *talk* about it a lot. (In this context, his tool use in the 1992 scenario could have been a great shock revelation, or his mating ritual in the 1996 version might actually have trumped the endlessly rehashed synchro-swim, which by now has been Xeroxed into impotency.) Ever since 1996, the question of how to redesign the Creature to compete in the *Alien-Predator* market has remained a hot topic. One makeover gave him backward-jointed birdy legs and a tiny head on the end of a long, serpentine neck … and overlooks the fact that the Creature—arguably the progenitor of rubber monster suits as we know them today—should not be messed into unrecognizability.

For all practical purposes, the most successful *Creature* remake to date has been *Anaconda* (1997)—yes, that giant snake movie. Its breathtaking use of location photography proves why the Amazon is the place to shoot mythic tales of Gill Men, and the cool Randy Edleman score is terrific just the way it is. Danny Trejo takes the place of the hapless Luis and Tomás as First Reel Victim; Eric Stolz updates Whit Bissell by spending the back half of the movie in a bandaged-up semi-coma; and Jon Voight cross-breeds the Richard Denning role with the crazed "Pete Hazard" from 1992, and adds a bizarre accent. The West Brazilian port of Manaus, site of the Instituto de Biología Marítima in the original film, is the point of departure for this film's ramshackle boat, the *Michaela*. The movie's climax was even shot in a legendary Los Angeles monster movie location: the Arboretum, home of such '50s classics as *Teenage Cave Man*. *Anaconda* owes its entire look, feel and pacing to its 1954 predecessor; in fact, one could easily cut out the laughable CGI serpent, give Rick Baker a quick call, shoot a week's worth of insert footage with the same cast—and a recognizable Gill Man—and a serviceable *Creature* remake could be film-canned in record time.

In July 2006, Universal Studios registered the domain name creaturefromtheblacklagoon.com on behalf of the remake. (Since then, the studio has removed its name and the domain has gone to a link farm.)

About remakes, and management, Jack Arnold had this to say:

> In planning to do the remake of *The Incredible Shrinking Man*, they never approached me. They never approached Richard Matheson … and then they complained to me that they were having trouble getting a good script! Then I was brought up to the people at Universal, but it's not the same Universal, and the people who are running it don't know anything about me. Many of them are not even movie *fans*; they're just businesspeople.
>
> Management has changed. Dealmakers are now running the studios. It's become very effete; they now depend on all the marketing gimmicks of Madison Avenue. MCA [Universal's parent company at the time] is run by ex-agents. They have the least amount of imagination it is possible for a human being to have, but they are *sensational* businesspeople. They charge their secretaries and the crews for parking; it's taken out of their salaries. The parking lot for the crew is on the other side of the lot, which is so damned far you certainly can't walk it … so they have a bus, which costs a quarter. The studio tour makes more money than their pictures do. Thousands of people come through every day, and the tours have precedence—they can drive that damned bus right through the middle of your shot and you have to stop and wait until they pass, y'know? I jokingly

told Lew Wasserman he missed a bet—they should have put in pay toilets! He didn't think it was funny, though.

They are the most successful operation in the motion picture business, today, and everybody hates to work there! It's a sardine factory, and I've had a great many fights with them, so they're not very happy with me. I won't sign any contracts with them, because it's not worth it. I'd get aggravated to death.

The piece was originally published in *Fangoria* #125 (August 1993) under the title "Old Green Eyes Is Back (Not!)." An updated version was published in *Filmfax* #73 (June–July 1999) under the above title and was reprinted in Schow's book of essays *Wild Hairs*, published by Babbage Press in 2000. This longer, even-more-updated version appears here for the first time.

Chapter Notes

Chapter 1

1. His surname on-screen in *Creature from the Black Lagoon* and *Revenge of the Creature* (1955) is Welbourne, but on-screen in other movies it's spelled Welborn, and I've seen a letter he wrote to a Universal production manager and signed "Charles S. Welborn."

2. Most of Figueroa's movies were made for south-of-the-border companies, but he also lensed such gringo-friendly titles as *The Fugitive* (1947, with del Rio), *Kelly's Heroes*, *Two Mules for Sister Sara* (both 1970) and director John Huston's *The Night of the Iguana* (1964) and *Under the Volcano* (1984). Figueroa received an Oscar nomination for *Iguana*.

3. In 1960 Zimm moved with his wife Molly to Hilo, Hawaii; he returned to California after her death in 1995. A decade later, 96-year-old Zimm, last surviving member of the key *Creature* team, died of pneumonia at his Westwood home. In June 2009, around the time of what would have been Zimm's 100th birthday, his son Frank Zimring, a University of California at Berkeley law professor, commemorated the date by having the Palace Theater in Hilo show the Zimm-scripted triple-feature of *Jeopardy*, *Creature* and *The Prodigal*. Admission was free.

    Frank Zimring tells me that his dad landed the *Black Lagoon* writing job because Universal owed him five weeks for an option they bought and then didn't pursue, and that Universal liked the *Black Lagoon* writing he did, but because Zimm had no film credits, wouldn't trust him to do the screenplay. "My father was not happy with being kept from doing the screenplay and with a number of elements in the final script. It left a bad taste in his mouth and he talked about asking to have his name taken off the film. But a senior and very successful writer at the Guild told him, 'Maury, I wouldn't do that if I were you,' and he didn't."

4. Without wishing to imply that More Monster = Better Movie, compare this to the finished film in which we get our first teaser (the Gill Man's webfooted prints on the beach) at 2:15 and a gander at the Gill Man's hand at 3:50; the action begins with his mostly off-camera attack on Luis and Tomas seven minutes later, and he becomes a full-fledged member of the cast of on-camera characters just after the one-third point.

5. Early press items about the forthcoming film made it sound very different from the monster movie that eventually developed; for example, columnist Edwin Schallert on March 21, 1953, wrote that Alland's proposed feature *The Black Lagoon* will be "about nature's dead ends, and will deal with an expedition up the Amazon to discover a type of human being whose evolution was completed in a different than normal way."

    In the collection of Robert Skotak is a copy of *Black Lagoon*'s revised second-draft screenplay, previously owned by Alland. In it, next to this dialogue exchange…

    > KAY: What was it like under there? [underwater in the Black Lagoon]
    > REED: A world of enchantment.

    … Alland put a large asterisk. Based on the way it's drawn with emphasis, *and* based on his conversations with Alland, Skotak interprets this as a big "Yes!" Said Skotak:
    > I think Alland was always wanting more of a Cocteau *Beauty and the Beast* feeling to the film—sad creature, enchanting undersea realm, an unattainable love, etc., but with scares. *Creature from the Black Lagoon* and *It Came from Outer Space* were his genuine favorites at Universal in that era. I also interviewed Jack Arnold about these films, and he never seemed quite as engaged as Alland about the intent of them.

    On another page of that script, as they first enter the lagoon, Reed says, "The Black Lagoon," and Kay follows that with a whispered line, "The beautiful lagoon." Alland has handwritten the word *awe* next to her words. Don't know if that adds anything, other than that he seemed keen on some nuance to the "horror movie" approach, keen on *not* characterizing the lagoon only as some standard "spooky-creepy" place, but a place of wonder, or some such.

    I'd have to say that Alland was one of those on the short list of interview subjects who had a really accurate memory, much of this apparent from the accuracy of the details he could talk about in regards to things many others would never seem to remember about, say, early versions of the films they were involved with. Much of this became clear to me after discussing the original version of *This Island Earth*. He had no copy for reference, but was able, some 30 or so years later, to point out some very specific details, solely from memory. (However, I feel he was certainly exaggerating in giving Harry Essex just about a big zero when discussing Essex's contribution to *It Came from Outer Space* [1953]. Obviously Bradbury's treatment needed a bit more work than just the assignment of scene numbers, etc.)

6. In the mid–1980s, during a visit to the Academy's Margaret Herrick Library in Beverly Hills, I heard the name "Leo Lieberman" called out by a librarian and, recognizing it, I introduced myself and briefly chatted with him. Unfortunately, at that point all I knew about him was that he had done some writing on a pair of 1957 Roger Corman movies, *Carnival Rock* and *Sorority Girl*. My discovery that he was one of the uncredited cogs in the *Black Lagoon* writing machine was then still years away. Born March 12, 1916, he died just over 84 years later, in 2000.

    In one of Robert Skotak's conversations with Alland, they raised the subject of

Lieberman's *Black Lagoon* contribution—if any. "I just recall that Alland did not find the guy the least bit useful in the process," Skotak told me. "Alland found him to be more of a nuisance, perhaps put there via the nepotism route. He had a very low opinion of Lieberman and was not happy that he was forced by the studio to take him in on the film. For what it's worth, Franklin Coen [who wrote Alland's *This Island Earth et al.*] was one of the few writers at Universal that Alland truly loved and respected. And Coen had nothing but endless praise for Alland and Alland's respect for writers—good writers—a rarity in Hollywood, it would seem."

7. In my Alland interview, the producer spoke highly of Ross' contribution to *Black Lagoon*: "Arthur Ross was the guy who did the best job—particularly once he found out that we were going to be able to shoot underwater. He really wanted to rewrite the whole thing and take full advantage of the underwater possibilities. So with encouragement from me, we went back into the script and did that."

8. The script suggests that the Institute be established via a long shot of Florida's Marine Studios, with the ocean in the background. That's where much of *Revenge of the Creature* would be shot.

9. Another title on the short (and it should be shorter) list of Essex's directing credits: *Mad at the World* (1955), made by the Ida Lupino–Collier Young indie company The Filmakers. It was "The True Story of Today's Teen-Age Hoodlums!" according to its posters ... with the teenage wolf pack played by actors (Stanley Clements, Paul Dubov, Joseph Turkel) ranging in age from late twenties to *late thirties*. Dubov, born during World War I, is older than some of the authority figures on the trail of his "teenage" character! After *Mad at the World*, Essex gave himself a 17-year break from directing, then inflicted *Octaman* (1973) and *The Cremators* (1972) on audiences.

10. In the summer of 1953 while *Black Lagoon* was in the process of being scripted, RKO released the documentary *The Sea Around Us*, based on marine biologist Rachel Carson's bestseller about ocean life. Like our favorite merman movie, it begins in misty outer space with a voice intoning, "In the beginning, God created the heavens and the Earth, and the Earth was without form and void." A fireball can be seen in the distance, spiraling through space and throwing off blazing fragments; the way it comes at the camera and explodes makes you think of 3-D (even though the movie is flat). Then we're shown, and told, about the cooling of the Earth, the way rain fell for centuries, etc. (The *Motion Picture Exhibitor* reviewer marveled, "Portrayed brilliantly are the creation of the earth and the oceans.") In short, there's not a lot about this Oscar-winning documentary's opener that *doesn't* make you think of the corresponding scene in *Black Lagoon*. William Alland told me that having the story of Creation as *Black Lagoon*'s introductory segment was his idea, and that he never saw *The Sea Around Us*.

11. The coelacanth may have missed its shot at sci-fi movie immortality in *Black Lagoon* but this prehistoric fish would return in director Arnold's 1958 *Monster on the Campus*.

12. Was a Creature suit with a tail ever made? "Underwater Gill Man" Ricou Browning has said that no Creature costume ever had a tail, and for many fans, it's "Case closed!" right there. But according to Bud Westmore, yes there *was* a Creature with a tail. In the two-page *Collier's* magazine story "Monsters Made to Order" (December 10, 1954), Westmore described an early costume: "We gave him two arms with crab claws, and we first had him with a tail and a built-in engine to operate it, so he could swish a man off his feet. But that interfered with his swimming, so we cut it out." Perhaps the monster outfit he describes is the one mentioned in the minutes of Universal's July 14, 1953, Studio Operating Committee meeting: "We are shooting underwater tests tomorrow of the 'lagoon man' in both 3-D and 2-D." This was weeks before anyone at Universal had ever heard of Ricou Browning, and vice versa.

13. Researcher Scott Gallinghouse has informed me that, according to Nims' high school yearbook, his favorite saying at that young age was, "It won't be long now"— an expression which, taken another way, couldn't do a better job of encapsulating the Hollywood career of a man with a passion for turning drawn-out movies into shorter ones!

14. Hand-on-shoulder shots then became a fixture in Universal's monster pictures: John Agar, Lori Nelson and Pat Powers were on the receiving end in *Revenge of the Creature*, Agar again in *Tarantula* (1955), David Janssen in *Cult of the Cobra* (1955), Craig Stevens in *The Deadly Mantis* (1957), Joanna Moore in *Monster on the Campus* (1958) and maybe more. *Deadly Mantis* director Nathan Juran even used it in his non-Universals *The Brain from Planet Arous*, *Attack of the 50 Foot Woman* and *The 7th Voyage of Sinbad* (all 1958).

15. Over the past several decades, sci-fi movie historian Robert Skotak has touched on *Creature from the Black Lagoon* in interviews with various Universal veterans, and he says that one of the things he gleaned about the film was "how great a degree William Alland was an all-around creative force behind it. [Universal executive] James Pratt and several others backed that up pretty strongly."

16. Alland is in rare form in this 41-minute doc, talking about his show biz career from its earliest days (at three years old, he played a *girl* in a tent show production of *Ten Nights in a Bar-Room*) through his Orson Welles years and his stint at Universal. It's a special feature on Alpha Home Video's DVD of the Alland-produced and -directed *Look in Any Window* (1961).

17. The Nims-Alland memo pointed out the need for a shot of the Gill Man following the boat, so that audiences wouldn't think there were *two* Gill Men— one at the geological camp, one in the Black Lagoon. And such a shot was apparently filmed but then cut out after the movie was scored; you can hear the music jump ahead a few notes when the movie gets to the spot where that shot would have been seen.

Come to think of it, why *did* the Gill Man happen to be at the geological camp, far from his lagoon, for the occasion of the discovery of the skeleton fossil? A mystical premonition that the bones of an ancestor were about to be unearthed?

18. The brief encounter between the Gill Man and the machete-wielding Garu, as described by Essex, is good and grisly, with the monster seizing and crushing the native's hand, clawing open his face and then lifting and flinging him into the camera for our 3-D benefit. In the several letters that passed back and forth between Universal and MPAA censor Joseph Breen, this appears to have been the only action scene that prompted Breen to remind the studio to avoid "objectionable gruesomeness."

19. Those two lines were written for inclusion in the scene after the Gill Man smashes the *Rita* rowboat. Here they are, in context:

> REED: And he'll keep trying to come aboard until he gets what he wants.
> WILLIAMS (scanning the water, hopefully): Let him ... (turning back to Reed) It'll still give us a chance to take him.

Notes—Chapter 1

REED (with finality): Can't you understand he's after Kay?

Even though the dialogue was disallowed by Breen, it *was* used when the scene was shot. But ultimately it was not heard in the movie.

20. Also discussed in the letter: the possibility of working out with *Life* magazine an arrangement by which Peter Stackpole (1913–97), one of *Life*'s original four staff photographers, would be given a three-week leave of absence to shoot still photographs during the filming of *Black Lagoon*'s underwater sequences. (Stackpole, an expert swimmer, had cameras equipped for underwater use.) Israel was aware that Stackpole's participation would not only yield Universal some first-rate stills, but also insure a *Life* magazine layout on the movie. For whatever reason, Stackpole did not get involved.

21. Scarier than anything in *Creature from the Black Lagoon*: Ball's injury and subsequent cancer treatments weren't covered by workman's compensation or insurance—even though the accident took place at her workplace as she rehearsed for a role! But, as of the day of her meeting with Thomas at any rate, Universal was keeping her on salary and picking up the tab for the treatments.

22. On what might have been his *very* first Wakulla visit, he watched a bit of the shooting of a Johnny Weissmuller Tarzan movie—probably either *Tarzan's Secret Treasure* or *Tarzan's New York Adventure* (1942).

23. In *The Wonders of Wakulla Springs*, *What a Picnic!* is followed by a portion of Rice's *Amphibious Fighters* (1943), made in color at Wakulla Springs at the height of World War II. Showing soldiers from Camp Gordon Johnston putting on an impressive mock battle, *Amphibious Fighters* went on to win an Academy Award for Best Short Subject.

24. One that Browning has forgotten was William Alland, who was not only there (according to Universal's records, and to him), but also got wet seeing the bottom-of-Wakulla sights. He told me,

> I had never been in scuba gear in my life and I was given no instructions. "Scotty" said, "Here, put this on and come on down." Nobody told me to make sure not to hold my breath, even though holding your breath can be very dangerous. When people start to come *up* [after scuba diving], the instinct is to hold your breath. But that'll explode your lungs—you're supposed to continue to breathe in and out normally. Nobody told me that [*laughs*]! "Scotty" and I went down together and looked at all these locations—as a matter of fact, we brought film back to the studio, and the brass saw me and "Scotty" swimming through the water together. In those days, I was ready to do anything.… When it comes to being stupid enough not to have much fear, that's me!

25. At age 14, Chris Mueller, Jr., was asked by his father, "What do you want to be when you grow up?" and, typical of 14-year-olds, the boy's an-

Chris Mueller, Jr., the sculptor of the Black Lagoon Gill Man's head, had a long Hollywood career that included contributions to several classics, including The Thief of Bagdad (1940). Here the giant genie (Rex Ingram) reclines on the steps of the Temple of the Dawn, a miniature sculpted by Mueller.

swer was a wisecrack: "A garbage man!" Smart-mouthed kids didn't go over big in the early 1900s so before you could say "Crazy Goole," the father got him a job as an apprentice in the shop of an architectural sculptor and modeler. Truth be told, though, the father probably would have plunked Jr. there no matter *what* answer the kid gave: Architectural sculpting and modeling had been in the Mueller family blood for 500 years. Chris Jr. was five when his father first started giving him clay and encouraging him to sculpt.

The above bio info—and a lot of what's to come—came from the October 15, 1974, issue of *JJG Reports*, some kind of newsletter, printed in Santa Clara, California, and apparently devoted to local carpenters, sculptors, landscapers, etc. It goes on to say that during Mueller's five-year apprenticeship, he

> was exposed to the best men and works of the profession on the Pacific Coast—through Old World masters who worked in every known architectural style. He studied on his own, and attended the California School of Fine Arts in San Francisco and the San Francisco Architectural Club. At age 19 Chris went to work for himself, his apprenticeship completed; he never wanted for work as gradually the men who taught him so well passed on and there became fewer men who could [fill] the demand for this type of work.

The call for artists like Mueller dwindled with the coming of the Great Depression, so in 1936 he relocated to Hollywood and began working in movies. According to *JJG Reports*, "Chris has done immeasurable research for the natural animal reproductions, monsters and rare special effects he has created; as he puts it, he 'lives the animal' before he reproduces or creates it." (The Gill Man too?) Mueller movie credits mentioned in *JJG Reports* include "architectural modeling for *Camelot* [1967], the execution of the decorative features on the Harmonia Garden and other

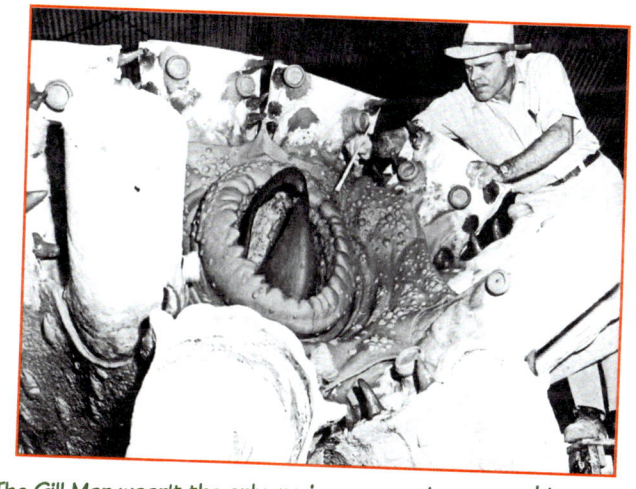

The Gill Man wasn't the only movie sea monster we need to be thankful to Chris Mueller, Jr., for: He was also part of the team that made the giant squid for 20000 Leagues Under the Sea (1954). In this behind-the-scenes shot he's working on the mouth and beak.

sets for *Hello, Dolly!* [1969], the giant squid in *20000 Leagues Under the Sea* [1954]" and his then-latest, *The Island at the Top of the World* (1974). Mueller's friend Bob Burns adds a few more screen accomplishments: the miniature of the Temple of the Dawn and its giant goddess statue in Alexander and Zoltan Korda's *The Thief of Bagdad* (1940) and two talking snakes (the treasure chamber–guarding White Cobra and the river snake Kaa) in the Kordas' *Jungle Book* (1942). The snakes were made of latex rubber over flexible wire armatures. Also for *Jungle Book*, Mueller built the miniature and full-size versions of the lost city's temple and, as a narrator calls it, "the barrel-bellied mugger, the crocodile." On the monster front, says Burns, Mueller made the Frankenstein headpiece and Wolf Man nose (and more) for *Abbott and Costello Meet Frankenstein* (1948), the Hyde mask and the "mouse-man" head (and more) for *Abbott and Costello Meet Dr. Jekyll and Mr. Hyde* (1953) and the Tyrannosaurus Rex for *The Land Unknown* (1957). He also sculpted ornate bric-a-brac for buildings, animals for Disney parks and so many other accomplishments that scratching the surface here is all I'm prepared to do.

Mueller died and then, some time later, his wife Helen. Burns said, "After Helen died, the city had a sale of everything in the house. Unfortunately, no one told me about it and I missed out on it. The real sad thing is, Helen had left to me in her will everything that Chris had stored in a rented garage: all his research material, his books on artwork, sketches and little sculpts he had done, the fossilized Gill Man claw from *Black Lagoon* and so on.

Chris Mueller, Jr., puts the finishing touches on a lion sculpt for Epcot at Disneyworld in 1980.

However, the will was never found. Pretty odd, I think."

26. One of the king-sized actors considered for the on-land Creature job already had several monster roles in his Hollywood past: a pair of giant beasts in *Flash Gordon* (1936), Petro the werewolf in *The Mad Monster* (1942) and, most memorably, the Frankenstein Monster in *House of Frankenstein* (1944), *House of Dracula* (1945) and *Abbott and Costello Meet Frankenstein* (1948). But 6'5" Glenn Strange turned down the Gill Man job because he felt it entailed too much work in the water.

27. Vaughn's memo also describes recent experiments to determine what substance to use in scenes involving rotenone. Pure cream mixed with aluminum looked too inky; pure cream looked okay for use in underwater shots. However, for shots of rotenone on the water's surface, he wrote that cream-with-aluminum "will be used for the value of the luminous glow." According to Vaughn's memo, propmaker Fred Knoth was presently adapting an oxygen tank into a rotenone gun.

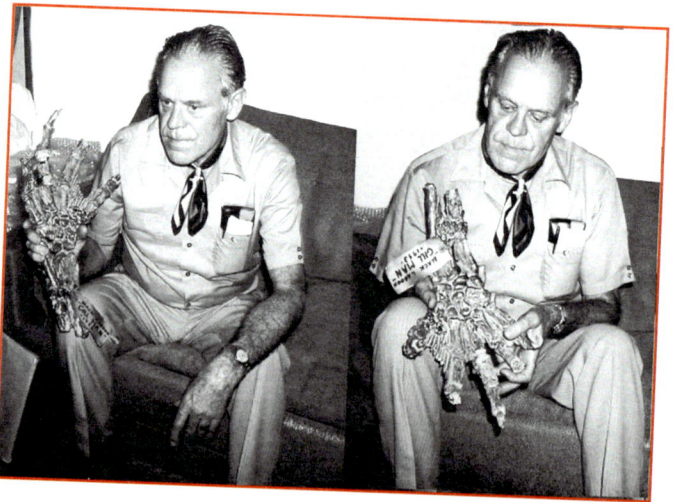

More than one Gill Man skeleton claw was made (Hollywood standard operating procedure, in case one got broken during production); Chris Mueller, Jr., kept an extra after filming wrapped, and in July 1973 brought it along on a visit to Bob Burns' home. "It ended up in Japan with a collector," said Burns. "I saw a photo of it in a Japanese magazine and it looked pretty broken up with pieces missing."

28. Mueller sculpted the head of the Land Creature over a bust of Ben Chapman and the head of the Underwater Creature over a bust of Browning. Chapman's head was bigger than Browning's, so if you put pictures of the two heads side by side you can see a few small differences; but watching the movie, you'd never notice.

29. In the 1948 comedy *Texas, Brooklyn & Heaven*, Patrick is briefly seen as one in a line of pretty girls working in a Coney Island sideshow; the barker calls them "water nymphs" and then goes down the line asking their names. Presumably they're all giving their real names because when he gets to Patrick, she answers, "Mil Patrick." Unfortunately, there's no hoped-for follow-up scene with "Mil" and the other ladies *doing* their mermaid-like act—although that would have been *so* appropriate for a future collaborator on the Gill Man outfit.

30. At least one other person tried to cut himself a fat slice of Creature credit: According to Jack Arnold, he co-designed the Gill Man suit. "It was Jack Kevan and I," he said in a June 1977 interview with David J. Schow. "We didn't know what the hell to make and tried everything.... Everything we did looked like winter underwear once it got wet.... [O]ne day, I thought, 'Gee, if we put a gill-head on it, and fins, and give him scales....' So I called Jack and said, 'Can we make a suit using this?' and I gave him a rough sketch, and Jack refined it, and that's how that got started."

31. This saved Universal more than a few bucks: Lovejoy was going to be paid $25,000 and Carlson got about half that. To see Universal's #1 and #2 choices for the *Black Lagoon* lead in a movie together, check out the indie *The Sound of Fury* (1950), a powerful melodrama with "action so realistic that one feels as if being present in a real scene of mob rule" (*Harrison's Reports*). The fact-based film stars Lovejoy as a jobless family man who out of desperation teams with stick-up artist Lloyd Bridges, and is on hand when Bridges unexpectedly murders a helpless man. Carlson plays a columnist for the city's "yellow rag" newspaper, a decent guy who makes an error of judgment and writes columns that prejudge the two men guilty—columns that inflame the locals. As a lynch mob gathers to storm the jail, Lovejoy and Carlson act opposite each other for the first and only time in the movie, through Lovejoy's cell door bars, both characters filled with shame over the consequences of their actions.

32. In her September 1 column, Hopper pointed out that "team work is becoming a policy at U-I" with writer Essex, producer Alland and director Arnold following their *It Came from Outer Space* success with *Black Lagoon* and producer Aaron Rosenberg, star James Stewart and director Anthony Mann currently doing their *third* picture together, *The Far Country* (1955). Carlson's subsequent addition to the *Black Lagoon* cast made it even more of an *It Came from Outer Space* "team reunion."

33. Ben Chapman's Gill Man helmet had removable eyeballs but Browning's did not. You can't tell that Browning's head has no eyes because the shadow of the brow always makes the eyes pits of darkness.

34. William Alland told me that he recorded the narration, and maybe he did, but I don't think what he recorded found its way into the movie. To me, the narrator sounds exactly like actor Richard Cutting, who provided a radio announcer's voice in *It Came from Outer Space* (1953). Cutting had fair-sized on-camera roles in Universal's *The Monolith Monsters* (1957) and *Monster on the Campus* (1958).

35. In *It Came from Outer Space*, Carlson's never-been-kissed scientist character freezes up and ruins the moment when his gal-pal Ellen (Barbara Rush) gets in kissing-close; and in *Black Lagoon*, Carlson's Dr. Reed is apparently shacked up with the girl. There's no middle ground with this guy!

Incidentally, this implication that Reed and Kay are cohabitating was caught by some preview audience members who expressed their disapproval via Preview Comment Cards. In at least one early draft of the script, Reed makes it known that he and Kay will be married soon, "Maybe when we get back to the States, next week." In that draft, consequently, Mark Williams' obvious resentment of their relationship is that-much-more offensive.

36. In 1968's *The Power*, Carlson played a character with identical concerns: Prof. Norman E. Van Zandt, head of a space program department trying to determine why one man will live and another man will die under the stresses that will be encountered in outer space. Even his speeches on the subject sound the same. In everything but name, Van Zandt is an older, higher-on-the-totem-pole David Reed.

In *The Creature Walks Among Us*, crazy Dr. Barton (Jeff Morrow) sees experimental surgery on the Gill Man as the first step toward getting Man ready for life in outer space. *Revenge of the Creature* is the only movie in the Gillogy where eventual space travel isn't the head scientist's motivation.

37. Notice that with neither native does the Gill Man instigate the violence: Luis throws the lantern, and Tomas grabs and swings his machete, before they run afoul of the claw. Noted jurisprudent David Schecter assures me that the Gill Man would be protected under the "Stand Your Ground" law of the Amazon and that no jury on Earth … well, no jury in Brazil, anyway … would hand down a conviction.

38. Script description of the world under the water: "What we see now is a veritable fairyland of the under-sea. Overhead, the sun tries feebly to force its way through, only to spend itself against this shadowy world.… [Williams is seen] swimming strongly … deeper…. He moves around sharp coral teeth, lacy fans, roots, the greens and blues of the crystal clear lake water, and seemingly out into audience."

39. The way the Creature unexpectedly pops into view from the bottom of the frame is in direct contrast to our easy-does-it first-looks at most previous Universal monsters. Think back to the shots where we first saw Dracula, the Frankenstein Monster, the Mummy, the Wolf Man *et al.*, all of which seem carefully designed *not* to unduly startle audience members, and compare them to the Gill Man's out-of-nowhere, jack-in-the-box entrance—which even comes with loud musical stinger. (One script explicitly calls for this moment to be a startler: "His appearance should be sudden and played for its maximum shock effect.") For another Universal horror movie moment so obviously intended to lift viewers out of their seats, you might have to go back as far as the unmasking scene in Lon Chaney's 1925 *The Phantom of the Opera*.

In addition to the take we see in the movie, the Florida unit also shot a few takes in which the Gill Man is more aggressive (or playful, or *some*thing): Instead of simply popping up to *watch* Williams, he pops out from a hiding place under a rock and tries to *grab* him. Williams, by unexpectedly turning to swim back in the direction from which he came, avoids being seized, and he swims away unaware of what just happened.

40. It was always planned for the bathing suit "reveal" to be a show-stopper moment: Back in the Zimm treatment, after Kay removes her robe, Zimm's next paragraph is just one sentence long: "The girl's got everything—and her swimsuit makes quite a showcase!")

41. "[A] reflex-type camera and light unit" to be exact, according to an August 1954 article on *Creature* in the magazine *The Skin Diver*.

42. Writer-producer-director Greg Nicotero's eight-minute black-and-white spoof *The United Monster Talent Agency* (2010) opens with a fun recreation of *Black Lagoon*'s climactic grotto scene with Kay (Cerina Vincent) on the rock, Reed (Sam Page) to the rescue and the Creature (Carey Jones) making an entrance complete with Bah-Bah-Bahhh! The Creature is closing in on Kay when a director (Frank Darabont) yells *cut* and we viewers realize we're watching the shooting of a movie scene. One of this book's authors, David J. Schow, is seen as the cameraman. Read more about it in the Marginalia section of Chapter Three, *The Creature Walks Among Us*.

43. New York's no-nonsense critics gave *Western Waters*, a comedy about flatboat pioneering down the Ohio River in 1800, the reviews you'd expect them to give a 24-year-old's play. (Carlson wrote it when he was even younger, a University of Minnesota student.) One critic wrote (in an unsourced clipping), "[I]n tone it is bedlam and cacophony," and *Women's Wear Daily* called it "a play of scant consequence.… [Carlson's] opus is written with more sincerity than skill. His direction of his play also left much to be desired." The *New York World Telegram* laid it on the line by labeling it "so ridiculous as to be almost painful."

Western Waters lasted seven performances—longer than *Black Lagoon* screenwriter Harry Essex's three-act *Something for Nothing* which, at a theater four blocks away, had recently closed after only *two* performances! Essex co-wrote the farce about a family trying to solve a series of picture puzzles and win a $100,000 contest; a few reviewers thought it might squeak by after some additional polishing but others were pretty negative: "[T]he situations are shopworn and the dialog is commonplace and dull" (*Women's Wear Daily*); "poorly constructed and amateurishly written" (*New York World-Telegram*); "Another of those incredibly stupid comedies that should never come to production" (*New York Daily News*). *Variety*'s thumbs-down review ran after it had closed, the paper printing it just for the record. How bad *was* it? A few weeks after it closed, Helen Hayes' manager Harry Essex wrote a letter for publication in the *New York World-Telegram* to say he was *not* the Harry Essex of *Something for Nothing*!

44. Carlson looked to be all set to play "Golden Boy" Joe Bonaparte, a brash New York East Side Italian who goes from violins (he wants to play professionally) to violence (in the prizefight ring). But at the eleventh hour, Carlson's commitment to the Broadway show *Stars in Your Eyes* kept him from the movie role. Twenty-year-old Holden landed the job and, overnight, became *Hollywood's* "golden boy" while Carlson, stars in *his* eyes, got permanently left behind. Like Carlson, Holden also had well-known battles with John Barleycorn, and in fact died in 1981 as a result of his boozing: In the bedroom of his Santa Monica apartment, he took a drunken fall and bashed his forehead on the sharp edge of a bedside table with enough force that the table damaged the wall behind it. The damage to Holden was worse: a gash that penetrated to the skull. Lying in bed, he tried to staunch the bleeding with Kleenex tissues before rolling off onto the floor, where he bled to death. He was a loner, so not until four or five days later was his body discovered by the apartment manager.

45. His first movie after the honeymoon was supposed to be Selznick-International's *Waterloo Bridge* with Vivien Leigh, but that ended up an MGM production, and with*out* Carlson.

46. RICHARD DUTOIT CARLSON (the name on his Los Angeles National Cemetery grave marker) died in 1977. Thirteen years later, MONA—HIS WIFE (her name on that same tombstone) was buried next to him.

47. According to *Variety*'s *Psychic Killer* review, Adams did "fine things with [the role], making it one of the rare honorable outings for an actress in films this year." *Cue* magazine called the Jim Hutton starrer a movie for viewers with "subnormal intelligence." Danton, co-writer of the script, included an in-joke for his ex's benefit: Her character, talking about her past, says, "I come from a small town in Arkansas, you probably never even heard of it. [*With gumbo-thick Southern accent:*] Blytheville!" Blytheville, Arkansas, is where Adams spent eight of her growing-up years.

48. In *Queen of the Mob*, Denning played one of Ma's (Blanche Yurka) larcenous sons, fatally shot up by cops as he and his brothers try to rob a store for the money to buy her a Christmas present. Funnily enough, the actor who played some of his best early roles in these fact-based crook movies had had his name shortened to Denning by Paramount because, it was felt, Denninger sounded too much like Dillinger (as in infamous gangster John).

49. Amusingly for *Black Lagoon* fans, Richard Carlson and Denning were two points in a romantic triangle in the studio's Anne Shirley-starring *West Point Widow* (1941).

50. From *The Hollywood Reporter*'s review of *The Magnificent Matador*: "[A] standout performance is given by Richard Denning as the loser in the romantic triangle. He plays what amounts to the heavy in the film and does it with real finesse."

51. The show's creator–executive producer Leonard Freeman liked his little in-jokes so in the pilot episode, there's a character named McAnkers, and a few episodes later, villain Ricardo Montalban's daughter is named Deedee (the Dennings' daughter's nickname).

52. But not in *Variety*'s annals. They critiqued *Santa* twice in 1932, their first reviewer complaining, "From American production standards it's pitiful…. [It] looks as though Antonio Moreno just walked through the job." When the paper assessed *Santa* a second time a few months later, the movie—and Moreno—were still low in their estimation: "Antonio Moreno, having a Hollywood background, should have his head bowed low over the job he handed in as director."

53. And some of his co-workers forgot even *that* (Chapman's name). Quoted in the book *The Westmores of Hollywood*, Richard Carlson recalled his *Creature* experience and credited *Ricou Browning* with playing the Gill Man in the Universal scenes: "Once inside the outfit Ricou Browning turned in one hell of a performance…. [Behind the mask], Browning let us know with his eyes that he realized he was a lonely, ugly, sad creature…. He loved Julie spiritually while I merely loved her carnally. He deserved her more than I did, and every graceful, fantastic move [Browning] made inside his monster suit, and what he did with his face inside that head, made the whole ridiculous thing believable." The book's author Frank Westmore worked on the movie at Universal and apparently he too had forgotten Chapman's name. *And* the fact that you couldn't see the Creature actor's eyes.

54. One of Chapman's wilder stories: Universal's mischievous makeup guys making a full-mast wang for the Gill Man! Longtime Creature and Chapman fan Joe "Sorko" Schovitz told me, "I'll never forget his telling (as only Ben could do it) of how the appendage matched the suit as far as texture, scales, color, etc. He'd say, 'It was beautiful,' 'It was as big as your forearm' and 'It looked like a baby's arm holding an apple!' He said that some photos were taken, but once someone upstairs [a studio executive] got wind of it, everything—including the Amazonian appendage—was confiscated and destroyed." Another fan recalls Chapman adding that he "terrorized his co-workers on the set with it." Chapman never told this story to me or to Bob Burns or to Davids Schow or Skal or in any interviews, apparently saving it for waaaay off-the-record party-type situations. To quote Henry Silva in *Amazon Women on the Moon* (1987), "Bullshit … or not?"

55. In 2012, the Stolen Valor Act was struck down by the Supreme Court in a 6-to-3 decision.

56. Right around this same time, Ray Harryhausen was there studying the movements of cephalopod mollusks in preparation for his upcoming *It Came from Beneath the Sea* (1955).

57. Burson (1919–2006) was a pioneer stuntwoman best-known for her work in Westerns; "I started rodeoing when I was seven, first riding calves and later doing trick riding," she said in a 1995 *Chicago Tribune* interview. She began her career in science fiction, doubling an actress playing a Martian in the 1945 serial *The Purple Monster Strikes*, but kept coming back to the Westerns, enough to eventually receive a Golden Boot award. "After rodeoing," she told the *Chicago Tribune*, "stunt work seemed like whipped cream."

58. Adams drew the line when it came to actually jumping off the *Rita*: "Despite my expertise in the water, I probably prevented one potential mishap from occurring when I was asked if I could dive off the boat for the shot that leads to the 'underwater ballet' scene. I firmly told them '*No,*' as I had never learned how to dive as a youth, and I wasn't about to learn in my late twenties with the cameras rolling. So a stunt double [Helen Morgan] did the beautiful dive in my place."

59. The skeleton hand prop was sculpted by Chris Mueller, who based the fingers on crab claws, "and then the rest he just made up," said Bob Burns. The thing set Universal back $210 ($180 for material and $30 for labor) but reaching out of the 3-D screen it looks like a million bucks; as David J. Schow mentions elsewhere in this chapter, at *Creature*'s 2013 showing at the Motion Picture Academy, the shot of the claw protruding from the rock wall was applauded. There may be a tip of the hat to that shot in *Jaws 3-D* (1983): In that movie's Sea World lagoon, there's a "sunken Spanish galleon" and the prop skeleton of a crew member whose bony hand identically reaches out in 3-D.

60. Stern doesn't get a single mention in Adams' autobiography *The Lucky Southern Star: Reflections from the Black Lagoon* but he wasn't around to notice: He died at L.A.'s Cedars-Sinai Medical Center a few months prior to the book's 2011 debut at the Egyptian Theatre on Hollywood Boulevard.

61. Browning had at least two Creature suits: That same day, October 14, Universal sent their second unit lads a telegram reading, "Monster Suit #2 left tonight air freight marked Hold at Tallahassee airport for pick-up."

62. Jack Arnold was thousands of miles away when *Black Lagoon*'s underwater scenes were shot but, thinking that we fans would never know that, he'd tell interviewers not only that he directed them but that he went underwater with the cast and crew to do so. Some of his lies were funnier than others: Talking to Dana M. Reemes (*Directed by Jack Arnold*), he said that when Ricou Browning was in dire need of air, Browning would convey that to Arnold "by going completely limp. Then he'd swim over to this air hose, then swim back into the scene and we'd continue filming." Okay, let's see if I have this straight: Whenever a swimmer was desperate for air, he first wasted precious seconds "going completely limp" and then, while all his coworkers idly watched, made a desperate swim to fetch the air hose himself? On what planet was *this* safety system devised, Jack?

Lying unfortunately goes with the territory in the land of make-believe, Hollywood, but Arnold seemed never to tire of trying to take every last ounce of credit away from the people (in this case, Welbourne and Havens) who actually did the work.

63. To get a look at an early example of underwater movie photography, and simultaneously scratch another title off your Universal Sci-Fi Must-See List, check out the studio's 1916 *Twenty Thousand Leagues Under the Sea*: Its Davy Jones' Locker scenes were shot by brothers Ernest and George Williamson, "who alone have solved the secret of under-the-ocean photography" (according to a card in the opening credits). This commingled adaptation of Jules Verne's *Twenty Thousand Leagues Under the Sea* and *The Mysterious Island* cost nearly $500,000 and was made over a two-year period, with subsea scenes shot in the Bahamas (the submarine *Nautilus*' Capt. Nemo *et al.* do a lot of walking around on the bottom, shoot at sharks, etc.). *The New York Times*' Christmas Day 1916 review called it a "spectacular" photoplay with "interesting and thrilling" underwater footage. Your 21st-century mileage may vary.

64. This shot would have preceded the scene in which she joins Dr. Thompson on deck as he stands guard over the caged Gill Man. The scene works better with*out* that shot, because viewers (and Dr. Thompson) mistakenly think that the off-camera racket she makes coming up on deck is Gill Man activity.

65. The ship made its debut in the Brando *Mutiny* and was subsequently seen in other movies, including one or two of the *Pirates of the Caribbean*s. She sank 90 miles off the North Carolina coast during 2012's Hurricane Sandy. The captain and a female crew member died but the 14 others aboard were rescued.

66. Ricou Browning told me, "Unionwise in those days, they had a rule where, if a studio came to Florida with a cameraman from California, they had to also hire a cameraman from Florida. The Florida guy they hired to match [Californian] 'Scotty' Welbourne was Cliff Poland, a real nice guy and a very good cameraman. He didn't go underwater on *Black Lagoon* but when the camera got flooded a couple of times, he was very important by helping 'Scotty' and the crew take it apart and put it back together and get it ready to go again." Poland (1916–2008) was, by the 1960s, a Florida-based d.p.; his credits include *Honeymoon of Horror* (1964), *Around the World Under the Sea* (1966), *Mission Mars* (1968), *Fireball Jungle* (1969), *Hello Down There* (1969), *Stanley* (1972), *Salty*

In some shots, tubes ran up into the Gill Man helmet, expanding and contracting hidden air bladders that made the gills move out and in. As the New York Herald Tribune reviewer rightly put it, "[T]he makeup man has done his best to endow the creature with logical loathsomeness."

(1973) and dozens of episodes of the Browning-created TV series *Flipper*.

67. Throughout the shooting of Gill Man scenes, the moviemakers regularly ran rubber tubes into the Creature head for this purpose. Chapman told me that under the gills, "there were little 'balloons' or air pockets. On the other end of the hose, there was somebody sitting off-camera with a little hand pump. We coordinated and worked together to create the effect. I would open my mouth and gasp at the same time that he would pump the gills; that way, it looked like the gasping was what made the gills flare out." In *Collier's* magazine, Bud Westmore said the Gill Man's pulsating gills "supplied a menacing type of movement." Maybe every other fan can see them moving, but except for the final-reel *Rita* scene where the Gill Man walks into a screen-filling closeup, I can't.

68. The name of the guy in the Creature suit in early scenes *might* be Ray Irvin: One Universal memo, aggravatingly undated, lists Irvin *and* Chapman as "Gill Man (Land)." Stuntman Regis Parton, who played both the Metaluna Mutants in *This Island Earth* and also one of the Mole People, recalled for interviewer Robert Skotak that he briefly wore the Gill Man suit on-camera. But Parton's name appears nowhere in the *Black Lagoon* (or *Revenge* or *Creature Walks*) production paperwork I've seen. My gut feeling is that, on one of the movies, he participated in the scaly-monster equivalent of a wardrobe test.

69. Chapman also didn't like being in the water that night. "Let me tell you, it was freezing," he told me. "And I do mean *freezing*, up in the hills, in the back lot there.... Of course they had hot soup, they had heaters, hoses that would pump warm water. And I got off *easy* compared to Richard Carlson and Richard Denning—they were in the water just like I was, but they didn't have a foam rubber suit on, they were in their bathing suits!"

70. Merrilee Kazarian told me that Chapman wasn't married at the time. The "wife" mentioned by *Life* was his French live-in girlfriend, the "seven-year-old son" *her* son Nicky. "Ben called his girlfriends 'my wife'—sort of a Tahitian thing!" Merrilee explained.

"Ben was only officially married twice, once when he was a kid, 17 or so, and their baby was stillborn. He didn't officially marry again until he was about 48; their son, Ben F. Chapman III, was born when he was 49! Ben was married to Wife #2 for only a short time."

71. For the record, Corliss' other five are *Tabu* (1931), *Gojira* (1954), *Moby Dick* (1956), *The Abyss* (1989) and, naturally, *Jaws*.

72. "The Creature was initially stunt work," Browning told interviewer Michael Michalski, "with some reactions and actions from the guy on the topside [Chapman] walking around with his arms up in the air. You couldn't really see any acting."

73. Yes, Wakulla is home to alligators—but when I asked Ricou Browning about working in a body of water where alligators live, I got a "Yeah ... what's your point?"–type shrug! "They weren't really a concern, because we were so busy doing our jobs that we didn't even pay any attention to them."

74. At the very end of the shot where Zee runs up to the Gill Man, notice that the Gill Man starts to get in position to lift him. "Creech" *does* lift Reed overhead in the finale; he also gorilla-presses Charlie (Robert Hoy) in *Revenge of the Creature* and Dr. Barton (Jeff Morrow) in *The Creature Walks Among Us.*

75. In my audio commentary on the 2000 DVD of *Creature from the Black Lagoon*, I said that the shot with the telephone pole was the first thing Jack Arnold shot on the morning of the first day of production. *Wrong.* I screwed up. The first shot of the first day was a different entering-the-Lagoon shot.

76. Little Susan's visits to Universal were not always that traumatic; in fact, she "loved going to Universal with [Alland] and did it every chance that I could. We lived in the Valley and this was 60 years ago, there was no Ventura Freeway then. We would go to work in his sports car and back then, with no smog, none of that kind of stuff, I could smell the orange blossoms on the way in. He would take me with him to the soundstages of movies that he was working on, or to the daily rushes of whatever it was he was shooting, and to the commissary for lunch where I would see actors and actresses in their costumes and makeup. There was a lot of glitz!

"I *loved* it—but I also *didn't* like it, because on the back lot of the studio you'd walk for a few yards and you were in Hawaii, and then a few more yards and you'd be in downtown London in the 1800s, and then a few more yards somewhere *else*. All these places looked great from the front but there was no 'backs' to them, they were all phony. Seeing how they [moviemakers] did things, I thought, 'Well, this is really phony. I don't really want to have anything to do with this myself.'" And she didn't; she became a teacher (now retired). The only time she ever worked on a movie was when, as a high schooler, she was a secretary of sorts on the only movie Alland ever directed, the low-budget *Look in Any Window* (1961).

77. At that depth, *Black Lagoon* still photographer Bruce Mozert told me, "the pressure in your ears is unbelievable. It's *exactly* like somebody's takin' nails and nailin' 'em in your eardrums. *Oh!*, it hurts!"

78. Malde, a bit player and a stand-in for actors Jack Oakie, Tony Curtis and Kirk Douglas, got some newspaper attention in 1972 when he crashed his car into another car in a Hollywood intersection, then drove over a 26-year-old bicyclist and sped away, dragging him for a mile-plus before two highway patrolmen got him to stop. A tow truck had to lift the car so that the bicyclist and his bike could be disentangled from the undercarriage. Malde, 67, was booked on suspicion of manslaughter.

79. According to a Universal publicity item, "the familiar Hollywood superstition that tragedy always travels in threes" came true when *Black Lagoon* assistant cameraman Kyme Meade was knocked off-balance by a moving camera crane, crashed through a 2 × 4 wooden barrier and fell ten feet into a deep water tank.

80. Notice, as Carlson surfaces and climbs the ladder, a "look box" bobbing in the water. These boxes, with bottoms of clear glass or clear plastic, are used by people on the surface to get a better look at what's in the water below. It's a nice touch that the moviemakers bothered to add this prop, for the benefit of the one-in-a-million viewer who'd spot it and know what it was. A topside down-through-the-look-box shot of Reed coming up toward the surface of Morajo Bay was on the Florida unit's to-do list but may not have gotten done.

81. Fans of werewolf movies may get a kick out of knowing that eye, ear and throat specialist Andrews is regularly mentioned in studies of the moon's effects on human behavior: By studying the outcome of 1000 surgical procedures, he gathered evidence that over four-fifths of post-operative bleeding crises occurred nearer the full and the new moon, although fewer operations were performed at those times. His findings, published in *The Journal of the Florida Medical Association* and also covered in *Time* magazine, lent credence to the often-derided bit of English folklore that, like ocean tides, the flow of a man's blood is governed by the phases of the moon.

82. To try and learn how the Creature-on-fire scenes were done in *Black Lagoon* and *Creature Walks* now that probably everyone who had a hand in them has passed, I turned to fellow '50s monster movie buff Robert Skotak—who also happens to be a two-time Oscar winner for visual effects (for 1986's *Aliens* and 1991's *Terminator 2: Judgment Day*). He emailed me, "I consulted with my brother Dennis on all of this, and it took us a while to not only co-

ordinate, but reach consensus. We looked at several different transfers. Ironically, old tapes [pre-digital enhancements and fix-ups] are the most reliable in terms of showing how these films originally looked. Writing about these things without having a fully detailed, accurate record at hand of what, how and when things went on can make one cautious about stating things as absolute fact. But, given what records to which I've had access, what interviews I've conducted with principals involved and what I know as an effects supervisor, the following should be pretty accurate." He continued,

> I have to say, in regards to the scene on the deck of the *Rita* in which the Creature is set on fire by Thompson, I find it amazing that such a dramatic scene could be accomplished with but two visual-special effects shots. Well, in fact, probably only one was actually accomplished on the single day on which the shots had been scheduled, though I have reason to believe two were *attempted*.
>
> First, the closeup shot of the Creature as a lantern is smashed on his head. Ben Chapman is on record as reporting that he was never set on fire. He recalled that he pantomimed reactions as if set on fire, thrashing about and jumping into the water, the idea being that a stuntman would copy his actions—after viewing and studying the processed footage—then be set on fire while wearing a black, fire-resistant (asbestos, likely) suit, to be photographed and, finally, optically combined, by optical effects supervisor Roswell Hoffman, with Chapman's footage.
>
> Chapman's "as-if-on-fire" performance was photographed in the late afternoon of the very last day of the live action shoot. The lantern toss, Scene 333 in Harry Essex's second revised shooting script, was photographed by the main unit, with Chapman reacting violently, thrashing over left to right and backing away from the 3-D camera, with a bit of reactive "firelight" cast on him by off-screen stage lights.
>
> A second shot—Scene 334 in the same shooting script—has the Creature engulfed in flame and then hurdling the rail and diving into the water. Again, the idea for the lantern and "water-jump" shots at the time is that a stuntman would duplicate this action some time later, wearing a black asbestos suit that was dressed as a very rough mock-up of the Creature, meaning only a few of the basic shapes of the face, etc., would be glued to the fireproof suit. Once these straightforward, non-pyro elements were photographed, the optical department would sync the action and combine Chapman's "non-fire" performance with the stuntman's "on-fire-against-black" performance into single matched, cohesive images.
>
> The first thing Hoffman would likely have done in the following days would be to make a simple superimposition (double exposure) of the closeup lantern-shatter shot, combining Chapman's thrashing action with the asbestos-stunt-fire element, in which Al Wyatt the stuntman matched as best he could Chapman's actions. Here is where I suspect that it became pretty clear that it would take a *lot* of post work to get the two performances to line up and, indeed, that turned out to be true: A study of the final shot in the film illustrates what a mess they had on hand. It is immediately obvious that a great deal of doctoring in the optical printer was required to even come close to bringing the two elements together. Another issue: A flame bar had been placed behind Wyatt to help outline and create (via a hand-traced a.k.a. rotoscoped matte) a workable silhouette of the black suit separate from the black background environment in which the fire had been photographed. The flame bar appears to have been hand-held and rather loosely moved about in an attempt to follow Wyatt's body movements. A lot of mismatching in the hand-held moves was obvious. As a result, the hard, linear edge of the bar repeatedly revealed itself out of alignment with the action. Much rotoscope retouching was required in an attempt to minimize the problem but unfortunately it remained still visible in the final film. On the other hand, the frantic blurring of the action helped the shot pass. Few in the audience were probably aware of the errors in the final shot—there was too much drama and action for anyone to notice!
>
> The wider shot—Chapman diving off the *Rita* into the water—came off perfectly, a terrific shot in the film. How was it done? Think about it: If a double-pass were to be used in which another person—meaning stuntman Wyatt—was to be set on fire while attempting to copy *every* action, every single movement, then every single movement plus all the related factors would have to line up exactly, meaning the distance of subject—the Creature—to the camera, the body positions, the speed of his movement and positions of his arms and legs in every single frame; the strength, height and timing of his leap; the angle of his trajectory to the camera and to the water; the contact-point of the jump relative to the edge of the *Rita*'s rail, all these matching points numerous and complex, and all of this to be done without a video-mixer to check accuracy as compared to the previously shot footage of Chapman. Then factor in having to precisely match the pan and tilt to follow the action established in Chapman's footage … *and* all performed in three-dimensional space where every point in space had to match! Kind of a "yikes!" Really, a near-impossible task at that time. Especially on a low budget, with little time and only standard equipment available.
>
> Once it was clear, upon viewing the results of the quick double-exposure test of Wyatt attempting to match Chapman's performance in the lantern-burn shot, in which lining up two separately shot actions would be extremely time-consuming to perfect, a simpler approach was deemed necessary: Go back to the Process Stage, where the *Rita* and jungle backdrop had been held in position in the water, and shoot the Creature on fire, *live*. The factor working in their favor for this potentially dangerous stunt was that the shot was very short. Mere seconds. And simple: a step or two and a jump into the water.
>
> My best guess is that, several weeks after the main, live-action unit had wrapped, an asbestos suit was made to look more like the Creature than it had in the lantern shot, by using appliqués of additional freshly cast pieces pulled from molds of the creature suit. A full Creature face, full hands and feet, etc. As to when it was shot, it appears very likely in-around the third week in November of that year. Wyatt would have donned the improved Creature suit, portions of which would have been coated with flammable gel (essentially a thick form of contact cement), set alight and photographed in action. With Wyatt properly protected in this asbestos fire-suit, the fiery leap would have been a safe and simple way to capture the very dramatic and much-needed action. The shot is so perfect that it hardly seems possible that it was a "combination shot" wedding two performances. The "mess" that had resulted from trying this in with the lantern shot adds further to this likelihood.

(According to Army Archerd's December 4, 1953, *Variety* column, Wyatt received burns doing these trick shots.) "Stan" Horsley was the cameraman on what Universal paperwork calls "'Gill Man on Fire' and 'Gill Man on Fire Jumps in Water' Trick Shots." Six-foot-three Al Wyatt, a son of Kentucky and an expert horseman, did well in the stunt business, doubled some top stars (including one of his best friends, Jeff Chandler) and got his share of acting gigs along the way. He worked without credit on *The Haunted Palace* (1963), almost certainly as the stunt double in a scene where Elisha Cook, Jr.'s character runs and collapses in the street with the back of his cape-like coat ablaze. Eventually Wyatt graduated to stunt coordinator and second unit director, and even associate-produced a couple Filipino-made George Montgomery pictures. Wyatt received the first Golden Boot Award for Stuntmen and is in the Hollywood Stuntman's Hall of Fame. Blood clots led to the amputation of a leg in the late 1980s, and he died in his Panorama City, California, home in 1992.

83. "Did you feel that your career was at risk if you didn't give the right answers?" I asked Alland in 1995. "Not only did I feel it, I was *told* it!" he laughed. "Edward Muhl, who was the head of production, called me in and said, 'Bill, we *love* you, but I have to tell you, if you don't cooperate with that committee, you're through!'"

84. Israel adds that he met Patrick that afternoon and admits, "I have great misgivings about what will happen in the eastern office when this gal walks in. I am sure Charley [Simonelli] will have nothing on his mind but one thing until you manage to get her out to Detroit."

85. Detroit moviegoers had the opportunity to see Patrick as well as another "*Creature* celebrity," Julie Adams. According to researcher Robert J. Kiss, Adams' Detroit appearance got some brief national coverage by way of Dorothy Kilgallen's column of February 25 in which she romantically linked Adams and her companion at the Detroit opening, Charles Simonelli—a relationship which had been "revealed" earlier in the month (February 2) by Earl Wilson in his syndicated *New York Post* column.

86. Her wardrobe apparently took a hit during her tour: The minutes of the Studio Operating Committee meeting of February 25, 1954, mention that Patrick "has returned to the studio and claims damage to her clothing to the extent of some $400. Mr. Israel has requested that she bring the clothes in for determination of the extent of damage by our Wardrobe Department."

87. Living well is the best revenge, and Patrick did just that. In addition to continued work on both sides of the camera, she married the Creature-sized (6'5") Lee Trent, once a radio, movie and TV actor but now a business entrepreneur successful enough for his missus' comings and goings to rate a mention in the California society pages. In the late '60s and early '70s, photos of the elegant lady at one gala, charity event or pageant after another regularly appeared in print (and, one hopes, were regularly seen by Westmore, who by then was scrambling to keep his job at Universal). A Bombay-datelined *Variety* item from 1971 says that an Indian producer was proposing to make a movie about international brotherhood with Patrick in the lead.

According to researcher Robert J. Kiss, who provided much of this information, the last major press reports about her (from 1986) concerned her research into her father's role in the construction of Hearst Castle. Kiss writes, "The lone exception—gulp!—is in George Tobias obituaries from 1980, in which she is referred to without the 'Trent' at the end of her name, as Tobias' 'longtime friend Milicent Patrick' (a euphemism if ever there was one!)." Tobias, incidentally, was one of many actors Universal considered for the role of the boat captain in *Black Lagoon*.

88. Gill Man costume pieces were still stored in the makeup lab during the time Merlin was there for *Adrian Messenger*; "I had the fun of trying on the hands made for the Gill Man," the actor recalls.

89. Decades later, Merlin boiled Westmore in ink when he wrote *Shooting Montezuma*, a fictionalized novel about his *Adrian Messenger* experiences. In the novel, the makeup men give their boss Sunny Moreland (the Bud Westmore counterpart) "the middle-finger salute" every time he leaves the room, which Merlin said is what Chambers used to do to Bud. "In *Shooting Montezuma* I made a monster out of the character I modeled from Bud Westmore," the actor told me. "That was just my own childish kind of revenge."

90. Now as always, it's the job of *parents* (as well as censors) to make sure that kids aren't exposed to movie and TV entertainment that will traumatize them—and the William Allands did their job well: "My mom and dad thought *Creature from the Black Lagoon* would be *way* too scary for me," Susan Alland told me, "so I never saw it as a child." Ben Chapman's late-in-life companion Merrilee Kazarian, ten in 1954, was also denied the experience: "My sister and I really wanted to see it," she told me. "But our parents wouldn't let us because they thought it would be too frightening!"

91. In the *Boxoffice* magazine section "The Exhibitor Has His Say" (May 15, 1954), Donald Donahue of the Novato Theatre in Novata, California, weighed in on *Project M-7*: "If, by any chance, you

In addition to her behind-the-scenes work in the 1950s, Milicent Patrick also acted on TV series including The Roy Rogers Show, Ramar of the Jungle, Lawman *and* The Restless Gun *(pictured).*

Julie Adams acted opposite many of Hollywood's top stars, did some marvelous work on TV and dazzled theater audiences. But she also did Creature from the Black Lagoon, *goes to autograph shows and lets the Gill Man drink Tiki piña coladas through a Crazy Straw, and darned if that hasn't trumped all. Ben Chapman joins in the nuttiness (courtesy Cortlandt "The Witch's Dungeon" Hull).*

have some enemies in town, book this one in and ask them to attend a free show. Lock the doors and make them sit through this little epic. What torture it is! This holds the all-time record for walkouts. To get a date on *Creature [from the Black Lagoon]* I was saddled with *Project M-7*—U-I is so ethical in their business practices."

92. Poor Bela!

93. All the front-of-theater (and top-of-marquee) stuff heralding *Creature from the Black Lagoon* must have been provided by the *Seven Year Itch* folks: The Trans-Lux 52nd Street was not playing *Creature from the Black Lagoon* at the time. In fact, they probably never played it. According to researcher Robert J. Kiss, in September 1954 when that scene was shot, the Trans-Lux was playing MGM's *Lili* (1953), "just as it had done the week before, and just as it would go on to do the week after the *Seven Year Itch* filming—indeed, *Lili* had opened at the theater in March 1953; was in its eightieth week there the night the *Seven Year Itch* scene was shot, and would *continue* to play there until some way into 1955!" In a newspaper column by the Trans-Lux's manager Wally Beach, he wrote that when he learned that *Black Lagoon*, not *Lili*, would be the title on the marquee, he protested and wanted to know why. He was then made aware that *Black Lagoon* was a story point in *The Seven Year Itch*.

94. *The Los Angeles Times*' Don Heckman reviewed Mancini's July 27, 1991, Hollywood Bowl concert and noted that the audience not only heard familiar Mancini melodies ("Peter Gunn," "Charade," "Days of Wine and Roses," etc.) but at least one unusual inclusion:

> One of the most interesting pieces was one of the most unexpected. Mancini dug way back into his Universal Studios past to uncover a cue he composed for *Creature From the Black Lagoon*, atmospherically titled "Monster Gets Mark." It was pure, '50s movie music, completely unlike what we have come to expect from Mancini, but totally fascinating in its illustration of his very early ability to bring vigor and color to the most mundane assignments.
>
> … The Philharmonic sounded relaxed and comfortable with the program's less-than-demanding scores. Mancini's opening "Strings on Fire" and a few of the inner workings of the *Black Lagoon* cue were the only items requiring much more than cursory attention.

Chapter 2

1. As a trivial aside, at least one draft of the *Creature from the Black Lagoon* script suggested that the Instituto de Biología Marítima be established via a long shot of Marine Studios, with the ocean in the background.

2. From the "Strange Bedfellows" Dept.: Four years (almost to the day) later, Universal released the Berkeley-scripted *Revenge of the Creature* … on a double-bill with the Collins-scripted *Cult of the Cobra*!

3. When *Skin Diver* magazine reported that Universal was planning a *Black Lagoon* sequel, they quoted *some*body at the studio as saying that in the new movie, the Gill Man "will be much bigger than the original guy." Getting the wrong idea, the *Skin Diver* writer concluded, "[I]t seems we may yet see something approaching an underwater King Kong before they're through shooting."

4. "As far as I was concerned, [William Alland] was a fine man," Ben "The Reel Gill Man" Chapman said in our 1992 interview. He continued,

> But evidently he didn't care for *me*, because I wasn't even considered when it came time to do the second Creature picture. I hope this doesn't sound like I'm letting my ego run away with me, but I thought I did a hell of a job on *Creature* and why *wouldn't* they have me on the second? But, hey, it was their movie.… I did come back to them about doing the second one and they said, "No, we're going to go with somebody else." That was the end of that. I've never been one to cry over spilled milk. Johnny [Lamb] and I were very dear friends. If I remember correctly, John told me they still had my old Gill Man suits and they were trying to find guys that would fit into 'em. John and I were built exactly the same—same height, same weight, same measurements.

5. Marineland, Marine Studios—why is there so much alternating between the two when people talk about it? Well, simply because it *is* confusing. In a nutshell: The marine attraction itself was named Marine Studios and on the land adjacent to it was built the "town" of Marineland—"town" in quotes because in the early days, it had a single-digit population. So many people mistakenly called the attraction Marineland instead of Marine Studios that by 1961 it was obvious that it was better to switch than fight, and the place was renamed Marineland of Florida.

6. There was also Merian C. Cooper, the legendary adventure and Hollywood heavyweight—and a product of Jacksonville, up the road from Marineland a piece. How funny that the co-writer, -producer and -director of *King Kong* should have his movie's plot copied by filmmakers working in his own theme park!

7. A 1941 newspaper article on Marine Studios says that the 300-pound Grumpy would "browbeat his fellows so much in order to get more than his share of food" that it became necessary to muzzle him.

8. The 1942 closing of the seaquarium and the release of all its specimens was documented in the newsreel *Let 'Em Go Alive*. According to Whitney's *High Peaks*, the Coast Guard personnel at Marine Studios made a contribution to the war effort "by developing a shark repellent which aviators could attach to their uniforms; if shot down and dumped in the sea, the repellent kept sharks away."

9. *Motion Picture Exhibitor* said that in *Adventure in Baltimore*, "Agar makes up in masculine appeal what he lacks in acting ability." *The New York Times* concurred: "John Agar makes [his character] little more than a subnormal goof." Talking to *Psychotronic*'s Dennis Daniel about the two movies in which he appeared with his wife, Agar said, "She was very supportive of me during the making of both those films and eased a lot of tension. Regardless of what people say, Shirley Temple, to me, was and will always be a very fine lady. She's the mother of our daughter and I have nothing but the highest respect for her."

10. To the best of my knowledge, Agar didn't rebut much of what Temple wrote about him—but he did speak up regarding *this* charge. In his posthumously published book *On the Good Ship Hollywood* he said, "Shirley has made a statement, in her own book, that I was not present at the hospital when [Linda Susan] was born. That is untrue. I *was* there.…, I was absolutely, positively at the hospital when she was born."

11. Or … maybe not. John Stephens, who helped cast some of the early Schenck-Koch movies, told me that the company never had *any* actor under contract, and that any news items about Agar being under consideration must have been planted by Agar's agent or publicist, just to keep his name in the papers. Stephens adds, "The only person [Schenck-Koch] *ever* tried to sign to a contract was Elvis Presley, when he first started. I'll never forget calling up

Col. Parker and he got on the phone and he was very pleasant and I told him about Schenck-Koch and he said, 'Well, that's very nice.' (I wonder if he ever saw any of our movies [*laughs*]!) But then what he said was, 'We have a meeting with [producer] Hal Wallis, who's interested in Elvis. But if that doesn't work out, I'll certainly call you.' Well, we're still waiting!

"We had a good time with John on *Shield for Murder*, he was fine. Then I also worked with him on an episode of *Family Affair* [Stephens was the Brian Keith TV series' production supervisor]—John was a good friend of Brian's. John had a bad rap because of the drinking problem, a lot of people did, but I never had a problem with him at all. He was just a real good guy and a very, very good actor."

12. Porpoise, dolphin—why is there so much alternating between the two when people talk about Flippy? Marine Studios named him Flippy the "Educated" Porpoise, but I've read that he was actually not a porpoise but a dolphin—a bottlenose dolphin, to be precise. The Messinger-McGinnis book *Marineland* goes so far as to say that Marine Studios never exhibited porpoises. Other experts say that, yes, there *were* porpoises at Marine Studios. And blah blah blah blah blah. Marine Studios called Flippy a porpoise so for the sake of consistency, everywhere in this book where I can get away with it, I'm *also* calling him a porpoise even though that's wrong. Don't like it? Write a letter of complaint to Charlie Tuna care of McFarland & Company.

13. There are lots of the kinds of titles "we" like on Soule's long movie and TV résumé, including *The Day the Earth Stood Still* (1951), *This Island Earth* (1955), *Revenge of the Creature*'s co-feature *Cult of the Cobra* (1955) and more. As a TV cartoon voice actor, he had a long run (from the late 1960s until the '80s) playing Batman on various series.

14. One of the other things then on his mind was his simultaneous production of a movie he felt had tremendous potential, the Technicolor-CinemaScope *Chief Crazy Horse* (1955), shot in the Black Hills of the Dakotas where the historical events it dramatizes actually took place. Alland thought this story of the Sioux Indian leader could be an artistic triumph. "But [Universal] destroyed this thing, they put a miserable director [George Sherman] on it," Alland moaned to me before abruptly cutting himself off: "Oh, I don't even want to talk about it, it makes me sick." Victor Mature played the title role alongside Suzan Ball, the actress who very much wanted to play the lead in *Black Lagoon*; it was her first and only movie after the amputation of her leg.

15. Of course Jack Arnold later tried to horn in on it: Interviewed by Dana M. Reemes for the book *Directed by Jack Arnold*, he said that he, the producer and the writers got together to cook up a plot, and the result of their brainstorming was the realization "The only natural thing to do was to capture him and bring him back alive." Actually, Alland had suggested the "bring 'em back alive" storyline in "The Sea Monster" all the way back in 1952.

16. Well, dupey, poor-quality stock footage of a crocodile, anyway—the same stock footage seen (in color) in Universal's African jungle adventure *Tanganyika* (1954), and probably 50 other movies. In the *Revenge* script, a manatee is the cause of the false alarm.

17. Marine Studios' small rectangular receiving tank was a flume situated between two large oceanaria, one circular and the other rectangular. The circular one was for the dolphins and the rectangular one was for what Sally Baskin calls reef fish: "the sharks, angelfish, barracuda, pompano, amberjack, the rays, the moray eels and so on." After a stunned shark (or a Gill Man) had been walked in the receiving tank and was now "hot" (able to swim again), the tank's underwater gateway to the rectangular oceanarium would be opened so that it could pass through. The rectangular tank used for underwater filming in *Revenge* was 100' × 40' and 18' deep with a capacity of 450,000 gallons of seawater.

At the other end of the receiving tank was the underwater gateway to the circular tank: After a dolphin had been placed in the receiving tank in order to acclimate it, it was then passed through *that* opening. All three tanks were surrounded by open-air promenades where park visitors could look down into the water. Between the oceanaria and the beach was the "filter house" through which Atlantic Ocean water passed; sand, shells, etc., were sifted out before the water went into the oceanaria.

18. Speaking of Gargantua…. In the May 5 version of the screenplay, there's a Black Lagoon night scene where Joe and Johnson put the unconscious Gill Man in a *Rita II* tank. Then Johnson sends a wireless message to the Ocean Harbor manager: "Mission accomplished. Return to Manaus in morning. Fly directly home. Don't spare the adjectives. This is the greatest attraction since Gargantua."

In the Black Lagoon prologue, Gill Man hunter Johnson refers to Ocean Harbor as "a conservative institution" but in the movie there are indications that the Ocean Harbor folks might have more show biz than ichthyology in their blood, mainly the stuck-on-overdrive press agent Lou Gibson ("The hotels are booked for 50 miles around here! I've got the radio! The TV!"). Then, too, Johnson (in that same opening scene) alludes to the fact that Ocean Harbor has counted their Gill Men before they hatched and already publicized his impending capture; like a carny, Johnson even refers to Ocean Harbor's announcement as "circus[sing]" the story. It's also interesting that there seem to be no scientists at Ocean Harbor interested in studying the Gill Man, as Clete and Helen come from outside—and apparently both on their own initiative and their own dime!

19. Monster Kid extraordinaire Mike Brunas commented on the Classic Horror Film Board (www.monsterkid.com), "One minor point that always irritated me is the aftermath of Joe's death at the hands of the Gill Man. Here's the second romantic lead who was given plenty of time to connect with the audience on some basic level yet his death barely registers with any of the other characters. Within minutes [of screen time,] Clete and Helen are taking a carefree boat trip. I know the movie was intended as Saturday matinee filler but what an emotional disconnect. To me, it distills everything wrong there is in the movie: It's designed as one big cartoon."

Actually, the boat trip scene is even more off-putting than Brunas indicates: No grief for Joe is expressed but Helen *is* unhappy over her missing dog!

20. "My dad used to go down to that stockyard and try to keep his meat packing business going," Agar told me. "He had angina, and all this pressure put on him caused his early demise—he died before he reached his 41st birthday, and he left my mom loaded with four kids at the age of 38. I was 14—this was 1935."

21. Several years before "discovering" *Revenge of the Creature* star Agar, Selznick "discovered" *Creature from the Black Lagoon* star Richard Carlson. In the early years of his career, Agar did all his movies on loanout from Selznick, never appearing in a Selznick movie.

22. "[John Agar] was really having a

hard time in those years," Lori Nelson said on the *Revenge of the Creature* DVD audio commentary, "and then he met and married Loretta, and Loretta was just the best thing in the world that ever happened to him. What a doll. They were a wonderful pair and they were so much in love."

23. Ben Chapman claims to have played a small part in the latter, but try to find him.

24. She still looked like a kid, though. Richard Carlson could play Julie Adams' love interest in *Black Lagoon* but when he played with Lori in the same-year *All I Desire*, he was her father!

25. After completing *Outlaw's Son*, Cooper and Nelson wrote a Western, *Young Gunsmoke*, as a starring vehicle for themselves and submitted it to Howard W. Koch. "Howard really liked it and he was going to do it," she told me, "and he wanted us to do some rewrites. But as youth will have it, we never did get around to it."

26. In *Harpoon*, the actor was top-billed as John Bromfield, having dropped the "sissy" name Farron. I've never seen the movie but, if *New York Times* stuffed-shirt reviewer Bosley Crowther can be trusted, it sounds pretty dire: He cites the "painfully amateurish" direction and acting, and adds, "One might almost suspect this film of being an old silent job, dubbed with dialogue adapted from the original subtitles."

27. Born in suburban Philadelphia, Thomas was eight or nine when her eye was caught by a girl dancer's costume and she thought, "I'd like to have one of those pretty things. I guess I have to take dancing lessons in order to *get* one." She told me that her first TV dancing jobs were on the New York–based series *Four Star Revue* (later retitled *All Star Revue*): "I worked on that show all the time and in 1951, when they decided to move to the West Coast, I thought, 'What am I gonna do?' So I went to [executive producer] Pete Barnum, the big mucky-muck at the time, and he said, 'I can't promise you a job and I can't pay to get you there, but if you should suddenly appear out there, we'll see what we can do.' So I jumped on my first airplane and went to California and I've been here ever since." In the Esther Williams vehicle *Million Dollar Mermaid* (1952), she swam in a big production number, "the one with the red and yellow smoke. That was my first movie, with the choreographer Busby Berkeley shooting guns in the rafters as cues for camera and what have you. It was quite an experience." Her first movies as a dancer were *Road to Bali* (1952) and *Here Come the Girls* (1953), she danced the can-can in 3-D in *House of Wax* (1953), was a Goldwyn Girl in *Guys and Dolls* (1955) and, most pertinently here, waterskied in *Easy to Love* (1953), another Esther Williams movie, this one with John Bromfield fourth-billed. "John was there and he spotted me and thought, '*That's* pretty cute.' And I thought, 'Well, *he's* pretty cute,' and that was the beginning of a big romance that led to a wedding."

28. "Jim Griffith was one of my dearest friends," Bromfield told Aaker, "and he kept me and everyone else in stitches pulling tricks, mostly on me. He loved to ask me who someone was, with a sketchy description, just before we were about to film so that it would bother me throughout the filming."

29. Like Merian C. Cooper, mentioned above, Burden also had a *Kong* connection: The explorer-naturalist was part of a 1926 expedition to the island of Komodo that brought back live Komodo dragons that were exhibited at the Bronx Zoo. Cooper read about these exploits in Burden's book *Dragon Lizards of Komodo: An Expedition to the Lost World of the Dutch East Indies* (1927) and combined them with ideas of his own in the run-up to the writing of *King Kong*. Try reading about Burden's trip to that "lost world" and the two dragons he captured and placed in the Bronx Zoo, where they were seen by thousands, without thinking of the Gill Man and Ocean Harbor.

If you're a monster movie nut, this ought to be full-circle enough to make your head spin: Burden's "lost world of the Dutch East Indies" adventures partly inspired Cooper to make *King Kong* while Gabriel Figueroa's "lost world of the man-fish of the Amazon" tale, *plus King Kong*, inspired William Alland to make *Creature* and *Revenge*. And now here's Alland making *Revenge* at Marine Studios, whose founders included Cooper and Burden! In fact, Burden was still president of Marine Studios in 1954 when *Revenge* was shot there.

30. At the end of Flippy's *Revenge* performance, the loudspeaker announcer says, "All right, Flippy. You may now return to your private quarters, and *thank* you!" Why "private quarters"? You may be sorry you asked! In a scientific study on dolphin behavior published in 1948, Marine Studios curator Arthur McBride and psychologist Donald Hebb wrote that, among the institution's male dolphins, "there is a good deal of masturbation, on the floor of the tank and against other males. One male had the habit of holding his erect penis in the jet of the water intake for prolonged intervals. The males also show a good deal of sex play with sharks and turtles, with the appearance of attempted copulation. With the turtle as sex object, the penis is inserted into the soft tissues at the rear of the shell." Gregg Mitman wrote in his book *Reel Nature* that Flippy himself "was known among Marine Studios personnel for his ceaseless 'masturbatory practices.' … [O]ceanariums knew that successfully managing the dolphin's career depended on keeping the dolphin's private sexual life out of public sight, both in the tanks and in the popular media."

31. Ricou Browning created the character of Flipper, the lovable and courageous dolphin who starred in two movies (*Flipper*, 1963, and *Flipper's New Adventure*, 1964, both big moneymakers) and a mid–60s TV series. It wouldn't be hard to jump to the conclusion that the world-famous Flippy was an inspiration, but Ricou's interest in the marine mammals predated the "Educated" One. He told me that some time in the mid-1950s when he was employed in the Silver Springs public relations department,

> I got the idea of going to South America and capturing freshwater dolphins. My boss the public relations manager, who was Bill Ray, agreed. An expedition was formed and we went there, seven or eight men. We went to Bogota, Colombia, and from there we flew south in a cargo plane to a little town called Leticia, which is on the Amazon, and then we went outside of the city, downriver, and put up a camp that we operated out of. We brought three back … one died on the airplane, and two survived. We put 'em in Silver Springs and they were kinda "my pets." I worked with 'em and trained 'em and fooled around with 'em for a number of months. They lived a year or so and then *they* passed away. They had something called "parasites of the brain," it was in their spinal columns and it moved up into their heads and it killed them. It was something they had before we brought them to Silver Springs. Anyway, I fell in love with them.
>
> Then, one day years later, I came home and the kids were watching *Lassie* on TV and I sat down with them and I was watching it, and it just dawned on me: "Why not do a movie or something about a boy and a dolphin?" And that's where *Flipper* started.

32. Cathy, the dolphin star of TV's *Flipper*, died not long after the series ended, and one of her trainers Richard O'Brien later said, "She just lost the will to live through boredom and a broken heart. It was just as if she had committed suicide.... Dolphins are sonic creatures and live in a world of sound, so keeping them in a pool is like putting a bucket over their heads."

33. Bob Burns said that Hennesy's Gill Man suit was not as "wearer-friendly" as those created for the previous Creature movie: The Browning and Chapman outfits were made in multiple pieces, and therefore had what are called flex gaps near the elbows, shoulders and knees. These flex gaps gave Ricou and Ben a bit of freedom and mobility. But Hennesy's molded *one-piece* body suit was very uncomfortable and gave him *no* freedom.

34. Finstad added, "There was an absurd, Fellini quality to the illusion of Natalie being under the protection of a studio welfare worker [Hennesy], when she was sexually involved off-set with the 43-year-old director [Nicholas Ray]."

35. According to Sally Baskin, "The fish were fed by a diver in an old hardhat diving suit who would go down with a metal basket full of fish." Over three minutes of the Pete Smith short *Marine Circus* is devoted to highly entertaining footage showing us an attendant doing just that.

36. Hennesy also told me that he looked back upon his oceanarium scene as "kind of a frightening experience, because not many people have been in a tank like that, with large sharks and sea turtles and barracudas and sawfish. There was no chance to prepare for that or anything, we just had to do it."

37. *Revenge* was not Browning's first time working at Marine Studios: Some years prior, perhaps as early as 1947, he was part of a troupe that made a short subject there. "They were shooting girls wearing bathing suits and various costumes, a fashion show, *above* water," he told me. "Then they would shoot girls doing the same thing, *under*water. I was the safety person for the girls."

38. Welbourne, the movie's d.p., would let someone else man the camera when they were shooting topside but underwater he operated it himself. In the oceanarium he was usually accompanied by four to six members of the technical crew, among them assistant cameraman Walter Bluemel, special effects man Frank Brendel and grip Jack Flesher. In addition to their technical duties, these others had the constant chore of waving, shoving or beating away the larger denizens of the tank when either unwittingly or purposefully they seemed to be menacing the actors or just got in the way. Then, too, there were local underwater swimmers Charles McNabb, Shirley Woolery (Ricou Browning's four-years-older sister, working her one and only Gill Man movie) *et al*. These "utility swimmers" also multi-tasked: helping to shoo fish, tending air hoses for principals who were in the water without aqualungs, etc.

39. Like Wakulla Springs, Silver Springs gets its water from a sub-aquatic cave that pumps it out at 5000 gallons per second. About a year and a half before *Revenge* began production, the cave was entered by scuba divers Charles McNabb and Frank Den Bleyker; the former was one of Ricou Browning's safety divers on all three Creature movies, and the latter was one on *Black Lagoon*. After twice being forced back, McNabb got in on his third try, with Den Bleyker following. The first thing on the inside was a 30-foot-high chamber with passages leading off on both sides. They discovered near the entrance a bone from a mastodon, extinct in Florida for 10,000 years.

40. When we see "bullets" hitting the water, they're actually marbles fired out of a "marble gun," said Browning. He described a marble gun as a row of four- or five-foot-long tubes, side by side. "They would put a marble in one end of each tube, like you would an old musket, and then they would load whatever they shoot it with [presumably some kind of detonating powder] in the back side of it. Then they would touch a wire to each one of 'em, and each time they'd touch it, it would fire that tube. They would have five or ten tubes and they could shoot either real fast, like a machine-gun, or individually. I don't know exactly how it worked, but that's how I guessed it worked." He said it probably wouldn't have hurt him if, while underwater, he had been hit by a marble, "because when it hits the water, it loses its power quickly."

41. Silver Springs isn't as deep as Wakulla Springs, and you can tell. In *Creature*, parts of the Black Lagoon seemed to be bottomless; in *Revenge*, when Joe goes into the water to secure the net, the bottom is just below the boat. A minute later, as Johnson fires his rifle and the Gill Man quickly swims away, the monster is in the small space between the top of the weeds and the surface of the water; his kicking feet are practically breaking the surface. During the river scene where the Gill Man is paralleling surface swimmers Clete and Helen, there's barely any space for him between them and the weeds. For *The Creature Walks Among Us* the moviemakers returned to Wakulla Springs and atoned for *Revenge* by getting some of the best underwater shots of the series.

42. A son of St. Augustine, Carl "Bogie" Selph worked at Marine Studios right from its beginning (1938); his widow Gloria told me that he was the boss over the employees (other than the office staff): ticket ladies, divers, groundskeepers, etc. Gloria and their son were extras in *Revenge* and Carl appeared in the simultaneously made *The Return of the Creature* (see Chapter 5, "Aquatic Kith and Kin").

43. One evening not long before the Universal location party's departure from Marineland, all of its members were guests at a beach party arranged by W.F. Rolleston, vice-president and general manager of Marine Studios. Attendees included players Agar, Nelson, Bromfield and Robert B. Williams, 40 members of the business

At a Marineland beach party with many of the Revenge cast and crew members in attendance, Ricou Browning grabs a bite to eat. When Tom Weaver emailed him this nearly 60-year-old photo and he saw it for the first time ever, he wrote back, "Good-looking sucker!" Indeed! (courtesy Sally Baskin).

and technical crew, and a half dozen of Marine Studios' top personnel.

44. In the Technicolor *Marine Circus*, we can see the Marine Studios tanks' blue water under blue skies and puffy white clouds, not to mention all the multi-hued fish; it makes you wish that *Revenge* was in color. But it was generally so gray and rainy when the filmmakers were there in June and July 1954 that shooting would have taken a month of Sundays if they worked only on beautiful days.

45. Arnold says in Dana M. Reemes' book *Directed by Jack Arnold*, "I assigned a grip with a club whose only job was to keep the damn turtle away from the Gill Man." For a look at one such "damn turtle" in full Annoying Mode, watch Pete Smith's *Marine Circus* where a fish-feeding hardhat diver resorts to slaps and shoves to deter a dangerous-looking loggerhead turtle named Grumpy.

46. Sally Baskin has a fun memory of Browning's Gill Man regularly getting out of the oceanarium and then "squeezing himself, to try to reduce the weight of the water the suit had absorbed." I mentioned this to Browning, who remembered doing it: "Yes, I would squeeze myself to make water pour out of the suit so it would be less heavy, *and*, so that I would not track water all over the place." In a 1983 newspaper story on Browning, the interviewer kiddingly wrote that, when wet, the Creature outfit "weighed more than a pickup truck"; he also described how long it took Browning to get into the suit and how hard it was for him to see. He then summed it all up nicely: "Creaturing, if you get the drift, could make for an extraordinarily long day."

47. Well, yes they had, but who can fault him for not knowing?: Back in the 1910s, a number of features were shot in St. Augustine—including 1915's *Life Without Soul*, one of the earliest movie versions of *Frankenstein*.

48. This recap of the Unlocked Door Story is the way Nelson told it to me the first time. She told it slightly differently, but with every salient point intact, when she, Bob Burns and I subsequently did a *Revenge* commentary for Universal's "Legacy Collection" DVD of the Gill Man trilogy.

49. At my request (i.e., hounding), Hart recently watched *A Global Affair* for perhaps the first time ever and, as it played on TCM, rocked in her chair at the awfulness of the thing. "I just wanted to get to my scene so I could stop watching it!" she told me. "The shots were set up just like a TV show … boring closeups, no editing of close-medium-long shots. The direction stunk. It's hard to believe the director did feature films 'cause this felt just like TV. AIP pictures are easier to watch!"

50. The original *Porpoise* and its collection team are seen in the aforementioned *Marine Circus*: Narrator Pete Smith jokingly calls the men "marine talent scouts" going out in search of "new actors" for the Marine Studios tanks. We see a tranquilized shark being pulled into the live well of the boat (Smith calls it the "casting office"); we next see the shark, still "needle-nutty" as Smith puts it, aloft in a water-filled Marine Studios cradle, and then in the back of a truck heading up the driveway toward the shark's next stop, the receiving tank (Smith calls it "his glorified fishbowl"). According to Smith, this 11-feet-plus shark is now (1939) the largest in captivity.

The boat seen in *Marine Circus*, the first *Porpoise*, was sold during World War II. The *Porpoise II* came along in 1948, and then was replaced by the *Porpoise III* in 1954. The latter was the first boat not adapted from a standard craft, according to the Messinger-McGinnis book *Marineland*: "She was built specifically for the capture and transport of live specimens. The 46-foot trawler was a larger, more seaworthy craft, allowing collecting operations to be extended out to the Gulf Stream." The *Porpoise III* was christened on May 17, the same day that William Alland and Jack Arnold left for Florida to scout locations. According to David Redman, who started working in Marine Studios' marketing department in 1957, the collection boat trips were often to the Bahamas where the attraction had an agreement with the British government.

51. According to Universal publicity, St. Augustine's *three* leading commercial photographers are in the movie: Beery, Jack Brandon and Harry Neill. I couldn't confirm the appearance of the latter two.

52. Regarding living near a lighthouse, he added, "I could go anywhere in the county I wanted to without fear of getting lost, because when it was time to go home I only had to climb a tree and look, and I knew which way to go!" The lighthouse is supposedly haunted; according to a tour guide, several visitors to the tower have told of being touched or having their hair pulled by unseen hands. It was the subject of an episode of the Sci-Fi Channel's *Ghost Hunters*.

53. Between silent movie days and *Revenge of the Creature*, there *was* at least one more movie partly shot in St. Augustine, the soldiers-vs.-Seminoles actioner *Distant Drums* (1951), and Beery Sr. was an extra in that movie as well: He played the part of a dead Indian in a scene shot at Castillo de San Marcos, aka "The Old Fort." Others making brief appearances: Ginger Stanley, also an extra, and 16-year-old Bob Burns, soon to become the world's #1 Gill Man fan! Spray-painted with Indian makeup and wearing a black wig, leather loincloth and moccasins, he was one of several Indian kids who ran up to Gary Cooper as he (Cooper) rode a horse into their camp. The scene, photographed on the Warners back lot thousands of miles from Florida where the rest of the movie was shot, didn't make it into the final print.

54. Universal paid $75 to insure the dog for full mortality; it was valued at $2500 and attended by its owner Henry East. East, one of Hollywood's top dog trainers, got his start in the silent era, and by 1938 had 70 trained dogs working in the movies. One of his most famous pup pupils: Asta of MGM's *Thin Man* series.

55. The production paperwork features a sketchy description of a camera set-up which gives me a feeling that at one point they positioned the 3-D camera high above the tank and tried to get a down-shot of Flippy shooting up out of the water and into the lens—a great idea. In *Jaws 3-D*, there *is* a down-shot like that, with a Shamu-type orca comin' at ya.

56. According to Universal publicity, in the background in the beach scene are four men and four women playing with a big ball, and the women include blondes Faye Weathersby, Miss St. Augustine of 1952, and Melissa Butcher, Miss St. Augustine of 1953. But the on-screen background action doesn't really match the publicity department's description of it, so who knows if the beauty queens are really in the scene or not.

57. Youngster Sally Baskin also appeared on-camera in that scene, running in and out of the shot with her mother Mildred holding her by one hand and a man (whom Sally now doesn't recognize) holding the other. Sally watched most or all of the Marineland filming and wasn't scared of the Creature "because I knew Ricou was in the suit. People would come by and look at the Creature and they were all in awe of him, and if I were standing there, all of a sudden he'd grab me. And, being as theatrical as I was, I'd start going

Twelve-year-old Sally Baskin got ten bucks (an extra's pay) for running away from the Creature, and kept her pay stub as a souvenir.

[*in a scared voice*], "Oh! Oh! The monster's got me!'—when all the time, he and I were in hysterics, laughing." Sally also recalls that, in order to work as an extra, she (at 12) had to get a Social Security card! "I've still got my check stub in my scrapbook from my one day as an extra. Ten dollars. I thought I was rich!" Seven dollars and eighty cents, actually.

58. Blooper: When Joe topples into the oceanarium, Clete is right behind him; the Gill Man kills Joe on the spot, then squats on the oceanarium bottom and shoots up to the surface. Therefore, he should burst up out of the water at the exact spot where Clete is standing. Instead he comes up on the opposite side of the oceanarium.

59. Well, aside from the full-screen "thank you" in the movie's opening credits: "We gratefully acknowledge the generous cooperation extended to us by the Marine Studios of Marineland, Florida, where scenes for this production were photographed."

60. The Daily Production Reports for that day ends with the note, "'Scotty' wanted me to tell you this night shooting was done under protest because he had no Arc—which they could not use because there was no operator for it."

61. Yes, the Lobster House is in Jacksonville and the city we see on the opposite side of the river is *also* Jacksonville; the river divides the city.

62. Like everybody else on our planet, Hennesy lacked an infallible memory, misremembering this'n'that *Revenge*-wise, and even giving different interviewers entirely different versions: To some he said that he never saw *Revenge* until the 2000s, while to others he claimed to have been one of the *first* people ever to see it, at a sneak preview where he got physical with a rowdy in the row in front of him. He may even have inaccurately recalled the Lobster House near-drowning incident he describes above. Print interviewers have run Hennesy's story past Ricou Browning, who always pooh-poohs it. Browning told me, "Tom Hennesy did not wear lead weights in his Creature suit. Being made of sponge rubber and latex, it was of course very buoyant, so he couldn't have gone under the water. If he'd *wanted* to go down and stay underwater, he couldn't have no matter *how* much he tried, because of the buoyancy. The only danger was that if the pickup boats had missed seeing him on the surface, he could have gone out towards the open waters." Ginger Stanley thinks that Hennesy may have hit the panic button once he got in the water but didn't want to admit that in his interviews. Read her description of the incident in Chapter 6, "Creature Conversations."

63. Wellll ... his first *on-screen* movie acting. Universal had already given him several voice-only chores, looping and doing wild lines for 1954's *Francis Joins the Wacs*, *Sign of the Pagan* and *Bengal Brigade*.

64. During the buildup, the Gill Man comes up behind the unsuspecting Charlie and reaches out for him, but at the last second Charlie kneels down and momentarily thwarts the monster. The Gill Man has a couple moments like this in the movie (he's pulling himself aboard the *Porpoise III* until it unexpectedly moves and he drops off, he starts climbing onto the Lobster House patio just as Clete and Helen walk away, etc.), all very reminiscent of Kharis the mummy, another frustrated monster known for his near-misses and potential victims who "escape" without even knowing they *are* escaping.

65. Pevney told me he wanted to direct 3-D movies but Universal wouldn't let him: "Universal said, '3-D is gonna *die*, it's just a *fad*. It's nothing for *you*, Joe!' They considered me a 'women's director' at that time. Therefore I started to find whatever action pictures I could get, like *Away All Boats* [1956], *anything*!"

In 1965 Pevney directed the *Munsters* episode "Love Comes to Mockingbird Heights," in which TV's "First Family of Fright" is looking forward to a visit from their Uncle Gilbert from "the old country" (Transylvania). At the end, as every Baby Boomer Monster Kid vividly remembers, Uncle Gilbert turns out to be the Creature from the Black Lagoon, dressed in an old-fashioned suit, hat and scarf. Richard Hale, the 70-something actor playing the part, was probably cast for his theatrical voice and delivery; he wears a Gill Man head (without the pop-in eyes), gloves and feet. As a fadeout gag, water gushes out of the mask when Herman (Fred Gwynne) slaps him on the back.

66. In an email to me, Creature fan extraordinaire David J. Schow vented about the "extreme overload of cutesy-pie animals; it is to puke, from Flippy to the rats to Neal the chimp (who smiles like Agar) to Lori's dog ... I thought I had my wires crossed with Animal Planet. And none of them adds anything to the movie."

67. In *Revenge* the Gill Man is in the receiving tank when we notice his aversion to flashbulbs; in the script but not the movie, the announcer tells his listeners, "Apparently the primeval monster is frightened of light for it stands in the center of the tank shielding its eyes from it—just as its ancestor millions of years ago must have done when it emerged from the water and saw the light of the sun for the first time."

68. Maybe Berkeley also gave some of *Creature from the Black Lagoon*'s script drafts a fast skim: His *Revenge* finale, with police and mobilized citizens tracking the Gill Man, is right out of Maurice Zimm's December 1952 *Black Lagoon* treatment. (In Zimm's *Black Lagoon*, military Jeeps with mounted searchlights scour the beach area for the monster.)

69. In *Revenge*'s Black Lagoon opening, the Gill Man swims away from the *Rita II* as Johnson's rifle bullets streak past him in the water. That same shot is used at the end as the Gill Man swims away from the police bullets, so *Revenge* even reuses footage from *itself*!

70. Sci-fi producer Alland went from his "desert-tropical phase" (*It Came from Outer Space*, the Creature movies, *Tarantula*) to his "snow and ice period" (*The Mole People*, *The Deadly Mantis*), and also made a movie that combined both: *The Land Unknown* (1957), in which three Navy men and a woman reporter find themselves stranded in a hot'n'humid *Lost World*–like jungle, complete with dinosaurs, far below the Antarctic surface.

Like the Gill Man trilogy, *Land Unknown* also had unmistakable echoes of everybody's favorite giant-gorilla movie: Kong had always been "king of his world," as Carl Denham put it, and the king of the Land Unknown is a scientist reduced to savagery (Henry Brandon) who teaches the dinosaurs fear and can scare them away by sounding a horn. Like Kong, he kidnaps the girl, brings her to his cave lair, and tries to fight off her would-be rescuers once they get past the lake's submerged, long-necked monster (*à la Kong*'s lake-dwelling Brontosaurus). Alland told me that *The Land Unknown* was based on a script by "an oldtimer who had been involved with the making of *King Kong*."

71. I have a feeling that Marine Studios' puffed-up, "Dignity! Always dignity!" attitude about itself went back right to the beginning days when the Pete Smith short *Marine Circus* was made there: Probably at the marine attraction's insistence, Smith's narration sometimes slips out of jokester mode and he becomes uncharacteristically "straight" and informative. When dealing with Universal on *Revenge*, it again seemed as though they were determined *not* to be perceived as merely a roadside sea zoo. Gregg Mitman confirmed my suspicions when he wrote in his book *Reel Nature* that W. Douglas Burden "took great pains to distance Marine Studios from the carnivalesque atmosphere that surrounded nineteenth-century animal exhibits such as the beluga whale kept, if only briefly, at P.T. Barnum's Aquariel Gardens and trained to pull a woman in a cart around the edge of the tank."

72. Hollywood had indeed jumped *off* the three-dimensional bandwagon. In fact, around the time that *Revenge*'s added scenes were being shot, Warners released their 3-D Randolph Scott Western *The Bounty Hunter*—in 2-D. Back in mid–1953 Warners had gone to the trouble and expense of giving it "the depth treatment" but by mid–1954 they apparently considered the fad dead and felt there was no upside to making 3-D prints available. The "left-right elements" still exist today, but the stereoscopic version has never been publicly seen. Other movies made in 3-D but released flat include *Top Banana*, *Jivaro*, *Dragonfly Squadron* (all 1954) and *Son of Sinbad* (1955).

Revenge was the last tri-dimensional film of the '50s. In *Directed by Jack Arnold*, Arnold said that the gimmick's demise wasn't a failure of technique but of showmanship:

Properly exhibited, the 3-D effect of these films is superb. But projecting 3-D is tricky business. If the projectors are a frame or two out of synch it will tear your eyes out. We had our guys in the main houses to make sure there was enough light on the screen and the shutters were synched. But by the time we made our third 3-D picture all the smaller studios were making them too, and they didn't have the manpower to supervise the exhibitors. People got headaches, and the studios gave up on 3-D.

73. Universal was free to do this, as the censors' office had informed them that they didn't consider the killings done by the Gill Man a crime.

74. According to a New York–dateline item in the April 1, 1955, *Hollywood Reporter*, "Indicating that the 3-D vogue is not entirely dead yet, U-I reports more than 200 theaters already have booked its triple-dimension version of *Revenge of the Creature*, with many situations doing outstanding business. First week's results at the Paramount Theatre, Denver, were the best since *The Glenn Miller Story* [1954]. In Detroit the picture is headed for a new U-I house record at the Broadway Capitol." On April 19 the paper revealed in a page-one follow-up story, "As a result of the success of the 3-D version of *Revenge of the Creature* in its early engagements, U-I has concluded that 3-D still has considerable public interest on a limited scale, and the studio is considering several other properties in that medium, it was stated yesterday by Alfred E. Daff, executive v-p. Though exhibitors were given a choice of playing [*Revenge*] in 3-D or standard version, the majority of playdates so far have been in 3-D. This bears out U-I in its policy of making pictures of all types and for every kind of screen and theater, Daff stated, believing that there is a market for every type of film."

75. *Revenge of the Creature* was Charles S. Welbourne's first assignment as a full d.p. (in *and* out of the water) and various notations on *Revenge*'s Production Reports make it clear that he tried to go the extra mile on the assignment. He was born Charles Scott *Welborn* [*sic*] on May 14, 1907, in Buncombe County, North Carolina; the family moved to Los Angeles when "Scotty" was still a child. After about ten years in Warner Brothers' still department, he became the department head and then, during wartime, a photographer with the rank of major with the U.S. Army. In 1939 he married Victoria Vinton, an actress whose finest hours had been in Poverty Row Westerns; their 1953 divorce was awarded with Welbourne *in absentia* due to "currently being in Florida" (he'd just finished *Black Lagoon*'s underwater scenes). "Yes, 'Scotty' *was* in the middle of getting a divorce at that time," Ricou Browning told me. "His mental attitude was … he was upset, quite a bit."

Welbourne's other d.p. credits include 1957's *The Monster That Challenged the World* (the underwater scenes), 1962's *The Three Stooges Meet Hercules* and dozens of episodes of TV's *Dennis the Menace*. During the shooting of the Jamaican-made *Manfish* (1956) with John Bromfield, Welbourne had a whirlwind romance with cast member Tessa Prendergast, a Jamaican actress-singer, and married her, the union lasting until 1958. In 1962, former model and bit-part actress Lois James became the next Mrs. Welbourne; in 1979 she became his widow when he died in Valley Village, Los Angeles.

76. William Alland didn't fail to notice that "Jungle Sam" Katzman's stock footage–filled *It Came* fared as well or better moneywise as his (Alland's) more deluxe sci-fi offerings and he figured it wouldn't hurt to tighten the purse strings on his own monster movies. This ushered in the era of the stock footage fests *The Mole People*, *The Deadly Mantis* and *The Land Unknown*.

Chapter 3

1. This action scene was a bit more exciting (or at least more *fiery*) in a subsequent draft: As the burning Gill Man goes over the side, a barrel of fuel oil spills onto the deck and into the water and ignites. In the water, the Gill Man is caught in these surface flames until he swims down to escape them.

2. Ross apparently couldn't decide *what* cars he wanted: In a July 13 draft, it's now a Thunderbird convertible for Marcia and a Lincoln sedan for Dr. Barton. In the movie, the Bartons drive to the yacht landing in a 1955 Chrysler New Yorker convertible, Marcia behind the wheel (the script called for an insert shot of the speedometer with the needle a little past 90) and passenger Barton doing a slow burn.

3. Ross consistently calls the Creature's enclosure "the rotunda" throughout his series of scripts, and the word carried over into behind-the-scenes Universal paperwork (for example, a post-production October 4, 1955, work order: "Strike rotunda and fencing and entry gates and posts and fence and sentry house"). But since rotundas are usually domed, and can also refer to round rooms within a building, I'm avoiding reader confusion by calling it a stockade.

4. Actually, he hadn't yet begun working on pictures on that level; in 1955 when *The Creature Walks Among Us* was made, Arnold directed *Tarantula*, the Western *Red Sundown* with Rory Calhoun and the crook drama *Outside the Law* with Ray Danton and Leigh Snowden. But, interviewed 20-something years after the fact, he shouldn't be faulted for that kind of timeline slip-up. Incidentally, *Outside the Law* may have played in at least one theater as *Creature Walks*' co-feature, creating a Leigh Snowden double bill. And Snowden's *Creature Walks* character's musical theme, the Henry Mancini–written "Perfect Wife?," heard in the Creature movie when she reminisces, is also played during her *Outside the Law* character's trips down Memory Lane. It's as if it's Leigh Snowden's music, following her from movie to movie!

5. Sherwood *may* have worked for Arnold at some point but I sure can't determine what picture or pictures that would be … or, given Arnold's predisposition for blowing smoke, if Sherwood had ever worked for him at all pre–1955.

6. Oh, what a surprise!

7. The third Gill Man movie was also a step-up for Robert E. Smith: It was his first picture as a full art director. Ten years later, he was an Oscar nominee (Best Art Direction–Set Decoration, Black-and-White) for 1965's *King Rat*.

8. Alland, a good "company man," didn't allow *Black Lagoon* to have an ending where the Gill Man is definitively destroyed, because he foresaw that the movie might be popular enough to rate sequels. But apparently he didn't want to be the producer to *make* those sequels!

9. According to monster movie music buff Mike Brunas, "*House of Horrors* and *The Brute Man* [two 'Creeper' movies from 1946] have the same main title music; the main title music from *The Mummy's Ghost* [1944] is heard again, with minor variations, in *The Mummy's Curse*; and *Son of Frankenstein*'s [1939] main title music is heard again, with variations, in *House of Dracula* [1945]. The *Frankenstein Meets the Wolf Man* [1943] main title music starts off with the beginning of *The Wolf Man*'s [1941] main title and segues into the main title from *The Ghost of Frankenstein* [1942]."

10. Morteno was in better shape in an early script draft where his visitors find him mending a sprawled-out fishing net near his ramshackle hut. The bones of his left hand appear to have been crumpled by some "terrible crushing instrument." Speaking in Portuguese throughout the scene, he tells the same story as in the eventual movie but ends with, "I joined with the Seminole for it attacked one of their people one day…. When a gun was fired at it…. But I give up…. They go on…. They keep looking…. They keep on looking for it…. They want to kill it…. They saw it last…. But it seems to hide from sight … just up the coastline."

But wait—there's more! (Ross must have thought he was writing a two-hour movie.) The Barton party proceeds upcoast, enters an island bay off the Everglades, gets in a flatboat and beaches at a nearly hidden Seminole village. A few non–English-speaking Seminole Indians appear. Dr. Simpson opens a kit and shows them a sectional drawing, a profile and full view of the Creature. One Indian nods and gestures for the group to follow him to a spot where a partly crushed canoe has been half-hidden in the brush to rot. The Indian then goes into charades mode, indicating the Creature drawing, pretending to be canoeing, pretending to be raising a rifle and firing, pointing at the fleshy part of his own arm and then gesturing to the Creature drawing once more—conveying that they shot and wounded the monster. A darkened stain in the boat is pointed out to Simpson, who squats to look at it and says, "Dried blood all right. Could be the Creature's."

But wait—there's *more*! (Ross probably had writer's cramp by the end of this assignment.) In a later script (mid–July), Morteno's injuries are more serious: He's got the bum leg, his right side is mangled, and his right arm hangs limply. "You will—make me—well?" he asks his visitors in a pleading tone of voice. At the end of the scene, Morgan professionally examines his crippled side, then stands up abruptly, sympathy on his face. In answer to the questioning looks of Morteno and his wife, he says only "I'm sorry" and begins to walk out. As he reaches the door, he stops, takes some bills from his pocket, puts them on a little table and, without a backward glance, exits.

11. Fans complain that much of *Creature Walks*' underwater footage of the Creature is from the first movie, and it is, but he's in at least one new shot where he's easy to miss: At 19:40 on the DVD, as the three divers swim left to right, notice the Creature spying on them from his place of hiding in the background.

12. This is the movie's first action, at nearly the midpoint mark, and it duplicates a shock moment in Arthur Ross' second-draft *Black Lagoon* screenplay: On their first night in the lagoon, Reed and Kay are standing in the bow of the boat when, "with a terrible churning of water," the Creature quickly rears up out of the water and knocks a lantern from Reed's hand.

A few moments after the *Creature Walks* Gill Man smashes the searchlight, we see a patch of surging bubbles on the water's surface, moving quickly toward the camera (indicating the Gill Man's underwater approach). But notice that the concentric ripples around the bubbles are moving *in*, *toward* the bubbles. That's because it's a patch-of-bubbles-moving-*away*-from-the-camera shot from *Black Lagoon* (indicating the Gill Man's underwater retreat), run in reverse.

13. Bob Skotak's examination of the Gill Man-on-fire scene from *Black Lagoon* can be found at note 82 from Chapter 1; here he describes how he believes *Creature Walks*' burning Creature scene was done:

> The Creature-set-afire effects in the third film spurs fewer questions as to approach and execution. From a "forensic" standpoint, for *Creature Walks* it's a bit easier to sort out how and what was done for one simple reason: There exist fewer statements and less information on the making of the film and, for that reason alone, there are fewer "contradictions" on record to sprinkle doubts on the very logical, reasonable conclusions that can be made at this late date, following a focused cinematic "dissection" of the Creature-pyro sequence.
>
> There are three Creature-on-fire shots, one shot more than in the first film's pyro sequence, the reason being the interaction between characters and the Creature and the setting are more complex: Here, there are more characters involved, and they are all in close proximity on a small boat. Those parameters dictated breaking up the action a bit more, especially considering the smaller budget than the first film: A longer, more continuous-action pyro-effects shot was not affordable. Breaking the action into more pieces, more individual cuts, was a logical solution.

The first shot follows the Creature accidentally pouring gasoline on his entire body. In it, a lit kerosene lamp is tossed at him, igniting the gasoline. The Creature goes up in hot flames, as his arms flail about. Perhaps having learned a lesson from the first film which illustrated the difficulty of trying to sync the frantic movement of an actor in two different takes, director Sherwood and the effects supervisors simplified the Creature's actions: not as much thrashing side to side. Most of the action would be carried out by having the stuntman mostly flail only his hands and arms. With this live action "plate" completed, a separate element could be—and was—shot at a later date (most likely, in order for the stuntman to study the basic action of the actor on film, once processed) at which time an asbestos-suited version of the Creature was set alight. The difference here is that the decision was made to more or less hide the entire middle of the Creature—torso, head and legs—in a thick column of fire. Thick and wide enough to hide most of his action within and behind the fire, in a successful effort to avoid any tight synchronization of movements between the Creature photographed on the set and the burning, asbestos-covered Creature photographed later. The completed optical composite included a double exposure of the lamp flying in for a few frames along with a bright flash of a fiery explosion—a larger scale one likely lifted as library stock footage from *This Island Earth*—to make the transition to the full-on, burning Creature. So, in the final image, viewers would catch general, vague-ish glimpses of the burning Creature moving about within the fire, while clearly seeing only the Creature's claws thrashing about on either side of the central fire column. For such a brief cut, an entirely effective solution.

The second cut is wider, showing the Creature standing in the small boat on fire. Here, the stuntman playing the Creature was shot on the set, on the boat, reacting to the fire, moving to some extent—enough to provide "life" so as to not appear static, but not enough to create, as in the first film, movements hard to replicate later. An element of the Creature on fire—the stunt performer again, in asbestos suit—was filmed separately on another day and composited atop the Creature.

In his second cut, optical supervisor Roswell Hoffman used rotoscoping to integrate the fire into the boat in and around the characters in the boat. In particular, he "opened up" a space between the burning Creature's knees and lower legs via a rotoscoped matte to allow the actors to be seen, as well as to better create a discernable outline of the thing's body. The fact that the boat rocks slightly during this action imparts a note of believability, since opticals like this—attempted long before the existence of digital tracking technology—generally required that everything on the set be locked down. This all worked well in the shot, since the ever-changing nature of fire offers a certain degree of a forgiving looseness in matching action.

In the final shot of the three, the Creature, still on fire, topples into the water. Having sold the action in the first two shots, a relatively simple solution appears here: First the actors were filmed on the boat with either the actor playing the Creature or, likely, just a mock-up dummy of the creature—posed at the near edge of the side rail, being toppled into the water. With the actors out of the boat, a second exposure was done, this time with a "dummy" also posed on the near rail of the boat, set afire, and also toppled into the water. The optical printer wed the two images. Though well-done, there is a noticeable exposure "pop" as the optical transits from optical double-exposure to non-optical as the action of the creature splashing into the water finishes up.

What was also quite well-done in this sequence, is the blending of motion picture and/or still plates of the "swamp and jungle" background with the foreground set and actors. Here, a rear-projection screen can be seen, when closely examined, actually set right *into* the water, with very well-matched exposures nearly flawlessly bringing both projected image and real set believably together, creating an environment more convincing than the first film's use of an occasionally obvious painted jungle backing.

14. *Pacific Stars and Stripes* reviewer Al Ricketts described the situation quite humorously, writing that the burned Gill Man is fortunate "that there are four doctors in the house. They quickly discover that their parboiled prize has lungs, and with a cut here and a stitch there, the docs soon have them pumping."

15. Whenever Barton and Morgan start going at it, Borg and Johnson shut up like a couple of clams, to the point where you forget they're even in the room. (The characters are such ciphers, you keep forgetting they're even in the *movie*!) Which is not to disparage either actor; the problem for them was the script and, maybe, the director. When I asked Maurice Manson about newbie feature director Sherwood, he said, "I remember the one question I put to him. You know, these damn scripts are not very heavy on character, they're all two-dimensional. And I asked, 'Well, now, what kind of a character is this doctor that I'm playing? How do you see him?' And he said, '*Welllll* … he's *a nice guy*.' *That* gave me a big clue [*laughs*]! And that's about all I can say about him!"

16. Lissa Morrow told me, "My father wrote a few stories about his experiences as a child, growing up in a mortician's place of business. I've read them. The writing was descriptive and pretty good, but I'm reading and reading and reading, and there's no plot [*laughs*]!" In 1956, when Morrow's father died at age 87, his *New York Times* obituary said that he was believed to be the New York area's oldest practicing undertaker.

17. According to columnist Edwin Schallert (January 21, 1953), *The Robe* almost came to the screen ten years earlier, and Morrow had been pencilled in for a part back *then*.

Then in 1953, *The Robe was* made, and Morrow came out to Hollywood from New York to play his part. He stayed in a Beverly Hills hotel and, *being* a New Yorker, was content to hoof it (get around on foot). He had let his beard grow for *The Robe* and in that era, a hairy-faced fellow on shanks' mare in the Hills of Beverly was a magnet for Johnny Law. Sure enough, the day came when he was stopped by a minion of the law and asked for identification. Morrow, who didn't yet have a driver's license, could produce no ID that satisfied the officer, and tried to prove that he was an actor by pulling from his wallet a small photograph of himself as Dick Tracy, a character he'd played on radio. But the gun in his hand in the photo made things *worse*, and the next thing he knew, he was en route to the precinct house! It took a phone call to 20th Century–Fox and confirmation that he was an actor to get Morrow off the hook.

18. "It was a calculated risk," Jeff told *Brooklyn Daily Eagle* interviewer Jane Corby in March 1954. "Burton and I used swords specially made, with aluminum blades and hilts, weighing three and a half pounds apiece instead of the six and a half pounds they would have weighed if made of steel. They still could be dangerous weapons. It was a hard fight because we had to be careful—we might not miss each other, by accident."

19. There's a little Dr. Barton in Morrow's *World in My Corner* character, a wealthy industrialist who takes an interest in aspiring boxer Audie Murphy and allows him to train on his Long Island estate; does he have Audie's best interests at heart, or a sinister plan to dominate him as he does everyone with whom he associates (including his own daughter Barbara Rush)? We never quite find out for sure but we suspect the latter because Morrow plays it with that crazy Dr. Barton-ish bearing and flashing eyes, giving the impression that danger may lie just below the respectable façade. In his *Video Watchdog* article "They Did Science!," Larry Blamire wrote, "With his heavy eyebrows and 8 o'-clock shadow, [Morrow] had a rugged face that seemed to come right off an old pulp cover. He didn't so much act it, he just looked like he could kick the circuits out of a metal walking behemoth with piston-like legs."

20. The actor told me, "'Rex' meant King [in Latin] and G. stood for George—King George Reason was my father's name!"

21. Talking to me about landing his role in *Taza*, he said, "[Universal] tested me, and they seemed to be very excited about the results. It was a rape scene with Barbara Rush—which, needless to say, was exciting to *me* [*laughs*]!"

22. *Lady Godiva of Coventry* (1955), featuring fourth-billed Reason as the son of English earl Torin Thatcher, was the screen debut of Rex's lookalike-soundalike brother Rhodes, who was hired as a stuntman. It may also be the *only* title they have in common.

23. One of his last roles was an episode of *Perry Mason* in which he and co-star Jeff Morrow, playing stage actors, have a swordfight as part of a *Romeo and Juliet* rehearsal; Reason is later accused of the on-stage, in-the-dark murder of Morrow. If you think Morrow was a better actor than Reason based on *This Island Earth* and *Creature Walks,* reinforce that opinion by watching them do Shakespeare!

24. Shirley Ann was Rex's third wife. The first Mrs. Reason was the mother of his children; the second Mrs. Reason was Miss Universe contestant and showgirl Sanita Pelkey, who also had a few movie credits, among them *Missile to the Moon* (1958) and *Ghost of Dragstrip Hollow* (1959). In August 1962 they secretly tied the knot; in August 1963 she started *untying* it, suing him for divorce and charging him with cruelty. "She was of Italian descent," said Shirley Ann, "and Rex said he got tired of eating spaghetti for breakfast, lunch and dinner [*laughs*]. Plus, he would bring her to these spiritual lectures, and she would fall asleep. That didn't go well with Rex. So it didn't last."

25. As if the 36-24-36 knockout wasn't already beautiful enough, Universal absorbed part of the cost of some dental work, as they also did for contractees Mara Corday and Dani Crayne.

26. In Mike Barnum's *Classic Images* interview with Reason, the actor said that Snowden "seemed happy and proud to be a part of [*Creature Walks*]." Ina remembers that Reason was fond of Leigh and came to their apartment several times.

27. The Continos' friend Bove dedicated it to "Leigh Snowden Contino—one of the finest, gentlest and most beautiful women who ever lived."

28. A dead ringer for Snowden, Mary became Miss Nevada in 1977 and was the first runner-up in the Miss USA pageant later that year.

29. In *Dick Contino's Blues*, a bit of fiction by crime writer James Ellroy of *L.A. Confidential* fame, it's 1958 and Contino, fed up with his draft dodger tag, cooks up a publicity stunt: He and his singer-friend Chrissy will be "kidnapped" at gunpoint by masked "psychos," and then "escape," and the headlines will goose both their careers. But a serial killer, the West Hollywood Whipcord, unexpectedly deals himself in on this put-up job. In the novelette as in real life, Contino is married to Leigh Snowden, who's stoic and "can-do" but very much a sideline character. At a point in the story when Contino is about to star opposite a beautiful actress in a B-movie, Snowden warns him, "Don't let that chipped-toothed vixen French-kiss you during your love scenes, or I will fucking *kill* you both."

30. In this Screen Gems–Hammer Films collaboration, a critically ill sculptor (Richard Bull) looks to Baron Frankenstein (Diffring) for medical help, but the baron says he can do nothing—when in fact he *wants* the sculptor to die so that he (the baron) can then steal his brain and put it in his monster (Megowan). Like the burned Gill Man, the sculptor finds himself in a whole 'nother body because of a mad surgeon; like the Gill Man, he's shot by the surgeon and then chases him with murderous intent; and like the Gill Man, he purposely ends his own existence, throwing himself into a grave that fills in and smothers him.

31. In 1951, when President Truman went on a four-day cruise down the Potomac and in Chesapeake Bay on the yacht *Williamsburg*, the press followed on the *Vagabondia III*. With tongue very much in cheek, the Associated Press' Ed Creagh wrote a humorous article about the "sacrifice" the newsmen were making:

[T]he hardships those White House correspondents have to put up with would wring tears from the eyes of a drill sergeant.

Picture their plight, if you can bear it: five long days of being cooped up on a 102-foot floating prison called *Vagabondia III*, with only one television set, scarcely a dozen servants, hardly enough showers and bathtubs to accommodate a Kiwanis convention.

Would you believe it? Only one butler's pantry.

32. Monster Kids will remember McMahon better as *The Thing from Another World*'s (1951) out-of-patience USAF Gen. Fogarty, forever shouting at visitors to his Anchorage office, "*Close the door!*" He was again seen as military men in *The Day the Earth Stood Still* (1951), *It Conquered the World* (1956) and *The Deadly Mantis* (1957).

33. Funnily enough, the same thing evidently happened to Alland: According to the Mercury Theatre's John Houseman, in his memoir *Run-through*, Alland in his early Mercury days was called Vakhtangov and "hung around day and night, working lights, holding book, sweeping, prompting, moving pianos, talking too much and making himself generally indispensable. In exchange for these services, at some time in the middle of the night, he had extracted a promise of employment in the theater. Orson was not one to remember such a commitment. He had quite forgotten Vakhtangov's existence." But Alland persisted and eventually got a job.

34. A defining speech from Marcia is part of this scene in an early screenplay draft. She says of her husband, "He was trying to change me—to think as he thinks—speak as he wants … to be remade into some—some perfect thing … some secret … terrible secret ideal he desires." As she stares intently at her listener, she continues, "To fail—and be hated for failing.… Not to know any more what I really want—to be sure of—to be free … not … to"—and then she falters.

35. Megowan was similarly bandaged on August 31, the first day of the heat wave, when the set was *not* air conditioned.

On the audio commentary of the 2004 DVD release of *Creature Walks*, Bob Burns pointed out that in addition to Gill Man head, hands and feet and sailcloth suit, Megowan was also padded to look bigger (especially the Hulk-like shoulders), probably with foam rubber. "Shooting out in the sunlight—he does a lot of stuff outside—he had to just cremate in that thing. From wearing gorilla suits, I know how hot it gets if you're out in the sun."

36. I don't know if it's the angle or the lighting or *what*, but as the Creature walks down the corridor toward camera, he actually looks a little like a mutant cross between Don Megowan and Rod Cameron. I wonder if, to provide the more-human Creature face, the makeup boys cast a life mask of Megowan and then proceeded to give it Gill Man characteristics. Speaking of Cameron, he and Megowan looked strikingly alike at the time—so alike that they were cast as brothers in one of Republic's last movies, *The Man Who Died Twice* (1958).

37. With soap opera–like plot threads encompassing marital discord, imagined infidelity, paranoia, etc., *Creature Walks* has a whole different vibe and seems a bit more "grown-up" than the Saturday matinee popcorn-munchers *Black Lagoon* and *Revenge*. How much the Bickering Bartons actually add to the movie is a whole 'nother question. Wanda Hale wrote in her *New York Daily News* review, "Dr. Barton is dictatorial, highly explosive, and he is insanely jealous of his beautiful blonde wife. His behavior is the tipoff as to what will become of him." If made by Universal a couple decades earlier, a pre–Code *Creature Walks* coulda-shoulda starred Lionel Atwill as Barton.

38. The moviemakers used other tricks to disguise the fact that all the yacht scenes with actors were strictly soundstage. In some scenes of characters on the stern deck, the camera gently rocks up and down throughout. And in several yacht interior scenes (in the lab, salon, Marcia's stateroom and the Creature's cabin), patches of through-the-window-slats "sunshine" visible on background walls slowly, almost imperceptibly move up and down as they would on a ship at sea. Some of the yacht sets have ceilings visible in low-angle shots.

39. In an early draft of the script, there's a half-alike scene: In a small and very isolated community with a Bay landing, we see the Creature get off the yacht. As a canvas-topped truck waits, he debarks via gangplank, silently watched by his captors, whose guns are under their jackets and ready for use. There's fear on the faces of the local onlookers; one woman holds her child to her; a horse shies and rears. As quickly as possible, the Creature's captors get him into the truck, drop the flap and speed away. In a different draft, the only local witnesses are a fisherman, two children and a dog who snarls and backs away a bit. The fisherman and his kids are seen again in this draft's finale; a description of *that* scene is the final entry in this chapter's "Other Script-to-Screen Changes" section.

40. It's fun, if one is enough of a movie nerd, to scrutinize assistant directors' reports for the causes of blown takes. In the case of *Creature Walks*, they also include an actor bumping his head making a through-a-doorway entrance, another suffering from frog-in-throat-itis, one dropping a hypodermic needle, another hitting the yacht corridor's wall-mounted fire extinguisher, and the fumble-footed Creature tripping on the Ranch's exterior stairway and slipping during his hill ascent. Plus, on soundstage sets, there were the unexpected movie debuts of a fly, a moth and, in the salon party scene where Morrow is drunkenly ranting ("Change the metabolism and *man* will change!"), a wasp.

41. All but one ended up on the cutting room floor; in the movie, the rest of the trip is represented by a succession of nicely photographed long shots of the Florida extras in a dinghy under a glowering sky.

42. But is the "good stuff" all that good? The waterway scene has a nice suspenseful buildup, with the unexpected screeches of a bird and other jungle noises keeping viewers on edge. But the Gill Man's attack on the men in the dinghy is a bust: He has the element of surprise going for him and yet doesn't get in a single lick, and even douses him*self* in gasoline in a semi-comical way. After his many battering encounters with Man, the Gill Man seems to have "slowed a step," as they say in sports lingo.

43. The trailer provides us with the uninterrupted "A" camera shot of the Creature smashing the doors, flipping the dresser and entering the room. It also features a more distant long shot of the Creature mangling and shoving open the stockade door.

44. Telling the story to *Photon*'s Mark McGee, Morrow said, "Don Megowan [was] a big, husky guy, but he's not *that* strong, you know—to be able to pick me up over his head—so they had me on wires with four men at the controls." Over the years, the wires have become more visible as the home video releases get sharper.

45. In 2004, Glenn Erickson, the online world's esteemed DVD Savant, reviewed Universal's new *Creature from the Black Lagoon* Legacy Collection and mentioned in his coverage of *Creature Walks*: "[Director] Sherwood manages the best-directed scene in the whole trilogy when the Creature invades the mansion house to punish the abusive Jeff Morrow. Excellent blocking shows the monster paralleling Morrow through a series of rooms, and he spots his prey out of the corner of his eye at the same time we do. The Creature barrels through a window to cut off Morrow's escape. The simple action scene is beautifully laid out for maximum involvement."

46. Part of this scene was deleted from the movie. The italicized lines below were the cutting room casualties, replaced by an unneeded, interruptive long shot of the yacht:

> BARTON: [The Creature is] boxing himself into a corner.
> MORGAN: 'Could be the other way around.
> GRANT: Not a chance.
> MORGAN: *Did you ever read the report of the first expeditions?*
> GRANT: *I don't <u>read</u> about hunting—I do it.*
> MORGAN: *You would've found it very instructive. The Creature built a barricade of logs to keep the ship in the lagoon. Logs that weren't there when the boat went into the lagoon.* (Looks around.) *It was a region like this—from another age ... the Devonian Age of half-land, half-water islands.* He knows his way around places like this.

In the movie, the pilot house scene ends with Morgan saying, "Now ... *we'll* wait for *him*," and we dissolve to a nighttime long shot of the yacht at anchor, and then cut to a shot of Barton, Morgan, Borg and Johnson in the lab eying the Fishscope (Morgan: "Well, it's apparent he doesn't intend to attack on *our* terms"); the impression we get is that very little time has elapsed. But a short transitional scene, also cut, made it clear that the wait was much longer: Between the pilot house scene and lab scene, there was to have been a scene shot by the second unit in Florida: the yacht at anchor under a high-noon sun as Morgan (played by a local) walks to the bow and surveys the surrounding scenery. They even got a Morgan's-eye view of the shoreline, the camera panning left to right and then right to left, with no life visible.

At 78 minutes, *Creature Walks* is the shortest *Creature* movie (*Black Lagoon* was 79, *Revenge* 82). But if they had used this footage, plus some other bits 'n' pieces that were photographed and then junked, *Creature Walks* would probably be the *longest* of the three.

47. On *Black Lagoon*, Al Wyatt was the stuntman who donned a Gill Man suit of sorts and was set afire in post-production trick shots; perhaps he did the honors in *Creature Walks* as well.

48. "In *Creature Walks* I hated what they did to the poor guy and how he just became a big Tor Johnson lookalike," Charles Thaxton wrote about the series-ender's ending in a Classic Horror Film Board thread. "I always liked to think that when he reached the water his gills would return eventually and he's still out there somewhere." Is there a Monster Kid alive who hasn't also had that same thought?

Incidentally, the three Creature movies are like all four of the early 1940s Frankenstein movies: When the monster dies, it's over, **THE END**, thanks for comin'. No wrapping-up-loose-ends scene, no Morris the Explainer, no last-second bit of comic relief to leave 'em laughin', no *nuthin'* beyond that point. In fact, a shot of the apparently dead or about-to-die Creature is the final image in every film.

49. In the interests of full disclosure, I have to point out that I'm ass-u-me-ing that it's Roberson in those two shots: Megowan was there too that day. But why would Universal hire Roberson and have him there and then not let him appear on camera?

50. Maurice Manson told me that the lit kerosene lamp "landed at my ankles and the cuff of my pants caught on fire, and I had to jump overboard! But it didn't cause any serious damage."

51. Morrow told interviewer Mark McGee in *Photon*, "[T]here's a scene in the picture where the Creature tips us over in a boat. Well, those studio tanks are usually warm when you get there at seven o'clock, but by ten in the evening when you're ready to shoot, it can get pretty cold. I don't drink that often, but there's usually someone there with some brandy and, let me tell you, it really warms you up."

52. Playing the minute, uncredited role of a secretary in *The Price of Fear*: Jeff Morrow's wife Anna Karen. It might have been her first-ever movie appearance.

53. The Season One *Flipper* episode "Flipper's Monster" was not Browning's idea even though it's about the making of a movie with a Gill Man–type monster in Coral Key, Florida (the series' setting); Browning's name appears in the credits four times, as co-creator of the series, as "Associate Producer in Charge of Underwater Operations," as director, and for playing the title role! It begins with a scene of the beastie submerged beneath an unsuspecting brunette swimmer (guest star Wende Wagner), reaching out for her feet (*à la* the memorable *Black Lagoon* scene) and then pulling her under. It turns out that we're watching a movie being made: The monster and the girl are being photographed in a swimming pool. At the end of this pre-credits sequence, Browning removes the monster head just before the fade-to-black and we get to see his two-toned (blond and black hair) '60s look. Later, when monster scenes are being shot on the sea floor, Flipper thinks the monster is a threat to the girl and swims to her rescue, leading to complications and conflict in the episode's second half. The on-land scenes near Flipper's pen were shot at the Miami Seaquarium; the scenes set on boats were done just south of there, in Biscayne Bay; and the underwater scenes were shot off Nassau in the Bahamas. During one underwater scene we get a real good look at a camera slate which, storyline-wise, should have the name of the monster movie on it, but instead it gives the name of the movie as *Flipper*, "R. Browning" as director, "L. Boren" as cameraman, and has the date 11/26/62 on it! The cameraman on the episode was Clifford Poland, a member of the Wakulla *Black Lagoon* camera crew in 1953. Flipper's Monster has the Monster of Piedras Blancas head, hands (originally Mole People hands) and feet (originally Metaluna Mutant feet). It seems safe to assume that they all had to have come from Jack Kevan, but Browning told me that all the costume pieces were shipped to them in the Bahamas; he had no part in making any arrangements for them and didn't even know at the time that some or all were Kevan-connected. Browning hose-breathed in order to stay underwater as the monster, and again bubbles visibly seeped out of the top of the head.

54. There are 12 cues in *Let's Kill Uncle* that derive from Universal's sci-fi and horror films, including *Black Lagoon*, *Creature Walks*, *This Island Earth* and *The Incredible Shrinking Man*, the latter being used to highlight a tarantula sequence, probably not a coincidence given that there was also a hairy spider in that Jack Arnold sci-fi picture. In the semi–sci-fi category, there's even a bit of Rosen's "Salvage of the Lady Luck," which plays a significant role in the first two Gill Man films. On the totally non–sci-fi front, *Let's Kill Uncle* borrows from the thrillers *Man Afraid* (1957), *Midnight Lace* and *Portrait in Black* (1960). Also plundered for the Castle picture was some of Stein's orig-

Ricou Browning as the title character in the Flipper *series' "Flipper's Monster," going after pretty Wende Wagner. Swimmer-diver-surfer-actress Wagner did her own underwater work in the episode.*

inal underscore for the 1956 Esther Williams non-swimming thriller *The Unguarded Moment*, the soap opera *Written on the Wind* (1956), comedies *The Private War of Major Benson* (1955), *Everything But the Truth*, *The Toy Tiger* (1956) and other pictures. Despite Stein being the author of only about 38 percent of *Let's Kill Uncle*'s music (none of it written for the film), for some ridiculous reason he still managed to receive an on-screen composer's credit. This is rather amusing considering Stein seldom got a composer's credit when he actually *did* write most of the music in a picture. Stein certainly would have gotten a good laugh out of the fact that some of his obituaries mentioned that this was the last film he scored.

55. Mancini's same melody also serves as the love theme in Jack Arnold's crime drama *Outside the Law* (1956), made a few months after *Creature Walks*, with "Perfect Wife?" being used three times in that picture. The movie co-stars the Creature's third girlfriend, Leigh Snowden, and Ray Danton, who in real life was married to Julie Adams, the Creature's first girlfriend. *Outside the Law* sports an interesting score in that the first part of the picture was mostly tracked with Mancini's music, while the second part was almost entirely tracked with Salter's music. Perhaps each composer worked on his own half of the movie, but regardless, there was obviously no attempt to try to fashion any sort of consistent sound in this particular score. The film's soundtrack also contained a few tracked cues by Skinner and Stein as well as three original Mexican source music cues courtesy of Stanley Wilson and Mancini.

Outside the Law re-used 12 cues from *Black Lagoon* and *Creature Walks*, not to mention many other tracked pieces that found their way into various horror movies the studio produced, including Mancini's music from *Four Guns to the Border*, *Johnny Dark* (1954), *The Far Country* and *Smoke Signal* (1955). Not surprisingly, all of the Creature music came courtesy of Mancini's pieces, as Salter's consistent use of the blaring Creature theme made most of his Gill Man music inappropriate for *Outside the Law*.

Chapter 5

1. In Hollywood trade papers, the movie was initially called simply *Curucu*. Later it became *Beast of the Amazon* and ultimately *Curucu, Beast of the Amazon*. Rybnick and Kay's company Jewell Enterprises was also responsible for *Untamed Women* (1952), the Americanized *Godzilla, King of the Monsters!* (1956), *Love Slaves of the Amazons* (1957), *Girls on the Loose* (1958) and others.

2. Beverly backed out of her commitment to star in Roger Corman's *The Oklahoma Woman* (1956) in order to accept *Curucu* and the getaway-from-Hollywood that went with it. While she was in Brazil, a gal-pal stayed at her apartment—and one night woke as a male intruder began choking her! The attacker fled when she cried out. The smart money says it was Richard Garland, who couldn't have known that Beverly had gone off on location and must have thought he was choking *her*.

3. After a long career of dancing in movies and on TV, Thomas spent years working on three-camera TV sitcoms (standing in for Shelley Fabares on *Coach* and for Mimi Kennedy on *Dharma & Greg*). "After that, I didn't pick up the phone [to look for work] and the phone never rang, so I thought, 'Well, this is *it*.' I worked 'til I was almost 73." She died in 2013.

4. *Piedras Blancas* star Don Sullivan told *Monsters from the Vault* interviewer Bryan Senn, "Jeanne Carmen, as I understand it—it may or may not be true—put up the money for that movie. I think she was engaged to somebody in Texas who was very wealthy, and in order to keep her happy or whatever, they said, 'We'll back the movie'; or maybe they were trying to make money, I don't know." Sullivan also mentioned that he and Carmen reunited at a 2007 celebrity autograph show in California ("I couldn't believe she looked so great") and three months later he heard that she was dead: "She had leukemia and didn't tell anybody about it."

5. Robert Skotak told me,

The sequel script was written and, I seem to recall, a heavily revised second draft. It was written by the late creature-effects guy Mark Williams: He re-sculpted and cast a new monster head (and shoulders, I think) that matched the original as best as could be done given the limited photo reference available of certain views of it. I think there was talk about trying to get Les Tremayne for a part. It's all pretty vague in my memory now. The only thing I recall about the story is that it was similar to the original, in other words, it took place in a small town with horrible killings by the monster.

Some of this came from a kind of lark trip Mark and I took to the original town where the film was shot where we ran into a couple people who were either in the original film, or knew people who were. My brother Dennis and I had an opening in our work schedules and thought it would be fun to work on a little project like that, plus the fact that, at that time, Mark was a good friend.

I was never much of a fan of the original other than the fact that I liked the locale, and I thought the monster pretty extreme and weird, more of an "alien" than sea creature. I remain a fan of Jack Kevan and his work, so that too was a factor.

Chapter 6

1. "That catfish and others were all over the springs," Browning told me. "That one learned that the girls were feeding bread to the fish and he or she wanted some, and kept coming around." He didn't reveal whether he himself was responsible for its "miraculous" disappearance, but he did happen to mention, "We had catfish for dinner."

2. In Florida, and apparently in Argentina also: On Christmas Day 2013, swimmers in the Paraná River were attacked by a huge school of flesh-eating piranhas. There were at least 20 children among the injured, some losing parts of their fingers or toes before they could get back to shore and escape the feeding frenzy. But according to a paramedic, within a half-hour many of the beachgoers were back in the water. Apparently they share Ginger's attitude: "You *kind of* know they're there, but you ignore it."

3. According to *Tampa Bay Times* writer Beth N. Gray in a July 2012 story, Stanley, Browning and several others became the first to be "remembered permanently" in the new Hall of Fame: "Granite tiles engraved with the names of the first eight inductees will hang in the park's famous mermaid theater and eventually will serve as the cornerstone for a museum that's been long in the planning." This first batch of honorees also included the late Newton Perry (natch), the synchronized swimming group The Aqua Belles, veteran mermaids Genie Young and Barbara Wynns, and others. "There will be more" in the future, promised Weeki Wachee Springs marketing and public relations director John Athanason.

Accepting on behalf of Newt Perry was his daughter Delee, who told me,

> Ricou was on one side of this big auditorium and I was on the other side, and I waved to him and I really wanted to get over to see him, but just then, the program got started. Then after it was over, I was kinda swamped by a lot of the older mermaids who remembered me when I was a little girl. I was very anxious to get over to see Ricou, and I was talking to the older mermaids trying to excuse myself, and I looked over and Ricou wasn't there any more. I was crushed, I thought he must have left. Then I turned around and there he was: He had walked *allll* the way around to the other side of the auditorium and came down the stairs, just to say hello to me. I was tickled absolutely to death. Oh … my … *gosh*, I couldn't get over it. Like all older people, he doesn't get around as well as he did when he was young, so the fact that he walked all that way to see me … it just melted my heart.

Delee's parents Newt and Dot Perry started the Perry Swim School in 1955, Delee runs it today and she looks to her grandkids to be "the fourth generation of Perry swimmers, teachers and champions." Newt began teaching people how to swim in 1923 so the family is now in its tenth decade of providing that service.

4. According to the *Revenge* press release quoted above, *Return* was shown "on the last day of the U-I troupe's stay at Marineland," which was Saturday, July 24; the Universal folks left that day at four p.m. and Gannon recalls that the wrap party did take place in the afternoon. If Gannon is correct that he got the idea to make *Return* when the wrap party was six days away, then it was written on July 18 and 19, shot on July 20 and 21, the film was sent to New York to be developed on July 22, it came back to Florida developed on July 23, *Return* was dubbed and scored on the evening of July 23 and the morning of July 24, and shown on July 24.

5. Brothers Dorrell and Stuart McGowan wrote, produced and directed *Snowfire*; Megowan played Mike McGowan; and Mike's daughters Mollie and Melodie McGowan were played by Dorrell's daughters Mollie McGowan, 8, and Melodie McGowan, 12. Dorrell and Stuart also regularly cast Megowan in their TV series *Death Valley Days*.

Chapter 8

1. Around this time Mick shot and edited several "Making of" documentary shorts, notably of the remake of *The Thing* and *Gremlins*, as well as hosting his own monster movie program on Theta Cable Television (then known as L.A.'s "Z Channel") featuring interviews with everybody from Steven Spielberg to Richard Crenna. Subsequently he became a noted writer-director in his own right.

2. All quotations attributed to Arnold are from an unpublished interview I conducted in 1977.

3. Kneale's *Creature* script was the first of two commissioned by Universal during his brief flirtation with that studio in the early '80s; the other was a first draft on *Halloween III: Season of the Witch*.

4. This is the only time a character name from the original film trilogy repeats in any of the remake scripts; Whit Bissell's character in *Creature from the Black Lagoon* was Dr. Edwin Thompson.

5. I should know, since I was the one Guillermo asked to write the script.

Index

Numbers in *bold italics* indicate pages with photographs.

Aaker, Everett 164, 165, 375
Abbott, Bud 49, 99–100
Abbott, Norman 100
Abbott and Costello Go to Mars (1953) 84, 115, 116, 125
Abbott and Costello Meet Dr. Jekyll and Mr. Hyde (1953) 42, 99–100, 115, 116, 207, 366
Abbott and Costello Meet Frankenstein (1948) 113, 207, 366
Abbott and Costello Meet the Invisible Man (1951) 115, 116
Abbott and Costello Meet the Keystone Kops (1955) 115
Abbott and Costello Meet the Mummy (1955) 115, *209*, 211
Abraham, Marc 360
The Abyss (1989) 370
Accordion Man: The Legendary Dick Contino (book) 250
Ackerman, Forrest 49
Acuna, Frank 105
Adam Had Four Sons (1941) 54
Adams, Julie 1–7, *1*, *2*, *4*, *5*, *6*, *7*, *19*, 36, 40–41, 42–43, *46*, 51–53, *52*, 59, 62, 64, 65, 66–67, *67*, *70*, 70, 72, 76, *76*, 77–78, 79, 80, 81, 82, 83, 84, *84*, 86, 89, 92, 93, 94, 99, 103, *110*, 111, *124*, 128, 134, *134*, 136, 160, 220, 224, 247, 296, 319, 328, 329, 330, 351, 352, 368–69, 372, *372*, 375, 385
Adams, Ron 309
Adventure in Baltimore (1949) 147, 373
Adventures of Captain Marvel (1941) 80
The Affairs of Martha (1942) 49–50
Against All Flags (1952) *41*, 42, 130
Agar, John 51, 146–48, *147*, 150, 156–59, *157*, *158*, *168*, 177–78, 180–81, 182, 183, *183*, 184, 185, *186*, 187, 189, 190, 191, 192, *192*, 193, 194, *195*, 196, 198, 200, 205, 208, 211, 224, 243, 251, 284, 295, 296, 307, 312, 331, 332, 364, 373, 374–75, 376
Agar, Linda Susan 147, 157, 373
Agar, Loretta 157, *157*, 194, 375

Águilas frente al sol (1932) 59
The Alamo (1960) 171, 172
Alda, Robert 97
Aldrich, Robert 248
All I Desire (1953) 160, 162, 375
All That Heaven Allows (1955) 248, 282
Alland, Susan 82, 370, 372
Alland, William 4, 13, 14, 18, 19, 20, 21, 29, 30, 31, 32, 35, 40, 41, 69, 70, 71, 73, 82, 84, 86, 87, 88, 89, 92, 94, 134, 141, 144, 150, *150*, 151–52, 173, 182, 195, 200, 207, 229, 234, 235, 257, 258, 259, 268, 276, 279, *280*, 283–84, 363–64, 365, 367, 370, 372, 373, 374, 375, 377, 378, 379, 380, 382
Allen, Steve 209
The Alligator People (1959) 119
Aloma of the South Seas (1941) 65
Alton, John 26
Amazing Stories (magazine) 49
America's First Network TV Censor (book) 100
Amfitheatrof, Daniele 112
Amphibious Fighters (1943) 365
Anaconda (1997) 360
Anders, Merry 161
Anderson, Arthur 151–52
Anderson, Judith 240
Anderson, Mitchell 211
Andrews, Edson J. 86, 370
Angeli, Pier 316
Anka, Paul 171
Ankers, Evelyn 49, 54, *55*, 56, *56*, 57, 368
Antoine, Le Roi 124
Archerd, Army 86, 171
Armstrong, Bess 211
Arnaz, Desi 55, 165
Arnold, Jack *2*, 3–4, 20, 31, 39, 40, 64, 65, 66, 72, 70, 73, 78–79, 80, 83, *84*, 86, 92, 93, 94, 102, 104, 117, 119, 129, 134, 137, 141, 143, 148, 151, 173, 174, 175, 176, *177*, 178–79, 181–82, 183, 184, 187, 189, 191, 193, 194, 195, 196, 199, 201, 206, 223, 224, 225, 234, 235, 273, 276, 283, 284, 332, 350, 353, 360–61, 363, 364, 366, 367, 369, 370, 374, 377, 379, 380
Arvidson, Frank 314

Assignment: Underwater (TV) 252
Asta (dog) 377
"The Astounding B Monster" *see* Baumann, Marty
Athanason, John 385
Attack of the 50 Foot Woman (1958) 259, 364
Auntie Mame (stage) 53

Back to the Black Lagoon (2000) 77, 208
Back to the Future Part III (1990) 211
Bacon, James 281
Badman's Territory (1946) *167*
Bainbridge, William 60
Bait (1954) 158
Baker, Charlie 88
Baker, Rick *316*, 353
Ball, Edward 37
Ball, Lucille 55, 165
Ball, Suzan 36, 365, 374
Balogh, Elmer *26*
Band of Angels (1957) 245
Baram, Marcus 142
Barker, Lex 59
Barnum, Mike 245, 246, 382
Barnum, Pete 375
The Barretts of Wimpole Street (stage) 240
Barsby, Jack 118
Barsi, Judith 211
Barton, Don 212
Basehart, Richard 110
Baskin, Mildred 144, 146, 180, *180*, 377
Baskin, Norton 146
Baskin, Sally 144, 146, 176, 179, 180, 181, *181*, 184, 187, 188, 189, 190, 208, 214, 374, 376, 377–78
Baskin, Tom 144, 146
Battle at Apache Pass (1952) 130
Baumann, Marty 247, 351
The Beachcomber (TV) 256
The Beast from 20,000 Fathoms (1953) 104, 112
The Beast of Hollow Mountain (1956) 118
Bedoya, Alfonso 105
Beery, Jere, Jr. *158*, 185, 189, 192, 306
Beery, Jere, Sr. 184–85, 191, 352, 377

Bela Lugosi Meets a Brooklyn Gorilla (1952) 80
Belfer, Hal 125
Ben-Hur (1925) 36
Benchley, Robert 147
Bend of the River (1952) 53, 107, 112, 117, 132, 160
Benet, Brenda 182
Bengal Brigade (1954) 378
Benny, Jack 247, 248
Bergen, Brooksie 71, 75
Berkeley, Busby *375*
Berkeley, Martin 141, 142–43, 152, 200, 212, 213, 224, 225, 373, 378
Berkeley, William D. 142–43
Berwick, Irvin 207, 312, 313, 314
Berwick, Wayne 313, 314
Beswick, Doug *316*
Betz, Jack *68*, 71, *74*, 75, *81*, 82, 329
Beyond the Blue Horizon (1942) 54, *54*
Beyond Tomorrow (1940) 49
Big Jake (1971) 171, 172, 251, 254
Billy Budd (stage) 241
Biondi, Guy 100
Birch, Paul 53
Bissell, Whit 6, 64, 67, *70*, 86, 87, 105, 350, 386
Bissette, Steve 350
Black Beauty (1946) 55
The Black Castle (1952) 13, 116, 130–31
The Black Lagoon Bugle (newsletter) 349–52
The Black Scorpion (1957) 53
The Black Shield of Falworth (1954) 102
Blackmer, Judeena 179, 189, 190, *190*, 209
Blackmer, Sidney 189
Blaisdell, Paul 137, *161*
Blamire, Larry 51, 156, 309, 382
Blazing Barriers (1937) 167
Bleckner, Jeff 356
Bluemel, Walter *80*, 376
Blyth, Ann *36*, 37
Bob Burns' Monster Kid Memories (book) 111
Bodeen, DeWitt 58
Bond, Ward 142
Bonestell, Chesley 104
Bonzo Goes to College (1952) 20
The Bounty Hunter (1954) 379

387

INDEX

Bove, Ben 250, 382
Boyette, Patsy 69, 321
Bradbury, Ray 20, 30, 103, 142, 317, 363
The Brain from Planet Arous (1958) 364
Brandon, Henry 379
Breen, Joseph 35, 194, 364–65
Breland, Keller 169
Brendel, Frank 376
Bride of Frankenstein (1935) 135
Briggs, Joe Bob 349, 351
Bright Victory (1951) 3, 52
Briskin, Fred 182
Broadway to Hollywood (TV) 96
Bromfield, John 148, *148*, 150, 163–66, *164*, *165*, *174*, 181, 185, 186, *186*, 187, *188*, 191, 199, 205, 208, 223, 224, *225*, 310, *310*, 311, *311*, 312, 375, 376, 379
Bromfield, Louis 163
Brooks, Foster 343
Browning, "Buddy" 38, 39
Browning, Ricou 2, *2*, *4*, 6, 7, *15*, *17*, *19*, *20*, *21*, *23*, *32*, *33*, 35, 38–39, *38*, 40, 41, 42–43, *43*, 44, 53, 62, 64–65, 67–69, 70, 71, *71*, *72*, 73, 75, 76, 77, 78, *78*, *81*, 82, *82*, 86, 93, 104–6, 134, 136, 137, 143, *155*, 173, 174, 175, *175*, 176, 177, *177*, 178, 182, 183, *183*, 184, 185, 187, 188, 189, *189*, 191, 192, 193, 194, 207, 208, 211–12, 236, *238*, 260, *260*, 262, *262*, *263*, 264, 274, 276, 279, 281, 283, 284, *284*, 296, 297, 306, 315, 319, 321, 325, 326, 327, 328, 329, 330, 331, 332, 333, 334, 335, 337, 351, 364, 365, 366, 367, 368, 369, 370, 375, 376, *376*, 377–78, 379, 384, *384*, 385, 386
Browning, Ricou, Jr. 39, *175*
Brunas, John 196
Brunas, Mike *253*, 374, 380
Buck, Frank 168
Burden, W. Douglas 144, 145, 146, 168, 338, 375, 379
Burkhart, Lillian 181
Burns, Bob 40, 41, 42, *62*, 74, 98, 102, 109, 110–11, 144, 172, 182, 209, 266, 351, 366, 368, 369, 376, 377, 383
Burns, Kathy 110–11
Burson, Polly 64, 79, *79*, 368
Burton, Richard 241–42, 381
Bush, James 49
Butcher, Melissa 377
Butterflies Are Free (stage) 53
Buttolph, David 112

Caesar, Sid 283
Caine, Michael 211
Calhoun, Rory 53
Calvet, Corinne 164–65, *164*
Camelot (1967) 365
Cameron, Rod 383
Campfire Conversations Complete (book) 172–73
Cape Fear (1962) 243
The Caper of the Golden Bulls (1967) 168

Capone, Al 142
Captain Lightfoot (1955) 98, 242
Carcaba, John 179, 190
Carling, Foster 118
Carlson, Mona 47, 49, 50, *50*, 368
Carlson, Richard 5, 43–44, *44*, *46*, 47–51, *48*, *49*, *50*, 54, 55, 64, 66, *67*, 70, *70*, 72, 75, 80, 83, 84, *84*, 86, 89, 91, 92, 93, 94, 100, 104, 109, *124*, *134*, 136, 167, 224, 252, 284, 295, 317, 366, 367, 368, 370, 374
Carmen, Jeanne 314–15, *314*, 385
Carpenter, John 243, 355
Carrillo, Leo 105
Carroll, Harrison 66, 79, 84
Carson, Rachel 364
Carter, Everett 219, 220
Case, Tom 99, 144, 330
Castelnuovo-Tedesco, Mario 120, 289, 290
Castle, William 168
Castle of Frankenstein (magazine) 194–95, 198, 276, 316
The Cat Creeps (1930) 59
Cat on a Hot Tin Roof (stage) 251
Cavanagh, Paul 36
Chace, H. Haile 312
Chambers, John 99, 372
Chandler, Jeff 245
Chaney, Lon 367
Chang (1927) 144–45
Chaplin, Charlie 248
Chaplin, Charlie, Jr. 248
Chapman, Ben *5*, 6, *11*, 39, 52, 53, 57, 60–64, *60*, *61*, *62*, *63*, 65, 66, 70, 71, 72, 74–75, 75, 76–77, *76*, 78–79, *79*, 80–81, *81*, 83, 84, *84*, 85, 86, 87, *88*, 92, 94, *95*, 100, 106, 109, *119*, 136, 137, 170, 172, 185, 236, 272, 274, 276, 296, 351, 366, 367, 368, 369, 370, 371, 372, *372*, 373, 375, 376
Chapman, Ben F., III 62, 63, *63*, 64, 370
Chase, Barrie 259
Chase, Borden 259
Chase, Frank 259
Cheyenne (TV) 255–56
Chief Crazy Horse (1955) 201, 374
Child Star (book) 147, 148, 373
Chinatown (1974) 80
Christine, Virginia 268
Cinefantastique (magazine) 137
Cinemacabre (magazine) 243
The Cisco Kid (TV) 120
Citizen Kane (1941) 13, 152
City Beneath the Sea (1953) 117, 123–25, 126, 132, 216, 218, 220
Clark, Mamo 281
Classic Images (magazine) 166, 167, 245, 246, 382
Climax! (TV) 162
Clint Eastwood—A Biography (book) 195
Clint—The Life and Legend (book) 196

Clutch Cargo (TV) 197
Coach (TV) 385
Cockrum, Dave 350
Coen, Franklin 364
Cohen, Herman *56*
The Colgate Comedy Hour (TV) 99–100
Collier's (magazine) 40, 102, 108, 364, 369–70
Collins, Richard 142, 373
Comanche (1956) 167
The Comancheros (1961) *171*, 251, 253
Conan Doyle, Arthur 14, 353
Congo Crossing (1956) 257, 258, 259
Connolly, Mike 89
Conquest of Space (1955) 206
Considine, Tim 171
Conte, Richard 3
Contino, Dick 249, *249*, 250, 251, 291, 382
Cooper, Alice 84–85
Cooper, Ben 161, 375
Cooper, Gary 196
Cooper, Merian C. 144, 373, 375
Corday, Mara 273, 382
Corliss, Richard 77, 370
Corman, Roger 55
Cornell, Katharine 240
Costello, Lou 49, 99–100
Cousteau, Jacques 7, 20
Cowan, André 169
Cowan, Will 60
Cowden, Jack 284
Crawford, Broderick 255
Crayne, Dani 263, 382
The Creation of the Humanoids (1962) 256
Creature from the Black Lagoon (MagicImage book) 25
Creature from the Black Lagoon (1954) 1–7, *2*, *4*, *5*, 11–137, *11*, *14*, *15*, *17*, *19*, *20*, *21*, *23*, *24*, *25*, *26*, *29*, *30*, *32*, *33*, *35*, *43*, *44*, *46*, *61*, *65*, *67*, *68*, *70*, *71*, *72*, *73*, *74*, *75*, *76*, *78*, *79*, *80*, *81*, *82*, *83*, *84*, *85*, *88*, *95*, *96*, *98*, *101*, *103*, *119*, *124*, *134*, 141, 143, 144, 150, 151, 152, 154, 155, 166, 167, 170, 173, 176, 178, 185, 187, 192, 196, 197, 198, 200, 201, 203, 205, 207, 208, 212, 214, 215, 216, 217, 218, 219, 220, 221, 222, 223, 224, 225, 229, 230, 232, 236, 237, 245, 252, 257, 261, 262, 267, 270, 273, 276, 279, 280, 282, 283, 285, 286, 292, 294, 296, 295, 298, 303, 310, 312, 314, 315–16, 317, 319, 328–31, 337, 338, 349, 350, 351, 353, 355, 356, 357, 363, 364, 365, 366, 367, 368, 369, *369*, 370, 371, 372, 373, 374, 375, 376, 378, 379, 380, 383, 384, 385, 386
Creature from the Black Lagoon (1954 novelization) 352
Creature from the Black Lagoon (proposed remakes) 283, 353–61

Creature from the Black Lagoon— The Musical (stage) 111
The Creature Walks Among Us (1956) 24, 28, 36, 51, 79, 84, 102, 109, 112, 117, 151, 170, 197, 205, 208, 209, 211, 227–299, *227*, *230*, *231*, *233*, *235*, *236*, *237*, *238*, *239*, *242*, *258*, *260*, *261*, *262*, *263*, *264*, *265*, *266*, *267*, *268*, *269*, *270*, *271*, *273*, *274*, *275*, *277*, *278*, *279*, *280*, *281*, *290*, *291*, *293*, *296*, *299*, 303, 309, 312, 313, 334, 342, 344, 354, 357, 367, 370, 376, 379, 380–81, 382, 383–84, 385
Creature with the Atom Brain (1955) 53
The Cremators (1972) 109, 317, 318, 364
Crews, Stanley *68*, 69, 71, *74*
Crosswinds (1951) 35, 39
Crypt Orchids (book) 350
Cult of the Cobra (1955) 79, 118, 202, 204, 206, 364, 373
Curse of the Undead (1959) 114
Curtis, Tony *43*, 81
Curucu, Beast of the Amazon (1956) 165, 310–12, *310*, *311*, 385
Cutting, Richard 367

Daff, Alfred E. 379
Dahl, Arlene 59
The Dalton Gang (1949) 52
Dangerous When Wet (1953) 78
Daniel, Dennis 52, 86, 103, 373
Dante, Joe 309, 349
Danton, Mitchell 53
Danton, Ray 53, 368, 380, 385
Danton, Steven 53
Darabont, Frank 349, 352, 367
Darcel, Denise 344
Darrow, Henry 243
Darwin, Charles 229
Dassin, Jules 50
David, Irene 157
David, Lester 157
Davis, Jim 251
The Day of the Triffids (1963) 209
Day the World Ended (1956) 53, *56*, 161, *161*
The Deadly Mantis (1957) 118, 142, 218, 364, 378, 379
Deas, Shirley 258
Death Valley Days (TV) 386
De Laire, Diane 195, 208
del Rio, Dolores 13
Del Toro, Guillermo 349, 357, 386
Dempewolff, Richard F. 149
Den Bleyker, Frank *68*, 376
Denning, Dee 55, 57, 368
Denning, Pat 57
Denning, Richard 5, 36, *46*, 49, 53–57, *54*, 55, *56*, 64, 66, 70, *70*, 71, 75, 83, *84*, 86, 89, 106, 136, 166, 368, 370
Dennis the Menace (TV) 379
de Sainte Colombe, Paul 312
Destination Inner Space (1966) 137

Index

Destination Moon (1950) 133
Destry (1955) 150, 160, 205
Devil Bat's Daughter (1946) 98
The Devil's Brigade (1968) 347
Devil's Canyon (1953) 25
*Dexter, Maury 245–46, *246*
Dharma & Greg (TV) 385
Diamond, Jack 177, 186, 187
Diamond Lil (stage) 241
Dick Contino's Blues (novel) 382
Did They Mention the Music? (book) 289
Didion, Joan 172
Di Fate, Vincent 350, 351
Dillin, John 169
Dillinger, John 368
Dillman, Bradford 110
DiMaggio, Joe 108
Dionne, Sara 337
Directed by Jack Arnold (book) 173, 187, 196, 234, 353, 369, 374, 377, 379
Disneyland (TV) 255
Distant Drums (1951) 105, 377
Dodds, Edward 144
Doherty, Thomas 142
Dolan, Robert Emmett 117, 123
Domergue, Faith 245
Don Winslow of the Coast Guard (1943) 167
Donovan's Brain (1953) 101
Douglas, Diana 245
Douglas, Jerry 109
Douglas, Warren 48
Doyle, Ed 306, *306*, 307, *308*, 337, *338*, 339, 340
Dracula (1931) 163
Dracula vs. Frankenstein (1971) 133
Dragon Lizards of Komodo: An Expedition to the Lost World of the Dutch East Indies (1927) 375
Dragonfly Squadron (1954) 379
Driving Miss Daisy (stage) 53
Drums Across the River (1954) 127, 219
The Drunkard (stage) 166
Dubov, Paul 241, 364
The Duel at Silver Creek (1952) 127
Dunagan, Donnie 63
"The Dune Roller" (short story) 317, 318
The Dune Roller (unmade 1950s movie) 109
Dunn, Pete 313–14, *313*, *314*
du Pont, Alfred I. 37

Earth vs. the Flying Saucers (1956) 282
East, Henry 377
East of Sumatra (1953) 36, 117, 125, 129, 130, 216, 217
Eastwood, Clint 189, 195–96, 201, 211, 217, 224, 255, 280, 284, 343, 378
Easy to Love (1953) 375
Eberhardt, Norma 316
Eden, Barbara 161
Eegah (1962) 198
Efron, Zac 152
Eisner, Breck 359

Eisner, Michael 359
Elam, Jack 343
Elliot, Biff 25–26
Ellis, Paul *58*
Ellison, James 52, *52*
Ellroy, James 382
The Eloise McElhone Show (TV) 96
Englund, Robert 280–81
Erickson, Glenn 383
Escalante, Henry 65–66, 106
Essex, David 315
Essex, Harry 18, 20, 25–26, 29, 30–31, 32, 34, 92, 103, 104, 108, 283, 315, 316, 317–18, 363, 364, 367–68
Evans, Maurice 240
Ewell, Tom 108
Ewing, Don 107

Faber, Bob 274
Fairchild, Edgar 113
Family Affair (TV) 374
Famous Monsters of Filmland (magazine) 49, 57
Fangoria (magazine) 212, 350, 361
Fant, Julian 168, 180, 191–92
The Far Country (1955) 367
Father's Day (stage) 51
Feature Players: Stories Behind the Faces, Volume 2 (book) 240
Feldman, Charles J. 202
Ferry, Ray 57
Fields, W.C. 166
Fierro, Paul *267*
Fiesta (1941) *59*
The Fighting Kentuckian (1949) 272
Figueroa, Gabriel 13, 40, 363, 375
Film Fan Monthly (magazine) 56
Filmfax (magazine) 67, 167, 314, 361
Films in Review (magazine) 285
Finstad, Suzanne 171, 376
First Spaceship on Venus (1962) 133
Fisher, James 184
Fitzgerald, Michael 55
Five Kings (stage) 258, 259
Flame of Stamboul (1951) 166
Flash Gordon (1936) 366
Flesh and Fury (1952) 13
Flesher, Jack 376
Flipper *384*
Flipper (1963) 375
Flipper (TV) 283, 315, 369, 375–76, 384
Flipper's New Adventure (1964) 375
Flippy 148, 149, 168–70, *168*, *169*, 179, 187, 201, 280, 374, 375, 377, 378
The Flying Doctor (TV) 55
The Flying Serpent (1946) 98
Flynn, Errol *41*, 42, 54
Fontaine, John *see* Stone, Jeffrey
Forbidden (1953) 89
Forbidden Planet (1956) 282
Ford, John 59, 147, 157, 196
Forrest, Wolf 350

Fort Apache (1948) 147, 157
Forty Carats (stage) 53
Four Star Revue (TV) 375
Fox, Michael 48
Fox, Michael J. 211
Francis in the Navy (1955) 211, 248
Francis Joins the Wacs (1954) 102, 195, 215, 217–18, 378
Frank, Fred 40
Frank, Milo 159, 160
Frank, Susan 206
Frankenstein (1931) 1, 135, 268
Freeman, Leonard 368
Freeman, Mona 55
Fresco, Robert M. 31, 142, 156, 312
Freund, Karl 135
Frohn, Adolf 148–49, 168, 169
From Hell It Came (1957) 253
Frontier Gambler (1956) 165
Frumkes, Roy 285
Funicello, Annette 171
Furmanek, Bob 93

Gabor, Zsa Zsa 110
Gallinghouse, Scott 364
Gandee, Lyman 291
Gannon, Mike 177, 306–7, *306*, 308, 309, 310, 337–42, *338*, *341*, 386
Garbo, Greta 69
Garland, Beverly 163, 310, *310*, 311–12, *311*, 385
Garland, Richard 310, 385
Garner, James 248
Garris, Mick 349, 353, 386
Garroway, Dave 96
The Garry Moore Show (TV) 335, 336
Garth, Anabel 110
Gary, Lorraine 211
Gautier, Dick 251
Gaye, Lisa 60, 161
Gaynor, Janet 49
Gengerelli, Joseph A. 151
Gentry, Race 201
Gerard, Philip 96, 97, 273–74
Gershenson, Joseph *113*, 114, 115, 116, 117, 118, 120, 125, 215, 219, 222, 286, 290
Gertsman, Maury 281–82, 297, 298
Gertz, Irving 112, *112*, 114, 116, 118, 217, 218, 286, 289, 290, *290*, 293–94
The Ghost Breakers (1940) 49
Ghost Hunters (TV) 377
The Ghost of Frankenstein (1942) 117, 130, 131, 136, 201
The Giant Claw (1957) 243
Gilligan's Island (TV) 182
Girls in the Night (1953) 143
The Glass Key (1942) 54
The Glass Menagerie (stage) 53
The Glass Web (1953) 55, 117, 127, 143, 216, 217
The Glenn Miller Story (1954) 102, 144
Glickstein, Irving D. 201, 202
A Global Affair (1964) 182, 377
Goetz, William 21, 98
Gojira (1954) 116, 370

Golden Boy (1939) 49, 368
Golden Boy (stage) 49
The Golden Horde (1951) 117, 133
The Golden Mistress (1954) 148
Goldrup, Jim 240, 246
Goldrup, Tom 240, 246
Goldsmith, Joel S. 246
Golitzen, George 83
Gomes, Geoffrey L. 166, 167
Gomez, Thomas 105
Gonzales, John 306
Gordon, Bert I. 51
Gordon, William 35, 151
Gorgo (1961) 211
Gorilla at Large (1954) 210
Gourson, N. Edward 259
Gozier, Bernie 80, 81, 86, 106
Gray, Beth N. 385
The Great Diamond Robbery (1953) 102
The Great Sioux Uprising (1953) 117, 123
Green, Johnny 112
Gregg, Virginia 272
Griffith, D.W. 59
Griffith, James 165, 375
Guastini, Vincent 360
Guest, Lance 211
Gunsmoke (TV) 272
Gwynne, Anne 55

Haas, Hugo 158
Hackett, Buddy 92
Hadley, Joe 70
Hailey, Oliver 51
Hajos, Karl 112
Hale, Richard 378
Hall, James Norman 60
Hall, Jon 60
Halsey, Brett 197, *197*, 198
Hammond, Laurens 124
Hangman's Knot (1952) 55
Hansen, Myrna 263
Harmon, John 314
Harpoon (1948) 150, 164, 375
Harris, Jed 241
Harris, Timothy 356
Harryhausen, Ray 368
Hart, Susan 182, 377
Harvey, Laurence 248
Has Corinne Been a Good Girl? (book) 164
Hatton, Raymond 52
The Haunted Palace (1963) 372
Havens, Irma B. 73–74
Havens, James C. 43, 44, 64, 65, 73–74, 86, 93, 173, 234, 257, 259, 260, 328–29, 369
Haverick, Russ 186, 201
Hawaii Five-O (TV) 57, 61, 368
Hawaiian Nights (1954) 60
Hayden, Russell 52
Hayes, Allison *149*
Hayes, Helen 240
Hayward, Susan 54
Hebb, Donald 375
Hecht, Maude 179, 191
Helffrich, Stockton 100
Hello, Dolly! (1969) 366
Hello Down There (1969) 284
Hennesy, Tom 79, 144, 170–73, *170*, *171*, 172, 174, *174*, 175–76, 181, *183*, 184, *184*, 185–86,

186, 187, 190, *190*, 191, 192, *192*, 193–94, 196, 197, *197*, 198, *198*, 199, 209, 212, *223*, *225*, 272, 274, 296, 332–33, 376, 378
Herbert, F. Hugh 48
Herbert, Frederick 221
Here Come the Nelsons (1952) 120
Herz, William 152
Herzoff, Archie 87, 93, 94, 100, 197, 202
Hickey, Duke 100
Hickman, Beau 144
High Chaparral (TV) 197
High Peaks (book) 145, 373
Hoffman, Roswell 371, 381
Hold That Ghost (1941) 49, 49, 167
Holden, William 47–48, 49, 368
Hollywood Monster: A Walk Down Elm Street with the Man of Your Dreams (book) 280–81
Holmes, Taylor 240
Holton, Scot 317
Honeymoon (1947) 147
Hope, Bob 49
Hopper, Hedda 43–44, 47
Hopper, Jerry 49, 367
The Horror Show (1979) 135
Horsley, David S. 88, 371
Hot Rod Girl (1956) 161
House of Dracula (1945) 201, 366
House of Frankenstein (1944) 366
House of Wax (1953) 36
Houseman, John 382
How to Marry a Millionaire (TV) 161–62
Howard, Jane *see* Howarth, Betty Jane
Howarth, Betty Jane 199, 263
Howdy Doody (TV) 100
Hoy, Bruce 165
Hoy, Robert 197–98, *197*, 370
Hudson, Larry 267
Hudson, Rock 81, 160, 245, 252
Huebner, Mentor 353
Hughes, Kathleen 48
Hugo, Jeffrey 75
Humanoids from the Deep (1980) 137
Hunt, Marsha 49–50
Hunter, Ross 99, 252
Hunter, Tab 160

I Died a Thousand Times (1955) 161, 162
I Led 3 Lives (TV) 43, 50–51, *50*, 55, 100
I Love Lucy (TV) 55
I, the Jury (1953) 25–26
I, the Jury (novel) 26
I Was That Masked Man (book) 105
Ifukube, Akira 116
The Incredible Shrinking Man (1957) 118, 130, 133, 215, 294, 384
The Infinite Way (book) 246
Ingram, Rex *365*
Invasion of the Body Snatchers (1956) 282
The Invisible Man (1933) 111, 135

The Invisible Man Returns (1940) 222
The Invisible Ray (1936) 295
Ireland, John 312
The Iron Glove (1954) 102
Irvin, Ray 370
The Island at the Top of the World (1974) 366
The Island of Dr. Moreau (novel) 261
Island of Lost Souls (1933) 295
Island of the Lost (1967) 284
Israel, Sam 35, 88, 96, 97, 365, 372
It Came from Beneath the Sea (1955) 118, 206, 279, 368, 379
It Came from Outer Space (1953) 3, 20, 25, 29, 30, 31, 42, 43, 44, 47, 48, 51, 54, 66, 79, 92, 102, 103, 109, 111, 112, 116, 117, 118, 124, 129, 133, 136, 143, 192, 207, 214, 219, 280, 317, 363, 367, 378
It Grows on Trees (1952) 248
I've Lived Before (1956) 248

Jackson, Donald L. 89
Jackson, James, Jr. 260, *260*, 262, *262*, 263, *266*
Jackson, Peter 357
Jacobs, Dick 117, 288
James, Brandon 314–15
James, Lois 379
Jankiewicz, Pat 67, 316
Janssen, David 201, 235, 248, 364
Jaws (1975) 22, 116, 135, 136, 370
Jaws: The Revenge (1987) 211
Jaws 3-D (1983) 102, 210–11, 355, 369, 377
Jensen, Paul M. 208
Jeopardy (1953) 15
Jesse James Meets Frankenstein's Daughter (1966) 167, 251
Jim Thorpe—All-American (1951) 167
Jivaro (1954) 55, 379
The Joe Palooka Show (TV) 100
Joe Panther (1976) 284
Johnny Dark (1954) 102
Johnson, Erskine 203, 229, 280
Johnson, John J.J. 167
Jolson Sings Again (1949) 65
Jones, Carey *281*, 283, 352, 367
Jones, Harvey B. 107
Jones, Jennifer 157
Jones, Stan 165
Jonny Quest (TV) 167
Jubilee Trail (1954) 102
Julius Caesar (stage) 151
Jungle Book (1942) 366
Jungle Girl (1941) 80
Jungle Headhunters (1951) 34
Jungle Moon Men (1955) 61
Jupiter's Darling (1955) 35, 333–34, 337
Juran, Nathan 364

Kadler, Karen 263
Kaper, Bronislau 112, 116
Kardell, Lili 263
Karen, Anna 240, 241, *241*, *242*, 243, 280, 384

Karloff, Boris 100, 135, 295, 297
Kass, Herman 202
Katzman, Sam 253, 255, 282, 379
Kay, Richard 310, 385
Kaye, Charlotte 179
Kazan, Elia 142, 143
Kazarian, Merrilee 61–62, 63, *63*, 64, 370, 372
Keith, Brian 374
Kennedy, Arthur 3, 52
Kent, Ted J. 135
Kevan, Jack *14*, *15*, *23*, *26*, *33*, *36*, 40, 41, 42, 43, 94, 100, 105, 144, 175, 178, 206–7, *235*, 283, 312, 313, 314, 366, 384, 385
The Kid from Amarillo (1951) 255
Kikume, Al 80
Killers from Space (1954) 102
Kim, Evan 354
King Kong (1933) 14, 19, 24, 103, 116, 133–34, 135, 137, 150, 200, 222, 223, 224, 349, 373, 375, 379
King Kong vs. Godzilla (1963) 133
King of the Mounties (1942) 167
King Rat (1965) 380
Kings Row (1942) 159
Kintz, Greg 93
Kirkpatrick, Glenn 208
Kiss, Robert J. 101–2, 107, 201, 202–5, 205, 222, 277–79, 317, 372, 373
Kiss Me Deadly (1955) 248
Kiss of Fire (1955) 245, *246*, 247, 276
Kneale, Nigel 353, 354, 357, 360, 386
Knight, Fuzzy 52
Knoth, Fred 366
Koch, Howard W. 375
Kohner, Paul 59
Korda, Alexander 207, 366
Korda, Zoltan 366
Kovack, Nancy *257*
Kraus, John *26*
Krenek, Ernst 289
Kronos (1957) 243
Kulick, Dottie 70–71, *71*
Kurland, Gilbert 42, 71, 143, 144, 201, 207
Kyser, Kay 291

The Lady from the Sea (stage) 241
Lady Godiva of Coventry (1955) 382
The Lady Takes a Flyer (1958) 31
Laemmle, Carl 44, 254, 287
Lamb, John 144, 148, 174, 175, 176, 212, 373
Lamothe, Dan 62, 63, 64
Lamour, Dorothy *54*
The Land Unknown (1957) 118, 120, 130, 366, 378–79
Landau, Arthur 159
Landis, John 31, 349, 353, 357
Lange, Arthur 113
Lantz, Walter 343
Lapis, Joe 312
Lassie (TV) 375
Lathrop, Philip 312
Lava, William 112, 114, 118, 215,

216, *216*, 218, 219, 220, 221, 222, 288
The Lawless Breed (1953) 13, 53, 89
A Lawless Street (1955) 255
Lawrence, Earl E. 118
Leaming, Barbara 29
Lee, Christopher 210
Lee, Pinky 60
The Leech Woman (1960) 114
Le Fevre, Ned 196–97
Let 'Em Go Alive (newsreel) 373
Let's Kill Uncle (1966) 119, 168, 288, 384–85
Lewis, Al 99
Lewis, Jerry 161
Liberace 105
Lieberman, Leo 20, 21, 26, 30, 363–64
Life (magazine) 27, 77, 104, 146, 151, 352, 365, 370
Life Without Soul (1915) 377
Li'l Abner (TV production) 252
Lili (1953) 373
Lilley, Tim 172
Lippert, Robert L. 245
The List of Adrian Messenger (1963) 99, 372
Little Women (unmade movie) 157
The Lively Set (1964) 31
Livingston, Jeff 209, 273, 274
Lloyd, Christopher 211
Lockwood, Gary 170, 171–72
Loh Tseng Tsai 151
Long, Richard 36, 245
Long Day's Journey into Night (stage) 53
Look in Any Window (1961) 364, 370
The Looters (1955) 53
Lopez, Perry 79–80, 84, 106
Lord, Jack 57
Lost Horizon (1973) 99
Lost in Alaska (1952) 115
Lost Skeleton of Cadavra (2001) 309
The Lost World (1925) 14
The Lost World (novel) 14, 353
The Lost World (unmade movie version) 353
The Lost World: Jurassic Park (1997) 354
Lovecraft, H.P. 110
Lovejoy, Frank 36, 43, 366, 367
The Loves of Carmen (1948) 65
Loving You (1957) 291
The Lucky Southern Star: Reflections from the Black Lagoon (book) 40, 42–43, 51, 53, 70, 77–78, 83, 352, 369
Lugosi, Bela 104, 282
Lux Video Theatre (TV) 248
Lyons, Cliff 66

Ma and Pa Kettle at Home (1954) 102
Ma and Pa Kettle at the Fair (1952) 160
Ma and Pa Kettle at Waikiki (1955) 160, 205, 211
Macbeth (stage) 240
MacCorkindale, Simon 210

Index

MacLane, Barton 55
Mad at the World (1955) 364
The Mad Doctor of Market Street (1942) 80
The Mad Monster (1942) 366
The Madmen of Mandoras (1963) 167
The Magnetic Monster (1953) 47, 48, 51
The Magnificent Matador (1955) 55, 368
Magnificent Obsession (1954) 102, 252
Mahoney, Jock 248
Makelim, Hal R. 158
Malde, Otto 84, 370
Malone, Bill *110*, 111, 351
The Man from Bitter Ridge (1955) 199
Man of a Thousand Faces (1957) 207
Man of Conflict (1953) 157–58
The Man Who Died Twice (1958) 383
The Man Who Pursued Rosebud: William Alland on His Career in Theatre and Film (2010) 31, 70, 364
Man Without a Gun (TV) 245
Man Without a Star (1955) 150
Mancini, Henry 112, *113*, 114, 115, 116, 117, 118, 120, 121, 123, 124, 125, 126, 128, 129–30, 133, 136, 215, 217, 218, 219, 220, 221, 222, 265, 284, 286, 288–89, *289*, 291, 292, 373, 380, 385
Manfish (1956) 165, 379
Mank, Greg 57
Mann, Anthony 367
Mann, Johnny 162
Manson, Maurice *231*, 235, *237*, 257, 258–59, 265, 267, *267*, *270*, 272, 273, 381, 384
Marcellino, Nick 99
Marine Circus (1939) 146, 376, 377, 379
Marine Corps Times (newspaper) 62, 63
Marineland (book) 146, 168, 374, 377
Marlowe, Hugh 110
Marsh, Tani 60
Marshal Morgan and the Tokyo Police (1961) 165
Marshall, Tony *see* Willcox, Charles
Martin, Dean 161
Marton, Andrew 245
Marx, Groucho 59
Marx, Harpo 59
Mary, Mary (stage) 53
Mason, Sydney 72, 196
Maté, Rudolph 3
Matheson, Richard 211
Mathews, Kerwin 316
Matinee (1993) 309
Maury, Lou 118
Maxwell, Charles 114
The Maze (1953) 47, 51
McBride, Arthur 375
McCallum, David 282
McClelland, Doug 56

McCoy, Dixie 175, 188, 191
McCreery, Mark "Crash" 359
McGee, Mark 206, 383, 384
McGilligan, Patrick 196
McGinnis, Terran 146, 168, 374, 377
McGowan, Dorrell 386
McGowan, Melodie 386
McGowan, Mollie 386
McGowan, Stuart 386
McKay, Christian 152
McKee, Iain 152
McLintock! (1963) 172
McMahon, David 258, 269, 382
McNabb, Charles 68, 69, *69*, 176, 207, 321, 376
Me and Orson Welles (2008) 152
Meade, Kyme 370
Mechanix Illustrated (magazine) 107–8
Meeker, Ralph 109
Megowan, Alva 256, 344, 346
Megowan, Bette 254, 255, 256, *342*, 343, 344, 345, 346
Megowan, Don 79, *231*, *233*, 236, *236*, *238*, *239*, 252, 254–57, *254*, *255*, *256*, *257*, 259, 261, 264, *264*, *266*, 268, *268*, *269*, 270, *270*, 271–72, *271*, 274, *280*, *291*, *293*, 296, *296*, 298, *299*, 342–47, *342*, *343*, 386, 382, 383, 384
Megowan, Greg 254–55, 256, 343, 344, 345, 346, 347
Megowan, Lelia Dale 342, *343*
Megowan, Vikki 255, 257, 274, 342–47, *342*, *345*
Men of the Fighting Lady (1954) 43
Menjou, Adolphe 142
Mercury Theatre on the Air (radio) 151
Merlin, Jan 99, 372
The Mermaids of Tiburon (1962) 212
Messinger, Cheryl 146, 168, 374, 377
MGM on Location (short) 207
Michael Shayne (TV) 55
Michalski, Michael 370
The Midnight Story (1957) 294
A Midsummer Night's Dream (stage) 240
Mighty Joe Young (1949) 167
Miller, Marvin 194
Million Dollar Mermaid (1952) 375
Mineo, Sal 171
Minor, Mike 111
The Miracle of the Hills (1959) 246, *246*
Mission Over Korea (1953) 245
The Mississippi Gambler (1953) 3, 107
Mr. & Mrs. North (radio) 55
Mr. & Mrs. North (TV) 55
Mr. No Legs (1979) 284
Mr. Peabody and the Mermaid (1948) 36, 37, 117, 123
Mister Roberts (1955) 171
Mr. Terrific (TV) 182
Mitchum, Robert 53

Mitman, Gregg 144, 169, 183, 375, 379
The Mob (1951) 255
Moby Dick (1956) 370
Moffitt, Jack 276
Mogambo (1953) 74
Mohawk (1956) 161
The Mole People (1956) 115, 120, 130, 167, 250, 378, 379
Molieri, Liliane 208
Mom, Can I Keep Her? (1998) 162
The Monolith Monsters (1957) 31, 117, 119, 129, 273, 288, 289, 290
Monroe, Marilyn 108–9, 247, 248, 252
Monster Bash (magazine) 309
Monster from Green Hell (1958) 251
The Monster of Piedras Blancas (1959) 137, 207, 283, 312–15, *313*, *314*, 384, 385
The Monster of Piedras Blancas (unmade sequel) 385
Monster on the Campus (1958) 114, 127, 129, 192, 364
The Monster That Challenged the World (1957) 379
Monsters from the Vault (magazine) 385
Moore, Clayton 105
Moore, Joanna 364
Moreno, Antonio 6, 36, 57–60, *57*, *58*, *59*, 64, 70, *70*, 85–86, 89, 92, 368
Morgan, Helen 369
Morrow, Jeff 229, *230*, *231*, 235, *237*, 240–44, *241*, *242*, *244*, 252, 257, 258, 261, *265*, *267*, 268, *268*, 269, *269*, 270, 271, 272, 273, 280, *291*, *293*, 294, 295, *296*, 370, 381–82, 383, 384
Morrow, Lissa 240, 241, 242, 243, 244, 280, 381
Moser, Mike 317
Mozert, Bruce 75, 78, 86, 327, 328, 335, 370
Mueller, Chris, Jr. 26, 29, 40, 41, 42, 109, 110, 111, 365–66, *365*, *366*, 369
Muhl, Edward 41, 92, 245, 372
Mulhare, Edward 282
The Mummy (1932) 135
The Mummy (1959) 210
The Mummy's Curse (1944) 268
The Mummy's Hand (1940) 105, 209, 282
The Mummy's Tomb (1942) 209
The Munsters (TV) 99, 378
The Munsters' Revenge (1981) 283
Murphy, Audie 382
Mussallem, Wallace 187–88, *188*
Mutiny on the Bounty (1935) 60, 281
Mutiny on the Bounty (1962) 74, 369
Mutiny on the Bounty (novel) 60
My Favorite Husband (radio) 55
My Friend Irma Goes West (1950) 252

Naked Paradise (1957) 55
Nalder, Reggie 171
Nash, Mike 38, 70
Natasha—A Biography of Natalie Wood (book) 171
Neal, Patricia 59
Nellie 212
Nelson, Lori 53, 149–50, *149*, *155*, 159–63, *159*, *160*, *161*, *162*, *163*, *168*, 172, 177–78, 180–82, *181*, 183, *183*, 184, 185, *186*, 187, 188–89, 191, 192, *192*, 193, 194, 197, *197*, 198, *198*, 199, 205, 208, 209, 212, 220, *223*, 224, 247, 295, 296, 307, 331, 364, 375, 376, 377
Nelson, Robert 150, *195*, 196
The Net (1953) *see Project M-7*
Never Say Never Again (1983) 284
Newman, Kim 349
Newsom, Ted 314
Nichols, Harman W. 107
Nicotero, Greg 283, 351–52, 367
Night Gallery (TV) 53, *109*, 110
Nims, Ernest 20, 29, 30, 31, 32, 364
No Name on the Bullet (1959) 273
Novarro, Ramon 36
Nuzzi, Nick 218–19

O'Brian, Hugh 248
O'Brien, Richard 376
Octaman (1971) 34, 212, 283, 315–18, *316*, *317*, 364
Odell, Rosemary 4
Odets, Clifford 49
Okefenokee (1959) 314
The Oklahoma Woman (1956) 385
The Old Fashioned Way (1934) 166
On an Island with You (1948) 71
On the Good Ship Hollywood (book) 158, 373
Once in a Lifetime (stage) 240
One Million B.C. (1940) 54, 281
Ortiz, Fernando Morales 59
O'Sullivan, Maureen 38
The Outer Limits (TV) *108*, 109, 282–83
Outlaw's Son (1957) 161, 375
Outside the Law (1956) 129, 292–93, 380, 385

Pace, Terry 196
Pacific Stars and Stripes (newspaper) 51, 190, 205, 381
Pagan Love Song (1950) 60
Page, Sam 367
The Painted Stallion (1937) 216
Paiva, Nestor 6, 36, 64, *70*, 86, 89, 91, 105, 136, 166–68, *166*, *167*, 186, 187, *188*, 199, 208, 222, 224, 280
Palance, Jack 42, *246*
Palmer, Dawson 110
Palmer, Gregg 35, 36, 235, 245, 251–54, *253*, 259, 260, 262, 264, *264*, 268, 269, *269*, 270, 272, 273

Pardners (1956) 161, 242
Parducci, Rudolph *26*
Parker, Eddie 209
Parker, Tom 374
Parton, Regis 370
Patrick, Cynthia 250
Patrick, Milicent 41–42, *41*, *42*, 95–98, *95*, *96*, *97*, *98*, 137, 366, 372, *372*
Paxton, Bill 359
Payne, John 39
Peanut Circus (TV) 100
Peet, Clarence *255*
Pelkey, Sanita 382
Penal Law (stage) 240
The Penalty (1941) 142
Perils of Nyoka (1942) 80
Perkins, Anthony 135
Perry, Delee 105, 333, 386
Perry, Dot 386
Perry, Newt 37–38, *37*, 39, 67, 105, 320, 321, 333, 385, 386
Perry Mason (TV) 382
Pershing, John J. 159
Persons in Hiding (1939) 54
Peters, Ken 200
Petrie, Flinders 105
Petschnikoff, Sergei 40, 42
Pevney, Joseph 199, 200, 378
The Phantom of the Opera (1925) 367
Phantom of the Rue Morgue (1954) 100, 102
Phiefer, John *26*
The Phil Silvers Show (TV) 67, 282
Philbrick, Herbert *50*, 51
Phillips, Bill 355, 356, 357
Phipps, William 87
Photon (magazine) 51, 206, 383, 384
Pichel, Irving 37
"Pickman's Model" (story) 110
The Pied Piper of Hamelin (1957) 161
Pillow Talk (1959) 273
Pinson, Allen 66
Pittsburgh (1942) 222
Playboy (magazine) 45
Pleasence, Donald 243
Poindexter, Ina 248, 249, *249*, 250, 382
Poland, Cliff 369, 384
Posse from Hell (1961) 119
Powell, William 37
The Power (1968) 367
Power, Tyrone 3
Powers, Clayton 192, 306, 307, 337, *338*, 339, 340, 341, 342
Powers, Pat 185, 191, 192, 209, 306, 307, *308*, 337, 339, 364
Pratt, James 41, 364
Pratt, Sherman 144
Prendergast, Tessa 379
Presley, Elvis 373–74
Previn, Charles 114
The Price of Fear (1956) 277, 278, 384
The Prime of Miss Jean Brodie (stage) 53
Prince of Darkness (1987) 243
Prince Valiant (1954) 255
The Prodigal (1955) 15

Prohaska, Janos 110
Prohaska, Robert *109*, 110
Project M-7 (1953) 102, 372–73
Psychic Killer (1975) 53, 368
The Psychotronic Encyclopedia of Film (book) 317
Psychotronic Video (magazine) 52, 103, 373
The Purple Monster Strikes (1945) 368

Queen of the Mob (1940) 54, 368

Rackmil, Milton R. 89
Rails Into Laramie (1954) 144
Rainer, Luise 241
Ramar of the Jungle (TV) 100
Ramsay, Clark 87, 93, 95–96, 97–98, 209, 273, 274
Randolph, Donald 36
Rappaport, Frederick 54
Rasumny, Mikhail 105
Rathbone, Basil 240
Ratner, Brett 359
Raw Edge (1956) 245, 273
Rawhide (TV) 196
The Rawhide Years (1956) 222
Rawley, James *231*, 235–36, 257, *265*, *267*, 270, 272, 273, 280–81
Rawlings, Marjorie Kinnan 146
Ray, Bill 334, 335, 375
Ray, Fred Olen 162
Ray, Nicholas 376
Reason, Rex 35, 36, 51, *231*, 235, *239*, 244–47, *244*, *246*, 252, 257, 260, 261, 263, *265*, *267*, 269, 270, 271, 272, 273, *274*, 276, 284, *290*, *291*, *293*, 294, 295–96, 382
Reason, Rhodes 244, 382
Reason, Shirley Ann 246–47, 382
The Rebel Set (1959) 253
Rebel Without a Cause (1955) 171
Red, Hot and Blue (1949) 52
Red Sundown (1956) 380
The Redhead from Wyoming (1953) 117, 133, 221
Redman, David 306, 309, 377
Redwing, Rodd 79, 80, 84, 106
Reedall, Mark 330
Reel Nature—America's Romance with Wildlife on Film (book) 144, 169, 183, 375, 379
Reemes, Dana M. 173, 234, 353, 369, 374, 377
Reiner, Joe 162, *163*
Reitman, Ivan 356
Reminisce (magazine) 260, 263
Rennick, Jonny 60
Rettig, Tommy 171
The Return of the Creature (1954) 192, 305–10, *308*, 337–42, *338*, 376, 386
Revenge of the Creature (1955) 28, 31, 51, 53, 69, *69*, 72, 79, 84, 87, 109, 112, 117, 124, 126, 127, 139–225, *141*, *144*, *148*, *149*, *153*, *155*, *168*, *169*, *170*, *173*, *174*, *175*, *177*, *178*, *179*, *180*, *181*, *183*, *184*, *186*, *188*, *190*, *191*, *192*, *195*, *197*, *198*, *204*, *206*, *223*, *225*, 229, 235, 236, 251, 270, 278, 279, 280, 286, 288, 303, 305–6, 307, 308, 309, 310, 331–33, 337, 338, 339, 340, 341, 386, 349, 350, 352, 354, 355, 363, 364, 367, 370, 373, 374, 375, 376, *376*, 377, 378, 379, 383, 384
Reynolds, Burt 162
Reynolds, William 201
Rhodes, Grandon 151, 184
Rhythm of the Islands (1943) *166*
Rice, Grantland 38, 365
Richard's Almanac (TV) 50
Ricketts, Al 51, 189–90, 205, 381
Ride Clear of Diablo (1954) 102, 117, 127, 218, 219
Riders to the Stars (1954) 48, 51
Riesner, Dean 109
Rinsch, Carl Eric 360
Roach, Hal 54
Roach, Hal, Jr. 54, 253
The Roaring 20's (TV) 246
The Robe (1953) 241–42, 381
Roberson, Chuck 272, *272*, 273, *273*, *281*, 384
Roberts, Bart *see* Reason, Rex
Robinson, Bill "Bojangles" 147
Robson, Mark 3
Rode, Alan K. 63
Rodriguez, Robert 360
Roemheld, Heinz 114, 115, 118, 222, 286, 287, *287*, 291, 292, 293
Rolleston, W.F. 201, 306, 340, 376
Romeo and Juliet (stage) 240
Rondell, Ronnie 234
Roosty (stage) 142
Rope of Sand (1949) 164
Rosen, Milton 112, 113, 117, 118, 124, 125, 126, *126*, 127, 215, 217, 218, 219, 220
Rosenberg, Aaron 367
Rosenstein, Sophie 160
Rosenthal, Jeannie 259
Ross, Arthur 18, 20–21, 22, 25, 26, 28, 30–31, 92, 136, 229, 230, 232, 261–62, 267, 274, 276, 281, 282, 285, 298, 357, 364, 379, 380
Ross, Gary 357, 359–60
Ross, Joe E. 282
Rozsa, Miklos 112
Ruby Gentry (1952) 287
Run-through (book) 382
Running Wild (1955) 129
Rush, Barbara 245, 367, 382
Rybnick, Harry 310, 385

The Sad Horse (1959) 247
St. Joan (stage) 240
St. Oegger, Joan 5
Saleh, Dennis 102
Sally and Saint Anne (1952) 116
Salter, Hans J. 112, 114, 115, 117, 118, 122–23, *123*, 127, 128, 129, 130, 131, 132, 133, 136, 215, 218, 219, 221, 222, 286, 288, 292, 385
Salty (1973) 284
Sands of Iwo Jima (1949) 157

Santa (1932) 59, 368
Sarafian, Tedi 357
Saskatchewan (1954) 59, 102, 144
Sawtell, Paul 112, 114
Saxon, John 201
Scala, Gia 263
Scarlet Angel (1952) 55
Scary Monsters (magazine) 314
Schallert, Edwin 26, 141, 254, 255, 363, 381
Scharf, Walter 112
Schary, Dore 245
Schickel, Richard 135, 195
Schlesinger, Mike 172, 212
Schnee, Thelma 109
Schovitz, Joe "Sorko" 368
Schow, David J. 78, 111, 230, 234, *281*, 283, 349–61, 366, 367, 368, 369, 378
Schulberg, Budd 31
Schwarzwald, Milton 114
Schweitzer, Albert 232
Science Fiction Gold: Film Classics of the 50s (book) 102
Scott, Randolph 379
Scott, Ridley 360
Scream of the Wolf (1974) 344
The Sea Around Us (book) 364
The Sea Around Us (1953) 364
Sea Hunt (TV) 212, 251–52, 284
The Searchers (1956) 59
Sears, Fred F. 255
Secret Sins of the Father (1994) 162
Selph, Carl 177, 306, 340, 376
Selph, Gloria 177, 180, 376
Selznick, David O. 49, 147, 156–57, 159, 374
Senn, Bryan 385
Serling, Rod 110
The Seven Year Itch (1955) 108–9, 373
The Seven Year Itch (stage) 108
The Seventh Commandment (1961) 314
The 7th Voyage of Sinbad (1958) 364
Sharp, Alex 270, *271*
She Wore a Yellow Ribbon (1949) 157
Sheffield, Johnny 71, 207
Shepard, Jim 45
The Sheriff of Cochise (TV) 165
Sherman, George 374
Sherman, Luanna 312
Sherwood, John 234–35, 257, 258, 259, 263, 266, 271, 273, 281, 298, 380, 381, 383
Shield for Murder (1954) 148, 374
The Shirley Temple Story (book) 157
The Shoemaker's Holiday (stage) 151
Shooting Montezuma (novel) 372
The Shootist (1976) 253, 272
Showdown at Abilene (1956) 129
Shurlock, Geoffrey M. 269, 281
Sierra (1950) 66
Sign of the Pagan (1954) 42, 222, 242, 378
The Silent World (book) 20, 21
Sill, Robert 177, 186–87, 208

Index

Silvers, Phil 282
Simmons, Floyd 196
Simmons, Jean 241
Simmons, Richard Alan 199
Simonelli, Charles 95, 96, 97, 372
Sinatra, Frank 248
Sincerely Yours (1955) 161
Siodmak, Curt 48, 310, 312
Sirk, Douglas 160
Six Bridges to Cross (1955) 1, 53, 215
The Six Million Dollar Man (TV) 61
Skal, David J. 368
Skelton, Red 197
The Skin Diver (magazine) 45, 70, 108, 367, 373
Skinner, Frank 112, 113, 114, 132, 217, 222, 264
Skinner, Ruth 262, *262*, 334
Skotak, Dennis 314, 370–71, 385
Skotak, Robert 84, 88, 102, 314, 363–64, 370–71, 380–81, 385
Sky King (TV) 100
Slim Carter (1957) 53
Smith, Alexis 59
Smith, Pete 146, 377, 379
Smith, Robert E. 380
Smoke Signal (1955) 245
Snowden, Leigh 235, *236*, *239*, *242*, 247–51, *249*, *250*, *251*, 257, 262, 263, *264*, *265*, *266*, 267, 268, 269, *274*, *275*, *290*, 291, 295, 296, 334, 380, 382, 385
Snowfire (1958) 344, 386
Snyder, William E. 64, 65, 134, 135, 352
Sole-Smith, Virginia 337
Something for Nothing (stage) 367–68
Sommers, Stephen 357
Son of Frankenstein (1939) 63, 136
The Son of Kong (1933) 222
Son of Sinbad (1955) 379
A Song Is Born (1948) 41
Sorry, Wrong Number (1948) 164
Soule, Olan 151, 374
The Sound of Fury (1950) 366–67
South Pacific (stage) 151
Southwest Passage (1954) 25
Soylent Green (1973) 99
Space Angel (TV) 197
The Space Children (1958) 31, 192
Space Patrol (TV) 317
Spielberg, Steven 135
Spillane, Mickey 25, 26
The Spirit Is Willing (1967) 168
Spooks! (1953) 102
Stackpole, Peter 365
Stader, Paul 269–70, *271*
The Stand at Apache River (1953) 1, 20
Stanley, Ginger 2, 6, 39, 53, 75, 77, 77, 78, *78*, 82, 105, 134, 136, 176, 178–79, *178*, 182, 192, 193, 276, 319–37, *320*, *321*, *322*, *323*, *324*, *325*, *326*, *327*, *330*, *332*, *333*, *334*, *335*, *336*, 351, 377, 378, 385

Stanwyck, Barbara 15
Stapley, Richard 47–48
Star in the Dust (1956) 196
Starlog (magazine) 60, 243, 316
Stars in Your Eyes (stage) 368
The Steel Jungle (1956) 80
Steele, Brian 359
Stein, Eddie 88
Stein, Herman 45, 112, *112*, 113, 114, 115, 116, 117, 118, 119, 120–21, *120*, 122, 124, 125, 126, 130, 133, 136, 152, 215, 216, 217, 218, 219, 220, 221, 222, 236, 286–87, 288, 292, 385
Steiner, Max 116
Step Down to Terror (1958) 114
Stephens, Harvey 150–51
Stephens, John 373
Stern, Leonard 66–67, 369
Stevens, Craig 59, 364
Stevens, Leith 133
Stevens, Warren 243
Stevenson, Robert Louis 13
Stewart, James 3, 160, 367
Stone, Jeffrey 164–65
Storm Over Tibet (1952) *244*, 245
The Story of Ruth (1960) 242
Stover, George 243
Strange, Glenn 100, 366
The Strange Door (1951) 47, 116, 120, 130–31, 200
The Stranger (1946) 29
Strangler of the Swamp (1946) 98
The Street Is My Beat (1966) 314
Strimpell, Stephen 182
Stroud, Don 64
Struzan, Drew 352
Stuart, Barbara 248, 251
Stumar, Charles 135
Suckling, Sir John 155
Sullivan, Barry 15
Sullivan, Don 385
Sunday Dinner for a Soldier (1944) 71
Swartz, James V. 312
Sweet Bird of Youth (stage) 162
Swires, Steve 316
Symmes, Dan 212

Tabu (1931) 370
Tales of Frankenstein (TV pilot) 255, *255*, 297, 382
Tales of Tomorrow (TV) 318
Tamiroff, Akim 105
Tamkin, David 114, 118
Tanganyika (1954) 88, 242, 292, 374
Tap Roots (1948) 265
Tarantula (1955) 31, 35, 79, 117, 118, 120, 127, 130, 142, 156, 167, 182, 192, 196, 211, 219, 221, 251, 266, 280, 282, 364, 378, 380
Target Earth (1954) 53, *56*
Tarzan and the Valley of Gold (1966) 346, *257*
Tarzan Finds a Son! (1939) 207
Tarzan's Secret Treasure (1941) 37, 38
Taylor, Don 59
Taza, Son of Cochise (1954) 102, 245, 252, 382

Tea and Sympathy (stage) 258
Temple, Shirley 146–48, *147*, 156, 157, 159, 181, 373
Terrell, Ken 270, *271*
Texas, Brooklyn & Heaven (1948) 366
That's My Boy (1951) 252
Thaxton, Charles 384
Them! (1954) 102, 112, 116
There's Always Tomorrow (1956) 222
They Came to Destroy the Earth (unmade movie) 312
The Thief of Bagdad (1940) *365*, 366
The Thing from Another World (1951) 91, 111–12, 382
The Thing That Couldn't Die (1958) 119–20, 121, 129
This Island Earth 88, 95, 118, 120, 133, 206, 217, 222, 235, 242, 243, 245, 266, 276, 280, 295, 363, 364, 370, 382, 384
Thomas, Bob 36, 93, 95, 103, 160, 365
Thomas, Larri 165, *165*, 311–12, 375, 385
Thompson, Edward 105
Thompson, Jesse 258
Thompson, Wes 88
The Three Stooges in Orbit (1962) 167
The Three Stooges Meet Hercules (1962) 379
Thriller (TV) 171
Thunder on the Hill (1951) 117, 131
Thunder Over Hawaii see *Naked Paradise*
Thunderball (1965) 284
Tillotson, Mary Ellen 166
Timbrell, Hilmer J. "Tiny" 291
Time (magazine) 77, 370
The Time of Their Lives (1946) 113
Tinney, Robert Lee "Sonny" 176, 178, *178*, 331, 334
Tiomkin, Dimitri 111
To Hell and Back (1955) 282
To the Shores of Tripoli (1942) 74
Tobey, Kenneth 243
Tobias, George 105, 372
Toch, Ernst 290
The Today Show (TV) 96
Tolstoy, Ilya 144, 145, 338
Tomahawk (1951) 117, 131
Tonight! Lincoln vs. Douglas (stage) 243
The Tonight Show (TV) 209
Top Banana (1954) 379
Toren, Marta 59
Tormented (1960) 51
Tors, Ivan 51
Touch of Evil (1958) 29
Tovar, Lupita 59
The Treasure of Lost Canyon (1952) 13
Tremayne, Les 385
Trent, Lee 372
Trog (1970) 232
Truman, Harry S 382
Tseng Tsai, Loh 151
Tucker, Forrest 39

Twelfth Night (stage) 240
Twenty Thousand Leagues Under the Sea (1916) 369
20000 Leagues Under the Sea (1954) 143, 206, *365*, 366
The Twilight Zone (TV) 243
The Two Jakes (1990) 80

Underwater! (1955) 160, 205
The Underwater City (1962) 53
Union Pacific (TV) 243
The United Monster Talent Agency (2010) *281*, 283, 351–52, 367
Unknown Island (1948) 53, *55*
Untamed Frontier (1952) 36, 131
Untamed Youth (1957) 161
U.S. Marshal (TV) 165

Vakhtangov, Yevgeny 151
Valentino, Rudolph 36
Van Doren, Mamie 60, 161
Van Dyke, Dick 335, 336
Van Helsing (2004) 357
Vaughn, James T. 40, 71, 83, 366
Vickers, Lu 337
Video Watchdog (magazine) 51, 156, 382
Vincent, Cerina 352, 367
Vinton, Victoria 379
Vogel, Mike 275
The Voice of the Millions (1912) 59
La Voluntad del Muerto (1930) *58*, 59
von Stroheim, Erich, Jr. 243
Voyage to the Bottom of the Sea (TV) 110, 212

Wagner, Wende 384, *384*
Wake of the Red Witch (1948) 60
Walker, Clint *236*, 255–56, 343
Walking My Baby Back Home (1953) 102
Wallis, Hal B. 164, 374
Walls, Joe 270, *271*
Walsh, Raoul 3, 13, 53
Walters, Barbara 335–36
War Arrow (1953) 102
"The War of the Worlds" (1938 radio broadcast) 92
The War Wagon (1967) 172
Ward, Edward 112, 114
Washburn, Sherwood L. 229, 231
Wasserman, Lew 361
Watson, Richard O. 180
Wayne, David 59
Wayne, Ethan 171
Wayne, John 60, 142, 147, 157, 158, 171, *171*, 172, 251, 253–54, 272
Wayne, Patrick 171
Weathersby, Faye 377
Weaver, Jon *253*
Weaver, Tom *244*
Week-end with Father (1951) 55
Weeki Wachee: City of Mermaids: A History of One of Florida's Oldest Roadside Attractions (book) 337
Wehking, Steve 184
Wehling, Robert 198
Wehmeyer, Ernest B. 102

Weinberg, Roger 40
Weingrod, Herschel 356
Weissmuller, Johnny 38, 61, 333
Welbourne, "Scotty" 6–7, 39, 40, 42–43, 44, 64, 67, 69–70, *69*, 71, 73, *80*, 86, 93, 94, 134, 135, 143, 148, 150, 173, 177, 194, 205, 222, 223, 224, 257, *261*, 264–65, 297, 298, 328, 329, 331, 365, 369, 376, 378, 379
Welch, William 110
Weldon, Michael 317
Welles, Orson 13, 29, 40, 92, 151–52, 258–59, 382
Wells, Dick 260, 262, *262*, 263, 264
Wells, H.G. 261
The Werewolf (1956) 255, 344
West, Mae 241
West of the Brazos (1950) *52*
West Point Widow (1941) 368
Western Clippings (magazine) 48, 55
Western Waters (stage) 49, 367
Westmore, Bud *2*, 4, *17*, *19*, *26*, *29*, *33*, 39–40, 41, *41*, 42, 94–99, 103, 144, 202, 206, 207, *235*, 364, 370, 372
Westmore, Dorothy 98
Westmore, Ern 97, 98
Westmore, Frank 40, 98–99, 368
Westmore, George 98
Westmore, Monte 98
Westmore, Perc 98, 99
Westmore, Wally 98, 99
The Westmores of Hollywood (book) 40, 98–99, 368
What a Picnic! (1945) 38, 365
What Makes Sammy Run? (novel) 31
White, Taylor 351
The White Album (book) 172
White Christmas (1954) 102
Whitman, Stuart 110
Whitney, Cornelius Vanderbilt 144, 145, 168–69, 309, 338, 341, 373
Whitney, Marylou 309, 341
Who Was That Lady I Saw You With? (stage) *162*
Wild Hairs (book) 361
Wilder, Billy 108
Willcox, Charles 106–7
Williams, Bill *236*
Williams, Esther 78, 333–34, 375
Williams, John 116
Williams, Mark 385
Williams, Robert B. 150, 184, 187, *188*, 191, 199, 224, 376
Williams, Wade 317–18
Williamson, Ernest 369
Williamson, George 369
Willock, Dave 151, 184, 186, 224, 280
Willson, Henry 246
Wilson, Earl 164, 372
Wilson, F. Paul 351
Wilson, Gahan 350
Wilson, Stanley 118
Wingfield, Mark 84
Wings (1927) 196
Wings of the Hawk (1953) 6, 59
Winter Carnival (1939) 49
The Wizard of Oz (1939) 207
The Wolf Man (1941) 117, 131, 136
The Wolfman (2010) 360
Women of the Prehistoric Planet (1966) 133
The Wonders of Wakulla Springs (documentary) 38, 365
Wood, Natalie 171, 376
Woolery, Shirley 179, 321, 376
The World in His Arms (1952) 41, 92, 112
World in My Corner (1956) 242
Wray, Fay 150, 223
Wrightson, Bernie 350
Wyatt, Al 371–72
Wyman, Jane 252

Yankee Buccaneer (1952) 130, 132
Yankee Doodle Dandy (1942) 287
Yankee Pasha (1954) 144
The Yearling (1946) 105
The Yearling (novel) 146
You Can't Cheat an Honest Man (1939) 215, 218–19
You'll Find Out (1940) 291
Young, Bill 192
Young, Jack N. 106
Young, W.A. 151, 265
Young Gunsmoke (unmade movie) 375
The Young in Heart (1938) 49
Your Show (TV) 96
Your Show Time (TV) 52
Yrigoyen, Joe 270, *271*

Zaat (1971) 212
Zacherley 210
Zanuck, Darryl F. 164
Zeisl, Eric 112, 222
Zendar, Fred *68*, *74*, 86
Zimm, Maurice 14–15, 18, 19, 20, 21, 25, 26, 30, 40, 105, 110, 141, 363, 367, 378
Zimmer, Dolph 207
Zimring, Frank 363
Zombies of Mora Tau (1957) 251, 253